These United States: *The Questions of Our Past*

4th edition

These United States

The Questions of Our Past

Volume II: since 1865

Irwin Unger

New York University

Portraits and Documents by DEBI UNGER

PRENTICE HALL
Englewood Cliffs, New Jersey 07632

LIBRARY OF CONGRESS
Library of Congress Cataloging-in-Publication Data

Unger, Irwin.
  These United States: the questions of our past/Irwin Unger:
  portraits and documents by Debi Unger   p.   cm.
  Includes bibliographies and indexes.
  Contents: v. 1. To 1877— v. 2. Since 1865.
  ISBN 0-13-942038-X (v. 1). ISBN 0-13-942079-7 (v. 2)
  1. United States—History.   I. Unger, Debi.   II. Title.
E178.1.U54 1989
973—dc 19   88-21912
                                                  CIP

To Rita and Mickey, Libby and Arnie, Phyllis and Jerry, and Norma and David—once more

Editorial / production supervision: Marina Harrison
Interior design: Anne T. Bonanno
Manufacturing buyer: Ed O'Dougherty
Cover design: Paul Agule
Photo editor: Lorinda Morris-Nantz
Photo researcher: Barbara Schultz
Cover art: *The Lost Bet,* Lithograph by Julius Kessler (after Joseph
  Klir, Paris), 1893.
  Courtesy Library of Congress

© 1989, 1986, 1982, 1978 by Prentice-Hall, Inc.
A Division of Simon & Schuster
Englewood Cliffs, New Jersey 07632

Printed in the United States of America
10 9 8 7 6 5 4 3 2 1

ISBN 0-13-942079-7

Prentice-Hall International (UK) Limited, *London*
Prentice-Hall of Australia Pty. Limited, *Sydney*
Prentice-Hall Canada Inc., *Toronto*
Prentice-Hall Hispanoamericana, S.A., *Mexico*
Prentice-Hall of India Private Limited, *New Delhi*
Prentice-Hall of Japan, Inc., *Tokyo*
Simon & Schuster Asia Pte. Ltd., *Singapore*
Editora Prentice-Hall do Brasil, Ltda., *Rio de Janeiro*

Contents

20
Republicans and Democrats

21
The American Empire

22
Culture in the Age of the Dynamo

23
Progressivism

24
World War I

Preface

THIS FOURTH EDITION OF *These United States* is an improved and updated version of a text that first appeared ten years ago. Much has happened in that decade to the nation and to historians' understanding of the nation's past. In this latest version I have attempted to incorporate these new events and new insights, bringing the story down to the present and at the same time reconsidering some of the interpretations adopted in previous editions. I have especially revised the material on colonial society and the colonial economy, and introduced a discussion of new views of Jeffersonian democracy absent from the third edition. The new edition also contains a number of new "portraits"; volume two has a complete new chapter on the "Reagan Revolution"; there are updated and expanded bibliographies. Finally, I have carefully reviewed every sentence and paragraph of *These United States* for ease of reading, clarity, and smoothness. I hope it shows.

These substantive changes notwithstanding, users of the fourth edition will, perhaps, be most immediately impressed by the work's new physical appearance. Now, for the first time, the volumes will be in four color, allowing us to present pictures far more vividly than in the past. Though a text must convey its lessons primarily through words, lively illustrations can, of course, be immensely helpful in carrying young readers along as well as conveying an idea or a thought effectively. That, at least, is our hope.

Despite the changes, we have retained the special features that marked the approach of *These United States* from the outset. We continue to use "questions of our past" as the central organizing principle for each chapter. As before, the material following each "question" attempts to answer it. But not at the expense of coverage. Each chapter also contains all of the narrative and description of the standard "core" text. In effect, the student and instructor get "two for the price of one."

As in previous editions, *These United States* goes beyond the traditional text in its coverage of social change and popular culture. It covers not only politics, diplomacy, and wars; it also deals with social classes, families, children, sports, entertainment, the way people worked, their health, living standards and many other topics that have now become part of the new social history. While avoiding technical jargon, it discusses economic growth, social mobility, and the clash of ideologies. It also seeks to inform its readers of groups, such as blacks and women, who used to be left out of the history books, while at the same time confirming the critical importance of elites in determining the course of public events.

Here, then, is the fourth edition of *These United States: The Questions of Our Past*. It is an improved version and, to repeat a previous preface, "we hope that readers will be even more pleased with the new . . . than they were with the old."

Acknowledgments

Like all authors I have profited from the kindness and help of many people. First, I wish to thank my colleague, Professor Patricia U. Bonomi, who provided me with a quick course in the newest historiography and bibliography of the colonial era and the early republic. I have also, once again, profited from the close readings of the previous edition by several scholars: Alfred Alexander, Evergreen Valley College; Randolph Campbell, North Texas State University; R. Beeler Satterfield, Lamar University; Edward Schapsmeier, Illinois State University; and Ronald Zarcone, Ever- green Valley College. Although I did not always accept their suggestions, I invariably learned something useful from their critiques. I also wish to thank Marina Harrison, my production editor, for her quiet efficiency, and James Tully, my copyeditor, for his careful and thoughtful review of the whole manu- script.

These United States: *The Questions of Our Past*

Chapter 16

Reconstruction

What Went Wrong?

1863   Lincoln announces his "ten-percent plan" for reconstruction

1863–65   Arkansas and Louisiana accept Lincoln's conditions but Congress does not readmit them to the Union

1864   Lincoln vetoes Congress's Wade-Davis Reconstruction Bill

1865   Johnson succeeds Lincoln • The Freedmen's Bureau is established • Congress overrides Johnson's veto of the Civil Rights Act • Johnson announces his Reconstruction plan • All-white southern legislatures begin to pass "Black Codes" • The Thirteenth Amendment

1866   Congress adopts the Fourteenth Amendment, but it is not ratified until 1868 • The Ku Klux Klan is formed • Tennessee is readmitted to the Union

1867   Congress passes the first of four Reconstruction Acts • Tenure of Office Act • Johnson suspends Secretary of War Edwin Stanton

1868   Johnson is impeached by the House and acquitted in the Senate • Arkansas, North Carolina, South Carolina, Alabama, Florida, and Louisiana are readmitted to the Union • Ulysses S. Grant elected president

1869   Woman suffrage associations are organized in response to women's disappointment with the Fourteenth Amendment

1870   Virginia, Mississippi, Texas, and Georgia are readmitted to the Union

1870, 1871   Congress passes Force Bills

1875   Blacks are guaranteed access to public places by Congress • Mississippi "redeemers" successfully oust black and white Republican officeholders

1876   Presidential election between Rutherford B. Hayes and Samuel J. Tilden

1877   Compromise of 1877: Hayes is chosen as president, and all remaining federal troops are withdrawn from the South

By 1880   The share-crop system of agriculture is well established in the South

Almost no one has had anything good to say about Reconstruction, the process by which the South was restored to the Union. Contemporaries judged it a colossal failure. To most southern whites Reconstruction was a time when Dixie was subjected to a cruel northern occupation and civilization itself was submerged under an avalanche of black barbarism. For the ex-slaves—or freedmen, as they were called—the period of 1865–1877 started with the bright promise of true freedom and prosperity, but ended in bitter disappointment with most blacks still on the bottom rung of southern society. Contemporary northerners, too, generally deplored these years. They had thought the Reconstruction program would change the South. But it had not succeeded, and most of them were relieved when the last federal troops withdrew in 1877 and the white South once more governed itself.

Americans in later years have not generally thought well of Reconstruction either. From the 1890s to the 1940s most historians assumed that the Republicans who controlled Washington and the southern state capitals were moved by the desire for revenge. Liberal scholars of the following generation, rejected this view, but they believed the chance to modernize and liberalize southern society had been missed because the North had neither will nor conviction sufficient to take the bold steps needed. Recently some younger historians have declared that by failing to provide land and power to the freedmen, the Reconstruction process nullified much of the advantage of emancipation. In this view, the North sold out the black people, leaving them little better off than before the Civil War.

Obviously, then, from almost every point of view, Reconstruction has seemed a failure. What went wrong? And was it as bad as most critics have believed?

The Legacy of War

A month or so after Appomattox, Whitelaw Reid, a correspondent for the Republican *Cincinnati Gazette*, went south to see what the war had done to Dixie. Strongly antisouthern, Reid was inclined to belittle claims of southern distress, but even he was struck by the devastation he encountered. Hanover Junction, near Richmond, Reid reported, "presented little but standing chimneys and the debris of destroyed buildings. Along the [rail]road a pile of smoky brick and mortar seemed a regularly recognized sign of what had once been a depot." Not a platform or water tank had been left, he wrote, and efforts to get the road in running order were often the only improvements visible for miles. Young pines covered the old fields of wheat and corn, and the crumbling remains of defense works could be seen everywhere.

Others gave similar descriptions. Wherever northern and southern armies had fought, every manmade object bore the scars. Interior South Carolina, hard hit by General Sherman's army, "looked for many miles like a broad black streak of ruin and desolation." In the Shenandoah Valley of Virginia between Winchester and Harrisonburg, scarcely a horse, pig, chicken, or cow remained alive. Southern cities, too, were devastated. Columbia, capital of South Carolina, was a blackened wasteland with not a store standing in the business district. Atlanta, Richmond, Selma, and other southern towns were also devastated.

Human losses were appalling. Of the South's white male population of 2.5 million in 1860, a quarter of a million (10 percent) had died of battle wounds or disease. Most of these were young men who represented the region's most vigorous and creative resource. Of those who survived, some were maimed; many were worn out emotionally. "A more completely crushed country I have seldom witnessed," a Yankee officer in the occupation force wrote the United States attorney general.

The South's economic institutions were also wrecked. Its banking structure, based on now-worthless Confederate bonds, had collapsed. Personal savings had been wiped out when Confederate currency lost its value. Even more crushing, the region's labor system was in ruins. Slavery as an economic institution—and as a social one—was dead, but no one knew what to replace it with. Many blacks remained on the farms and plantations and continued to plant, cultivate, and harvest. Many others—whether to test their new-found freedom, hunt for long-lost relatives, or just to take their first holiday—wandered the roads or flocked to the cities, abandoning the land that had traditionally sustained the South's economy.

The physical and institutional destruction of the war was matched by its emotional damage. People in both sections harbored deep resentments. After struggling for independence against the "tyrannical government in Washington" and "northern dominance" for four years, white southerners could not help feeling apprehensive, angry, and deeply disappointed. Now, even more than in 1860, a weak South would be dominated by the North, whose arrogance and power were reinforced by victory and unchecked by any need to compromise. Northerners, for their part, would not easily forget the sacrifices and losses they had suffered in putting down what they considered the illegal and unwarranted rebellion; nor would they easily forgive the "atrocities" committed by the Confederacy. At Andersonville, Georgia, for example, during July 1864, 31,000 Union prisoners had been confined in a sixteen-acre stockade, sheltered only by tents and fed on scanty rations. As many as 3,000 prisoners had died in a month—100 a day. It did not matter that the prisoners'

guards received the same rations, that southern prisoners in northern camps were not treated much better, or that bad conditions were made worse by Yankee captives who preyed on their own comrades. To the northern public the Confederate officials, and especially the camp commandant, Captain Henry Wirz, were beasts who must be punished. Regarding the South as a whole, John Sherman, an Ohio Republican, spoke for many northerners: "We should not only brand the leading rebels with infamy, but the whole rebellion should wear a badge of the penitentiary, so that for this generation at least, no man who has taken part in it would dare to justify or palliate it."

The American people, then, faced a gigantic task of physical, political, and emotional restoration. By the usual measure, the period of restoration, or Reconstruction, lasted for some twelve years, until 1877. It was a time of upheaval and controversy, as well as new beginnings. In its own day the problems associated with Reconstruction dominated the political and intellectual life of the country, and they have fascinated and repelled Americans ever since.

Richmond, Virginia, the Confederate capital, being abandoned by the Jefferson Davis government in the last days of the war.

Issues and Attitudes

It is difficult even today to draw a balanced picture of Reconstruction. Many issues—racial inequality, southern poverty, sectional antipathies—are still with us. During Reconstruction people were even more deeply concerned with the role of blacks in the restored nation and the proper relation of the South to the rest of the United States. All agreed that racial and political readjustments were necessary. But how to make them deeply divided the American people, North and South, white and black, Republican and Democrat.

The positions that people took fell roughly into five categories: Radical Republican, northern conservative, southern conservative, southern Unionist, and southern freedmen. Let us allow each of these groups to speak for itself. The speeches that follow are fabricated, but they show what these groups of Americans felt about Reconstruction and wanted to see come out of it. Because they controlled so much of the process, let us start with the Radical Republicans.

Radical Republicans. "The South must be made to recognize its sins, and southerners must acknowledge that now that they have been defeated, they can no longer decide their own fate. It is now in the hands of the victorious North. Southerners can avoid our anger and show they are prepared to be readmitted as citizens of the United States in a number of ways. At the very least, they must reject their former leaders and choose new ones who have not been connected with the Confederacy. They can take oaths of loyalty to the United States. They can reject all attempts to repay the Confederate debt incurred in an unjust cause. Most important of all, they can accept the fact that the former slaves are now free and must be treated as the political equals of whites.

"Many former slaves worked and fought for the Union, and we must now help them through the difficult transition to full freedom. As to how this end can best be accomplished, not all of us are agreed. A few of us hold that it will be necessary for the freedmen to get land so they can support themselves independently. But all of us believe that at the very minimum the freedmen must have the vote and, during the early stages of the change, must be protected against starvation and exploitation. No doubt they will be grateful for the efforts of their Republican friends in defeating the slave power, destroying slavery, and defending them against those who will not accept the new situation. This gratitude will incline them to vote Republican. And that is all to the good. The Republican party

is the great hope of the nation. It is the party of freedom and economic progress. It is not afraid to use government to encourage that progress. In a word, it is the party that has, since its founding, proved that it is the best embodiment of both the nation's moral and practical sense."

Northern Conservatives. "We, the northern conservatives, are generally of the old Democratic persuasion. Most of us opposed secession and supported the war. But we agree that now that the war is over and secession defeated, we must forget the past. Let southerners—white southerners, that is—determine their own fate. It is in the best American tradition to let local communities decide their own course without undue interference from the national government. Let us confirm this great principle of local self-determination, and short of a few guarantees for Unionists and blacks, let us allow the South back into the Union on its own terms.

"We must not try to force black suffrage or social equality down the throats of the former Confederates. Almost all white Americans believe that Negroes are ill-equipped to exercise the rights of citizens. The Radicals insist on giving them the vote only because they want to secure continued control of the national government. They want to guarantee the predominance of the values and goals of the Northeast, the nation's commercial-industrial capital, against the very different interests and goals of the country's agricultural West and South. It is clearly hypocritical of the supposed champions of the freedmen to be so timid in supporting Negro suffrage in the northern states, where such a stand is politically unpopular and where there are too few Negroes to add to their voting strength. We must reject such hypocrisy and restore peace and tranquillity to the nation as quickly and completely as possible."

Southern Conservatives. "The war we fought and lost was for a noble cause, and it brought out the best in our southern people. We must never forget the sacrifice and heroism of the gallant men in gray. Perhaps secession was a mistake, but that fact will never diminish the tragic grandeur of our struggle.

"But let us now get back to the business of daily living. We of the South must be allowed to resume our traditional political relations with the rest of the states. We must be free to determine our own fate with a minimum of conditions. Above all, we must be permitted to steer our own course on race relations. The 'carpetbaggers' who come down from the North looking for easy money, and the southern renegade 'scalawags' lusting for power, are self-serving and contemptible. They do not understand or accept southern traditions.

"True, we must recognize that Negroes are no longer slaves and we must make certain concessions to their private rights, but in the public realm these must be limited by their capacities. Above all, Negroes must not be allowed to exercise political power. They are not the equal of whites. They are ignorant, lazy, improvident, and intellectually inferior. They can be duped and deceived by their professed 'friends' into supporting the Republican party, but actually their interests will be best served by those who have always been the leaders of southern society and who remain the Negroes' natural protectors. Nature dictates that the freedmen of the South remain in subordination, that they accept their humble economic stations and political inferiority, for that is the only way they can function at all."

Southern Unionists. "At long last we are free to speak our minds! For four long years we have been persecuted and intimidated by the secessionists. Now that they have been defeated, we deserve recognition and favor. Unfortunately the rebels are still in the majority. They say they have accepted the new circumstances of the South, but many of them have not, and we are in a vulnerable position. At the very least we must be protected by our northern friends against hostile unreconciled rebels. Moreover, we should be rewarded for our loyalty to the Union with an important place in the new order.

"We do not all agree about the role of the Negroes in the South's future, but many of us recognize that they are entitled to equal political rights now that they are free. Given the vote, they will inevitably—and rightly—look to us for leadership. Ex-rebels may call us scalawags and worse; that is to be expected. But we can help transform the South from a sleepy backward region dominated by the former planter class into a bustling, thriving region of farms, factories, and cities."

Southern Freedmen. "We are now free men and women and must be accorded all the privileges of free people as expressed in the Declaration of Independence. We contributed mightily to Union victory in war and have earned the right to be treated as equals. We are also the largest group in the South truly loyal to the Union. Southern whites, with few exceptions, cannot be trusted. They are unreconciled to defeat, and if the North fails to protect us and guarantee our rights as free men and women, these ex-Confederates will

once more seize power and nullify the Union victory. The federal government, then, must continue for an indefinite period to wield a strong hand in the process of southern Reconstruction.

"We do not expect white southerners to accept us as social equals; but we must have legal equality and full civil rights, including, of course, the right to vote. We must also have economic independence, which means the right to sell our labor in the open market *and* the right to our own land. Thousands of the South's best acres, abandoned by disloyal owners during the war, are controlled either by the Freedmen's Bureau or by the army. Giving us this land would enable us to secure our independence and prevent our being kept in permanently subordinate positions. We also deserve access to education. Literacy is an important tool for achieving economic independence. If the cost of a public school system means that southern state taxes must rise, so be it."

Several of these positions overlapped. Radical Republicans and black freedmen, for example, often agreed on measures to guarantee a successful transition. The position of northern conservatives overlapped that of southern conservatives. But it would clearly be difficult to reconcile those people who wanted to return to prewar conditions as quickly as possible and those who hoped to make social transformation a requirement for readmitting the South to the Union. The diversity of opinion boded ill for the effort to bring together the nation's separated halves. In the next dozen years there would be fierce battles between the contending parties, some almost as passionate as the war itself.

Presidential Reconstruction

Even before Lee's surrender at Appomattox in 1865, the Union government had been forced to consider the question of reconstruction. As Union troops advanced into the South, the Lincoln administration was confronted with the problem of how to govern the conquered territory. Military administration might suffice for a while; but it ran counter to the American tradition of civilian rule, and wherever possible the government sought to restore some civilian control.

Lincoln's Ten-Percent Plan. Lincoln tried to tailor his approach to each state's situation. In general, however, he started by appointing a civilian governor, supported by the military commander and whatever loyal residents the governor could find. In December 1863 he unveiled his "ten-percent plan," which provided that a former Confederate state would be readmitted to the Union when a number of citizens equal to 10 percent of those who had voted in the 1860 presidential election took an oath to support the Constitution and establish a state government that accepted the end of slavery.

Many Republicans felt that Lincoln was being too generous, and in July 1864 Congress responded to his scheme with the Wade-Davis Bill. This legislation required that before a new state government could be formed, a *majority* of the white male citizens must pledge to support the federal Constitution. If they did so, the provisional governor would call a state constitutional convention. The governor could exclude anyone who had fought as a Confederate soldier or had held

An idealized portrait of Andrew Johnson. His photographs show a coarser featured man and probably convey a better sense of what sort of person he was.

public office during the Confederate period. Lincoln vetoed the Wade-Davis Bill; but in his usual flexible— if confusing—way, he said that he did not object to it as an alternative to his own plan. Needless to say, no southern state chose to reorganize by the more stringent congressional blueprint. Tennessee, Arkansas, Virginia, and Louisiana accepted the terms of the president's ten-percent plan, however, and Lincoln proclaimed them back in the Union.

Johnson's Plan. Lincoln's assassination altered the course of political reconstruction profoundly. Had he lived, his standing, popularity, and flexibility might have induced Congress to accept major portions of his plan. Still, even he would have encountered difficulty. The war had swollen federal executive power beyond its former limits, and at the end of the conflict Congress certainly would have reasserted itself by fighting to control so vital a program as Reconstruction. It seems unlikely that either side would have had its way entirely.

Lincoln's successor, Andrew Johnson, had to deal with this inevitable clash between Congress and the chief executive. Unfortunately, lacking Lincoln's prestige and political skill, Johnson handled the situation badly. Though he was the same age and from the same southern yeoman background as Lincoln, Johnson was a very different man. Lincoln's family left the slave South when he was a boy, and Abe grew up in the free state of Indiana. Later, as a respected Illinois lawyer, he developed a strong ego and came to appreciate the diverse views of a free society. Johnson, on the other hand, grew up in North Carolina, settled in yeoman-dominated eastern Tennessee, and worked as a simple tailor before entering politics. He was never personally secure, and his lack of self-confidence made him boastful of his humble beginnings and susceptible to flattery. His insecurity, combined with the antiblack and antiaristocratic sentiments of his home region, goes far to explain both his insensitivity to the plight of blacks and his initial hostility to the southern planter class. Johnson's pro–states' rights views also hampered his efforts to solve the unprecedented problems of the postwar period.

Moreover, Johnson was a rigid man, one who often lashed out at his opponents. He could be cajoled out of a position; but when defied directly, he refused to budge. This stubborness, in turn, often forced his opponents into positions more extreme than their original stands. More than any other factor, Johnson's inability to compromise discouraged the moderates in Congress and drove many into the waiting arms of

Black Reconstruction

Black southerners were not passive participants in the Reconstruction process. In the South they joined the militia companies and the Union Leagues, as well as the Republican party. They also spoke out against their enemies and appealed to their white northern friends for support. The following is an early instance of such an appeal. It is a statement adopted by a black convention held in Virginia in August 1865, soon after the end of the war. Note how many of the things the delegates asked their white allies for were actually granted.

"We, the undersigned members of a Convention of colored citizens of the State of Virginia, would respectfully represent that, although we have been held as slaves, and denied all recognition as a constituent of your nationality for almost the entire period of the duration of your Government, and that by *your permission* we have been denied either home or country, and deprived of the dearest rights of human nature: yet when you and our immediate oppressors met in deadly conflict on the field of battle—the one to destroy and the other to save your Government and nationality, we, with scarce an exception, in our inmost souls espoused your cause, and watched, and prayed, and waited, and labored for your success. . . .

"When the contest waxed long, and the result hung doubtfully, you appealed to us for help, and how well we answered is written in the rosters of the two hundred thousand colored troops now enrolled in your service; and as to our undying devotion to your cause, let the uniform acclamation of escaped prisoners, 'whenever we saw a black face we felt sure of a friend,' answer.

"Well, the war is over, the rebellion is 'put down,' and we are *declared* free! Four fifths of our enemies are paroled or amnestied, and the other fifth are being pardoned, and the President has . . . left us entirely at the mercy of these subjugated but unconverted rebels, in *everything* save the privilege of bringing us, our wives, and little ones, to the auction block. . . . We *know* these men—know them *well*—and we assure you that, with the majority of them, loyalty is only 'lip deep,' and that their professions of loyalty are used as a cover to the cherished design of getting restored to their former relations with the Federal Government, and then, by all sorts of 'unfriendly legislation,' to render the freedom you have given us more intolerable than the slavery they intended for us.

"We warn you in time that our only safety is in keeping them under Governors of the *military persuasion* until you have so amended the Federal Constitution that it will prohibit the States from making any distinction between citizens on account of race or color. In one word, the only salvation for us besides the power of the Government is in the *possession of the ballot.* Give us this and we will protect ourselves. . . .

"We are 'sheep in the midst of wolves,' and nothing but the military arm of the Government prevents us and all the *truly* loyal white men from being driven from the land of our birth. Do not then, we beseech you, give to one of these 'wayward sisters' the rights they abandoned and forfeited when they rebelled until you have secured *our* rights by the aforementioned amendment to the Constitution. . . .

"Trusting that you will not be deaf to the appeal herein made, nor unmindful of the warnings which the malignity of the rebels are constantly giving you, and that you will rise to the height of being just for the sake of justice, we remain yours for our flag, our country, and humanity."

Radicals like Thaddeus Stevens, Charles Sumner, and Benjamin F. Wade.

The president's characteristics become apparent only gradually, however. At first, Republican leaders responded to Johnson very favorably. Moderates and Radicals alike respected his plucky fight against secessionists when he was military governor of Tennessee. The Radicals, having heard him remark that "treason . . . must be made infamous and traitors . . . punished," were certain he would be tougher on the South than Lincoln. The "accession of Johnson will prove a Godsend to the country," Congressman George W. Julian wrote soon after Lincoln's assassination.

The new president's first important act of Reconstruction was to pardon large groups of southerners who were willing to take an oath of loyalty to the Union. Excluded from the pardon was the planter class, defined as all those whose taxable property exceeded $20,000. Those not admitted to the general pardon could apply individually to the president, but the Radicals did not expect Johnson to be lenient. The power to pardon would prove important, for unpardoned

A Historical Portrait

Thaddeus Stevens

His enemies in the South accused him of murder, adultery, misanthropy, and treason. His friends in the North considered him a sterling defender of democracy and freedom. His admirers called him "the old Commoner" after the eloquent and witty William Pitt, leader of the British House of Commons. Detractors called him "old Clubfoot" because of his congenital deformity. This man who attracted scandal and controversy all his life was Thaddeus Stevens, leader during Reconstruction of the Radical Republicans in the House of Representatives.

Born in April 1792, Stevens was the second son of a sometime farmer, surveyor, wrestler, and shoemaker who disappeared permanently after the birth of his fourth son. His mother, Sarah, was a religious, strong-willed, and energetic woman who ran the farm and taught her sons reading from the Bible. It was she who showed Thaddeus how to fight failure and finally overcome it. She was a firm believer in the value of education, moving her four fatherless children to Peacham, Vermont, when an academy was founded there.

Thaddeus was a bright boy who justified his mother's faith in him. He was also rebellious, a trait that lasted his entire life. As a senior at the academy, he took part in a theatrical performance "by candlelight," an activity expressly forbidden by the stern puritan headmaster. After signing "articles of submission" stating that he regretted his misdeed, he was allowed to finish school. He graduated from Dartmouth in 1814, and in his commencement speech he defended luxury and wealth, claiming they were necessary for progress. Paradoxically, Stevens later attacked the South as a bastion of entrenched privilege and inequality.

In 1815 he went to York, Pennsylvania, where he taught for a year at the local academy and continued his study of law, begun in Vermont. Although the county insisted on a two years' residency requirement for admission to the bar, Stevens thought he was ready after a year because of his previous training. The lawyers of York did not like him and were unwilling to grant him a dispensation, so he crossed the border to Maryland. Here he answered a few questions on Blackstone's *Commentaries*, and a few on evidence and pleading, gave the judge two bottles of Madeira, and received his certification.

Stevens liked Pennsylvania, but did not want to return to York, where he had been snubbed. Instead, he opened his law office in Gettysburg. After a hard first year with few clients, he defended a mentally defective farmhand who had murdered a constable, using insanity as his plea. This was not a recognized defense at the time, and Stevens lost his case. He won himself a reputation for genius and boldness, however, and business poured into his office. He quickly bought himself a horse, a house and property in town, and a farm for his mother in Vermont. By 1830 he had become the largest property owner in the county, had invested in an iron business, and had been elected president of the Borough Council.

During his Gettysburg years Stevens survived an attack of typhoid fever that left him completely bald and added to his feelings of physical inferiority. Although he had many chances to marry, he rejected them all, feeling that his baldness and lameness made him unattractive and that any woman who wanted him must have reasons other than love.

Stevens also became an enthusiastic Anti-Mason, in part because of his rejection at Dartmouth and in York by secret societies. In 1831, in a speech at Hagerstown, Maryland, he attacked the Masons as corrupt, accused them of encouraging crime, and charged them with attempting to stop "the regular action of government." Jacob Lefever, a leading Mason and the owner of a Gettysburg newspaper, who had long been printing anonymous letters blaming Stevens for his supposed part in two recent murders, printed the Hagerstown speech in its entirety with a comment suggesting that Stevens had "blood" on his "skirts." Stevens sued him for criminal libel and damages. Lefever was sentenced to three months in jail and ordered to pay $1,500 in damages.

Despite the Masons' attacks, the Gettysburg townspeople elected Stevens to the state legislature, where he initiated much anti-Masonic legislation. He also made fiery speeches in behalf of an act to extend the free school system of Philadelphia to the entire state. His defense of education for all continued as long as he lived. Just a month before his death he introduced a bill in the House of Representatives "to establish a system of schools for the District of Columbia which shall serve as a model for similar institutions throughout the Union."

While still serving in the Pennsylvania legislature, Stevens became active in the antislavery cause, founding a colonization society and presenting a report in favor of abolishing slavery and the slave trade in the District of Columbia. At the state's constitutional convention in 1837 he refused to sign the final version of the constitution because it restricted suffrage to white males. He also acted as lawyer for fugitive slaves from other states hiding in the Pennsylvania hills. He was, by now, widely recognized as one of the state's foremost abolitionists.

In 1842 Stevens found himself at a personal low point. He had lost his seat in the state legislature and was deeply in debt because of business reverses, losses on massive election bets, and the failure of clients and friends to repay loans. To add to his troubles he was faced with a paternity suit brought by the father of an unmarried woman, a man whom he considered a friend. He was eventually cleared of this charge, but was embittered by this betrayal and his experiences in Gettysburg generally. He moved his residence and law offices to Lancaster, where he regained his fortunes and his reputation as the state's most accomplished lawyer. Here he also acquired a mulatto housekeeper, Lydia Hamilton Smith, who worked for Stevens until he died. People speculated about their relationship; his enemies snidely referred to her as "Mrs. Stevens."

In 1848 Stevens was elected to Congress as a Whig. In Washington he immediately gained a reputation as a firebrand. He denounced slavery as accursed, criminal, and shameful, and condemned northerners who permitted its continuance as fiercely as the southerners who practiced it. His House colleagues, from both sections, were often shocked by his abusive and offensive language, believing it better "suited to a fishmarket" than to the halls of Congress. He fought vigorously against both the Compromise of 1850 and the Fugitive Slave Act. After the shattering defeat of Winfield Scott, the Whig candidate for president in 1852, Stevens left

Congress and returned to Lancaster to attend to his legal practice and iron business. Having no legitimate children of his own, he also devoted himself to his nephews, Thaddeus and Alanson.

Though out of Congress, Stevens remained involved in politics, taking an active part in the birth of the Republican party in Pennsylvania. In 1858 he was returned to Congress as a Republican, winning 75 percent of the votes in Lancaster County. In 1860 Stevens was a delegate to the Republican national convention. He was mentioned for a cabinet post after Lincoln's victory at the polls, but instead stayed in the House, where he became chairman of the powerful Ways and Means Committee. A month after Lincoln's inauguration Confederate troops fired on Fort Sumter, precipitating the War Between the States. Stevens's committee gave the administration staunch support on financial matters. He was largely responsible for the Internal Revenue Act of 1862, which taxed almost every article produced by the Union. He favored the greenback paper currency, issued directly by the United States and backed by the credit of the country rather than by gold.

During the war Stevens was remorseless toward the South. He favored confiscation of captured enemy property and called for war without mercy. Some thought this was in retaliation for the destruction of his iron works during Lee's invasion of Pennsylvania in 1863. He introduced a bill calling for general emancipation, with compensation for loyal slaveholders and the freeing of slaves who wanted to leave their masters or who aided in "quelling the rebellion." Stevens favored generals who opposed slavery, believing that such men fought better. He hated George McClellan for his indecisiveness and was pleased when Lincoln fired him.

It was on Reconstruction that Stevens left his greatest mark. He and Charles Sumner were the two most prominent Radical Republicans—a group that favored strict terms for southern readmission to the Union, strong measures to guarantee the rights of the freedmen, and vigorous federal intervention to further economic progress. The Radicals had not been satisfied with Lincoln's lenient "ten-percent plan" for readmitting the seceded states to the Union. The harsher Wade-Davis Bill pleased Stevens no better; it was still too lenient.

When Andrew Johnson became president after Lincoln's assassination, Stevens hoped he would join the Radicals. On the surface, Johnson looked like an ally. A former senator from Tennessee, he had remained loyal to the Union and had fought against secessionists as military governor of the state. Both Stevens and Johnson had strong sympathies for the underdog, but where Stevens championed blacks, Johnson limited his compassion to poor whites. Less than two months after Johnson took office Stevens was permanently disillusioned with the president, considering his plans dangerous and his actions "insane." When Johnson proceeded to reconstruct the Union according to his own lenient design, Stevens and his fellow Radical Republicans determined to take over Reconstruction themselves.

On December 1, 1865, Stevens called together twenty-five supporters to propose a joint committee of both houses of Congress on Reconstruction. The committee would study the condition of the "so-called Confederate States of America," and no member elected to Congress would be admitted until the committee had made its report. When the full Republican caucus met the next night, it unanimously adopted this proposal. When Congress convened later that month, no southerner was

A Historical Portrait (*continued*)

seated and the Joint Committee of Fifteen on Reconstruction was established. As chairman of the House faction, Stevens was the dominant member of the committee. He intended to reduce the South to a "territorial condition" and treat it as a "conquered province" over which Congress would have complete control. He also was determined to guarantee the political and, if possible, the social rights of the freedmen. In 1865 and 1866 Stevens urged confiscation of land owned by rich ex-confederates and the transfer of forty acres of this property to each adult ex-slave. Not only would this provide the freedmen with a secure economic position in the South, it would also humble the proud southern elite that Stevens believed had brought the horrors of a brothers' war on the nation.

Stevens saw Johnson as the chief obstacle to the Radicals' policies and determined to get him. In early 1867 he secured passage of the Tenure of Office Act stripping the president of the authority to remove high officeholders who favored congressional Reconstruction. The Radicals also passed a measure requiring the president to issue orders to the army through the general of the army, Ulysses S. Grant, who could not be dismissed without the Senate's consent. The law was intended to filter all orders concerning Reconstruction through Grant, now a supporter of the Radical position.

This legislation set the stage for the impeachment of Andrew Johnson when the president refused to keep Edwin Stanton, a Radical, in his cabinet and ordered him to resign in February 1868. Stevens was in his middle seventies and in poor health by now, but he actively took part in the impeachment proceedings. He bypassed the Judiciary Committee and reported a resolution out of his own Committee on Reconstruction to impeach the president for violating the Tenure of Office Act. "Old Thaddeus Stevens," wrote a contemporary political commentator, "is still keeping himself alive only by the hope of sometime scalping Andrew Johnson . . . and watches with a feverish and bilious eye from behind the rampart of his Reconstruction laws the least movement of the enemy." The House voted for impeachment 126 to 47, but when the Senate tried Johnson for high crimes and misdemeanors, the necessary two-thirds majority for conviction fell short by one vote.

Stevens lived only ten weeks after the trial. Many said that his disappointment speeded his decline. This was not true, however. In the short period before his death he continued to work for Reconstruction, a free public school system for the District of Columbia, various railroad bills, and the purchase of Alaska. He died in August 1868 and rested in state in front of Lincoln's statue on the Capitol Rotunda, attended by an honor guard of black soldiers from Massachusetts. After his burial in Lancaster, the Republican party, in a spectacular gesture of respect, formally nominated him for Congress. So loyal were his constituents that he won in November!

Stevens made many fierce enemies during his lifetime. For many years after his death their views of him were widely accepted and he was remembered as an ill-tempered, vindictive, and punitive man who set back the course of sectional reconciliation. Now, following the "second Reconstruction" of the 1950s and 1960s, "the old Commoner" appears as a statesman ahead of his times and an often admirable defender of racial justice. He, of course, preferred to be seen as a great egalitarian. The inscription he chose for his tombstone testifies to his deep concern for all humanity, regardless of race:

I repose in this quiet and secluded
   spot,
Not from any natural preference
   for solitude
But, finding other Cemeteries lim-
   ited as to Race by Charter
   Rules,
I have chose this that I might
   illustrate in my death
The Principles which I advocated
Through a long life:
EQUALITY OF MAN BEFORE HIS
   Creator.

---

southerners could not vote, hold office, or reacquire property seized by the federal government during the war.

During his first eight months of office Johnson had a free hand in formulating Reconstruction policy. Congress was not in session when Lincoln died in April, and was not due to meet until December. A wiser man, especially one who had served in both the Senate and House, as Johnson had, might have called Congress into special session and consulted its members about Reconstruction policy. But Johnson took the easy way out and acted on his own.

The president put his eight free months to good use. In May, on the same day he issued the general pardons, he also revealed his Reconstruction policy. The Johnson plan provided that a provisional governor, appointed by the president, would call a state constitutional convention whose delegates would be chosen by those who had taken the prescribed loyalty oath. Johnson made it clear that he expected the conventions to refuse to pay the Confederate debt, and he recommended that they give the vote to educated blacks. Otherwise he gave them almost a free hand to decide what sort of governments their states would have. Once having complied with these lenient conditions, the states would be readmitted to the Union. Congress, Johnson assumed, would accept the result when it assembled in December.

In the next few months, each of the unreconstructed states held elections for a convention and adopted a new state constitution. Each acknowledged the end of slavery and all, except South Carolina, pledged not to pay debts incurred in supporting the Confederate war effort. No state conceded blacks the vote, however. Soon afterward, they held statewide elections for governor and other officials and chose state legislators and delegates to Congress. Satisfied that the states had met his conditions, Johnson ordered that the powers exercised by his provisional governors be transferred to the newly elected state officials.

The Johnson Governments. For several months the "Johnson governments" operated without restraint from Washington. Their deeds dismayed many northerners, strengthened the Radicals, and destroyed any possibility that Congress would accept the president's Reconstruction policy.

Two things, especially, offended northern Republicans. In the elections for state and federal offices southern voters turned frequently to former Confederates for leadership. To the upcoming Congress they elected four Confederate generals, five Confederate colonels, six Confederate cabinet officers, fifty-eight Confederate congressmen, and Alexander H. Stephens, who had been vice president of the Confederate State of America. Many newly elected state and local officials, too, had been active in the secession governments. These men all qualified for office because they had received pardons from the president. Whatever the hater of the planter elite had originally felt, it was clear by the end of 1865 that Johnson could not resist the appeal of these men when they came to him hat in hand and asked for forgiveness.

It was natural for white southerners to turn to former secessionists when choosing their leaders. To have done otherwise would have been to acknowledge a completely new order, a course that few communities ever accept willingly, and none in so short a time. But this blatant display of Confederate sympathies offended many northerners. Besides, it was only one of the "unforgivable" offenses resulting from the Johnson plan. Not only did the Johnson governments refuse to allow even a few blacks to vote; they also tried to permanently fix the status of blacks in southern society as an inferior one. In the so-called Black Codes the new state governments extended to the freedmen some rights previously reserved for the South's free population. Marriages between blacks, including earlier slave marriages, were legalized; freedmen were allowed to buy, own, and transfer property; and they were given the right, generally, to appear, plead, and testify in

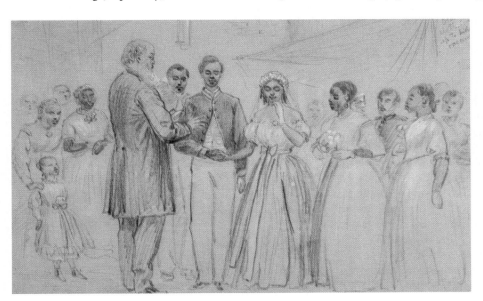

One of the real advances afforded by the emancipation was the legal recognition of black marriages. After 1865 black men and women seized the opportunity to solemnize relationships begun under slavery or to contract new ones. Officiating at this wedding is a chaplain from the Freedmen's Bureau.

court. But the Black Codes also placed the freedmen in a position of distinct legal inferiority to whites. Blacks could not enter into work contracts freely: These were subject to elaborate regulations supervised by a judge. Blacks had to conform to prescribed agricultural work rules. Those who desired to work at a trade, or anything besides farming, had to meet strict apprenticeship standards and, in many areas, to obtain a license. Any black man not gainfully employed might be treated as a vagrant and imprisoned or sentenced to hard labor. In Mississippi fines were imposed for idleness and for a long list of petty offenses; blacks who could not pay these might be hired out to anyone who would reimburse the local authorities for their labor. Blacks were also commonly forbidden to carry arms. They could be punished for a given crime more severely than white people. In some states the Black Codes even restricted where they could live and own property.

Many northerners saw little difference between these laws and the prewar slave codes. Republicans were deeply angered. The *Chicago Tribune* declared that the people of the North would turn one of the worst offending states, Mississippi, into a "frog pond" before they would allow its Black Code "to disgrace one foot of soil in which the bones of our soldiers sleep and over which the flag of freedom flies." Another critic called the codes "an outrage against civilization." Even some white southerners feared that the new legislation had gone too far and would provoke the North into a harsh response. Meanwhile, congressmen were receiving almost daily reports from southern white Unionists that the former secessionists were crowing about how they once again had the upper hand and would make life difficult for their Unionist opponents.

Congress Takes Over

By the time Congress assembled on December 4, 1865, the Republican majority—moderates as well as Radicals—were seething with anger at the Johnson governments. Many were also beginning to have second thoughts about the president himself, who was showing too much sympathy for ex-Confederates. When the southern delegations appeared in Washington seeking admission to the Congress, its irritated leaders refused to seat them and determined to take over the task of managing Reconstruction.

On the first day of the session Congress established the Joint Committee on Reconstruction to oversee all measures concerned with restoring the South to the Union. This committee consisted of fifteen senators and representatives, three of them Democrats, whose views ranged all the way from moderate to radical. Under the leadership of the sardonic Thaddeus Stevens of Pennsylvania, it soon became a vehicle for the Radicals.

The first act of congressional Reconstruction was a bill to extend the life of the Freedmen's Bureau and widen its authority. Established in March 1865, the bureau provided aid to refugees, both white and black. It distributed rations, found employment for freedmen, and supplied transportation home for those who had been displaced by the war. It had established hospitals and schools and had drawn up guidelines for bringing exslaves into the free labor market. In enlarging the bureau's scope, Congress gave it "military protection and jurisdiction" over all cases involving discrimination against freedmen.

Republican moderates considered the Freedmen's Bureau Bill a relatively mild measure justified by the South's apparent stubbornness, but Johnson refused to sign it. His stated grounds were that the military provisions of the measure took away the authority of existing civilian agencies. Many Republicans correctly interpreted his veto as resistance to a strict Reconstruction policy and an attempt to retain executive control of the restoration process.

The fight over the Freedmen's Bureau was the opening round of a struggle that lasted until the end of Johnson's term, with each new battle driving more and more moderates into the Radical camp. Soon after his veto, Johnson further offended the Republican leaders by calling Stevens and Senator Charles Sumner of Massachusetts "traitors" and "opponents of the fundamental principle of government." Still the moderates comtinued to hope that the president would accept reasonable proposals to protect the freedmen. With this in mind, Lyman Trumbull of Illinois submitted a civil rights bill to Congress that defined United States citizenship to include blacks and declared that all citizens must be accorded the "full and equal benefit of all laws and proceedings for the security of person and property. . . ." Most Republicans considered the bill a judicious measure and endorsed it. Nevertheless, the president responded with another veto. This time virtually all Republicans thought the president had gone too far, and Congress promptly overrode the veto.

The Fourteenth Amendment. While Congress and Johnson were fighting for supremacy, the joint committee set to work on a comprehensive plan for Reconstruction. The Thirteenth Amendment to the Constitution, adopted in December 1865, had confirmed Lincoln's Emancipation Proclamation of 1863 and officially abolished slavery, but it did nothing to make freedmen equal to whites under the law. The federal courts were clearly not too sympathetic to Republican policies. In the 1866 Milligan case, for example, they declared illegal the imposition of martial law on civilians in Indiana, a decision that went against the tough line Lincoln had taken toward antiwar Copperheads. The decision suggested that the courts were inclined to defend local rights against federal power. Who could say what they might do when they came to pass on Republican civil rights legislation? The joint committee's first effort, therefore, was to propose a Fourteenth Amendment to the Constitution that would define United States citizenship and guarantee individual rights. A constitutional amendment would place these rights beyond the power of contravention by the courts, the president, or the state governments.

As finally hammered out and submitted to the states, the Fourteenth Amendment was not all that the most radical of the Republican leaders desired. Congress had the chance to declare unconstitutional all political discrimination on racial grounds. Instead, it deferred to conservative opinion and continuing

northern racial prejudice by passing an evasive measure. Rather than giving the vote to all men, it merely declared that whenever a state denied any portion of its adult male population the right to vote, the representation of that state in Congress would be reduced proportionately. The South, with its large black population, would now have a powerful incentive to grant black men full voting rights, while the northern states, with few black residents, could continue to deny them their rights without serious penalty. Not until after the adoption of the Fifteenth Amendment (1870) were "race, color, and previous condition of servitude" eliminated as grounds for denying anyone the vote.

In addition to its voting provision, the Fourteenth Amendment defined national citizenship. It also excluded from state and federal office anyone who had taken an oath to uphold the constitution and had then engaged in "insurrection and rebellion." Moreover, it declared the federal debt a sacred obligation of the American people. The most important clause of the amendment extended the protection of the Constitution to citizens whose rights might be threatened by state governments. The original federal Bill of Rights had limited the power only of the federal government over citizens. Now the Constitution would limit the states as well. No state, this important provision de-

Reconstruction of the South, 1865–1877

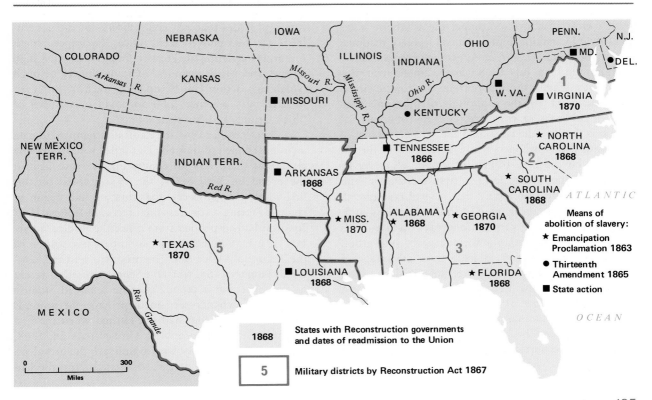

Means of abolition of slavery:

★ Emancipation Proclamation 1863

● Thirteenth Amendment 1865

■ State action

1868 — States with Reconstruction governments and dates of readmission to the Union

5 — Military districts by Reconstruction Act 1867

clared, could "make or enforce any law which shall abridge the privileges or immunities of citizens of the United States; nor shall any state deprive any person of life, liberty, or property, without due process of law; nor deny to any person within its jurisdiction the equal protection of the laws."

In specifically restricting the franchise to males, the Fourteenth Amendment was a severe disappointment to women's rights reformers, many of whom had hoped that Union victory would result in suffrage for women as well as blacks. With ratification of the Fourteenth Amendment, the Constitution itself now implicitly denied women the vote, and a new amendment would be required to allow women to vote in federal elections. This setback split the women's rights advocates between those who supported black suffrage even if it was restricted to males and those who decided that they could no longer allow the struggle for racial justice to delay women's progress to full citizenship. By 1870 two women's rights groups, the more militant, New York-based National Woman Suffrage Association (led by Elizabeth Cady Stanton and Susan B. Anthony) and the more conservative, Boston-based American Woman Suffrage Association (led by Lucy Stone and Thomas Wentworth Higginson), had been organized.

The First Reconstruction Act.

The passage of the Fourteenth Amendment in June 1866 was followed by a concerted effort to compel the southern states to ratify it by making approval a condition of readmission to the Union. Despite congressional pressure, however, not until late July 1868 was the amendment ratified. Meanwhile, the supporters of congressional Reconstruction and the supporters of Johnson's plan vied for public endorsement. In the 1866 congressional elections the president adopted the unusual policy of stumping the North personally to win votes for his position. He did little to help his cause. Wherever he went, his opponents heckled him mercilessly and goaded him into rash replies that seemed undignified. In the end the Radicals won a decisive victory—anti-Johnson Republicans carried Congress by a two-thirds majority. Radical legislation would now be veto-proof.

The new Congress quickly took advantage of its mandate. In March 1867, over the president's veto, Congress passed the Reconstruction Act. The most comprehensive piece of congressional Reconstruction legislation, this measure voided the Johnson governments and divided the South into five military districts, each under the jurisdiction of a general and subject to martial law. The generals were to supervise a new constitution-making process in which blacks must be allowed to participate. Any constitution adopted by these conventions must uphold the principles that black men could vote but ex-Confederates would be excluded from both voting and officeholding. When a state had adopted a new constitution, and when it had ratified the Fourteenth Amendment and that amendment had become part of the federal Constitution, *then* that state would be allowed to seat its delegation in Congress. In the following months Congress passed several additional Reconstruction acts to reinforce the first and override southern delaying tactics.

Johnson Impeached.

Johnson did what he could to frustrate the Reconstruction Act of 1867. He appointed five military governors who he knew would interpret their powers narrowly to favor white conservatives rather than blacks and local Radicals. And he continued to use his pardoning power, enabling former rebels to regain control of lands that had been seized by the federal government.

Congress feared that Johnson would undermine its Reconstruction program through the hostile use of his executive powers. To hedge him in, it passed the Tenure of Office Act in March 1867, which prohibited the president from dismissing officials appointed with the advice and consent of the Senate without that body's approval. But its only sure weapon against the president's hostility was impeachment. The Constitution provides that all "civil officers" of the government can be removed from office "on Impeachment for, and Conviction of, Treason, Bribery, or other high Crimes and Misdemeanors." The machinery through which this action can be taken is unclear, but even murkier was whether Johnson could be accused of "high Crimes and Misdemeanors."

In December 1867 the Radicals attempted to pass an impeachment resolution. This failed when it became clear that there was no convincing evidence against the president. Well before the House voted on this first resolution, however, the situation had begun to change. During a congressional recess in August 1867 Johnson had suspended from office the Radical secretary of war, Edwin Stanton, in apparent violation of the Tenure of Office Act. The president restored Stanton in January 1868, when the Senate refused to accept his removal, but a month later he removed Stanton again. This defiance seemed to provide the grounds for impeachment that had not existed when the first resolution had been proposed. On February 24, 1868, the House formally resolved to impeach the president.

The impeachment trial, conducted before the Senate sitting as a court, was the show trial of the century. The major charge against the president was his "unlawful" removal of Stanton. Attorney General Henry Stanbery, the president's counsel, based his defense on the fact that Stanton had been appointed by Lincoln, not Johnson. Consequently, Stanbery argued, he was not covered by the Tenure of Office Act. In any case, the law was probably unconstitutional, and it was the right of the president to test it by violating it and bringing it before the courts. Furthermore, Stanton was still in office (he had refused to leave), so no law had actually been broken.

During the six weeks of the trial intense excitement reigned in Washington and the country. Radicals insisted that acquittal would be a victory for rebels and traitors. The president had frustrated the clearly expressed will of the nation's duly elected legislators by pardoning rebels wholesale and by appointing officials to administer the Reconstruction Act who would not carry it out as they were required to. He must be stopped. Democrats and Johnson's remaining moderate supporters within Republican ranks claimed that conviction would mean that Congress had successfully usurped the power of the executive branch. The president's defenders also noted that his removal would have political consequences. The man next in line for the presidency was the president pro tempore of the Senate, the truculent Radical Benjamin Wade.

When the decision finally came on May 16, 1868, Johnson was acquitted by one vote. He should not have been impeached in the first place. There can be no question that he was stubborn, at times undignified, and that he used his executive power to impede Congress. Nor is there much dispute among scholars today that his policies were misguided. In a parliamentary system like Britain's he would probably have been removed by a legislative vote of no confidence. But the Founding Fathers had deliberately created an independently elected executive with the right to disagree with Congress. It seems unlikely that they intended impeachment to serve as a way to remove an official from office except for breaking the law or for gross incapacity. Through impeachment, then, the Radicals were actually seeking to change the Constitution.

Reconstruction in the South

Johnson's term came to an end soon after. There is evidence that the president had been trying since 1866 to win the favor of the Democrats, his former party, in order to secure the Democratic nomination in 1868. But instead they turned to Horatio Seymour, the wartime governor of New York. The Republicans chose General Ulysses S. Grant. On a platform that simultaneously promised justice for southern Unionists and freedmen and peace between the sections, Grant won a decisive victory.

By the time the new president was inaugurated, the governments organized under the congressional Reconstruction acts—composed of white and black Republicans and decidedly Radical in temper—had

In August 1866 Johnson announced that "peace, order, tranquility, and civil authority now exist . . . in the United States." Dissatisfied with Johnson's idea of peace and order, the House voted his impeachment less than two years later. Here a packed gallery follows the trial of the century.

been admitted to the Union, and the Fourteenth Amendment had been incorporated into the Constitution. In a narrow legal sense, Reconstruction was now complete. But in fact, the situation in the newly restored states remained uncertain and tense.

Economic Recovery. Several important changes had taken place in the South since April 1865. Physical reconstruction had proceeded at a rapid pace. Southern railroads were quickly rebuilt after Appomattox and then extended to additional regions. Between 1865 and 1879, 7,000 miles of track were added to the southern rail network. Much of the needed capital was supplied by investors in the North and in Britain, who anticipated a more favorable business climate in the South. The southern state governments, both the Johnson regimes and the ones established under Congress's formula, also contributed, going heavily into debt to lend money to railroad enterprises. Industry also recovered. In 1860 southern cotton mills boasted 300,000 spindles. By 1880 these had increased to over 530,000. Between the same two dates southern manufactures as a whole increased in value almost 55 percent.

Many southerners had expected even more spectacular advances. Now that slavery was dead and the plantation class that had discouraged manufacturing was out of favor, the South, some felt, would flourish industrially. Until the 1880s such hopes were largely unrealized. Still, the rebound of industry and transportation from immediate postwar lows was remarkable.

During the period 1865–1877 agriculture continued to be the chief element in the southern economy, and the war did little to shift southern agriculture from its traditional emphasis on corn and cotton. If anything, cotton became even more important after 1865 than before the war. For a year or two after Appomattox cotton prices remained high. Though cotton was taxed heavily by the federal government—vengefully, southerners believed—high cotton prices helped put money into the pockets of a needy people. It took years to restore cotton production to prewar levels, but by 1878 the South's cotton output had almost reached its prewar peak. Thereafter, it grew steadily, and by the 1890s the region was producing twice as many bales as in 1859.

Tenantry and Sharecropping. By the end of the century the social basis of southern agriculture had been thoroughly transformed. Before the war, defenders of slavery had denied that blacks could function in a free labor market. During the war the Treasury Department, under Secretary Chase's prompting, put this the-

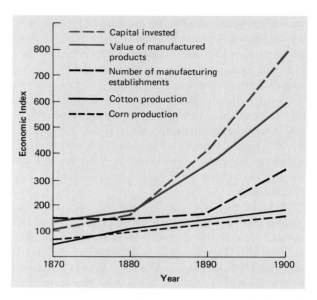

The economic recovery of former confederate states, 1870–1900

Note: Indexed at 1860 = 100
Source: *Twelfth Census of the United States, 1900: Agriculture.*

ory to the test in an interesting experiment in the South Carolina Sea Islands near Port Royal. The experiment demonstrated that when ex-slaves were given land, they made successful farmers. A similar experiment undertaken by Grant at Davis Bend, Mississippi, also proved successful. Unfortunately, neither test benefited the freedmen. The Port Royal venture collapsed when the Treasury Department failed to transfer land title to the freedmen as it had promised, selling the abandoned Sea Island property to the highest bidder instead. The Davis Bend property was returned to planters armed with pardons from President Johnson.

The efforts to create a class of black farm owners in the South did not cease with these two instances. After 1865 Thaddeus Stevens and other Republicans in Congress advocated giving freedmen lands confiscated from "rebels" during the war. Only landowning could protect blacks against exploitation and keep them from being reinslaved, Stevens and people of like mind insisted. Former slaves themselves yearned to become landowners. "We all know that the colored people want land," a South Carolina carpetbagger declared. "Night and day they think and dream of it. It is their all and all." Whitelaw Reid in his trip south quoted an old black man: "What's de use of bein' free if you don't own land enough to be buried? Might juss as well stay slave all yo days."

Wishes were often transformed into vivid expectations. Many blacks, hearing the opinions of Stevens and his colleagues, came to believe that the government intended to give them "forty acres and a mule" and were bitterly disappointed when it proved untrue. Some acreage was turned over to freedmen. Radical-controlled South Carolina set up a program to sell land on easy terms to exslaves. By 1890 the state Land Commission had given some 2,000 black families title to their own farms. In 1866, Congress passed the Southern Homestead Act, providing free land for blacks and whites alike on the federal domain in the former slave states.

In the end, however, a large black yeomen class failed to appear. The lands available in the South for homesteading were isolated and infertile, and few if any black families were able to make a success of farming them. Congress might have followed Stevens's advice and turned over all seized Confederate land to the freedmen. It might even have "nationalized" all southern land and redistributed it as various revolutionary governments have done in our time. But ultimately the Radicals were not so very radical, and their respect for private property rights—even those of ex-rebels—took precedence over their concern for the freedmen. Most were certain that the ballot offered sufficient protection to the freedmen; a social revolution was not needed.

There was another way that freedmen might have become landowners: Black southerners might have accumulated some money and bought land. Southern land prices were low in the 1870s, and a few hundred dollars could have bought a black family a small farm. In 1865, Congress chartered the Freedmen's Bank to support such black self-help efforts. But the bank was poorly managed and could not withstand the financial Panic of 1873. When it closed its doors the following year, it took with it over $3 million of hard-won savings from thousands of black depositors.

Though few southern blacks ever became yeoman farmers, they did remain on the land. For a short while after Appomattox most worked for wages under contracts supervised by the Freedmen's Bureau. But this system pleased neither blacks nor their employers. Cash was difficult for landowners to find in the months following the war, so money wages were hard to pay. The bureau tried to guarantee payment, but employers often fell behind in their obligations anyway. The freedmen, of course, resented such treatment and also disliked the harshness with which some bureau agents enforced labor contracts against them. Still more unsatisfactory from the freedmen's point of view was the return to gang work and the planters' close supervision of every aspect of their labor and their lives. The system reminded them too much of slavery and seemed a mockery of freedom.

Out of this mutual dissatisfaction with wage-paid agricultural labor emerged a tenant farmer system that by 1880 had become characteristic of the South. Tenantry took many forms and included whites as well as blacks. Thousands of Confederate privates returned home to become, not successful planters, but tenants on lands owned by former slaveholders. Tenants might pay rent either in cash or in part of the crop, typically cotton. Though the system was not as desirable as ownership, a cash tenant was at least free from constant supervision and sometimes could save enough to buy land.

The greater number of tenants farmers, however, especially among the freedmen, were sharecroppers, who turned over their crops to the landowner in exchange for either half the proceeds or perhaps two-thirds if the tenant did not have to borrow mule and plow from the landlord. Linked to sharecropping was the crop-lien system, a credit arrangement by which a storekeeper (who sometimes was also the landlord)

The status of farm operators in former slave states, 1900

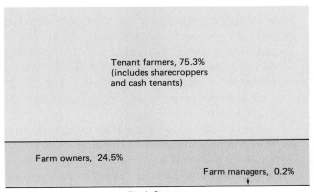

Tenant farmers, 75.3% (includes sharecroppers and cash tenants)

Farm owners, 24.5%

Farm managers, 0.2%

Black Status

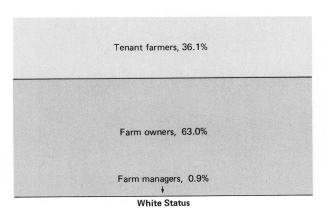

Tenant farmers, 36.1%

Farm owners, 63.0%

Farm managers, 0.9%

White Status

would extend credit to the tenant for supplies during the crop-growing season. When the harvest came and the cotton was sold, the tenant would then repay the debt. Buying on credit was expensive since it included an interest charge. It also gave dishonest storekeepers a chance to cheat. Because they kept the books, they had the upper hand and often juggled the debits and credits to suit themselves. Tenants who could not meet their debts could not change the merchant they dealt with; they remained tied to him almost like serfs.

The freedmen's lot represented a missed opportunity for the nation. This is not to say that freedom was no better than slavery. Some blacks managed to become landowners despite all the difficulties. Most were released from the degradation of close personal supervision by whites. Economically they were better off as sharecroppers than as slaves. Roger Ransom and Richard Sutch conclude in a recent study that whereas slaves received in food, clothing, housing, medical attention, about 20 percent of what they produced for their masters, sharecroppers obtained a full

They were free, but the economic condition of most black sharecroppers and tenant farmers was not dramatically better than that of slaves. Redistribution of confiscated plantation lands might have improved their lot, but the government, which gave millions of acres to railroads, was not so generous to its newest citizens.

half of their total output. In addition, blacks were now able to make decisions about their lives that they never were allowed to make before. Almost all decided that black women would no longer work in the fields; like white women, they would stay home and become proper housewives and mothers. Unfortunately, these gains were a one-time advance, made just after the war. Thereafter, while the country as a whole became richer, black living standards remained stagnant.

Indeed, the sharecrop–crop-lien system proved to be an economic trap for the entire lower South. Because they did not own the land, sharecroppers had no incentive to improve it. Landlords, too, had little incentive, for they could only hope to recover a portion of the greater output that might come from additional capital investment. This arrangement also tied the South to a one-crop system and prevented diversification. As one sharecropper complained in the 1880s: "We ought to plant less [cotton and tobacco] and more grain and grasses, but how are we to do it; the man who furnishes us with rations at 50 percent interest won't let us; he wants money crops planted." Failure to diversify produced serious soil exhaustion that could only be offset by expensive additions of fertilizers. Worse still, cotton prices steadily declined for a generation after 1865, pulling down the entire cotton-tied Southern rural economy. Farms in the North and West, though they, too, had problems, came to look neater and more prosperous after 1865. Meanwhile, travelers in the rural South told of weed-choked farmyards, sagging unpainted shacks, and ragged, discouraged-looking people, black and white. With each year the South fell further behind the rest of the nation in almost every measure of material and social well-being: literacy, infant mortality, and per-capita income.

Cultural Change. Whatever the long-term economic effects, the end of slavery brought immense social and cultural gains for black Americans. Black men and women enjoyed a new freedom of movement, which some exercised by going to the cities or escaping to more prosperous parts of the country. At the end of Reconstruction several thousand blacks left the lower South and moved north or west. A particularly large movement of "exodusters" to Kansas after 1878 alarmed southern white leaders, who feared that the South might lose its labor force.

The end of slavery freed blacks to express themselves as never before. Slavery had not destroyed black culture, but it had made it difficult for blacks to demonstrate the full range of their talents and to exercise their organizational abilities. The end of formal bondage released energies previously held in check. Blacks withdrew from white churches in large numbers and formed their own. Particularly successful were the Baptists and Methodists. By 1870 there were 500,000 black Baptists; in 1876 the African Methodist Episcopal church had 200,000 members. These churches gave talented former slaves an opportunity to demonstrate leadership beyond anything previously possible. Unlike politics, which was largely closed to talented black men after 1877, the ministry continued to provide leadership opportunities.

The end of slavery also expanded educational opportunities for blacks. Before the war slaves had been legally denied education. After 1865 northern philanthropists seized on Dixie as missionary territory. As one Yankee benefactor remarked, South Carolina needed only "freedom and education" to become "another Massachusetts." In the months after Appomattox hundreds of Yankee teachers, hoping to uplift a benighted region, went South to establish schools and bring the blessings of literacy. The Freedmen's Bureau also labored to end illiteracy and sought to train blacks in trades. The most permanent impact was achieved by self-help. Before long every southern state, under Radical guidance, had made some provision for educating black children. The southern educational system long remained segregated (except for a time in the cosmopolitan city of New Orleans) and poor; yet the schools managed to make a dent in ignorance. By 1880 a quarter of all blacks could read and write; twenty years later the figure had risen to half. College training for blacks, nonexistent in the South before 1860, became available. No blacks were admitted to the established southern state universities, but southern state governments founded separate black colleges and universites. Meanwhile, the Freedmen's Bureau and white philanthropists helped charter such strong back private colleges as Atlanta University, Fisk in Tennessee, and Howard in Washington, D.C. Black education—indeed, all southern education—had a long way to go before it caught up with the North; but compared with the accomplishments before 1860, the gains of the generation following the war were truly impressive.

Yet segregation remained a central fact of life in the South. In 1875 Congress passed a strongly worded Civil Rights Act guaranteeing to all persons, regardless of color, "the full and equal enjoyment of all the accommodations . . . of inns, public conveyances . . . , theaters, and other places of public amusement"; but separation and social inequality persisted. In most communities trains, buses, and theaters had white and black sections. In private life the racial spheres were even more exclusive, and blacks were almost never invited to the homes of white people. Even southern Radicals seldom treated blacks as social equals.

The Southern Radical Governments.

To black Americans at the time, however, the greatest disappointment of Reconstruction was its political failure. Accepting blacks as political equals and even, in the case of black officials, as superiors was completely alien to the established values and customs of the white South.

Yet the governments set up under the 1867 Reconstruction Act allowed blacks an important role in local governments. They voted in the elections supervised by the five regional military commanders, and many were returned to office as state legislators and in other official capacities. Blacks did not, however, dominate the Radical Republican state regimes that congressional Reconstruction brought to power. Even in South Carolina, where blacks outnumbered whites in the total population, they held only a minority of leadership positions.

One of the persistent myths of Reconstruction is that black political leaders during the years of Republican rule were unusually corrupt or incompetent. Among the fifteen black southerners elected to Congress were a number of exceptionally intelligent, educated, and able men. Senator Blanche K. Bruce of Mississippi was an effective legislator who, had he been white, would have been a power in the land. On the level of state government, black officials ranged from excellent to poor. All in all, as legislators and politicians, their record did not noticeably diverge from the contemporary white southern average.

It used to be said, too, that white Republicans were a deplorable bunch of dishonest opportunists. This view is also invalid. Some of the white Radicals who ruled the postwar South were idealists who were committed to establishing a new order. Most were probably practical realists who believed it to the South's advantage to accept change. Carpetbaggers—northerners who came South after the war—were not all adventurers interested only in quick gains. Some had sincerely cast their lot with their new communities. And numbered among the native southern scalawags were many former Unionists and a large portion of the South's business class, as well as planters who before the war had voted Whig. These people were attracted to the Republican party because they approved of its commercial and industrial policies, because of their traditional Whiggish differences with the Democrats, or because

When the Freedmen's Bureau set up schools for blacks, former slaves of all ages flocked to them. Wrote Booker T. Washington, "It was a whole race trying to go to school." The Snow Hill School, here, abandoned classical education in favor of industrial training, which was deemed more appropriate to black needs.

of humanitarian considerations. In any case, they were not the tiny minority of the white population that we would expect if they had been merely dissatisfied troublemakers. In 1872, for example, 20 percent of the South's white voters were Republicans.

In general, the Radical-dominated southern state governments were remarkably effective and reasonably honest. Of course, measured by the standards of the tightfisted prewar South, they were big spenders and ran up huge debts. But the job of rebuilding and adjusting to the new circumstances required a great deal of money. The new governments contributed freely to railroads and other businesses. They established the South's first state-supported school systems and sharply increased public spending for poor relief, prisons, and state hospitals. Though still far behind the North in providing social services, under Radical rule the South began to catch up with the nineteenth century.

The new Radical governments were also more democratic than the prewar regimes. The state constitutions adopted under congressional Reconstruction made many previously appointive offices elective and gave yeoman farmers better representation in the legislature than they had had before the war. They also gave the vote to white males who did not meet the old property qualifications. The new state governments reduced the number of crimes punishable by death,

and granted married women more secure control over their property, as the North had done before 1860.

"Redemption." Despite these accomplishments, many white southerners despised the radical regimes and accused them of corruption. Some were in fact corrupt, but generally no more than was normal in state affairs during those years. Southern conservatives also disliked the reforms they initiated, because they were new, because they seemed to be Yankee-inspired, and because they were expensive. Landlords, in particular, denounced the new programs because they raised taxes on real estate. But above all, conservatives found it difficult to accept the Republican-dominated state governments because they were part of the new racial regime. After 250 years of regarding blacks as inherently inferior, the white South could not easily agree to changes that declared a black person the political equal of a white one.

A fierce struggle for political control soon developed in the South between the forces of the new era and those of the old. Radical Union Leagues helped to rally black and scalawag voters in support of Republican candidates for state and local offices. The Radicals also had influential friends in Washington, and after 1869, when Grant became president, they had the support of the federal executive branch. For a while they succeeded in holding on to office, especially in states where they were most firmly entrenched—Alabama, Mississippi, Texas, Florida, Louisiana, and South Carolina. But in the end they could not match the experience, self-confidence, and ruthlessness of the defenders of bygone times, who hoped to "redeem" the South from "Black Republicanism."

A major weapon of the "redeemers" was the Ku Klux Klan. Formed in 1866 by young Confederate veterans primarily as a social club, the Klan quickly became an antiblack, anti-Radical organization. At the outset it used fear and superstition to intimidate blacks. Hooded, mounted Klansmen would swoop down at night on isolated cabins, making fearsome noises and firing guns. Later they resorted to more violent methods. The Klansmen burned black homes, attacked and beat black militiamen, ambushed both white and black Radical leaders, and lynched blacks accused of crimes.

At its height in the late 1860s, the Klan went virtually unchecked. Then in 1870 and 1871 Congress passed three Force Bills, which collectively declared "armed combinations" and the Klan's terrorist activities illegal. Designed to enforce Reconstruction programs, the bills gave the president the right to prosecute in federal courts those who prevented qualified persons from voting. Grant invoked the measures in nine South Carolina counties, and soon hundreds were indicted for Klan activities.

The Klan quickly declined, but by the 1870s racism was thoroughly institutionalized in Democratic politics. The determination of southern conservatives to render blacks submissive and to take control of the South away from Radicals and their supporters persisted. The redeemers abandoned hooded robes and night rides, but not other forms of intimidation. Typical of their approach was the successful effort in 1875 to return Mississippi to conservative control. There the redeemers ostracized the scalawags and drove many white Republicans to abandon politics or change their party. One who gave in to their tactics, Colonel James Lusk, told a black fellow Republican: "No white man can live in the South in the future and act with any other than the Democratic party unless he is willing and prepared to live a life of social isolation and remain in political oblivion."

Black voters could not be so easily forced to abandon the party that had served them so well, but here tougher tactics were often effective. Blacks who continued to vote Republican were denied jobs or fired from those they had. More stubborn black Republicans were threatened with violence. During the 1875 state election thousands of white Democrats armed themselves with rifles and shotguns, and then, to make the message clear, entered the names of black Republicans in "dead books." In Vicksburg, Yazoo City, and other Mississippi towns blacks were shot and killed in pre-election fights.

The campaign worked. The Democrats captured the Mississippi legislature and elected the only state official running for office. The Republican governor, Adelburt Ames, faced with impeachment by the new legislature, agreed to resign. Mississippi had been "redeemed." Similar processes took place in most of the other states, so that by 1876 only Louisiana, Florida, and South Carolina remained under Republican administrations—and these regimes stayed in power only because they were protected by federal troops.

The End of Reconstruction. Clearly the redeemers were effective tacticians and organizers. But if the commitment of northerners to Radical rule in the South had not been weakening, the redeemers would not

Secret societies like the Knights of the White Camelia, the Pale Faces, and the Knights of the Ku Klux Klan organized to frustrate Reconstruction. Describing itself as an "institution of Chivalry, Humanity, Mercy, and Patriotism," the Klan violently intimidated blacks.

"The negroes of the South are free—
free as air," says the parliamentary Wat-
terson. This is what the *State*, a well-
known Democratic organ of Tennessee,
says, in huge capitals on the subject:
"Let it be known before the election that
the farmers have agreed to spot every
leading Radical negro in the county, and
treat him as an enemy for all time to come.
The rotten ring must and shall be broken
at any and all cost. The Democrats have
determined to withdraw all employment
from their enemies. Let this fact be
known."

Southern black voters after 1865 were alternately courted and coerced by white politicians. The Democrats found force more necessary than did the Republicans to win
black votes. In this Radical Republican cartoon two Democrats (the one at right looking
remarkably like Jefferson Davis) make no pretense of winning "hearts and minds."

have succeeded. The decline of northerners' determination had several sources. To an increasingly large number of Republicans, it began to seem that the defense
of the black man was merely an excuse for continued
domination by the corrupt wing of their party. Whenever a new scandal was uncovered in the Grant administration—and there were many—it would be blotted
out by an appeal to Republican unity against the ex-
rebels, a process usually referred to as "waving the
bloody shirt." The problem of how to deal with the
blacks and their oppressors always seemed to justify
continued Republican ascendancy. By the middle of
the 1870s many who had once supported the Republican party concluded that abandoning the blacks and
their friends in the South was better than continuing
to uphold a corrupt party.

Fatigue and racism also played their parts. How
long, many northerners asked, could the country invest

energy and money to sustain a system that the "best
elements" of southern society opposed? Clearly, they
said, blacks would never make good citizens, and there
was no point in continuing the hopeless battle. Such
arguments were reinforced by a growing conviction
among northern commercial and industrial groups that
peace in the South would be better for business than
the political agitation that constantly disturbed the
nation.

The end came in 1876. In the presidential election
of that year the Democrats nominated Samuel J. Tilden
of New York, a stuffy but honest corporation lawyer.
The Republican candidate was Rutherford B. Hayes,
the equally upright and unapproachable governor of
Ohio. The Democratic platform promised to withdraw
federal troops from the South and endorsed traditional
Democratic low-tariff, small-government positions.
The Republicans declared that they would never aban-

don the black man and would continue to support positive government, a protective tariff, and "sound money."

The election was so close that the results were challenged. The Democrats claimed they had carried New York, New Jersey, Connecticut, Indiana, and the entire South. The Republicans insisted that the votes of Florida, Louisiana, and South Carolina—the "unredeemed" states—rightfully belonged to them. They also challenged one Democratic vote in Oregon, where electors had split between the two candidates. As in 1824, the election was thrown into the House of Representatives. For the next four months the country's political life was in an uproar as the politicians tried to settle the issue before Inauguration Day in March 1877.

Both sides brought every weapon to bear on the dispute—propaganda, legal maneuvering, congressional commissions, and threats of violence. Some historians believe that one hidden but vitally important issue during the disputed election period was railroads. The Republicans had favored government land grants to encourage completion of the national rail network.

The Democrats, however, disliked federal aid, and on many occasions leading northern Democrats had attacked the land-grant policy. At the time of the disputed election, a major grant of special importance to southern commercial and business interests was being considered in Congress. The beneficiary of this gift was the Texas and Pacific Railroad, designed to connect New Orleans and other important southern cities with the Pacific Coast. The rail link, it was believed, would bring wealth to many communities in the South. A Democratic administration, of course, would remove the troops from the remaining unredeemed states and end Reconstruction, but it would also certainly oppose the Texas and Pacific rail project. This reasoning, it is said, led influential southern leaders, many of whom were former Whigs with little love for the Democrats, to seek a bargain with the Republicans. In return for a promise to remove the troops, to give some high political office to southerners, and to support a Texas and Pacific land grant, southerners in the House of Representatives agreed to support Republican Hayes. Many scholars believe that this bargain, known as

Election of 1876

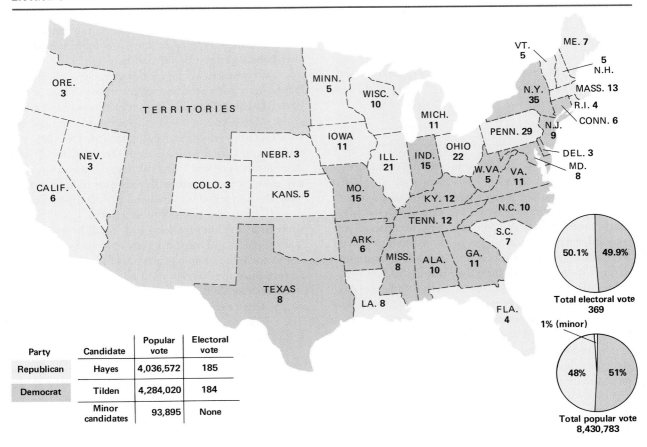

Party	Candidate	Popular vote	Electoral vote
Republican	Hayes	4,036,572	185
Democrat	Tilden	4,284,020	184
	Minor candidates	93,895	None

Total electoral vote 369

Total popular vote 8,430,783

The Compromise of 1877 was a political deal; Hayes was only elected when he, in effect, made promises to end Reconstruction. Neither southern Democrats nor northern Republicans wanted their dealing made public, so they met in secret sessions like this.

the Compromise of 1877, gave Hayes the election. Others deny that such a wide-ranging agreement occurred. Instead, they argue, the southerners merely traded electoral votes for removing federal troops from the South. There was no economic deal. In any event, soon after Hayes's inauguration as nineteenth president of the United States, the last federal troops were withdrawn from the South. The redeemers quickly moved in. Reconstruction was over.

Conclusions

Reconstruction was not an unrelieved disaster. During these momentous years southerners repaired the physical devastation of the war and reestablished their states' constitutional relations with the Union. Meanwhile, black southerners were able to create for themselves important new islands of freedom—freedom to move, freedom to establish social and cultural institutions of their own, freedom for black women to leave the fields. Also on the credit side were the Radical-sponsored Fourteenth and Fifteenth amendments. Once implanted in the Constitution, they would become the bases for a "second Reconstruction" in our own day.

Yet there is much that is dismaying about Reconstruction. In general, Americans of the era failed to meet the great challenges that faced them. Instead of a prosperous black yeomanry, the South would be left with a mass of impoverished semipeons who for generations would be a reproach to America's proud claims of prosperity and equality. Instead of political democracy, Reconstruction would bequeath a legacy of sectional fraud, intimidation, and shameless racial exclusion. Rather than accelerating southern economic growth, Reconstruction would chain the South to a declining staple crop agriculture and leave it ever further behind the rest of the nation.

Who was to blame for this debacle? One answer is that Americans were trapped by the past. Deep-seated prejudices and memories of slavery blinded most white southerners—and many northerners—to the need for racial justice. Traditional individualism and the commitment to self-help obscured the fact that the special circumstances of black dependence resulting from slavery called for imaginative government aid. And there were the accidents of events and personalities. Would Lincoln have seen realities more clearly? Certainly the succession of Andrew Johnson, a stubborn man of limited vision and conventional racial views, did nothing to solve the unique problems of the day. Refusing to recognize the North's need to exact some penance from the defeated South, he needlessly antagonized even moderates and drove them into the Radical camp. The result was a legacy of sectional hatred that poisoned American political life for generations.

Meanwhile, the nation was turning away from the intractable "southern problem" to what many citizens believed were more important matters. The South and Reconstruction became increasingly remote as the country at large experienced a surge of economic expansion that dwarfed anything of the past.

For Further Reading

Eric L. McKitrick. *Andrew Johnson and Reconstruction* (1960)

Andrew Johnson's personality is emphasized in this study of Reconstruction. McKitrick says that Johnson was easily flattered and irrationally stubborn when defied. Most serious of his deficiencies, however, was that he failed to see that the North needed evidence of southern contrition before it could forgive and allow a return to normal relations between the sections.

Clement Eaton. *The Waning of the Old South Civilization, 1860–1880* (1968)

An excellent short summary of life among the common people and the planter elite in 1860, the effect of the war on southern culture, the postwar white adjustment to freed blacks, economic recovery, and the "cultural lag" especially evident in small towns and rural areas. Eaton concludes that the New South retained much of the old, especially its devotion to states' rights, white supremacy, and the cult of southern womanhood. In the brief generation since this book was written, much has changed, however.

Albion W. Tourgée. *A Fool's Errand: A Novel of the South During Reconstruction* (1879). Edited by George M. Frederickson (1966)

An autobiographical novel by a "carpetbagger" lawyer from Ohio who settled in North Carolina after the Civil War. As a Radical superior court judge, Tourgée was hated by white conservatives for his attempts to bring Ku Klux Klan leaders to justice. His estimate of the role of idealistic carpetbaggers is summed up in his title.

Allen W. Trelease. *White Terror: The Ku Klux Klan Conspiracy and Southern Reconstruction* (1971)

The big, definitive study of the first Klan after the Civil War. This is a potent indictment of the KKK and all its doings.

Joel Williamson. *After Slavery: The Negro in South Carolina During Reconstruction, 1861–1877* (1965)

In this detailed, interesting study of race relations in one key Reconstruction state, Williamson concludes that racial segregation was not wholly a product of "redemption." He also deals with efforts by South Carolina Radicals to provide "land for the landless."

Willie Lee Rose. *Rehearsal for Reconstruction: The Port Royal Experiment* (1964)

The efforts of the northerners who attempted to give the former Sea Island slaves their masters' land are tragicomic in Rose's account. Ultimately the ex-slaves lost the rich cotton lands to their former owners. Yet the temporary success of the Port Royal experiment tells us what might have been if the northern commitment to black freedom and racial justice had been stronger.

Roger Ransom and Richard Sutch. *One Kind of Freedom: The Economic Consequences of Emancipation* (1977)

An important book by two "cliometricians" about how emancipation affected the economic well-being of the freedmen and the South as a whole. Has an interesting discussion of the sharecrop–crop-lien system.

LaWanda Cox and John Cox. *Politics, Principles, and Prejudice, 1865–1866: Dilemma of Reconstruction America* (1963)

A study of presidential Reconstruction that gives the Radicals much credit for idealism and suggests how much politics actually entered into Andrew Johnson's decisions. Reverses the older pattern of blaming the Radicals and praising Johnson.

Leon Litwack. *Been in the Storm So Long: The Aftermath of Slavery* (1980)

Professor Litwack tells us—at somewhat excessive length—what black men and women felt about the new world of freedom after 1863. He shows that their reactions were amazingly diverse and often contradictory.

Herbert Gutman. *The Black Family in Slavery and Freedom, 1750–1925* (1976)

Excellent social history, not only of the slavery period, but also of the postslavery experience of black families.

Kenneth Stampp. *The Era of Reconstruction, 1865–1877* (1965)

An excellent overall view of the "new" Reconstruction history. Stampp attacks the myth that Reconstruction meant federal tyranny and "Negro rule." He considers the failure to redistribute property to the freedmen a mistake, but believes the Radicals were governed by idealism rather than greed or pure politics.

C. Vann Woodward. *Reunion and Reaction: The Compromise of 1877 and the End of Reconstruction* (1951)

The dean of southern historians concludes that the agreement to end the presidential election dispute of 1876/1877 was not a bargain made purely in the interest of political peace and orderly government. Rather, it was a behind-the-scenes agreement to exchange continued Republican supremacy for major economic favors to southern business groups. Not all scholars buy his thesis.

Chapter 17

The Triumph of Industrialism

What Were the Causes, What Were the Costs?

1862, 1864   Pacific Railroad Acts

1866   The National Labor Union is established

1869   The Knights of Labor

1873   The Slaughterhouse cases • Financial panic; unemployment climbs to 12 percent

1877   The Compromise of 1877: Rutherford B. Hayes elected president • U.S. Supreme Court decides the Granger cases • Socialist Labor party is established

1880   James A. Garfield elected president

1881   Garfield assassinated; Chester A. Arthur becomes president

1882   John D. Rockefeller forms the first "trust," but it is dissolved by Ohio courts • Edison's first electric generating station opens in New York • The San Mateo case

1884   Grover Cleveland elected president

1886   Haymarket Riot in Chicago • Samuel Gompers founds the American Federation of Labor (AFL) • *Santa Clara Co.* v. *Southern Pacific Railroad*

1888   Benjamin Harrison elected president

1890   Sherman Antitrust Act

1892   Grover Cleveland elected president for the second time • Populist party is established

1893   Sherman Silver Purchase Act is repealed • The American Railway Union is organized by Eugene V. Debs

1894   Pullman strike is ended by federal troops

1895   E. C. *Knight* case weakens Sherman Antitrust Act

1896   William McKinley elected president

1897   *Maximum Freight Rates* case

1901   McKinley is assassinated; Theodore Roosevelt becomes president • Eugene V. Debs's Socialist party is founded

1904—12   Socialist party membership increases to 130,000

1913   Federal Reserve System established

A lmost every portion of the economy grew at breakneck speed during the post–Civil War period. Mining, construction, agriculture—all showed remarkable gains. Yet the most impressive advance was in industry. The farm sector of the economy in 1869 produced over 22.2 percent of the nation's income. By 1910 it had fallen to under 19 percent, not because agriculture failed to grow, but simply because it could not keep up with manufacturing.

What caused the sharp post–Civil War acceleration in economic growth? Did the United States or the American people suddenly exhibit some special quality that made the difference? Or was the enormous economic success spurred by a combination of diverse factors? And did the American people pay a price for the impressive advance? Or was the growth essentially cost-free? Let us start our inquiry by investigating the causes of the economic acceleration during the years following 1865. We shall then consider what price, if any, Americans paid.

Captains of Industry

If the average educated American were asked to explain the country's late-nineteenth-century economic surge, he or she would probably point to men like Andrew Carnegie, John D. Rockefeller, and "Commodore" Vanderbilt as the principal agents. Even against the gaudy and boisterous background of the era we call the Gilded Age, the image of these big-business tycoons stands out vividly. The image is, in many ways, a negative one: The business leaders of this period were "robber barons" who held the nation for ransom to amass their great fortunes; they were crude and vulgar men who flaunted their wealth and their bad taste. Yet to this day many Americans will readily concede that these men almost single-handedly made the United States an industrial giant. Are they right?

A close look at the extraordinary economic achievement of the Gilded Age shows that the great entrepreneurs—those who organized, managed, and assumed the risks of business—were indeed important elements in the nation's spectacular economic success. Entrepreneurship is a major element in virtually all economic growth. To increase an economy's output, it is not enough to add more materials, labor, and machines to the economic mix. Growth also requires advances in the initiating, coordinating, and managerial functions to start new businesses and improve old ones. The ability to detect an important economic need, cut costs of production to a minimum, tap new sources of savings, recruit and manage labor, recognize and inspire new talent—these entrepreneurial skills are not common or easy to marshal. When a given society is able to bring these talents to bear, the economy will almost certainly advance more quickly than before.

Gustavus Swift and the Organizing Function. To understand the role of entrepreneurship in the economic growth and change of the post–Civil War period, let us consider several examples. A good place to start is the meat-packing industry.

Before the Civil War a few western cities like Cincinnati were important meat-packing centers. Hogs and cattle were slaughtered on a large scale and pickled in brine to supply merchant seamen and slaves with salt pork and beef. Most fresh meat, however, came from local butchers as it spoiled too quickly to be sent from suppliers to distant markets. Live animals could be shipped by rail or driven on the hoof to city consumers, but they often lost much weight or were injured or killed in transit. Then, in the generation following the Civil War, three developments helped transform the business of supplying the public with meat. First, an increasing proportion of Americans came to live in cities, distant from the farms and from the major meat-producing areas of the country. Second, an expanding railroad network made the products of the prairies and plains of the West more accessible to urban consumers. Third, in the 1870s refrigerated railroad cars appeared, allowing chilled fresh beef and pork to be shipped long distances without spoilage.

One of the first men to recognize the new possibilities that these changes opened up for the meat industry was Gustavus Swift, a New Englander who came to Chicago as a cattle buyer in the 1870s. Swift saw the advantages of slaughtering cattle close to the grass and corn of the West and shipping the trimmed product to eastern consumers. Such a system would eliminate

the losses in shipping live cattle; more important, centralized processing would be more economical. Much of the slaughtering could be mechanized, thereby reducing labor costs, and the animal parts that were normally discarded could be sold to make medicines, sausage casings, fertilizers, leather, and other by-products. (It would be said of the great hog butchers of the late nineteenth century that they used every part of the pig but the squeal.)

Swift sent his first chilled beef east by refrigerator car in the mid-1870s. At first he encountered stiff resistance to the unfamiliar product from consumers and from local retailers alike. But in a few years, joined by other packers like Philip D. Armour, Michael Cudahy, and Nelson Morris, he was shipping millions of pounds of meat annually from his Chicago plants

Entrepreneur Gustavus Swift created a new industry and expanded a national market by bringing western meat to eastern cities. Swift's "dissembly lines" for dressing beef and pork and his improvements of the refrigerator car made more meat available at lower prices to more people.

Industry, 1860–1890.

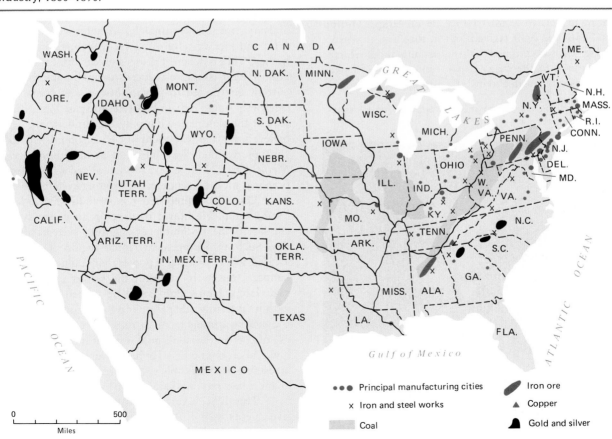

and marketing it through a network of branch houses and agents. In 1875 the Chicago packers slaughtered 250,000 cattle; in 1880, 500,000; in 1890, a million.

Thomas Edison and Technological Innovation. Swift's contribution to the economic advance of the period consisted primarily of improving the organization of an existing industry. Thomas Edison developed new technology, adapted it to public needs, and created several whole new industries.

We think of Edison today as an inventor of gadgets—and indeed he was. He improved the telephone and the telegraph, and invented the motion picture camera, the phonograph, and the incandescent light bulb. Yet he was far more than an inspired tinkerer; he was also a first-rate entrepreneur whose skills immeasurably improved the quality of American life and launched a giant new business.

At the beginning of the nineteenth century Americans worked and played almost entirely during daylight hours, and the rhythms of life closely corresponded to the seasonal length of the day. At night city streets were dark. Private homes were also unlighted after daylight, or at most dimly lighted, except on special occasions or if the owners were well off and could afford expensive candles or whale oil lamps. During the 1850s gas light arrived, but it, too, was expensive and its use was confined to the upper and middle classes and limited to the larger urban centers, where it was economically feasible to install costly pipes and meters.

Thomas Edison, one of the most inspired of America's inspired tinkerers.

The new petroleum industry changed this picture. In the 1840s and 1850s, "rock oil" was a substance extracted from streams and used as a medicine. Its value as an illuminant was understood, but no one was certain that it could be collected in large enough quantities to be useful for lighting. Then, in 1859, a group of businessmen hired E. L. Drake, a former railroad conductor with some knowledge of well drilling, to try to extract oil from the ground in western Pennsylvania. After several weeks of effort Drake struck a major oil pool, proving that it was possible to guarantee a steady supply of the substance. Thereafter, what had been a quack medical remedy became a household necessity. Refined into kerosene, petroleum quickly replaced whale oil and candles as the nation's major source of home lighting.

Kerosene was especially valuable as an illuminant in rural areas, and indeed it is still used on isolated farms and backwoods camps today. But from the outset, the risk of fire in congested city homes, and in stores, hotels, and restaurants, made it unwelcome in the major urban centers. By the 1870s it was widely recognized that electricity would not have this drawback. In fact, it was regularly used already, in the form of arc lights, for illuminating stage productions and city streets. Unfortunately, arc lights were too powerful and too wasteful of power to be used in private homes. This is where Edison saw his opportunity. If electric light could be reduced to small packages and current distributed to private homes and businesses, electricity would replace kerosene and gas. Many scientists at the time, knowing only the brilliant arc light, believed that the feat could not be accomplished. Edison ignored their warnings and at his laboratory in Menlo Park, New Jersey, pushed ahead to develop a practical incandescent electric lighting system.

Edison was interested in more than efficient long-lasting lamp. He hoped to develop an entire system similar to the profitable gas-lighting systems of the day. Such an arrangement would require a centrally located source of electric power that could serve many lamps, a means to transmit the power efficiently to each lamp, lamps that could be turned on and off without affecting other lamps on the circuit, and finally, a metering arrangement to measure each customer's use of current. Edison's goal was not merely technical; it was also commercial. He had to lure customers from an established workable system—gas—to his own, and at the same time make a profit for private investors.

This difficult enterprise aroused Edison's impressive talents as both businessman and inventor. After securing dependable financial backing, he worked out the technical specifications for an efficient and economically feasible lighting system—with the aid of a trained mathematician. Once he had developed a usable carbon filament for his glass lamp, he built a central generating station on Pearl Street near New York City's financial district, where his success would be sure to attract the attention of the nation's money men. He also developed a simple metering system that enabled the Edison Company to assess charges against users.

The Pearl Street station began operation on September 4, 1882, and was a brilliant success. During the next few years the Edison Company opened other stations in Boston, Philadelphia, and Chicago. Before long the incandescent lamp had almost totally replaced gas light in towns and cities. In a few years the nation's cities were alive with light, and urban Americans stayed up later to read, talk, dine, and generally enjoy themselves. Eventually electricity came to the farms and rural areas. A whole way of life had been revolutionized by one man's skill, insight, and enterprise.

Andrew Carnegie and Cost Consciousness.
Careful cost analysis and ruthless cost cutting were the hallmarks of Andrew Carnegie's entrepreneurship.

Carnegie was the essential self-made man. After arriving in the United States with his familiy in 1848, the thirteen-year-old Scottish lad first worked in a Pittsburgh textile factory replacing broken threads on the spinning spools for $1.20 a week. In the 1850s, after a stint as a telegraph operator, Carnegie became an assistant to Thomas A. Scott, vice president of the Pennsylvania Railroad. Scott was one of the most creative railway executives of his day. The railroads—with their thousands of employees, millions of dollars of capital, and complex financing and rate-setting problems, as well as their enormous territorial extent—were the first truly modern business organizations. From Scott, Carnegie learned how to deal with a large-scale enterprise and how to save thousands by squeezing pennies.

Carnegie was not an inventor like Edison. He worked with existing technology and processes, but made them show a profit. When he moved from railroading to bridge building and then to iron and steel making during the 1860s, men like Abram Hewitt and Eber Ward had already begun to make steel with the new Bessemer and open-hearth processes. Carnegie was more than willing to spend money on promising investments, and he seized on the new steel-making methods for his Pittsburgh-based Edgar Thomson Works. He was never content with the status quo, however. When new improvements came along, he adapted them, disre-

Andrew Carnegie at the height of his power and fame.

garding the costs of scrapping his older but still usable equipment. He ran his furnaces, hearths, and converters full-blast regardless of replacement costs, and did not let up even when orders tumbled during hard times. He also cut expenses ruthlessly and kept down labor costs by mechanizing as many processes as he could. When faced with the prospect of paying dearly for high-quality coke produced by another firm, Carnegie bought a major coke company and acquired along the way its president, the shrewd Henry Clay Frick, as a partner. Later he bought his own ore fields in the newly opened Mesabi Range of Minnesota. Carnegie recruited a corps of driving young executives and then held them strictly accountable for every penny spent producing steel. One of these men later said: "You [were] expected always to get it ten cents cheaper the next year or the next month." Within a few years Carnegie and his associates had lowered the price of steel enough for it to replace iron, wood, and stone in construction, thus paving the way for marvels of engineering never before conceived.

Of all the so-called robber barons, Carnegie was probably the most civic-minded. Like the others, he was convinced that high wages meant low profits, but he also believed that rich men were custodians of wealth for society at large. Before he died, the "Star-spangled Scotsman" gave away much of his immense fortune for libraries and to charitable institutions, research foundations, and endowments for peace and international understanding. And his charity was genuine: In Carnegie's day, before the income tax, philanthropy was not tax-deductible.

Capital Creation and J. P. Morgan.
Swift, Edison, and Carnegie faced the problem of raising money to invest in blast furnaces, meat-packing plants, and power stations. Where did these funds come from? Ultimately the source of any money for capital investment must be savings. Swift and Carnegie relied largely on their own savings, derived from the profits of previous and existing enterprises. Many businesspeople, however, were forced to tap the pools of savings set aside by other people.

Fortunately, the savings rate was exceptionally high in the era, far higher than in our own day. People saved because it was enjoined by religion; they also saved because there was no other way to provide for old age, disease, or accident. Substantial inequalities of wealth and income also help explain the high savings rate. Rich men and women were particularly able to save because their incomes far exceeded their day-to-day needs. These savings usually represented the profits they earned by employing labor. They had money to invest because other people received lower wages and incomes than might otherwise have been possible. Thus millions of ordinary wage earners surrendered part of their income to speed economic expansion, though they were seldom consulted directly about the process. In effect, in a society where inequalities of wealth and income existed, a large proportion of the public involuntarily contributed to economic growth.

Piling up savings is not enough, however. These savings must be channeled into the hands of entrepreneurs who have the will and the skill to use them effectively. When the saver and the investor are the same person—as in the case of Carnegie and Swift—there is little problem. But what if the two are different individuals? It is here that various investment institutions come into play.

One of those institutions was the stock market located on New York's Wall Street, where stocks and other securities issued by corporations had been bought and sold since the late eighteenth century. Selling stock was potentially a very useful device for tapping the savings of people with capital. Those who bought "shares" in a business corporation were part owners of the firm and received a portion of its profits without risking losses beyond the extent of their share purchase (limited liability). This system should have been an effective way for entrepreneurs to raise capital, but its value was seriously reduced by the fact that by the end of the nineteenth century the stock exchange had become a sort of gambling casino where speculators—"bulls" and "bears"—bought and sold shares, not to gain profits from corporate earnings, but to make killings in "corners," "raids," and other get-rich-quick maneuvers. Prudent people with capital looked aghast at these risky and shady doings and stayed away from the stock market.

A more successful way to channel savings to investors during these years was through the banks. By using other people's savings deposits or simply by establishing a line of credit for borrowers, bankers were able to provide funds to investors who met their standards of creditworthiness. But the nation's banking structure had serious weaknesses. The National Banking Acts of 1863 and 1864 had created a single, uniform bank note issue and had made this secure by backing it with government bonds. The national banking system was a major advance over the old state bank system, but it had substantial drawbacks. Banks with national charters were not allowed to take land as security for loans, a restriction that limited their value for farmers who only had their land to offer as collateral. Nor could they easily increase the country's money supply to take care of seasonal needs or the steady, long-term growth of the economy, since the amount of their paper money issues depended on their holdings of a limited volume of government bonds. Lacking a central bank of last resort that might provide extra funds when needed, the national banking system was also unable to deal effectively with financial panics or other sudden crises. Not until the Federal Reserve System was established in 1913 were many of these problems solved.

Despite these flaws the regular commercial banks that formed the national banking system served to bring savers and investors together satisfactorily, especially where small amounts of capital were needed. For large-scale capital investment, however, the most effective agent was the investment banker. The need for investment bankers was especially urgent during the Gilded Age, when explosive urban growth and rapidly expanding railroads and industry created an extraordinary need for capital.

Investment banks were generally not part of the national banking system and did not normally engage in the day-to-day business of commercial banking. Instead, they dealt with large borrowers, either government agencies or industrial and transportation promoters interested in raising enormous amounts of capital.

Investment banking did not appear abruptly in the Gilded Age. Before the Civil War a few banking firms had begun to serve as middlemen between the

J. P. Morgan. He had a bulbous red nose—carefully obscured in this portrait.

gan reinforced investor confidence by placing one or more of his partners on the new firm's board of directors. When the new company issued stock to expand its operations, people with money found these attractive investments. In this way hundreds of millions of dollars were conveyed from rich savers—including many English, French, and Dutch capitalists—to American enterprises.

Once accustomed to buying stock, investors became enthusiastic about the new way of putting their money to use. By the end of the century the stock exchange on New York's Wall Street had become a major money market where those with funds to invest in industry came together with those who needed these funds. By 1910 billions of dollars of stock were being bought and sold annually on Wall Street. Much of this trading was gambling, as in the past. But a good deal of it was a constructive meeting of savers who wanted safe returns and promoters who could put these savings to productive use.

The Spoilers

Clearly the entrepreneurship of Swift, Edison, Carnegie, Morgan, and others like them benefited the American people by providing new or cheaper products or by aiding investment. Though most nineteenth-century businessmen had limited social sympathies and were not above sharp dealing, they helped to some degree to increase the income of many Americans. Not all business leaders, however, were constructive innovators. Some were primarily spoilers who got rich by manipulating finance while taking advantage of investors' gullibility, bribing politicians, ruthlessly snuffing out competitors, or devising ways to rig prices. Among these spoilers were Jay Gould and John D. Rockefeller.

The Railroads and Jay Gould. The Civil War had delayed railroad construction, but after 1865 the country turned with a will to the task of conquering time and distance with rails and locomotives. In 1865 there were about 35,000 miles of track in the United States. By 1873, after an enormous spurt of construction encouraged by government aid, this mileage had doubled. During the depression years of 1873 through 1879 the railroads grew slowly. Then came the prosperous 1880s, and by 1890 the country had 167,000 miles of track. By 1910, when the rail network was largely complete, America was tied together by 240,000 miles of steel track.

Much of the new construction occurred in the

government and savers. They bought government bonds, thus guaranteeing the treasury the money it needed, and then peddled the bonds to the public. During the war Jay Cooke and Company had assumed many of the risks of selling the giant Union issues of "five-twenty" bonds that had financed the Union army and navy. Cooke's success in this enterprise helped make him the leading investment banker of the day and encouraged him to move into private investment banking after the war. In the 1870s he became the financial agent of the Northern Pacific Railroad, but Cooke became too deeply involved. When the public stopped buying Northern Pacific securities, Cooke and Company went bankrupt, bringing on the Panic of 1873 and six years of hard times.

The public's experience with Cooke reinforced its suspicion of stocks and the stock market. But things began to change in the 1880s, largely because of the work of J. P. Morgan. Morgan often said that his chief asset was his reputation. The public trusted him with its money. Building on this trust, Morgan was able to engineer a flock of major corporate mergers that created new giant firms. These mergers encouraged investor confidence by improving the profitability of the constituent companies, which no longer had to face "cutthroat" competition and could, because of their increased size, take advantage of the economies and savings that came with large-scale enterprise. Mor-

older regions of the country. In the years immediately following the war, promoters created trunk lines such as the New York Central and the Baltimore and Ohio that allowed freight and passengers to move from the Atlantic to the Midwest without changing from one road to another. Chicago, St. Louis, Kansas City, and Omaha became major rail centers, and from these points other promoters began to push west and south over the rapidly developing prairies. The most spectacular growth, however, occurred in the transcontinentals. In 1869 construction teams from the Central Pacific, driving eastward from Sacramento, and from the Union Pacific, driving west from Omaha, met at Promontory Point in northern Utah, completing the first Atlantic-Pacific railroad connection. By 1890 five major railroads connected the Atlantic to the Pacific coast.

Railroad efficiency was also vastly increased. Relatively cheap steel rails produced by Carnegie and his competitors soon replaced the older iron tracks, allowing the railroads to run larger, more efficient locomotives and cars. Heavier trains created serious braking problems, but these were solved with the adoption of George Westinghouse's air brake in the 1880s. Track gauges—the distances between rails—were standardized in these years so that passengers and freight need not be shifted from one set of cars to another. Meanwhile, George Pullman had invented a new passenger car that was an ordinary coach by day but could be converted into a comfortable sleeping car by night.

Several scholars have warned against exaggerating the impact of the railroads on the late-nineteenth-century American economy, but most interpreters believe it was immense. Cheap, all-weather transportation accelerated the decline in shipping costs that had begun during the pre–Civil War period, opening vast new regions to economic exploitation. Lower transport costs allowed commodities to be produced in the most efficient locations and then shipped to consumers all over the country. They enabled each region to specialize in what it did best and exchange its products for those of other regions, further lowering consumer costs. The creation of an integrated national market raised the country's total output per capita substantially.

Some of the people who helped bring this process about were farseeing, creative individuals who risked their own fortunes in opening new areas to settlement. James J. Hill, for example, the promoter of the Great Northern connecting St. Paul with Puget Sound, built his road without the great federal subsidies behind the other transcontinentals. Hill, rightfully called the "Empire Builder," was an uncommon man. Many of the railroad promoters of the age were neither as civic-minded nor as creative as Hill. Most notorious of all was Jay Gould.

Gould was a railroad man, but he built no railroads. Instead he made a great fortune by manipulating their financial structure and leaving them debt-ridden and ruined. In 1867 Gould and his friend James Fisk became directors of the Erie Railroad. They were supposed to be allies of Cornelius ("Commodore") Vanderbilt, who wished to add the Erie to his own New York Central and gain a stranglehold on New York City's western traffic. Vanderbilt began to buy up Erie stock, hoping to acquire a controlling interest.

The new directors, joined by the notorious speculator Daniel Drew, betrayed Vanderbilt. Drew, especially, was a master of "stock watering." As a cattle drover before the Civil War, he had often driven his herds long distances without allowing them to drink, and then, just before arriving at market, let them have as much water as they wanted. When sold to the butchers by weight, the bloated animals brought Drew a handsome profit. Now he and his confederates "watered" the Erie Railroad stock by issuing vast amounts of new securities unjustified by any increase in the railroad's earning capacity. They dumped these shares on the market. The unsuspecting Commodore bought and bought, but could not manage to buy enough to gain control of the railroad. Eventually Vanderbilt discovered the deception and sought help from the courts; the Erie Ring leaders did the same. For months the two groups fought bitter legal battles, culminating in Gould's wholesale bribery of the New York State legislature to legalize his acts. Soon Gould lost interest in the Erie and moved on to greener pastures. But the railroad, stuck with millions of shares of watered stock, was never the same. As he turned to new endeavors, Gould jeered: "There ain't nothing more in Erie."

John D. Rockefeller and Monopoly. The career of John D. Rockefeller illustrates another form of business abuse common during these years: monopoly. His manipulations also highlight a general characteristic of the era: Business operated in a permissive legal atmosphere in which the rules were either unclear or unformulated. Some of Rockefeller's actions were not strictly illegal at the time, however unfair or ethically suspect.

Rockefeller's business arena was the oil-refining industry. After Drake's discovery in western Pennsylvania, the oil industry had boomed. Prospectors swarmed all over the East and soon discovered oil in western New York, West Virginia, Ohio, and Indiana. By the mid-1870s California, too, had begun to produce pe-

John D. Rockefeller's first oil refinery in Cleveland, Ohio, about 1869.

troleum in commercial amounts. The new sources of supply soon generated spectacular growth in the refining industry, which converted crude oil into kerosene, wax, and lubricants. By the early 1870s the refining companies had begun to concentrate near Cleveland, Ohio, a region close to the eastern oil fields and with unusually good transportation to the country's major population centers.

The refining industry was risky. For a few thousand dollars anyone could set up a simple plant to produce kerosene. As more and more firms entered the business, profits fell to the vanishing point, and many refineries went bankrupt. The intense competition undoubtedly kept prices low and benefited the consumer, but from the refiners' point of view, the results were disastrous.

The petroleum refiners were not the only business people injured by cutthroat competition. In the 1870s the railroads, too, found themselves slashing rates on competitive lines to stay in business. In that decade passenger fares between New York and Chicago dropped dramatically; first-class freight rates over the same route dropped by two-thirds or more. Business people, not surprisingly, found this risky regime hard to bear and sought to do something about it. Consolidation of several firms under one controlling firm was a common response among railroad entrepreneurs. In

the 1870s they also tried the "pool," an agreement among several roads with competing routes to divide the traffic according to a formula and not try to win additional traffic by cutting rates. Invariably these agreements broke down when one firm or another found it advantageous to break the pool. Because their legality was at best dubious, the pools could not be enforced by law. Industrial firms also tried the pool and several variants, but with similar dubious results.

Rockefeller's campaign to reduce competition in his own industry was more successful than most. In 1870 he and his partners established the Standard Oil Company of Ohio. With a million dollars invested in stills, pipelines, storage tanks, and other equipment, Standard soon became one of the largest refining companies in the country. The technical and managerial skills of the Standard people were important factors in their firm's prosperity. Equally significant, however, was Rockefeller's ability to squeeze cheap rates from the railroads for shipping crude and refined oil. So competitive was the refining business that even a small saving on transportation costs could give one producer an edge over the others. Taking advantage of the railroads' own fierce competition, Rockefeller arranged to provide large-scale shipments of Standard products by a given railroad in return for rebates that would reduce Standard's shipping charges far below the published rates. As a result, Standard Oil grew at the expense of its competitors—many of whom were forced to sell out to their aggressive opponent—and with each spurt of growth further increased its ability to squeeze favorable terms out of the railroad companies.

By 1872 Rockefeller controlled about one-fourth of the country's entire refining capacity. Thereafter, Standard Oil went on to establish a virtual monopoly of American petroleum refining. By 1880 it controlled between 90 and 95 percent of the country's refining capacity and 92 percent of the crude oil supply of the Appalachian area, the major oil region at the time. In 1882 Rockefeller and his associates formed the first "trust," a company that owned the securities of subsidiary firms and controlled their operations.

Rockefeller's trust was dissolved by the Ohio courts on the grounds that it violated the rights of owners of the individual firms and was "a virtual monopoly of the business of producing petroleum . . . to control the price." But the Standard people reorganized under a New Jersey law that legalized a rather similar device, the holding company. Thereafter, Standard's share of the industry declined somewhat, but as late as 1911, when the United States Supreme Court ordered the parent holding company dissolved into thirty separate firms, it was still by far the largest producer of refined oil and crude petroleum in the world.

The post–Civil War business leaders were, then, both wreckers and builders. It would be difficult to consider business leadership a major factor in late-nineteenth-century economic growth if all business leaders had resembled Jay Gould or John D. Rockefeller. But others such as Carnegie, Edison, Swift, and Morgan clearly helped accelerate economic growth.

The Intellectual Foundation

Entrepreneurship was only one component of the economic advances of the Gilded Age. Another was a system of values congenial to material growth.

Not all the mine, railroad, and factory workers enthusiastically supported the era's economic developments. Indeed, a substantial minority were reluctant participants. Yet, to an amazing degree, they and the rest of the American public endorsed private profit, hard work, and economic progress.

In part this support can be explained by the realities of Gilded Age American society. As we shall see, the growing economy, however imperfect, did permit a fair degree of improvement in the economic status and income of average wage earners, and a certain amount of movement up the social ladder for their children. These improvements reinforced the faith of ordinary people in the system. But actual experience was not the whole of it. Faith in the system was buttressed by a mass of ideology, myth, and propaganda that sang the praises—and the inevitability—of the social and economic status quo.

The Work Ethic. Many American workers wholeheartedly accepted the teachings of the work ethic. A residue of the colonial Puritan notion that the elect who were destined to be saved would be detectable by their material success, this ethic proclaimed the virtues of hard work, sobriety, and a willingness to sacrifice present advantages for future gains. Idleness in this view was both socially undesirable and morally corrupting. Hard work, moreover, was likely to pay off. Success was not a matter of mere good luck, proclaimed the purveyors of the work ethic. According to the famous McGuffey *Readers*, the enormously successful reading texts of the period: "He who would thrive, must rise at five; he who has thriven, may lie to seven." All of American history, announced the apostles of hard work, demonstrated the effects of enterprise. In biographies and novels, especially those of William M. Thayer and Horatio Alger, the rewards of the work ethic were dramatized. Especially popular were the success tales of Alger, a literary hack who wrote 119 books, most of them for young people. In fact, Alger's heroes usually achieve success more by sheer luck than by persistent labor. In one Alger story, for example, "ragged Dick" rescues a child from drowning and is rewarded with a job by the child's father—a banker, it turns out. In another story, the hero finds an enormous gold nugget. Yet the lesson Alger conveyed was that toil was both good and rewarding. His heroes, however lucky, are also youths who glory in work. Tom Thatcher is "a sturdy boy of sixteen with bright eyes and smiling, sun-burned face. His shirt sleeves were rolled up, displaying a pair of muscular arms. His hands were brown, and soiled with labor. It was clear that here was no whitehanded young aristocrat." Raised on a steady diet of such edifying tales and myths, millions of Americans were prepared to accept the virtues of the contemporary economic system.

The Defense of Inequality. The work ethic no doubt helped to inculcate values and habits that were useful to employers. Indirectly it also justified unequal rewards, for if hard work was the way to achieve riches, then what divided rich from poor was the quality and intensity of their effort, not birth or luck. But there were more direct defenses of the inequalities of wealth as well.

Until close to the end of the century the Protestant ministry often defended the disparities between rich and poor. Henry Ward Beecher told an audience during the 1870s depression: "I do not say that a dollar a day is enough to support . . . a man and five children if a man would insist on smoking and drinking beer. . . . But the man who cannot live on bread and water is not fit to live." In his lecture *Acres of Diamonds*, Baptist minister Russell Conwell delivered the message that material riches were a sign of God's approval, if honestly earned. For the Christian to reject riches was a mistake, for riches allowed the Christian to aid others. Conwell was an enormously popular speaker. During the Gilded Age he traveled to every part of the country and gave his standard talk 6,000 times to many thousands of listeners.

The ministers were not alone in defending the economic inequalities of the time. In the colleges and universities, on the editorial boards of newspapers and magazines, writers, academics, and journalists saw virtues in the competitive spirit of the age and the unavoidable success of some and failure of others. To defend inequality, these men drew on either the ideas of Adam Smith and other economists of eighteenth- and early-nineteenth-century Britain or the newer ideas of Charles Darwin.

Adam Smith and his disciples, writing at the dawn of the Industrial Revolution, sought to demonstrate how free competition—by offering rewards to enterprise, skill, and talent—inevitably spurred innovation and growth. One consequence of such free competition was no doubt inequality, they admitted, and perhaps this was unfortunate. But the alternative was worse. For government to seek to interfere in favor of the weak would be to check progress by discouraging ability and would, in addition, make economic decisions a plaything of politicians. Laissez-faire (hands off) was the best policy toward the economy.

Defenders of inequality had used these arguments to bolster their position long before the Civil War. After 1865 they could also turn to social Darwinism to make their case.

Social Darwinism was an attempt to apply the ideas of the English naturalist Charles Darwin to the social realm. In his momentous work *Origin of Species*, first published in 1859, Darwin posited a mechanism to account for the emergence of the great diversity of the world's plant and animal species. This mechanism was competition among all creatures for the limited means of survival. In this incessant battle, individuals who were stronger, quicker, more intelligent, or more aggressive—in a word, the "fittest"—survived to reproduce their kind. The others died, and their lines ceased. Bit by bit, through this struggle to survive, all animal and plant life, including humans, had evolved.

To social Darwinists it seemed clear that what applied to the biological world also applied to society: Competition and the "survival of the fittest" constituted the only way to achieve progress. For humankind to advance, competition must be encouraged, not discouraged, even if this meant accepting gross social disparities and apparent evils. Every attempt of softhearted philanthropists to interfere with the evolutionary process by reducing the advantage of the fittest and improving the position of the weak was shortsighted and mistaken. "Let it be understood," wrote

Horatio Alger, writer of "pulp" novels, was the apostle of the work ethic and its myth of success in late-nineteenth-century America. The title page of his *Fame and Fortune* suggests that newsboys and shoeshine boys have their feet on the first rungs of the ladder of success.

RAGGED DICK SERIES
BY
HORATIO ALGER JR.

FAME AND FORTUNE

Yale professor William Graham Sumner, "that we cannot go outside this alternative: liberty, inequality, survival of the fittest; not liberty, equality, survival of the unfittest." Sometimes this insistence on laissez-faire was carried to preposterous extremes. Herbert Spencer, the English philosopher who traveled extensively through the United States and helped popularize social Darwinist ideas, believed that laws to aid the poor, to provide publicly supported education, to regulate housing, to provide cheap mail service, even to protect citizens against medical quackery were all misguided and certain to lead to social disaster.

It is not clear how seriously the business community took social Darwinism; after all, many of these same men were busily organizing pools and trusts to reduce competition and demanding government aid. Yet at times businessmen echoed the slogans of the professors and philosophers. Rockefeller reportedly told a Sunday school audience that "the growth of a large business is merely the survival of the fittest. . . . The American Beauty rose can be produced in the splendor and fragrance which brings cheer to its beholder only by sacrificing the early buds which grow up around it." Even Andrew Carnegie, an atypical business tycoon in so many ways, accepted the necessity for inequality on Darwinian grounds. In his famous work *The Gospel of Wealth*, he startled the reading public by declaring that rich men were only "stewards of wealth" who must give it all back to society, but Carnegie also wrote: "We accept and welcome . . . great inequality of environment; the concentration of business, industrial and commercial, in the hands of a few; and the law of competition between these as being not only beneficial, but essential to the future of the race."

Students of society cannot be certain how ideas such as social Darwinism actually affect human actions and social change. Some believe that ideas possess only limited capacity to influence those who perceive them as contrary to their own advantage. Certainly business people were capable of ignoring their own laissez-faire precepts when it suited their purposes. Other scholars credit ideas with the power to create myths that obscure people's view of their true interests. It is difficult to choose between these positions. Yet it is probably true that in many cases, where they did not fly in the face of clear, firsthand experience, the defense of hard work and inequality, and the propaganda for the self-made man were accepted by workers. These ideas in turn undoubtedly reduced discontent and helped create a disciplined labor force that contributed to economic growth after 1865.

The Role of Government

Anyone who believes the entrepreneurs of this era solely responsible for economic progress must explain away the vital part played by government. The federal government stimulated the economy by direct investment, by grants, by tariffs, and by giving business the freedom to do virtually all that it wished. Without this help, growth would have been slower.

Government Aid. At times Washington invested directly in the physical improvements the nation needed. The federal government appropriated funds for post offices, docks, and canal locks, and dredged river channels. In 1874 James B. Eads, already famous for his steel bridge across the Mississippi at East St. Louis, designed federally financed jetties that deepened the lower Mississippi and helped preserve New Orleans's role as a major ocean port. Each year Congress supported such enterprises by a flock of "rivers and harbors" bills. In 1867 these took $1.2 million from the taxpayers' pockets; by 1895 they took almost $20 million. Local governments, too—by paving streets, constructing sewers, and building hospitals, schools, reservoirs, and aqueducts—contributed to the country's growth.

An especially important federal contribution to Gilded Age economic growth was friendly tax policy. After the 1870s the tariff—in effect a tax on consumers—rose virtually without pause until the twentieth century, providing a wall behind which investors could initiate new industries without fear of more efficient foreign competition. Internal taxes also favored investors. For most of this period, import duties and excises on tobacco, whiskey, beer, wine, and other items were the main sources of federal funds. The tax system was quite *regressive*; that is, it took a larger portion of the income of the poor than of the rich. During the period 1861–72 the federal government imposed an income tax, a *progressive* tax that rose proportionally with higher income. Had it remained, the income tax would have placed more of the tax burden on those able to afford it. But it was dropped as part of the postwar retreat from heavy taxation; when it was revived again in 1894, it was quickly declared unconstitutional by the Supreme Court. Local governments raised most of their revenues by taxing property, an equally regressive practice. All told, the tax burden fell disproportionately on farmers and on people at the lower end of the income ladder, constituting a kind of subsidy to the rich and the corporations. The system was not just, but it probably stimulated economic growth: The

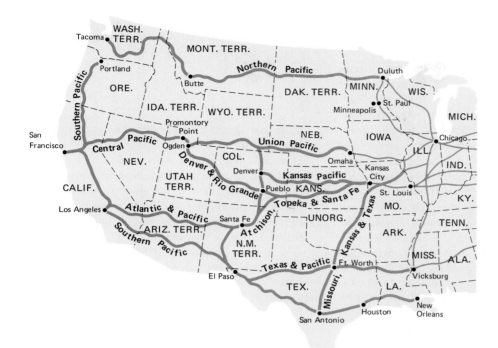

Railroads, 1850–1900

rich were left with substantial sums to invest in land, securities, or business enterprises.

During the post–Civil War decades such wartime Republican initiatives as the Homestead Act (1862), which gave western land to those willing to settle it, and the Morrill Land Grant College Act (1862), which endowed agricultural colleges, stimulated greater agricultural productivity. Federal railroad legislation had even weightier consequences. By 1871, under the terms of the Pacific Railroad Acts (1862 and 1864) and several later measures, the federal government had given private railroad companies over 130 million acres of land in the trans–Mississippi West, about one-tenth of the entire public domain. This vast empire included timber, minerals, and some of the most fertile soil on earth. Individual states contributed 49 million additional acres from their public lands. This huge block of real estate—larger than the state of Texas—was a vital source of funds for the railroads. People with savings, especially rural folk, who would not buy the stocks and bonds of the railroads, did buy their land. Thousands were attracted west to take up farms on railroad lands. Their contribution to the roads' coffers was immense. The average price at which the railroads sold their land was about $3.30 an acre, bringing the promoters about $435 million in much-needed funds.

The wisdom of the railroad land-grant policy has been debated for many years. Some historians call it a giant giveaway that deprived the American people of a large part of their heritage in order to benefit a few. Railroad promoters certainly made money from the land grants, but the government and the public also benefited: The grants accelerated growth of the West, reduced charges for transporting government goods—a requirement written into each of the grants— and enhanced prices of the land retained by the government adjacent to the railroads. Most important, the policy speeded the process of linking the country together by rail. If the railroads had not had land to sell, few private capitalists would have put their money in ventures so risky as railroads thrown across hundreds of miles of empty space, much of it arid and— until the railroads arrived—virtually worthless. Without the land grants, economic development would have been slower.

Hands Off. Each of these examples—tariff, tax policy, railroad land grants—is an instance of government's contributing directly to economic development. Eventually, through the federal courts, it also contributed immensely in indirect ways as well.

The courts' development of a strong probusiness

attitude unfolded slowly. Between 1865 and 1880 the federal courts took the position that the states could restrict the exercise of private property rights in order to protect the health, welfare, or morals of citizens. In the Slaughterhouse cases of 1873, for example, the Supreme Court rejected the contention that the Fourteenth Amendment, which had been passed to safeguard the political rights of black freedmen against state encroachment, also protected the profits and property of individuals and corporations against state regulation. In the Granger cases (notably *Munn* v. *Illinois*) of 1877, it upheld the right of Illinois to establish maximum rates for storing grain on the grounds that a state, under its legitimate police powers, could regulate any business that embraced "a public interest."

In the 1880s, however, the federal courts began to limit the power of state legislatures to intervene in economic transactions to protect citizens. In the *San Mateo* case (1882) and the *Santa Clara* case (1886)—both involving efforts by California to regulate railroads—the Supreme Court reversed its earlier position. The Fourteenth Amendment, it now declared, applied to "persons" besides those suffering legal discrimination owing to race; those whose economic interests were injured by state law were also entitled to federal protection. Moreover, the Court said that corporations were legal "persons" and hence protected by the Fourteenth Amendment. Corporations, too, could claim that they had been deprived of rights by a state "without due process" and could expect the federal government to intervene on their behalf. Thereafter, it became difficult for state legislatures to regulate business.

Having restricted the states' right to regulate private business, the federal courts soon clamped down on the federal government, too. In the *Maximum Freight Rates* case (1897), for example, the Supreme Court limited the power of the Interstate Commerce Commission to set federal railroad rates, and in the *E. C. Knight* case (1895), it weakened the Sherman Antitrust Act (1890), a federal measure designed to prevent monopoly.

By 1900, then, the federal courts had established a lopsided hands-off policy toward business enterprise, subordinating the states' regulatory power to federal law on the one hand, and then crippling Congress's right to regulate. The federal government could help business through tariffs, railroad land grants, investments, and tax policies; but it could not limit business by imposing any commitment to the public welfare. The policy ignored social justice, and later generations would condemn it harshly. But it also created an atmosphere in which those with money to invest felt confident that they could count on good returns for their risks. By rewarding entrepreneurs, it encouraged economic expansion.

The Wage Earner

In discussing the triumph of industry after 1865, we have considered causes. What about consequences? How did laboring men and women, those who tended machines, who went down into the mines, who sawed the wood and dug the foundations, who stoked the furnaces and engines—how did these people fare as the nation accelerated its output, and how did they respond to what they experienced?

If we look only at the cold statistics, the lot of Gilded Age wage earners appears moderately good. Their incomes were growing. Average real wages and annual earnings rose substantially in the half century following the Civil War. One economist has estimated that hourly wages and earnings for American industrial workers, allowing for changes in the purchasing power of the dollar, increased by 50 percent between 1860 and 1890. Another concludes that during the next twenty-five years the increase was another 37 percent. Even omitting individual improvements in skill and increasing experience, then, industrial workers between 1865 and 1914 almost doubled their real income.

But these statistics tell only part of the story. They are only averages, and so mask a great deal of variation. They also disregard many other aspects of the working person's life in this era of pell-mell economic change.

Social Mobility and Financial Rewards. White males made up a majority of the labor force in this era, and we will examine them first. There was a definite cycle in the working lives of most white male wage earners. During their late teens, when they took their first jobs, they received the typical wages of unskilled "laborers." A majority, however, raised their skill levels over the years, and by their late forties or early fifties were earning considerably more than they had twenty or thirty years before. And there was another factor at work that white male workers could count on to improve their lot: social mobility. The data available on social mobility among white American working men, though somewhat ambiguous, suggest overall that movement from unskilled to semiskilled and even to skilled jobs was fairly common, although such mobility varied greatly, depending on the decade and the worker's community, ethnic background, and even religion.

Steam-driven trip-hammers stamped out metal parts for reapers and other farm machinery at the McCormick factory in Chicago. Machines like these increased workers' productivity, but they also added immeasurably to the hazards of wage earners' lives.

It was exceedingly difficult, however, for a poor boy to become a millionaire. The great tycoons of the Gilded Age were almost all native-born Protestants of old American stock whose fathers were themselves middle class or rich and who received far better educations than the average American.

Horatio Alger and the other myth-makers were apologizing for a system that did not invariably pay off. On the other hand, the popularity of their myths depended on many Americans' seeing mobility all around them or actually enjoying it themselves. As the social historian Herbert Gutman has said in a study of mobility in Paterson, New Jersey: "So many successful manufacturers who had begun as workers walked the streets of that city . . . that it [was] not hard to believe that 'hard work' resulted in spectacular material and social improvement."

Financial rewards as well as mobility varied among workers. Although the average wage in 1900 was $483 a year, carpenters, masons, and other skilled construction workers often earned as much as $1,250 annually. In 1880, when "laborers" were getting an average of $1.32 a day, blacksmiths received $2.31, locomotive engineers $2.15, and machinists $2.45. The wages of federal employees, clerical workers, and western miners were also above the national average. Agricultural workers, even when we take into account that they were commonly fed and housed by their employers, were always poorly paid. In the aptly named "sweated trades" of the big-city garment industry, working people were squeezed hard by their employers—struggling small businessmen who showed little consideration for those whose wages represented their major cost of production.

One reason for low wages in the garment industry was the presence of many women workers. Very few women in these years received wages comparable to those of adult men. A typical woman's wage was the dollar or two a week earned by female domestics who washed, cooked, sewed, and ironed in middle-class

Much of the unskilled labor force of early twentieth-century America was foreign-born—like these Russian steel workers in Homestead, Pennsylvania, in 1907.

homes; women piece-workers in New York and Chicago garment loft factories received under a dollar a day. Fortunately, the picture was not as bleak as these figures suggest. Most women eventually married and ceased to be part of the labor market. Yet for the "spinster" who had to support herself or the widow with young children, such wages were scandalous.

Black Americans were also paid well below the average. Most were sharecroppers in the South, but the few who had left the farms for the mills or factories were almost all relegated to low-paying, dead-end jobs regardless of their education, skills, or talents. Immigrants, too, at least until they acquired skills and an adequate command of English, received lower wages than skilled and native-born white workers.

Living and Working Conditions. For families at the bottom of the wage pyramid, life was hard. Few Americans went hungry, but many wage earners fought a constant battle to maintain a decent living standard and achieve a little comfort. In 1883 the large family of a railroad brakeman in Joliet, Illinois, reportedly ate chiefly bread, molasses, and potatoes. The family's clothes, a contemporary investigator noted, were "ragged" and the children "half-dressed and dirty." A witness before a Senate committee in 1883 described the home of the typical Pennsylvania coal miner as consisting of two rooms, one upstairs and one down. "The houses are built in long rows without paint on the outside," he reported. "The kitchen furniture consists

of a stove and some dishes, a few chairs and a table. They have no carpets on the floor. . . ."

Matters improved over the next generation, as we have seen, and life expectancies as well as income increased. In the industrial state of Massachusetts the average life expectancy of a newborn infant increased from about forty-two years in 1880 to about forty-five in 1920. Much of this improvement reflected lower infant mortality rates, but adults, too, benefited from the advancing living standards. In 1850, twenty-year-old males could count on living a trifle over forty more years; in 1920 they could look forward to about forty-five more years. In the same period the improvement in life expectancies for twenty-year-old women was slightly greater.

Despite these advances the *quality* of the wage earner's life, regardless of income, remained unsatisfactory from a modern viewpoint. Factory hours dropped from about sixty-six a week in 1850 to sixty in 1890. Yet the length of the workday remained a trial for most workers. "I get so exhausted that I can scarcely drag myself home when night comes," exclaimed a woman worker in a Massachusetts mill. A working man knew "nothing but work, eat, and sleep," and was "little better than a horse," declared one Pennsylvania factory employee.

Even when hours became shorter, there was the dreary monotony to contend with. Much industrial work consisted merely of repetitive, simple manipulations. At one Chicago packing house at the end of

Women were the most harshly exploited adult workers during the Gilded Age and the early twentieth century. In light industries like the garment trade—much of it located in New York City—"sweatshops," such as this, where immigrant women labored, were common.

Many American working-class families lived on the edge of subsistence, slipping into poverty if the economy declined or their families grew too large. Heads of families like this one worked sixty to seventy hours a week, only to drag themselves back to bare, cramped homes.

the century, five men were needed to handle just the tail of a steer—two to skin it, another two to cut it off, and one to throw it into a box. How could such mindless work provide any satisfaction? One middle-class reformer who tried factory work in the 1890s summed up the feelings of most industrial wage earners: "There is for us in our work none of the joy of responsibility, only the dull monotony of grinding toil, with the longing for the signal to quit work, and for our wages at the end of the week."

In some ways "progress" made the worker's life worse, not better. Rapid technological change made many skills obsolete. Although the job market as a whole expanded enormously in this period, skilled hands often found themselves replaced by machines. In the iron industry, for example, Andrew Carnegie and Henry Clay Frick pushed relentlessly for new ways to reduce the number of skilled workers in the mills. They succeeded in bringing down production costs, but only at a high price to their workers. Some were discharged; many who remained were forced to accept semiskilled or unskilled work, which reduced their income and made their jobs more monotonous. Some employers adopted Taylorism—that is, the ideas of Frederick W. Taylor, an industrial engineer who had developed his theories while trying to increase the efficiency of the work force at the Midvale Steel Company. Taylor was certain that machine tenders, like machines, could be made to work more effectively if the physical operations they performed were carefully examined and timed. By doing so, wasted motion could be eliminated and output raised. Workers often charged that implementation of Taylorism resulted in speed-ups that made their lives on the job more hectic and difficult.

Industrial work was also unsafe and unhealthful. Even at the end of the era few people understood the effects on health of chemicals, pollutants, dust, and other contaminants. Thousands suffered from chronic illness brought on by industrial conditions. Thousands more died young from silicosis (a lung disease caused by inhalation of rock dust), tuberculosis, cancer, heart conditions, and other work-induced diseases. Industrial accidents were epidemic. Unsafe machinery, mine gases, and explosive, dust-laden air maimed and killed many. Between 1870 and 1910 there were almost 4,000 injuries or deaths at Carnegie's South Works alone. In 1917 the nation's industrial casualty list was 11,000 killed and 1.4 million wounded.

Society did little or nothing to offset the fearful toll. Before 1900, common law held that if a "fellow servant" was responsible for a job injury, the employer was not liable for damages. And even if injury resulted

Mechanization made factory labor both more routine and more dangerous. If a man became disabled, his family had to struggle desperately to survive. Without government assistance, injury and unemployment were disastrous.

from direct employer neglect or carelessness, injured workers or their families had to sue to receive compensation. Few could take such an expensive course. Some prosperous working people were able to buy private insurance; but when the chief wage earner was killed or lost the ability to hold a job, most families faced a grim future indeed.

In addition to accidents and sickness, workers had to contend with unemployment produced by periodic hard times. Between 1870 and 1900 there were two serious slumps and several lesser ones. In the first and last of these (1873–1879 and 1893–1897) the proportion of the labor force unemployed ran to over 12 percent, a figure not equaled until the 1930s. During these lean years many working-class families had difficulty keeping a roof over their heads and decent clothes on their backs. Beggars swarmed the streets, and hoboes and tramps rode the rails from town to town looking for work.

Averaged out throughout the Gilded Age, unemployment reduced workers' total income only about 7 percent below a full-employment level. But this burden, too, was not equally shared. For older workers, for blacks, for many unskilled immigrants, depressions were especially disastrous. Considered marginal by employers, they were the first to be fired and the last to be rehired. For the least employable members of the labor force, hard times sometimes meant permanent idleness.

Old age also presented economic hazards for working people. There were no pension systems. Men and women who became too old to work usually had little to fall back on if they lacked personal savings. Private charity was often degrading and stingy. Many aging parents moved in with their children. If retired workers presented a less serious problem for society as a whole during this period than today, it was because men and women had more children to support them, and fewer lived to their later, nonworking years.

To understand the conditions of the American wage earner during the Gilded Age, it is essential to make distinctions. White, male, native-born skilled workers were the nation's "labor-aristocrats"; many lived in decent comfort, owned their own homes, ate well, and enjoyed some comforts, even a few luxuries. Like all other workers, they were subject to job insecurity and danger and worked long hours; but generally they had reason to praise their society and the economic system that made their moderately comfortable lives possible. It is difficult to calculate the size of this labor elite, but it probably represented between a third and a half of the total nonfarm labor force.

For the other members of the armies of labor— women, blacks, and unskilled, recent immigrants—life was not only precarious but often meager and harsh. The families of the unskilled made up for the primary breadwinner's low wages to some extent by sending everyone to work—young and old, male and female. The prevalence of child labor was one reflection of this need. But this arrangement was a high price to pay for survival. In sum, even though unskilled American workers were probably better off than their equivalents abroad, their lives were not only insecure but also pinched. Life was getting better, but there was still a long way to go before people at the base of the income pyramid could say that America had fulfilled its age-old promise of abundance.

Working-Class Protest

Given these failings of the economic system, it is not surprising that wage earners expressed discontent. Much of their protest, as always, took the form of vague mutterings, loud talk, and antisocial behavior.

But there were organized expressions of discontent as well. These took three forms: trade unionism, political activism, and utopianism.

Trade unionists accepted the capitalist system— though often with reservations—and sought higher wages, better working conditions, and shorter hours through collective bargaining. To achieve their ends, they endorsed strikes, boycotts of employers' goods, and work slowdowns when necessary. Political activists sometimes favored labor parties to fight for the eight-hour workday, paper money, workers' compensation for one-the-job injury, safety legislation, and child-labor laws. More radical political activists—whether socialist or anarchist—sought to replace private capitalism with a "cooperative commonwealth." In their ideal society property would be held in common and the profit motive would disappear; but they did not seek to dismantle the industrial system itself or turn back the clock. In contrast, those who took the third approach, utopianism, hoped to convert the industrial worker into either a farmer or a small manufacturer. This position expressed a nostalgic yearning for a past in which almost all Americans had been farmers or some other kind of self-employed producer.

Until the 1880s a combination of moderate political action and utopianism dominated the American labor movement. Between 1865 and 1873, when employees' power in the job market was at its height because times were good and labor scarce, trade unions like those of the iron molders, typographers, and machinists and blacksmiths squeezed some concessions on wages and hours out of employers. The National Labor Union (NLU) sought to combine reform of the capitalist system through political activism with utopian goals. Formed by Boston machinist Ira Steward in 1866 as the first nationwide labor federation, the NLU at first devoted itself to securing the eight-hour day through state law. Steward believed that the triumph of the eight-hour principle would not only make life on the job more tolerable but also help to liberate wage earners from bondage. Under William Sylvis, Steward's successor as NLU president, the union embraced a scheme by which the federal government would issue large amounts of paper money that could be lent to groups of workers so that they could become self-employed small businesspeople. These "producers' cooperatives" would enable working people to escape the lowly status of wage earners and become small producers in their own right.

The Depression of the Seventies. The Panic of 1873 and the depression that followed made jobs hard to get and hurt the trade union movement. Employers, finding that they could hire desperate unemployed men and women willing to accept any terms, became less tolerant of "troublemakers." In 1873, after trying to convert itself into a national labor party, the NLU collapsed. Union membership nationwide declined from about 300,000 in 1873 to some 50,000 in 1878.

The mid-1870s were a time of bitter labor strife. In January 1874 New York City police charged into a crowd of unemployed workers assembled in Tompkins Square to protest hard times, injuring many. The following year was marked by the sensational trial of the so-called Molly Maguires for the murders of coal mine managers in eastern Pennsylvania and for acts of violence against the mine owners' property. To this day it is not clear whether the violence resulted from class hatreds or ethnic tensions between the Irish Catholic miners and their Welsh and Scottish Protestant bosses. Some scholars believe that the sensational evidence against the Mollies, collected by an agent of the Pinkertons, a private detective agency employed by the owners, was largely concocted so that the principal mine owners could break a miners' union. In any case, when ten Mollies were hanged and another fourteen sent to jail, many middle-class Americans saw their suspicions of labor organizations confirmed.

The middle-class public suffered a still worse shock in 1877 when the eastern and midwestern railroads, to protect their profits in the face of declining business, cut their workers' wages and increased their hours. In Baltimore in mid-July the angry workers began to picket; the police dispersed them. Soon after, Baltimore and Ohio workers seized the railroad's terminal and yards at Martinsburg, West Virginia. This spontaneous uprising quickly spread to Pittsburgh, Chicago, Buffalo, and points west, involving several major railroads and thousands of workers. For two weeks it looked as if the country was in the throes of a revolution. In Baltimore militia fired on a mob of workers and youths, killing ten. In Buffalo strikers seized the facilities of the Lake Shore and Erie railroads. In Pittsburgh rioters burned hundreds of freight cars, the Union Depot, and machine shops; looted stores; and engaged in a pitched gun battle with militia. Frightened by these signs of "red revolution," governors and local officials called out state troops and deputized volunteers. The governor of Maryland, panicked by the Martinsburg seizure, called for and got federal troops, one of the earliest examples of such use. By early August the violence had ended, but many conservative Americans were convinced that they had narrowly escaped a major social revolution.

The Knights of Labor. With the return of prosperity in 1878–1879, labor discontent once more took the form of orderly organizing. The chief beneficiary of the new mood was the Noble Order of the Knights of Labor, a body created in 1869 by a group of Philadelphia tailors led by Uriah S. Stephens. During the mid-1870s the Knights had done little more than survive, but with the return of good times they began to prosper.

At first the Knights operated more like a secret lodge or fraternal order than an ordinary trade union. They provided a setting for social activity and offered life insurance, burial plots, and other benefits to compensate for the uncertainties of the wage earners' life. If they had any general labor policy, it was to encourage producers' cooperatives.

In the early 1880s, under the leadership of Terence V. Powderly, the Knights responded to improved times and the enhanced leverage on employers that resulted. Abandoning their longer-range reform goals, they confronted employers with wage demands backed by strikes or threats of strikes. In March 1885, the

The Knights of Labor had problems dealing with race prejudice among its members. Terence Powderly (here introduced by black Knight Frank M. Farrell) was not bigoted, but he had to placate southern members. In the end the Knights endorsed the "civil and political equality" of all citizens, but pledged to avoid interfering in southern "social relations."

Knights forced Jay Gould's Southwest Railroad to cancel a 10 percent wage cut. In the strength of this victory over a hated Gould, the union attracted throngs of new members. In the next two years membership leaped from a little over 100,000 to almost 730,000.

Here was an opportunity to create a powerful labor movement, but the chance was missed. Powderly and the Knights' other leaders never could decide whether they were organizing a trade union, a lodge, a reform association, or a political pressure group. Nor could they decide whether to recruit black members. Powderly endorsed organizing among black workers, but he denied that he endorsed racial equality and insisted that black members be confined to segregated locals. The Knights could not sustain the momentum of the mid-1880s and lost many of the new members.

The final blow to the Gilded Age trade union movement came with the 1886 Haymarket Riot in Chicago. During the spring of 1886 Chicago was a turbulent city of factories, railroad yards, meat-packing plants, and large commercial enterprises. At the vast McCormick Harvester Company, one of the city's largest employers, company officials had locked out 1,400 members of the Knights of Labor for demanding an eight-hour day and a $2 daily wage. On May 3, when the company tried to bring in "scabs" to replace the union men, the workers attacked the strikebreakers; the police fired on the workers.

The McCormick dispute marked the climax of a five-year citywide struggle for the eight-hour day, led by the Knights and by an assortment of socialists and labor leaders, that had deeply disturbed Chicago's labor relations. One element in the inflammable mixture was the anarchists, a group of radicals dedicated to destroying all government, along with private property and the wage system. Though few in number, the anarchists had supporters among the city's large German population. Following the police attack at McCormick, August Spies, a leading anarchist, issued a circular in German calling on the city's wage earners to "rise in your might . . . and destroy the hideous monster [of capitalism] that seeks to destroy you." The response of the conservative daily press was equally alarmist and overwrought. "A Wild Mob's Work; Wrought Up to a Frenzy by Anarchist Harangues, They Attack Employees" was the headline in the *Chicago Tribune*.

On the evening of May 4, at the anarchists' call, 3,000 men and women gathered at the Haymarket on the city's West Side. The crowd was disappointing. Many who might have come were frightened away

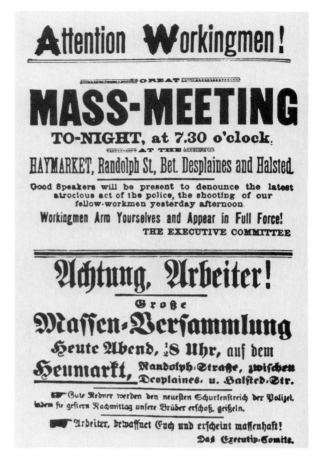

The labor troubles in Chicago in 1886 were heightened by the activities of a small group of anarchists. The group's fervor is captured in this handbill—in both English and German—for the meeting that would become the Haymarket Riot.

by Spies's inflammatory words. Yet the meeting was relatively orderly, and the crowd had begun to thin out when the police tried to disperse the small remnant. At this point someone threw a bomb, which exploded among the advancing police. When the smoke cleared, seventy policemen lay wounded. Eventually seven died from the blast.

The forces of law and order reacted blindly and violently. No one ever discovered who threw the bomb, but the public and the authorities blamed the anarchists and, by extension, all "labor agitators," whether radical or not. Hundreds of men were hustled off to jail, and ten anarchists were indicted for conspiracy to commit murder. Seven were sentenced to death after a trial that failed to establish their direct connection with the massacre. In late 1887, four were hanged.

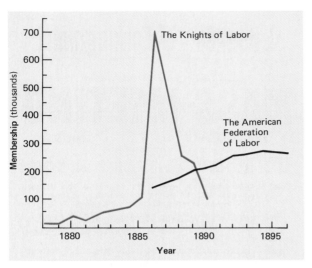

The passing of the Knights of Labor
Source: *Leo Wolman*, The Growth of American Trade Unions (1924).

The public outrage at the Chicago bombing shook the whole labor movement. Middle-class people, already convinced by the Molly Maguire trial and the 1877 riots that labor unions were violence-prone, now condemned all labor unions, even the most moderate and peaceful. To the already weakened Knights, the Haymarket affair was disastrous. Recruiting dried up; timid members quit. The Knights survived for another decade and a half, but after 1886 the union became a shadow of what it had been at its peak.

American Federation of Labor. As the Knights sank, the American Federation of Labor (AFL) rose. Established in 1886 by ex-socialists, including Adolph Strasser, Peter J. Maguire, and Samuel Gompers, the AFL concentrated its efforts on native-born workers in the skilled crafts. As its name suggests, the AFL was a federation of unions. Each of these represented workers in a specific trade such as tailors, bakers, typographers, cigar makers, carpenters, or bricklayers. Individuals could belong to the AFL only through their own trade union.

The AFL succeeded for several reasons. First, it confined its organizing efforts to skilled workers. These were the most easily organized because they were not easily fired. A factory owner could replace floor sweepers, machine tenders, and other untrained hands if they demanded too much, but a construction company could not hire carpenters or bricklayers off the street, nor could a printer easily replace its press operators and typesetters. When skilled laborers demanded higher wages, threatened to strike, or insisted that a

union be recognized as their bargaining agent, employers had to take them seriously.

The AFL was successful also because it abandoned utopian goals and avoided politics. Gompers and his lieutenants, though they had once been socialists, believed that political radicalism was dangerous to the labor movement. Skilled workers, they noted, were wary of radical politics, and any hint of extremism frightened the middle class. The blow that the Haymarket Riot had dealt the Knights of Labor convinced the AFL leaders that direct action, radical or not, was unsafe. Moreover, if the state were encouraged to become involved in labor-management relations, as socialists demanded, it might pass measures harmful to labor or seek to impose its decisions on labor disputes. Through the courts the government could easily suppress strikes, boycotts, or other labor actions by injunctions and by citing union leaders for contempt.

Gompers, who served as AFL president almost continuously until his death in 1924, favored "volunteerism" and "pure and simple" trade unionism as the best policies for the AFL. Unions would improve labor conditions by collective bargaining, resorting to strikes if necessary. Workers themselves would be encouraged to vote for labor's political friends, but beyond that, political involvement would be avoided. Seeking to abolish the capitalist system was simply not realistic. It was foolish, Gompers declared, to suppose that people could

> go to bed one night under the present system and tomorrow morning wake up with a revolution in full blast, and the next day organize a heaven on earth. That is not the way that progress is made; that is not the way . . . social evolution is brought about. We are solving the problem day after day. As we get an hour's more leisure every day it means millions of golden hours of opportunities to the human family. As we get 25 cents a day wage increase, it means another solution, another problem solved, and brings us nearer the time when a greater degree of social justice and fair dealing will obtain among men.

Joined with this moderate philosophy was a pragmatic program. The AFL fought to extract an eight-hour day from employers along with higher wages and better job conditions. It demanded that employers recognize the union as the "collective bargaining" agent for their employees. Eventually it tried to get a union shop—that is, a promise by management that union membership be a precondition for hiring workers.

Armed with this philosophy and program, the AFL forged ahead, particularly when prosperity re-

The son of a London cigar maker, Samuel Gompers established the American Federation of Labor in 1886. Although he was once a socialist, he came to believe labor's problems should be solved through negotiation with employers, using, if needed, the weapons of strikes and boycotts.

turned after the depression of the mid-1890s. Battling against strong opposition by employers, who branded every effort to achieve collective bargaining an interference with the rights of private property, the federation made substantial gains. In 1904 it claimed 1.6 million members out of a total of some 2 million union members in the country. By 1914 it had over 2 million workers in its affiliated unions out of 2.7 million union members altogether. A large majority of blue-collar industrial workers, particularly the unskilled, remained outside the protection that unions conferred; so did most black workers and women. But by the eve of World War I, Gompers and the AFL were powers to be reckoned with in national life.

The Socialist Alternative. Forced to fight conservative employers on the right, the AFL also had to fend off socialists on the left. Before the Civil War, "socialism" and "communism" had sometimes been used as synonyms for the philosophies of utopian communitarians like Charles Fourier and Robert Owen. The socialism of the late nineteenth century, however, was largely Marxist.

Marxism was a body of political beliefs and a theory of society that would exert enormous influence. In his famous book *Das Kapital* (1867), and in other works, Karl Marx had written that material, or economic, relations had always determined human interests and actions. All institutions and values derived ultimately from the way goods were produced and distributed. The religion, family structure, government, literature, arts, and philosophy of a given era reflected that era's fundamental economic institutions. Marx also believed that each economic era was marked by a dominant class. Those who controlled the means of production—whether land, as in feudal times, or capital thereafter—had power, manipulated institutions to further their own ends, and enjoyed the good things of life while others got the leavings.

According to the Marxist interpretation of history, capitalism in its early stages had been a progressive force that had dramatically increased the world's wealth. During this period of vitality, capitalists (the bourgeoisie), like other ruling classes, were able to control and dominate all the social, cultural, and political institutions of their society. All these were used to bolster the capitalist system, and even those people who were not beneficiaries of capitalism found it difficult to deny its legitimacy.

But this situation, Marx said, could not last. By the mid-nineteenth century capitalism had generated within itself certain "contradictions." Capitalists need consumers. But by limiting the working class (the proletariat) to bare subsistence wages, capitalists had limited their own markets. As the working class became progressively poorer, capitalist societies increasingly were finding themselves with goods that no one would buy. In the near future. Marx predicted, capitalist economies would experience ever more frequent and more serious depressions, and these crises would further undermine the workers' conditions. Eventually they would become "class conscious." They would see their common interests; abandon the ethnic, cultural, religious, and national differences that had kept them apart; and become militant revolutionaries. The "class struggle" would worsen. Finally, the masses would seize the railroads, factories, farms, and banks and nationalize the means of production and distribution. Government, now an agent of the proleteriat, would own and manage all.

The profits, formerly skimmed off by the capitalists, would be used to benefit the masses. Under the new socialist system there would no longer be exploiter and exploited, powerful and powerless. Instead, there would be only one class, the working class, and within it all would be equal. With the class struggle ended and capitalist contradictions eliminated, humanity would prosper as never before under a regime of economic and social justice for all.

To thousands of men and women the Marxist vision was an inspiration. It appealed to the oppressed by holding out hope of a world in which they would enjoy the abundance and freedom supposedly reserved for the rich under capitalism. Its promise of a perfectly harmonious society appealed to intellectuals by offering a substitute for their lost religious faith. It spoke to artists, writers, and romantic rebels by promising an antidote to what they saw as the crude and vulgar world of bourgeois values.

In the Gilded Age the Marxists competed with several other socialist groups for the allegiance of wage earners and middle-class dissenters. For a while many Americans were attracted to the Nationalist clubs organized by the journalist Edward Bellamy. In *Looking Backward* (1888), Bellamy told of a young man who awakened in the Boston of the year 2000 and found society transformed into a cooperative commonwealth where abundance, cooperation, and leisure had superseded scarcity, competition, and drudgery. An enormous best-seller for a while, *Looking Backward* made socialism of an undogmatic sort temporarily respectable for thousands of middle-class people.

Also prominent for a while were the anarchists, whose activities in the Haymarket Riot have been mentioned. Members of the so-called Black International (in contrast with the Marxist Red International), anarchists believed that every effort to regiment or coerce human beings was a denial of freedom. Capitalism was evil, but so was any state or government, no matter which class controlled it. In place of the all-powerful workers' state envisioned by the Marxists, anarchists would substitute voluntary associations of people organized around their jobs. These associations would own the factories, mines, and tools and would cooperate to produce a benevolent and just society.

Although noncoercive in their philosophy, the anarchists were anything but gentle in their tactics. They believed in direct action to destroy the capitalist state. In Europe and America they were notorious for assassinating public officials and throwing bombs to make their antiauthoritarian point.

The Homestead Strike. Prior to the Haymarket bombing the anarchists and socialists had won small working-class followings in the major industrial centers. At first there were several competing socialist groups; but after its founding in 1877, the Socialist Labor party, under the brilliant but abrasive Daniel De Leon, became the chief socialist organization. As we have seen, the public reaction to the Haymarket Riot injured trade unionism; it also damaged the various anticapitalist parties, and for several years they languished as little more than debating societies.

A further blow to labor fell in July 1893 as labor and management came together in a searing, violent clash at the Carnegie steel plant at Homestead, Pennsylvania. The issue was new technology. Carnegie and Frick had introduced the most modern labor-saving machinery. Claiming that the new equipment would enhance productivity and thus wages for those who worked by the piece, Frick announced that piece rates would be reduced. The Amalgamated Association of Iron and Steel Workers, representing a small group of the most skilled men, refused to accept the new arrangement. At the end of June 1892, joined by the unskilled workers, they went on strike and sealed off the plant.

Frick had no intention of allowing the strikers to close down the Homestead works and advertised for strikebreakers. But how was he to get the new employees to the idle machines? The locked-out workers were sure to block the way. To solve this problem Frick hired 300 armed Pinkerton agents and sent them in two barges up the Monongahela River, which ran along the edge of the Homestead works. Early on the morning of July 6 the Pinkertons tried to slip by the guards posted by the strikers, but they were detected. The strikers let go with rifles and pistols; the Pinkertons returned the fire until the strikers poured oil on the water and lit it. At this point, rather than be burned alive, the Pinkertons surrendered in return for safe conduct. As they departed for the railway station, however, they were badly beaten. All told, five strikers and three Pinkertons died in the savage melee.

Five days later the governor of Pennsylvania sent 8,000 militiamen to the plant and returned it to the company. The Amalgamated then offered to surrender its economic demands in return for recognition of its right to serve as the bargaining agent for the workers. Frick refused. "Under no circumstances will we have any further dealings with the Amalgamated Association," he declared. "This is final." This arrogant attitude, combined with the use of Pinkertons, brought

This contemporary scene shows the Carnegie Homestead works in Pennsylvania as they appeared at the time of the great strike of 1892. In each corner of this prostrike engraving are scenes showing the "defeat and capture of the Pinkerton invaders."

public opinion to the side of the strikers. Though he supported Frick, Carnegie was dismayed by the mayhem and might have forced concessions. But a young anarchist, Alexander Berkman, outraged at Frick, went to his office and shot and stabbed him repeatedly. Frick survived, but public opinion quickly turned against the strikers, ending all possibility of compromise. As one union man noted: "The bullet from Berkman's pistol went straight through the heart of the Homestead strike."

Depression, Pullman, and Socialist Revival.   The depression following the Panic of 1893 encouraged further labor violence and gave socialism a renewed impetus. As in the 1870s, unemployment soared and

thousands of idle workers tramped the streets or "rode the rails" looking for work. Employers sought to maintain profits and avoid losses by cutting wages. Like all depressions in capitalist societies, that of the 1890s undermined confidence in the system and aroused dissent.

By creating a new charismatic leader, the Pullman strike of 1894 became an important turning point in the history of American socialism. Pullman, the inventor of the sleeping car, had established his giant factory outside Chicago and surrounded it with a model community for his employees. With its tree-lined streets, cream-colored brick houses, its gardens and parks, the town of Pullman was a physically attractive place. It was also a repressive place. Pullman insisted on making his town moral, obedient, and profitable. He forbade

Pullman Workers' Grievances

The workers in George Pullman's Palace Car Company went on strike in June 1894 after years of accumulated grievances. These included not only the typical labor issues of wages and hours, but also those involving the community of Pullman, the company town where most of the workers lived. The selection below is from a statement issued by the forty-six-member Pullman employee grievance committee to the American Railway Union, the union many Pullman workers had recently joined. It was designed to explain the Pullman workers' decision to strike and to appeal to the ARU for support.

"In stating . . . our grievances it is hard to tell where to begin. You all must know that the proximate cause of our strike was the discharge of two members of our grievance committee the day after George M. Pullman, himself, and Thomas H. Wickes, his second vice-president, had guaranteed them absolute immunity. The more remote causes are still imminent. Five reductions in wages, in work, and in conditions of employment swept through the shops at Pullman between May and December, 1893. The last was the most severe, amounting to nearly 30 percent, and our rents had not fallen. We owed Pullman $70,000 . . . [on] May 11. We owe him twice as much as today. He does not evict us for two reasons: One, the force of popular sentiment and public opinion; the other because he hopes to starve us out, to break . . . the back of the American Railway Union, and to deduct from our miserable wages when we are forced to return to him the last dollar we owe him for the occupancy of his houses.

"Rents all over the city [of Chicago] . . . have fallen, in some cases to one-half. Residences, compared with which ours are hovels, can be had a few miles away at the prices we have been contributing to make a millionaire a billionaire. What we pay $15 for in Pullman is leased for $8 in Roseland; and remember that just as no man or woman of our 4,000 toilers has ever felt the friendly pressure of George M. Pullman's hand, so no man or woman of us all has ever owned or can ever hope to own one inch of George M. Pullman's land. Why, even the very streets are his. His ground has never been platted of record, and today he may debar any man . . . from walking in his highways. . . .

"Pullman, both the man and the town, is an ulcer on the body politic. He owns the houses, the school-houses, and churches of God in the town he gave his once humble name. The revenue he derives from these, the wages that he pays out with one hand . . . he takes back with the other. . . . He is able by this to bid under any contract car shop in this country. His competitors in business, to meet this, must reduce the wages of their men. This gives him the excuse to reduce ours to conform to the market. . . . And thus the merry war . . . goes on, and it will go on, brothers, forever, unless you, the American Railway Union, stop it; crush it out.

"Our town is beautiful. In all these thirteen years no word of scandal has arisen against one of our women, young or old. What city of 20,000 persons can show the like . . . ? We are peaceable; we are orderly. . . . But George M. Pullman . . . is patiently . . . waiting . . . to see us starve. . . .

"George M. Pullman . . . has cut our wages from 30 to 70 percent. . . . [He] has caused to be paid in the last year the regular quarterly dividend of 2 percent on his stock. . . . [He] . . . took three contracts on which he lost . . . $5,000. Because he loved us? No. Because it was cheaper to lose a little money in his freight car and his coach shop than to let his workingmen go, but that petty loss . . . was his excuse for effecting a gigantic reduction of wages in every department of his great works, of cutting men and boys and girls with equal zeal. . . .

"We will make you proud of us, brothers, if you will give us the hand we need. . . . Teach arrogant grinders of the faces of the poor that there is still a God in Israel, and if need be a Jehovah—a God of battles. . . ."

liquor, spied on his employees, fired workers for running against the candidates he favored for local office, and charged high rents and utility rates. Pullman considered himself a benevolent man, but he acted like a feudal lord of the manor.

In the summer of 1893, when orders for new Pullman "palace cars" began to fall off, Pullman began to fire workers and cut wages while refusing to reduce rents and utility rates. To defend themselves, Pullman workers began to join the newly organized American Railway Union (ARU) led by a tall, lanky Indianan, Eugene V. Debs. On May 11, 1894, after several unsuccessful attempts to negotiate with Pullman officials, over 3,000 employees walked off the job and asked for ARU supports. Debs tried to persuade the Pullman management to talk. When his efforts failed, he reluctantly ordered the ARU switchmen to refuse to attach Pullman cars to trains. The railroad officials responded by dismissing the defiant switchmen. The ARU struck back. By July 1 all twenty-four railroads operating out of Chicago, the nation's rail hub, had shut down.

Despite their anger, the strikers were restrained and orderly. Yet the shutdown of the country's major transportation system frightened the middle-class public. The *Chicago Herald* charged: "If the strike should be successful the owners of the railroad property . . . would have to surrender . . . future control to the class of labor agitators and strike conspirators who have formed the Debs Railway Union."

Hoping to break the strike and smash the union, the General Managers Association, representing the major railroads entering and leaving Chicago, hired strikebreakers and asked the federal government for aid, claiming that it was Washington's responsibility to guarantee delivery of the mail, which had slowed in many places when the trains ceased to run. In Attorney General Richard Olney the railroad had a friend in government. A hot-tempered former railroad lawyer who despised labor leaders, Olney quickly ordered federal marshals to Chicago. He also convinced a federal judge to issue an injunction that ordered the union to cease the strike or be "in contempt of court." The following day, July 3, over the protests of Illinois governor John P. Altgeld, who denied that there was sufficient disorder to require federal intervention, President Grover Cleveland ordered the entire garrison of Fort Sheridan to the city to prevent violence.

The presence of troops and federal marshals infuriated the strikers, and the railway yards were swept by a wave of shootings and arson. The federal authorities cracked down, arresting Debs and other ARU officials on July 17 for violating the court injunction. Deprived of their leaders, the men gave up and gradually went back to work.

Debs went to prison for six months and thereafter turned against capitalism. In 1897 he became a founder of the Socialist Party of America, an organization that would win a far larger following than De Leon's Socialist Labor party. During the remainder of his life, Debs would embody both the best and the worst in American socialism. Generous, humane, and fiery in defense of justice, he was also a stubborn visionary who lacked the ability to manage a party racked by bitter internal disagreements. Despite his failings, under Deb's leadership the Socialist Party of America grew rapidly before World War I, winning the support of many German and Jewish wage earners and even some rural and small-town people in the Midwest. It also attracted many prominent authors, ministers, and professional people. Between 1904 and 1912 the party increased its dues-paying membership from 20,000 to 130,000; in 1912 Debs received 900,000 votes, 6 percent of the total, when he ran for president. The party did even better on the local level, electing several congressmen and a half-dozen mayors in cities like Scranton, Milwaukee, and Syracuse.

Still, the Socialist Party of America never captured the support of a majority of American wage

A poster for one of Eugene Debs's earlier presidential campaigns.

A Historical Portrait

Eugene V. Debs

For a generation, Eugene V. Debs was the soul of the socialist movement in America. There were other prominent socialists, but no one else so fired the imaginations and raised the hopes of those who accepted the socialist vision at the beginning of the twentieth century.

Deb's American birth was important for the party and movement he headed. Far too many socialist leaders and followers were foreign-born. With his midwestern twang and rangy build, Debs seemed typically American. Actually, his family roots did not go very deep in American soil. His father and mother were both immigrants from Alsace, the German-speaking province of France, who had arrived at Terre Haute in western Indiana in 1851.

Born in 1855, Eugene enjoyed a moderately prosperous middle-class childhood, attending the local private academy and clerking in his father's grocery store. Though his parents were not needy and opposed his decision, Eugene quit school at fourteen to become an unskilled worker for the Vandalia Railroad.

Over the next four years Debs rose to the rank of fireman, but then lost his job during the depression of the mid-1870s. Fortunately, his father succeeded in getting him placed as a clerk in the prosperous wholesale grocery business of a friend. Debs retained a foot in the blue-collar camp by joining the Vigo Lodge of the recently formed Brotherhood of Locomotive Fireman. Yet the lodge was more a fraternal organization like the Masons or Elks than a modern trade union. It was certainly not a militant, class-conscious organization. In 1878, the year after the violent railroad strikes, Debs would tell an approving Brotherhood convention that the firemen's interests were "closely aligned with those of their employers."

The young man of twenty still believed in social harmony as an ideal. One of his friends was William McKeen, president of the Terre Haute and Indianapolis Railroad. Debs praised McKeen as a benevolent employer. McKeen in turn supported Debs when he ran for city clerk on the Democratic ticket in 1879, and again when he ran for the Indiana State Assembly in 1884. During these years the Republican *Express* called the rising young politician "the blue-eyed boy of destiny." In 1885 Debs capped his worldly success by marrying Kate Bauer, daughter of a prosperous Terre Haute druggist.

Despite his upward mobility, Debs refused to abandon his union work. In 1880 he became national secretary-treasurer of the Locomotive Firemen's Brotherhood. He also served as editor of its journal. His ambitious, status-conscious wife kept urging him to accept various business offers, but Debs continued to travel around the country on Brotherhood business. The marriage was not a happy one. The couple could not have children, and this affliction left a gap. Kate Debs took solace in buying a luxurious house in Terre Haute with the proceeds from an inheritance and furnishing it elaborately. She never liked her husband's union and political associates; they were not respectable. Her obsession with material things would prove embarrassing to the country's leading socialist in later years.

During the later 1880s the increasing impersonality of labor-management relations and the erosion of skilled workers' status by new labor-simplifying technology affected Debs's social views. The event that finally liberated him from his earlier ideal of social harmony was the Firemen's strike in 1888/1889 against the Chicago, Burlington, and Quincy Railroad. The workers were unable to cooperate against an alliance between the railroad and the courts, and they were defeated. The experience convinced Debs that unless working people pulled together, they would never improve their position relative to capital.

In 1893 Debs helped organize the American Railway Union and became its first president. The ARU was soon embroiled in a major strike against James J. Hill's Great Northern Railroad. The following year Debs brought his union into the Pullman strike on the side of the Pullman Palace Car workers. Accused of defying a federal court injunction to stop impeding the mails, Debs and other ARU officials were sentenced to prison terms. The union suffered a blow from which it never fully recovered.

Despite a later myth that Debs himself encouraged, he did not at this time become a socialist. He did emerge from six months in Woodstock prison with a more radical evaluation of American society, yet in 1896 he campaigned for Bryan, the Democratic–free-silver candidate for President. Bryan's defeat pushed Debs over the line, however, and in January 1897 he told his associates at the ARU that "the issue is Socialism versus Capitalism. I am for Socialism because I am for humanity." Debs soon maneuvered the remnants of the ARU into forming the

Social Democracy of America.

Between 1897 and 1900 Debs came to accept the orthodox socialist class-conflict version of history and politics and became a major figure in the socialist movement. In 1900 the newly formed Social Democratic party nominated him for president, and in 1901 he helped forge the Socialist Party of America out of a collection of socialist splinter groups and factions.

For the next two decades Debs remained the leading figure in the American socialist movement. He was the Socialist party candidate for president in 1904, 1908, 1912, and again in 1920, the last year running his campaign from prison. In the 1912 campaign he received almost a million votes, over 6 percent of the total cast. Debs was a powerful speaker who could hold an audience in his grasp for hours while alternately excoriating capitalism and evoking glowing images of the future Cooperative Commonwealth. Millions, including many who would not "throw away" their votes on a third-party candidate, adored him. To many Americans of the day, he personified the heroic and humane socialist ideal.

Yet within the socialist movement Debs had his critics and opponents. To his right within the party there was Victor Berger of Milwaukee and Morris Hillquit of New York. Both were foreign-born, yet both represented moderate positions. They believed it essential for socialists to work within the existing conservative labor unions, seeking to gain control by influencing members' views. They also believed that socialists must support reform programs in order to appeal to discontented members of the middle class as well as to blue-collar workers.

Debs led the left wing, which endorsed separate radical unions in competition with the American Federation of Labor, was more skeptical of reform, and more "proletarian" in its sympathies than the right wing. Yet Debs had his critics to the left, too. These were people like "Big Bill" Haywood of the Industrial Workers of the World (IWW), who advocated industrial sabotage, the general strike, and overtly confrontationist tactics to bring capitalism to its knees. Debs tried to mediate between these extremes. He did not always succeed, but his charisma and popularity with the rank-and-file members managed to preserve the formal unity of the party.

World War I was a catastrophe for the socialists and for Debs. Some prominent socialists left the party to support the Allied cause even before American entrance into the war, and more resigned when, in April 1917, shortly after America's declaration of war against Germany, the party announced its opposition to the war. During the war the mood of intolerance and superpatriotism led to official repression of socialist publications, government raids on party offices, vigilante actions against socialists, and the arrest and imprisonment of socialist leaders on charges of subversion and attempts to discourage men from registering for the draft. In June 1918, following a speech critical of the United States, Debs was indicted by the federal government for violating the 1917 Espionage Act. He used his trial as an effective forum for his ideas, but he was sentenced to ten years in prison and sent to Atlanta Penitentiary to serve his term.

During the two years Debs actually spent in prison, the party he had helped to found underwent drastic changes. In the decade preceding 1917 more and more of the party membership came to consist of recent immigrants from Finland, Russia, and other parts of eastern Europe. When the Bolsheviks took power in Russia in late 1917, many of these immigrants hailed the event and insisted that the party endorse the Revolution. Before long the "foreign-language federations," with their far-left allegiances, formed a caucus within the party and sought to seize power. In March 1919 the Bolshevik leaders in Moscow ordered the formation of the Third International, with the slogan "Back to Marx" and the name "Communist." One of the first directives issued by the International's leaders was that each of the organized Socialist parties divest itself of any bourgeois, right-wing elements. This encouraged the foreign-language federations to split off from Debs's Socialist party and organize what came to be the American Communist party, leaving behind a depleted and demoralized rump.

At first Debs supported the radicals, but then, while still in prison, he changed his mind. After his release from Atlanta in December 1921, he returned to Terre Haute to be greeted by 25,000 cheering supporters. By this time the early hope that the Socialist party might become a major agent of fundamental change had evaporated. In 1924, recognizing the depleted energies of the party, Debs supported Robert LaFollette's presidential bid on the Farmer-Labor ticket. For this he was bitterly attacked by his former left-wing comrades, now mostly Communists.

Debs had never been a healthy man. Over the years he had suffered numerous breakdowns from mysterious ailments and had taken a series of "cures" at sanitariums. On October 20, 1926, following a massive heart attack, he died in Chicago and his body was brought to Terre Haute. Thousands came to pay their respects, trailing through the parlor of the Debs's house to view the coffin. Eugene's brother Theodore, Theodore's wife and daughter, and other family members greeted the mourners. Debs's widow, Kate, remained upstairs in her room, however. To the very end she could not help expressing her disapproval of her husband's disreputable associates.

earners. Unlike the French, Italian, German, and British Socialist parties, it never truly challenged the leading moderate parties for control. Some scholars have blamed this comparative failure on the Socialists' tendency to fight among themselves over minor points of Marxist theory. Others contend that American capitalism was too self-confident, too competent, and too powerful to be successfully challenged. Another view emphasizes the power of cultural indoctrination, such as the Horatio Alger myth or the work ethic, to dissuade American workers from accepting radical ideas.

The most convincing answer, however, points in a different direction. No doubt factionalism and strong capitalist resistance weakened the Socialist party in the United States; but European socialists, who faced the same difficulties, prospered. In contrast to European workers, however, American wage earners, especially the native-born, were not class-conscious. Well paid by comparison with industrial workers in other lands and just a generation or two off the farm, they expected to prosper and move up the social ladder. Many owned some property and could not accept a philosophy that predicted inevitable class conflict and the increasing misery of wage earners under capitalism. Immigrant workers were not much better as potential recruits for socialism. Most had difficulty enough adjusting to American cities and American industry without making further trouble for themselves, and they avoided "labor agitators." Despite their initially low status, they, too, expected to rise socially and economically. All told, the relative prosperity of the United States and people's expectations for improvement were strong antidotes to radical politics. As the German sociologist Werner Sombart noted at the turn of the century, socialist "utopias" in America inevitably foundered "on the reefs of roast beef and apple pie."

Conclusions

As we consider the reasons for the nation's economic surge a century ago, several distinct factors come into view. Creative industrial tycoons gave a strong push to America's forward leap. Their skill, intelligence, drive, and even ruthlessness furthered the growth that propelled the Republic far past its rivals. But besides the builders who added to the nation's efficiency, innovation, and technology, there were the spoilers who milked the achievements of others solely for their own advantage. And the tycoons—builders or spoilers—could not have created an industrial nation alone. Working people, accepting the conventional wisdom of the age, labored hard, believing that success and security would reward their efforts. It is also clear that without government's substantial contributions, despite the theories of laissez-faire and social Darwinism, progress would have been far slower.

Clearly many of the men and women who lived through these tumultuous years were ground down by the great economic machine they were helping to build. The pain they experienced was expressed in the violence of the Pullman, Homestead, and railway strikes, and in the organized political efforts meant to effect change. Yet we must not exaggerate the extent or depth of discontent among wage earners. Many found their lives satisfactory and, with reason, looked forward to better times. Despite the agitation and the occasional violence, it remains true that most Americans retained their faith in the "system" and refused to accept radical solutions to the problems they faced. This ultimate faith was expressed in the continued vitality of the economy and the mainstream political parties and in the growth of cities and the nation as a whole.

For Further Reading

Edward C. Kirkland. *Dream and Thought in the Business Community, 1860–1900* (1956)
> This intellectual history of Gilded Age businessmen is based on their private correspondence, congressional testimony, and published writings. Seeking to avoid stereotypes, Kirkland presents their thoughts on the economy, government, the civil service, public schools, philanthropy, and the universities.

Matthew Josephson. *Edison* (1959)
> According to Josephson, Edison's Menlo Park laboratory was his greatest invention: It was the first industrial research laboratory, applying scientific theory and technical knowledge to practical problems.

Harold C. Livesay. *Andrew Carnegie and the Rise of Big Business* (1975)
> This small jewel of a book makes Carnegie's role in the post–Civil War economic surge clear. It is not a full biography, but it makes the economic man and his accomplishments come alive.

Frederick Lewis Allen. *The Great Pierpont Morgan* (1949)

A breezy, entertaining biography of Morgan that succeeds in defining his place in American economic life. Allen makes complex financial deals easy to understand.

Irvin G. Wyllie. *The Self-Made Man in America: The Myth of Rags to Riches* (1954)

Wyllie follows the myth of the self-made individual from colonial times to 1929. He describes the continuing power of the myth in the face of some hard statistics suggesting that to go from rags to riches was a rare achievement.

Theodore Dreiser. *The Financier* (1912)

The hero of this novel is modeled after the Gilded Age streetcar magnate Charles Yerkes. A superb historical document: Dreiser understands the sort of driven and aggressive man Yerkes was and perceives the relationship between business and politics in this era. Dreiser actually admires Yerkes for his powerful will.

Herbert Gutman. *Work, Culture, and Society in Industrializing America* (1976)

A collection of essays, written at different times, by a leading social historian. It emphasizes the experience of working-class life in the half century following 1865. An important, though uneven, book.

Stephen Thernstrom. *Progress and Poverty: Social Mobility in a Nineteenth-Century City* (1964); and *The Other Bostonians: Poverty and Progress in the American Metropolis* (1973)

The first of these two books deals with Newburyport, Massachusetts; the second with Boston. Both seek to determine the extent of social mobility for working people and the middle class in nineteenth-century America. In Newburyport, a small city, Thernstrom finds that movement up the social and occupational ladder for wage earners was modest and difficult, though it took place. In Boston, on the other hand, it was remarkably easy, especially for native-born Americans, Northern Europeans Protestant immigrants, and Jews, though slower for blacks and Irish Catholics. Both studies are important.

Stanley Buder. *Pullman: An Experiment in Industrial Order and Community Planning, 1880–1930* (1967)

This is as much an urban as a labor history. It tells the story of the town of Pullman and views it as an example of unsuccessful paternalism.

David Montgomery. *Beyond Equality: Labor and the Radical Republicans, 1862–1872* (1967)

An interesting attempt to connect the Gilded Age labor movement to the egalitarian ideas of the 1860s Radical Republicans.

Daniel Walkowitz. *Worker City, Company Town: Iron and Cotton Worker Protest in Troy and Cahoes, New York, 1855–1884* (1978)

A study of two New York industrial towns with different ethnic mixes and with different property distribution patterns. Walkowitz links the differing response to labor conditions of each wage earner community to its distinctive social milieu. Though seemingly narrow in scope, the study makes for interesting reading.

David Brody. *Steelworkers in America: The Nonunion Era* (1960)

Brody shows not only what produced discontent among American steelworkers before 1919, but also what encouraged labor's stability and acquiescence. A model study.

Harold C. Livesay. *Samuel Gompers and Organized Labor in America* (1978)

Another good biography by Livesay, this time of a leading labor statesman. The book goes beyond biography, however, and tells us much of the evolving labor movement, particularly the AFL, during the years 1890 to 1920.

Daniel T. Rogers. *The Work Ethic in Industrial America, 1850–1920* (1975)

Examines the intellectual defense of hard work and steady application that accompanied industrialization in the United States.

Daniel Bell. *Marxian Socialism in the United States* (1962)

Bell, although at one time a Marxist himself, was critical of socialism by the time he wrote this brief book. Though one must keep his biases in mind, this short history of American socialism is valuable.

Nick Salvatore. *Eugene V. Debs: Citizen and Socialist* (1982)

This is the best biography of Debs. Written by a scholar sympathetic to, but not uncritical of, the Socialist leader.

Charles Francis Adams, Jr., and Henry Adams. *Chapters of Erie* (1866)

The classic account of the chicanery of Jay Gould and his confederates. Written by patrician descendants of two presidents who themselves knew the Gilded Age business community.

Maury Klein, *The Life and Legend of Jay Gould* (1986)

Professor Klein attempts the difficult here: rehabilitating the reputation of Jay Gould. And almost pulls it off.

Chapter 18

The Gilded Age City

What Did It Offer, and to Whom?

1860–1910   American cities, as defined by the Census, increase in number from 392 to 2,220

1871   The Great Chicago Fire

1872   New York's Boss Tweed is indicted and jailed

1878   Asphalt paving introduced in Washington, D.C.

1880   Salvation Army introduced from England • James A. Garfield elected president

1881   Garfield assassinated; Chester A. Arthur becomes president

1882   Chinese Exclusion Act passed in response to organized labor's fear of cheap labor

1884   Grover Cleveland elected president

1888   Benjamin Harrison elected president

1892   Cleveland elected president for the second time

1894   Immigration Restriction League • Coxey's Army marches on Washington to protest unemployment

1896   William McKinley elected president

1897   First subway line is built, in Boston

1899–1904   Mayor Samuel "Golden Rule" Jones institutes municipal ownership of utilities in Toledo

1900–10   Eight million immigrants arrive

1901   McKinley assassinated; Theodore Roosevelt becomes president

1907   Congress appoints Dillingham Commission to investigate immigration

1914   Birth control advocate Margaret Sanger is forced to leave the country

The city has been a central element in civilization for perhaps 5,000 years. In fact, cities seem to "equal" civilization, for it has been in urban settings that humanity has produced most of the ideas, artifacts, art, and science that we identify as essential marks of civilized life.

Always in the past, however, city populations have been a rather small part of any society; until the years following the Civil War, the United States was no exception to this rule. As late as 1860 only 20 percent of the nation's population was urban. The most heavily urbanized sections of the nation were the New England and Middle Atlantic areas, where industrialization had already seized hold and thousands of farm people, both native- and foreign-born, had been drawn to the factories, docks, and countinghouses of both old towns and new ones. Elsewhere, particularly in the West and the South, most Americans continued to live on villages and farms.

The Civil War slowed city growth somewhat, but thereafter it resumed at a breakneck pace. Between 1860 and 1910 the number of "urban places" increased from 392 to over 2,200. In 1860 New York and Philadelphia were the only American cities with more than half a million inhabitants. By 1910 these communities, along with the "prairie colossus," Chicago, had over a million residents each, and five other cities had grown to 500,000 people. During that fifty-year stretch the urban share of the country's population went from 20 to 46 percent. The Northeast remained the most urban part of the nation: Massachusetts and Rhode Island were about 90 percent urban; Connecticut, New York, New Jersey, and Pennsylvania were over 60 percent urban. But urbanization had spread far beyond the areas that had first felt the pull of industry and commerce. In the Midwest, Illinois, Ohio, Michigan, Wisconsin, Indiana, Missouri, and Minnesota were almost 46 percent urban—the 1910 national average. The Far West and Pacific coast were not far behind, and by 1910 Colorado, Washington, and California were all either ahead or just behind the national average.

What forces explain this rapid urban growth? What brought millions of people from the farms of America and from distant regions of the world to the cities of the United States in these years? And how did the millions of new urban dwellers fare in their new homes?

Immigration

One major factor that set urban populations soaring in the half century following the Civil War was the influx of foreign-born newcomers. In the 1880s more than 5 million people entered the United States. The severe depression of the 1890s reduced the number of immigrants substantially, but between 1900 and 1910 over 8 million additional foreigners arrived. Many of these people eventually returned home, either disappointed or so successful that they could live well in the "old country" on what they had made here. Yet most immigrants, by far, remained in America, and by the end of the century most of them made the cities their home.

America's Attractions. Like previous immigrants, Gilded Age arrivals came because of both "pushes" and "pulls." The chief "pull" of America, for late-nineteenth-century immigrants as for their predecessors, was economic. Immigrants from every land were attracted by the possibility of improving themselves in some material way. Only a minority were drawn by America's reputation for religious and political freedom. Through letters from previous arrivals and from the newspapers and magazines in their native lands, immigrants were remarkably well informed about American economic conditions. During hard times in the United States, such as the mid-1890s, foreigners stayed home. During good times, such as the 1880s and the first decade of the twentieth century, the flow of immigrants became a flood.

America actively encouraged immigration. During the 1850s western mining companies had brought in Chinese workers to dig for gold in California and Nevada. In the 1860s the Central Pacific Railroad imported 10,000 Chinese to help construct the first transcontinental line. After its completion many of these laborers remained to build other western railroads and to swell the populations of San Francisco,

Sacramento, Denver, and other towns. In Texas, Arizona, New Mexico, California, and Colorado, railroad employers recruited many Mexicans from across the border to work on repair and construction crews; many others came to work the orchards and the cotton, lettuce, and tomato fields.

The railroads encouraged immigration in other ways, too. Anxious to convert their land grants into cash, they sent agents abroad to advertise farms in the West. With their flyers and offers of cheap land and help in getting started as farmers, the railroads attracted thousands of immigrants.

The business recruiter was also active in the East. The Contract Labor Law of 1864 had authorized employers to hire foreign workers under an agreement that guaranteed passage money, a specified wage, and defined working conditions. Actually, the law had little effect. Only a few hundred skilled workers were brought to the United States under its provisions, and after pressure from labor unions, Congress passed the Foran Act (1885) repealing it.

More important was the *padrone* system that was used to recruit Italian labor for eastern mines, factories, and construction projects. *Padroni* were Italian-American middlemen, frequently connected with small immigrant banking firms, who signed up gangs of Italian laborers in southern Italy at fixed wages and paid for the workers' passage. In the United States the *padrone* contracted with an American employer to supply workers at a sum that gave him a substantial profit. In the early years, when the United States was still an unfamiliar destination for Italians, the system was useful in providing immigrants with food, board, and advice. The *padroni*, however, often took advantage of the trusting men they recruited, charging them high prices for what they provided while keeping them in virtual slavery. Fortunately, when the Italian-American community had put down firm roots and would-be immigrants could turn to relatives and friends for advice and help, the system declined.

Though immigration was to some extent "guided," then, the great majority of European arrivals needed little encouragement to join the burgeoning industrial market of America. Letters from relatives and friends, talks with townspeople back in the "old country" for a visit, or information supplied by government agencies and shipping companies was enough to draw people by the thousands to Genoa, Trieste, Bremen, Le Havre, Odessa, Salonika, Oslo, or Liverpool to take ship for the United States.

Despite the obvious attractions of America, fewer immigrants would have crossed the Atlantic or the Pacific if not for the plummeting prices of ocean fares and the growing speed of ocean travel. Here the steamship made the difference. During the 1860s the introduction of large and fast steam vessels with auxiliary sail reduced translatlantic crossing times from as long as three months to as little as ten days. A dozen shipping companies—British, German, Italian, Dutch, and French, as well as American—soon entered the transatlantic trade, and their fierce competition quickly brought passenger rates down.

The Push: The New Immigrants. Like the "pull" to America, the "push" was predominantly economic. Until the 1890s most European immigrants came from nothern Europe—Britain, Germany, and Scandinavia. In each of these countries agriculture had been hurt by competition from the newer grain-growing regions of Canada, the United States, Argentina, and Australia. Unable to compete with the lower production costs in these new lands, European landlords squeezed out the peasants and introduced machinery. To make matters worse, the 1870s and 1880s were times of severe drought in parts of western and central Europe. Overseas competition, combined with nature's ill favor, drove thousands of Swedes, Germans, and Britons to seek havens in the United States.

The push from northern Europe soon slackened. By the 1890s northern European agriculture had adjusted to the overseas competition. At the same time, rapid industrialization in Sweden and Germany, plus falling birthrates throughout northern Europe, provided new opportunities for displaced farm people in their own nations' factories and mines. Meanwhile, growing militarism in Germany led to official efforts to discourage the emigration of young men. British emigration continued; but more and more, the Irish, Scottish, English, and Welsh found the British "dominions"—Canada, Australia, New Zealand, and South Africa—more attractive than the United States.

After 1890 a wave of immigrants from southern and eastern Europe more than offset this northern European decline. These so-called New Immigrants were a diverse lot. Many were Slavic peoples—Czechs and Bohemians, Poles, Ukrainians, Slovaks, Serbs, Croatians, Ruthenians, and Russians—from the Hapsburg Empire (Austria-Hungary) or from Russia, the empire of the Romanov czars. Many were southern Europeans, with the largest number from Italy, though there were many Greeks as well. Other eastern Europeans included Hungarians and Rumanians. From the Turkish dominions came Armenians and Syrians. A large group of New Immigrants consisted of Jews from either Austria-

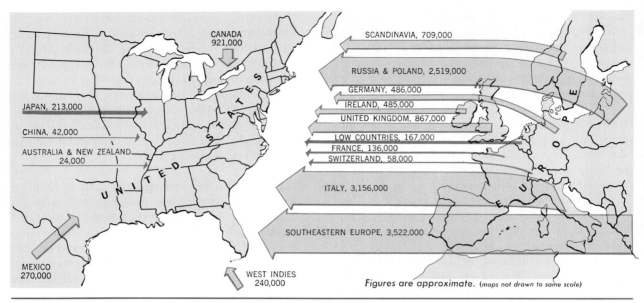

Sources of immigrants, 1900–1920

Map labels:
- CANADA 921,000
- SCANDINAVIA, 709,000
- RUSSIA & POLAND, 2,519,000
- GERMANY, 486,000
- IRELAND, 485,000
- UNITED KINGDOM, 867,000
- LOW COUNTRIES, 167,000
- FRANCE, 136,000
- SWITZERLAND, 58,000
- JAPAN, 213,000
- CHINA, 42,000
- AUSTRALIA & NEW ZEALAND 24,000
- ITALY, 3,156,000
- SOUTHEASTERN EUROPE, 3,522,000
- MEXICO 270,000
- WEST INDIES 240,000
- Figures are approximate. (maps not drawn to same scale)

Hungary or imperial Russia. Many of the Slavs and virtually all the Italians were Roman Catholic, and for the first time there were substantial numbers of Orthodox Catholics among the new arrivals.

Until late in the century America had meant little to these people. It was too far away and too expensive to reach. Besides, the Hapsburgs, the Romanovs, and the Ottoman Turks had refused to allow their subject peoples to leave for fear of reducing their military forces or their tax rolls. Toward the end of the century Austria, Russia, and Turkey abandoned their opposition to emigration. At the same time, as we have seen, ocean passage rates and travel time declined sharply. In addition, the blight of overseas agricultural competition, which had attacked the countries farther west a decade or so earlier, finally spread to eastern Europe.

Though the push was largely economic, political and religious factors also played a part in propelling people from the czarist and Ottoman lands across the Atlantic. No country in Europe was as backward, as illiberal, and as authoritarian as Russia. The czars often treated non-Russian subjects harshly. After 1870 thousands of German Pietists, who had settled in southern Russia during the eighteenth century, fled when the czars withdrew their privileges. A much larger group of refugees from the czars' domains were Jews who had resided in Russian lands since the Middle Ages. Never treated as full equals, they had managed to survive as craftworkers, innkeepers, small merchants, and

manufacturers. After 1880, however, a wave of laws excluded them from public office, universities, agricultural pursuits, the professions, and other activities. The government also incited anti-Jewish riots (pogroms) that resulted in hundreds of deaths and the devastation of whole communities. Meanwhile, in the Ottoman Empire, the Turkish government began to persecute brutally its Christian Syrian and Armenian minorities.

These changes produced a drastic shift in the source of the immigrant streams: Most now came from southern and eastern Europe. In 1880 a mere 17,000 immigrants to the United States came from Austria-Hungary; by 1907 there were almost 340,000. Only 5,000 Russian subjects immigrated to America in 1880; in 1907 over 225,000 arrived. In 1880 some 12,000 Italians came to the United States; in 1907, over 285,000. Northern European immigration showed the opposite trend: In 1880 the number from Britain, Germany, and Scandinavia totaled 295,000; by 1907, when total immigration was almost three times as great, it was down to 199,000.

From Farms to Cities. The ocean crossing remained unpleasant for poorer immigrants until well into the twentieth century. Unable to pay for private cabins, they traveled below decks in "steerage," jammed in with hundreds of others. Rough seas brought seasickness. At times cholera epidemics swept the ships, killing

Were poor immigrants a resource? Steel king Andrew Carnegie, himself an immigrant, believed they were. In fact, he estimated that each one was worth $1,500. Immigrants labored in mines and mills, built railroads and bridges, farmed the land, and bought products of the nation's factories.

scores and so frightening American officials that the federal government imposed quarantines, shutting down all transatlantic immigration for substantial periods.

Most European immigrants came through New York, Boston, New Orleans, Baltimore, or Philadelphia. Before 1892 most New York–bound immigrants passed through Castle Garden, a facility established at the tip of Manhattan Island by New York State officials. In 1892 the federal government took over the responsibility for receiving immigrants and replaced Castle Garden with a new facility at Ellis Island in New York harbor. Here new immigrants were asked their names, ages, occupations, places of origin, literacy, and financial status. They were also examined by doctors to see that they were not carriers of infectious diseases. At Ellis Island, too, immigrants first made contact with the many societies established by their compatriots to offer advice and services and to keep them out of the hands of swindlers eager to cheat "greenhorns" of their money and possessions.

Once in America, the immigrants had to consider their ultimate destinations. During the 1870s and 1880s thousands of Germans, Scandinavians, Poles, and Bohemians went to the wheat regions of Minnesota, the Dakotas, Nebraska, and Kansas, where they bought land from the railroads. Then, as the nation shifted from an agricultural to an industrial economy,

the immigrants were increasingly drawn to the cities and their factories.

Specific immigrant groups tended to concentrate in certain industries. There were several reasons for this: because their compatriots who had come to America earlier worked in the particular industry, because it was related to a business they were familiar with, or because they had settled in a region dominated by one industry. French Canadians crossed the border from Quebec to the nearby New England textile towns, where they displaced many of the Irish, who had earlier replaced the New England mill girls. Jews from Russia and Poland who had been skilled tailors in Europe entered the garment industry of New York, Rochester, and Chicago. Italians, coming from a land notable for stonemasons and workers in marble, concentrated in the construction industry; Slavs entered mining and heavy industry; the Portuguese from maritime Portugal and the Azores moved into the New England fishing industry.

Nativism. The new pattern of immigration that emerged toward the end of the century disturbed many Americans. Some deplored the immigrants' urban concentration, seeing it as a deterrent to their assimilation into the mainstream of American life. Concentrated in tight-knit ghettos, they would be slow to lose their alien ways and become "good Americans." Immigrant organizations were also concerned, and Jewish and Catholic organizations sought to encourage recent arrivals among their coreligionists to avoid the cities and settle in rural areas. Many native Americans resented the unfamiliar appearance and ways of the newcomers. The novelist Henry James, visiting Boston after spending many years in Europe, felt out of place as he walked the city's streets. While strolling on fashionable Beacon Hill one Sunday, James observed groups of men and women in their best clothes walking and "enjoying their leisure." "No sound of English . . . escaped their lips; the great number spoke some rude form of Italian, the others some outlandish dialect unknown to me. . . . The types and faces bore them out; the people before me were gross aliens to a man, and they were in serene and triumphant possession."

The resentment was not confined to elite, old-stock Americans. The New Immigrants frequently clashed with the Old Immigrants of the pre–Civil War generation or with their half-assimilated children. In 1877, during the hard times that followed the Panic of 1873, Irish-American workers in San Francisco attacked Chinese businesses and the docks of the Pacific Mail Steamship Company, the firm they held responsible for importing the "coolie" immigrants from Asia to undercut their wages. Local businessmen organized a Committee of Public Safety and with the aid of federal authorities stopped the rioting, but not before four men had died. Soon afterward Denis Kearney, a native of Ireland's County Cork, helped organize the Workingmen's Party of California, an organization dedicated to improving the lot of the city's working people, but also committed to eliminating the Chinese from the community. Kearney denounced the rich railroad and mining magnates of California, but his speeches usually ended with the cry: "And whatever happens, the Chinese must go!"

The anti-Chinese movement in California was not unique. Spokesmen for organized labor feared "coolie labor," and indeed any cheap labor, whether from Europe or Asia. Passage of the Foran Act in 1885, repealing the Contract Labor Law of 1864, was largely the result of trade-union pressure. In 1882 similar pressure induced Congress to pass the Chinese Exclusion Act prohibiting the immigration of Chinese laborers for ten years. This measure was renewed several times, and Chinese exclusion was made permanent in 1902. Not until 1943 were foreign-born Chinese allowed to take up legal permanent residence in the United States.

Anti-immigrant sentiment in these years, however, was not primarily economic in origin. Most native-born Americans had little to fear from the New Immigrants, for they generally took the low-paid, unskilled, dirty jobs that no one else wanted. Nativist feelings, rather, had roots that were largely cultural. No American denied that the country was composed of past immigrants and their descendants. But many native-born people were certain that the New Immigrants were inferior to the immigrants of the past. They seemed more alien and illiterate. They came, it was said, from more backward lands where democratic institutions were unknown. A larger proportion of them were Catholic or Jewish, and hence further removed than earlier arrivals from the American Protestant tradition. They were responsible for the increased disorder, violence, and vice of the cities. The New Immigrants, moreover, did not intend to stay, the critics said. Many were birds of passage, men without wives or families, who would make their fortunes in America and return to their native lands. They refused to go to the farms, the indictment continued, congregating instead in the big cities, where they retained their foreign ways, turned to crime, and succumbed to insanity, epilepsy, or other nervous or emotional disorders that severely taxed local health facilities.

The hostile response to immigrants was reinforced at the turn of the century by the racist theories of men like Josiah Strong and Madison Grant, who proclaimed the natural superiority of "Nordics" over "Mediterraneans," "Alpines," and other darker-haired, darker-eyed white people of southern and eastern Europe. Racist ideology and traditional prejudice against foreigners led in 1907 to the appointment by Congress of the Dillingham Commission to investigate immigration. Its voluminous report confirmed all the common negative stereotypes. The commission described the Old Immigrants as "ideal farmers" and people "imbued with sympathy for our ideals and . . . democratic institutions." By contrast, the more recently arrived southern and eastern Europeans were "different in temperament and civilization from ourselves." Serbo-Croatians had "savage manners," Poles were "high-strung," southern Italians had "not attained distinguished success as farmers." Generally, the report endorsed the common view of the inferiority of the New Immigrants and branded them undesirable.

The Dillingham Commission's report was full of errors. It disregarded the differences among nationalities except when these could be held to their discredit. But the new arrivals were not all alike. The illiteracy rate was high among Italians, low among Bohemians. Greeks returned to their homeland in some numbers, but few Jews of the czar's vast empire did, for Russia was violently anti-Semitic. Many New Immigrants were unskilled; but the Armenians were more skilled than the Germans arriving in the same period.

Whatever the reality, many old-stock Americans continued to believe in the inferiority of the most recent immigrants and supported nativist organizations that were dedicated to reducing the flow of immigrants or limiting their role and that of their children in American public life. In the 1880s and 1890s, the American Protective Association (APA) demanded that noncitizens be excluded from political power and attacked "the diabolical works of the Roman Catholic church." In 1894 a group of New England blue bloods organized the Immigration Restriction League with a program to impose literacy tests on the new arrivals, many of whom, the League believed, could not pass such a test. The League was blunt in expressing its goals. According to one prominent member, Americans must decide whether the country was "to be peopled by British, German, and Scandinavian stock, historically free, energetic, progressive, or by Slav, Latin, and Asiatic races, historically downtrodden, atavistic and stagnant."

The League accomplished little before the 1920s.

A large unidentified office, about 1900. An increasingly complex society needed more literate white-collar workers, and so proved willing to finance high school education out of public funds.

In 1896, and again in 1913 and 1915, Congress passed measures requiring that all immigrants be able to read and write either English or their own language. Each time, however, the president vetoed the measure. Though many Americans feared the foreign deluge, others opposed restriction. Business people resisted an end to the seemingly inexhaustible supply of cheap labor, and the National Association of Manufacturers constantly lobbied against restrictions on immigration. Old-fashioned liberals, who prized America's tradition as a haven for the world's poor and oppressed, also fought efforts to end free immigration. In the end the doors remained open. Though Congress whittled away at free movement from Europe by passing laws excluding immigrants with chronic diseases, those with records as criminals or prostitutes, and those with known anarchist views, drastic limitations on transatlantic immigrants would wait until a later day.

"Buckwheats" and "Hayseeds." City streets were crowded not only with the foreign-born; they were also jammed with men and women straight off the nation's farms. Just as there were "pushes" and "pulls" in the movement of immigrants to America, there were similar factors in the exodus from the nation's farms and villages to Gilded Age cities.

The lure of the city for rural people is a persistent theme in the history of the Western world. Cities were no doubt wicked; they were dangerous. But they were also vivid places where life was full of excitement and color. Compared with the sleepy village or farm, the city—with its well-stocked stores, its bustle, its amuse-ments, its street life, and its brilliant lights—was a joy. The novelist Hamlin Garland recalled that everything about Chicago was interesting when he arrived there as a young farm boy: "Nothing was commonplace, nothing ugly." In *The City*, a 1909 play by popular playwright Clyde Fitch, one character exclaims: "Who wants to smell new-mown hay, if he can breathe gasoline on Fifth Avenue instead!"

But besides the urban glamor, there were irresistible economic pulls. Jobs, of course, were primary. Thousands of young rural people came to the cities to work as clerks, secretaries, bookkeepers, and salespeople. Farm boys also were drawn to the mills and factories to tend machines, stoke furnaces, and supervise other hands. At his plants in Pennsylvania Andrew Carnegie liked to hire "buckwheats," lads from the nearby countryside. These young men, he believed, made the best workers in the mills. For young Americans with special career interests, the cities were indispensable. To talented musicians, artists, writers, actors, or performers of any kind, only the largest cities of the land could provide the training, the experience, and the appreciative audience they needed and craved.

The push also applied to rural youths—"hayseeds" in the vocabulary of the day. If the cities were fascinating, the farms and villages often were not. Hamlin Garland wrote about the "sordidness, dullness, triviality, and . . . endless drudgeries" of rural life. In his short story "Up the Coulee" one of his characters complains: "Anything under God's heavens is better'n farmin'." But even if a farm youth wanted to stay and till the soil, it was often difficult. Because farm

families were large, rural fathers could not provide land for all their sons. There was the option of going west, but as we shall see, through much of the late nineteenth century, agriculture was a depressed industry even on the newer western lands.

In the Northeast the farmers' problems were compounded. With the completion of the transportation network, it became ever more difficult for the old, rocky fields of New England and the Middle Atlantic states to compete with the rich soils of the Plains and the prairies. In certain places northeastern farmers were able to adjust to the new competition. In many areas, however, they and their children simply abandoned the land that their ancestors had occupied for generations and went off to the nearest big city. As the census of 1890 showed, the counties in two-fifths of Pennsylvania, one-fourth of New Jersey, about five-sixths of New York, and a very large part of New England had declined in population during the 1880s. A French visitor who traveled through Pennsylvania and New England in the early 1890s noted: "Sloven farms alternate with vast acreages of territory, half forest, half pasturage." Farm buildings "partly in ruins testify at once to the former prosperity of agriculture and to its present collapse."

The Urban Setting

The Physical Environment. Whether from Italy or Iowa, Austria or Alabama, all newcomers found urban life in the Gilded Age replete with problems. American cities in the years immediately following the Civil War were generally brutal, dirty, congested places. The streets were unpleasant. Many cities had miles of dirt roads, dusty in summer, muddy in winter, and filthy at all times owing to the large numbers of horses. Nor was the sky above any better. The soft coal used for heating and industrial fuel darkened city air with soot. In the 1890s the ash from its steel and glass factories often brought twilight at midday to Pittsburgh.

Until the end of the century few American cities had adequate public water supplies or decent sewer or street-cleaning services. In 1880 Baltimore, with 330,000 people, had "no sewers to speak of . . . , all chamber slops [being] deposited in cess pools or privy vaults." A newspaper report on Chicago in the same year declared with unusual directness that "the air stinks." Just after the Civil War, Memphis was described as an open sewer.

Housing presented the most serious urban prob-

This floor plan of a "dumbbell" tenement explains the name but leaves much unsaid. Each unheated apartment housed at least one family, allowing the landlord to charge rent for as many as 700 people in a single block of dumbbells. The "hall" was less than three feet wide, and the light shafts—often used to dispose of garbage—were a fire hazard. Like most tenements, the dumbbell had a way of looking dilapidated as soon as it was built.

lem. Newcomers to the city struggled to find decent dwellings at cheap prices. Many were forced to take the dilapidated houses formerly occupied by the middle class, who had fled the squalor and congestion of the inner city. The originally spacious rooms of these older

The Boston Poor

Not every city dweller in the Gilded Age, not even every working-class person, was miserably housed, of course. But in this era, when rural Americans and immigrants poured into the country's cities, decent living accommodations are denied many people. For decades following the Civil War few middle-class Americans worried much about the "slums." But then, toward the end of the century, a new urban reform movement appeared, led by men and women who believed that much of the cities' misery could be blamed on the wretched hovels imposed on the urban poor. One such reformer was Benjamin O. Flower, a Boston journalist and publisher. The following is a description of Boston's North End from a book-length report called *Civilization's Inferno* that Flower wrote in 1893.

"The first building we entered faced a narrow street. The hallway was as dark as the air was foul or the walls filthy. Not a ray or shimmer of light fell through transom or sky-light. The stairs were narrow and worn. By the aid of matches we were able to grope our way along, and also observe more that was pleasant to behold. It was apparent that the hallways or stairs were seldom surprised by water, while pure, fresh air was evidently as much a stranger as fresh paint. After ascending several flights, we entered a room of undreamed of wretchedness. On the floor lay a sick man. He was rather fine looking, with an intelligent face, bright eyes, and a countenance indicative of force of character. No sign of dissipation, but an expression of sadness, or rather a look of dumb resignation peered from his expressive eyes. . . . There, for two years, he had lain on a wretched pallet of rags seeing his faithful wife tirelessly sewing, hour by hour and day by day, and knowing full well that health, life and hope were hourly slipping from her. This poor woman supports the invalid husband, her two children and herself, by making pants for leading Boston clothiers. No rest, no surcease, a perpetual grind from early dawn often far into the night. . . . Eviction, sickness, starvation—such are ever-present spectres, while every year marks the steady encroachment of disease, and the lowering of the register of vitality. . . .

"The next place visited was the attic of a tenement building even more wretched than the one just described. The general aspects of these houses, however, are all much the same, the chief difference being in the degrees of filth and squalor present. Here in an attic lives a poor widow with three children, a little boy and two little girls. They live by making pants at starvation wages. Since the youngest child was two and a half years old she has been daily engaged in overcasting the long seams of garments made by her mother. . . . There, on a little stool, she sat, her fingers moving as rapidly and in as unerring a manner as an old experienced needle-woman.

"Among the places we visited were a number of cellars or burrows. We descended several steps into dark, narrow passageways, leading to cold, damp rooms, in many of which no direct ray of sunshine ever creeps. We entered one room containing a bed, cooking stove, rack of dirty clothes and some broken chairs. On the bed lay a man who had been ill for three months with rheumatism. This family consists of father, mother and a daughter in her teens, *all of whom are compelled to occupy one bed.* They eat, cook, live, and sleep in this wretched cellar and pay over fifty dollars a year in rent. This is a typical illustration of life in this underground world.

"In another similar cellar or burrow, we found a mother and seven boys and girls, some of them quite large, *all sleeping in two medium-sized beds in one room*; this apartment is also their kitchen. . . . Their rent is two dollars a week. The cellar is damp and cold; the air is stifling. Nothing can be imagined more favorable to contagion both physical and moral than such dens as these. Ethical exaltation or spiritual growth is impossible with such an environment. It is not strange that the slums breed criminals, which require vast sums yearly to punish after evil has been perpetrated; but to me it is an ever-increasing source of wonder that society should be so short-sighted and neglectful of the condition of its exiles, when the outlay of a much smaller sum would ensure a prevention of a large proportion of the crime that emanates from the slums; while, at the same time, it would mean a new world of life, happiness, and measureless possibilities for the thousands who now exist in hopeless gloom. . . ."

structures were cut up into small, cramped apartments for people who could pay only $8 or $10 a month for rent. Others found room in shoddily constructed new buildings. In New York at the end of the century over a million people lived in tenements of five to six stories with shallow air shafts on either side to provide a little light to interior rooms. These structures, called "dumbbell tenements" because their floor plans revealed a long, narrow waist where the air shafts were placed, had only one bathroom for every twenty inhabitants, a situation that endangered the health and undermined the comfort of the inhabitants. Chicago, too, was full of substandard housing. Although the Great Fire of 1871 created the opportunity to construct comfortable apartments for working people, the city permitted builders to throw up block after block of shanties and ugly two-decker flats on the burned-over land.

As cities grew, it became increasingly difficult for people to get to stores, workplaces, and recreation areas. Congested downtowns, full of wagons, carriages, and pedestrians, made the movement of goods a nightmare. Long before the era of the automobile, downtown city streets experienced colossal traffic jams.

Well before the Civil War the country's largest urban centers had ceased to be "walking cities," in which everything was accessible for people moving on foot, and had adopted the horse-drawn "omnibus" and, a little later, the horse-drawn streetcar on rails. After the war many more communities expanded beyond comfortable walking-city size and adopted animal power. Using a horse-drawn vehicle was faster than walking, but it had many drawbacks. The cars were often crowded and stuffy. Riders were packed in like "smoked hams in a corner grocery." In 1864 a newspaper described a streetcar trip as an experience in "martyrdom." Public transportation also compounded the sanitation problem. The thousands of horses trotting the city streets created enormous piles of waste, and the resulting smells and clouds of flies made the summer, especially, an ordeal for city dwellers.

The Immigrant Adjustment. Newcomers to the city also faced a harsh and disruptive social environment. For foreign immigrants the challenge was particularly severe because they had to make a double adjustment, acquiring the ways of both America and the city simultaneously. Most eastern and southern European immigrants were rural peasants who found the cities alien places. Here were no one-story cottages, but multifloor apartment dwellings. Here you did not light your candle or oil lamp or cut wood for your cooking stove; you turned on a switch or stopcock and paid utility bills to the gas or electric company. In Chicago, Cleveland, or New York, you did not throw your garbage to the pigs; you placed it in refuse cans for the sanitation department. And how different it was to earn a living and get from place to place! Immigrants, in a word, had to abandon the familiar customs and practices of Europe's rural villages and learn how to survive in the vast impersonal metropolis.

For some groups social and institutional adjustment was especially difficult. Southern Italians, for example, had no tradition of group cooperation. At home loyalty had been given to the family and the village, not to the larger society. Even the Italian nation, a recent political creation, did not evoke a strong shared response. In America, however, being Italian set one apart and forced one to acknowledge a group identity. Unused to self-help and communal associations, Italian immigrants from diverse regions had to learn for the first time to cooperate. It has been said that people from Naples, Calabria, and Sicily became Italians only in America.

Some groups were spared the double adjustment. The Jews, in particular, had already become acclimated to town life before they arrived. In both Russia and Austria-Hungary, many had been town dwellers with occupations readily transferable to the cities of America. In addition, they had a strong group cohesion forged through centuries of persecution. Unlike the Italians, they brought to America associations and fraternal groups to help ease their adjustment.

The economic problems were the most urgent ones the immigrants encountered in the American "urban wilderness." Most groups of newcomers included a professional and business class. The Jews in the garment industry not only worked as cutters and sewing machine operators but also owned the shops. Italians became building contractors employing Italian workers. Because all groups retained a strong loyalty to the customs, cuisine, and language of their native land, a few enterprising people with a little capital established restaurants, groceries, theaters, bookstores, and assorted businesses catering to their fellow countrymen and women. The newcomers also preferred to turn to their own kind for professional help, and immigrant doctors, lawyers, priests, and rabbis found ample demand for their services. By 1914 the typical American city was crowded with signs in Polish, Italian, Yiddish, Chinese, Spanish, and other languages that advertised the wares of ethnic shopkeepers and the services of ethnic professionals.

Most of the cities' foreign-born remained unskilled or semiskilled workers. Yet social mobility studies of the Gilded Age city paint a mixed picture. In Boston the British and other northern Europeans, as well as the Jews, moved up rather rapidly from unskilled to skilled jobs; some even graduated into the ranks of business or the professions. The Irish and Italians, in contrast, lagged behind both native American newcomers to Boston and more mobile immigrant groups. In New York, on the other hand, according to one study, both Jews and Italians moved ahead almost equally fast and both achieved large gains in income and status in a rather short time. In Atlanta immigrants raised their status with remarkable speed, says one scholar, far faster than the city's large black population.

The crucial factor affecting the immigrants' economic progress apparently was education. Those who were illiterate or who could not speak English were easily exploited. The people who had nothing to sell but physical brawn stayed on the bottom rungs of the economic ladder. Immigrants understood the importance of education very well and flocked to night schools where, after a hard day's work, they attempted to learn English and reading and writing. The more enterprising or energetic succeeded. Others failed, defeated by age, bad luck, or personal inadequacy. Those who did not, or could not, acquire a basic education generally remained part of the large mass of urban poor.

Pressures on the Family. The traditional father-dominated, home-centered family suffered in the city. On the farms and in the small towns fathers worked close to the rest of the family. As the cities spread out, the physical distance between work and home grew even greater. The advent of the horse-drawn streetcar enabled many of the more prosperous working-class men to commute to work. Although the "streetcar suburbs"

provided space for recreation and some of the pleasantness of the countryside, the long commuting time meant that a man spent longer periods than ever away from his wife and children. With fathers so often absent, young men, in particular, lost close contact with a model of how to deal with the adult world, and many found the process of adjusting to work and adulthood more difficult than in earlier times.

The gap between generations encouraged by city life was even greater among immigrants than among the native-born. The children of European peasants and laborers encountered very different customs and habits from those their parents had known in the "old country." Growing up in the city streets and attending American schools, the second generation often developed drastically different values. Girls picked up attitudes that were at odds with strict European views of the proper role for unmarried women. Children who knew English and felt familiar with American life fared better in the new environment and could use the language more effectively than their parents. Boys often found work when their fathers could not. Adolescence is at best a turbulent time of revolt against parental control; in the cultural clash between foreign-born parents and native-born children, families were frequently shaken to their foundations.

The city not only weakened the structure of the family but also reduced its size. It took a lot of money to raise children in the city. Farmhouses could sprawl

One of Ash Can School's pictures of city streets. George Luks' *Hester Street,* a portrait of New York's Lower East Side in 1905.

almost indefinitely without affecting the family's expenses for shelter. But in the cities working-class families could not afford large apartments and painful congestion was common. Benjamin Flower, a philanthropist-editor, described a woman and her seven children who lived in one room in Boston's North End. In 1899 housing expert Lawrence Veiller noted a New York tenement block of four- and six-story dwellings in which almost 3,000 people lived in thirty-nine buildings.

Nor were children the economic asset in the city that they were in the country, where they were an important part of the work force. Working-class urban families were forced to put their children to work at odd jobs. Some children worked alongside their parents at garment making or some other "sweated" trade conducted in the home. But compulsory education laws and the difficulties of finding wage-paying work for boys and girls meant that they were not as self-supporting as rural children.

The cost of raising a family in the city encouraged family limitation. Fertility rates in the United States had been declining for generations in both towns and countryside. Toward the end of the nineteenth century the constraints of the urban environment provided new incentives to familiy limitation.

The growing trend toward smaller families offended social conservatives. Moralists and religious leaders frequently denounced efforts to disseminate birth-control information as sinful. In 1873, at the urging of "purity" crusader Anthony Comstock, Congress classified birth-control information as obscene and excluded it from the mails. Toward the end of the century, however, Margaret Sanger, a visiting nurse on New York's East Side, launched a campaign to provide poor women with scientific birth-control information. Defenders of old-fashioned morality attacked Sanger, and denounced the whole family-limitation movement as "race suicide." Sanger persisted but was forced to flee the country in 1914 for distributing the pamphlet *Family Limitation*. She later returned and organized the American Birth Control League, which became the leading agency of the birth-control movement in the United States.

Margaret Sanger's effort, initially directed at the slum family, achieved its greatest success among middle-class women and those working-class women most anxious to move into the middle class. Its effect on their lives was profound. With fewer children in the family, they were relieved from long years of childbearing and child nurture. Together with new laborsaving devices for the home such as the gas range and hot piped-in water, the decline in family size freed many women from lifelong household drudgery. Some directed their released energies to civic work or self-improvement. Women's clubs, literary societies, and discussion groups proliferated and became potent forces for political and social reform in the early twentieth century.

Changes in family responsibility also enabled

For poor immigrant families, privacy was unknown. Whole families shared a single bed, and they squeezed boarders into their homes for extra income. Children frequently worked long hours at some "home industry" with their parents to bring in enough income to support the family.

Most immigrant children learned to read and write and to understand the ways of their new country in public and parochial schools. But parents like this Italian immigrant father also helped their children acquire the skills needed to get ahead in the new land.

middle-class women to join the labor force in growing numbers. Until late in the nineteenth century few middle-class women worked outside the home, since schoolteaching aside, the jobs available to them were largely in domestic service or low-paid factory work. By the 1890s, however, urban service jobs were expanding rapidly, and thousands of middle-class women could become retail salesclerks, bookkeepers, typists, bank tellers, and secretaries. By 1914 city streets were thronged with working women going to and from their jobs in downtown offices and stores.

Family limitation had mixed social consequences. In smaller families children were less often neglected. And with fewer mouths to feed, the family was more prosperous. Children could be allowed to stay in school until they were better prepared for the "race of life." Married women often found their lives more rewarding and the bonds of marriage less confining.

But the change in family size also had a dark side. The family as an institution lost some of its cohesion. In 1867, when divorce laws were strict and divorced people ostracized, only 10,000 divorces were granted in the entire country. By 1907, as a result of divorce-law reforms and the more permissive moral climate, there were 72,000 divorces, a rate over three times as great per capita. Whether viewed as a social calamity or liberation, divorce had become a more widely accepted feature of American life.

Crime, Vice, and Loneliness. All newcomers to the American Gilded Age city encountered social pathologies. Cities were schools of crime and disorder, with gangs of cardsharps, pickpockets, purse snatchers, and thieves. Then as now, poor people were the major victims of city crime. They were also its chief perpetrators, especially of violent crimes. A city disease, crime was also a way of "making it" in America. Street boys stole from stores, passers-by, and drunks. In Chicago, an observer noted, the newsboys who gathered in the courtyard of the Hearst Building to pick up the evening papers were also petty thieves.

Those young men, it seems, usually gambled away what they stole, but other slum dwellers used their illegal gains to get ahead. Crime, in sociologist Daniel Bell's phrase, was a "queer ladder of social mobility" for some of the urban poor. It was also typically American: it fit the American ideal of self-employment and called forth the "manly" virtues of courage and physical skill.

Prostitution also plagued the cities of this period. The Gilded Age was a particularly prudish era in sexual

A pioneer in the birth-control movement of the early twentieth century, Margaret Sanger offended traditionalists and inspired reformers. In 1914 she was indicted for violating the laws against obscenity by mailing birth control information. Here she poses for photographers after her arraignment at court.

matters. Except in the medical profession, the physical relations between men and women were seldom discussed by decent people. "Good" women were expected to be indifferent to sex. By itself this distaste for sex might have encouraged prostitution; but in addition the cities attracted multitudes of young women looking for jobs and respectable marriages. Although many achieved their goals, others failed and fell prey to madams, shady saloonkeepers, and others who took them in and led—or forced—them into prostitution. Periodically, reformers and crusaders would rise up against the "white slave" trade and close the brothels, but they would generally spring up again.

Respectable people disapproved of the city saloon, but it, too, met an urgent urban social need. American cities were lonely places for the thousands of men and women who arrived without family or friends. To offset the isolation of their lives, newcomers to the city joined lodges, church organizations, ethnic societies, and veterans' groups. In the 1890s settlement houses, where the poor could find educational and recreational facilities, helped create community feeling in the city neighborhoods. The local tavern often served the same purpose. Church leaders and moralists might rail, but to many isolated men the saloon was where they could find companionship for the price of a glass of beer.

The saloon, the settlement house, the fraternal order, and the ethnic society proved inadequate in providing moral and emotional support for city dwellers, especially those without families. Even the churches often failed. Catholics and Jews were quick to provide for their own religious needs, and every immigrant quarter was dotted with small churches and synagogues. But Protestants often neglected their less-fortunate members. With their base in older rural America, the Protestant denominations frequently found it difficult to understand or cope with the problems of city dwellers.

Disturbed by the demoralization in the city centers, in the 1880s Protestant reformers launched the Charity Organization movement. Hundreds of middle-class women became volunteer "friendly visitors" to slum families to advise them how to save, how to use their money, how to dress, and how to keep clean; they accomplished little. The Salvation Army was more successful in aiding the cities' outcasts. It set up hundreds of soup kitchens, shelters, lodging houses, and "rescue missions" in the rundown areas of many cities to provide meals and a place to stay for the homeless. The YMCA and YWCA also sought to help. But none of these efforts solved the problems created in the cities

by the breakdown of traditional ties to family, neighbors, and other social groups. By the end of the century every city had its "skid row," where lonely men and women in cheap rooming houses lived out narrow lives amid squalid surroundings.

Suburbanization.   In part the failure to deal successfully with the problems of the city was the consequence of suburbanization. Many middle-class, old-stock Americans chose to escape the problems of congestion, decrepit housing, noise—and newcomers—by leaving them behind and fleeing to new, middle-class neighborhoods. The earliest suburbs appeared in the 1850s when the railroads first provided fast connections between country home and city office for a small group of prosperous merchants. The coming of the streeetcars in the post–Civil War period made it possible for less affluent folk to buy suburban private homes. Richer people could afford large, detached private houses with sizable backyards and front lawns. The lower-middle-class and skilled blue-collar workers made do with two- or three-family dwellings such as those constructed in Boston's "streetcar suburbs" of Roxbury and Dorchester. With another family or two to pay rent, a clerk, foreman, or skilled machinist could afford to live along the tree-shaded avenue of a suburb rather than on the grimy streets of downtown.

The suburbanization of these years was not a mass movement; that would come with the advent of the motor car in the 1920s. But it did make a dent in city congestion. In Milwaukee, for example, 34 percent of the population lived within a mile of the city's business core in 1880; by 1900 this figure had fallen to some 17 percent. During much of the nineteenth century the cities kept these people as taxpayers by annexing the suburbs and so maintained their solvency. After 1920, when the suburbs resisted political union with the central cities, the exodus of the middle class would have serious social and economic consequences for those who remained behind.

City Government

Contemporaries might argue over the social and physical virtues of cities, but few cared to defend their politics. Lord James Bryce, an English observer of Gilded Age America, in fact considered American cities "the worst governed in Christendom."

The critics' chief target was the city machines—political organizations designed to perpetuate a faction or party in office. Each machine was led by a "boss," who might or might not serve as mayor but who, regardless of his official title, dominated the city government. Beneath the boss was a collection of faithful aides—the ward or precinct captains ("ward heelers") and various rank-and-file hangers-on—who performed the machine's essential functions of mobilizing the vote for its mayoral and city council candidates. The machines kept the loyalty of their retainers by providing them with jobs, often sinecures that paid well but did not require serious effort or any demonstrated competence.

The purpose of the machine was to win and retain office. But for what? Reformers, champions of "good government," insisted that the machine's only goal was to milk the city treasury or to confer favors on business people and purveyors of vice for the personal gain of its members. The boss and his henchmen, they said, were at heart little more than racketeers. And their methods were no more savory than their goals. Machines, the reformers noted, won the support of voters by wholesale bribery and corruption. They paid the poor $5 or $10 each for their votes; they stuffed ballot boxes with false returns; they brought in "floaters" from other communities to vote in city elections; they illegally naturalized aliens to cast ballots for the machine and against its opponents. In short, as "good-government" people saw it, the machines were essentially diseased organs that had to be cut out of the body politic if city life was to be improved.

The Machine in Action. The reformers were not entirely fair. The machines performed important functions that could not be handled by the more formal institutions of the day. New York in the 1870s illustrates how they operated and why they became so deeply entrenched.

In the years immediately following the Civil War, the country's largest city was governed by a confused jumble of overlapping agencies. It had a board of aldermen, a board of councilmen, twelve supervisors, and a separate board of education—all with power to make decisions in various spheres without the mayor's approval. The police commissioners were appointed not by the mayor or by any city agency but by the governor of the state, as were the commissioners of Central Park and of the fire department. The system was a "hodgepodge," declared James Parton, a contemporary critic, that made New York virtually ungovernable.

Into this confusion stepped William Marcy Tweed. Tweed was not the gross, predatory figure depicted in the savage cartoons of reformer Thomas Nast. Neither was he the model of an upright public servant. Tweed and his henchmen bilked the city treasury of millions of dollars collected largely in the form of kickbacks from private contractors, who provided the city with overpriced material and services and then secretly returned some of their fees to the machine and its leaders. In building the fabulously expensive New York County Courthouse, for example, three-fourths of the total cost of $12 million represented profit to the ring composed of Tweed and the other officials of Tammany Hall, the New York Democratic machine. One estimate puts the ring's total thefts at between $45 million and $200 million.

Reformer Thomas Nast was to plague Tammany Hall's Boss Tweed long after Tweed's imprisonment. Years later, after Tweed had escaped abroad, Spanish authorities arrested him on kidnapping charges. Apparently they had seen an old Nast cartoon showing Tweed beating a child.

A Historical Portrait

Abraham Ruef

In 1883, Abraham Ruef graduated from the University of California at Berkeley with a senior thesis called *Purity in Politics*. At Hastings Law School he and some friends founded the Municipal Reform League to study city problems and find ways of solving them. Twenty years later, as boss of the San Francisco Republican machine, Ruef pleaded guilty to charges of extortion and spent four years at San Quentin prison.

This reformer-turned-boss was born in San Francisco in 1864, two years after his parents emigrated from France. Though the son of immigrants, Ruef's childhood was affluent. His father became a successful storekeeper on Market Street and a real estate dealer who listed himself in the city directory as "capitalist." Abraham himself was a precocious student who spoke seven languages and graduated from Berkeley with high honors and a major in Greek and Latin.

Ruef stumbled into politics. In 1886 he was admitted to the California bar and opened a law office in the Bay city. Soon after, he found himself at a Republican club meeting in his home district attended by only two others—a boardinghouse owner and a saloonkeeper, the two district leaders. The two men, Ruef later claimed, told him that the large, intelligent crowd that had attended had just left, and they induced him to write a newspaper article describing the successful party gathering. Whether out of appreciation of the young lawyer's literary imagination or his pliability, they soon made Ruef captain of two Republican precincts and got him elected a delegate to the municipal convention of 1886. Ruef's political career was launched.

San Francisco's leading Republicans soon noticed this bright, cocky lawyer who considered himself "a young political genius, educated at a University; born master of the ward game, but with the ideals of a cultured mind." They may have bridled at his pretensions, but his seniors in the machine found his cultivation and refinement a welcome contrast to the vulgarity and ignorance of the typical machine hack. As for Ruef, he realized the value of the machine in bringing him into contact with public officials, judges, and successful fellow lawyers. Before long he began to dream of becoming United States senator.

Though initially Ruef preferred the good-government faction of the party, he soon judged the reformers "apathetic" and "drifted" to the side of the machine. "Whatever ideals I once had," he later confessed, "were relegated to the background." Ruef quickly became the local Republican boss of San Francisco's Latin Quarter, the raffish and bohemian district of the Bay city.

Boss Ruef displayed all the skills and talents of his breed. He systematically developed the different ways he could collect votes. He joined every social club he could find. He understood the endless demands of the district's people for charity and bought tickets to every benefit. He cultivated the judges at the police court so he could help his constituents in trouble with the law. He also made friends with the city's tax assessors to help local business people and property owners when tax time came around. He even established useful contacts at the coroner's office so he could get a death report changed to suit a political ally.

Ruef understood that every function of government provided an opportunity to do a favor for a constituent. But he also had other political assets. His sense of humor endeared him to the voters. On one occasion at a political rally, he noticed that the audience had a supply of eggs to throw at him when he got up to speak. "Throw all the . . . eggs at one time," Ruef told the crowd, "so that we can get down to business."

In 1901 Ruef founded the Republican Primary League to help influence the course of an important three-way mayoral contest. The city had just weathered a huge dockworkers', sailors', and teamsters' strike that had idled 40,000 workers and tied up 200 ships in the harbor. When Mayor James D. Phelen finally decided to call in the police to protect strikebreakers, a riot had broken out that ended in bloodshed. The strikers, outraged at the use of police, formed a new party of their own—the Union Labor party—to take control of the city government, and received the support of William Randolph Hearst's powerful paper, *The Examiner*.

Ruef allied his League with the new party and then hand-picked his friend and client Eugene Schmitz as its candidate. A violinist, composer, and director of the Columbia Theater orchestra, Schmitz qualified as a friend of organized labor as president of the local musicians' union. Meanwhile, the Republicans, dominated by the Southern Pacific Railroad, had picked city auditor Asa Wells as their candidate; the Democrats chose a member of Phelen's entourage, Joseph S. Tobin.

Schmitz's campaign, managed by Ruef, emphasized fair play for labor, public ownership of utilities, and economy in government. Energized by deep working-class resentments against the recent police brutality, the Union Labor party won. Schmitz's fellow musicians expressed their elation at the results by parading around the city playing their instruments with gusto. But no one was more pleased than Ruef. The new party, he wrote, would be "a spark . . . which would kindle the entire nation. . . . [It would be] a throne for Schmitz as Mayor, as Governor— as president of the United States. Behind that throne, I saw myself its power, local, state—nation. . . ." Schmitz, in office, did not actually seek city ownership of public utilities, yet labor did benefit from his friendly attitude. During the streetcar strike in 1902 working people considered his role "fair and fearless." His tight rein on the police allowed labor to win this dispute and many later ones. Under Mayor Schmitz San Francisco would earn the reputation as the "tightest closed-shop town" in the United States. In 1903 the violinist-Mayor won a resounding reelection.

As Schmitz prospered, so did Ruef. During the day the "Curly Boss" could be found in his law offices, putting in long hours. At night he held court at the Pup, a French restaurant downtown. Ruef did not drink or smoke, but he was vain and drove a sporty automobile he called the "Green Lizard." He never married, and his nocturnal headquarters were said by his enemies to be an "institutionalized house of assignation."

Much was also said about his political morals. Both at his office and at the restaurant, Ruef allegedly collected bribes camouflaged as payments for legal services, from the United Railroad, the Pacific State Telephone and Telegraph Company, and the Home Telegraph Company, in exchange for political favors. He and his friends also collected tribute from dairies, real estate brokers, insurance adjusters, auctioneers, produce dealers, and proprietors of restaurants, theaters, gambling houses, saloons, and brothels.

By 1903 the good-government forces, led by Fremont Older, the reformist editor of the *San Francisco Bulletin* and friend of former Mayor Phelen, had determined to oust Schmitz and break Ruef's grip on the city government. The two men, Older insisted, were false friends of the working people and were utterly corrupt. Soon editorials were appearing in the *Bulletin* almost daily, attacking the "boodlers" and "grafters" who were running the Bay city. Older's denunciations of Ruef spared nothing. Even his legal work for the city's prominent French restaurants was immoral. These establishments, he noted, had family eating rooms with good food on the first floor, but no respectable woman would be seen on the second, with their private dining rooms, or on the third, with their accommodations for prostitutes and their clients.

The campaign of Older, Phelen, progressive reformers, and antilabor city businessmen to dump Schmitz in 1906 failed; the Mayor won a smashing reelection victory. But Older persisted. Later that year he visited President Theodore Roosevelt in Washington and procured the services of Francis J. Heney, special assistant to the United States attorney general. With the support of Rudolph Spreckles, one of the city's most prominent business leaders, Older and his friends raised $100,000 to investigate Ruef's deal to build an electric trolley streetcar line. Aside from their suspicion that it was a corrupt deal, they also objected to the overhead wires that they claimed would mar the city's natural beauty. At the same time they proposed on alternate scheme of their own: streetcars powered by an underground moving cable.

The earthquake and fire that ravaged the Bay Area in April 1906 drove the corruption and transit system issues from people's minds. Schmitz proved to be an able leader in the crisis, and Ruef served on the Committeee on Reconstruction. For the moment it seemed that all hostilities would be suspended. But while the city remained preoccupied with reconstruction, Ruef's associates got an ordinance passed authorizing their overhead trolley streetcar. When the public discovered the coup there was a huge outcry amplified by new allegations of money distributed to secure a favorable telephone company franchise. Ruef's plans for building a "greater" San Francisco, charged a city newspaper, were essentially "plans for a greater Ruef."

By this time Older and his associates felt they had enough evidence to proceed to trial. Some of this evidence had been obtained by a "sting" operation wherein an agent for the reformers had enticed some of the city's supervisors into taking bribes and then promising them immunity in return for testimony against the boss. Ruef tried to forestall the trial, but in November 1906, he, Schmitz, and a flock of their colleagues were indicted for graft.

In exchange for partial immunity, Ruef confessed and implicated several prominent California business leaders in his deals. This did not help him. Chief Prosecutor Heney decided that the confession was entirely self-serving and untrue, and withdrew the immunity offer. The trial was one of the most sensational on record. Prosecution documents were rifled, witnesses suborned, jurors bribed, and incriminating evidence hidden away. A supervisor's house was blown up, and the chief prosecutor was shot in the courtroom by a juror he had revealed to be a former convict. Someone even kidnapped Older and spirited him away to Santa Barbara, but the kidnapper lost his nerve and refused to carry

A Historical Portrait (*continued*)

out his commission to kill him. Heney was eventually replaced by a young California lawyer, Hiram Johnson, who later went on to become Governor of the state and a leading progressive in the United States Senate.

In the end the prosecutors obtained only four convictions. Three of these were reversed, and only Ruef ended up going to jail. On March 7, 1911 he entered San Quentin to begin his sentence of fourteen years.

Agitation for his release began almost immediately. Many people felt that with corruption so pervasive in San Francisco, it was unfair to single out Ruef. Foremost among the doubters was Fremont Older, who had been so instrumental in getting Ruef convicted. Older apparently had come to believe that Ruef had been victimized by a corrupt political environment for which all the citizens of San Francisco were to blame. He also felt that the prosecution had used tactics as despicable as those of the defense, especially reneging on the promise to grant Ruef partial

immunity. A few months after Ruef entered San Quentin, Older visited him, asked his forgiveness, and promised to work for his parole.

As part of his release strategy, Ruef would write his memoirs, which Older would publish in the *Bulletin*. Older believed that Ruef was fully repentant, and further, that the series would have educational value for readers. In May 1912, the paper ran the first installment of Ruef's "The Road I Traveled: An Autobiographic Account of My Career from University to Prison, with an Intimate Recital of the Corrupt Alliance between Big Business and Politics in San Francisco." In September, when the account reached the period of the trial, the memoirs stopped. Older had decided that if Ruef's side were published it would raise too many hackles and weaken the public sympathy that had been aroused. Instead, Ruef began a new series entitled "Civic Conditions and Suggested Remedies," in which the corrupt boss proposed a series of civic reforms.

Ruef spent three more years in prison. While he was in jail Older served as custodian of his estate, and appeared at San Quentin to take him home the day he was released. Ruef returned to the Bay city in the fall of 1915 and spent the rest of his life there, devoting all his time to the real estate business. Although he never reentered politics, his name would appear in the press from time to time in connection with various business schemes, like his project to remove the alcohol from wine without destroying its taste, or his more successful venture, a restaurant at Fisherman's Wharf. At one point he was charged with renting one of his hotel properties to a prostitution ring, but he proved that he had evicted these tenants as soon as he discovered their business.

By the 1920s Ruef had restored most of his fortune. In the Depression, however, he suffered severe business reverses. When he died of a heart attack on February 29, 1936, he was bankrupt.

But Tweed and his Tammany henchmen did not take without giving. Tweed made the chaotic, aimless political system of New York respond to the pressing needs of its citizens. Did shippers need improved docks? Tweed would get new powers for the city to build them. Did working people need a rapid transit system? Tweed would see that transit promoters could acquire private property for the right-of-way. Did households need new sewers or a better water supply? Tweed would use his influence in the state capital so that the city could borrow to provide them.

Other cities had versions of Tweed. In St. Louis Ed Butler was the conduit through which most of the urban captial improvements flowed. In Philadelphia the ring under boss David Martin organized the granting of contracts for city services in an efficient and orderly manner. Chicago's Republican boss, William Lorimer, helped the city obtain streetcar lines and ex-

panded gas services. In Cincinnati boss George B. Cox stemmed the social disorganization that set in after 1880 and provided the city with remarkably efficient administration.

The machines were not only useful devices for getting new sewers, improved lighting, and transit lines; they were also informal welfare organizations, providing services today supplied by local, state, and national governments. Although cities of that time had official almshouses, orphanages, hospitals for the insane, and even refuges for drunkards, these were dreary and oppressive places avoided by the poor. Churches and private philanthropic organizations also sought to help the poor, yet their aid remained grossly inadequate for such large numbers of needy.

The machines helped offset the failings of the contemporary welfare system. Because they controlled massive amounts of patronage, they could find jobs for the unemployed in the police department, the fire department, the schools, or the sanitation service. Civil service rules seldom applied to these jobs, and the local ward captains reserved them for their favorites. The machines also supplemented the incomes of the poor—providing coal during the winter, turkeys at Thanksgiving and Christmas, and free medical services—and fed money into private charities. During his term as state senator, Tweed pressured the New York legislature into appropriating funds for the Catholic charities and parochial schools that many of his poor city constituents relied on.

The city machines were also buffers between the poor citizen and the law. Much of what was accounted illegal in the contemporary American cities was victimless crime: gambling, drinking on Sunday, "blood" sports such as cockfighting or bare-knuckled boxing, and sex for money. Not all Americans believed that

these activities should be considered illegal, and many continued to engage in them. When, during a sudden surge of civic virtue, the authorities clamped down on saloons, gambling, or vice, people were arrested for practices that they considered at worst venial sins. Where could they turn for help? The obvious answer was the precinct captain, who could "speak to" the judge. Even better, the machine could crush the spasm of virtue in the first place. City machines were understanding of human weaknesses, as reformers seldom were, and overlooked small transgressions that did not unduly disturb public order.

The machines, then, often functioned both as social service organizations and as buffers between city people and the abrasions of city life. As Tammany leader George Washington Plunkitt explained, a ward captain was always obliging: "He will go to the police courts to put in a good word for the drunks and disor-

The ward captain, or "heeler," was the neighborhood leader of the Gilded Age city machine. His job was to disperse the benefits that the machine used to win and keep voters' loyalty. Shown here is the annual outing of Tammany Hall's Timothy D. Sullivan Association on a summer day in New York.

derlies or pay their fines, if a good word is not effective. He will feed the hungry and help bury the dead." Martin Lomasney, a Boston machine leader, explained it more philosophically: "I think that there's got to be in every ward somebody that any bloke can come to—no matter what he's done—and get help. *Help, you understand; none of your law and justice, but help.*"

"Goo-Goos." Of course the machines were not purely altruistic. In return for these services they expected gratitude that could be turned into votes at election time, as well as a certain acceptance of graft and corruption. The public's acquiescence was finite. Eventually Tweed, for example, ran up bills that the voters would not tolerate. When a disgruntled former Tammany leader decided to tell all, the commercial and financial leaders of the city, joined by good-government reformers ("goo-goos" to their enemies) and an outraged citizenry, mounted a campaign to cut Tweed down. In the election of 1871, although Tweed himself was reelected to the state senate, most of his cronies lost their races for state and local office. In 1872 the reformers elected to the mayor's office William F. Havemeyer, a wealthy sugar refiner and one of their own. Tweed himself was indicted on criminal charges and sent to jail. On his release he was rearrested to stand trial in a civil action to recover the sums he had stolen. He fled to Spain, was returned to New York, and sent to jail again, where he died in disgrace in 1878.

For the next few years the reformers attempted to run the city on economical and honest principles. They cut back on hundreds of patronage positions in the city service departments and eliminated many construction projects. Thousands of workers lost their jobs. With Tweed no longer in Albany to manage the necessary legislation, the state ceased to appropriate money for private and religious charities. Ticket fixing, "talking to" judges, and gifts of coal and turkeys also stopped, as did the tolerance for the petty law bending of working-class life. This moralism and the cuts in patronage and services cost the reformers the support of the poor, and bossism soon returned in the form of "Honest" John Kelley. As leader of Tammany Hall, Kelley was a more reputable man than Tweed; but he, too, anchored the machine squarely on the support of the city poor and dispensed favors and services with a ready hand.

The pattern of spendthrift machine followed by tightfisted reformers and spendthrift machine again was repeated over and over in American cities during the Gilded Age. The poor preferred openhandedness to economy, ethical tolerance to the moralism of the reformers. If municipal reform movements before the 1890s were generally short-lived, it was due as much to the reformers' limitations as to any perversity on the part of city voters.

A Better Place to Live

Many of the difficulties faced by city dwellers after the Civil War were the result of extraordinary growth that outran the capacity of cities to solve their problems. Urban citizens had to turn to makeshifts, including the city machines, to meet their needs. They often had to accept inferior facilities and services as well. By the 1880s, when the cities finally began to catch up with their problems, city life began to improve.

Physical Improvement. A part of the advance was the upgrading of the physical environment. The introduction of asphalt in the 1870s made city streets cleaner and safer. Asphalt was cheaper than cobblestone or brick and more durable than wood blocks; it soon became the standard paving material for cities.

Waste-disposal problems were not as easily solved; yet as the years passed, matters improved. In 1887 Los Angeles, a city without a major river to use for dumping waste, built a sewage treatment plant. Chicago stopped the pollution of Lake Michigan, the source of its drinking water, by reversing the direction of the Chicago River so that it flowed into the Mississippi. In the landlocked Midwest several cities turned to incinerators to dispose of waste. Most of these schemes only postponed the difficulties or imposed them on some other community. But they were better than those that had preceded them.

One of the great urban triumphs of the age was the provision of pure water. By the time of the Civil War many cities had systems for piping water into homes. After the war, following the discoveries of Koch and Pasteur that bacteria are powerful disease-causing agents, cities began to filter and chlorinate their water. By the time of World War I, every American city had pure drinking water, and death rates from cholera, typhoid, and other water-borne diseases plummeted. Combined with milk pasteurization and other new health measures, these advances drastically reduced urban mortality rates, especially among the young.

New Ideas in Housing and Architecture. The most intractable urban problem—the lack of adequate housing for the working class—became the concern of philanthropists during the 1870s. Alfred T. White, a successful Brooklyn businessman and engineer, became convinced that landlords' profits and decent housing for the poor were compatible. Pursuing "philanthropy and 5 percent," he completed his Home Buildings near the Brooklyn waterfront in 1877. These attractive structures accommodated forty families in apartments two rooms deep, ensuring good light and ventilation; they included a bathroom for each family. Although his projects attracted the attention of civic-minded men and women all over the country, White's experiment did not revolutionize building practices. Developers continued to throw up jerry-built structures that crammed human beings into dank, dark apartments with few amenities.

Clearly better design was not enough; but until the 1890s philanthropists had no other approach. Then, as part of the emerging "progressive" mood, reformers began to mobilize the power of government to protect the urban citizen against the unrestrained profit motive. In New York, the community with the worst housing problem, reformers secured a series of state tenement laws culminating in the measure of 1901, which outlawed the dumbbell structure and established more stringent minimum housing guidelines. Chicago, too, revised its housing code in 1898 and 1902 to impose higher standards on builders. Still, housing for the poor continued to be overcrowded and squalid.

Architects, philanthropists, and reformers soon began to focus their attention on improving other city facilities. Before the 1890s American cities had few open spaces. Office buildings, city halls, and courthouses were often ugly structures scattered about the downtown areas without plan or order. Above the city streets unsightly tangles of telegraph and telephone wires crisscrossed the sky. Many city streets were blighted by elevated trains that clattered overhead and plunged the surface below into gloom.

A few cities had escaped the blight. Following the Civil War Washington was transformed from a village of shanties to a spacious, tree-lined city appropriate for a national capital. New York had reserved land for the great Central Park in the heart of Manhattan, designed by the landscape architects Frederick Law Olmsted and Calvert Vaux. Kansas City constructed a $10 million system of parks and boulevards. Most cities, however, had not shown such foresight and had sold their open land to developers, who covered it with solid blocks of apartment houses or office buildings.

Toward the end of the century new attitudes began to gain public acceptance. The change was ushered in by the White City, which was erected in Chicago to house the Columbian Exposition of 1893. Inspired by its gleaming neoclassical structures, architects and urban planners launched the City Beautiful Movement to bring aesthetic order and distinction to American cities. During the next generation scores of American cities built elaborate civic centers composed of neoclassical buildings to house city agencies. These structures, usually grouped around a large landscaped plaza, provided spacious open areas for urban dwellers in Cleveland, San Francisco, St. Louis, San Diego, and other cities.

This period also saw the birth of the skyscraper as a characteristic American architectural expression. The offspring of technology and economics, the skyscraper conserved downtown land by combining the new technology of steel, which permitted tall structures without space-wasting thick walls, and the electric elevator. Although it started as an engineering innovation, it soon became a distinctive architectural style, worthy of aesthetic consideration.

City Transit. Transportation also improved as the century approached its end. In the 1870s New York had built its first "el," short for elevated railway, a steam railroad raised on columns above the city streets. Chicago and other cities had quickly followed suit. The el was fast, but it was also dirty and unsightly. Pedestrians on the street below were treated to a steady rain of soot and ash, while the el structure created a ribbon of blight along every avenue it traversed.

Help came during the 1870s. The cable car, first adopted in San Francisco in 1872 to meet the special needs of that unusually hilly city, was an early attempt to provide a clean transport system for city-dwellers. Traction for the cable car was supplied by great revolving reels that pulled long cables running beneath the street. Each car was attached to the moving cable by a grip that reached down through a slot between the car's wheels. Then, in the late 1880s, Frank Sprague, a naval engineer and former colleague of Edison's, built the first electric streetcar system in Richmond, Virginia. The Sprague streetcar drew its power from an overhead "trolley" held against a power wire by a spring arrangement. Fast, smooth, and nonpolluting, the electric trolley car was an immediate success. By 1895, 850 lines were operating, carrying passengers from home to office, stores, factory, and amusement parks. Many longer interurban lines connected towns and cities in a dense network that blanketed the popu-

In general, the "White City" at the 1893 Chicago World's Fair aped ancient Rome. This view of the "Grand Court" makes it look like Venice.

lous East and parts of the metropolitan West. Especially admired was the system of "red cars" that stretched like spokes from the central hub of Los Angeles to the surrounding satellite communities.

The final improvement was the subway, which combined electric traction with an underground right-of-way unobstructed by pedestrians or other traffic. Boston became the first city to acquire an underground transit system when it dug a mile-and-a-half tunnel for its trolleys under its downtown streets in 1897. New York opened the first true underground railroad in 1904 when it completed the first fifteen-mile stretch of what would eventually become the most extensive subway system in the world. Philadelphia and Chicago, too, acquired subways before World War I.

Schools for Newcomers.
As the country approached the new century, cities also began to cope better with the mass of newcomers who poured in from every part of the world. The major agency for Americanizing the new arrivals was the city school system.

When we look back at urban schools of the Gilded Age, we are struck by their strict discipline, narrow view of subject matter, and limited physical facilities. Nonetheless, they were successful in teaching the basic skills that society needed. Unlike today, the schools in large cities performed better than those in rural areas.

Americanizing the immigrants and their children was a difficult and impressive accomplishment of the

schools. A cultural gap often existed between the children in city classrooms and their teachers. At times the teachers literally did not speak the pupils' language, and textbooks made no concessions to the pupils' backgrounds. Yet many immigrant children overcame this gap. Mary Antin, a young Russian-Jewish immigrant, writing in 1912, told how the Boston schools had made her into a "good American." Mary sat "rigid with attention" as her teacher read the story of the Revolutionary War. As she learned "how the patriots planned the Revolution, and the women gave their sons to die in battle, and the battle led to victory, and the rejoicing people set up the Republic," it dawned on her "what was meant by *my country*." She, too, was an American citizen, and the insight changed her life.

Not every immigrant child was so successfully Americanized. Many, finding the schools alien and uncongenial, resisted their influence. Some dissenters believed the schools were taking away the children's sense of their own heritage and leaving them stranded between two cultures. Horace Kallen, a prominent teacher and social philosopher, conceived an alternative approach to the problem of American social and cultural diversity. His "cultural pluralism" celebrated a "democracy of nationalities, co-operating voluntarily and autonomously in the enterprise of [American] self-realization through the perfection of men according to their kind." He hoped men and women of diverse backgrounds could retain their heritages while sharing important common values and attitudes. Few schools in these years heeded Kallen's advice, yet they managed on the whole to ease the transition from immigrant to American.

Reform with a Heart.
The contribution that the schools made toward easing the cities' social problems was supplemented by other advances. The most comprehensive effort took the form of a new kind of humane political reform. During the 1870s and 1880s, as we have seen, urban reformers had emphasized economy and efficiency over social justice and had often offended the urban poor. If any group of city politicians was concerned with the well-being of the city masses, it was the bosses who ran the machines. This division—shady politicians with a heart and honest reformers with a ledger—did not entirely cease with the advent of the new century. During the Progressive Era that began in the mid-1890s, one group of reformers continued to be more concerned with economy and efficiency than with social justice, as we shall see in Chapter 23.

But there was another thread to the urban reform

As time passed, conditions in the cities began to improve. Streetcars, for instance, increased job possibilities for poorer citizens by making transportation to areas far from their homes faster and easier. These vehicles needed tracks in the street so horses could pull them more easily.

New York at about the turn of the century. Note the three simultaneous means of transportation.

movement that developed in the 1890s. As public-spirited citizens became aware of the failings of the Gilded Age city and of previous reform philosophies, they began to acquire a more sophisticated understanding of what had to be done. The result was compassionate urban reform and a movement for social justice in cities like Detroit, Cleveland, Toledo, and Milwaukee.

In Detroit, Mayor Hazen Pingree was the agent of the new reform. Pingree was a rich but self-made manufacturer of shoes. Although of Protestant Yankee background himself, he rode into office as the reform mayor of multilingual and predominantly Catholic Detroit in 1890 following the indictment of several Democratic aldermen for taking bribes.

At first Pingree differed from the traditional reformers more in style than in substance. Although he emphasized reducing "the extravagant rate of taxation," he was not a rigid puritan. He avoided the usual goo-goo attacks on the voters' cultural preferences. In the style of the old ward leaders, he launched his first campaign by a round of drinks with the boys at Baltimore Red's Saloon.

Pingree soon learned, however, that his constituents required more than social tolerance. They also demanded that he acknowledge their economic needs. Pingree became their champion against "the interests." He attacked the street railway monopoly for its high fares and reactionary labor policies. During an 1891 street-railway strike, the mayor sided with the strikers against the company. Following the 1893 Panic, he initiated a much-publicized "potato-patch" plan by which the city turned over vacant lots to needy families so that they could raise vegetables to help support themselves. The mayor also shifted some of the city's tax burden from Detroit's consumers to the corporations that did business with the city.

Toledo's equivalent of Pingree was the colorful Samuel ("Golden Rule") Jones. Jones began a program of city ownership of water, gas, and electric utilities; put to a popular vote such questions as extending city franchises to private companies; and inaugurated a major expansion of the system of parks, playgrounds, and municipal baths. Like Pingree, Jones refused to go along with the conventional reformers' prejudice against working-class customs, amusements, and even vices. He rejected demands that he close the saloons and put drunks in jail. When local ministers asked him to drive prostitutes out of the city, he asked them pointedly: "To where?"

For reform groups in Milwaukee, too, efficiency was less important than the general welfare. Until the mid-1890s the city's reformers had been of the tradi-

tional goo-goo type. But during the hard times following 1893, when the utility companies tried to raise their rates while refusing to pay local taxes, reformers' attitudes changed. Outraged by the arrogance of the state's utility tycoons, they sought allies among the working class in a concerted attack on privilege. A decade and a half later the Socialists took control of the city from the middle-class reformers when Emil Seidel became mayor and instituted a regime that combined good government and social justice. During the years of Socialist control the city enacted a minimum wage for all city employees and established a permanent committee on unemployment. In addition, Seidel expanded the public concert program, established commissions on tuberculosis and child welfare, and encouraged the use of the public schools for after-hours social, civic, and neighborhood clubs.

Conclusions

During the half century following the Civil War, American cities exerted a powerful pull on the peoples of the world. Glamor, culture, excitement, and, above all, jobs drew millions of rural men and women, foreigners and natives, to the cities of the country. For a while the deluge overwhelmed many urban centers. City services and facilities were poor, making life for the newcomers uncomfortable and unhealthy. City government, designed for a simpler era, was inadequate, so political machines took over. Newcomers found city life unsettling and damaging to individual personality and to family structure. Poverty and crime were the consequences of this unsettled life, and there were few social services that could help.

American cities never became paradises. But by the early years of the twentieth century, they were better places to live than they had been a half-century before. Billions of dollars were spent for sewers, streets, aqueducts, and other municipal services, improving the health and comfort of citizens. Electric streetcars and subways brought fast, clean, and relatively comfortable transportation. Best of all, new leadership by people with a strong sense of responsibility toward the voters made government more efficient without sacrificing the values and interests of the great mass of working-class citizens. Many problems remained; in later years much that was gained would be lost. But for a while, around the year 1910, the American city had become an interesting, a relatively livable, place. In 1905 the reformer Frederic C. Howe could call the American city "the hope of democracy."

For Further Reading

Maury Klein and Harvey A. Kantor. *Prisoners of Progress* (1976)

The authors briskly describe American industrialization and the growth of cities between 1850 and 1920. They depict the clash of cultures in the city and describe the lives of the rich, the poor, and the in-between. They also deal with city planning and urban reform movements of the day. Well illustrated.

Sam B. Warner. *Streetcar Suburbs: The Process of Growth in Boston, 1870–1900* (1962)

Originally separate towns, Roxbury, West Roxbury, and Dorchester were bound to Boston by the streetcar after the Civil War. Public transportation thereafter molded their physical and social structure. Warner describes the developing economic and social segregation of city and suburbs as the middle and upper classes left Boston, spurred on by the "rural ideal."

Thomas Kessner. *The Golden Door: Italian and Jewish Immigrant Mobility in New York City, 1880–1915* (1977)

A case study of urban social mobility for two important New Immigrant groups. In lucid prose that makes this careful statistical study easy reading, Kessner demonstrates extraordinary material progress for Gilded Age immigrants in the nation's largest metropolis.

Philip Taylor. *The Distant Magnet: European Immigration to the U.S.A.* (1971)

This volume by an English scholar deals with European immigration to the United States for the whole period from 1830 to 1930. It is especailly good on the European "pushes" of immigration.

Stanford Lyman. *Chinese Americans* (1974)

A brief treatment of the Chinese-American experience by a sociologist. Tells of the constant tension in Chinese-American's between desires for community and ethnic integrity on the one hand and for acceptance in the wider world of Caucasian America on the other.

Matt S. Meier and Feliciano Rivera. *The Chicanos: A History of Mexican Americans* (1972)

A brief survey of the whole sweep of Mexican-American history. Described by one reviewer as "coherent and readable."

John Higham. *Strangers in the Land: Patterns of American Nativism, 1860–1925* (1955)

An interesting account of anti-immigrant attitudes and movements from the Civil War to the end of unrestricted European immigration in the mid-1920s. Higham demonstrates how the European immigrant often became a scapegoat when Americans suffered a loss of confidence as a result of depression, war, or some other crisis.

Abraham Cahan. *The Rise of David Levinsky* (1917)

One of the best of the immigrant novels. Written by a Jewish immigrant journalist and editor who came to New York's Lower East Side, it vividly describes sweatshops, problems between the established German Jews and the newer arrivals from eastern Europe, and conflicts between generations in immigrant families. For David Levinsky the materialism of American life and its moral and ethical confusion are mixed with opportunity, intellectual stimulation, and financial success.

Seymour Mandelbaum. *Boss Tweed's New York* (1965)

Tweed was not a good man, but he *was* a useful one—as Professor Mandelbaum shows in this study of Thomas Nast's favorite villain. Using his "communications" model of urban bossism in the late nineteenth century, the author shows how Tweed brought together various important groups in New York to get things done.

Zane Miller. *Boss Cox's Cincinnati* (1968)

Cox, too, was useful, but more enlightened and honest than Tweed. In this description of Cox's achievements Miller makes Cincinnati's boss into a rather admirable character.

Humbert Nelli. *The Italians in Chicago, 1880–1930* (1970)

A model study of an urban ethnic group of the New Immigration following 1880. Nelli disposes of many stereotypes, especially the one of ethnic solidarity. His south Italians find that they are Italian only after they have lived for several years in Chicago.

Melvin Holli. *Reform in Detroit: Hazen Pingree and Urban Politics* (1969)

Pingree was the "potato-patch mayor" of Detroit who fought the transit magnates and brought reform with a heart to his city. A well-written and interesting study of late Gilded Age urban reform.

Theodore Dreiser. *Sister Carrie* (1900)

Sister Carrie recounts the experiences of a young rural woman who comes to Chicago to make her fortune. She succeeds—by choosing, and using, the right lovers. An early exponent of naturalism in fiction, Drieser was concerned mostly with the battle between primitive drives and moral principles within each of us. Along the way he tells us much about the urban jungle of the Gilded Age. The novel was banned for indecency when it first appeared.

Chapter 19

The Trans-Missouri West

Another Colony?

"I PAY FOR ALL."

1849	Bureau of Indian Affairs formed
1851	Federal government begins negotiating treaties for small Indian reservations in place of "the Indian Frontier"
1862	The Homestead Act • The Morrill Land Grant College Act
1864	The Chivington Massacre at Sand Creek • Lincoln reelected
1865	Sioux War on the Plains • Lincoln assassinated; Andrew Johnson becomes president
1866	"Long drive" of cattle, from Texas to railroad sites to expand market to East begins
1867	Federal peace Commission creates reform policies to assimilate Indians to white civilization • Patrons of Husbandry founded
1868	Ulysses S. Grant elected president
1873	The Timber Culture Act
1876	Custer's Last Stand at Little Big Horn
1877	Rutherford B. Hayes becomes president • The Desert Land Act
1880	James A. Garfield elected president
1881	Garfield assassinated; Chester A. Arthur becomes president
1884	Grover Cleveland elected president
1887	The Dawes Severalty Act designed to make Indians individual landowners • Severe winter destroys cattle boom on the Plains
1888	Benjamin Harrison elected president
1890	Massacre at Wounded Knee Creek
1892	Cleveland elected president for the second time
1893	Financial panic begins depression
1896	Presidential election between "goldbugs" and "silverites"; McKinley elected president over Bryan
1901	McKinley assassinated; Theodore Roosevelt becomes president
1902	The National Reclamation (Newlands) Act is passed to develop irrigation
1904	Roosevelt elected president
1905	The California Fruit Growers' Exchange introduces Sunkist products

merica has had many "Wests." During most of the colonial period, the West was the forested region beyond the settled Atlantic coastal plain. On the eve of the American Revolution, the West was the great valley across the Appalachian Mountains. For the generation preceding the Civil War, it was the land past the Mississippi. The "last West" of 1865 to 1910 was the vast expanse of territory stretching from the Missouri River to the Pacific Ocean.

In the last West, as on America's previous frontiers, people with a basically European culture came into contact with an unfamiliar social and natural environment. As they adapted to western realities, the settlers often came to resent the power the East held over the country and their lives. Easterners, they felt, did not understand the country's newest region or its problems; they were only interested in milking the frontier and its people. Between the Civil War and the turn of the century, many western Americans came to view themselves as inhabitants of a colony, exploited by people who lived thousands of miles away.

To a certain extent, the last West *was* treated as a colony of the East. Western mining companies held their board meetings in New York or Chicago, not in Denver, Butte, or Boise. The great cattle ranches of the Great Plains and Great Basin were often owned by Bostonians, New Yorkers, or even French and English investors. Indian policies and land policies were not made in "the territories"; they were made in Washington by people who did not seem to understand either Indians or western needs or wishes. When a cartoonist in the 1890s pictured America straddled by a huge cow grazing on the Plains and being milked in New York, westerners nodded knowingly.

The men and women who settled the trans-Missouri West would eventually feel almost as alienated from Washington, D.C., Boston, and Chicago as the white colonists of Massachusetts and Virginia had from the England of George III. Eventually, in alliance with the South, they would rise up in a major political revolt against the more urban East. Unlike the Revolution 120 years before, the uprising would fail and discontent would subside. Yet for a while the nation would be startled by the sectional resentment it revealed.

How did this East-West relationship develop? What was the basis for western discontent following the Civil War?

Settlement of the Last West

The Land. The last West was a vast and diverse area of about 1.2 million square miles, approximately two-fifths of the entire nation. Its eastern third, the Great Plains, is a level plateau gradually rising toward the west like a table tilted up at one end. In its eastern portion—through the central Dakotas, Kansas, Nebraska, Oklahoma, and Texas—rainfall in normal years is twenty inches or more, sufficient for grain crops. West of this band a few elevated spots such as the Black Hills of South Dakota catch the moisture-laden winds coming from the west. Elsewhere the rainfall in the western part of the Great Plains is usually too scanty for ordinary farming. Before the land was settled, except for stream borders and a few favored spots where trees grew, the ground was covered with grass—long grass in the more humid eastern parts, short grass in the drier western half. Without trees or hills, the area lacks shelter from constant winds that often bring fierce blizzards in winter and turn grass and grain to dry straw in a few days during blazing hot summers.

As settlers moved west across the Great Plains, 600 miles west of the Missouri River, they suddenly encountered a great escarpment rising like a wall—the lofty, forested Rocky Mountains. The Rockies form the eastern rim of several shallow but extensive basins. The largest is the Great Basin, which consists of most of present-day Nevada, western Utah, northern Arizona, and the extreme southeast of California. This region is almost a true desert. Besides the Colorado, there are few rivers with outlets to the oceans. Before dams and irrigation, water flowed only briefly, after occasional cloudbursts. Rivers generally petered out into "sinks" or ended in shallow lakes that evaporated during the dry season, leaving behind white alkaline "flats."

The narrow band of the Cascade and Sierra Nevada mountains form the western rim of the harsh basin region. Their eastern slopes are arid, but the western slopes catch the moisture-laden Pacific winds and are heavily forested. Between the Cascade-Sierra and the coastal hills of Oregon, Washington, and California are several broad valleys: to the north, the valleys of Puget Sound and the Willamette River; to the south, in California, the great Central Valley.

Beyond the coast ranges, a narrow coastal plain, scarcely more than a thin ribbon of beach in many places, borders the Pacific. From San Francisco Bay northward, the climate of the Pacific coast region resembles that of northwestern Europe, with rainy, relatively warm winters and cool, drier summers. South of San Francisco, the climate is Mediterranean: warm all year with little cloud cover and only sparse winter rains.

Settlement Patterns. The settlers of the last West and their patterns of settlement were as varied as the land they had to adapt to. The earliest part of the last West to be settled was the Pacific coast. The fertile soils of the Willamette Valley of Oregon attracted midwestern farmers in the 1840s, and in the 1850s gold brought thousands to California by ship around Cape Horn or overland by wagon train. By 1860 two Pacific coast states had entered the Union: Oregon with 52,000 people and California with 380,000.

The Great Basin and Rocky Mountain regions were settled as much from the West as from the East.

During the 1850s the easy pickings in the Sierra gold streams of California had ended. Gold remained, but it was either buried under many layers of silt or embedded in quartz rock. Ordinary prospectors did not have the capital or expert knowledge to extract the metal from these deposits and were forced to leave gold mining to corporations. During the later 1850s and through the next decades, displaced California miners and prospectors spread through the Great Basin and Rocky Mountain regions from Mexico to Canada, their bedrolls, shovels, pans, supplies, and rifles piled on a burro or mule. News, or even rumors, of a strike brought them rushing from all directions to stake claims along reported gold streams. There they would join crowds of men, and a few women, from the East who were new to the game. Many of the gold-seekers were black; many more, especially among the Californians, were Mexican or of mixed Indian-white parentage; and there were many Celestials, as the Chinese were called. No one racial group had a monopoly of either the sweat or the luck of the mining frontier. As in California, only a few struck it rich. Most of the others drifted off in quest of new bonanzas.

The settlement patterns in the Great Plains was more conventional. Most settlers on the Plains came from the agricultural Mississippi Valley immediately to the east. These people were farmers and farmers' children seeking cheaper lands than those available

Railroads were not only transportation companies; they were also land-selling companies, as these brochures advertising cheap land in the Plains attest.

in the Midwest. During the 1880s Iowa, Missouri, and the five states of the Old Northwest lost a million of their sons and daughters to the Plains region.

Joining these ex-midwesterners were immigrants from Ireland, Canada, Germany, and Scandinavia, as well as former black slaves fleeing southern sharecropping. Travelers in the eastern part of Dakota Territory reported that Norwegian was spoken more often than English. And despite the initial hostility of white Kansans, black farmers eventually acquired some 20,000 acres of rich Kansas farmland.

Plains settlers usually came as individuals or members of family units, but part of the migration was sponsored or even subsidized by outside agencies. In the Great Basin, for example, Mormon missionaries were responsible for drawing thousands from the East and from Europe to Utah and the so-called Mormon Corridor, stretching from Idaho to Arizona. The transcontinental railroads attracted easterners and Europeans to their lands on the Plains by colorful brochures advertising $4-an-acre land, free seed, and free agricultural advice. In later years farmers would denounce the railroads for their greed and their exploitive practices. But the railroad companies were initially a big help to those who came west to farm the lands that Congress had granted them, and were an important factor in the settlement of the last West.

Indians of the Last West

To the Indian tribes of the trans-Missouri West, the whites were unwelcome intruders. The Great Plains alone were inhabited by over 125,000 Indians in mid-century. About 75,000 of these were former woodland people—including the Blackfoot, Assiniboine, Sioux, Cheyenne, Arapaho, Crow, Shoshone, Pawnee, Kiowa, and Comanche—who had moved into the Plains from the East several hundred years before and adopted nomadic ways. These tribes shared the Plains with an almost equal number of Indians of the so-called Five Civilized Tribes (Cherokee, Choctaw, Chickasaw, Creek, and Seminole), who had been transplanted by government order before the Civil War from their traditional lands in the Southeast. In the Oregon region there were some 25,000 Nez Percé, Spokane, Yakima, Cayuse, Chinook, Nisqually, and other peoples. Texas contained 25,000 Lipan, Apache, and Comanche Indians; while in California and New Mexico Territory there were 150,000 Native Americans, distributed among the Ute, Pueblo, Navajo, Apache, Paiute, Yuma, Mojave, Modoc, and a flock of smaller coastal tribes,

collectively called "Mission Indians," who had been gathered by the Spanish friars into settlements centering around mission churches during the preceding century.

The Western Cultures. These Indians, like those farther east, were diverse in their cultures, economies, religion, and political arrangements. The Navajo and Apache of the Far Southwest were mostly nomadic hunters, though they practiced some agriculture as well. They acquired much of their food by stealing the sheep, goats, and horses of their neighbors, Indian and white. Along the Rio Grande and its tributaries were the Hopi, Zuñi, and other "Pueblo" peoples, who practiced irrigation agriculture and lived in villages of adobe and stone structures that resembled modern apartment houses. The Hopi and Zuñi had warded off the Spaniards and the Mexicans during the eighteenth and early nineteenth centuries and, by adopting policies of passive resistance, would manage to fend off American influences, too. As a consequence, unlike many other tribes, they were able to avoid the social and cultural breakdown that whites generally brought.

The Indians of the Northwest—the Oregon-Washington region—included the coastal fishing peoples, who consumed salmon, traveled the sea in hollowed-out canoes, lived in timber lodges, wore clothing made of bark, and engaged in elaborate social ceremonies (potlatches) that involved competitive destruction of physical wealth to establish social status. To their east were tribes like the Nez Percé, whose material culture was transitional between that of the Plains and that of the coastal peoples. The Nez Percé lived in brush lodges, wore skin garments, and both fished for salmon and hunted elk, deer, and mountain sheep for food.

The Plains Indians were the classic "Indians" of American frontier legend: tall, bronzed, with straight black hair, high cheekbones, and prominent curved noses. At the eastern fringes of the Plains some tribes practiced agriculture. Farther west, where the rainfall diminishes, they were nomadic hunters.

These western Plains Indians were formidable opponents. They traveled light. Their homes were skin-sided teepees that could be folded up in minutes and loaded on a pony to be set up again miles away. Unlike the Indians of the East, people such as these could not be subdued by burning their crops and destroying their villages; they grew no crops, and did not live in settled communities.

The vast buffalo herds provided the Plains Indians with almost everything they needed to survive. They ate buffalo steaks and tongues; they made their

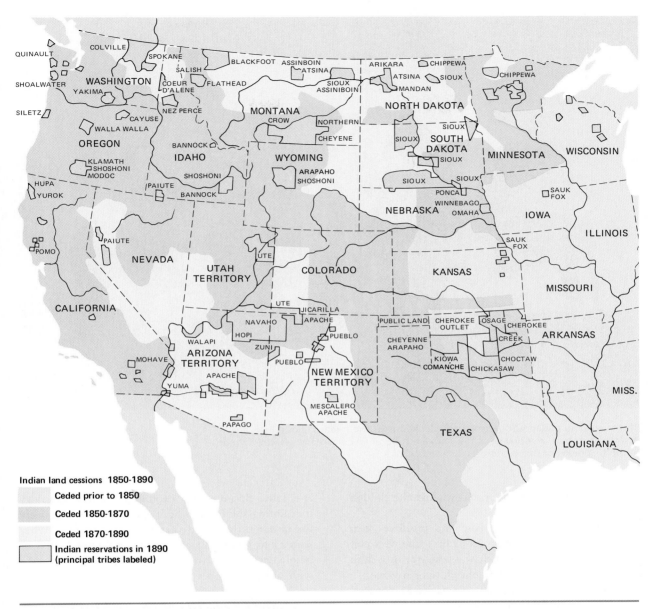

Indian relations beyond the Mississippi, 1850–1890

Indian land cessions 1850–1890

Ceded prior to 1850

Ceded 1850–1870

Ceded 1870–1890

Indian reservations in 1890 (principal tribes labeled)

clothing and their teepees of buffalo hides; buffalo "chips" (droppings) were their fuel; and buffalo sinews provided their cord and string. The guns and horses that they had acquired from Europeans generations before made buffalo hunting easier and enabled the Plains Indians to increase their range and prosperity. They also made them formidable adversaries. By the time the westward-moving Americans encountered the Plains tribes, they enjoyed little military advantage over them except numbers.

Conflicting Views. Indian and non-Indian societies were separated by a wide cultural gulf. White society emphasized individual rights and goals. The individual took precedence over the group. By contrast, Indians generally subordinated personal ambitions to the tribe's needs and goals. The identity of the individual was largely merged with that of the tribe. The tribe took precedence over the individual even when it came to parent-children relationships. As one Indian shaman told a French Jesuit missionary: "You French people

This is what an Indian war party actually looked like. The Indians shown here are Atsinas, members of a branch of the Arapaho tribe of Plains Indians, photographed at the beginning of this century by Edward Curtis.

love only your own children; but we love the children of our tribe."

Attitudes toward the land and resources were also different. The white settlers who came west conceived of land as an object. It was a source of wealth, a means to an end. Much like a plow or a wagon, it could be owned, bought, sold, bequeathed, inherited, and used up by an individual owner. Most Indians saw land as part of the sacred world. Men must live in peace with that world, must live in balance with nature. Resources must not be squandered. Land was also the collective possession of either tribe, family, or clan. If an individual had any special claim to a piece of land, it was only because he or she used it. Land left idle could be redistributed among other members of the tribe.

The nomadic ways of the western Plains tribes compounded Indian-white differences over land ownership. Nomads must wander in search of food and cannot respect artificial boundaries established by deeds and laws. Because they exploit the land *extensively* for hunting and food gathering, rather than *intensively* for farming, they need vast amounts of space. What seemed to whites an enormous surplus of land was barely enough to provide a Cheyenne or a Sioux tribe with sufficient food.

Washington, the Indians, and the Settlers. In dealing with the Indians, the federal government often showed no more understanding of Indian realities than the whites who went west. Until 1871 the Washington authorities accepted the fiction that the tribes were independent Indian "nations" that, like other soverign states, could be dealt with through diplomatic negotiations and treaties. This view was useful to white Americans because the disparity in power between the United States and the individual tribes made it possible to impose conditions that favored whites. In exchange for some blankets, food, tools, a few rifles, or a little cash, the Indians were pressured into surrendering vast streteches of valuable land. If the government could not extract the agreement it wanted from the current Indian leaders, it would find some dissident group it could bribe to deal with. Federal authorities would then announce that the agreement reached with the malcontents represented the collective will of the tribe. Nor did the federal government respect the treaties it signed with the Indians as it did those concluded with foreign nations. When local western interests—miners, ranchers, farmers—found a treaty inconvenient, they often succeeded in getting the government to violate it. At times the whole treaty system seemed nothing more than a facade for exploitation. As a governor of Georgia once expressed it: "Treaties were expedients by which ignorant, intractable, and savage people were induced without bloodshed to yield up what civilized people had the right to possess by virtue of that command of the Creator delivered to man upon his foundation—be fruitful, multiply, and replenish the earth, and subdue it."

Until the 1850s the federal government had tried to maintain a permanent Indian frontier beyond the Mississippi. But the opening of California and Oregon to settlers soon made a shambles of the plan, and the government replaced it with the "reservation" policy. In place of a solid wall of Indian communities blocking off white settlement and passage westward, the tribes would be concentrated in compact tracts. Here, supposedly, they would be protected from white exploiters and taught the ways of agriculture and other "civilized" arts and practices.

In the 1850s the new policy was incorporated into a collection of treaties negotiated with the tribes by the commissioner of Indian affairs, who headed the Indian Bureau, a division of the Interior Department. Under these treaties, the tribes agreed to surrender much of the land they claimed in exchange for clear title to a smaller piece and payments of cash and other gifts. The reservation policy was accompanied by serious troubles. White settlers on the scene often begrudged the Indians even the reduced plots of ground the treaties gave them, while many of the Indians fiercely resisted the government's efforts to deprive them of their traditional range.

The most important of these treaties were those concluded with the Plains tribes at Forts Laramie and Atkinson in 1851 and 1853, respectively. Under their terms, the Indians promised to dwell in peace with the whites and with one another forever and to allow the whites to build roads through their territory. The treaties also defined precisely the boundaries of each tribe's lands. These boundaries would later become the bases of the Plains reservations.

Indians and the Civil War. During the Civil War the last West became a battlefield bewteen Indians and whites, as well as Union and Confederate sympathizers. The war temporarily depleted the West of troops, but then more blue-clad soldiers than ever appeared in the Plains and the Great Basin. The Union volunteers were better fighters than the lackluster regulars they replaced. Those from the West itself, moreover, were often fiercely anti-Indian, and their operations against the tribes would be pursued with a new ruthlessness. Meanwhile, the war notwithstanding, whites continued to move into the last West, attracted by a succession of gold strikes in the Pacific Northwest, the eastern flank of the Sierra Nevada, and the foothills of the Rockies.

The war was particularly destructive for the Civilized Tribes of Indian Territory (Oklahoma). Many of these Indians owned slaves and sympathized with the South. A minority favored the Union. Whatever their preferences, the Indians resisted the attempt to involve them in the whites' quarrels. But they could not prevent their lands from becoming a battleground. At one point Cherokees wearing Confederate uniforms fought Cherokees wearing Union blue, and in the bloody clashes hundreds died. In the end the Civilized Tribes became useful allies of the Confederacy, and several regiments of Creek, Seminole, and Cherokee fought with the Confederate forces at the Battle of Pea Ridge in 1862.

The war years also proved disastrous for the western Indians elsewhere. In Minnesota the growing discontent of the Sioux with the reservation policy boiled over into a major Indian War that cut a bloody swathe through the new state. Meanwhile, in the Far Southwest, General James Carleton and Kit Carson, colonel of the New Mexico volunteers, clashed with the restless Navajo and forced them to settle down at Bosque Redondo reservation, a barren region where many died of exposure, disease, and malnutrition. In Colorado Territory the wartime Indian "troubles" culminated in the notorious Chivington Massacre.

This dreadful event was rooted in territorial politics. The Colorado Cheyenne had proved reluctant to surrender title to their lands and withdraw to reservations in the southern part of the territory. Their stubborn resistance enraged territorial governor John Evans and Colonel John M. Chivington of the Colorado volunteers. Both men nursed political ambitions, and saw the Indians as impediments to the territory's progress toward statehood and national political roles for themselves.

Warfare broke out in Colorado in the spring of 1864 when Cheyenne chief Black Kettle refused to settle down on the reservation assigned his people some years before. By the summer, however, Black Kettle was willing to settle the issues between the Cheyenne and the government and had arranged what the Indians considered a successful agreement. Unfortunately, the peaceful outcome did not satisfy many Coloradans, who believed the Indians insufficiently chastised. These people ridiculed Chivington and his regiment, the "Bloodless Third," for their inactivity against the Indians. Chivington soon showed that he was as fierce an Indian fighter as anyone could wish. On November 29, at dawn, the Third Volunteers swooped down on Black Kettle's sleeping camp of 500 Indians at Sand Creek. The Indians tried to escape, but they were hunted down and slaughtered. The militia shot and killed 200 of the unsuspecting Cheyenne, two-thirds of them women and children, and scalped and mutilated many. The victors of Sand Creek paraded through the streets of Denver to the cheers of the citizens. "Colorado soldiers have again covered themselves with glory," trumpeted the *Rocky Mountain News*.

On the northern plains, too, the government tried to apply a military solution to the "Indian problem" during the war years. Here General John Pope, the man responsible for the Union debacle at the Second Battle of Bull Run, treated all the tribes as enemies, and after Sand Creek, many of them were. In the spring of 1865, just as the Confederacy began its death throes, the Sioux, Cheyenne, and Arapaho went on the offensive, burning ranches and stagecoach stations, plundering wagon trains, tearing up telegraph wire, and stealing cattle. Pope sent massive forces with ponderous supply columns to subdue the Indians. The Indians easily eluded the soldiers, while the troops in turn suffered much from the bitter Plains weather. In the end the campaign petered out with little accomplished, except that the Indians by this time were weary of the struggle and ready to make peace.

Developing an Indian Policy. The end of the Civil War marked a change in the government's Indian policy. The Radical Republicans who came to power after 1865 were far more committed than most white Americans to a policy of racial justice. Though this attitude largely applied to southern black freedmen, it carried over to the western Indians to some extent. Also, the Chivington Massacre had shocked the eastern public

and convinced many sensitive men and women that major reforms were essential.

These new attitudes opened a major sectional gap. Easterners might now be convinced that a "peace policy" was the best approach to the Indian problem, but recent events had only confirmed westerners in their conviction that the government was not determined enough to put down the Indian menace. When Senator James R. Doolittle of Wisconsin arrived in Denver in the summer of 1865 to represent the Senate Indian Committee, he quickly learned how wide the East-West rift was. At a public meeting in Denver's opera house Doolittle attempted to explain the peace position that was now taking hold in the East. Should the Indians, he asked, be firmly placed on reservations and taught to support themselves or should they be exterminated? Doolittle assumed that the question answered itself. But, as he later reported, his rhetorical question was followed by "such a shout as is never heared unless upon some battle field—'Exterminate them! Exterminate them!' "

The new approach also produced a gap between civilians and the military. Having seen what force could do against an implacable white enemy, the victorious Union generals saw no reason why it should not be used against a lesser foe, the Indians. The divisions in opinion widened when Red Cloud's Cheyenne, Arapaho, and Sioux warriors ambushed a detachment of U.S. troops under Captain William Fetterman in late 1866 near Fort Kearny in Nebraska. Fetterman and his whole force of eight men were killed.

In the end the peace advocates and the reformers prevailed. In 1867 Congress established a commission to try to end violence on the Plains. The commissioner's attitudes were those that would mark reformers' views for the next half-century. They wanted peace with the Indians and hoped to see them prosperous and content. But this meant that the Indians must conform to white ways. The reformers saw the reservation policy as a progressive system that would compel the Indians to surrender their nomadic life, settle down as farmers, and shift from "barbarism" to "civilization." To help the Indians assimilate white culture, the government would provide schools to teach them English, agriculture, and mechanical skills, and would bring them the blessings of the Christian faith. Until they became self-supporting, they would be supplied with food, blankets, tools, and clothing. There was another side to this apparent generosity: A thoroughgoing reservation policy would open large tracts of Indians lands to white settlers.

The commissioners met with the Kiowa, Comanche, Cheyenne, and Arapaho in 1867 and, after bribes, threats, and cajolery, induced them to accept reservations in western Oklahoma on lands confiscated by the Civilized Tribes as punishment for their support of the Confederacy. The next year the Sioux signed the Treaty of 1868 at Laramie, Wyoming. In exchange for the government's abandonment of a mining road through their lands and the usual promise of blankets, rations, and other handouts, they agreed to lay down their arms and accept a reservation in western South Dakota. Federal officials extracted similar agreements from the Shoshone, the Bannock of Wyoming and Idaho, and the Navajo and Apache of Arizona and New Mexico.

The peace policy did not work any better than previous strategies. Whites continued to covet Indian lands and encroached on the reservations. The government itself violated the agreements, often failing to come through with the promised food and blankets. The efforts to Christianize the Indians offended their religious sensibilities. To make matters worse, the Bureau of Indian Affairs soon became a hotbed of corruption. The commissioner of Indian affairs was invariably a political appointee, almost always a party hack. He and his agents often used money allotted for Indian supplies to line their own pockets. Effective administration was further undermined by the division of responsibility between civilian officials and the army. Gradually the peace policy broke down and violent confrontation between the army and the Indians once more became a chronic element in Indian-white relations in the last West.

The Final Indian Wars. One of the gravest blows to the Indians' survival and autonomy was the destruction of the great buffalo herds they depended on. The slaughter of the buffalo was not a deliberate effort to subdue the Indians. Many were killed to supply meat for the crews working on the trans-continental railroads that began to cross the Plains soon after the

Most of the treaties between the United States government and the Indian nations were coerced. In this stiffly posed 1867 photograph, Louis Bogy, commissioner of Indian Affairs, apparently interprets the terms of the treaty in his left hand to chiefs of the Sauk and Fox tribes, who lived in the upper Mississippi Valley. The Indians finally surrendered 157,000 acres of their fertile lands in exchange for $26,574 and about three times as much less desirable land in Oklahoma.

war ended. Others fell to "sportsmen" who came to the Plains to stalk the great beasts for the thrill of it. Eventually, random slaughter gave way to more purposeful and profitable hunting to satisfy the demand for leather and buffalo robes. During the 1870s buffalo hunting became a major Plains industry and it was clear to everyone that the buffalo would not survive. "From the way the carcasses are strewn over the vast plains," wrote a traveler in these years, "the American bison will soon be numbered among things of the past." He was almost right. By 1883, 13 million animals had been destroyed. When an eastern museum expedition arrived on the Plains that year to obtain specimens for its collection, it found only 200 animals still alive.

The destruction of the buffalo virtually ended the Plains Indians' nomadic ways. Without the herds the Indians became ever more dependent on the government for handouts, or else were forced to take up an alien agricultural way of life to support themselves. Yet for a generation more many would resist giving up their traditional life. With each passing year their overall resentment against the reservation policy mounted.

Restlessness induced by the reservation policy was reinforced during the last years of the nineteenth century by a chain of white provocations. In the mid-1870s, gold prospectors invaded the Sioux reservation in the Black Hills of South Dakota. At first the federal authorities tried to exclude the whites. When the prospectors persisted, the government attempted to buy back or lease Sioux lands containing the gold diggings. The Indians defied the authorities and were declared renegades.

The Sioux turned for leadership to Sitting Bull, a chieftain of imposing appearance and fierce determination who had long spurned the white man's gifts and promises. Sitting Bull had only contempt for the Sioux who had accepted life on the reservations. "You are fools to make yourselves slaves to a piece of fat bacon, some hardtack, and a little sugar and coffee," he taunted his weak-willed brothers. Allied with Chief Crazy Horse, he encouraged the rebels and was soon being pursued by soldiers under the command of General Alfred Terry. On June 25, 1876, a detachment of Terry's troops led by the reckless George Custer attacked the Sioux camp at the Little Bighorn River. Sitting Bull's warriors were waiting and pounced on Custer's men. By the time Terry's forces came to the rescue, Colonel Custer and all 264 of his men were dead.

Though an immense moral victory for the Indians, Custer's defeat ultimately hurt their cause. More

An army inspector and his family pose with a group of Indians. The exploitation of the Plains Indians did not stop with their removal to reservations. Many died awaiting money the government promised for their support. Sitting Bull was reduced to traveling with Buffalo Bill Cody's Wild West Show.

soldiers flooded into the Plains, and the government forced the Sioux to surrender much of the Black Hills region to the whites. During the next fourteen years almost all the tribes as yet untamed were compelled to accept confinement on the reservations. But discontent continued to seethe. The final pitched battle—though not the last violence—of the 400-year Indian-white war in North America took place in December 1890 at Wounded Knee Creek on the Sioux reservation in South Dakota.

The Indians at Wounded Knee had gathered for religious purposes. The chronic resentments among the Sioux and other Plains tribes had encouraged an Indian revival movement spread by a Paiute Indian prophet named Wavoka. Wavoka preached a new religion that promised the Indians a paradise where they would be free of the whites and where they would live forever in peace and prosperity amidst their ancestors, without sickness or suffering. This Indian Garden of Eden could be attained by practicing love, hard work, and peace with the whites, and by participating in the Ghost Dance, a ceremony of spiritual renewal emphasizing singing and dancing to the point of trance.

The Ghost-Dance religion appealed tremendously to the despairing Plains Indians, for it promised liberation from white oppression and a bright new age. The movement worried the white authorities who, despite its professions of peace, saw it as a possible incitement to violence. Their nervousness converted a possibility into a reality. When the commander of the U.S. Seventh Cavalry tried to disarm a group of Sioux at Wounded Knee, someone fired several shots. A bitter hand-to-hand fight ensued. When the Indians broke through the army's line, the troops fired at them with hotchkiss cannon, killing at least 150, including many women and children.

The New Reformers. After 1870 Congress and the federal authorities became increasingly convinced that the solution to the Indian problem was assimilation. During these years influential congressmen and their constituents, particularly in the East, became aroused to the plight of the Indians by the writings of Helen Hunt Jackson. Her 1881 book, *A Century of Dishonor,*

In this vivid portrait of Sitting Bull we can see the determination and strength that led to the United States cavalry's greatest defeat—Custer's disaster at Little Big Horn in 1876.

recounted the doleful record of American Indian policy since independence and created a large public in favor of reform.

The active Indian reformers of the 1870–1900 period—people like former antislavery leaders Wendell Phillips and Harriet Beecher Stowe, and explorer-anthropologist John Wesley Powell—were well-meaning men and women who found the western Indians worthy objects of their compassion and social consciences. But like the peace commissioners of 1867, they had little regard for traditional Indian ways. Even Powell, who described the reservations as "pen[s] where a horde of savages are to be fed with flour and beef, to be supplied with government blankets from the Government bounty, and to be furnished with paint and gew-gaws by the greed of traders," saw no substitute for "civilizing" the Indians.

The Indian reformers were influential people who succeeded in getting their views incorporated into major new legislation. To train Indians in white ways, Congress established special Indian schools both on the reservations and off. There Indian children were separated from their language and their culture and taught to read and write English and learn trades that presumably would help them prosper on the reservations.

The reformers also succeeded in getting the land laws changed to suit their theories of Indian assimilation. The Dawes Severalty Act of 1887 gave the president the power to order Indian lands surveyed and divided into 160-acre plots. These would be allotted to each head of family, with additional amounts for minor children. If the land was suitable only for grazing, the plot size could be doubled.

The law broke with Indian tradition. Each adult male Indian was to become an individual landowner; the tribe would no longer own the land collectively. Indians would, it was hoped, become independent farmers on the white American model. To help ensure that the Indians would not quickly lose their land to sharpers, it was to be held in trust tax-free for twenty-five years. Individuals who took the allotments would in time become citizens of the United States and no longer be considered members of autonomous Indian "nations." The Dawes Act did not cover the Five Civilized Tribes, but under the Curtis Act of 1898 similar measures were applied to them.

Easterners and westerners generally welcomed the Dawes and Curtis acts, but for different reasons. The humanitarian reformers, with their assimilationist views, called the Dawes Act the "Emancipation Proclamation for the Indian." Westerners rejoiced because

A Historical Portrait

Sitting Bull

Sitting Bull was the son of Returns-Again, a chief of the Hunkpapa, a tribe of the Teton, the western division of the proud Sioux Nation. Born in 1831 in what is now South Dakota, the young boy was first called Slow. The name described his deliberate way of doing things. Even as an infant, for example, he would examine carefully a piece of food placed in his hand before putting it in his mouth.

Slow got his adult name when he was fourteen. The Sioux were a warlike people. Their clashes with their Indian neighbors were often motivated by their quest for horses. They were also a vital part of Sioux culture with much of the tribe's life taken up with war dances, preparations for war, lamenting for the dead and wounded, and distributing spoils.

The fighting itself was a glorious sport. Sioux braves achieved status by striking the first blow, or *coup*, against an enemy in battle, whether the blow was a mere touch with a stick or an actual thrust with a weapon. Yet it was a bloody sport. Once the *coup* had been achieved, the Sioux fought to kill and spared neither men, women, nor children. They often mutilated their victims by removing, ears, scalps, fingers, or genitals as souvenirs of their successes.

It was on a raiding expedition against the Crow in 1845 that Slow made his first *coup*, and in recognition he was given the new adult name *Ta-tan'-ka I-yo-ta'-ke*, Sitting Bull. At fourteen the Indian lad was a man.

Thereafter Sitting Bull rose in the esteem and affection of his people as a brave, vigorous, and generous man. His first contact with whites came in 1864 at Kildeer Mountains in present-day North Dakota when the western Sioux clashed with army troops on a punitive expedition following Indian attacks on settlers in Minnesota. Thirty Indians died in a series of skirmishes with the soldiers, but most escaped. Sitting Bull, present in the thick of the fight, was not impressed with the quality of the white fighting men. They did "not know how to fight," he said. "They are not lively enough. They stand still and run straight; it is easy to shoot them."

After the Sand Creek Massacre of 1864, the Sioux joined the Cheyenne for a campaign along the Platte River to avenge Chivington's bloodbath. During the fighting Sitting Bull proved his prowess against the whites and soon was recognized as a chief not only of his own Hunkpapa, but also of other western Sioux tribes.

For a time in the mid-1860s Sitting Bull directed the aggressive energies of the Sioux against his Indian foes, the Crows, Mandans, Flatheads, Hohe, and Rees. But he did not forget the white danger. Sitting Bull had become a leader of the "hostiles," the Indians who resisted the whites' reservation policy. The Indians, he believed, must be allowed to continue their nomadic, hunting ways, and must never agree to settle down to farm or take the white man's food, blankets, and other handouts. In these immediate postwar years, like other leaders of the northern Plains tribes, he demanded that the whites close their road across the northern Plains, burn and evacuate the forts in the region, stop the steamboats from ascending the Missouri and its tributaries, and expel all white intruders except traders.

The Sioux got much of what they wanted in the Treaty of 1868, a document that reflected the conciliatory mood of the post–civil War peace policy. Under this agreement the government abandoned its road through the new Great Sioux Reservation, promised to destroy its forts within the Sioux lands and exclude all whites, except those who obtained tribal permission to settle or pass through. But in return the Indians agreed to abandon their nomadic life and settle down on the reservation near the Indian agencies where they were under protection and supervision of the white Indian agent.

Despite the government's concessions Sitting Bull refused to surrender the old ways. In 1869 he led his warriors on raiding expeditions against the Crows and the Flatheads in which many warriors fell. He refused to settle near the Indian agency. In 1872 and 1873 the Sioux skirmished with soldiers escorting Northern Pacific Railroad surveying parties through Sioux lands. After these incidents Sitting Bull and his friend Crazy Horse, of the Oglala Sioux, resolved to adopt a new policy toward whites: "If they come shooting, shoot back."

One of the white officers in these battles was General George Armstrong Custer, a brave, but flamboyant and foolhardy, veteran of the Civil War. In 1874 General Philip Sheridan, of Civil War cavalry fame, sent Custer with a thousand soldiers, along with miners and journalists, to explore the Black Hills region of the Sioux reservation, where, rumors had it, there were rich gold deposits. The Indians protested that this expedition violated the Treaty of 1868, but the authorities refused to yield.

The reconnaissance had tragic

consequences. Custer's miners confirmed that there was gold in the Black Hills streams, though not in lavish amounts. The expedition also found fertile, well-watered land, and abundant timber in the region's valleys and mountain slopes. Custer's report, though cautious, was like a lightning bolt in a dry forest. The country was in the midst of a severe business recession with thousands unemployed. News of the Black Hills' resources set off a rush of miners and would-be settlers to the Dakota region that resembled California in 1849.

The influx of whites clearly violated the Treaty of 1868, and the Indians loudly protested. The army made a half-hearted attempt to drive out the miners, but in the end allowed them to stay. Instead, in 1875, the government decided to negotiate a new treaty that would remove the Black Hills from Sioux control. The government's incentive was an extension of the period of federal aid and handouts. Under the 1868 agreement this was supposed to last for a limited time while the Indians transformed themselves into settled farmers. The process had failed; the Sioux and other buffalo hunters despised farming as unworthy of true men. Unfortunately, the buffalo on which their nomadic existence had depended were fast disappearing. They found cattle herding more congenial, but it did not provide sufficient food and money for them to become self-supporting. Taking advantage of the Indians' continued need for government largess, federal officials, at a meeting with the Sioux at the Red Cloud agency, offered to give the Indians $400,000 a year for mining rights in the Black Hills or $6 million for their outright sale. Sitting Bull, one of the chiefs present, had already rejected any surrender of Indian lands and the meeting failed to accomplish anything.

The government now decided to use force. In December 1875 the Secretary of the Interior ordered all Indians to report to the reservation agencies or face the government's displeasure. In 1876, after the hostile Sioux had failed to comply, General George Crook sent several expeditions to break their will. Prime target during the spring foray was the camp where Sitting Bull and Crazy Horse had gathered under their command Sioux from almost every tribe as well as hundreds of other Plains Indians who hated both the white man and the reservation policy. In mid-June, Crook's men fought an inconclusive battle at the Rosebud River with Sioux and Cheyenne led by Crazy Horse.

The second punitive expedition produced the greatest military disaster in the long history of the western Indian wars. This foray was led by General Alfred Terry, with Custer second in command. When Terry reached the Tongue River he divided the Seventh Cavalry into two columns, one under Custer, and ordered it to advance on the Indian camp.

Custer did not know that he was about to poke his nose into a hornet's nest. Ten thousand to 12,000 Indians, including 4,000 fighting men, were encamped near the Little Bighorn River. Custer's force numbered a scant 500 men, and he further weakened his command by placing almost two-thirds of it under other officers, Major Marcus Reno and Captain Thomas Weir.

Early on the afternoon of June 25, 1876, the 140 dismounted cavalrymen of Reno's force approached the Indian encampment. The Sioux and Cheyenne attacked, forcing Reno back. Meanwhile, Custer and his men advanced on the camp from the north. The Indians were desperate to protect their women and children and fell on the soldiers with ferocity. Much of the fighting was hand-to-hand, a whirling confusion of shouts and shots enveloped in a dust cloud stirred up by frantic men and lunging horses. This time the Indians ignored *coups* and fought to kill from the start. Reno heard the sounds and saw the smoke of battle, but he did not come to his superior's rescue. In a brief, savage hour Custer and all 264 of his men lay dead. It was the greatest victory that the Plains Indians had ever won over the white men.

The victory at the Little Bighorn could not alter the fate of the Plains tribes. Though there was some talk of forming an Indian confederacy that would stop the encroachment of the whites, this never came about. Nor would it have made any difference. There were thousands of whites to replace every one of Custer's fallen men.

In the wake of "Custer's last stand" another Indian commission forced the Sioux to surrender the Black Hills and accept other onerous revisions of the 1868 Treaty. The original treaty had solemnly promised that there would be no changes unless three-fourths of the adult Indian males had agreed. This provision was simply ignored and the government pronounced the new treaty in effect when the principal chiefs had signed it.

Sitting Bull and his hostiles remained at large and were not a party to this pact. During the winter following the Little Bighorn battle the army continued its campaign to force Sitting Bull and his followers to settle down. At one point General Nelson Miles and Sitting Bull parleyed face-to-face and the chief told the general that no white man had ever loved an Indian and that no true Indian had ever failed to hate the white man. Despite Sitting Bull's belligerent response, Miles succeeded in detaching several thousand Indians from the hostile group. Even Crazy Horse defected, but Sitting Bull refused and fled across the border into Canada where the Americans could not touch him.

During the next few years Sitting Bull and his followers remained encamped just north of the international boundary, making occasional raids across the border to hunt buffalo and attack white settlers. Finally, in 1881, their resolve undermined by hunger and exhaustion with incessant fighting, the chief and his remaining followers surrendered to the American authorities.

For a time they were placed under guard at Fort Randall, in South Dakota, and then moved to the Standing Rock agency on the Sioux reservation. During his last years Sitting Bull remained a thorn in the government's side. He demanded extra rations and cattle, even horses and buggies, for himself and his followers. In 1889, when the government once more revised the treaty with the Sioux, further reducing their lands, he again resisted, though this time with words rather than arrows or bullets. Soon after, he took up and encouraged among his people the new Ghost-Dance religion.

As preached by the Paiute Indian prophet Wovoka, the Ghost Dance was a peaceful faith. in Sitting Bull's version, however, the new Indian messiah, when he returned to earth in 1891, would exterminate the white man. It is not clear whether Sitting Bull believed the Ghost-Dance prophecy, or whether he was only seeking to use it to restore his authority among the Sioux, but it frightened the already nervous white authorities.

On December 15, 1890, the reservation police, a force made up of "tame" Indians, came to arrest Sitting Bull for continuing to encourage the Ghost-Dance ceremonies. As he was preparing to accompany them, the old chief shouted "I'm not going. Come on! Take action!" At this signal, Catch-the-Bear, one of his followers, fired a shot that hit Lieutenant Bull Head in the right side. The lieutenant fired back, hitting Sitting Bull. A confused melee followed, and at the end Sitting Bull lay dead.

Scholars often date the end of the nineteenth-century Indian Wars from the Wounded Knee massacre of December 29, 1890. In fact, the wars had really ended two weeks before when the great Hunkpapa chief, Sitting Bull, the fierce defender of his people's heritage, fell before the bullets of the tame Indians wearing the white man's uniform.

the laws reduced tribal holdings and allowed them to acquire additional Indian lands. For the Indians, the results were almost entirely negative. Government agents often prevented them from claiming the best lands. The long-term exemption of Indian lands from taxation led several states to refuse to provide schools and other services to Indians, and despite its promises, Congress did not come through with adequate funds to offset this loss.

As agencies of "civilization," too, the acts were failures. The tribes lost their cohesion without many Indians becoming strong, self-sustaining individuals. Caught between two cultures, Indians often turned to drink, petty crime, and idleness. Though the twenty-five-year trust period written into the original laws, supposedly protected the Indians from sharpers, the laws were amended so often that many Indians lost their property to speculators for a song. Between 1887 and 1934, Indian-owned lands were reduced from 139 million to 47 million acres. Without means or livelihoods, many Indians became charges of the public authorities.

By the 1920s it had become clear that the reformist Indian policies adopted after 1870 were bankrupt. A number of white Americans, most notably the progressive social reformer John Collier, began to perceive that forced assimilation degraded the Indians' heritage and deprived them of their culture without providing a satisfactory alternative. Working through the American Indian Defense Association, Collier and his supporters demanded the end of the Dawes policy, the guarantee of basic civil rights to Indians, limited self-government on the reservations, the end of government paternalism, and the preservation and encouragement of Indian traditions and culture. When Collier became commissioner of Indian affairs in 1933, he promptly set about changing Indian policy. The chief legislative embodiment of his work was the Wheeler-Howard Act of 1934, which repealed the allotment policy, recognized the right of Indians to organize for "the purposes of local self-government and economic enterprise," and stated that the future goal of Indian education should be to "promote the study of Indian civilization, arts, crafts, skills, and traditions."

Passage of this Indian Reorganization Act did not solve all the Indians' problems. Indians continued to be poor; infant mortality rates on the reservations remained appalling; Indians were still treated, espe-

Dawes Act

From the perspective of white reformers, the Dawes Severalty Act of 1887 was an ideal, long-overdue measure that would assimilate the tribal Indians into the mainstream of American life. It would, Amherst College's benevolent president Merrill E. Gates declared, make the Indian "intelligently selfish." It would get him "out of the blanket and into trousers—and trousers with a pocket in them, and with a pocket *that aches to be filled with dollars!*" The actual effects were different, but the measure stands as a monument to the good intentions of white reformers toward the country's native American peoples.

"*An act to provide for the allotment of lands in severalty to Indians on the various reservations, and to extend the protection of the laws of the United States and the Territories over the Indians, and for various other purposes.*

"*Be it enacted*, That in all cases where any tribe or band of Indians has been, or hereafter shall be, located upon any reservation created for their use, either by treaty stipulation or by virtue of an act of Congress or executive order setting apart the same for their use, the President of the United States be, and he hereby is, authorized, whenever in his opinion any reservation, or any part thereof of such Indians is advantageous for agriculture and grazing purposes to cause said reservation, or any part thereof, to be surveyed, or resurveyed if necessary, and to allot the lands in said reservation in severalty to any Indian located thereon in quantities as follows:

"To each head of a family, one-quarter of a section;

"To each single person over eighteen years of age, one-eighth of a section; and,

"To each orphan child under eighteen years of age, one-eighth of a section; and,

"To each other single person under eighteen years now living, or who may be born prior to the date of the order of the President directing an allotment of the lands embraced in any reservation, one-sixteenth of a section; . . .

"SEC. 5. That upon the approval of the allotments provided for in this act by the Secretary of the Interior, he shall . . . declare that the United States does and will hold the land thus allotted, for the period of twenty-five years, in trust for the sole use and benefit of the Indian to whom such allotment shall have been made, . . . and that at the expiration of said period the United States will convey the same by patent to said Indian, or his heirs, . . . discharged of such trust and free of all charge or encumbrance whatsoever. . . .

"SEC. 6. That upon the completion of said allotments and the patenting of the lands to said allottees, each and every member of the respective bands or tribes of Indians to whom allotments have been made shall have the benefit of and be subject to the laws, both civil and criminal, of the State or Territory in which they may reside; . . . And every Indian born within the territorial limits of the United States who has voluntarily taken up, within said limits, his residence separate and apart from any tribe of Indians therein, and had adopted the habits of civilized life, is hereby declared to be a citizen of the United States, and is entitled to all the rights, privileges, and immunities of such citizens, whether said Indian has been or not, by birth or otherwise, a member of any tribe of Indians within the territorial limits of the United States without in any manner impairing or otherwise affecting the right of any such Indian to tribal or other property. . . ."

cially in the West, as second-class citizens; there was little that intervened to reduce the erosive effect of white culture on Indian values. But by 1934 it could be said that mainstream America was finally seeking to reverse the damaging trends of the past.

The Mining Frontier

The gold seekers whose invasion of Indian lands in the mid-1870s had tripped off the Sioux uprising were pioneers of a new mining frontier. This was a special type of community development common in the mountain West and it left its imprint on the social development of the region and on the collective American imagination.

Mining Communities. The spillover of prospectors from the California gold streams first reached north into British Columbia. In 1859 the search was deflected to the region around Pike's Peak in western Colorado. In a few months a new town, Denver, appeared under the shadow of the Rocky Mountains. Soon afterward two prospectors in the mountains surrounding the Carson River valley in northwestern Nevada Territory hit "pay dirt." Called the Comstock Lode after a gabby drifter who claimed to be its discoverer, the strike was one of the richest on record. The district immediately became the magnet for thousands of California miners, and Virginia City—a settlement of tents, lean-tos, and prefabricated frame structures—rose mushroomlike from the desert in a few weeks.

The Comstock Lode discovery was followed by strikes on the Snake River in northwestern Idaho. In 1863 gold was found at Last Chance Gulch in west-central Montana. The next major precious metal strike was that in the Black Hills of South Dakota during the 1870s. Coeur d'Alene in northern Idaho followed in the early 1880s. This was the last of the major rushes in the contiguous forty-eight states. But at the very end of the century fabulous finds would be made in the Canadian Yukon and in Alaska, the last mining frontier.

The mining communities that grew up around the strikes were the setting for a way of life that has become a part of the American legend. They were places of great variety where every nation, race, and class could be found. The California diggings, reported Louisa Clappe, were "a perambulating picture gallery" where one could hear English, French, Spanish, German, Italian, and many Indian tongues spoken on the streets.

Crime was common in these frontier communities. The gamblers and hangers-on who followed the gold frontier were often unruly men and women. But violence and theft also flowed from the refusal of the federal government to provide either laws or law enforcement. The western answer was the vigilance committee, a group of local worthies who, without benefit of legal trial, hanged the worst of the troublemakers as an example to the rest.

Slow in providing law enforcement officers for the territories, the federal government was even slower in responding to demands for statehood in the mining regions. When Congress failed to act, the Colorado settlers in 1859 organized the Territory of Jefferson with an elected governor and legislature. Congress rejected this initiative, and not until 1876, when the community was well beyond the frontier stage, did it admit Colorado to statehood.

Big Business and Mining. The tent camps and the vigilance committees were only passing phases of the western mining boomtowns. In some cases the next stage was abandonment. In scores of communities, when the richer ores gave out, the miners, storekeepers, and camp followers departed, leaving ghost towns of rusting machinery, decaying buildings, and empty mine shafts.

Many mining communities, however, became permanent towns and cities. Denver, Lewiston, Coeur d'Alene, and Butte developed into substantial places with schools, churches, opera houses, and police forces. The mining industry also stimulated the growth of regional supply, shipping, and outfitting centers such as Seattle, Spokane, and Tucson.

The change from raw mining camp to sedate city seldom took place without a major shift in the mining business that sustained the local economy. As in California in an earlier period, after the loose nuggets

At the California gold diggings women were almost as scarce as the precious metal, and "good" women, at least, were almost as highly prized. This unusual photograph was taken at Auburn, in the Sierra foothills, in 1852.

Creede, Colorado, was a silver boom town in the Rockies, springing up in a canyon so narrow there was only room for one main street. After silver was discovered there in 1890, Creede grew by several hundred people a day; by 1900 it was a virtual ghost town.

and flakes had been skimmed off by men panning the streams and washing earth through cradles, gold mining became a heavy industry that required deep shafts and expensive machinery. Refineries were needed to extract silver from its ores. Still more expensive to produce were the copper and lead found here and there throughout the Great Basin and Rocky Mountains regions. These ores required deep mines, crushers, and complex chemical processes—operations that depended on heavy infusions of capital, trained mining engineers, technicians and chemists, and a permanent force of wage-earning miners and smelter workers.

The capital needed by the postpioneer mining industry was seldom available from local sources. Much of the costs of sinking shafts and erecting mills and refineries in the fabulous Comstock Lode district, for example, came from San Francisco capitalists. These men extracted millions from the Comstock, and with the proceeds built great mansions on Nob Hill overlooking the beautiful city on San Francisco Bay. One Californian who made a fortune in Nevada silver was George Hearst, whose son, William Randolph, would become a powerful New York press lord at

the end of the century. In the 1880s Meyer Guggenheim, a lace manufacturer of Philadelphia, began to invest in the Leadville silver district of Colorado and soon became a major economic force in the state. In Montana the copper kings—William A. Clark, Marcus Daly, and Frederick Heinze—built Butte into a major copper-smelting center. Clark represented local capital, but Daly was allied with the Anaconda Copper Company, an eastern corporation with many English investors. Phelps Dodge, a New York firm, owned large copper mines and refineries in Arizona.

During the last years of the century, eastern capitalists fought bitterly over control of the western mining interests. Chief antagonists were Daniel Guggenheim, son of Meyer, and Henry H. Rogers, an early associate of John D. Rockefeller, whose American Smelting and Refining Company (ASARCO) sought to establish a monopoly of copper smelting by absorbing the Guggenheim interests. The Guggenheims fought back. After the dust had cleared, Daniel Guggenheim and his brothers controlled ASARCO, which they ruled from headquarters in New York City.

Although outside control over local resources

would later fan westerners' discontent, the opening of the western mines added enormously to the country's resources. By 1900 the United States was one of the world's largest producers of gold, silver, copper, lead, and zinc. Politically and financially, the production of gold and silver would be of immense significance. The flood of gold would facilitate the adoption of the international gold standard. But at the same time, the even greater proportional increase in silver would depress its price relative to gold and profoundly disturb the nation's monetary affairs.

The Cattle Kingdom

Just east of the mining regions another economic frontier was taking shape. During the two decades that followed the Ciivl War, cattle raising became the major activity of the Great Plains, attracting eastern and even European investors and creating a way of life that would become a vivid part of the American legend.

Longhorns and Long Drives. The Plains cattle industry began in the Texas grasslands, where, before the Civil War, Mexican ranchers had pastured immense herds of wild, rangy animals. When Americans entered the south Texas area, they brought new breeds of cattle with them. These mingled with the Spanish-Mexican variety to produce the famed Texas longhorn, a wiry, resourceful creature that could survive winter on the open grasslands by digging through the snow with its hooves to the dried grass beneath.

The Civil War cut off the Texas cattle industry from its major markets—eastern leather manufactures and New Orleans beef buyers. During these years the cattle ran wild on the Texas grasslands, and by 1866 there were an estimated 5 million head on the state's southern prairies. Meanwhile, the rest of the country, having slaughtered vast herds of cattle to meet the Union army's needs, was starved for beef. In Texas, cattle were selling for $4 a head, while in the eastern cities they were worth as much as $40 and $50. Returning Confederate veterans saw this imbalance and soon after Appomattox began to consider ways of getting Texas cattle to eastern consumers.

By this time the Missouri Pacific Railroad had reached Sedalia, Missouri, 700 miles north of San Antonio, the heart of the Texas cattle country. If cattle could be driven on the hoof to the railhead, they could then be shipped east. At this point a group of Texas ranchers and Iowa and Kansas businessmen saw their opportunity and in March 1866 launched the first of the classic "long drives" of range cattle, the first step in satisfying the insatiable eastern market for beef and hides.

The Texas cattle drives became annual affairs. In a standard drive, a half-dozen mounted "cowboys" under a "trail boss" guided each band of a thousand or so unruly longhorns across open country accompanied by "chuckwagons" to carry food and equipment and a "horse wrangler" to care for the mounts. The way was often beset with difficulties. Besides mud, swollen streams, and rough terrain, there were hostile humans to contend with. The Sedalia Trail passed through Indian territory where resentful tribesmen often stampeded the herds. Even more troublesome were Missouri farmers, who feared that the invading longhorns carried the dread Texas fever and would infect their own cattle. Turning out in force, they engaged in shootouts with the Texans. Despite these obstacles, cattle that got through sold for $35 a head in Sedalia, providing a clear profit for the ranchers.

It did not take long for an enterprising businessman to see how the system could be improved. In 1867 a cattle dealer from Illinois, Joseph G. McCoy, established a depot at Abilene in central Kansas along the Kansas-Pacific Railroad, where "the country was entirely unsettled, well watered, [and with] excellent grass." There ranchers could pen their animals and arrange for their sale to buyers, who would then ship them east by rail. The route north to Abilene by way of the Chisholm Trail passed through country farther west than the Sedalia Trail and avoided irate farmers. Between 1867 and 1871 some 1.5 million head of Texas cattle were driven to Abilene for shipment east.

The day of the Chisholm Trail was brief. The railroads brought farmers and settlers who opposed the Texas cattle drive. When the area around Abilene became too densely populated, the drive was deflected farther west to Ellsworth on the Kansas-Pacific line. Later the "cow towns" of Newton and Dodge City were developed along the Santa Fe Railroad.

The Kansas cow towns, like the mining camps, were rowdy places. It was hard to maintain law and order among the transient "cow poke" population. Cowboys were a diverse lot of ex-Confederate and ex-Union soldiers, former slaves, Mexicans, and Indians who rode the range twelve hours a day looking for strays. At spring roundup they worked hard roping and branding the unmarked calves. On the long drives cowboys spent as many as four months in the saddle, keeping the cattle moving and preventing stampedes. The work was dirty, hard, lonely, and unhealthy. No wonder that when he was paid several months' wages

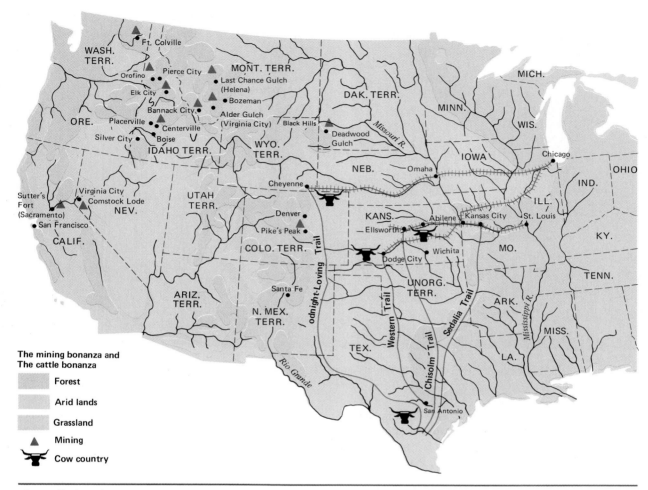

The mining bonanza and
The cattle bonanza

- Forest
- Arid lands
- Grassland
- ▲ Mining
- 🐂 Cow country

The cattle kingdom

in Dodge City or Abilene at the end of the long drive, the cowboy went on a roaring spree—drinking, gambling, and sometimes shooting up the town.

Boom and Bust. Stimulated by expanding markets, the Texas cattle industry soon spread over a large part of the Lone Star State. Then, as the railroad penetrated the central and northern Plains, thousands of Texas cattle were driven north to stock the newly accessible region. By the early 1870s the central and northern Plains were covered with ranches.

As fully developed during the late 1870s and early 1880s, the range cattle industry of Colorado, Wyoming, Montana, Idaho, and the western Dakotas relied on free use of the public land and on weather mild enough for the cattle to graze outdoors on the open range all year. The cattle used the public domain at no cost to the ranchers, who, in effect, was subsidized

by the government with free land, grass, and water. All the ranchers had to do was wait while their cattle increased and put on weight. In the spring they rounded up their herds, branded the calves, and shipped the mature animals east at a good profit.

The profits and the free, adventurous, and individualistic ranch life attracted many to the Plains. For a decade the cattle kingdom flourished. "Cotton was once crowned king," exulted a contemporary editor, "but grass is now." Some would-be ranchers, like the lively young New Yorker Theodore Roosevelt, came out from the East. Others came from Europe. Englishmen and Scots, particularly, were attracted to the rancher's life. And other outsiders who did not come themselves sent their capital. When a committee of Parliament reported profits in American ranching of 33 percent, money from Britain poured in by the millions. In 1883 twenty cattle-raising corporations capi-

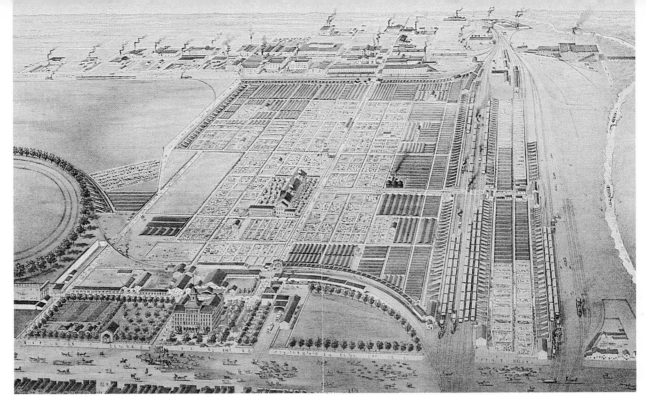

Union Stockyards in Chicago in 1878, as the city was becoming "hog butcher to the world."

talized at $12 million were formed in Wyoming alone.

By 1885 farsighted people began to suspect trouble ahead. Each year the range grass became thinner as more and more cattle grazed on the Plains. To prevent personal disaster, ranchers began to fence off areas of range with barbed wire—invented in 1874—though this was illegal on publicly owned land. They also formed livestock associations to regulate the number of cattle grazed, exclude intruders, and protect the cattle against rustlers and wolves. Despite these efforts, by the mid-1880s the Plains were overstocked. So numerous were cattle shipments that prices began to tumble. Some ranchers, seeing the handwriting on the wall, sold off their herds and got out, further depressing prices.

Then nature struck. From 1875 to 1885 the weather had been unusually mild and rainy on the northern Plains. In 1886 it changed. That summer was hot and dry; by fall the cattle, lacking decent forage, were weak. In November the blizzards came. January 1887 was the worst winter month that anyone could remember, with record snows and temperatures dipping at times to seventy degrees below zero. Thousands of cattle were buried alive by the drifts. Others froze to death standing upright. Unable to get to the grass beneath the snow, crazed cattle poured into the streets

of several settled communities and tried to eat everything in sight. When the terrible winter ended, hundreds of carcasses were carried down the streams by the spring freshets, bearing with them the fortunes of their owners.

The cattle industry survived on the Plains, but it was never the same. Many of the cattle corporations went bankrupt, a process that drove out a lot of distant eastern and European investors who could not supervise their investments closely. Under the control of local people the industry was transformed. Even more land than before was fenced in. Ranchers began to raise hay for winter feed and replace the wiry longhorns with Herefords and other breeds that would produce more meat per animal. Some ranchers, recognizing that sheep were hardier than cattle, turned to wool production, though others fought the sheep invasion as a threat. The life of the cowboy changed, too. Now he spent less time in the saddle and more digging post holes and stringing barbed wire. The cowboy became a "ranch hand." Meanwhile, wheat farmers began to intrude from the east, driving the cattlemen into the more isolated portions of the Plains. The ranching industry survived, but as a smaller, more localized, and more rational industry than during the heyday of the open range.

Western Land Policies

Cattle ranchers were not the only people to capitalize on liberal land policies. The federal government—always vital in determining who got land and how it was used—played a particularly important role in the apportionment of land in the last West, for almost all of it was public domain, acquired by war, purchase, or treaty. From 1862 to the end of the century, Congress gave away or sold vast amounts of these western lands under inconsistent policies designed to satisfy a variety of interests. In the end the small western farmers who were supposed to benefit from these policies felt betrayed, and were convinced that outside speculators and the government's distance from western realities were responsible.

Land Acts of the 1860s. From the earliest years of the republic, Jeffersonians, hoping to perpetuate the "sturdy yeomen" they considered the nation's backbone, had joined with those representing small farmers' interests to push policies that would provide cheap or free land in small parcels to settlers. These people achieved one of their long-established goals when, in 1862, Congress passed the Homestead Act. This measure provided that any adult head of family could acquire 160 acres of government land free of cost, except a small fee, if the family resided on the land for five years and introduced "improvements."

Only a fraction of the public domain ever got into the hands of small farmers free of charge. At the same time it was giving land to settlers, the government was also handing out vast parcels for other public purposes. In the same year that Congress passed the Homestead law, for example, it also approved the Morrill Land Grant College Act conferring on each state part of the public domain in proportion to its population, to be used to support state-run colleges for agriculture. Paradoxically, this act granted the most land to the populous eastern and older midwestern states, where agriculture was less important than industry. The railroad land grants were another example of such "national interest" policies. In addition, the federal government handed out land to encourage the building of wagon roads and gave away millions of acres to states entering the Union after 1862.

While it was handing out parcels of land, presumably to benefit settlers and the nation as a whole, the federal government continued to sell land at auction to the highest bidder. In 1862 some 84 million acres of federal lands were on the market for cash. Those who spoke for the western farmers complained that free homesteads were largely an illusion. Much of the best land was available only by cash purchase from the railroads, the states, or the federal government. Between 1862 and 1904 only some 147 million acres of land passed to farmers under the Homestead Act; more than 610 million acres were sold for cash.

Nor was the Homestead Act itself without abuses. Technically, every homesteader was supposed

"Doing a land office business" has become a cliché for holding a fabulously successful sale. In this 1885 photograph of the United States Land Office in Garden City, Kansas, we can see where the phrase originated.

to "improve" the land and reside on it before taking legal title. Actually, many people who filed a claim made only the slightest show of improving the property before "proving up." Another fraudulent practice was for employers to order their hired hands to file claims and then, when the land became theirs, buy it from them for a purely nominal amount. Many farmers, ranchers, and timber magnates thus acquired considerably more than the 160 acres that the Homestead Act envisioned.

Acts Tailored to Western Land Problems. The Homestead Act also took no account of the special land problems of the dry Great Plains and Great Basin. In the humid East and parts of the Midwest 160 acres were sufficient to support a farm family, for yields per acre were high where rainfall was abundant. West of the ninety-eighth meridian, however, rain was sparse and crop yields were low. The 160-acre allotment was too small for the "dryfarming" cultivator on the eastern edge of the Plains; for the rancher who grazed hungry cattle in the drier portions of the region, it was impossible, because each animal required 40 acres of grazing land to survive.

Following the Civil War Congress passed a series of measures to deal with the special land problems of the West. One, the Timber Culture Act of 1873, allowed farmers with 160-acre homesteads to take out papers on another 160 acres of adjacent land on the condition that they agree to plant trees on some portion of it. In theory, trees would encourage rain and so make the plains less arid. In reality, the tree-planting provision was largely ignored; the effect was to give Plains farmers about 10 million additional acres of dry land.

The Desert Land Act of 1877 was also designed to accommodate the land laws to the arid West. Most scholars, however, consider it a giveaway to the cattle companies. Under its provisions lands could be bought for a down payment of 25 cents per acre if the purchaser agreed to irrigate a full section (640 acres) within three years. After irrigating the section the purchaser could pay an additional dollar per acre and own the whole purchase. Unfortunately the law allowed purchasers to assign the acreage to others even before they had met the irrigation requirement. Thousands of acres thus passed to the cattle companies with few public benefits.

Still another measure, the Timber and Stone Act of 1878, violated the spirit of the Homestead Act. The law applied to lands "unfit for cultivation" and "valuable chiefly for timber or stone." After declaring that the land in question contained no valuable minerals, any citizen could buy up to 160 acres at $2.50 an acre. Few small farmers benefited from the law. Instead, through various forms of fraud, vast tracts ended up in the hands of large timber companies.

A final major law designed to take into consideration the special climatic needs of the West was the National Reclamation, or Newlands, Act of 1902. It provided that a reclamation fund be established with proceeds from federal land sales in arid states and territories, the fund to be used for building dams, water channels, and other irrigation facilities in these states. The public lands so irrigated would be reserved for small farmers in tracts of 160 acres under the same provisions as the 1862 Homestead Act. Water users were to pay water-use fees and reimburse the government for its capital outlays over a ten-year period. The reclamation fund, thus renewed, would become available for other projects in succeeding years.

The Newlands Act was one of Congress's more successful western land measures. Under it a score of dams were constructed, including Roosevelt Dam in Arizona and Idaho's Arrowrock Dam, and thousands of acres were irrigated and reclaimed from the desert. Less successful than the engineering feats were the social results. Many settlers found that they could not pay the government's charges. Much of the land passed to large holders, though periodically the government sought to provide relief for the hard-pressed small farmers.

To many western citizens, the land laws seemed generally to benefit land speculators and midwestern cities, while the western family farmer got the crumbs off the table. Indeed, there were some large corporate farms in the wheat lands of the Northwest, and certainly much of the country's mineral and timber lands fell into the hands of corporations. But the greatest speculators were actually the small farmers themselves, who often took more land then they needed and reaped large profits on the excess when they sold it. Nevertheless, the legend of the evil outside land speculator helped shape much of the political reaction of the later nineteenth century. Here was still another reason to denounce the East and demand relief from eastern "oppression."

Farming in the Last West

Indians, miners, cattlemen—all these groups could show how eastern policies and interests were inappropriate to western needs. For the Indians, certainly, the

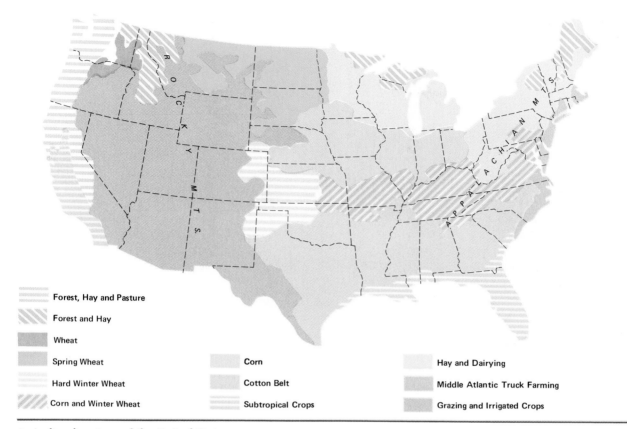

Agricultural regions of the United States

Legend:
- Forest, Hay and Pasture
- Forest and Hay
- Wheat
- Spring Wheat
- Hard Winter Wheat
- Corn and Winter Wheat
- Corn
- Cotton Belt
- Subtropical Crops
- Hay and Dairying
- Middle Atlantic Truck Farming
- Grazing and Irrigated Crops

inadequacies were devastating. But the farmers' discontent ultimately became the most visible.

Plains Agriculture. The Great Plains presented special problems to the would-be farmer. Along its eastern fringes precipitation was adequate for cultivation methods familiar in older farming regions to the east. Elsewhere, although ground water was too far beneath the surface to be raised by ordinary wells, the constant winds made the region ideal for windmill-powered pumps. During the 1880s they became an almost universal means of raising water. Another way to conquer aridity was by "dry farming"—planting seeds far apart and covering growing plants with a dust mulch after each rainfall to preserve moisture. Farmers also adopted new drought-resistant types of grain, some brought from Russia.

Even in areas of adequate rainfall, immigrants from the East found difficulties they had not encountered back home. The most serious was the absence of stone and timber. Except for some cottonwoods, willows, and hackberries along stream banks, there were few trees on the Plains. Furthermore, the soils were deep and generally stone-free. What materials could the farmer use for fencing, for building barns and a house?

During the 1860s agricultural experts touted hedging as a method of fencing off cultivated fields. But before hedging could become widely adopted, barbed wire was invented. A barbed-wire fence required only a few timber uprights; the rest was iron wire, a few rolls of which could enclose hundreds of acres. One contemporary listed the advantages of barbed wire: It "takes no room, exhausts no soil, shades no vegetation, is proof against high winds, makes no snowdrifts, and is both durable and cheap."

To solve the shortages in housing material, early Plains settlers used bricks of sod cut from the thick Plains grass. These were piled up to make walls along the edges of deep holes dug into the ground. The roof of such a house was also sod, placed on brush and cottonwoood rafters. Warm in winter and cool in summer, these half-buried structures were also dirty, and during heavy rains they leaked badly. Yet they served some families for many years and were even used for schoolhouses and other public buildings. Eventually,

Mechanized agriculture in the West was encouraged by the absence of trees. In eastern Washington State in 1900 wheat was harvested efficiently by enormous combines drawn by huge teams of horses.

when the railroads came, timber from the East and Far West made frame structures possible. In time the houses of the Plains began to resemble those in the Midwest.

The Plains environment presented still other problems. In 1874 swarms of grasshoppers descended on the region from the Dakotas to Texas, consuming grain, vegetables, bark, clothes, and even the handles of plows and pitchforks. During the 1870s and early 1880s, however, rainfall was generally sufficient in the region, and with the confinement of the Indians to reservations and the arrival of the railroads, people swarmed into western Kansas, Nebraska, and the Dakotas to grow grain for the East and Europe. Then the late 1880s ushered in a decade of extremely dry conditions. Crops drooped and died, and whatever survived the parching winds was consumed by insects. Farmers and their families fled the searing sun during the early 1890s and returned east with the sides of their wagons sardonically inscribed: "In God We Trusted; In Kansas We Busted!"

Yet many farmers persisted and ultimately prospered. Once labor shortages—another chronic problem on the Plains—had been solved by the invention of special harvesting and threshing machines, Plains farm-

ing became enormously productive. It was *extensive* agriculture that cultivated vast acreages using little labor. It focused on wheat, the crop best suited to grasslands and, owing to its durability, to production far from consumers. By 1899 the United States was producing over 600 million bushels of wheat a year, much of it from the Plains. In 1870 the wheat belt had been centered in the older Midwest. By 1899 Minnesota, North Dakota, South Dakota, and Kansas were among the top five wheat producers.

Pacific Coast Agriculture. As the Plains became the nation's wheat belt, the Pacific coast emerged as the region that supplied the country's fruits and vegetables. California land was initially used for cattle ranching and wheat production, often on "bonanza" farms of more than a thousand acres. The Pacific Northwest states, too, at first concentrated on grain and cattle, though never on such a large scale as California.

Gradually, as transportation to the East improved and it became possible to preserve perishables by refrigeration, agriculture on the Pacific coast became more diversified, taking advantage of the region's mild climate. Oregon began to supply the San Francisco market with apples, pears, peaches, plums, and grapes.

In Washington the arrival of the Northern Pacific Railroad in the 1880s stimulated the production of apples and pears in the state's eastern valleys.

Meanwhile, California was developing into a significant specialty agricultural region. Grapes had been grown there long before the Americans arrived, but in the 1860s and later, after the arrival of German and then Italian immigrants, the wine industry grew rapidly. During the 1870s and 1880s the vineyards were almost wiped out by an insect pest, but were saved when resistant grapevine species were developed. By 1900 California produced 19 million gallons of wine, over 80 percent of American output.

Citrus fruit, too, had been grown in California during the Spanish period. The fruit, however, was inferior and consumed only locally. Then in the 1870s Brazilian navel oranges were introduced on irrigated fields in southern California. When refrigeration came in the 1880s, navels picked during the early winter could be shipped all the way to the East Coast. Summer-ripeniing Valencia oranges, introduced somewhat later, enabled the growers to produce year-round.

The citrus industry at first was plagued by haphazard marketing. Shipments spoiled or got lost; at times the market was glutted, at other times it was undersupplied. To deal with these problems, the growers tried to form cooperatives during the 1880s. The middlemen who marketed the crop blocked this effort, but then in 1893 the growers organized the Southern California Fruit Exchange, which later became the California Fruit Growers' Exchange and marketed its product under the brand name Sunkist. The Exchange brought stability to the industry.

Farm Discontent and Western Revolt

Viewed from a broad economic perspective, the development of American agriculture during the generation following the Civil War was a success story. In quantity, acreage, output per person and per acre, the results were spectacular. Largely because of the mechanized farms of the Plains, wheat production tripled between 1860 and 1899. In the older Midwest, states like Illinois and Iowa shifted from wheat to hogs and cattle, feeding them on the country's huge corn harvests—840 million bushels of corn in 1860, 2.7 billion bushels in 1900. In cotton and livestock the increases were equally dramatic. The nation's farm labor force continued to rise in absolute numbers until 1910, but the increase in farmers was far smaller than the expansion in their output, for new technology, new plant science, the land-grant colleges, and the Department of Agriculture all helped to increase productivity at a rapid pace. The result was that the United States became an agricultural cornucopia, capable of producing cheap grain, meat, and fiber, not only for its own exploding urban population, but also for much of the industrializing Atlantic world. So efficient was American farm production and marketing that it undermined British, French, and German cultivators and led to loud European demands for protection against the "American menace."

And yet there was another tale that competed with this agricultural success story: The post–Civil War American Farmers were discontented and were in full-scale revolt against the perceived oppression of rural

Wheat and cotton prices in the Gilded Age
Source: Historical Statistics of the United States, Colonial Times to 1970.

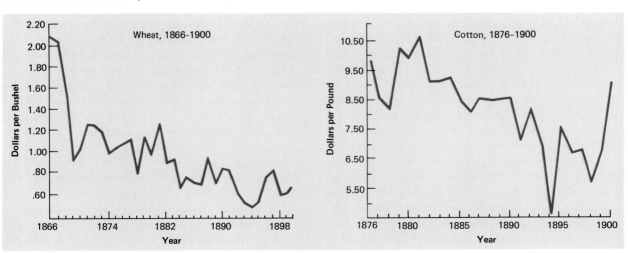

America by the rich and the powerful residing in the cities.

Farm Problems. The grievances behind the insurgency were broad-ranging in their scope. According to farm spokespersons, farmers were victimized by bankers and mortgage companies that kept interest rates high and squeezed farmers and other borrowers and debtors through "hard money" policies that restricted the country's money supply. The typical American farm, they claimed, was mortgaged to the hilt, and the moneylenders and bankers showed no mercy in foreclosing when the farmer could not pay. Farm advocates also insisted that the prices of the goods that cultivators bought were kept artificially high by tariffs and monopoly practices, whereas prices they received for their crops fell steadily. They charged that middlemen's costs—for transporting their products to market, for storing their grain, for milling their flour, and ginning their cotton—all rose during this period. The parasitic railroads, farm processors, grain and cotton brokers, and all the others grew fat while they grew poor. Beyond these economic grievances, spokespersons for "agrarianism' expressed fears that those who "fed them all," the nation's cultivators, were losing influence and the new "money power" was in the driver's seat.

Today, economic historians are puzzled by the charges leveled by farm advocates during these last years of the nineteenth century. For one thing, they note, farmers did not all fare alike economically. Pacific coast farmers prospered by adopting fruit and vegetable crops. Prairie farmers of Iowa and Illinois switched from wheat to corn and hogs and made decent profits. East Coast and Great Lakes truck and dairy farmers found profitable markets.

As for claims of financial oppression, this too is puzzling. It is true that interest rates were higher in the West and South—the country's premier farm areas—than in the Northeast. But this difference can be explained by the shortage of savings in the two staple-crop regions and the higher risks of farming than manufacturing or commerce. Nor were American farm borrowers poor peasants turning to moneylenders to stave off starvation. Most of the money that farmers borrowed was for barns, fences, plows, harvesters, and other improvements, all items that were needed to increase productivity and income. The loans they contracted were, in effect, no different from the loans of any other small businessperson. Nor were the oppressive farm mortgages as universal as the critics claimed. Even in the wheat belt, no more than 39 percent of the farms were burdened with mortgages in 1890, though the figure was higher in Kansas and Nebraska. As for the legendary wicked urge to foreclose, this was not common. The banks and the mortgage companies that lent farmers money were not interested in acquiring farm acreage; they often extended the repayment terms of loans more than once to avoid having to foreclose.

The claims that falling prices were contrived deliberately by a cabal of bankers and money power monopolists to squeeze the nation's "producers" were equally dubious. All prices fell during the generation following the Civil War. This meant the prices the farmers paid as well as those they received. Not only did wheat, cotton, pork, beef, and tobacco decline, but so too did iron, coal, clothing, railroad and interest rates, farm machinery, barbed wire, and lumber. There is no good evidence that the "terms of trade" between the producers of food and fiber and the providers of the services and manufactured goods that they used shifted significantly against the nation's rural tillers in these years. Moreover, the price declines were not only an American phenomenon; they were common to the entire world. If there was a conspiracy to force down prices, the conspiracy was evidently worldwide in its scope.

Nor is it clear that monetary forces were responsible for the great deflation of the late nineteenth century. This was an era when *real* costs were going down. Each year the furnaces that created steel, the locomotives and boxcars that hauled freight, and the plows and combines that produced grain became more efficient and their products less expensive in terms of labor and matériel. Even the middlemen's real costs declined owing to greater efficiency. When, in the 1890s, the Russians sought to make their grain more competitive in the world market, they sent a delegation to the United States to learn how American brokers and grain handlers managed to get the American wheat crop to market at such low cost. Some scholars do believe that late-nineteenth-century price declines can be traced to a slow increase in the money supply. But few believe that this was deliberately engineered by a collection of conspirators. And in any event, the case for excessively slow money growth is not proven.

Agrarianism. And yet we are left with the reality of turbulent farm discontent in the generation following the Civil War. How can we explain it?

First, let us note that the agrarian insurgency of the period was confined primarily to the wheat- and cotton-growing areas. Dairy farmers, corn-hog farmers, and truck farmers were generally proof against the insurgent appeal. In large part this was because they sold their products to domestic consumers in the fast-growing cities. Though their prices declined like all others, they were more stable than many.

Stability—or rather its absence—is one possible answer to the riddle of insurgency in the wheat and cotton belts. Grain and cotton farmers were subject to a degree of uncertainty that other producers did not experience. These cultivators sold their crops in a world market where they competed fiercely with other nations. Europeans bought not only the grain of the American prairies and plains, but also the wheat of Canada, Australia, Argentina, and Russia. They bought cotton from the American South; they also could buy it from Egypt, India, and Brazil. By the end of the nineteenth century the entire world was knit together in a single market for nonperishable agricultural goods, and prices were established by countless impersonal transactions between buyers and sellers.

The system was a tremendous boon to consumers. Everywhere they benefited from the declining cost of food and fabric. But, of course, however successful in lowering their own costs of production to offset world price declines, farmers would have been better off if prices had risen. Of greater significance, however, was the painful experience of price instability. The American farmer's own output was only one factor affecting world crop prices. A bumper wheat crop in the American Plains could be expected to lower world grain prices. But it might be more than offset by a dearth in, say, Argentina, that would push prices up. And, of course, the reverse might also occur: An American farmer, expecting good prices after a short crop, might be bitterly disappointed if Australia or the Russian Ukraine had a bounteous harvest. The net effect was that farmers found themselves on a rollercoaster over which they could exercise no control. The villains were actually impersonal market forces, but these were not as satisfactory as flesh-and-blood people of the sort that farmers saw or heard about every day—the bankers, railroad officials, politician, and farm machinery manufacturers.

Clearly, like the wage earners discussed in Chapters 17 and 18, American farmers as a group faced difficult problems adjusting to the demands and circumstances of a new industrialized, urbanized era. Some of their problems were exaggerated, but some were also real. No one could deny the distress of sharecroppers in the South, penalized often by a vicious social and racial system that placed them at the mercy of powerful and privileged planters and landowners. Land in America, moreover, bore a disproportionate share of the national tax burden; personal property and personal income was lightly taxed or exempt. Though railroad rates generally went down, in noncompetitive areas, often in the West and South, the railroad managers tried to make up for the "cutthroat" competition on major trunk lines by charging all that the local traffic would bear. Finally, agriculture as a way of life had lost standing. More and more the cities had seized on the imaginations of Americans. This explained, in part, the exodus of the young from the rural areas. It also accounted for the increasing references to "rubes," "hayseeds," and "appleknockers" in the metropolitan press.

Moved by such forces and feelings, in the generation following the Civil War farm advocates launched a campaign to arouse the sympathy of the nation for a war against the oppressors and exploiters. Claiming to speak for the entire rural community, and playing on resonant Jeffersonian chords, they created a social philosophy based on agrarian distress and rural rights that can best be labeled *agrarianism*.

Agrarianism exalted the farmer as the only true citizen, the backbone of the nation, the heart of the "producing masses." Agrarians gradually expanded the concept to include the ever-growing number of wage earners and sought to construct a farmer-labor alliance of producers, whose plight was said to be shared by the nation as a whole. On the other side, agrarians personalized the enemy as the "money power" or the "bloated middlemen." These "plutocrats," they said, had seized control of the economy and through various hidden financial arrangements had imposed their will on the nation. The United States was fast becoming the land of a rich few and an impoverished, exploited, and powerless many.

Though agrarian advocates sought to universalize their protest, much of their indictment had a sectional edge. Both the Great Plains and the South regarded themselves as colonies in bondage to the "East." It was the East that was the source of credit, and it was eastern moneylenders and bankers who charged the high interest rates the "producing sections" paid. The railroads had their headquarters in Boston, New York, Philadelphia, or Chicago, and it was in these eastern and large midwestern cities that the freight rates that squeezed cotton and wheat farmers were set. Easterners—or Europeans—also owned the land and marketed the crops, the agrarians said. The farm-machinery manufacturers, the barbed-wire producers, and the other industrialists who made the equipment western and southern farmers needed to survive were easterners with headquarters in Chicago, Indianapolis, or Richmond. Futhermore, the East dominated the major political parties and through them the government. Policies regarding the Indians, finance, money, tariffs, and land were not made by the people of the West and South, who were most directly concerned. They were made, agrarians claimed, by the representatives of the eastern "money interests," who sought only their own gain.

Whether true or false, whether exaggerated or exact, the agrarian indictment of plutocracy and the East had become a powerful political force by the end of the century. The discontents that built up over the years in the West and South emerged in a series of political movements from the 1870s until the end of the 1890s. Like socialism among wage earners, these were all reactions against the perceived abuses that accompanied the great economic and social changes that marked the era.

Agrarian reformism differed from socialism in many ways, however. First, though like Marxism it considered labor the source of all value, it was distinctly American in origin, borrowing heavily from the Jefferson-Jackson emphasis on the small landholder and the "producer." Second, though the agrarian reformers sought to win support among eastern wage earners, their appeal fed largely on southern and western discontents, especially those of cultivators. Finally, the agrarian reformers were never enemies of private property and a profit system. Their complaint was with the way capitalism had supposedly been rigged in favor of the few and against the many. Their desire was not to end profit and property but to make sure that the benefits of both were more widely distributed among the masses of the people.

The Grangers.

To solve their problems, some farmers during the Gilded Age, like some wage earners, turned to collective action. In the early 1870s they flocked to local "Granges" of the Patrons of Husbandry, a social-fraternal order founded in 1876. At first the Granges were primarily social and educational organizations. Farm life was isolated and lonely, and farmers and their wives welcomed the chance to socialize and listen to lectures at the local Grange hall.

As midwestern farmers became increasingly dependent on middlemen and railroads, the Grangers became politically active. Joining with many eastern merchants and business people who also disliked the railroads' high and often arbitrary freight charges, they supported state laws to regulate railroad companies and grain elevator firms. In states like Illinois, Iowa, Wisconsin, and Minnesota, where political power was balanced between the major parties, the pro-Granger men in the state legislatures were able to enact the regulatory laws the Patrons of Husbandry supported.

The patrons were also active in various cooperative ventures to improve the economic standing of farmers. In several midwestern states Grange agents negotiated purchases of large quantities of supplies from merchants or manufacturers at special low prices and passed these savings along to Grange members. In 1872 a group of merchants formed Montgomery Ward and Company for the purpose of dealing with the Grangers. Grange agents also secured price reductions from some farm machinery manufacturers. Efforts to *produce* farm machinery cooperatively failed, however; the managers of Grange manufacturing enterprises lacked experience and were unable to meet the aggressive competition of established private firms.

The Alliances.

By the late 1870s the Grange had ceased to be anything more than a social-educational organization, but farmers did not abandon political or economic organization. New agrarian alliances soon appeared that were more militant than the Patrons of Husbandry.

The Alliance movement began in the mid-1870s when small rancher-farmers in central Texas organized a secret club to catch horse thieves, collect stray cattle, and fight the large ranchers who ignored the rights of their smaller neighbors. The scheme soon spread to the rest of the state and grew in strength and ambition. In 1886 the Texas Alliance, borrowing ideas from the Greenback party of 1884, revealed a program calling for opposition to landholding by foreigners, for stiff taxes on railroads, and for paper money. These political demands threatened to split the Alliance until Charles W. Macune brought the opposing sides together.

Macune went on to become a major leader in a regional Southern Alliance that incorporated the Arkansas Wheel and a large Colored Alliance composed of black tenant farmers and sharecroppers. By 1890 the Southern Aliance had a million members.

Farm discontent in the prairies and Great Plains led to similar efforts. By 1890 the Northwest Alliance, organized a decade earlier, had expanded to fifteen states, with particularly heavy concentration of membership in Kansas, Nebraska, the Dakotas, and Minnesota.

Toward the end of the 1880s the Alliances began

This poster shows farmers as living a potentially idyllic existence. Their actual position was much less fortunate, and they created Granges to push for political solutions to their problems. Although "Granger Laws" eventually regulated railroad and grain elevator rates, farm problems remained severe through the end of the century.

to emphasize politics rather than cooperatives. Alliance-affiliated candidates running on platforms favoring the "producers" over the bankers, merchants, and manufacturers won election as either Democrats or Republicans to state legislatures in the South and West. In several states they captured one of the major parties and compelled it to endorse farmers' programs. But the Alliance-controlled state legislatures achieved relatively little. They enacted some legislation regulating railroads and businesses, but these measures were largely ineffective. Alliance-dominated state governments were frequently led by political novices who were easily outmaneuvered by the seasoned politicians

of the regular parties. When the Alliance leaders were not simply duped, they were sometimes handicapped by a limited vision of what government could or should do. Too often, in the words of the Tennessee Alliance, they considered the "Jeffersonian noninterference theory of government" to be the "wisest" and refused to employ state power in positive ways.

Frustrated by their initial experiences with politics, Alliance leaders concluded that the fault lay in relying on the Democrats and Republicans. Instead, the farmers should organize their own party, one that would be free of the old-line politicos, who seemed indifferent at heart to the needs of rural people

Conclusions

The development of the last American frontier made an enormous difference in the nation's history. The exploitation of the trans-Missouri West added immense resources to the country's economic base. The cattle frontier also added to the raw material for American literature and legend. For the American Indian, development of this area was the final defeat in almost three centuries of bitter conflict with people of Old World origins.

The last West was also the focus for the last truly serious threat of sectional disunity. Along with the cotton South, it was indeed in some ways a colony of the Northeast. Eastern money controlled its resources; eastern attitudes affected its Indian policy; eastern politicians decided its political fate. By the end of the century, moreover, western and southern grievances had created a sense of apartness, of distinctiveness, that contributed to a mighty political revolt. This sense was reinforced and given focus by a group of agrarian thinkers who drew their ideas from the Jefferson-Jackson tradition of the early Republic. Scholars may argue over the validity of western grievances or whether western leaders properly identified the causes of their section's difficulties. But there can be no question that by 1890 in the West and the South a vast wave of discontent was gathering. Before the new century began, it would sweep over the nation, threatening to push aside long-standing political alignments and shift the country's balance of power.

For Further Reading

Walter P. Webb. *The Great Plains* (1931)

> The classic study of the Great Plains. Describes the physical environment of the Plains region, its native inhabitants, and the efforts of people of European ancestry to conquer it. Webb shows the important ways in which geography and climate modified transplanted institutions.

Fred A. Shannon. *The Farmer's Last Frontier: Agriculture, 1860–1897* (1945)

> This older work is still the indispensable study of agriculture in the generation following the Civil War. Shannon is more than a scholar in this book; he is also an advocate of southern and western farmers in their struggles with the railroads, the manufacturers, and middlemen. In some ways *The Farmer's Last Frontier* is the baseline from which all later works on the post–Civil War "farm problem" are derived.

Allan G. Bogue. *Money at Interest: The Farm Mortgage on the Middle Border* (1955); and *From Prairie to Corn Belt* (1963)

> Two revisionist treatments of the post–Civil War farmer's difficulties. Bogue denies that eastern moneylenders were greedy or made excessive profits from western farmers. He also claims that corn belt farmers did very well for themselves in the late nineteenth century. Neither of these books should be read for recreation.

Everett Dick. *The Sod-House Frontier, 1854–1890* (1954)

> The subtitle of this book is: "A Social History of the Northern Plains from the Creation of Kansas & Nebraska to the Admission of the Dakotas." It summarizes quite well the contents of the work. This is old-fashioned social history—and it is lively.

Rodman W. Paul. *Mining Frontiers of the Far West, 1948–1880* (1963)

> This brief book combines excellent scholarship with a sense of the romantic aspect of the great western mining bonanzas. Has first-rate illustrations.

R. K. Andrist. *The Long Death: The Last Days of the Plains Indians* (1964)

> A skillful overview of the tragic destruction of the Plains tribes by the encroachment of "civilization." The work of a talented journalist.

Robert W. Mardock. *Reformers and the American Indian* (1970)

> Surveys the Indian reformers through to the Dawes Act of 1887. Mardock ties their efforts to the anti-slavery movement that most of them had participated in. They were sincere, he says, but their vision was limited and culture-bound.

Ernest Staples Osgood. *The Day of the Cattlemen* (1929).

> Old, but good. A brief study of the range cattle industry of the northern Plains, this is 250 pages of instruction and entertainment.

Robert Dykstra. *The Cattle Towns* (1968)

> This book is an up-to-date, unromantic, but interesting study of the cattle towns—Dodge City, Abilene, Ellsworth, Caldwell, and Wichita—between 1876 and 1885. Written by an urban historian, it emphasizes the nature of town life in the cattle communities and talks as much of dry-goods merchants as of cowboys and dance-hall girls.

Gene M. Gressley. *Bankers and Cattlemen* (1966)

> The subtitle of this book is "The Stocks-and-Bonds, Havana-Cigar, Mahogany-and-Leather Side of the Cowboy Era." That is as good a description as

one could find of this study of the western cattle industry from 1870 to 1900.

John D. Hicks. *The Populist Revolt: A History of the Farmers' Alliance and the People's Party* (1931)
> This is the standard older treatment of late-nineteenth-century agrarian insurgency. Hicks sees the Populists as the forerunners of twentieth-century American liberalism.

Hamlin Garland. *Main-Travelled Roads* (1891)
> The characters in this collection of short stories are pitiful victims of a harsh environment and unjust laws. Garland, who settled with his parents on the Iowa prairie, learned early that "farming is not entirely made up of berrying, tossing the new-mown hay, and singing "The Old Oaken Bucket' on the porch by moonlight."

Frank Norris. *The Octopus* (1901)
> The fortunes of western farmers were tied to the railroads, the grain elevator operators, the Chicago Board of Trade, and the weather. In this description of California wheat growers in the Central Valley, the Southern Pacific Railroad is depicted as "a giant parasite fattening upon the lifeblood of an entire commonwealth."

Robert Utley. *The Last Days of the Sioux Nation* (1963)
> The best, most complete treatment we have of the Ghost-Dance uprising and the Wounded Knee massacre.

Chapter 20

Republicans and Democrats

What Made Gilded Age Politics Work?

1861 The United States goes off gold standard

1873 With the Coinage Act, or the "Crime of '73," Congress drops silver from the coinage system

1875 The "Whiskey Ring" scandal

1877 Rutherford B. Hayes is elected president in Compromise of 1877

1878 The Bland-Allison Act

1879 The United States returns to gold standard

1880s More than 80 percent of the electorate turns out to vote in presidential elections

1880 James A. Garfield elected president

1881–82 The "Star Route" scandals

1881 Garfield is assassinated; Chester A. Arthur becomes president

1883 The Pendleton Act establishes the Civil Service Commission

1884 Grover Cleveland elected president

1886 *Wabash, St. Louis and Pacific Railway Co. v. Illinois*

1887 The Interstate Commerce Act creates the Interstate Commerce Commission (ICC)

1888 Benjamin Harrison elected president

1890 The Sherman Silver Purchase Act • The Sherman Antitrust Act • The McKinley Tariff Act

1892 People's party (Populist) is formed • Grover Cleveland elected president for the second time

1893 Financial panic leads to depression

1894 The Wilson-Gorman Tariff Act

1896 William McKinley elected president, defeating William Jennings Bryan

1897 Almost half of federal employees are under Civil Service rules

The Gilded Age, so the story goes, was the era of triumphant Republicanism. The party that won the Civil War retained its tight hold on the nation's decision-making processes and succeeded time and again in electing its candidates to office against a divided and demoralized Democratic opposition. The reasons for Republican success were both ideological and practical, this view holds. The "Grand Old Party" (GOP) was the party of big business and relied on the support of the great postwar tycoons for the financial means to achieve electoral victory. In return it handed out favors lavishly in the form of tariffs, land grants, and other probusiness measures. In this version of the period, the Democrats, hampered by their record of opposition during the Civil War, remained a minority party whose appeal lay with those voters, both rural and urban, who opposed the strong-running currents of industrialism that seemed to be conquering the nation.

This interpretation emphasizes the economic basis for party politics. Men voted for one party or the other because it expressed their economic interests and they expected their party's program to benefit them in material ways. By implication the Republicans were consistent winners because more Americans found their program of encouraging industrial growth to their liking, whereas the Democrats, identified with traditional rural values, seemed backward-looking and unprogressive. This view also implies a class separation of the parties. The Republicans, it says, were the party of the prosperous; the Democrats, the party of the poor, the unsuccessful, and the dispossessed.

These generalizations collide head-on with the real facts of Gilded Age politics. One of the most striking characteristics of the political system between the end of Reconstruction and the 1890s was the failure of either party to dominate national politics. True, every president during these years except Grover Cleveland was a Republican, but almost all federal elections were close. In 1880 Republican James Garfield defeated his Democratic opponent, Winfield Scott Hancock, by only 7,000 popular votes. Four years later Cleveland, a Democrat, defeated James G. Blaine by under 25,000 votes out of 10 million cast. Only for three short periods during this era did the same party control the presidency and both houses of Congress. In only one congressional election between 1878 and 1888 inclusively did more than 2 percentage points separate the total Democratic and Republican votes.

On the local level the picture was more complex. In parts of northern New England and regions elsewhere settled by New Englanders, the Republicans were consistently in firm control. The South, except for a few Republican pockets mostly in the old Unionist regions, was solidly Democratic. In these areas one party almost totally dominated the local political scene.

On the whole, however, the close political contests of the Gilded Age not only refute the notion that there was a minority party and a majority party; they also call into question the view that the parties represented distinct and antagonistic economic interests. If one party—the Republicans—represented big business, and the other—the Democrats—the mass of the people who did not benefit from the legislation demanded by big business, how could the Republicans ever have won? How many businessmen—big or little—were there in the country? Surely not enough to guarantee Republican success even 50 percent of the time. As most voters were either small farmers or wage earners, something is also clearly wrong with the idea that the country was divided into rich Republicans and poor Democrats. But is this commonsense deduction confirmed by the facts? And if it is—if Gilded Age politics was not a contest between the rich and the poor—what did the parties stand for?

The Economic Issues

As we saw in Chapters 17 and 18, the Gilded Age was a time of headlong industrialization and urbanization. People were moving from country to city, from East to West, and from agriculture to industry and commerce. The lives of millions of men and women were being transformed both for good and for ill. Social inequality, slums, depressions, the difficulties of adjusting to urban life, and many other new issues arising out of the pell-mell economic transformation were being thrust to the surface of national life. Reflecting these crosscurrents, three important economic issues

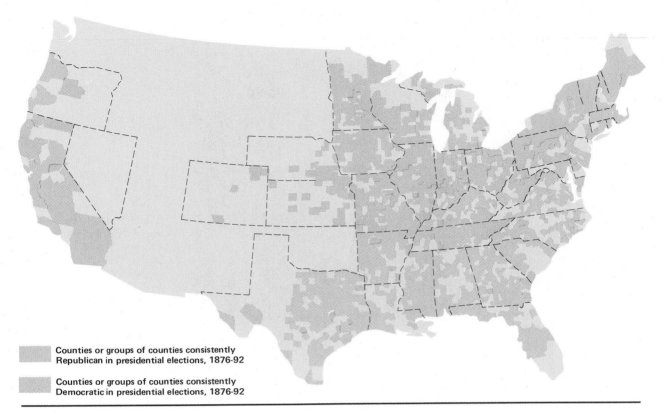

Counts or groups of counties consistently Republican in presidential elections, 1876-92

Counties or groups of counties consistently Democratic in presidential elections, 1876-92

Consistency of the vote, 1876–1892

entered political discourse: the tariff, money, and government regulation of private enterprise. None of these clearly divided the nation along party lines.

The Tariff. Traditionally, the Democrats were the party of free trade; the Republicans the party that endorsed protection of domestic industry. In the years immediately following the Civil War, however, the two parties seldom confronted one another directly on the tariff issue. Both were too divided internally. Western Republicans, more closely tied to agriculture than industry, were less enthusiastic about a high tariff than were eastern Republicans. Pennsylvania Democrats, who represented the state with the largest commitment to heavy industry, were almost invariably protectionists, unlike Democrats from, say, commercial New York or agricultural Mississippi.

During Reconstruction and for some years thereafter, tariff rates gradually rose to levels never reached before. But not until 1888 did the tariff become a contested issue in a presidential campaign. The 1888 election seems to confirm the traditional view of a big-business-oriented GOP and a mass-oriented Demo-

cratic party. Democratic President Grover Cleveland made "tariff reform"—that is, downward revision—the key plank in his reelection platform. The Republicans took a strong stand for the tariff and fought the campaign on the issue.

The Republican candidate, Benjamin Harrison of Indiana, was a former United States senator and the grandson of Old Tippecanoe, William Henry Harrison. A dignified figure with a gift for words, he was nonetheless colorless and lacking in warmth before crowds. One newspaper reporter called him "the man who never laughs." Provided by manufacturers with what then seemed unlimited funds, he waged a successful "front porch" campaign despite his austere personality. Delegations came to visit Harrison at his home in Indianapolis and listened to his prepared statements—usually homilies that played on religion, patriotism, and freedom—which were then disseminated to the country by the Republican party press. The strategy was hard on Harrison's front lawn, but the results demonstrated its political effectiveness. Harrison toppled the incumbent by winning an electoral college majority, although he fell behind Cleveland

The tariff failed as the central issue in the flagrantly corrupt election of 1888. Instead, such problems as the return of captured Confederate flags and Cleveland's veto of veterans' pension bills dominated debate. The Republican victory was narrow, especially in Indiana, where votes that had once cost only $5 sold for as much as $20.

by 100,000 popular votes. Apparently Republican protectionism had met Democratic free trade head-on and beaten it.

But if we look closely at the election of 1888, it becomes clear that it was neither a serious test of party commitment nor of public attitudes toward tariffs. Cleveland's running mate, Allen Thurman of Ohio, was a protectionist, and during the campaign Cleveland himself retreated from his antiprotectionist stand. "We have entered upon no crusade for free trade," he declared. The Democrats, if victorious, would arrange tariff schedules with the "utmost care for established interests and enterprise." The Republicans, too, wavered. In the industrial East they emphasized the high-tariff plank of their platform, but in the West they told the farmers that the GOP was the soul of moderation on the tariff.

Besides this waffling on issues, many other considerations affected the 1888 election. The age and feebleness of the Democratic vice presidential nominee, Allen Thurman, dismayed many voters. As usual, moreover, the Democrats of New York proved to be more interested in fighting one another than their common Republican foe. Finally, president Cleveland lost some usually Democratic Irish votes when the British minister to Washington, representing the traditional enemy of Irish patriots, foolishly allowed it to come out that he preferred Cleveland to Harrison. These factors make

it hard to demonstrate that Republican victory was a mandate for a high tariff—or for any other policy.

Never again during the Gilded Age did the tariff come as close as in 1888 to becoming a clear-cut election issue. The tariff reform bill initiated by Cleveland in 1888 ended as the McKinley Tariff of 1890, which set rates higher than ever before. In 1894, after Cleveland had returned to office, his administration attempted once more to lower rates. The Wilson-Gorman Tariff that resulted was the product of considerable lobbying in the Senate, where eastern Democrats imposed 634 amendments that effectively raised the duties. This bill was so gentle in its attack on protection that the disappointed president allowed it to become law without his signature.

Finance. National finance was another matter that might have separated the parties. But between 1865 and 1896 it seldom did. The issue was a complicated one. Some people, the advocates of "soft money," believed that the country's supply of money and credit was too restricted. A minority of the soft-money people favored reforming the banking system to make it more flexible and capable of expanding its issues and its credit. More of the soft-money group were Greenbackers, who believed the nation's economic problems were caused by a shortage of government-issued paper currency. There were still $400 million of the Civil War federal greenbacks in circulation, but this amount was fixed by law and was not enough for an expanding economy. With a static money supply and a growing volume of business transactions, the country, Greenbackers said, was experiencing a severe money shortage that deflated prices and raised interest rates. This deflation was harmful to farmers, industrial wage earners, and all debtors and borrowers.

On the other side were the advocates of "sound money" or "hard money," who deplored any attempt to inflate the currency. Their opponents, they said, were demagogues whose policies would shake the public's trust in the economic system and derange all commercial relations. The soft-money people were inflationists whose policies would push up the prices of all commodities and injure every citizen whose income was fixed. The hard-money people insisted that a fixed money and credit supply had to be maintained, and the best way to achieve this goal was to ensure that paper money—if needed at all—be made and kept redeemable for gold on demand at the banks and at the treasury. To the sound-money group the gold standard was the very foundation of the international economy, if not of modern civilization itself.

From the end of the Civil War to the end of the century, the hard-money and soft-money forces fought a series of battles. The first was over reducing the wartime issue of greenbacks and making them redeemable in gold. The soft-money forces prevented the former, but in 1879, under the prodding of hard-money groups, the country returned to the gold standard it had abandoned in 1861, thereby making all the federal greenbacks redeemable in gold on demand.

The second round of the long struggle, the battle over silver also ultimately went to the hard-money forces. Silver had been part of the nation's currency ever since Alexander Hamilton's day, when it was established along with gold as part of the coinage system. At that time it was legally exchangeable with gold at a ratio of fifteen ounces of silver to one of gold. In the 1830s the ratio was altered to sixteen to one. But this change was insufficient to match the relative value of the metals on the open market, where gold and silver were bought and sold like wheat, coal, or corn. Because the government's stated value of silver was lower than its price on the open market, it became profitable to melt down silver coins and sell them as metal. As a result, by 1860 the country was on an actual gold standard—that is, only gold circulated as coin, and only gold was actually used to back the country's paper money.

The discovery of huge silver deposits in the West after the Civil War lowered the price of silver relative to gold in world markets. By 1876 the official sixteen-to-one exchange rate now *overvalued* silver and made it the cheaper metal with which to pay debts. The soft-money men noted this development and also saw that silver's growing abundance offered the chance for the country to increase its money supply, stimulate the economy, lower interest rates, and raise all prices. Silver must, they declared, supersede gold as the world monetary standard.

Unfortunately, from the soft-money point of view, the potential benefits of abundant silver had been thrown away in 1873 when Congress had "demonetized" silver—dropped it from the coinage system. The soft-money advocates charged that this "Crime of '73" had been carried out by corrupt manipulators to frustrate debtors and "producers" while benefiting creditors and all those whose profits were advanced by high interest rates and price deflation. Especially implicated in the "crime," they held, were British bankers, who preferred this "expensive money" because it suited their creditor needs and advanced the interests of their own nation. These men, they said, had sent agents to Washington to bribe congressmen when the 1873 Coinage Act was being considered.

The money question, in its various forms, would disturb political life for a generation following the Civil War. But until 1896, when William Jennings Bryan made it the key Democratic plank in his first presidential race, it would not become a party issue. Greenbackers were to be found in both parties; so were "free silverites," who wanted silver "remonetized" at the old sixteen-to-one ratio. The same was true of gold-standard advocates: Some were Democrats, others Republicans. There was a slight bias toward the gold standard among Republicans and a bias toward the greenback–free-silver position among Democrats. But both parties had hard-money and soft-money wings.

Section rather than party or class was generally the distinguishing characteristic of the two groups. Western congressmen, either from the silver-mining area or from the debtor agricultural regions, tended to be soft-money men, as did representatives of the agricultural South, regardless of party. Democratic and Republican politicans from the commercial states and, by and large, the industrial regions of the northeast and the Midwest, concerned that greenbacks and free silver would push up the cost of living for wage earners and disturb business relations, favored the gold standard. The money question, then, *was* tied to economic interests, but it did not divide the nation along lines of rich and poor, Democrat and Republican.

The battle between the silverites and "gold-bugs" was politically joined at a number of points. In 1878 the silverites won a partial victory with the passage of the Bland-Allison Act, requiring the treasury to buy not less than $2 million nor more than $4 million of silver monthly and coin it into silver dollars at the old rate of sixteen ounces of silver to one of gold. The Bland-Allison Act was not a party issue: In the Senate 62 percent of the Republicans and 73 percent of the Democrats supported the bill. The volume of silver coin authorized by the Bland-Allison Act did expand the money supply by a small amount, but the inflationary effect was undetectable and the agitation for silver continued. In 1890, after the value of silver had fallen still further relative to gold, the silverites— now reinforced by a bipartisan group of senators from several newly admitted, far western mining states— succeeded in pushing another silver measure through Congress, the Sherman Silver Purchase Act. This law required that the treasury buy virtually the entire yearly domestic output of silver and turn it into silver certificates. But even this massive addition of silver to the currency did not topple the gold standard. With a gold reserve of $100 million, the treasury, under both Democratic and Republican secretaries, was able to redeem all currency—greenbacks, small coins, silver dollars, and the new silver certificates—in gold, thereby frustrating silverites' hopes. Not until after the Panic of 1893 did the accumulation of silver coin and silver certificates threaten to undermine the gold standard. At this point it was shored up and saved, with bipartisan support.

Government Regulation.

The third major economic issue of the Gilded Age was government regulation of private enterprise. This problem, too, did not divide the parties. Nor did it divide the American people. After the Supreme Court declared in the 1886 Wabash case that the state legislatures were incompetent to regulate interstate railroads, federal regulation seemed unavoidable and received wide support among farmers as well as among business interests who required cheap transportation to make profits. Even the railroads were not totally opposed to regulation. Far better to have some guidelines on rates and practices, the railroad leaders said, than the anarchy and cutthroat competition for freight and passengers that often prevailed in the transportation business.

Pushed by these allied forces and led by Senator Shelby Cullom of Illinois and Congressman John Reagan of Texas, Congress passed the Interstate Commerce Act in 1887. This measure established the first

federal regulatory body, the Interstate Commerce Commission (ICC). The ICC was given apparently ample powers. It could compel the railroads to desist from agreements to divide traffic to avoid competition, from discriminating among customers in setting rates, from charging more for short than for long hauls, and from granting the sorts of rebates and kickbacks that had helped make Rockefeller rich. The act also gave the ICC power to examine the books of railroad corporations and required the roads to file annual financial reports and adopt a uniform accounting system.

The law had some grave weaknesses, however. Time would show that all regulatory commissions tend toward co-option—taking on the principles and goals of the industries they were created to regulate. But the Interstate Commerce Act was particularly flawed. The ICC could not *set* rates, and its orders did not have the force of a court's. To compel a railroad to desist from some outlawed practice, the ICC had to institute proceedings before a federal judge. The federal courts turned out to be generally unfriendly to effective regulation. In the 1897 *Maximum Freight Rate* case the Supreme Court virtually annulled the Interstate Commerce Act.

What does the formation of the ICC tell us about Gilded Age politics? Although traditionally the Democrats favored a laissez-faire policy and the Republicans advocated strong government, the Interstate Commerce Act was a bipartisan law. Of the two original sponsors, Cullom was a Republican and Reagan a Democrat. The bill passed both houses of Congress by large margins, and yeas and nays cut across party lines.

The same bipartisanship applied to the other major federal law designed to place public reins on private business, the Sherman Antitrust Act of 1890. The Sherman Act was Congress's reaction to a wave of public anxiety over the dangers of monopoly. This fear went back to the earliest years of the republic, when Jeffersonians and Jacksonians had warned of concentrated economic power. After 1865 it inspired the western Greenbackers and farmers' groups to push for "Granger" legislation regulating railroad, grain elevator, and warehouse corporations.

In the Sherman Act of 1890 Congress responded to the public anxiety about trusts and monopolies by declaring illegal "every contract, combination in the form of trust or otherwise, or conspiracy, in restraint of trade or commerce among the several states, or with foreign nations." Anyone who made such an agreement was to be punished by a fine of up to $1,000 and a year in jail; anyone injured by such an agreement might sue for triple damages in the federal courts. The measure, like the Interstate Commerce Act, was scarcely one that separated the parties; The vote by which it was adopted in Congress fell one short of complete unanimity!

The conclusion is clear: The major economic issues of the Gilded Age were not party issues. This does not mean that economic matters played no role in Gilded Age party politics. That would be almost inconceivable. Both parties contained a variety of economic pressure groups—farmers, workers, bankers, merchants, industrialists—that fought for control. It was *within* the parties rather that *between* them that economic conflict took place, and until 1896 it proved impossible for any pressure group to dominate completely either the Democrats or the Republicans.

The American Love of Politics

Despite the absence of major differences between Democrats and Republicans on economic matters, American voters during the Gilded Age were passionate political participants. Voter turnouts during these years were enormous. Everywhere but the South, where thousands of black voters were effectively deprived of the right to vote after 1877 and where the Democratic nominee was the guaranteed victor, a far larger proportion of the eligible voters cast ballots than today. During the 1880s, for example, more than 80 percent of the voters went to the polls during presidential election years. In 1896 this figure soared to more than 95 percent in the five states of the Old Northwest—Ohio, Indiana, Illinois, Wisconsin, and Michigan. In local elections, too, the proportion of the eligible voters who voted was greater than today.

These citizens were not only enthusiastic participants; they were also dedicated partisans. "Independents" in those years were treated with contempt as people without spirit or commitment, and few voters were willing to accept the label. Obviously Americans considered it important whether one party or the other won. But given the party overlap on economic matters, the question is: Why?

Politics as Recreation. Entertainment was one force that helped drive the political machinery. Americans of this era enjoyed relatively little leisure time. Most worked on Saturdays, and even Sunday was not a day of rest for everyone. Besides the Fourth of July and Washington's Birthday, there were few legal holidays. Thanksgiving was not celebrated outside New England, while in New England, Christmas, considered a "papist" feast, was just another day in the calendar. A political rally gave working people one of the few occasions to take time off. Employers might not like it, but few dared say no when an American male citizen asserted his God-given right to hear a political speech.

Besides providing an excuse to avoid work, political campaigns were diverting. Gilded Age politics was a sport for both spectators and participants. In the absence of television, motion pictures, and professional athletics (except baseball, which had already become the national game), politics was a lively amusement. Contemporaries frequently acknowledged this fact. One reporter described a Republican political rally in Cambridge City, Indiana, in 1876 as "a spectacle no foreign fiesta could equal." Even though most peo-

Elections aroused extraordinary interest during the Gilded Age. This picture is of New York's Printing House Square on November 4, 1884. The thousands of spectators are awaiting the announcement of returns on the Cleveland-Blaine contest—despite the rain that may have helped Cleveland win.

ple could not hear the distant speaker, General Harrison, they were perfectly content, for it was "the holiday diversion, the crowds, the bravery of the procession, the music and the fun of the occasion they came chiefly to enjoy." As one late-nineteenth-century observer noted: "What theater is to the French, or the bull fight . . . to the Spanish, the hustings [election campaigns] and the ballot-box are to *our* people."

In part the excitement derived from the closeness of the contests, which, like a tight baseball pennant race, brought out the partisans of both sides in record numbers. When, after 1896, the Republicans forged far ahead of their Democratic rivals and the excitement declined, voter turnouts dropped off sharply.

Like all exciting and well-patronized spectator sports, Gilded Age politics had to have its stars, its heroes, its villains. Many of them were colorful characters. There was James G. Blaine, Republican senator from Maine, the "plumed knight," magnetic, charming, combative, brilliant, and corrupt. His sworn enemy, Roscoe Conkling, Republican senator from New York, was a strutting "turkey-gobbler," whose gorgeous plumage of yellow shoes, scarlet coat, waistcoat

One reason for enthusiastic political participation during the 1880s was the spectacle that politics provided. Here we see a gaslit parade staged for the St. Louis Democratic convention of 1888.

with gold lace, and green trousers entranced the voting public and amused his Senate colleagues. There was Thomas B. Reed, the 300-pound-speaker of the House. Ponderous in body but quick in mind, Reed was one of the wittiest men in America and tossed off aphorisms as funny as Mark Twain's: "A statesman is a dead politician"; "One with God is always a majority, but many a martyr has been burned at the stake while the votes were being counted." Men like these alternately delighted and dismayed the voting public and helped sustain the enthusiasm for the Gilded Age politics.

Politics as Morality Play. The metaphor of Gilded Age politics as a sport is useful up to a point. To some Americans—the "best men"—politics during these years seemed rather to be a profound moral drama. It was, these latter-day Puritans believed, a contest between good and evil. The evil was personified by the political rogues who had risen to the top after the Civil War and had perverted the once-virtuous Republic. The good was personified by men like themselves—disinterested, dedicated, scrupulous, and expert, who wished only the publiic good and who, if allowed to govern, would restore America to a state of grace.

Almost all the "best men" were young, though they included some survivors of antebellum reform battles. Many came from the country's most distinguished families: Charles Francis Adams, Jr., and his younger brother, Henry, were the grandsons of one president and great-grandsons of another. Several, however—such as the righteous Carl Schurz and the self-righteous E. L. Godkin—were self-made or foreign-born. Almost all were university educated; most were men of cultivation and refinement.

The "best men" disapproved of contemporary American political life. They believed that both parties were corrupt, and although they were generally nominal Republicans, they avoided partisan allegiance. Almost alone among the political active people of the era, they voted for candidates and platforms rather than parties and gloried in being "independent." Their tone was one of almost constant outrage—an attitude that often amused the general public. One subscriber to the independent *New York Evening Post* noted that she always felt safe with the paper on her doorstep: "It just lay there and growled all night."

However exaggerated or humorless the response of the "best men" to contemporary politics, their indignation had much to feed on. Scandal after scandal marred state and national politics in the Gilded Age.

In many states rings of dishonest businessmen united with corrupt politicians to control the legislatures. In New York the Erie Ring bought and sold legislators like cattle. In Pennsylvania it was said that when Thomas A. Scott, president of the Pennsylvania Railroad, finished his business with the state government, the legislature at Harrisburg adjourned. At the federal level the Whiskey Ring, an unholy alliance of federal officials and distillers, bilked the treasury of millions of dollars in revenue taxes. In 1881–82, the federal authorities uncovered a gang of Post Office personnel that awarded generous contracts to private parties to deliver mail to remote areas (the "Star Routes") in return for kickbacks.

Much of the corruption originated in the desire of businessmen to secure valuable favors that only government could confer. To this extent it is valid to interpret Gilded Age politics as an instrument that served the needs of an aggressive capitalist system. Sometimes, however, the politicians themselves initiated corrupt deals. An example of this were the "strike bills," making illegal some common business practice, that were constantly introduced in the state legislatures. The politicians never intended the bills to pass, but anxious businessmen were willing to pay good money to make certain they did not. After the sponsoring politicos had been properly paid off, the strike bills died quietly in committee.

Corruption spread even to elections. Every year, following some local or national political contest, the newspapers carried long accounts of bribery, stuffing of ballot boxes, illegal voting by aliens, and the use of "floaters," who, to tip a close election, crossed state lines to vote illegally. Most of the electoral chicanery took place in the cities and involved local offices. But there were also numerous instances of corruption in national elections, and not all occurred in large urban centers where the foreign-born could be blamed. In fact, one of the most flagrant instances of chronic electoral dishonesty in this era took place in Adams County, Ohio, a rural community composed mostly of old-stock Americans. There, beginning in the 1870s, virtually the entire voting population sold their votes to the highest bidder. Given the near parity of parties, it is likely that more than one presidential election was won by voting fraud.

The greatest failing of all, however, as seen by the independents, was the spoils system, which had first emerged during the Jackson era but had come to full flower during the Gilded Age. It grew out of a problem that Americans have never fully solved: How to pay for party government? Should the party system

be supported by ordinary citizens through small contributions and through voluntary labor? Must it be financed by the rich or by special-interest groups seeking to influence legislation? Or, as many Americans have recently come to believe, should it be supported by public funds?

Under the spoils system of the Gilded Age, parties were in effect financed by the government, though scarcely in the form advocated by reformers today. Government support in these years took the form of patronage, and vast amounts of patronage were available. Government was a major growth industry. Between 1865 and 1891 the federal payroll expanded from 53,000 to 166,000. Even the lowest-paid federal employees earned from two to three times the annual income of privately employed unskilled workers, and they normally spent only eight hours a day at their jobs, in contrast with the ten- to twelve-hour workdays common in private industry.

Men and women, not surprisingly, eagerly sought federal employment. Would-be officeholders worked hard for political candidates and expected patronage appointments in return. Once on the job, appointees were willing to contribute further effort and a portion of their salaries ("assessments") to keep their party in office lest the opposition deprive them of their positions.

The system was wasteful and often inefficient. Although government was becoming ever more complex and technical, the spoils system made flattery, party loyalty, and political knowhow the sole measures of merit. Moreover, when competent people did gain office, they seldom kept their jobs long enough to learn their duties and perfect their skills. At the beginning of each administration the civil service, and consequently the whole federal government, was immobilized while the president sorted out the patronage claims of party supporters all over the country. The spoils system also encouraged outright corruption. Men and women frequently paid cash for their jobs, and advertisements like the following were not uncommon in Washington newspapers during the 1880s:

WANTED—A GOVERNMENT CLERKSHIP at a salary of not less than $1,000 per annum. Will give $100 to anyone securing such a position.

WANTED—BY TWO YOUNG LADIES situations in Government office; will give first month's pay and $10 monthly as long as retained.

The independents condemned the spoils system and demanded civil service reform that would substitute merit (determined by examination) for party loy-

A Historical Portrait

James G. Blaine

James G. Blaine traveled two paths, wrote one of his biographers, "one in the daylight that was straight, one in the dark that was twisted as a ram's horn." An idol to millions in his day, Blaine epitomized to many others all that was venal and corrupt in American political life in the Gilded Age.

Blaine was born in Pennsylvania in 1830 of Irish stock. On his father's side he was descended from a line of Scotch-Irish Presbyterians who came to America from Ulster in the 1740s. His mother's family was Irish Catholic from County Donegal. James himself was raised as a Protestant, though his mother never forsook her Catholic faith. His mixed religious background would affect his career in an age when religion was an important determinant of political preference.

Almost from the outset the young Pennsylvanian exhibited the democratic politician's essential qualities: geniality, eloquence, humor, and an excellent memory for names and faces. At Washington College, which he entered at the startling age of thirteen, both his fellow students and his instructors thought him charming. People were drawn to him in a way that gave meaning to the popular adjective of the day: "magnetic."

After graduation, Blaine became an instructor of mathematics and classical languages at a military academy at Georgetown, Kentucky, where many of his students were as old as he was. It was there that he met Harriet Stanwood, a teacher at the local "female seminary," and married her in 1850. Harriet was a New Englander with family roots in Maine. The connection would prove as important as the marriage was happy.

In 1854, after a short stay in Philadelphia, Blaine was offered an opportunity by Harriet's brothers to edit the *Kennebec Journal*, and he left his native state to spend the rest of his career in Maine. Most ambitious young men went west to seek opportunity; Blaine reversed the direction.

Blaine's editorship of the *Journal* inevitably thrust him into politics because all newspapers were then closely affiliated with one of the two parties. He had arrived in Maine at the time when the Whigs, his original party, were breaking up. Blaine and the *Journal* soon became ardent Republicans, defending the new party's positions on slavery, the tariff, and the territorial issue. In 1859 he became chairman of the Maine Republican State Committee, a post he retained for over twenty years.

Maine was a small state at a far corner of the continent. But it had advantages for Republican politicians with national ambitions. It was a "rock-ribbed" Republican state and could be counted on to reelect its Repulican officeholders over and over again. In Congress this practice guaranteed seniority and national prominence.

In 1862, after three terms in the Maine legislature, Blaine was elected to the United States House of Representatives. He arrived in Washington the following year to take part in the exciting events of the Civil War and Reconstruction eras. Blaine was a Radical Republican who distrusted the "rebels" even after they had laid down their arms. He was not an extremist, however, and frequently clashed with Thaddeus Stevens, leader of the most militantly antisouthern Radical faction. Though

Blaine was willing to take strong positions, he kept the respect of his colleagues and in 1869 they elected him Speaker of the House, one of the most powerful positions in the federal government.

Blaine presided over the House with a degree of good nature and fairness that won the respect of even the Democrats. But he did make one enemy: the arrogant, supercilious, opinionated Republican congressman from Utica, New York, Roscoe Conkling. In 1866 Blaine and Conkling got into an argument over a bill to create a permanent provost marshal's office in the army. Conkling was sarcastic about Blaine's views on the issue under discussion. Blaine responded in kind, describing Conkling's "haughty disdain, his grandiloquent swell, his majestic, supereminent, turkey-gobbler strut," and concluding that the New Yorker, compared to the truly eloquent Henry Winter Davis to whom he had been likened, was as "mud to marble, dunghill to diamond, a singed cat to a Bengal tiger, a whining puppy to a roaring lion." Conkling never forgave Blaine, and the two men's enmity would affect the course of Gilded Age politics.

During Grant's administration (1869–1877) Blaine became leader of the Republican "Half-Breeds," along with James Garfield and John Sherman of Ohio, and George F. Hoar of Massachusetts. Slightly younger than the "Stalwarts," led by Conkling, John A. Logan of Illinois, Zachariah Chandler of Michigan, and Simon Cameron of Pennsylvania, the Half-Breeds were also less committed to defending traditional Republican obligations to the freedmen and to invoking the Civil War as the basis of party politics in the post-1865 period. But Half-Breed–Stalwart differences over policy were less important than their battles over patronage and appropriations.

It was during the 1876 presidential campaign that Blaine's reputation for financial honesty suffered its first serious blow. Grant's second term was over and he did not as yet harbor third-term ambitions. The field was wide open for another Republican and many believed Blaine the logical choice. But fate intervened when, in April 1876, a director of the Union Pacific Railroad reported that Blaine had received a permanent loan of $64,000 from the UP against the worthless collateral of some Little Rock and Fort Smith Railroad bonds. In effect, the Union Pacific had given Blaine a large gift of money.

The House committee appointed to investigate the charges soon received information that one James Mulligan had letters by Blaine that implied that the Maine congressman had accepted securities in return for favors to the railroad. When Mulligan came to Washington to testify, Blaine intercepted him at his hotel and walked off with the letters Mulligan had intended to give the committee. The following day Blaine himself wove the letters selectively into a brilliant speech on the House floor that obscured the most incriminating portions. The performance dazzled the public, and convinced his partisans that their hero had thoroughly vindicated himself.

But Blaine never fully cleared his name, and at the Republican convention in Cincinnati he saw the presidential nomination go to the governor of Ohio, the colorless but honest Rutherford B. Hayes. It was at Cincinnati that Robert Ingersoll, in the course of his nominating speech, used the phrase "the plumed knight" to describe Blaine. It became his nickname, often used with irony by his detractors.

In 1877 the Maine legislature sent Blaine to the United States Senate. Here he spent most of his time locked in battle with Conkling and positioning himself for 1880. As the struggle for the nomination began, it seemed like a contest between Grant, with his Stalwart supporters, and the Half-Breeds led by Blaine. In the end the Grant and Blaine forces deadlocked and the nomination—and the election—went to Garfield, a friend of Blaine's.

Blaine had not found the Senate as congenial as the House and he welcomed his appointment by Garfield as secretary of state. In the State Department Blaine was a diplomatic activist who believed that American influence in the Western Hemisphere and elsewhere must be expanded. His aggressive support of American interests abroad earned him the label "Jingo Jim." He also acted as Garfield's chief domestic adviser and used his influence to remove his Stalwart enemies from influential office. In New York this led to wholesale dismissals of Conkling's supporters. Whatever satisfaction Blaine felt at Conkling's discomfiture was short-lived. On July 2, 1881, an embittered Stalwart shot the president, who died two months later, leaving Chester A. Arthur, a New York Stalwart, as his successor. Blaine remained in office for a few months more but then resigned to return to private life and write his political memoirs.

As 1884 approached, the "Blaine legion" of loyal supporters once again prepared to make their idol president. This time they got further than ever before. Blaine won the party nomination at Chicago on the first ballot and, for the sake of party peace, chose Stalwart John Logan as his running mate. His opponent in the contest was Governor Grover Cleveland of New York.

To an unusual extent the race turned on Blaine's honesty. By now a substantial portion of the country's educated class, voters often nominally Republican, were "Mugwumps," who felt that the Republican party had lost its moral bearings and existed only for the sake of patronage and plunder. Cleveland was considered a reformer because as governor he had opposed the New York Democratic machine and conducted an honest state administration. The Mugwumps—led by Carl Schurz, former secretary of the interior; George William Curtis of *Harper's Weekly*; E. L. Godkin of the *Nation*; and others—attacked Blaine as corrupt and a spoilsman. No party, declared Schurz, had any right to expect victory at the polls "without respecting that vital condition of our greatness and glory, which is honest government."

At one point it looked as if the anti-Blaine forces would lose their moral advantage. In July a Buffalo newspaper published an article telling of Cleveland's illegitimate child. This revelation created utter dismay in the reformers' ranks until they rationalized it away as an isolated transgression and one that, in any event, lay in the private rather than the public sphere.

In September the Mugwumps found further ammunition to use against Blaine—a complete, uncensored transcript of the Mulligan Letters, including items not available in 1876. One was a letter from Warren Fisher, Jr., a promoter of the Little Rock and Fort Smith, dictated to Fisher by Blaine, absolving the then Speaker of all blame in the Union Pacific loan incident. Blaine's own letter requesting Fisher to help him had ended with the incriminating phrase "burn this letter." When the Fisher letter and the others were published in the anti-Blaine papers, they confirmed the worst suspicions, about Blaine's corrupt relations with the railroads.

In the end Blaine lost the election to Cleveland because the hotly contested state of New York went to the

A Historical Portrait   (*continued*)

Democrats. Many observers had expected Blaine to carry New York's Irish voters and with them the state. His Catholic lineage, his anti-British attitudes, and his personal warmth and charm were all supposed to be particularly appealing to Irish-Americans. Unfortunately he failed to reprove the disparaging "Rum, Romanism, and rebellion" charge made against the Democrats by the Reverend Samuel Burchard and consequently lost Irish votes. He had also offended many working men by appearing at "Balshazzar's Feast" in New York, a banquet given in his honor by some of the nation's best-hated "money kings." The two mistakes clearly lost him more than the 1,200 votes that gave the Empire State and the election to the Democrats.

Blaine was not finished with public life. Though his health was poor, he accepted the secretaryship of state once again when it was offered him by Benjamin Harrison in 1889. His second stint as secretary represents America's resumption of a vigorous foreign policy, now more in tune with the public mood. Blaine was especially interested in displacing Great Britain from economic leadership in Latin America, and to this end sought to create an informal "Pan-American" union with the United States as "elder sister."

Though his three years in the State Department under Harrison stand out from the low plain of nineteenth-century American diplomacy, the period was not personally fulfilling. The Blaines resided during the winters in a house close to the State Department, formerly owned by William Seward. They escaped the Washington summer heat at their home in Bar Harbor on the Maine coast. The Blaine's marriage remained happy, but tragedy struck when their eldest son, Walker, died of pneumonia at only thirty-five. Soon after, their eldest daughter, Alice, also died, and in a little over a year their second son, Emmons, was dead as well. Nor did Blaine find much satisfaction in his relations with his chief. Harrison was a distant and aloof man whose personality clashed with that of the outgoing, genial Blaine. In June 1892 Blaine resigned his post in a brief, cool letter. Harrison's acceptance was equally brief and formal. Neither man expressed any personal esteem for the other.

Blaine's health had been fast declining and he did not have many months left. The Blaines went to Bar Harbor for the summer of 1892 and then, in the fall, returned to the Seward House in Washington. Suffering from gout and Bright's disease, Blaine took to his bed. Bulletins about his health appeared in the newspapers and the faithful Blaine legion, who had worshiped the man for thirty years, gathered before his house to express their loyalty. He died on January 27, 1893, three days short of his sixty-third birthday. His life had indeed followed two paths, "one in the daylight" and "one in the dark."

---

alty, and tenure in office for constant rotation. But the spoils system was so deeply rooted in American politics that it was difficult to remove, although federal officials sometimes adopted merit schemes for their own departments or divisions. In 1871 President Grant established a commission to study a merit system and recommend a practical program of civil service reform. These moves accomplished nothing. Then, in 1883, after the assassination of President James Garfield by Charles Guiteau, a disappointed office seeker, Congress passed the first federal civil service law, the Pendleton Act. It forbade the assessment of federal employees, made appointments contingent on competitive examinations, and regularized promotions and linked them to demonstrated competence. Presidents Arthur and Cleveland placed some 20,000 federal jobs on the "classified list" of those covered by the new rules. By 1897, when William McKinley became president, 86,000 employees—almost half the federal civil service—were recruited by examination, promoted by merit, and protected by tenure.

The number of men and women who saw national politics as a battle between the forces of light and the forces of darkness never amounted to more than a small minority. But they were a very influential group. Through the pages of Edwin L. Godkin's *Nation* and other journals of criticism and opinion, their views entered the homes of the educated middle class. The independents became a sort of conscience for the nation, and few well-read Americans could entirely resist the feeling that what they supported was virtuous and what they opposed evil.

Both parties long resisted civil service reform, but after Garfield's assassination they could not ignore the clamor for change. The Pendleton Act, by establishing the merit system, made it difficult for politicians to favor members of their families, a practice lampooned in this 1890s cartoon.

The Bases for Party Affiliation

Viewing Gilded Age politics as an exciting game or as a moral drama tells us something about how and why the political system worked: Americans of this era may not have had much faith in the party system as a way to achieve their economic or material ends, but they did enjoy it as a spectacle. This interpretation does not tell us, however, what distinguished the average Democrat from the average Republican.

The Civil War Legacy.   The Civil War, its antecedents, its Reconstruction aftermath, and the long memories of these events helped forge links of loyalty to the parties. For at least a generation following Appomattox, sectional feelings remained an influential component of party loyalty. Republicans may have abandoned the black population of the South to the conservative white "redeemers," but they felt guilty about it and were quick to react when southern mistreatment of blacks became too blatant. As late as 1890 a Republican House of Representatives passed a "force bill" designed to reestablish federal supervision of national electors to guarantee that blacks were not totally disfranchised by the southern states. Southerners, too, remembered the past; when President Cleveland was bitterly attacked for returning captured Confederate

battle flags to southern state governments, they rushed to his defense.

Lingering sectional resentments, in both North and South, reinforced party distinctions. In the white South memories of "Black Republican" emancipation and Radical Reconstruction created a remarkable and long-lasting Democratic solidarity. Any white man who voted for a Republican became a traitor in the eyes of most white southerners. Thousands of transplanted white southerners in the old Midwest also voted Democratic. By contrast, black voters, though not numerous in either section, remembered their champions Abraham Lincoln and Thaddeus Stevens and were among the most loyal Republicans in the entire nation.

The North was not as "solid" as Dixie, but it was difficult for ex-Union soldiers to support the Democrats. Union veterans were bombarded by Republican "bloody shirt" speeches telling them, and erstwhile pro-Union citizens, that a vote for the Democrats was a vote for the South and the Confederacy. And Republicans used more substantial methods as well to hold Union veterans in their party. Prodded by the Union veterans' organization, the Grand Army of the Republic (GAR), successive Republican adminstrations appropriated millions of dollars in pensions for former Union soldiers and their dependents. By 1899 the total paid annually amounted to almost $157 million.

Religion, Race, and Nationality. With each passing year the political hold of the Civil War became fainter. Yet party loyalty remained intense, and only the most extraordinary scandal or the most lackluster candidate could drive the average voter away from his traditional party allegiance. What tied the voters to their parties so firmly?

Many historians now believe that ethnic and religious factors forged the tightest bonds of Gilded Age party loyalty. During these years the United States was an exceptionally diverse nation. By the 1880s the German, Irish, and Scandinavian immigrants of the 1830–1870 period had put down roots and had emerged as an important political force. In addition, there were now many second-generation, American-born children who combined an understanding of the American political system with a continuing loyalty to their ethnic and religious traditions. It is no surprise, then, that in the generation following the Civil War, cultural loyalties and tensions played a special role in political life.

Religion apparently shaped party loyalties more than nationality or ethnic background. Whatever their national origins, members of the "liturgical" churches, which emphasized "right belief" over personal regeneration, were generally Democrats. The most numerous of the liturgical church groups were the Catholics who since the days of Jefferson had found a political refuge in the more "popular" of the two parties. Led by religiously tolerant and pragmatic men, the Jeffersonians and then the Democrats had welcomed the Catholic French, Germans, and Irish who crossed the Atlantic before the Civil War, and had catered to their needs. These needs, in part, had been material and practical, and, as we have seen, the predominantly Democratic machines in the cities helped the immigrants with jobs, handouts, and legal aid.

Both parties played this game, but concessions to cultural differences were more difficult for the Republicans, and their Whig predecessors, to make. Catholics wanted more of America than material advantages. They also wanted freedom to pursue their religion, which meant not only formal freedom to worship but also a share of local taxes for Catholic parochial schools and the right of Catholic chaplains to serve in state hospitals and penal institutions. And they wanted the freedom to pursue their customs, which meant being able to consume wine, beer, and

This Republican cartoon, depicting Cleveland surrounded by Democratic leaders, enthusiastically waves the bloody shirt, reminding northerners of the supposed traitorious past of the Democratic party.

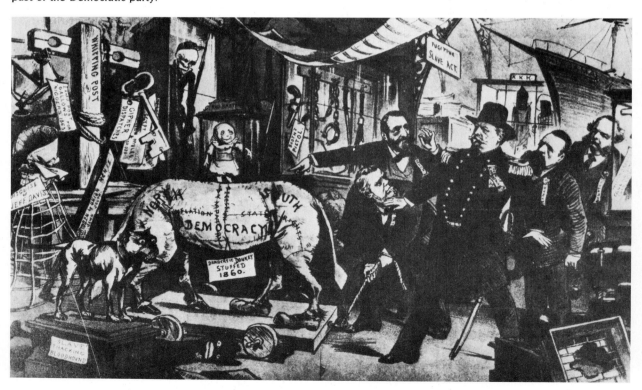

State aid to private Catholic schools won support from Tammany Hall, and Republicans charged the "Romish Church" was using the Democratic party to overthrow the American school system. Here Thomas Nast portrays crocodiles with Catholic bishops' miters attacking wholesome innocents, presumably Protestants, while Tammany bosses look on approvingly.

whiskey without excessive restriction and to enjoy a "Continental" Sunday without being harassed by the "blue laws" that shut down businesses, forbade work, and banned recreation in many American cities and towns on the Sabbath. Members of other churches that emphasized ritual and well-defined dogma shared these preferences with Catholics; thus Lutherans, Jews, Episcopalians, and Catholics were frequently allied. But the Catholics were the largest single bloc of liturgical voters in the country.

Republicans, like their Whig forebears, generally resisted the cultural and religious pressures of those from the liturgical faiths. The difficulty was not primarily bigotry or ill will but a latter-day puritanism that was an essential ingredient in the makeup of rank-and-file Republican voters. Both Whigs and Republicans, each party in its own day, represented evangelical America. Whig-Repulican voters were drawn heavily from members of churches that emphasized inner regeneration, personal reformation, and "right behavior." They were mostly native-born Baptists, Methodists, Presbyterians, and Congregationalists; but many were foreign-born Pietists who, like their native-born counterparts, tended to consider politics a vehicle for displaying and imposing their morality.

In the 1850s evangelicals had helped found the Republican party dedicated to the containment and ultimate extinction of sinful slavery. Through the remainder of the century Republican zeal for public and private virtue was expressed in demands for blue laws and restrictions on the manufacture and sale of liquor and on "blood" sports such as cockfighting and boxing. Republicans also insisted on strict separation of church and state, since the alternative, they felt, was to allow Catholic influence on public institutions.

Catholics, as well as many Episcopalians and Lutherans, resented these efforts to restrict their personal freedoms and limit their influence. Unlike evangelicals, they believed that what citizens did in their personal lives was no business of the state. They also believed that far too many state-supported institutions, though supposedly nonsectarian, were actually dominated by pietistic Protestants. The Democrats naturally took advantage of these resentments. In 1881 the Ohio state Democratic platform declared that the Democrats favored "the largest individual liberty consistent with public order, and . . . opposed legislation merely sumptuary." John ("Bathouse") Coughlin, a Chicago Democrat, warned the voters: "A Republican is a man who wants you t' go 't church every Sunday. A Democrat says if a man wants t' have a glass of beer on Sunday he can have it. Be Democrats unless you want t' be tied t' a church, a schoolhouse, or a Sunday school."

If political puritanism had stopped at the blue laws and equally mild expressions, it might not have polarized the voters. But it did not. In the 1880s the antiforeign, anti-Catholic American Protective Association (APA) demanded the exclusion of noncitizens from American political life, attacked "the diabolical works of the Roman Catholic Church," and pledged to fight for the "cause of Protestantism." During the

1890s the APA shouldered its way into several local campaigns as an unacknowledged, but not unrecognized, ally of the Republicans and a champion of "true Americanism" against "aliens" and "papists." However impatient liturgical voters might become at times with their traditional party allegiances, or however tempted to vote for a particularly attractive Republican candidate, this virulent anti-Catholic and antiforeign sentiment confirmed their view "that personal liberty . . . [was] surely only safe with the Democratic party in power."

Church affiliation and nationality determined not only the voters' party preferences but also those of officeholders. In the 1893 lower house of the Wisconsin legislature, for example, all eight German Catholics were Democrats, as were twelve of the fifteen Irish Catholics and ten of the thirteen German Lutherans. On the other hand, the Republicans were predominantly Scandinavian, British (English, Scottish, and Scotch-Irish), and Yankee Protestants. These ethnic differences between the two parties produced divergent voting patterns in the legislature. Wisconsin Democrats and Republicans agreed on most economic issues, but they fought over social questions. These disagreements were at times so sharp that the atypical Democratic legislator—say, a British Protestant—or the atypical Republican legislator—say, an Irish Catholic—might desert his party on a roll call concerning regulation of liquor or some similar issue to vote with British Protestant or Irish Catholic colleagues of the opposite party.

Although religion was a major determinant of political affiliation, its role in politics was not usually overt. Politicians recognized that religious conflict violated American ideals of tolerance and that bigotry was politically explosive. Yet local campaign for legislators, governors, and municipal officials were often thinly disguised confrontations of the opposing liturgical and evangelical points of view. The 1875 gubernatorial campaign in Ohio, for example, was fought ostensibly over the question of greenbacks and inflation. Actually, an important hidden issue was whether Catholic chaplains would be allowed to minister to Catholic convicts in the state prisons.

At other times the religious issue was undisguised. In Wisconsin in the 1890s German Lutherans criticized the Bennett Law, which required all children to attend schools where instruction was in English, seeing it as an attack on their German-language parochial schools. Catholics, with parochial schools of their own, joined the German Protestants in protesting the Republican-sponsored measure. For a while the Bennett Law controversy threatened to disrupt Wisconsin political life. Not until the Democrats repealed the bill was the issue laid to rest.

Religious differences were expressed more often in local political affairs than in national politics, largely because the federal government at the time had little to do with social issues such as liquor regulation, education, blue laws, and the other matters that impinged directly on the daily lives of citizens. Yet the national parties were as much defined by cultural-religious issues as the local parties. This effect can be explained by the structure of the party system during the Gilded Age. Far more than today, the major parties were built from the bottom up. Only in presidential election years did the national party machinery become more important than the state, city, and county organizations—and then, generally, only for the brief span of the presidential campaign. Between national elections *Democrat* and *Republican* were little more than labels for collections of state and local organizations. Almost always, the person who voted for a Republican for mayor, state legislator, or governor would also vote for a Republican for Congress and for president. The result was that the national parties were polarized along the same ethnic-religious axis as the local ones, regardless of presidential campaign issues.

The Election of 1884. Yet even national party politics were not entirely free from direct ethnic or religious confrontation, and at times religion became a significant issue in a national campaign. The most important of these occasions was the 1884 presidential contest between Grover Cleveland and James G. Blaine.

If any visible issue separated Cleveland and Blaine, it was honesty. In 1876 Blaine, the Republican nominee, had damaged his reputation badly by apparently using his power and influence as Speaker of the House of Representatives to procure a land grant for the Little Rock and Fort Smith Railroad. In a dramatic appearance before the House, Blaine had denied the charges against him and had seemed to show that certain incriminating letters from him to the railroad directors in fact proved his innocence. Reading selections from these so-called Mulligan Letters, Blaine created the impression that he had done nothing wrong, and he avoided disgrace. But the charges would not die. Blaine entered the 1884 presidential race with the smell of corruption clinging to him. Then Democratic headquarters in New York received a packet of new letters showing that Blaine's defense in 1876 had been a clever fraud. In mid-September, at the height of the campaign, these letters were published, setting off a major furor.

By contrast, Cleveland seemed above moral reproach, at least in his public life. As mayor of Buffalo and governor of New York, he had endeared himself to the advocates of clean government by taking a stand against the machine politicians and for honest, economical government. In 1884 this record won him the support of the "best men," who deserted the Republicans and worked for Cleveland's election. The Republicans called the turncoats Mugwumps—a derisive term supposedly of Indian origin.

Late in the campaign the Republicans discovered that as a young man Cleveland had fathered an illegitimate child. They were quick to publicize this personal transgression. During the last days of the campaign marching Republicans in New York chanted enthusiastically: "Ma! Ma! Where's my Pa? Gone to the White House, Ha! Ha! Ha!" The damaging effect of the revelation was blunted, however, by Cleveland's candid admission of his slip and by the fact that he had willingly provided financial support for the child.

Despite his clean political record and the support of the Mugwumps, Cleveland fell behind Blaine as the campaign neared its end. New York was the crucial state, and it seemed to be leaning to Blaine. In this situation the Irish vote could determine the winner. Blaine was a Republican, and the Irish did not normally vote Republican. But he was a Republican with a difference: Although a Protestant himself, his mother was a Catholic and his cousin the head of a convent. Moreover, as secretary of state during James Garfield's brief administration, Blaine had badgered and baited the British, had "twisted the lion's tail," a time-honored practice among politicans interested in cultivating the Irish vote. Combined with his personal charm, his kindness, and his verbal brilliance, these acts made him an attractive candidate even to those who seldom voted Republican.

Then, in the last days of the campaign, one of Blaine's supporters undermined his advantage with a foolish remark that deeply offended Catholic voters. The occasion was a meeting between the candidate and Protestant ministers in a hotel lobby in New York. The Reverend Samuel Burchard, in a short address greeting the candidate, remarked: "We are Republicans and don't propose to leave our party and identify with the party whose antecedents have been rum, Romanism, and rebellion." The statement, if we discount its obvious hostility, was an accurate description of the Democratic party, most of whose members were op-

The 1884 presidential campaign was particularly scandal-ridden. The Republicans thought they had a winning issue when they discovered that Democrat Grover Cleveland had fathered an illegitimate child. In the end Cleveland had less cause for dismay than this Republican cartoon suggests.

posed to strict liquor regulation, were Catholic, or were southerners. But it violated one of the basic commandments of American political life: Do not insult a man's religion. Blaine, tired and inattentive at this late stage in the campaign, failed to rebuke Burchard, and the remark went out over the wire services.

In a matter of hours gleeful Democrats were distributing Burchard's statement in handbills and posters, and it was plastered over all the newspapers. On Sunday, November 4, Catholic clergymen denounced the slur from their pulpits. On election day, the following Tuesday, Blaine lost New York state by 1,200 votes, and with it the election. The chagrined Republican later told some friends: "I should have carried New York by 10,000 if the weather had been clear on election day, and Dr. Burchard had been doing missionary work in Asia Minor or Cochin China."

Actually, it is not clear precisely what caused Blaine's defeat. Many things could have accounted for Cleveland's hairbreadth victory in New York. But whatever its practical significance, the Burchard slur suggests the power of religious and cultural biases, even at the national level, in Gilded Age politics.

Party Realignments

For fifty years cultural values and memories of the Civil War had forged bonds between the voters and the two major parties that were extraordinarily strong. But not every American believed that the Democrats and the Republicans exhausted the range of political possibility. By the 1890s, in fact, there were those who would be singing the words of a new political song: "Good-Bye, My Party, Good-Bye." The discontented westerners and southern farmers discussed in Chapter 19 would break away from the major parties, and in the process inadvertently create a new political era, one dominated by the Republicans.

The Populist Party. In 1892 leaders of the Farmers' Alliances and assorted political dissidents launched the People's Party of the U.S.A., or Populists, at a convention held at Omaha, Nebraska. The Populist leaders were agrarians representing a coalition of sections; the preamble to the new party's platform delivered

Women were particularly active in Populist politics. Mary Elizabeth Lease, a Kansas lawyer, was among the most effective Populist speakers. She caught the nation's attention when she told Midwest farm audiences to "raise less corn and more hell."

an agrarian message. The nation was on the verge of ruin as a result of wealth concentration and the power of bondholders, usurers, and millionaires, it said. "A vast conspiracy against mankind" had been "organized on two continents" and was "rapidly taking possession of the world." As a result of this conspiracy, the nation's money supply was totally inadequate for its business, and the consequences were "falling prices, the formation of combines nd rings, and the impoverishment of the producing class." The two traditional parties had let the people down. Now, in the impending political campaign, they proposed "to drown out the outcries of a plundered people with the uproar of a sham battle over the tariff, so that capitalists, corporations, national banks, rings, trusts, watered stock, the demonetization of silver, and the oppression of the usurers may be lost sight of."

The Populist platform itself called for "free and unlimited coinage of silver" at a sixteen-to-one ratio with gold, a money supply of at least $50 per capita, a graduated income tax, and a postal savings bank for small savers. To limit the power of the transportation and communications corporations, the Populists demanded government ownership of the railroads and of the telephone and telegraph systems. The party's land plank demanded that aliens and the railroads be compelled to give up excess land. A section tacked on as an afterthought called for the secret ballot, restrictions on immigration, and an eight-hour workday for government workers. Populists wanted the tools of direct democracy placed in the people's hands. Citizens should have the power to instigate laws directly by the initiative petition and the right to pass proposed legislation by actual referendum, without the need for Congress and the legislatures to act. And the voters should elect the president and United States senators directly; their choice should not be made by the electoral college or the state legislatures.

The Populist platform of 1892 was in many ways a forward-looking document. Several provisions foreshadowed the programs of the early-twentieth-century progressives and even the New Deal and the modern welfare state. Its overall thrust was the desire to make government more responsive to the popular will, limit the power of large corporations, and reduce some of the worst disparities of wealth. At the same time, it did not directly challenge the existing regime of private property. It is not surprising that several leading socialists of the day dismissed the Populists as a "bourgeois party" composed of petty agrarian capitalists.

As the delegates at Omaha adjourned, they faced the difficult task of convincing the voters to drop their

What's Wrong with the Major Parties

By the 1880s discontent with the major parties was growing among several groups in the nation. In the West and South the dissent was led by the Farmers' Alliances. Eventually the mood of dissatisfaction with the Democrats and Republicans exploded as the Populist Revolt of 1892–1896. The document below is by a leader of the Northern Farmers' Alliance and expresses the disenchantment of many agrarians with the two major parties. It is clear that the chief complaint of the writer is with the parties' financial principles.

"The Republican party was born of the spirit of opposition to chattel slavery. It was this principle that gave it life, vitality and power. While this contest was waging it was grand in its conception of right and justice. It taught the inconsistency of slavery growing on the tree of liberty, that the two could not be blended in one harmonious setting; that the cries of the mother who was compelled to part with her child did not harmonize with the songs of heaven; that the groans of the woman compelled to become a mother without being a wife, were not consistent with the teachings of Christianity; that this was intended by the fathers of American liberty to become, and indeed in truth, a free land; that it was a Union of States having a common interest, that it was a land of free churches, free schools and free men. When the contest for these principles was over, and chattel slavery went down amid the boom of artillery, the rattle of musketry and groans of the dying, the Republican party emerged from the conflict with a prestige and glory that commanded the admiration of the world. Flushed with victory, they said in the pride of their heart—like the king of Babylon—see, we have done all this.

"Then the work of despoiling began. . . . The glory of the Republican party has departed. Their bright sun has set in the hopeless misery which their financial policy has entailed upon an enterprising people. Their record on contraction of the currency, national banks, back salary steals, credit strengthening act, funding schemes and demonetization tendencies should have consigned them to political oblivion long ago, and would, but there was no power that promised any better, and the people were in the hands of corporations and combinations. . . .

". . . Since the war [the Democratic party has] aped the policy of the Republican party on every issue of vital interest to the great masses of the people. They have voted for contraction; they have favored national banks; they have aided the Republicans in their funding schemes; they have voted and worked to strike down silver; they have bowed to Baal; they have worshipped Mammon; they have built unto themselves false Gods, and set them on the hill-tops of freedom; they have courted aristocratic establishments; they have partaken of the spoils; they have received bribes; they have forsaken their principles,, and their glory is departed from them forever. . . ."

traditional allegiances and join their new political organization. The problem promised to be especially difficult in the South, where a third party could crack the white solidarity established by Democrats in the 1870s and maintained by their equally conservative successors, known as the Bourbons. Conservative whites feared that if the Populists successfully challenged the "lily white" Democratic party, blacks might regain a foothold in southern political life.

Some southern Populists were indeed eager to gain black votes. In Georgia Tom Watson promised black voters that if they stood "shoulder to shoulder" with the Populists, they would have "fair play and fair treatment as men and citizens, irrespective of color." In Texas two black men were elected to the Populist executive committee. In North Carolina blacks were given a visible role in the 1892 presidential campaign. But the Populist commitment to racial equality was limited. Populists in southern state legislatures did not differ noticeably from the Bourbons in their desire to keep blacks "in their place," nor were they particularly sensitive to the special social problems that blacks faced beyond those they shared with poor whites. In Tennessee the Alliance members of the legislature endorsed measures to eliminate remaining black voters from election rolls. Tom Watson's *People's Party Paper* supported proposals to segregate blacks from whites on the state's railroads.

In the 1892 presidential election the Populist candidate, James B. Weaver, a former Union general, conducted an energetic campaign. Unfortunately for the Populists' chances, sectional biases left from the Civil War were still strong. Weaver's Union record made him unwelcome in the South. The surviving southern

Republicans were willing to vote Populist, but most southern Democrats, whatever their economic or social sympathies, feared breaking the solid white front against restored black rule. On the western Plains the new party did better: In several states the Democrats, the weaker of the two parties, fused with the Populists and ran local candidates on joint "Popocrat" tickets while continuing to support Grover Cleveland for president. In several western states the Democrats merely stole the Populists' thunder by adopting platforms endorsing Populist principles. In the end the Populist ticket won over 15 percent of the vote in the Deep South and higher percentages in the silver-producing mountain states and parts of the Great Plains. Weaver received over 1 million to about 12 million votes cast, or about 8.5 percent. Cleveland won, but the Populist vote promised—or threatened—much for the future.

Unrest under Cleveland. Cleveland's second term (1893–1897) was marked by social unrest more stormy than anything the country had seen since the Civil War. In the spring of 1893 the stock market crashed, ushering in a devastating depression. Labor disturbances broke out in many parts of the country as workers struggled desperately to keep their jobs or prevent cuts in pay. It was this climate of fear and anger that set off the Pullman strike of 1894 (described in Chapter 17).

Another manifestation of the times was Coxey's Army, a march of the unemployed on Washington in 1894. Organized by Jacob S. Coxey, an ex-Greenbacker, the march sought to dramatize the plight of the jobless and advertise Coxey's scheme for a federal works program financed by a paper-money issue of $500 million. The experts ridiculed the idea, and when Coxey's 400 bedraggled men arrived in Washington, federal officials arrested their leaders for trampling the Capitol grass.

The reaction of the Cleveland administration to the distress of the laboring population was at best unimaginative. The president believed that Populist agitation and the government's piling up of silver—required by the Sherman Silver Purchase Act—had set off the Panic of 1893 and the resulting depression by frightening business and shaking public confidence in the ability of the government to pay its obligations in gold. Whether valid or not, in fact this fear was fast becoming a financial danger in itself. Hoarders were withdrawing more and more gold from the banks and the treasury, and before long the nation would be forced off the gold standard. To stop the gold drain and reassure public creditors, Cleveland pressured

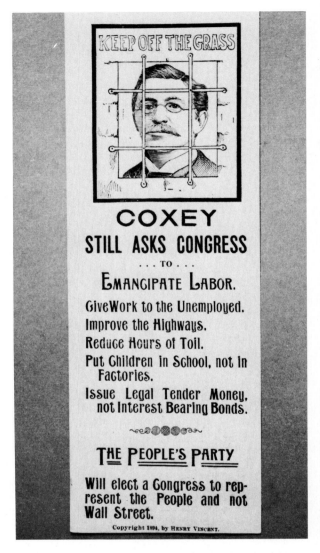

The Washington police arrested Jacob Coxey and several of his followers when they trespassed on the Capitol lawn. But he and his "army" had a serious program to end unemployment and promote economic recovery after the Panic of 1893.

Congress to repeal the Sherman Silver Act. Simultaneously he sought to shore up the treasury's gold reserve by selling bonds to the public for gold coin. The public bought the bonds, but then brought more paper money to the treasury to be redeemed for gold. Gold went in one treasury door and out the other. Ultimately, by getting the international investment bankers to guarantee delivery of foreign gold, Cleveland saved the gold standard, but his tactics only confirmed the belief of millions of southerners and westerners that J. P. Morgan, "Wall Street," and the European banking family of the Rothschilds owned the country.

It is against this background of depression, unemployment, and suspicious dealings with the international financiers that we must view the momentous election of 1896. By 1895 the country was restless and uneasy. Many Americans, especially in the West and South, believed that the United States was fast falling under the sway of the "money power." These sections could not be ignored. In the generation since the Civil War the South had regained some of its self-confidence and the West had become an important force in the nation's economic and political life. In 1889–1890, North Dakota, South Dakota, Montana, Washington, Idaho, and Wyoming had been admitted to the Union, adding to Congress twelve senators who endorsed the West's view of politics and increasing the political power of the silver-mine owners, the chief financial backers of free-silver candidates. For thirty years or more the country's social and economic institutions had been undergoing fundamental change as the United States moved from farming and rural life to industry and cities. Yet despite socialists, anarchists, Greenbackers, and now Populists, the country's political life had changed little. Would the forces of political change now succeed or be beaten back? In the end the American people rejected major alterations in the status quo, but only after a political battle that aroused, among conservative citizens, fears of anarchy and revolution.

"Bryan! Bryan! Bryan!" Despite the Populists, the arena in which the contending forces fought out their differences was the Democratic party. On one side were the Democratic gold bugs, mostly from the Northeast and the Midwest, who believed that civilization itself rode on the gold standard. On the other side were the many western and southern Democrats, who were equally convinced that humanity could survive and prosper only if silver were restored to the currency system. The Republicans also had silver and gold wings, representing western and eastern attitudes, respectively. But the proponents of silver were stronger among the Democrats.

In addition to their clashing financial views, silverites and goldbugs, particularly within the Democratic party, differed over more fundamental matters. Free-silver Democrats were often indistinguishable from Populists in their agrarian values, their support of direct democracy, of taxes to equalize wealth, and of government regulation of large corporations. Gold-

bug Democrats resembled the most conservative Republicans in their political and social views.

In June 1896, the Republicans nominated William McKinley of Ohio on a platform pledged to a high tariff, a gold standard (although promising to consider silver if acceptable by international agreement), and an aggressive foreign policy. The gold-standard plank was a bitter disappointment to the Republican silverites, and Senator Henry M. Teller of Colorado and his western friends walked out of the convention.

At the Democratic convention in Chicago the silverites were in the majority. Senator Richard ("Silver Dick") Bland of Missouri was the front-runner as the delegates arrived. But a young ex-congressman from Nebraska, William Jennings Bryan, was also a serious contender. The young Nebraskan had spent many months rounding up support for himself and silver, writing letters, speaking before silverite audiences and Democratic groups, and cultivating the Farmers' Alliances. Rising as the last speaker before the convention voted on whether to endorse a gold-standard or a free-silver platform, he launched into what is probably the most influential address in American political history.

Bryan preferred to avoid polarizing the nation and the party. In answer to the previous speaker, a defender of gold, he pointed out that the man who worked for wages, the "merchant at the crossroads store," the farmer, and the miner were also "businessmen." All were the same and must be treated the same. But then he made clear that the money question did indeed drive a sharp wedge between Americans. "We say not one word against those who live upon the Atlantic Coast, but the hardy pioneers who had braved all the dangers of the wilderness . . . are as deserving of the consideration of their party as any people in this country. . . . It is for these that we speak." He continued:

> You came to tell us that the great cities are in favor of the gold standard; we reply that the great cities rest upon our broad and fertile prairies. Burn down the cities and leave our farms, and the cities will spring up again as if by magic; but destroy our farms and the grass will grow in the streets of every city in the country.

Now followed the moving conclusion that gave the name "Cross of Gold" to the address. If the gold men insisted on the gold standard, the silverites, supported by the "producing masses" and the "toilers everywhere," would fight them to the end. Raising his hands to the sides of his head, with fingers extended, Bryan thundered: "You shall not press down upon the brow

The Issue — 1900
· LIBERTY ·
· JUSTICE ·
· HUMANITY ·

W.J. BRYAN

NO
CROWN
OF
THORNS

NO
CROSS
OF
GOLD

EQUAL RIGHTS TO ALL   SPECIAL PRIVILEGES TO NONE.

Though they criticized Bryan's religious rhetoric, the Republicans had their own pious slogan: "In God we trust, in Bryan we bust." The election's religious flavor is ironic because the issues of 1896 were, ultimately, economic.

of labor this crown of thorns, you shall not crucify mankind upon a cross of gold."

As Bryan finished, he stretched his arms out horizontally, as if crucified himself. For several seconds the crowd was silent, then it burst into frenzied shouts and cheers: "Bryan! Bryan! Bryan!" Amid flying hats and waving handkerchiefs, the delegates lifted the speaker onto their shoulders and carried him off the platform. On July 10, 1896, the Democrats chose Bryan as their candidate and Arthur Sewall, a silverite Maine businessman, as his running mate.

The Election of 1896. What would the Populists do now? At their convention in St. Louis soon after the Democrats had adjourned, they faced a dilemma. Bryan claimed to speak for social justice, but his emphasis was heavily on silver. Many Populists saw free silver as an exaggerated issue. What about popular election of senators, a progressive income tax, government ownership of railroads? According to the Populist journalist Henry Demarest Lloyd, silver was the "cowbird" of the insurgent movement. It would deposit its eggs in another bird's nest and when its young were born they would evict the offspring of the original parents. In effect, silver would crowd out the other issues.

Moreover, Bryan was a Democrat. To southern Populists, especially, the Democrats were the enemy. After fighting the Bourbons for so long, how could they now fuse with them on the candidate at the top of the ticket?

On the other hand, Bryan could win, whereas no Populist could. And, though not a Populist himself, he was a champion of the people and could be expected to fight for social reform. And besides, if he won with the Populists' support, he would be in their debt and they would undoubtedly occupy influential places in the new administration.

Despite misgivings, delegates to the St. Louis convention gave Bryan their nomination as president. Unable to support banker Arthur Sewall, however, they

Bryan ran for president three times. This is a poster from his 1900 second campaign, but you can still see echoes of the first in the slogans.

selected Georgia's fiery Tom Watson, one of their own, as their vice presidential nominee.

The campaign that followed was one of the bitterest on record. Both major parties split. A large group of conservative Democrats refused to endorse Bryan and organized a separate "gold" Democratic ticket with John M. Palmer of Illinois at its head. "Silver" Republicans endorsed the Democratic candidates, Bryan and Sewall.

Obviously the underdog, Bryan campaigned hard. Consciously or not, he sought to change the foundation of Gilded Age party alignments. Playing on the hard times, he labored to overcome evangelical allegiance to the Republicans by appealing to class and economic interests. With silver, he declared, times would get better, prosperity would return, and wealth inequalities would be reduced.

Bryan appealed to traditional Republicans by speaking the language that Americans of pious Protestant background understood. Bryan himself was a devout Protestant, raised on the Bible and old-time religion. His earliest ambition had been, he said, to be a Baptist minister; when he became a lawyer and a politician, he never ceased being a preacher. As the Cross of Gold speech implied, free silver to him was more than an economic position; it represented justice and virtue. Gold, on the other hand, was not just the metal of the creditors; it was the source of injustice and oppression. "Every great economic question," Bryan declared as he crisscrossed the country, was "in reality a great moral question." Through the Midwest he called on goldbug sinners to "repent." Wherever the Nebraskan went he was received as an evangelist. In the South and on his beloved prairies, the people treated his rallies like great religious camp meetings. The Democratic campaign of 1896 was a crusade.

The Republican campaign was a countercrusade. To conservative Americans, Bryan and his forces were dangerous radicals. Postmaster General William L. Wilson declared that the silver leaders were "socialists, anarchists and demagogues of a dangerous type. . . ." A writer to the *New York Times* asserted that "within six months of Bryan's election mobs would be rushing up and down our streets howling for bread," If Bryan tried to make the free-silver cause a moral issue, so did his opponents. Clergymen denounced free silver as immoral. The *Chicago Tribune* declared that the gold position was a matter of simple honesty. "It is in no respect a question of politics, but of moral princi-

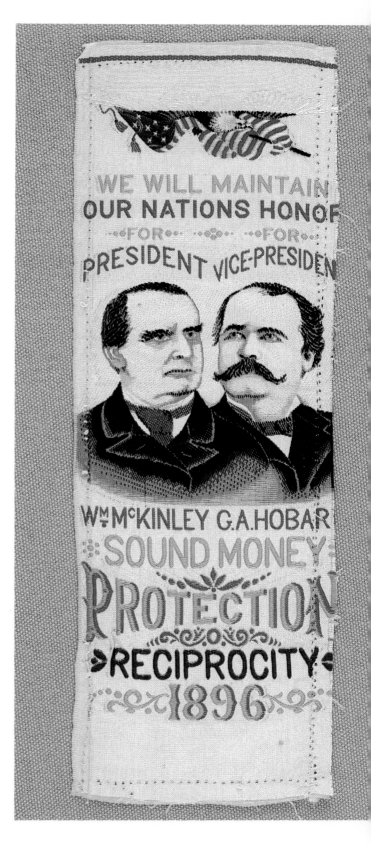

"Sound Money" was the Republican cry in 1896. But so was a higher tariff.

ple. It is taking the commandment, 'Thou Shalt not Steal,' which is a common text, and applying it to the Nation."

The goldbugs had the tremendous advantage of money. The Republican national chairman was Cleveland industrialist Mark Hanna, a close friend of McKinley. Hanna was spectacularly effective in convincing the business community to write checks for McKinley and other antisilver candidates. The one important business group that might have contributed to Bryan, the silver-mine owners of the mountain states, proved surprisingly stingy (the price of silver having dropped). To make up for the lack of money, Bryan had only his fierce energy and enormous eloquence.

In the end these were not enough. The public perceived the election as the most critical since 1860 and turned out in record numbers. But the consequence was a resounding defeat for Bryan. The Democratic candidate won 6.5 million popular and 176 electoral votes to McKinley's 7.1 million and 271.

The nature of the vote reveals much about the social and sectional tensions of the 1890s. In New England, the Middle Atlantic region, and the states of the Old Northwest where the Democrat Cleveland had done well in 1892, Bryan carried not a single state. On the Pacific coast he carried only Washington. In the Great Plains he did much better, taking Kansas, Nebraska, South Dakota, and Missouri. Bryan's real support, however, came from the South and the mountain states. In the South traditional Democratic voters joined with Populists to give Bryan the large majorities that Democratic candidates could invariably count on from the former Confederacy. In the mountain states, however, the Bryan sweep represented a major shift, best explained by the Democratic focus on silver.

If we look more closely at the details of the returns, it becomes even clearer that section rather than class determined how Americans voted in 1896. Despite Bryan's appeal to all "producers," city people voted strongly Republican, except in mining centers like Butte, Boise, and Denver, where those concerned over monetary issues made up an influential portion

The election of 1896

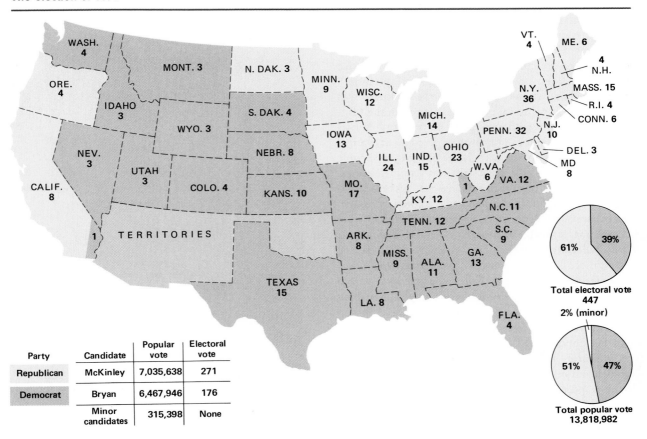

Party	Candidate	Popular vote	Electoral vote
Republican	McKinley	7,035,638	271
Democrat	Bryan	6,467,946	176
	Minor candidates	315,398	None

Total electoral vote 447

Total popular vote 13,818,982

of the population. One possible explanation for his failure to win city votes is that Bryan's evangelical fervor repelled many of the urban Catholics and Lutherans who usually voted Democratic. On the other side, Republicans who normally offended Catholic and other liturgical voters were careful to avoid stepping on ethnic toes. Instead, unity and tolerance were major Republican themes. "We have always practiced the Golden Rule," declared McKinley: "the best policy is to 'live and let live.' " There were also economic factors. Rather than splitting the rich from the poor, the self-employed and professional classes from the wage earners, the threat of free silver forged a bond across class lines. Eastern working men saw no advantage for themselves in cheap money. The Republican promise that a new tariff would bring prosperity and "the full dinner pail" seemed more likely than the millennium promised by Bryan.

Nor did Bryan appeal to all rural Americans. Wisconsin dairy farmers, California citrus growers, Iowa and Illinois corn-hog farmers, and New Jersey truck gardeners, for example, saw little reason to take a chance on free silver. Prices for pork, milk, cheese, oranges, and vegetables were good; these farmers had no desire to experiment with the country's monetary and financial system.

Scholarly partisans of Bryan had charged that the Republicans used coercion to win wage earner votes for McKinley. Republican employers, they say, threatened to fire Bryan supporters or close their own businesses if the Democrats won. There is indeed evidence of such business pressure. Bankers threatened to call in farm mortgages. The railroads declared they would be forced to shut down if foreign investors were scared away by free silver. Many businessmen were panicked by the free-silver issue and made extravagant statements expressing their fears. But this pressure was not decisive. In the end, Bryan and free silver lost because their appeal proved primarily southern and western.

Conclusions

The facts are clear: The Republican party did not dominate the political life of the nation during the Gilded Age; nor did the successes it scored imply the triumph of big business over agriculture, labor, and the other interests that made up the country's socioeconomic system. Americans were not indifferent to the economic questions raised by rapid industrialization: the tariff, currency backing, and government regulation of industry. But opposing groups worked within each party to achieve their ends.

In defining themselves politically, moreover, most American voters paid more attention to cultural and religious matters than to class or economic ones. The Democrats, as the party of cultural laissez-faire, appealed more to Catholic and other liturgical voters who preferred to keep politics out of private life. The GOP, as the party of "God and morality," to use a Democratic critic's phrase, appealed to those evangelical Protestant groups who saw politics as a vehicle for creating a more virtuous society. Section and race also defined the two Gilded Age parties. White southerners did not easily forget that the "Black Republicans" had crushed the Confederacy, abolished slavery, and tried to impose black suffrage. Northern Union veterans and southern blacks remembered the same things, but with greater affection and the opposite political effect.

Cultural values and these memories maintained the alignment of the parties in the Gilded Age, but the discontent of southerners and westerners disturbed that balance. When Bryan gave voice to many of their complaints as the Democratic candidate in 1896, he weakened the traditional party ties, alienating many Catholic and Lutheran voters as well as eastern workers. After 1896 the Republlcans would grow in strength.

That year also marked a change in farmers' fortunes. When prices for cotton and wheat began to rise after the 1896 election, western and southern cultivators lost interest in political insurgency. Farmers continued to be concerned about the abuses of middlemen and the high cost of credit; they still worried about the declining quality of rural life. But they ceased to talk of political revolt. By 1900 the Populist party was dead, and political insurgency as a sectional phenomenon was over.

Although the Populists had often been naive in their analyses and solutions, the problems of industrialization and urbanization they had complained about were real and did not go away. Serious social and economic abuses by the powerful, and the fundamental inequalities of wealth and power, continued. As the new century began, more and more eastern and urban Americans who had rejected Bryan would come to see that he and his supporters had grasped some important parts of the American reality. Populism foreshadowed the growth of twentieth-century liberalism. But first Americans would turn their attention to overseas affairs in a way that they had not since the earliest days of the republic.

For Further Reading

H. Wayne Morgan, editor. *The Gilded Age: A Reappraisal* (1970)

>Twelve contributors write on civil service reform, labor, the robber barons, science, the currency question, the party system, Populism, foreign policy, popular culture, and the arts. Morgan pulls together the threads with an introduction that emphasizes growing national unity.

Richard Jensen. *The Winning of the Midwest: Social and Political Conflict, 1888–1896* (1971)

>Using statistical data, Jensen demonstrates how political affiliations during the Gilded Age were often determined by social and religious values rather than by pocketbook issues. You will find this a challenging example of the "new" political history as practiced by historians armed with computers. For another good example of this genre, see Paul Kleppner, *The Cross of Culture: A Social Analysis of Midwestern Politics, 1850–1900 (1970)*

John G. Sprout. *"The Best Men": Liberal Reformers in the Gilded Age* (1968)

>A fine study of Gilded Age reform focusing on the Liberal Republican movement of 1872 and the later Mugwumps. Sprout sees these people as out of touch with the harsh realities of their time and he calls their brand of reform the "politics of nostalgia."

Irwin Unger. *The Greenback Era: A Social and Political History of American Finance, 1865–1879* (1964)

>Deals with post–Civil War finance as an example of who controlled political power in the Gilded Age. The author of *These United States* tends to be partial to this work.

David Rothman. *Politics and Power: The United States Senate, 1869–1901* (1966)

>Rothman shows how the United States Senate changed from a leaderless group of politicians during the Reconstruction era to a tightly organized and immensely powerful "millionaires' club" by the beginning of the twentieth century. He analyzes recruitment patterns for Senate seats, state party structures, and lobbying practices.

Morton Keller. *Affairs of State: Public Life in Late-Nineteenth-Century America* (1977)

>A meaty book, one that attempts to show how the social and economic transformation of the nation between 1865 and 1900 was reflected in its political life. Deals with changes in state as well as national government and with law as well as politics. Keller sees the Civil War as expanding the scope of government for some years following 1865.

Matthew Josephson. *The Politicos, 1865–1896* (1938)

>The classic older treatment of Gilded Age politics.

According to Josephson, the political leadership of the period was thoroughly unprincipled. Politicians either blackmailed businessmen for their own gain or, after the civil service reform of the 1880s, were the corrupt tools of big business.

Thomas Beer. *The Mauve Decade: American Life at the End of the Nineteenth Century* (1926)

>Another classic treatment of the Gilded Age. "Americans have no political ideas," writes Beer. "They follow leaders who attract them or know how to manage them. The kind of political leaders they like are human circuses." In other words, Beer endorses the concept that Gilded Age politics was a kind of spectator sport.

Allan Nevins. *Grover Cleveland: A Study in Courage* (1932)

>The Gilded Age has not inspired political biographers, despite the color of its politicians. The best political biography for the era remains this older work by a master of narrative history, Allan Nevins.

Mark Twain and Charles Dudley Warner. *The Gilded Age* (1873)

>Fictional Senator Dilworthy (modeled on a real senator, the corrupt Samuel C. Pomeroy of Kansas) exclaims: "I think I can say, and say with pride, that we have some legislatures that bring higher prices than any in the world." This satire of the "all-pervading speculativeness" in business life and corruption in politics gave the Gilded Age its name.

Mary R. Dearing. *Veterans in Politics: The Story of the G. A. R.* (1952)

>A study of the Civil War Union veterans' organization, the Grand Army of the Republic, as a political pressure group and a bulwark of the Republican party after 1865.

Richard Hofstadter. *The Age of Reform: From Bryan to FDR* (1955)

>The first third of this important and influential interpretation of American reform deals with Populism. Hofstadter sees Populism as a backward-looking movement of men and women who were trying to restore a vanished rural age. He says they were also much given to conspiracy theories to explain why the times were out of joint.

John D. Hicks. *The Populist Revolt: A History of the Farmers' Alliance and the People's party* (1931)

>This is the standard older treatment of late-nineteenth-century agrarian insurgency. Hicks sees the Populists as the forerunners of later liberalism.

Lawrence Goodwyn. *Democratic Promise: The Populist Movement in America* (1976)

An impassioned defense of the Populists against their detractors (such as Hofstadter). Despite the breadth of coverage implied by the title, this is really a study of southern Populism.

Louis W. Koenig. *Bryan: A Political Biography of William Jennings Bryan* (1971)

The best one-volume biography of Bryan. Fair without being enthusiastic. By a political scientist, but good nonetheless.

Paul Kleppner. *The Cross of Culture: A Social Analysis of Midwestern Politics 1850–1900* (1970)

Kleppner's book is the pioneer study of Gilded Age cultural politics. Interesting but not a conventional "good read."

Chapter 21

The American Empire

Why Did the United States Look Abroad?

1853–54   Commodore Perry opens American-Japanese trade

1867   Secretary of State Seward negotiates the purchase of Alaska and American control of the Midway Islands

1868   Ulysses S. Grant elected president

1869–70   Grant attempts to annex Santo Domingo

1877   Rutherford B. Hayes becomes president

1878   Coaling station at Pago Pago established

1880   James A. Garfield elected president

1881   Garfield is assassinated; Chester A. Arthur becomes president

1883   Congress appropriates funds to build modern naval vessels

1884   Grover Cleveland elected president

1887   The U. S. secures a naval base at Pearl Harbor

1888   Benjamin Harrison elected president

1890   The McKinley Tariff Act • Alfred Thayer Mahan's *The Influence of Sea Power upon History* published

1892   Grover Cleveland elected president

1893   American planters organize coup d'état in Hawaii • Frederick Jackson Turner's *The Significance of the Frontier in American History* published

1895   U. S. disputes British claims in Venezuela

1896   William McKinley elected president

1898   The *Maine* is sunk in Havana harbor • Congress declares war on Spain • Congress votes to annex Hawaii • Treaty of Paris: Spain surrenders the Philippines, Puerto Rico, and Guam, and frees Cuba

1899–1900   Secretary of State Hay writes the Open Door Notes • The Boxer Rebellion

1899–1902   Emilio Aguinaldo leads a guerrilla war against the American occupation of the Philippines

1901   McKinley assassinated; Theodore Roosevelt becomes president • The Platt Amendment affirms American right to intervene in Cuba • The Hay-Pauncefote Treaty allows the United States to build a Central American interocean waterway

1903   Hay–Bunau–Varilla Treaty gives the United States the Canal Zone

1904   Roosevelt states Monroe Doctrine Corollary

I n April 1898 Albert Beveridge, a young, ambitious Indiana Republican, spoke to Boston's Middlesex Club on the occasion of former President Grant's birthday. The Spanish-American War had just been declared, and although the fighting had scarcely begun, Beveridge looked ahead to what would follow the expected American victory.

> American factories are making more than the American people can use; American soil is producing more than they can consume. Fate has written our policy for us; the trade of the world must and shall be ours. . . . We shall establish trading posts throughout the world as distributing points for American products. We will cover the ocean with our merchant marine. We will build a navy to the measure of our greatness. Great colonies governing themselves, flying our flag and trading with us, will grow about our posts of trade. Our institutions will follow our flag on the wings of our commerce. And American law, American civilization, and the American flag will plant themselves on shores hitherto bloody and benighted, but by those agencies of God henceforth to be made beautiful and bright.

In this brief burst of oratory Beveridge summarized virtually every motive that contemporaries—and later scholars—would advance for America's overseas thrust during the generation following the Civil War. The American people needed markets for their surplus manufactures and farm products; they envisioned the glorious Stars and Stripes waving around the globe; they foresaw American civilization conferring immense benefits on the "benighted" peoples fortunate enough to fall under United States dominion. And all this was to be accomplished by the "agencies of God." Glory, Gold, and God all justified an American empire in 1898—as they had a Spanish empire in 1498 and a British empire in 1598.

The resemblance between historical phenomena 400 years apart is striking, and it is tempting to assume that not much had changed in the interval. But nineteenth-century Americans were not fifteenth-century Spaniards or sixteenth-century Englishmen. Even if they had the same general motives for expansion as their predecessors, these motives were expressed in different ways and were present in different proportions. How can we explain America's expansionist impulse during the years immediately preceding our own century?

The Background

Viewed one way, post–Civil War expansionism seems an extension of the American past. For 250 years following the first permanent settlements along the Atlantic coast, the American people had pushed steadily westward toward the Pacific. Americans often think of this movement as the filling in of an empty continent and the conquest of nature. But the vast interior of North America was not devoid of people: it was occupied by several million Indians, who resisted the settlers' thrust and were pushed aside. Parts of what later became the United States, moveover, were under the sovereignty of European nations, and Americans used aggressive diplomacy and military power to incorporate these areas into the United States. In one sense, then, the overseas thrust following 1865 was merely a continuation of what had preceded. Having run out of "Wests," expansionist Americans sought new frontiers on other continents and on the islands off their shores.

Besides noting this continuity with the past, any theory of post–Civil War expansionism must consider the immediate international context. Expansionism is an expression of unequal power. As the Western world's advantage over the underdeveloped world increased during the nineteenth century, the temptation to use that advantage grew irresistible. The closing decades of the century witnessed the last burst of European colonialism. In Africa, the Pacific Islands, and Indochina the European powers were on the move, seizing territory, until the remotest regions were firmly under European hegemony. All the great Western nations, as well as newly westernized Japan, vied for influence and trade in China, a vast but weak and disintegrating empire and a potentially rich market for industrial goods. America in these decades surpassed its competitors on every index of wealth; inevitably, this view holds, it felt the same urge as the other industrial nations to impose its will on others.

Post–Civil War expansionism clearly had an economic dimension. Marxist analysis asserts that modern imperialism can be explained as a way that strong, advanced capitalist nations avoid serious internal problems by preying on weak, precapitalist ones. In the Marxist view such advanced societies reach an economic saturation point through years of development. They have difficulties finding markets for their goods and outlets for their capital at home, and so turn to weaker societies to exploit. In this way—through imperialism—they are able to stave off social upheavals and achieve stability.

This description may fit European imperialism, but it clearly does not explain the American equivalent. Until well into the twentieth century the United States was itself more of an economic colony than an economic imperialist. Few Americans had investments abroad; rather, millions of European pounds, francs, and marks were invested in American railroads, government bonds, and land. Nor did the United States depend on foreign markets for its economic survival. The enormous American home market was far from saturated with goods. American agriculture, it is true, relied on foreign consumers; but the consumers were in countries such as Britain, France, and Germany. These nations were in no danger whatever of becoming America's colonies.

And yet we cannot dismiss economic motives entirely. Even though the American economy did not depend on foreign trade, much less colonies, during hard times like the late 1870s and the early 1890s, many business people, farmers, and politicians became fearful that unless the country could find overseas outlets for its surplus goods, it would be forced to keep its machines, factories, and labor force idle. It is the rhetoric of such periods that lends itself to the theories of Marxist economic determinists. In reality, business people and farmers seldom believed that actual colonies, politically controlled by Washington, were essential to the country's economic health; but they did demand that the American government do what it could to open markets for American goods abroad. Groups of intellectuals and some politicians then carried the prescription for prosperity one step further: Why not guarantee captive markets and outlets for surplus capital by actual political control? These men, few in number but often in positions of power and influence, would form a vanguard for imperialism after 1865.

The Beginnings of American Overseas Expansion

The story of American overseas expansion does not begin abruptly in 1865. Before the Civil War southerners had strongly favored the absorption of Spanish-controlled Cuba into the United States, and in 1854 President Pierce had offered Spain $130 million for the island. In the same decade American adventurers and soldiers of fortune had fomented revolutions in Central America with the purpose of annexing territory to the United States. In the Far East the United States had pursued an aggressive policy of encouraging American trade, which culminated in the two visits of Commodore Matthew Perry and an American naval squadron to Japan in 1853/54. Perry forced the Japanese government, virtually at gunpoint, to open its doors to foreign trade and traditional diplomatic relations.

The Civil War brought these expansionist activities to a sudden halt. Both South and North were too caught up in the battle for survival to concern themselves with overseas adventures. But after Appomattox, despite the continued distractions of Reconstruction, Americans once again looked with interest toward the surrounding oceans and the lands that dotted and bordered them.

Foreign Policy Under Seward. The man who gave concrete shape to this revived interest in the outside world between 1865 and 1869 was Secretary of State William Henry Seward, chief formulator of American foreign policy during the presidency of Andrew Johnson. Seward's interest in American expansion had its practical, strategic side. The Union's difficulties in dealing with the Confederate ships raiding northern commerce during the Civil War had convinced him that the United States must have naval bases and coaling stations scattered around its perimeter to fend off any future naval aggressor. But Seward's interest was also based on a romantic vision of a benevolent American empire resembling the Manifest Destiny of the 1840s. In 1867, in a burst of poetry surprising in a man so practical and businesslike, Seward announced:

> *Our nation with united interests blest,*
> *Not content to pose, shall sway the rest;*
> *Abroad our empire shall no limits know,*
> *But like the sea in boundless limits flow.*

Before he could consider expansion, however, Seward had to attend to the nagging problem of European intrusion into the Western Hemisphere. In 1863, while the United States was preoccupied by the Civil War, the French had established a puppet regime in Mexico under Archduke Maximilian of Austria, and had sent troops to support him against Mexican patriots led by Benito Juárez. The French occupation of Mexico was a clear challenge to the Monroe Doctrine of 1823, which stated that the United States would consider any attempt by the major European powers "to extend their system to any portion of this hemisphere as dangerous to our peace and safety." When the war ended, Seward told Napoleon III, the French emperor, that the United States would no longer tolerate Maximilian's rule in Mexico. Growing opposition at home, the cost of maintaining troops in America, and the threat of the seasoned Union army just across the border induced the French to withdraw their support of the puppet regime in 1867. Shortly thereafter, Maximilian was captured by Juárez's forces and executed.

Seward's success in expelling the French was applauded by the Mexican people. For once, the Monroe Doctrine had served Latin America as an effective shield against European aggression. Seward's fellow citizens were also delighted at having forced Napoleon III to abandon his ambitions in the Western Hemisphere.

But neither Latin Americans nor citizens of the United States greeted Seward's expansionist moves as warmly. Americans had other things on their minds than overseas possessions and were either indifferent or stubbornly opposed to empire building. When Seward tried to buy land for a coaling station in Santa Domingo (the Dominican Republic), Congress refused to support him. He also could not get Congress to approve a treaty to purchase the Danish West Indies (now the U.S. Virgin Islands). Critics of the secretary had a field day with these island-shopping trips. A mock advertisement in a New York newspaper ran: "A Few West India Islands Wanted.—Any distressed persons having a few islands to dispose of in the Spanish Main can find a purchaser by applying to Washington D.C. . . ." The only islands that Seward ever managed to acquire were specks of land a thousand miles west of Hawaii: the Midway group. Seward's only major success was Alaska.

"Seward's Folly." Alaska, in Russian hands for many years, had been exploited by the Russian-American Company for its furs. By the mid-nineteenth century the fur trade had begun to decline, and the Russian government faced the prospect of having to rescue the company from bankruptcy. It was also feared that

in a war with Great Britain, Russia would not be able to protect her distant colony. Uncertain of Alaska's defenses and unwilling to support it financially, the czar decided to sell it to the United States.

The American secretary of state was more than willing to talk terms. Seward saw Alaska not only as a base for American naval defense in any Pacific war but also as a way station to the Far East and the potential markets of China. But many outspoken Americans, including many in Congress, were opposed to acquiring a distant, unknown, and apparently worthless land. Those who had ridiculed Seward's Caribbean interests promptly labeled his new scheme "Seward's Folly" and the territory itself "Seward's Icebox." A weekly newspaper reported that the benefits of buying Russian America included a bracing climate, a promising ice crop, and cows that gave ice cream instead of milk. At the very least, many Americans felt, the $7.2 million that the Russians wanted was a high price for half a million square miles of mountains, ice, tundra, and scrub forest.

Seward responded with a major sales campaign. He secured testimonials from experts describing the region's vast resources. He collected statements from the newspapers of 1803 attacking the Louisiana Purchase to show his opponents as foolish, timid men

This 1867 cartoon showing President Johnson and Secretary of State Seward welcoming "our new senators" pokes fun at "Seward's Folly," the purchase of Alaska from Russia. Many Americans had little faith in Alaska's ability to become a modern community. (Note: the penguin on the left was not found in Alaska; it was an Antarctic bird!)

The battleship *Maine* was a product of the "new navalism" of the 1880s. This 1880 photograph shows it under construction at the Brooklyn Navy yard. Its building was an example not only of the change in America's international outlook, but also of the new technology of steel construction.

without vision or foresight. With the help of Charles Sumner, the influential chairman of the Senate Foreign Relations Committee, he induced the Senate to pass the treaty annexing Alaska. When the House of Representatives balked at appropriating the necessary money, the Russian minister plied the reluctant House members with cash. In the end it all worked out. On October 18, 1867, the American flag was raised over the Russian fort at Sitka. Alaska was now American territory.

A Stronger Navy. Then for almost two decades following Seward's retirement, the American people turned inward. In 1869/70 the Senate rejected President Grant's attempt to annex all of Santo Domingo, and thereafter the expansionist impulse subsided. During the 1870s and 1880s much of the nation's energy was consumed in filling in the rest of the continent with farms, railroads, mines, factories, and new cities and towns. With so much of the interior still undeveloped,

there seemed little reason to seek out new lands across the seas. So remote and unimportant did America's foreign relations appear that as late as 1889 the *New York Sun* could half seriously suggest doing away with the diplomatic service as "a costly humbug and sham" that did "no good to anybody."

Yet even during this low point of diplomacy, there were rumblings of a revived interest in foreign concerns and a new aggressiveness toward the outside world. At first the new mood manifested itself as anxiety about American naval impotence. Of the 1,900 vessels in the fleet in 1880, only 48 could fire a gun. Citizens began to wonder how the country could protect itself against attack.

In 1878 the new concern led to a treaty with the ruler of the island of Samoa establishing an American naval coaling station at Pago Pago. In 1883 Congress authorized four new steel ships capable of defending the country's coasts, adding the battleships *Texas* and *Maine* to the fleet in the next few years. These additions made Americans breathe a little easier, but the American navy remained primarily a defensive force.

Then, in the 1890s, the United States began to construct a high-seas fleet that could support an ambitious foreign policy. The inspiration for the "new navalism" was the writings of Captain Alfred Thayer Mahan, a career naval officer who in 1886 went to teach at the Naval War College at Newport, Rhode Island. Mahan believed that nations must either expand or die, and that naval power was the key to expansion. In *The Influence of Sea Power upon History*, published in 1890, he described how Britain had become the greatest nation in the world by seizing command of the seas. America must now strive to equal Great Britain or accept eventual decline.

Mahan's book enjoyed a great vogue. It confirmed the views of those who were ready to look outward; it convinced many who remained dubious of colonialism that the country must have a navy second to none. Spurred on by Mahan's ideas, during the 1890s the United States built numerous fast vessels with long cruising ranges, capable of meeting an enemy anywhere in the world. By the end of the decade the naval building program had created a high-seas fleet consisting of seventeen steel-sided battleships, along with six armored cruisers and numerous modern smaller craft.

"Jingo Jim" Blaine. Navalism, though a sign of change, did not end the country's isolationism, and Americans as a whole remained uninterested in foreign concerns. James G. Blaine, secretary of state under James Garfield (1881) and again under Benjamin Harrison (1889–1892) felt differently. Blaine was not a man to sit in his office and shuffle papers. Jingo Jim* was particularly interested in Latin America. Like many Americans since Monroe's day, he believed that the United States had a special big-brother role to play in the Western Hemisphere, and he advocated stronger ties among the nations of the New World, a policy he referred to as "Pan-Americanism."

Blaine's interest in Latin America combined altruism and economic gain in roughly equal parts. The United States imported from Latin American countries almost $100 million worth of goods more a year than it exported to them. Although it bought large quantities of foodstuffs and raw materials from its southern neigh-

bors, they continued to buy most of their manufactured goods from Europe. Blaine hoped to divert the flow of Latin American trade from Europe to the United States, but he feared that improved economic relations would be impossible if the Latin American nations continued to squabble constantly among themselves. If the United States could act as a peacemaker and a stabilizing influence in the Western Hemisphere, everyone would benefit. Good deeds would bring good profits.

In 1881, Blaine called an inter-American conference to meet in Washington to further these goals. Before it could assemble, President Garfield was assassinated. Blaine soon resigned as secretary of state, and his successor in the State Department canceled the conference. Blaine got another chance during the second round of his "spirited diplomacy" under President Benjamin Harrison. In October 1889 representatives of seventeen Latin American states convened in Washington at Blaine's invitation. The results, from Blaine's point of view, were mixed. The delegates rejected the secretary's pet project, a Western Hemisphere customs union designed to increase United States–Latin American trade and curtail trade with Europe. They also turned down his proposal for establishing procedures to handle inter-American disagreements. The conference was not a total failure, however. It set up the Pan American Union as a clearinghouse for distributing information and furthering cooperation between Latin America and the United States, and it provided a model for further hemispheric solidarity.

A New Frontier. Blaine's career suggests that even during this low point in diplomacy, Americans never completely lost their interest in international affairs. But a vague interest is a long way from expansionism. Then, in the last two decades of the century, thoughtful men and women began to reconsider fundamentally their country's place in the world.

The process was inspired by a paradoxical mixture of arrogance and fear. During the 1880s and 1890s a sense of crisis seized many middle-class Americans. The country was in turmoil. Populism, labor unrest, and growing radicalism were threatening the nation's stability. What was responsible for these dangers and what could be done about them? As they struggled for understanding, many people turned to political seers and social prophets for help. In these years they encountered a persistent theme: The United States had run out of physical space.

This new idea found several expressions. Its most influential spokesman was the historian Frederick Jack-

_____
*A *jingo* was an aggressive patriot willing to fight at the drop of a hat to protect the nation's interests. The term comes from a British song of the late 1870s expressing a combative attitude toward Russia during an international crisis.

Blaine was much beloved and much despised, about par for a Gilded Age politician.

son Turner who, in 1893, announced that the frontier experience was over. According to Turner the frontier had ended in 1890 when the Census Bureau had ceased to mark the line on its official maps where population dropped to less than two persons per square mile. For almost three centuries, he noted, the "West" had provided a constructive outlet for social discontents and had encouraged social and political democracy. Now it was gone and a vital chapter in American history had closed. Turner did not propose moving the American frontier overseas, but he raised in the minds of the educated the frightening prospect of growing inequality and social chaos if America could not find some altenative to continental expansion.

The Reverend Josiah Strong made the solution explicit. In his widely popular book *Our Country* (1885) he asserted that since the free land was gone, the United States would soon "approximate European conditions of life," marked by class conflict and gross inequality. To avoid these afflictions, America must leap the oceans and find new frontiers abroad where its civilization would have room to expand. "I believe it is fully in the hands of the Christians of the United States, during the next ten or fifteen years," wrote Strong, "to hasten or retard the coming of Christ's kingdom in the world by hundreds, and perhaps thousands, of years. We of this generation and nation oc-cupy the Gibraltar of the ages which commands the world's future." Though Strong's vision combined Protestant missionary zeal and American expansion-ism, his advocacy of expanded foreign missions was lost in the defense of American destiny.

Strong and Turner derived their insights from history and sociology; another group of expansionist thinkers extracted theirs from science, or pseudo-sci-ence. Social Darwinians, as we saw in Chapter 17, viewed the competition among nations and peoples as a necessary continuation of the struggle for survival that fueled biological evolution. In this struggle the strong would win and gain dominion and the weak would fail and be enslaved. The result might appear immoral and heartless, but it would further human progress.

At its most extreme, social Darwinism tipped over into the "scientific" racism of Madison Grant, John Fiske, John W. Burgess, and others. These men believed in the "natural superiority" of the Nordic and Anglo-Saxon peoples. Grant, who was associated with the Museum of Natural History in New York, used notions of the superiority of northern Europeans primarily to justify immigration restrictions. Other rac-ists insisted that this superiority gave Americans the right to rule "inferior peoples." Fiske, a philosopher and historian, noted that the Anglo-Saxons had always been conquerors. Now, in the nineteenth century, they could not give up their "sovereignty of the seas" and "their commercial supremacy." Burgess, a professor of political science at Columbia University, taught his students that people of English origin were particularly well suited to the establishment of national states and were destined to impose their political institutions on the rest of the world.

In future years, when Americans considered the morality of colonialism, they would ease their con-sciences by recalling the inherent "inferiority" of the world's brown-skinned and black-skinned races. Ironi-cally, racism could also be used to argue against main-taining colonies. When it came time to decide whether to keep the Philippines, the spoils of the Spanish-Ameri-can War, some of the most unashamed racists in the country advised against trying to incorporate the mil-lions of "little brown brothers" into the nation's body politic.

The Foreign Policy Elite. The Americans who read the works of Turner, Strong, Grant, and the other expansionist scholars belonged to the literate middle class. Their interest in foreign policy was probably marginal to their lives, and although their views were

A Historical Portrait

Alfred T. Mahan

No single person, of course, was responsible for American expansionism at the end of the nineteenth century. The events that culminated in the war with Spain in 1898 and the acquisition of an American empire are bound up in an intricate crisscross of forces, institutions, values, personalities, and accidental circumstances. Yet no explanation of the nation's post–Civil War outward thrust can ignore the role of a tall, balding, intellectual naval captain, Alfred Thayer Mahan.

Mahan's father was an army officer and engineering professor at the military academy at West Point when Alfred was born in 1840. If Alfred's story had been typical, he would have become an army officer himself. But Professor Mahan and his wife did not believe that a military life was desirable for their son and sent him to Columbia College in New York for a conventional education. Alfred, for his own part, had developed a fascination for the sea from his boyhood reading and defied his parents' wishes. In 1856 he convinced his local congressman to appoint him to the United States Naval Academy at Annapolis.

Acting Midshipman Mahan, with two years of college, was ahead of most of his classmates and was therefore given advanced standing at the academy. This advantage alone would have made him unpopular with his classmates, but in addition, Mahan was a reserved young man more interested in reading than in the rough games of the typical Annapolis cadet. He also had a priggish streak. Upperclassmen were expected to report lowerclassmen for infractions of the rules. However, they exempted themselves from the practice. Mahan insisted on treating his fellow seniors like everyone else, and was soon on speaking terms with few of them.

In June 1859 Mahan graduated from the academy and was assigned to the frigate *Congress* for his first long tour of sea duty. His experience on the *Congress* taught him much about ships and navies in the age of sail, knowledge that would be invaluable to him when he undertook his histories of sea power. While on station off the coast of Brazil, the crew of the *Congress* learned of the secession of the southern states and the ship quickly returned home.

Lieutenant Mahan spent most of the next four years on blockade duty off the Confederate coast. Though vital for Union victory, the duty was routine and monotonous. One event of the war stood out for Mahan, however. In December 1864, while serving with Admiral Dahlgren's squadron off Georgia, he was able to present his father's greeting to William Tecumseh Sherman, Professor Mahan's former student at "the Point," when his army reached Savannah after their march to the sea.

The end of the war was followed by the precipitous decline of the U.S. Navy. Appropriations were drastically cut and thousands of officers and men left the service. Ships were neither repaired nor replaced. By 1874, a military publication noted, the navy was "a heterogeneous collection of . . . trash."

During these years of retreat Mahan served aboard a succession of creaky vessels in Europe, the Far East, South America, and other places. In June 1872 he married Ellen Evans of New York. Like all navy wives, Mrs. Mahan was forced to accept her husband's long absences at sea, punctuated by leaves and occasional longer periods of shore duty. She was not happy with the arrangement, but she kept busy raising the Mahan children and serving as hostess when the captain was at home.

In these early postwar years Mahan was opposed to expansion and an aggressive foreign policy. During the 1884 Blaine–Cleveland presidential campaign, he thanked God that the jingoistic Blaine was not president. "If that magnetic statesman were in office, he wrote a friend, "I fancy that American diplomats would be running around in the [ships'] with lighted candles."

But American attitudes toward expansion, including Mahan's, would soon change. In 1885 Admiral Stephen Luce induced the navy to establish the United States Naval War College to help revitalize the service. This would be a sort of graduate school for commissioned naval officers where they would study naval history and tactics. Many old "sea dog" types opposed the scheme, and for its first decade the War College, located in Newport, Rhode Island, was under constant attack. But Luce prevailed and appointed Mahan to his faculty to teach naval tactics.

Mahan took most of a year off to prepare for his new task. During these months he read widely in naval and general history and took extensive notes for his forthcoming lectures. These notes his wife typed up until he had a large volume of 400 pages. The course proved a success. Mahan's own lectures at the War College were supplemented by talks of visiting scholars. One of these was the young civil service commissioner, Theodore Roosevelt, who had written a scholarly history of the naval War of 1812. The Mahan-Roosevelt encounter brought together two men who would become leaders in the new expansionism.

Despite the War College's success, its enemies managed to cut its budget and merge it with the adjacent Torpedo Station. Fortunately the emerging "new navalism" soon rescued both the War College and Mahan. In 1889 Harrison's secretary of the navy, Benjamin Tracy, induced Congress to make the War College a permanent navy installation with a new building for its own use at Newport. The supervisor of construction would be Captain Mahan.

Over the next few years, while Mahan was overseeing this project and giving lectures, he published the book that brought him fame. It was a study of how sea power had governed history during the years when Britain was establishing its overseas empire through its domination of the seas. The Influence of Sea Power upon History, 1660–1783 made an implicit plea not only for a powerful American navy but also for colonies. The road to glory for the United States, Mahan suggested, was the route that Britain had pioneered.

By this time Mahan had become an unabashed expansionist. He had formerly believed, he later noted, that colonies required large standing armies and that these in turn made free government difficult. But his study of Britain's experience had convinced him that great empires were created by navies, not armies, and this was not incompatible with democratic rule. He had also come to believe that the British Empire had benefited the peoples it had governed and ultimately the world. Surely a similar venture by the United States would have similar benevolent results. During the early 1890s, in a succession of articles and letters to newspapers, Mahan endorsed the construction of the new "dreadnought" type battleships, American annexation of Hawaii, the conversion of the Caribbean into an American lake, the construction of an isthmian canal across Panama, and other policies that became vital parts of the expansionist platform.

In 1892 Mahan completed a sequel to his first sea power book. The Influence of Sea Power upon the French Revolution and Empire, which recounted the effect of navies on the momentous events in Europe between 1793 and 1812. This work was even more influential than the first. Widely praised in the United States by the advocates of a bigger navy, it also evoked a strong response elsewhere. The young, headstrong German emperor Wilhelm considered it a masterpiece and had copies in translation placed in German naval libraries. Mahan's ideas helped to inspire the German naval expansion that so frightened and antagonized the British in the closing years of the century.

In 1893, despite the efforts of his many political friends and admirers to keep him ashore where he could pursue his scholarly studies, Captain Mahan was ordered to sea as commander of the cruiser Chicago under Admiral Henry Erban, head of the European station. The three-year tour of duty turned into a personal triumph. Wherever the ship docked, Mahan was feted. In England banquets, attended by members of the royal family, were given in his honor. Erban felt slighted and responded by submitting a negative report on his chief subordinate. The captain, he declared, was not interested in "ship life or matters," and he was "therefore not a good officer." Mahan protested against this evaluation, but in truth it was accurate.

The European tour was Mahan's last sea duty. He returned to the United States in 1895, and the following year retired from the navy to devote the remainder of his life to scholarship. In 1898 he returned to active duty for a short while to head the strategy board supervising naval operations in the war against Spain. The board actually had little influence on the course of events that led to the great American naval victories in the Philippines and off Cuba, but Mahan could take satisfaction in his part in the naval revival that had provided the country with the modern vessels that made the victories of Dewey and Sampson possible. In the debate over the peace Mahan was also an influential voice on the side of those who wanted to keep what America had seized from Spain.

Mahan spent his last years in New York City. He continued to lecture at the Newport War College and to write. In 1902 he was elected president of the American Historical Association, the historical guild's highest honor. Four years later, though on the retired list, he was promoted to the rank of rear admiral. In 1914 Mahan was induced by J. Franklin Jameson, a noted historian, to come to the Carnegie Institution of Washington as scholar-in-residence. This last chapter in his life did not last long. Mahan had been ill with a weak heart for some time, and on December 1, at the Washington naval hospital, he died.

The tributes and assessments quickly poured in. His friend, former president Theodore Roosevelt, called him "one of the greatest and most useful influences on American life." A foreign newspaper labeled him "the greatest naval historian of the nineteenth century." But the most pithy, and in some ways the most accurate, evaluation was one by a small-town paper: "The super-dreadnoughts are his children, and the roar of the 16" guns are but the echoes of his voice."

important, they did not directly affect foreign policy decision making. Closer to that process was what one scholar has called "the foreign policy elite." These were people scattered across the nation, who were seriously concerned with what went on in the world. Strategically located in government, journalism, the universities, the professions, and business, they influenced public opinion, Congress, and the State Department out of proportion to their numbers. Their concerns were not primarily economic but grew out of their cosmopolitanism and their interest in world affairs.

Many members of this elite were admirers of imperialist France or England, and French or English policies shaped their attitudes toward American foreign policy. To many it seemed a shame that the United States, as strong as any of the great European colonial powers, had so far held back. America's restraint, they said, had encouraged Europe to consider it unimportant in international affairs outside the Western Hemisphere. Few European countries, they noted, assigned ambassadors to Washington, being content with ministers or lesser diplomatic representatives. To the foreign policy elite, a colonial empire promised to end this inferiority and propel the United States into the ranks of the world powers, where it belonged.

Hawaii and Venezuela

Toward the end of the 1880s, then, expansionist sentiment and national assertiveness began to reemerge. Early in the 1890s the phrase "Manifest Destiny" began to appear once more in political platforms; in 1893 Congress created the rank of ambassador to replace that of minister. Yet for some years Americans' interest in overseas matters would continue to vacillate as the experience with Hawaii illustrates.

Ambivalence About Expansion. The strategic value of the Hawaiian Islands had been recognized ever since their discovery by Captain James Cook in 1778, and Americans had been active there for many years. In the early nineteenth century American merchant ships en route to China often stopped at the beautiful islands for fresh water and supplies. In 1820 the first American missionaries arrived and devoted themselves to bringing their Christian faith to the native Polynesian peoples. Whalers soon came to the island kingdom, and the whaling crews, long without women, helped to undo the missionaries' efforts to improve Hawaiian morals.

The sons of the missionaries, along with other American settlers attracted to the islands, made sugar growing rather than soul saving their chief concern and eventually came to own much of the land. The strong American presence and the strategic location of the island chain inevitably aroused the interest of the United States government. Seward soon added the annexation of Hawaii to his other ambitious schemes. But few Americans were interested and nothing was done. Then, in 1875, the United States agreed to allow Hawaiian sugar, unlike that from other foreign lands, to enter the United States duty free. As a result, the islands' sugar plantations expanded and their economy soon became dependent on the profitable American market. The Hawaiian government, meanwhile, came under the influence of the American planters and businessmen who had brought prosperity to the kingdom. In 1887 the United States renewed the sugar agreement and received the right to use Pearl Harbor as a naval base.

Suddenly the rosy Hawaiian economic situation changed. The McKinley Tariff of 1890 removed the duty on all sugar entering the United States, thus ending Hawaii's advantage over its competitors in the American market. The islands' economic boom collapsed. Almost simultaneously Queen Liliuokalani succeeded her brother to the Hawaiian throne, determined to restore much of the royal power he had surrendered to American advisers. The new queen was violently anti-American. Adopting the battle cry "Hawaii for the Hawaiians," she launched a campaign to end all foreign influence in her kingdom. In 1893 she proclaimed a new constitution that disfranchised all white men, except those married to native Hawaiian women, and gave the queen dictatorial powers.

The Americans in Hawaii now had both political and economic reasons for seeking annexation to their mother country. They promptly organized a "Committee of Safety," staged a coup d'etat, and established a provisional government with themselves in control. To intimidate Queen Liliuokalani, the American minister to Hawaii, John L. Stevens, on the pretext of protecting American property, stationed marines from the cruiser U.S.S. *Boston* outside the queen's palace.

Unable to counter this show of force, the queen abdicated. Stevens then proclaimed the islands an American protectorate and triumphantly wrote the State Department: "The Hawaiian pear is now fully ripe and this is the golden hour for the United States to pluck it." The provisional government soon applied for annexation to the United States, as Texas had sixty years before under similar circumstances.

Less than a month after the queen's overthrow, President Harrison signed an annexation treaty with representatives of the rebel government. Unfortunately for the annexationists, Grover Cleveland succeeded to the presidency before the Senate could act on the treaty. The new president—upright, principled, conscientious—was a figure from the nonexpansionist past. Reluctant to involve the country in a new policy of acquisition, he was also skeptical of the morality of the takeover by the American residents. Accordingly, he withdrew the treaty from the Senate and sent James H. Blount as his personal representative to the islands to investigate the circumstances of the queen's downfall.

Annexationists attacked Cleveland's scrupulous actions. A New York newspaper accused him of turning

Queen Lilivokalani was actually less benevolent than this picture suggests.

back "the hands of the dial of civilization." But when the Blount report arrived in Washington, it confirmed Cleveland's worst suspicions. Blount chastised Stevens for interfering in Hawaii's internal affairs and declared that a large majority of the native Hawaiian voters opposed annexation. Cleveland now determined to restore the queen to her throne. But when she declared her intention to decapitate the revolutionaries as soon as she could, he withdrew his support, allowed the Americans to remain in power, and recognized the provisional government as the Republic of Hawaii. Until its annexation to the United States in 1898, Hawaii remained an independent republic controlled by its American residents.

The Monroe Doctrine Reasserted. The Hawaiian affair points up the unassertive side of American public opinion and the cautious side of American foreign policy. But the jingoist, aggressive side soon took hold under the impact of depression, fears about the closing of the frontier, and the influence of Mahan, Strong, and the social Darwinists.

This more combative attitude was displayed in the Venezuela incident of 1895. Independent Venezuela and the English colony of British Guiana, both on the Caribbean northern shore of South America, had long disputed their common boundary. From the beginning of this controversy, the Venezuelans had sought American support and had taken pains to depict the British as callous aggressors against a weaker nation.

Matters came to a head in 1894 when the British government refused President Cleveland's offer to arbitrate the dispute. The American State Department had become suspicious that British machinations in Central America and French intrigue in Brazil showed renewed European interest in Latin American colonies. The Royal Navy had recently landed troops in Nicaragua and extracted $360,000 from its government on the pretext that the British consul had been insulted. The incident, made doubly offensive to Americans by the British admiral's remark that the Monroe Doctrine was a myth, had set off a strong anti-British response in the American press. The American government's anxiety was further increased by the realization that if the British won the boundary dispute with Venezuela, they would control the mouth of the Orinoco and gain commercial priority in the large area of the continent drained by that river. Britain's refusal to accept American good offices to settle the dispute only confirmed anti-British prejudices.

Not surprisingly, the United States sided with Venezuela. Early in 1895 Congress passed a resolution

Though Cleveland moved cautiously on the Hawaiian matter, he and Olney did not consult Venezuela before intervening in its border dispute with England. The cartoon is obviously an American view; a heroic Uncle Sam is defending the "poor" Latin Americans against attack by aggressive European powers.

denouncing British claims in Venezuela. Secretary of State Richard Olney backed the resolution in a strong letter to the American minister in London. Brusque and aggressive in Olney's usual manner, the note insisted that America's interest in the dispute was legitimate under the Monroe Doctrine. After defending the right of the United States to guarantee the independence of Latin American republics, the secretary launched into a blunt declaration of American power that startled the British. "Its infinite resources," he boasted, "combined with its isolated position render [the United States] the master of the situation and practically invulnerable against any or all other powers." Olney concluded by demanding that the issue be submitted to arbitration and that Britain respond before Congress met later in the year.

The British prime minister, Lord Salisbury, denied the applicability of the Monroe Doctrine and, offended by Olney's tone, rejected the call for arbitration with a brusqueness almost equal to Olney's. President Cleveland replied that if Britain refused arbitra-

tion, the United States would impose a boundary line and defend it militarily if necessary. Amid a wave of anti-British enthusiasm throughout the United States and Latin America, Congress approved Cleveland's plan and quickly appropriated $100,000 for a boundary commission. Anglophobes and jingoes eagerly anticipated war with Great Britain.

Fortunately for world peace, sober second thoughts soon took hold on both sides of the Atlantic. By now Britain had begun to fear an aggressive German empire that was challenging British and naval supremacy and had recently sided against the British in their dispute with the Boer settlers in South Africa. Rather than take on both the United States and Germany, Lord Salisbury chose to conciliate Washington. In the United States, once the initial excitement had passed, a peace faction composed of clergy, business leaders, financiers, and journalists prevailed. Britain and Venezuela eventually agreed to accept arbitration; but by the time a decision was handed down in 1899, the whole dispute had been virtually forgotten.

Cuba Libre

The second Cleveland administration (1893–1897) was a time of transition between an isolationist and a more expansionist attitude toward the rest of the world. The issue that triggered the shift in outlook was Cuba.

That rich island, as well as Puerto Rico, had remained under Spanish control long after the rest of Spain's once-great empire in the New World had disintegrated. The Cubans, however, were not satisfied to accept subordination to a declining European power. In 1868 they began a ten-year uprising to gain independence. Cuban rebels, some of them naturalized American citizens, appealed to the United States for help. But despite a number of minor diplomatic brushes with Spain, the United States refused to be drawn in, and the revolt eventually subsided.

Revolution in Cuba. For seventeen years the Cuban revolutionary spirit remained dormant. Then, in the early 1890s, harsh Spanish rule, its effects amplified by a severe crisis in the Cuban sugar industry, goaded the Cubans to revolt once again. This time the insurrectionists not only attacked Spanish soldiers and officials but also set fire to sugar plantations and cattle ranches, hoping that Spain would capitulate if nothing of value was left on the island. Cuban patriots living in the United States organized groups called "juntas" to aid the rebels and provoke trouble between Spain and the United States.

Spanish authorities under General Valeriano Weyler ("The Butcher") rounded up thousands of suspected rebels and sympathizers, including women and children, and confined them in concentration camps. Despite his reputation, Weyler did not intend mass murder, but unsanitary conditions and rebel interference with the food-supply systems made the concentration areas death camps. According to the American consul-general in Havana:

> Four hundred thousand self-supporting people, principally women and children [have been] transformed . . . into a multitude to be sustained by the contributions of others, or die of starvation, or of fevers resulting from low physical condition . . . without change of clothing and without food. Their homes were burned, their fields and plant beds destroyed and their livestock driven away or killed.

American Sympathies. As in all revolutions and civil wars, both sides were brutal and destructive, yet almost without exception the American people condemned Spain and supported the Cuban rebels. It used to be said that our sympathies were determined by our economic interests in the island. But there is little evidence to support this assertion.

Actually, most American business interests were opposed to political involvement in Cuba. With the depression of 1893–1897 just coming to an end, war was the last thing the business community wanted. Today we tend to see war as an economic stimulus, but in the late 1890s it seemed more likely to produce a financial panic and another depression. As relations with Spain worsened, the business press attacked any drastic action that would "impede the march of prosperity and put the country back many years."

Some farm spokespersons and part of the agricultural press did take a strong prointerventionist stand, but that they did so for economic reasons is doubtful. Even if farmers yearned for expanded overseas markets and generally favored an aggressive foreign policy, it is difficult to see what advantages they would have derived from war. Working people usually shared the views of their employers: A war with Spain would hurt business and therefore labor.

And yet by April 1898 most Americans—farmers, business people, wage earners, and others—favored intervening in Cuba despite the risk of war with Spain. Why? Clearly Americans were outraged at Spanish cruelty and sympathized with the Cuban underdogs. These feelings were reinforced by America's own anticolonialist past: The Cuban people seemed to be fighting the same battle for freedom that Americans had fought 120 years before.

But natural sympathies were not enough. During the nineteenth century Americans sympathized with virtually every foreign group they perceived as persecuted and with every anticolonial movement. Yet the United States had managed to avoid going to war against the oppressors. Fortunately for the Cuban rebels, American sympathies for them were strongly amplified by the activities of the "yellow press," especially William Randolph Hearst's *New York Journal* and Joseph Pulitzer's *New York World*. During the late 1890s the two press lords fought a bitter war in which truth took a back seat to circulation. Each sought to provide a daily diet of atrocity stories detailing Spanish brutality, for that sold papers. Both were unscrupulous, though Hearst was probably even less principled than his rival. According to one story, when an American artist sent to Cuba to illustrate the insurrection reported that things were quiet, Hearst shot back: "You furnish the pictures and I'll furnish the war."

An apostle of national prosperity, President McKinley was more interested in the country's recovery from the 1893 depression than in challenging Spain in Cuba. Here he is trying to keep the jingoes from killing the golden goose.

War Becomes Unavoidable.

Yet war seemed only a remote possibility when William McKinley was inaugurated in March 1897. The new president shared the business community's reluctance to jeopardize returning prosperity and declared in his inaugural address that war must be avoided "until every agency of peace has failed; peace is preferable to war in almost every contingency." But McKinley could not control events. Ordinary public opinion was running against him, and the foreign policy elite considered his course cowardly and unworthy. The young New Yorker Theodore Roosevelt, for one, believed McKinley was as spineless "as a chocolate éclair." Early in 1898 a key group of congressional Republicans agreed to push the president for a war resolution, promising to join with the Democrats and sponsor one themselves if he did not yield. The religious press, viewing the issue in Cuba as a fight betwen Cuban virtue and Spanish beastliness, also demanded that the American government intervene to end the atrocious situation.

The Spaniards seemed to be their own worst enemies during this period. In January 1898 the Spanish minister to the United States, Enrique Dupuy de Lôme, a well-meaning but indiscreet gentleman, wrote an imprudent letter to a friend in Cuba expressing his contempt for McKinley and admitting that Spain was negotiating in bad faith over a proposed trade treaty with America. A Cuban patriot stole the letter from the desk of the recipient in Havana and sent it to Hearst, who promptly published it in his newspapers. The outraged public demanded that de Lôme be sent home. The minister instantly resigned in hope of mending

the situation, but the damage was done. The American people now had even more reason than before to picture the Spaniards as arrogant and deceitful.

De Lôme's blunder was soon followed by an even bigger blow to Spanish-American relations. In

Shown is William Randolph Hearst, the young newspaper publisher who helped propel the United States into war in 1898.

January 1898 the American government sent the battleship *Maine* to Havana. The visit was officially "friendly"; the ship was only there to protect American lives and property following a serious local riot. The captain and the crew of the vessel were treated courteously by Spanish officials in Havana, though the visit naturally aroused some suspicion. Then, on February 15, a tremendous explosion rocked the ship, sending it to the bottom of the harbor with the loss of over 260 lives.

No one has ever solved the mystery of the *Maine*'s destruction. Spanish authorities disclaimed responsibility for the sinking. When American divers examined the hull of the ship, they concluded that the explosion had come from outside and could not be the result of a burst boiler, as the authorities in Havana implied. But neither they, nor anyone else, could determine who had done it.

Regardless of who or what sank the ship, most Americans considered it an act of war. Agreeing with Theodore Roosevelt's theory that the *Maine* had been "sunk by an act of dirty treachery on the part of the Spaniards," they demanded immediate retaliation. Jingoes had a field day. Mass rallies were held all over the country at news of the atrocity. People marched through the streets, chanting, "Remember the *Maine*. To Hell with Spain!" The yellow press, of course, insisted that Spain be punished with all the force of America's might.

McKinley could not resist the growing pressure to intervene. He promptly instructed the American minister in Madrid to demand that the Spanish government grant an armistice to the rebels and end the cruel concentration camp policy. Spain would have until October to accept these terms. If it did not, the United States would impose a settlement. The Spanish government was caught in a dilemma. To bow to the American ultimatum would antagonize many of its own citizens; if it refused to give in, it would certainly find itself at war with the United States. For a while it wavered,

A contemporary artist's horrific vision of what the destruction of the battleship *Maine* looked like.

but finally, on the advice of the pope, it agreed to grant an armistice and abolish the concentration camps.

Spain had given the United States virtually everything it had asked for, but it was not enough to avoid war. American opinion now would not be satisfied with anything less than an independent Cuba—"Cuba Libre." The president was still reluctant to intervene, but he, too, was caught in a dilemma. In Congress the pressure to declare war was becoming irresistible; even if he did not request a declaration of war, there were signs that Congress would go ahead without him. Moreover, if he held back, the Democrats would charge him with weakness and jeopardize his chances of winning reelection in 1900.

On April 11 McKinley sent a war message to Congress. The United States, he said, must protect the lives and property of American citizens and put an end to the "barbarities, bloodshed, starvation, and horrible miseries . . . right at [its] door." Intervention was justified, the president claimed, by the "very serious injury to commerce, trade, and business of our people, and by the wanton destruction of property and devastation of the island." In addition, it was of "utmost importance" to end a disturbance which was a "constant menace to our peace and entails upon this Government an enormous expense."

Considering the intensity of the war fever, Con-

gress acted surprisingly slowly. On April 19 it passed four resolutions defining the nation's war policy. They were: (1) that Cuba must be free; (2) that Spain must withdraw from the island; (3) that the president could use the armed forces to obtain these ends; and (4) that the United States would not annex Cuba. The commitment to nonannexation—the Teller Amendment—was approved without a dissenting vote. On April 25, 1898, Congress formally declared war on Spain.

The Spanish–American War

The war with Spain was short and cheap. Few American lives were lost; more soldiers died at Custer's Last Stand than from battle wounds in the entire Spanish-American conflict. Moreover, the war was over in a few months and peace concluded by December 1898. As wars go, this one was also a financial bargain: It cost the United States only $250 million. John Hay, the American secretary of state, called it a "splendid little war," and from the point of view of most Americans, the successes of their country's armed forces, particularly the navy, were splendid indeed.

Quick Victory. As assistant secretary of the navy, Theodore Roosevelt had anticipated war with Spain

The Spanish American War in the Caribbean

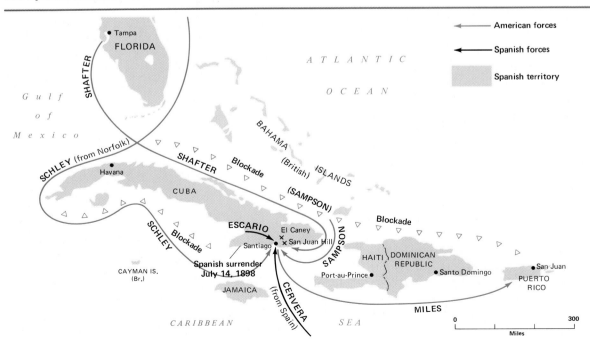

Dismounted black cavalry supporting the Rough Riders at the Battle of Qarimas near Santiago, Chile.

and prepared to attack Spain in the most exposed parts of its scattered empire. Acting in the absence of his superior, he had dispatched Commodore George Dewey and the Asiatic squadron to China even before McKinley delivered his war message. When Congress declared war, Dewey immediately sailed for the Philippines, a Spanish possession in the China Sea. Commanding six modern vessels of the new fleet, Dewey attacked and sank the whole Spanish Asiatic squadron in Manila Bay without losing a ship and hardly a man. The navy soon repeated Dewey's Pacific triumph in the Caribbean. In July the main United States naval detachment in Cuban waters smashed the Spanish squadron in a brief battle off Santiago. Again, American losses were minimal: one killed, one wounded.

The army's performance was considerably less impressive. For years its main job had been to contain and control the Indians in the West, and it was a comparatively small force. When war came, the War Department had to recruit and train a large number of volunteers, including Roosevelt's band of western cowboys and eastern gentlemen who enlisted as the "Rough Riders." Secretary of War Russell A.

Alger botched the job of organizing and supplying the new recruits. Amid incredible confusion, 17,000 ill-equipped soldiers were embarked from Tampa, Florida, and landed near Santiago in southeastern Cuba. After several sharp skirmishes, including the rough Riders' famous charge up San Juan Hill, the Americans captured the heights overlooking the city. On July 17, following the Spanish naval defeat, the Spanish military commander surrendered his troops. Soon afterward the American army occupied Puerto Rico without opposition.

The Spoils of War. By the end of July the Spanish government was ready to sue for peace. Delegates from the United States and Spain met in Paris in October to work out final details. Spain had already agreed to give Cuba its independence and to cede Puerto Rico and the Pacific island of Guam to the United States. The issue that blocked quick agreement was the fate of the Philippines. Although Dewey had sunk the Spanish Asiatic fleet and demolished Spanish power in the islands, he lacked troops and waited offshore for reinforcements before occupying Manila, the capital city.

Meanwhile, Britain and Germany assembled naval squadrons nearby, ostensibly to protect the interests of their citizens in the Philippines but actually to claim the islands if the United States proved indifferent.

Before the war few Americans had been interested in the Philippines; few even knew where they were. Now, suddenly, they found themselves up to their ears in international complications over these exotic islands. What should they do with them? Particularly disturbing were the designs of Germany. Since its unification twenty years before, it had become an aggressive colonial power, rummaging around for new territories all over the world. This lust had seldom disturbed Americans before, but the Philippines were a different matter. The United States had fought for the islands; the Germans had expended nothing for them. Why allow them to fall into undeserving hands?

Moral and practical considerations also encouraged the United States to hold on to the islands. Whatever the business community felt at the war's start, it was now convinced that the Philippines would be a useful base for establishing closer trade relations with China. In July 1898, moved by a new, war-generated expansionist fever, Congress had finally annexed Hawaii. Add the Philippines and the United States would have a convenient set of steppingstones across the Pacific to the Asian mainland. As Senator Henry Cabot Lodge noted, controlling the port of Manila would be "the thing which will give us the eastern trade." Many Americans also believed it would be inconsistent and irresponsible to have fought to free Cuba from Spanish tyranny and ignore the similar plight of the Filipinos. Besides, what a field for missionary effort the islands promised to be! Ignoring the fact that most Filipinos were already Catholics, McKinley found this opportunity to advance Christian civilization a compelling reason to hold on to the islands. He had been troubled by the fate of the Philippines and its people, he later told a church group, until in answer to his prayers for divine guidance he had suddenly seen what must be done:

> We could not give them back to Spain—that would be cowardly and dishonorable. . . . There was nothing left for us to do but take them all and to educate the Filipinos, and uplift and civilize them and Christianize them, and by God's grace do the very best by them, as our fellowmen for whom Christ also died.

After reaching this inspired and practical conclusion, McKinley told the American negotiators in Paris to insist that the whole island chain be given to the United States. Spain resisted at first, but in exchange for $20 million it surrendered the Phillippines, along with Puerto Rico and Guam, and at the same time confirmed Cuban independence.

The Anti-Imperialists. The Treaty of Paris, especially the provision ceding the Philippines, set off a storm of protest in the United States. Although the war had shifted American public opinion as a whole in the direction of imperialism, there were still many opponents of expansion. Mugwump reformers, who had fought for civil service and sound money during the 1880s, along with many intellectuals and clergymen, believed that colonies were immoral and expensive. America, these anti-imperialists were certain, would be denying its finest ideals and traditions if it continued

This 1899 German cartoon makes fun of a hypocritical Uncle Sam. Protesting against imperialism, he erects a diplomatic skyscraper that dwarfs the works of other western nations. The title means "either Caesar or Nothing!"

Anti-Imperialism

America's outward thrust during the last years of the nineteenth century did not go unchallenged at home. A sizable portion of the American people saw it as a violation of the country's most precious traditions and a dangerous precedent. In June 1898, people of this persuasion met in Chicago and formed the Anti-Imperialist League to fight what they considered the jingoism and aggressiveness of the expansionists. The following is the core of the Anti-Imperialist League platform adopted at the League's October 1899 Chicago convention.

"We hold that the policy known as imperialism is hostile to liberty and tends toward militarism, an evil from which it has been our glory to be free. We regret that it has become necessary in the land of Washington and Lincoln to reaffirm that all men, of whatever race or color, are entitled to life, liberty, and the pursuit of happiness. We maintain that governments derive their just powers from the consent of the governed. We insist that the subjugation of any people is 'criminal aggression' and open disloyalty to the distinctive principles of our Government. . . .

"The United States have always protested against the doctrine of international law which permits the sugjugation of the weak by the strong. A self-governing state cannot accept sovereignty over an unwilling people. The United States cannot act on the ancient heresy that might makes right.

"Imperialists assume that with the destruction of self-government in the Philippines by American hands, all opposition there will cease. This is a grievous error. Much as we abhor the war of 'criminal aggression' in the Philippines, greatly as we regret that the blood of Filipinos is on American hands, we more deeply resent the betrayal of American institutions at home. The real firing line is not the suburbs of Manila. The foe is of our own household. The attempt of 1861 was to divide the country. That of 1899 is to destroy its fundamental principles and noblest ideals. . . .

"We propose to contribute to the defeat of any person or party that stands for the forcible subjugation of any people. We shall oppose for reelection all who in the White House or in Congress betray American liberty in pursuit of un-American gains. . . .

"We hold, with Abraham Lincoln, that 'no man is good enough to govern another man without that man's consent. When the white man governs himself, that is self-government, but when he governs himself and also governs another man, that is more than self-government—that is despotism. . . . Those who deny freedom to others deserve it not for themselves, and under a just God cannot long retain it.'

"We cordially invite the consideration of all men and women who remain loyal to the Declaration of Independence and the Constitution of the United States."

the quest for colonies. "America had something better to offer mankind," lamented Professor Charles Eliot Norton of Harvard. "These aims she is now pursuing . . . [are a] desertion of ideals which were not selfish or limited in their application but which are of universal worth and validity." By searching for colonies, America had "lost her unique position as a potential leader in the progress of civilization" and had "taken her place simply as one of the grasping and selfish nations of the present day." Other anti-imperialists were more angry than sad about the nation's desertion of its ideals. "God damn the United States for its vile conduct in the Philippine Isles," wrote the philosopher William James. If the United States made the islands a colony, it would leave the Filipinos with nothing: we could "destroy their own ideals," he declared, "but we can't give them ours."

Not all anti-imperialists were idealistic, however, Carl Schurz, for instance, feared that racial problems would overwhelm the United States if it incorporated the Philippines and parts of the Caribbean into its domain. Could the nation, he asked, absorb "immense territories inhabited by white people of Spanish descent, by Indians, by negroes, mixed Spanish and Indians, mixed Spanish and negroes, Hawaiians, Hawaiian mixed blood, Spanish Philippinos, Malays, Tagals?" These people were "savages and half-savages": they were all "animated with the instinct, impulses and passions bred by the tropical sun." "What will become of American labor and the standards of American citizenship?"

The most active opponents of colonialism banded together to form the Anti-Imperialist League, which tried to prevent American negotiators from signing the Treaty of Paris. When this effort failed, the league turned its attention to the Senate, where the fight for ratification promised to be long and bitter. In the course of a few months it mailed thousands of propaganda pieces denouncing colonialism and badgered senators and other politicians to stop the treaty.

Ratification of the Treaty of Paris. In the end the anti-imperialists failed. Despite misgivings, most Americans favored the treaty and the new American policy it implied. The decision in the Senate, however, was certain to be very close, because the treaty's opponents needed only one vote more than a third of the upper chamber to defeat it. Under a barrage of cajolery, persuasion, and pressure from McKinley and other administration leaders, almost all Senate Republicans pledged to support the treaty. But Democratic votes, too, were needed for passage.

William Jennings Bryan seemed to hold the key to success. Though defeated in 1896 and now a private citizen, he continued to exert great influence among fellow Democrats. Bryan was not an imperialist, but he threw his support behind the treaty, believing that ending the war was more important than the details of the settlement. He naively assumed the United States would give the Philippines its freedom almost immediately. Enough Democrats went along with Bryan to carry the treaty 57 to 27, just one vote more than needed for ratification.

Imperial America

The Treaty of Paris did not end the controversy over expansionism. Bryan still opposed overseas colonies and hoped to make the election of 1900 a referendum favoring return to the country's old, nonimperial ways. But American presidential elections seldom revolve about a single issue. In the end, the election of 1900 turned on silver, reform, prosperity, and the achievements of the first McKinley administration. Bryan's resounding defeat revealed little of what the American

The United States in the Pacific, ca. 1900

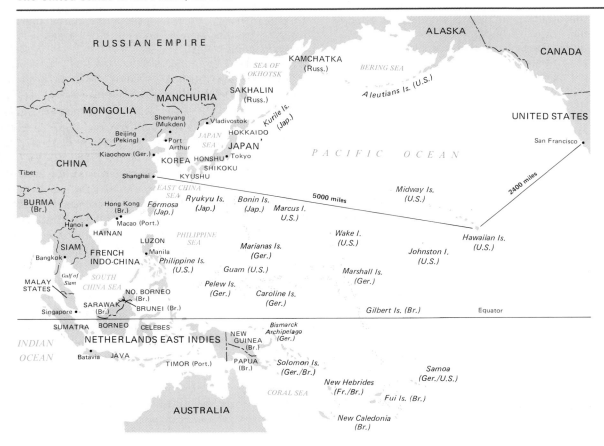

The American Navy, built during the 1880s and 1890s, destroying the Spanish fleet at Manila Bay during the Spanish-American War.

public felt about overseas expansion: Even the anti-imperialists split their votes between the two candidates.

Meanwhile, events in the Philippines were demonstrating the dangers and costs of America's new imperial course. Two days before ratification of the Spanish treaty, full-scale fighting broke out between the Filipinos, led by Emilio Aguinaldo, and the American forces attempting to establish American sovereignty on the islands. Eventually the United States was forced to fight a full-scale colonial war to put down the Filipino patriots. Not until mid-1902 were the 70,000 army regulars able to capture Aguinaldo and pacify the islands. The Philippines Insurrection was America's first land war in Asia, and like Vietnam in the 1960s, it was marked by savage atrocities on both sides.

In the years following 1902 the United States sought to make amends in the Philippines by introducing land reform, establishing local self-government, and improving educational facilities. In 1902 Congress created a Philippine legislative assembly, though the governor of the islands remained an American. But the ugly war experience was a disturbing one and made Americans all the more uneasy in the role of colonial power.

During the next twenty years the nation vacillated between its liberal and its imperial tendencies. In 1900, under the Foraker Act, Congress authorized limited self-government for Puerto Rico. By the Platt Amend-

ment to the Army Appropriation Bill of 1901, it directed the president to withdraw American forces from Cuba. Yet Cuba was not to be truly free. According to the Platt Amendment, it could not enter into any treaty that would impair its sovereignty, nor could it contract debts beyond its capacity to pay. Also, the United States might intervene in the island's internal affairs to maintain law and order. Until the outbreak of World War I the United States continued to waver, sometimes aggressively seeking overseas advantages, sometimes appearing indifferent to them, and at other times supporting weak nations against greedy European powers.

Relations with Latin America. The United States' attitude toward its closest neighbors in Latin America during these years was that of a strict older brother: It would protect them against outsiders, but they must behave or face American wrath. This policy worried and offended Latin Americans; Yankees considered it necessary for their peace of mind. The United States was the only great power in the Western Hemisphere, and Americans found this situation comfortable. Any hint that a European country was trying to extend its influence into the Western Hemisphere set off immediate alarm bells in Washington.

Sometimes this proprietary attitude operated to the advantage of America's smaller neighbors. Without United States protection, a number of the weaker Latin American states would almost certainly have fallen

The biggest engineering problems faced by the Panama Canal builders were the "cuts," the deep gorges that had to be sliced through the ridges across the Isthmus. This is a view of the difficult Culebra Cut.

again into the hands of one or another of the great European powers. Yet Latin America undoubtedly paid a high price for this protection. The United States insisted that its strategic, political, and economic interests came first, and often demonstrated this attitude in ways that left a legacy of resentment.

A characteristic instance of American highhandedness occurred in 1903. During the recent conflict with Spain the U.S.S. *Oregon* had taken many weeks to sail from Puget Sound around Cape Horn to come to the defense of the exposed and anxious East Coast. The ship's slow progress had underscored the advantages of the canal across the isthmus connecting North and South America. With the war over and America the uneasy owner of a new Pacific empire, a canal seemed even more vital.

Two obstacles blocked the way. The Clayton-Bulwer Treaty, signed with Great Britain in 1850, had denied the United States exclusive control over an isthmian canal. This hurdle was overcome by the 1901 Hay-Pauncefote Treaty with Britain, which gave sole right to the United States to build, control, and fortify a Central American waterway. Location was the second problem. Two routes were possible: one through Nicaragua and one at Panama. A factor favoring Panama was the enormous labor already expended by the

French, who, under the leadership of Ferdinand de Lesseps, builder of the Suez Canal, had been hacking and digging their way unsuccessfully through the fever-ridden jungles and mountains of the isthmus since the 1880s. When the French offered to sell their rights and equipment for $40 million, Congress accepted.

But another difficulty now loomed. Panama was part of Colombia. Before construction could begin, Colombia would have to agree to the arrangement. In January 1903 the United States concluded a treaty with Tomás Herrán, the Colombian minister in Washington, giving the South American republic a one-time $10 million payment and $250,000 annually for the rights to build the canal and to lease a canal zone six miles wide along the right-of-way for ninety-nine years. When the treaty reached the Colombian Senate, however, it was defeated. The Colombians had two major objections: The treaty gave the Americans too much power over a portion of their territory, and they saw no reason why they should not receive the $40 million that was promised to the French canal firm.

President Theodore Roosevelt considered the Colombians' action abominable. These people, he shouted, were "jack rabbits" and "contemptible little creatures." They were "imperiling their own future," and the United States might have to teach them a lesson for their own good. Equally upset were the agents of the French canal company, who saw the promised $40 million escaping their grasp, and those residents of Panama who looked forward to the prosperity that the canal would bring and feared that it would now be built in Nicaragua.

In the end, the French agents, the Panamanians, and Theodore Roosevelt combined to secure a Panama route. Although they had revolted against Colombia in the past, the Panamanians had never succeeded in gaining their independence. Now, encouraged and financed by the French canal company, they rose once again. Fortunately for the insurgents, the U.S.S. *Nashville*, an American warship, had conveniently arrived just a day before the revolt broke out and was docked at Colón on Panama's Caribbean coast. Inspired by this scarcely disguised support, the rebels quickly overcame the feeble Colombian military forces and in a matter of hours proclaimed an independent Panamanian republic. To no one's surprise, Roosevelt immediately concluded an accord with the new government. For the same financial terms offered Colombia, the United States was granted the right to build a canal through a ten-mile-wide zone where it would exercise "all the rights, power, and authority" it would possess "if it were the sovereign of the territory."

With the political details out of the way, work on the gigantic project began. Using mammoth steam shovels and thousands of black laborers drawn from the Caribbean islands, as well as better-paid whites from the United States, American engineers dug, blasted, and chopped their way across the isthmus. Hundreds of lives were lost to yellow fever until Colonel William C. Gorgas wiped out the mosquito-breeding places at Colón and Panama City and eliminated the disease from the isthmus. On August 15, 1914, the interocean canal connecting the Atlantic and Pacific, the dream of three centuries, was formally opened to world shipping.

Roosevelt also acted aggressively elsewhere in Latin America. Many of the smaller Latin American countries, he felt, had acted irresponsibly and thereby had endangered the safety of the hemisphere. Debt default and political chaos in the weaker countries were inviting European nations to intervene to protect their citizens and their investments. By American reasoning, if the Caribbean and Central American republics expected the United States to defend them against the European powers—as indeed they did—they could not expect their protector to ignore their misdeeds. In 1904, when several European nations threatened to blockade the Dominican Republic until it paid its debts, Roosevelt decided to lay down the law. In his "corollary" to the Monroe Doctrine, he announced that "chronic wrongdoing" by Latin American countries or political "impotence" that resulted in serious disorder might force the United States to "exercise . . . police power, and compel it to intervene in the offending nation's internal affairs." While the Roosevelt Corollary prevented takeovers by European nations, it also gave the United States an excuse to intrude at will into Latin American affairs.

The Open Door in China. The United States often took advantage of its power to overawe its weaker hemispheric neighbors, but its role in the Far East was, on the whole, more benign. After acquiring Hawaii and the Philippines, the nation eagerly awaited the opening of the supposedly vast China market. It never materialized: The Chinese people had neither the wealth nor the tastes for America's major exports.

Americans had long been fascinated with China, both as a land of mystery and as a vast potential market for American products. This elaborate display of Chinese splendor drew huge crowds at the St. Louis Exposition in 1904.

Nevertheless, Americans remained hopeful and were anxious to prevent China from being carved up by Japan and the major European powers into exclusive "spheres of influence" where others could not trade.

But American interest in China went beyond trade. Americans were fascinated by China's ancient civilization, art, and customs. They also considered the Celestial Empire a promising field for missionary effort. The first American missionaries had arrived in China before the Civil War, bringing Western science and learning along with Protestant Christianity. However contemptuous they were of Chinese "heathenism," the missionaries deeply sympathized with the long-suffering Chinese people and conveyed their compassionate feelings to pious churchgoers at home. By the end of the nineteenth century millions of Americans—notwithstanding considerable hostility to those Chinese living in the United States—considered China an arena for benevolence, not one for crass economic and political exploitation.

For many years American policy toward China was marked by this combination of self-interest and compassion. After China's defeat by Japan during the First Sino-Japanese War (1894–1895), the great powers renewed their demands for political and economic concessions. The United States, which had no designs on Chinese territory, feared that the Western nations would completely carve up the decaying empire, destroying Chinese sovereignty while excluding the United States commercially. Encouraged by the British, Secretary of State John Hay in 1899 sent notes to the major colonial powers asking for assurances that they would not demand special trading privileges in China. Most gave Hay evasive answers, but he chose to interpret these as acceptance of his "open door" principle, which rejected exclusive "spheres of influence" and held that all nations must be free to trade throughout China. In 1900, following suppression of the antiforeign Boxers by an international army, the United States converted the principle of economic parity to one of defending the Chinese nation against European annexation. In a circular letter of July 1900 Hay declared that it was "the policy of the United States government" to "bring about . . . peace to China" and to "preserve Chinese territorial and administrative entity. . . ."

The Open Door policy was a perfect mirror of American ambivalence. Unprepared by its history and traditions to take up the burdens and responsibilities of blatant colonialism, the United States sought to protect its share of the Chinese market in some less costly way than political control. At the same time, Americans

sincerely sympathized with the Chinese people and sought to preserve Chinese sovereignty. But whatever the motives, the concern of the United States for an independent China would serve on more than one occasion to keep it from being dismembered by the European colonial powers and Japan.

Conclusions

Many elements contributed to the outward thrust of the post–Civil War generation. The impulse that had carried the American people 3,000 miles across the North American continent continued to operate even after the Pacific was reached. Much as the earlier expansion had been fortified by the quest for gain, so the later one was reinforced by the desire for trade and expanded investment opportunities. Altruism, however misguided and arrogant, also influenced America's interest in foreign lands. Americans continued to believe that they had unique gifts—political freedom and material abundance—to offer other peoples. The American role in China, Hawaii, and the Philippines, in particular, expressed this mixture of the crass and the idealistic.

But post–Civil War expansionism also contained new ingredients. The desire to achieve big-power status by collecting colonies, as had the western European countries, augmented the older Manifest Destiny. So did the fear that now that continental expansion had ended, the United States must seek out new territory or cease to prosper and grow. The aggressiveness of the American government, particularly toward Latin America, reflected the new mood of big-power assertiveness: Great powers cut a wide swath in their own neighborhoods; they did not allow themselves to be defied by troublesome pygmies.

And yet Americans never wore the mantle of imperialism very comfortably. A rich nation of continental proportions, the United States needed to throw its weight around, but less so than nations that had fewer natural resources and smaller home markets. Less strongly impelled by necessity, the United States was also more restricted by its traditional liberal anticolonial values and by its fears that overseas acquisitions could not be incorporated into the Union as equal partners with the older states. In the new century just opening, the world would see many further instances of American forbearance and even generosity toward weaker nations combined with manifestations of self-serving interest, and would be puzzled by the course of the Great Republic.

For Further Reading

Walter LaFeber. *The New Empire: An Interpetation of American Expansion, 1860–1898* (1963)

> A study of late-nineteenth-century American expansionism by a scholar who believes that "economic forces [were] the most important causes" of the expansionist impulse.

Ernest R. May. *American Imperialism* (1968)

> May ascribes the major cause of American expansionism near the end of the nineteenth century to the appearance of a foreign policy elite inspired by the example of Britain, France, and Germany.

Walter Millis. *The Martial Spirit: A Study of Our War with Spain* (1931)

> A fine older narrative history of the origins, course, and results of the Spanish-American War. Millis sees the war's origins in the gradual development of a warlike spirit that derived from a mixture of boredom, greed, politics, and the yearning for glory.

Julius W. Pratt. *Expansionists of 1898: The Acquisition of Hawaii and the Spanish Islands* (1936)

> Pratt criticizes the view, common in his day, that the Spanish-American war was the work of business groups anxious to acquire markets. He gives far more credit to new currents of thought that he calls the "new Manifest Destiny."

Graham A. Cosmas. *An Army for Empire: The United States Army in the Spanish-American War* (1971)

> This study of the army and the War Department during the war with Spain seeks to refute the usual picture of bungling and general incompetence. Cosmas believes that, given the realities of time and the difficulties of tropical warfare, the army did rather well.

Kenton J. Clymer. *John Hay: The Gentleman as Diplomat* (1975)

> A study of Secretary of State John Hay's thought about such matters as race, expansion, England, and China. Clymer sees Hay as a patrician with a strong leaning to Britain. He denies that Hay's Open Door policy was primarily intended to protect China from rapacious foreign powers.

Margaret Leech. *In the Days of McKinley* (1959)

> A superb "life and times" of McKinley that emphasizes his presidential years. Leech spends much time on the relations between McKinley and his invalid wife, but she also deals colorfully with the events surrounding Cuba and the Spanish-American War.

Howard K. Beale. *Theodore Roosevelt and the Rise of America to World Power* (1956)

> An effective, if not always fair, attack on TR for his jingoism and imperialistic arrogance. In truth, TR is often condemned out of his own mouth.

Joseph Wisan. *The Cuban Crisis as Reflected in the New York Press* (1934)

> Wisan probably exaggerates the significance of the Hearst-Pultizer circulation battle in New York as a cause of the Spanish-American War. But his study of public opinion formation does tell us much about American values and prejudices, and how prowar groups played on them.

Frank A. Freidel. *Splendid Little War* (1958)

> The words and pictures of news correspondents, artists, and photographers tell the story of the war in Cuba. Freidel's 300 illustrations include some by Frederic Remington. Others are charming photographic efforts by cadets fresh out of Annapolis.

Robert Beisner. *Twelve Against Empire: The Anti-Imperialists, 1898–1900* (1968)

> Beisner studies twelve prominent Americans who opposed the Spanish-American War, including William James, "Czar" Thomas Reed, and Andrew Carnegie. All upper-class Republicans or former Mugwumps, they believed that acquiring unwilling colonies ran counter to American principles and would threaten democracy at home.

Leon Wolff. *Little Brown Brother* (1961)

> War in the Philippines lasted from 1898 to 1902, but after 1898 the United States fought not Spain but Filipino guerrillas. Wolff describes the methods army officers with Indian-fighting experience used to persuade "our little brown brothers" to accept American control. He also treats the growing controversy at home over army atrocities and the costs of the prolonged conflict.

Thomas J. McCormick. *China Market: America's Quest for Informal Empire, 1893–1901* (1967)

> In this New Left interpretation of American expansion in the Pacific, McCormick proposes that the government refused to solve the problems of overproduction by dealing with underconsumption at home. Instead, he says, the American economic and political leadership sought a tariff to promote exports and an Open Door agreement designed to assure American domination of the China market.

David C. McCulloch. *The Path Between the Seas: The Creation of the Panama Canal, 1870–1914* (1977)

> A lively account of the building of the great isthmian canal, from the early French effort to the final success under the auspices of the United States. Fine narrative history. McCulloch is an honest scholar who describes the greed, incompetence, and chicanery that accompanied the construction as well as the intelligence, hard work, and heroism.

Chapter 22

Culture in the Age of the Dynamo

Were Materialism and High Culture Compatible?

1851   The YMCA is established in the United States

1858   The National Association of Baseball Players is founded

1859   Darwin's *The Origin of Species* published in England

1870–82   Printing processes improve, enabling newspapers to print more news daily • The Associated Press and the United Press are founded • Pulitizer begins "yellow journalism" in the *New York World*

1870–90   American school of art, led by Winslow Homer

1876   American Library Association is founded and lobbies for local communities to support free public libraries

1880   William Le Baron Jenney designs the first skyscraper

1883   Brooklyn Bridge is completed • Metropolitan Opera House opens

1884   Mark Twain's *Huckleberry Finn* published

1893   The Chicago World's Fair

1895   Stephen Crane's *The Red Badge of Courage* published

1896   First showing of a commercial motion picture in a legitimate theater

1900   Theodore Dreiser's *Sister Carrie* published • "Tin Pan Alley" marks the beginning of the popular music trend • 240 Ph.D.s are awarded, beginning the expansion of graduate schools and professional education • Frank Lloyd Wright begins functional modernism in architecture

1903   First World Series

1904   Pragmatist philosopher John Dewey institutionalizes major changes in the education system • The Henri "Ashcan" school marks the trend toward modernism in painting

1913   The Armory exhibition exposes Americans to the works of Cézanne, Van Gogh, Picasso, and Duchamp, as well as the Henri group

1915   Over 80 percent of all children attend school as a result of compulsory attendance laws

I n the half century following the Civil War the United States, as we have seen, became a nation of cities and factories. Millions bent their energies to making money, developing skills, surviving, or getting ahead. It was an era when young men went to work at fourteen, spent ten or twelve hours a day on the job, and received no yearly vacation; when young women commonly devoted even longer hours to cooking, cleaning, and washing for large families.

In such a time few men and women could think of much more than the daily round. Ordinary Americans had little time and energy left for "the finer things"—for "serious" literature, music, art, and other so-called embellishments of life. Nor did people of wealth seem to be in any better shape to appreciate or pursue the arts. The American rich were not leisured gentlemen and ladies whose family wealth had been earned by some aggressive ancestor and who had themselves mellowed into "cultivation" and appreciation of beauty for its own sake. There were such people—survivors of colonial merchant families in the North and of the planter aristocracy in the South—but they had been superseded in numbers and wealth by the upstarts, the "new men"—the Rockefellers, Goulds, Carnegies, Swifts, Hearsts, and Guggenheims—who had clawed their way to the top of the economic pile and thrown the old elite into deep shadow.

Among the small intellectual class, especially in the opening years of the period, there was despair at the possibility of high cultural achievement in a nation so swamped with materialism. In 1874 Edwin L. Godkin, a transplanted Anglo-Irishman who edited the prestigious *Nation*, declared that his adopted country suffered from a "chromo civilization"; like the popular colored prints of the day (chromolithographs), its colors were gaudy and false.

To some, America's democracy seemed almost as hostile to cultivation and good taste as its materialism. In a famous passage the novelist Henry James made it clear why he had fled his homeland to live in England. The United States, he noted, "had no sovereign, no court, no personal loyalty, no church, . . . no diplomatic service, no country gentlemen, nor old country houses, . . . nor ivied ruins, no great universi-

ties. . . ." In short, it had few, if any, old, privileged institutions and few of the men and women that such institutions produced. These were the only interesting subjects to the writer, in James's view, and lacking them, America could never create a great literature.

James's critique was meant as a general indictment of America's cultural and intellectual potential. How could a society so immersed in wealth-getting, and so dedicated to equality at all costs, make room for the arts? How could it be expected to think creatively? How could Americans even find the leisure to amuse themselves? To critics such as James there was an irreconcilable conflict between materialism and culture, whether the "high" culture of sophisticated trained artists and thinkers or the popular culture of ordinary people.

And yet in the half century following Appomattox the United States experienced a cultural flowering that compares favorably with any that preceded or followed. The country produced a flood of authors, painters, architects, thinkers, and educators who made it one of the cultural centers of the Western world. There was also an exuberant and vigorous growth of "low" culture—the song, dance, theater, and amusements of average men and women—that became a powerful attraction to people of other lands.

How did the nation manage to avoid the dire predictions of such critics as Henry James? How did it manage to combine wealth-getting, industrialization, and urbanization with literature, painting, music, sports, educational progress, and the creation of new ideas? How did it manage to avoid a "chromo civilization"?

Literature

The Genteel Tradition. Post–Civil War Americans had an impressive literary heritage to build on. In the years between 1800 and 1860, in New England especially, the United States had experienced a literary birth that had astonished the world. But many of the outstanding figures of the prewar days did not survive the Civil War. Hawthorne, Cooper, Irving, Thoreau, and Poe were all dead by 1865. The aura of their reputations, however, persisted, so that New England, especially the Boston-Cambridge area, for some time continued to be the literary capital of the nation. Here were published two of the country's chief journals of culture—the *Atlantic Monthly* and the *North American Review*. Along with the *Nation* and *Harper's Weekly*, published in New York, these were the arbiters of literary taste among the small educated elite. The Boston-Cambridge area also was home to Longfellow, James Russell Lowell, and Charles Eliot Norton, all of whom taught at the country's most prestigious university, Harvard.

These men and these publications defended what the philosopher George Santayana would call the "genteel tradition" in literature. They believed that art, and especially fiction and poetry, must represent the spiritual, the pure, and the noble, for literature was a moral medium, not merely an aesthetic one. Literature should not report life as it actually was; that would include much that was sordid and mean. Rather, it must try to transform life into something higher and more refined. In poetry the genteel tradition called for pseudo-classical epics or romantic lyricism that imitated either the Roman poet Horace or the English romantics Keats and Shelley. The genteel novelist believed that nothing could be recounted that might offend the ears of a middle-class maiden. Lowell in fact declared that no man should write what he was unwilling for his young daughter to read. Evil existed in the fiction of the genteel authors, of course, but it was without detectable social cause, personified by evil men and women, and always, in the end, defeated. Sex was so buried under flowery romanticism that a traveler from another solar system who read a genteel novel might not have known that men and women were biologically different.

The exemplars of the genteel tradition included a few survivors from the great years of prewar New England, like Lowell, and also a new group of men. With the exception of Thomas Bailey Aldrich, whose sentimental *Story of a Bad Boy* (1870) is still read, these critics, poets, and novelists are deservedly forgotten. Yet for a while during the last thirty years of the nineteenth century, they sought to impose a set of values on American literary taste that denied all the great changes of the nation's recent history. One of them, George Boker, in 1882 expressed in verse his disapproval of Gilded Age America and his view that poets must defend traditional values:

> We poets hang upon the wheel
> Of Time's advancement; do our most

> To hide its inroads, and reveal
> The Splendors which the world has lost.

> Science and Avarice, arm and arm,
> Stride proudly through our abject time;
> And in their footsteps, wrangling, swarm
> Their own begotten broods of crime.

Regionalism. Even as Boker composed these lines, writers were beginning to challenge their genteel assumptions. The first fiction writers who defied post–Civil War gentility were authors who insisted on depicting American regional reality with all its coarse vigor and liveliness.

One of the new voices came from the mining camps of California and depicted a way of life that had just recently passed. In 1867 Bret Harte, a transplanted easterner who had come to California in 1854, published "The Luck of Roaring Camp," a short story, in the San Francisco–based *Overland Monthly*, a new magazine that he edited himself. The story concerned the hard-bitten miners and dance-hall girls of a Sierra mining camp who are bequeathed a baby. The plot was less important, however, than the cast of characters; each has a rough exterior and speaks the way people in the mining camps did indeed speak. Few are "good" people in the usual sense. It was this quality of apparent authenticity that made the story an instant sensation and Harte a celebrity. In the next few years his other stories about the mining camps, including "The Outcasts of Poker Flat," "The Idyl of Red Gulch," and "Tennessee's Partner," were widely applauded as examples of honesty in literature. In fact, much sentimentality remains in Harte's characters; even the most villainous and degraded have hearts of gold. Yet Harte's work was a milestone on the way to a more realistic literature.

Over the next few decades the vein of regionalism that Harte had first mined attracted other authors. The Midwest had Edward Eggleston, whose series of books—*The Hoosier Schoolmaster* (1871), *The Circuit Rider* (1874), *Roxy* (1878), and others—depicted rural Indiana with a sharp eye for local color and true ear for regional speech. In the South, George Washington Cable wrote brilliantly about Creole New Orleans in *Old Creole Days* (1879) and *The Grandissimes* (1880). The southern mountain people of the Great Smokies and the Cumberland plateau found their literary portraitist in Mary Noailles Murfree, who published under the pseudonym of Charles Egbert Craddock. Joel Chandler Harris wrote about poor Georgia whites and even poorer Georgia blacks. His "Uncle Remus" stories depicted black farmers honestly and accurately, though

Harris emphasized humor rather than the very real oppression that blacks labored under in the Gilded Age South. The East, too, had its local colorists. Sarah Orne Jewett began to write stories of the village and farm people of southern Maine during the 1860s. Her novel *The Country of the Pointed Firs* (1896) has been described as "the best piece of regional fiction to have come out of nineteenth century America." Another local colorist of the East was Mary Wilkins Freeman, whose stories dealt with the people of rural Massachusetts.

Mark Twain. The most talented of all the regional authors, one who far exceeded them in depth and universality, was Samuel Langhorne Clemens, alias Mark Twain. Mark Twain shared with the local colorists their love of dialect, their focus on rural and small-town "types," their humorous emphasis. A native of

By the time this photograph of Mark Twain was taken (1906), he had become an adored national monument. Nevertheless, he was a tortured man who never could reconcile his contempt for wealth with his need for luxury and worldly success.

Missouri, he fought briefly in the Confederate army, and then, in 1862, departed for the gold diggings at Virginia City, Nevada, where he became a reporter and feature writer for the *Territorial Enterprise.*

In 1864 Mark Twain went to California, where he achieved fame for a story using the same mining-camp material as Harte, "The Celebrated Jumping Frog of Calaveras County" (1865). But Twain was far more talented than Harte. Combining the traditions of the frontier tall-tale with an uncanny ear for speech, and at times a sense of the tragic, Mark Twain ultimately became an author of international stature. At the beginning of his career, however, he capitalized on his capacity to make people laugh. In books such as *Innocents Abroad* (1869) and on the lecture circuit, which occupied much of his time and earned him large fees, he joked, ridiculed, and in general seemed to be interested solely in amusing people.

Mark Twain's more serious side became evident in his later books. In three he turned to his own youth and to the upper South before the Civil War, describing the joys and the agonies of youth. The first of these, the novel *Tom Sawyer* (1876), is about a boy growing up in a town very much like Sam Clemens's Hannibal, Missouri. Tom is no paragon, but a realistic boy given to laziness and romantic dreaming, yet capable as well of loyalty and courage. *Life on the Mississippi* (1883) is a superb nonfiction account of the great days before the Civil War when the steamboat dominated commerce on the South's rivers and the steamboat captain was almost a Renaissance prince. Mark Twain's greatest novel, *Huckleberry Finn* (1885), was a sequel to *Tom Sawyer.* But Huck is a more interesting boy than Tom—less conventional, more genuine, less spoiled by romantic illusion, more spontaneous. The novel also is more sensitive to fundamental human issues. Huck helps Jim, a black slave, escape from bondage and refuses to betray him, though Huck is troubled by a sense that he is defying his own community. Clemens, though a southerner himself, portrayed Jim as an even braver, more manly personality than Huck.

Despite his genius and his willingness at times to choose truth over romantic convention, Mark Twain never fully escaped from the literary conventions of the Gilded Age. Even his best works contain much sentimentality and cheap farce. He eventually turned to vapid historical romance and developed a tendency to flaunt an adolescent melancholy. Only in *The Gilded Age* (1873), written in collaboration with Charles Dudley Warner, did he use contemporary industrial America as his theme. The novel recounts the adventures of a cast of sharpers, confidence men and women, and corrupt Washington politicians in the crass years immediately following the Civil War, when businessmen wanted favors and government had them to confer. The book caught the moral and aesthetic shoddiness of the day so well that it gave its name to the whole postwar era. Yet Mark Twain never repeated the performance, and while the nation marched rapidly into the industrial age, he continued to write about antebellum Missouri or England and France in the Middle Ages.

In his later years Mark Twain became a national institution much beloved by Americans. When he died in 1910, the nation sincerely mourned. Yet despite his fame and popularity, in many ways he was a tragic figure whose enormous talents never found a truly worthy theme.

Realism. As the century progressed, other men and women would come closer to fitting their talents to vital modern materials. Leader of the move toward realism was William Dean Howells, an Ohio-born author and editor who came to Boston in 1867 to become editor of the *Atlantic Monthly*. Howells was the first westerner to edit this pillar of New England gentility, and he brought a breath of fresh air to the publication. Though he never fully liberated himself from the prudishness of the day, Howells insisted on new principles for judging literature. A novel, he declared, must be "true to the motives, the impulses, the principles that shape the life of actual men and women." As editor and critic, he praised the work of such early American realists as John William De Forest, whose *Miss Ravenel's Conversion from Secession to Loyalty* (1866) has been described as the best Civil War novel ever written. He welcomed newer talents such as Hamlin Garland, whose bitter stories of western farm life, *Main-Travelled Roads*, appeared in 1891. He was also receptive to the realism of Émile Zola in France and Henrik Ibsen in Scandinavia, and introduced these authors to American readers.

A talented novelist in his own right, Howells practiced what he preached. In *The Rise of Silas Lapham* (1885) he described a self-made millionaire manufacturer who finds that his simple western ways cause social difficulties for himself and his family in Boston. The novel is one of the earliest portrayals of a businessman by an American author.

The violent Haymarket affair in Chicago produced a personal crisis for Howells. The sentencing to death of the five anarchists in 1887 seemed to him "civic murder" and awakened his social conscience. In his next business novel, *A Hazard of New Fortunes*

(1890), Howells's business characters are less amiable and sympathetic, and his canvas expands to include poor working people, a German-American socialist, and a violent streetcar strike. Howells never became a Marxist, but he did come to believe that unrestrained capitalism was not the most desirable economic system. In *A Traveler from Altruria* (1894) and *Through the Eye of the Needle* (1907), he built on Edward Bellamy's utopian novel *Looking Backward*, positing socialist alternatives to a dog-eat-dog economic system.

A major American literary figure not easy to classify is Henry James. James had an extraordinarily acute sense of the nuances in human relationships, and his characters are men and women in comfortable circumstances whose lives revolve about the subtleties of taste, class, and nationality and crises of personal integrity. His settings are generally European, but his characters are often American, and the tensions in many of his best works—*The American* (1877), *The Portrait of a Lady* (1881), *The Wings of the Dove* (1902), and *The Golden Bowl* (1904)—arise between simple but honest and intelligent Americans, often young women, and sophisticated but corrupt and devious Europeans. It is difficult at first glance to see in James's work much of Howells's realism. James seemed little interested in the vast social changes sweeping the Western world. Yet there is in his fiction none of the "picturesqueness" that his criticism of the American literary scene, as previously quoted, seems to prize, nor does he suffer from the false sentimentality of the genteel authors. His people, though well-bred and worldly, are recognizably real human beings with the complex personalities found in daily life.

Naturalism. As the end of the century approached, Howells's rather mild realism gave way to something more vigorous and more brutal—naturalism. Though the realists sought to describe the day-to-day world of work, class, and ordinary people doing ordinary, everyday things, they retained an essentially sunny view of life. Not so the naturalists. These authors saw life as sordid and vicious. Modern science and social science, they held, showed that all things were determined, subject neither to chance nor free will, and they applied this determinism to people. Men and women were mere atoms in the grip of forces beyond their control or even understanding, whose endings were generally tragic. Naturalist literature did not always have an urban setting; but almost invariably the naturalist writers focused on the emerging industrial-urban order, and even their rural characters are people whose lives are entangled in the vast social and economic changes that characterized the closing years of the nineteenth century.

One young writer who explored the relationship between large social currents and the lives of rural Americans was Hamlin Garland, a "son of the middle border," the prairie region undergoing momentous and jarring change during the 1870s and 1880s. In *Main-Travelled Roads* (1891) and *Prairie Folks* (1893), Garland told of the bitter failures and intense hardships of rural life, and of farm people crushed both by cruel nature and by even crueler human oppressors. Stephen Crane's *Maggie* (1893), subtitled *A Girl of the Streets*, is about a young woman in the slums of New York. Maggie is destroyed by the poverty, drunkenness, and crime of her environment. The picture is one of brutality and sordidness so frankly rendered that no publisher would risk it; Crane had to finance its publication himself under a pseudonym. Crane, who died young, would write one masterpiece, *The Red Badge of Courage* (1895), the story of a young boy in the Civil War experiencing his first taste of battle. Born in 1871, Crane had no firsthand knowledge of the war; but the tale is a magnificent evocation of courage, cowardice, death, and violence under fire.

Another naturalist novelist was Theodore Dreiser. An Indianan who came from a background of poverty and scandal himself, Dreiser was a crude stylist but a writer of great cumulative power. His characters, unlike Crane's Maggie, are often strong people; but they, too, are at the mercy of their circumstances, their appetites, their drives, their yearnings. Carrie, of *Sister Carrie* (1900), is an ambitious young woman who uses men, is corrupted by them, and then destroys them in turn as she climbs her way up the social ladder. The hero of *The Financier* (1912) and *The Titan* (1914), modeled after Charles Yerkes, is Frank Cowperwood, an unprincipled big businessman driven by a lust for power that allows nothing and no one to stand in his way; although he triumphs over all his enemies, he is no more master of his destiny than the tragic Maggie.

Other authors of these years who played on the theme of powerful forces molding people include two Californians, Frank Norris and Jack London. In *McTeague* (1899) Norris depicted a simple-minded San Francisco dentist who is gradually overwhelmed by material failure and tragically driven to murder. *Vandover and the Brute* (1914) is the tale of a man afflicted by illness who turns into a beastlike creature. *The Octopus* (1901) concerns the wheat farmers of California's Central Valley and their struggles with the railroad. Norris sympathized with the farmers, but as a

naturalist, he tried to avoid praise or blame. All the characters, heroes and villains alike, are in the grip of forces they cannot control. London, though an avowed socialist, worshiped the power of the individual, and in adventure books set in Alaska—*The Call of the Wild* (1903), *White Fang* (1905)—as well as in works dealing with driven men—*The Sea Wolf* (1904)—he glorified the superman. Modeled on philosopher Friedrich Nietzsche's "blond beast," these brutal, arrogant, commanding characters, acting like elemental forces, sweep lesser beings aside.

Painting and Architecture

In two other areas of the arts, painting and architecture, we encounter the same movement from romantic gentility to an honest attempt to come to terms with the emerging modern world. In both, as in literature, some of the results are lasting and impressive achievements.

Romanticism to Modernism. American painting during the 1860s and 1870s was dominated by borrowed European romanticism, and Europe of the "Old Masters" remained for many years the measure of good taste in painting. When the first American museums were established in the decades surrounding the Civil War, their collections were almost exclusively paintings by European artists of the Renaissance and the seventeenth century. By the 1870s rich Americans had begun to buy paintings, sculpture, and other art objects as a mark of "culture" and sophistication, but almost invariably these were the works of established figures. The enormous collections accumulated by J. P. Morgan, Henry Clay Frick, and others brought much-needed cash to impoverished European gentry with family pictures to sell, but they benefited living American artists scarcely at all.

At the beginning of the post–Civil War era most American painters received their training in France or Germany, where they learned to paint in the romantic manner. Men like James McNeill Whistler and John Singer Sargent in fact preferred Europe as their permanent homes. During the years from 1875 to 1890 a more distinctively American school appeared, led by Winslow Homer, John La Farge, and Thomas Eakins. At their best these men painted vigorously honest portraits of professional men, sportsmen, Americans at play. Their work was realistic in the sense that it was direct and vivid, but it was not contemporary. Its subject matter lacked relevance to the world in which the artists themselves lived.

These paintings by Winslow Homer (left) and John Sloan (below) reveal how the sensibilities of visual artists changed in the half century following the Civil War. In Homer's 1866 painting, the upper-middle-class subjects, the balanced composition, and the croquet game itself all reflect the genteel tradition that dominated American art. The "Ashcan" painter Sloan depicted urban working-class life without sentimentality or disapproval. The woman in this 1911 painting does not seem distressed by the large family wash.

As the twentieth century began, a new group of painters appeared who had come to terms with the emerging urban-industrial America. The core of this group consisted of Everett Shinn, George Luks, John Sloan, and William Glackens, all of whom had been newspaper illustrators in Philadelphia in the 1880s. Trained to capture events as news photographers do today, they developed a keen eye for city scenes and city types. In the early 1890s the Philadelphia group came under the tutelage of Robert Henri, a teacher at the Pennsylvania Academy of Fine Arts. Henri had received his training in Europe but had been influenced by the French impressionists rather than the earlier romantics. Impressionists avoided sharp lines and photographic realism. Instead they relied on the sort of visual shorthand that the eye in real life detects and the mind converts into reality. Toward the end of the decade Henri and his four disciples, one by one, moved to New York, where they were joined by Maurice Prendergast, Arthur B. Davies, and Ernest Lawson.

The Henri circle considered the conventional American painting of the day anemic and feeble, suitable for interior decoration, "merely an adjunct of plush and cut glass." Their own work they proclaimed as vigorous and real. Their subjects were certainly contemporary. They depicted prize fights, ordinary people waiting for taxis and streetcars, pigeons wheeling over tenement roofs, children at play in city streets, urban backyards, and the New York el at rush hour. Their technique often bordered on caricature. People were fat, frumpy, often coarse-looking. The critics attacked

their work as brutal and vulgar. When, in 1904, six of the group exhibited at the National Arts Club, a conservative critic described them as portraying "an outlook where nature is seen under her most lugubrious mood, where joyousness never enters . . . and where unhealthiness prevails to an alarming extent." Before

The Armory Show sponsors, recognizing how controversial their exhibition would be, tried to win friends by offering the press a free beefsteak dinner. The menu, signed by prominent sponsors, features the scandalous Duchamp painting, *Nude Descending a Staircase*.

long the Henri group was being derided as the "Ashcan school." Offended by the tight rein imposed on artists by the conservative National Academy of Design, which excluded them from its prestigious exhibitions, eight Ashcan painters held their own show at the Mac-Beth Gallery in New York in 1908. The show immortalized "the eight" and marked a new era in American painting.

In 1913 the Henri group, and the still more radical postimpressionists, sponsored a major showing of the best new European work at the Sixty-Ninth Regiment Armory in New York. Here for the first time a large number of Americans saw the works of Cézanne, Van Gogh, Picasso, and the cubists, who seemed to have abandoned representation entirely. The sensation of the show was Marcel Duchamp's *Nude Descending a Staircase*, a cubist painting that by a succession of closely overlapping flat plane figures suggested the motion of a woman walking from the top to the bottom of a flight of stairs. One critic called the Duchamp painting "an explosion in a shingle factory." Another

labeled the whole exhibit an exercise in "incomprehensibility combined with symptoms of paresis."

Despite the attacks, the Armory exhibit was an immensely influential event in American art. In New York and in the other cities where the paintings were shown, they attracted immense crowds. Most people came to smirk, but many stayed to marvel and appreciate. In all, 235 of the paintings were eventually sold, and American taste was given a tremendous push toward modernism.

Architecture. The years immediately following the Civil War found American architecture particularly out of tune with American life. Designers of public buildings were still making them look like Greek temples or combining elements of so many traditional European styles that no clear stylistic label could be given them. A similar eclecticism marked domestic architecture for the rich. French chateaux, Elizabethan half-timbered cottages, small Roman temples—or frequently mixtures of all three—were what rich businessmen commissioned. Meanwhile, the ordinary middle-class family bought a balloon-frame house constructed of wood uprights and siding stuck together with nails, and decorated, if at all, with wooden "gingerbread" trim.

By the 1880s and 1890s many critics had become disenchanted with American architecture. Charles Eliot Norton, professor of fine arts at Harvard, told his students that "we have, as a nation, painfully displayed our disregard of the ennobling influence of fine architecture upon national character." Norton and his colleagues were the equivalents of the genteel literary critics, who saw art as a means for improving public virtue. Yet what they endorsed was a higher level of performance than was common in their day.

To some extent the plea for a finer aesthetic in building was answered by a group of young men—including Stanford White, Charles McKim, Daniel Burnham, and William Robert Ware—who studied in Paris and returned with finely honed skills that enabled them to reproduce accurately the traditional styles of the past. They could design Renaissance and Elizabethan homes for the rich, as well as Gothic buildings for colleges. But, the critics asked, in what sense were these *American* buildings?

A few utilitarian objects had somehow escaped the almost universal blight of inappropriate overdecoration. At the 1876 centennial celebration in Philadelphia, the Corliss engine, a monster machine, had been admired not only for its power but also for its clean lines. The Brooklyn Bridge, completed in 1883, delighted almost everyone by its airy simplicity. But on the whole there was little relationship, in either building or household and industrial design, between the use of structures or objects and their appearance. Nor, as the 1870s ended, had architects yet taken new technology—cheap steel, electricity, and the telephone—into account.

The first signs of change came in the 1880s when a group of Chicago architects began to develop a new way of looking at building. During this decade the Windy City was caught up in a frenzy of construction, both to restore structures destroyed in the fire of 1871 and to build new ones to meet the space needs of the nation's fastest-growing metropolis. In the midst of this building boom William Le Baron Jenney designed the first true skyscraper.

There had been tall buildings in the past, of course, but these had been both expensive and impractical. Walls of high buildings had to be very thick at the base to bear the enormous weight of the masonry above. Windows on the lower stories had to be small, making it difficult to light interiors. The thick lower walls also reduced sharply the structure's usable space. Finally, the inconvenient stairs of high buildings made space at the top virtually unrentable.

The new buildings of Jenney, Louis Sullivan, Ernest Flagg, Cass Gilbert, and others used steel, electric light, and the electric elevator to get around these problems. Steel, especially, revolutionized construction. Instead of heavy, weight-bearing walls, architects needed only a frame of light, interlocked steel beams. To these they attached thin walls of brick or stone veneer. With electricity and fast elevators, such a building could provide convenient, usable space at much lower cost than an equivalent masonry structure. Because the skyscraper could be erected to virtually any height, designers could go up rather than out and so reduce the outlay on expensive downtown land.

At first skyscrapers, like other American structures, ignored the design implications of technology. They were decorated with classical pillars; many were made to look like overblown Gothic cathedrals. Gradually, however, a new attitude appeared that held that a structure's design and appearance should honestly reflect its function. In the words of Louis Sullivan, "Over all the coursing sun, *form ever follows function*, and that is the law." A building should not disguise its use, but proclaim it boldly and honestly. In line with this new perception, Henry Hobson Richardson designed structures like Marshall Field's wholesale warehouse (1885–1887)—square, simple, and solid, without fussy lines or details borrowed from traditional

European styles. Sullivan's best works were the Schiller Building (1891/92) in Chicago and St. Louis's Wainwright Building (1890/91).

Frank Lloyd Wright, Sullivan's pupil, translated his mentor's theories into domestic architecture. Wright had learned not only from Sullivan but also from the Japanese, whose simple, light domestic buildings with adjustable spaces he had observed at the 1893 Chicago World's Fair. After establishing his own Chicago office in 1894, Wright developed his ideas concerning the close relation of form, use, materials, and site. These ideas became the basis for his famous prairie houses—long, low structures to match the terrain of the flat Midwest. Wright broke with the past by avoiding traditional elements of exterior design,

Though they originated in Chicago, skyscrapers were quickly adopted in crowded Manhattan. In this view of the Flatiron Building on twenty-third street we can see the steel frame as yet incompletely encased by its masonry sheath.

and he built the homes of local stone and timber that suited their locations. Critics hailed Wright's work as strikingly innovative, yet at first few patrons came to him. Not until the 1920s did Wright's form of modernism begin to attract widespread public acclaim.

Popular Culture

It is possible, then, to trace the gradual response of artists to the realities of the American social and economic scene in the half century following the Civil War. A similar pattern of adaptation to an emerging urban-industrial environment can be observed in popular culture, entertainment, sports, and recreation.

Spectator Sports. As more and more Americans moved to the cities, they found that the world of play as well as the world of work had changed. Country people engaged in sports, of course. They swam, fished, played versions of baseball. Yet rural labor offered so many opportunities to exercise in the open air that

country residents had less reason to crave organized games than town people.

Smaller American urban centers were in some ways ideal places for sports. They had both many open spaces for games and enough people of like mind to make up teams. The largest cities, however, presented serious problems. True, there were both the people and the need for outdoor recreation, but space was often unavailable and so, too, was leisure. As we have seen, few American cities had preserved open space in their congested centers. Not until the very end of the nineteenth century did cities open playgrounds for children and add sports and exercise programs to school curricula. Insufficient leisure remained a deterrent to sports for a longer time. As late as 1890 the average workweek for American factory workers was sixty hours; until the mid-1920s it was still fifty. Few wage earners had paid vacations. Most worked every day except Sunday, and in many cities Protestant groups had succeeded in imposing blue laws that kept theaters and ball parks closed on the Sabbath. Only gradually as the old century gave way to the new did

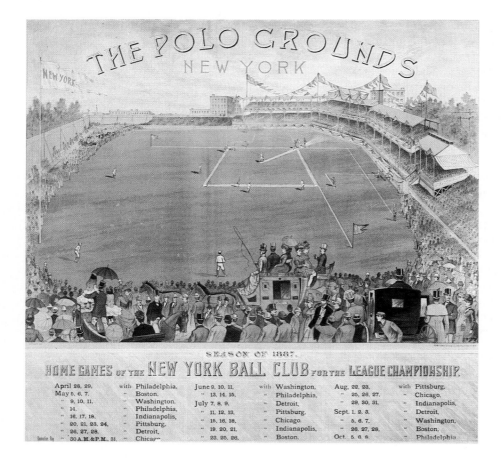

An 1887 poster advertising the New York Giants. Note at the bottom the list of home games. The "season" was much shorter a century ago.

pressure from Catholics, nonbelievers, and various secular groups force city officials to permit Sunday sports and amusements. Increasingly, sports became a part of city life. But city dwellers were mostly spectators rather than participants.

The one exception was the bicycle craze that followed the invention of the "safety" bicycle with two equal-sized wheels in place of the easily tipped older vehicle with a mammoth front wheel. During the 1890s thousands of men and women took Sunday bicycle trips to the country and began to demand that counties and states improve the nation's poor roads. But the bicycle fad was an exception. Most Americans watched professionals play rather than participating themselves.

The first of the nineteenth-century sports to be commercialized was baseball, a game that had developed out of a number of centuries-old children's games. By the 1850s amateur baseball clubs had become common in the cities and towns. Their matches soon attracted spectators, and reports of their encounters began to appear in the newspapers. Before long the teams were erecting high fences around their playing fields and charging spectators for admission to underwrite the cost of equipment, uniforms, and travel to rival communities.

The next steps in commercializing baseball came quickly. In 1858 the National Association of Baseball Players was organized, and in 1869 the Cincinnati Red Stockings began to pay salaries to players. In 1876 the National League of Professional Baseball Clubs—with teams in New York, Philadelphia, Hartford, Boston, Chicago, Louisville, Cincinnati, and St. Louis—superseded the amateur organization. In the next few years more teams joined the National League, and in 1899 a group of promoters organized the American League. The two leagues struggled for supremacy for a few years and then amicably agreed to coexist. In 1903 the champions of each met in the first World Series; the American League's Boston Red Sox beat the National League's Pittsburgh Pirates. Baseball attendance grew rapidly in the early part of the new century, and in the 1913 World Series gate receipts for the five games reached $326,000. In 1908 the popular song "Take Me Out to the Ball Game" marked the triumph of baseball as the country's most popular sport.

Football and boxing failed to match baseball's popularity during these years. Until the 1920s football remained a game played in colleges by amateurs and patronized by upper-middle-class people, often graduates of one of the schools. Yet toward the end of the

The bicycle craze of the 1890s, like its equivalents today, spawned hobbyist magazines.

century college rivalries had led to active recruiting of players, often poor sons of immigrants. By 1917 critics were charging that the supposedly amateur game had become commercialized with hidden subsidies to players, vulgar hoopla, and expensive stadiums—in addition to excessive violence.

Because of its brutality, boxing carried a stigma as a "blood" sport in these years. Few women and few respectable men attended matches, and in some cities boxing was forbidden. Yet the sport was popular among working men, especially recent immigrants and second-generation Americans in the big cities. When John L. Sullivan returned to his native Boston after knocking out Jake Kilrain in a harrowing seventy-five round, bare-knuckle fight in 1889, the city's Irish turned out in force to honor him.

The new spectator sports not only diverted city people but also filled them with pride. Professional sports were relatively democratic. The lists of outstanding players or champions record the growing assimilation and acceptance of newer-stock Americans. At the beginning the names are Anglo-Saxon; by the 1890s

New Yorkers in the 1890s amused themselves at Steeplechase Park in Coney Island. Almost every city in America had its equivalent in this era.

they are German and Irish; by 1910 or 1920 they are increasingly Italian, Spanish, and Jewish. Clearly, professional sports provided an escalator upward for each new European group in America.

Most professional sports retained the "color line," however. Black players were excluded from major league baseball and forced to play in black leagues, where salaries were low, equipment poor, and ballparks mere fenced fields. College football was somewhat more open in the North, though when northern teams played rivals in the South, they benched their black players in deference to southern prejudices. The least segregated major spectator sport was prize fighting; in 1908 Jack Johnson, a black man, defeated Tommy Burns, a white Canadian, to become heavyweight champion of the world. But even boxing was not free of prejudice. The white public resented Johnson's reign as champion and yearned for a "white hope" to defeat him. Johnson's unpopularity was magnified when he married a white woman. When he was defeated by Jess Willard, a white American, the white public cheered.

Women were even more restricted in their sports role than blacks. Prevailing American attitudes of the Gilded Age and the early twentieth century held sport to be a masculine occupation. Middle-class women shared in the bicycle craze of the 1890s and played genteel games like croquet and lawn tennis. Working

women and working-class housewives had little time for these, though some joined their husbands, brothers, and fathers in attending sports events. Women participated in professional sports exclusively as spectators. Nowhere in these years was there a professional women's team that attracted paying customers.

Mass Entertainment. Besides spectator sports, music, the theater, the circus, and the amusement park were ways in which city people in the half century following the Civil War filled their limited leisure time and softened the rough edges of their daily lives.

The amusement park was in part an outgrowth of the streetcar lines. In an effort to encourage weekend business, the traction companies established resorts on the outskirts of the towns they served. Chicago had Cheltenham Beach and later White City. Boston had Paragon Park; San Francisco, The Chutes; St. Louis, Forest Park Highlands; Philadelphia, Willow Grove; and New York, Coney Island. On Sundays city people flocked to these parks to hear concerts, watch balloon ascensions and bicycle races, and patronize the "rides," including the Ferris wheel, the roller coaster, and others. Here they ate hamburgers and frankfurters for the first time.

Before World War I "classical" music had not been fully absorbed into American life. The elite could hear symphonic music and opera in some cities, but it was music composed by foreigners and often performed by foreigners. Popular music was home grown. During the years after the Civil War, writing popular songs to be sold as sheet music that was played and sung at the parlor piano became a successful business for a score of composers. By 1900 most of the songwriters and their agents were located along New York's Twenty-eighth Street, and "Tin Pan Alley" had become the nickname for the lucrative popular music business.

Some of the most successful composers, Gussie Davis for one, were black. Others, including Edward Marks, Monroe Rosenberg, and Irving Berlin, were Jewish. During the 1890s black composers, especially Scott Joplin, introduced ragtime into popular music. "Rags" were instrumental pieces written for either piano or band, rather than pieces for singing. They combined elements of traditional white music with the syncopation of urban black music and the street music of the white underclass. In the hands of Joplin, a Texas-born black man with formal musical training, they were often complex, sophisticated works. Joplin wrote thirty-nine rags and was widely imitated by other composers, black and white alike.

Jazz, like ragtime, had roots in the black city ghettos. Its original home was New Orleans, where blacks had long been a vital part of the cultural scene. Black wind musicians played at funerals and other important occasions, both solemn and joyous, and freely improvised solos from traditional French and American marches and popular tunes, combining it with ragtime-style syncopation drawn from the black musical experience. Black singers and pianists also played in the raffish saloons of the New Orleans red-light district, Storeyville. Here one heard both ragtime and "the blues," a mournful vocal style related to rural black spirituals, but usually concerned with crime, betrayal, and sexual love.

When military authorities closed Storeyville in 1917, supposedly to protect servicemen from venereal disease, New Orleans musicians dispersed in all directions. Some became performers on the passenger steamboats, which still plied the Mississippi. Eventually they settled in the emerging black ghettos of Chicago, St. Louis, Memphis, Kansas City, and New York. Young white musicians came to hear the new "Jass" music and to imitate and adapt it, often by watering it down to suit respectable white middle-class tastes.

Popular music in this period was often presented with other entertainment on stage. In the minstrel shows, which dated from before the Civil War, songs, dances, and comedy acts exploited black stereotypes and black musical themes. There were a few all-black minstrel companies, but groups such as Christy's Minstrels were made up of white people who darkened their faces with burnt cork. The stereotype they presented showed black people always amiable and carefree. During the 1860s a hundred companies toured the country performing minstrel shows.

By the 1880s the minstrel show, rooted in an earlier, simpler era, had been replaced by vaudeville, which offered much greater variety. A typical vaudeville performance consisted of as many as thirty brief acts—dances, comic skits, songs, acrobatics, animal stunts, juggling, magic. Like the minstrel show, it was a showcase for popular songs. It also offered talented young men and women from newer immigrant stock—Jewish, Spanish, Italian, Irish—opportunities to win fame and fortune as performers. The vaudeville show was especially popular among the new urban audiences. They did not need to know English to enjoy a juggler or a magician, and the costumes and music created a glamorous image, briefly transforming the narrow, impoverished world of slum dwellers.

The motion picture was even better suited to the growing urban audience. Its basis was a set of technical advances that combined a flexible medium for photographic emulsions, a camera that could take a fast series of still frames, and a projector that could send these through a magnifying lens onto a screen to create the impression of live motion. Edison did much of the work in joining these elements, though at first he saw little but an amusing toy in his invention and was happy to license exhibitors to show thirty-second films in penny arcades. The first films were merely scenic views or bits of action—dancers, acrobats, boxers. Soon the exhibitors discovered more profit in such racy material as *Taking a Bath*, *What the Bootblack Saw*, and *Dolorita's Passion Dance*. Motion pictures began to tap a more general audience in 1896 when the first film was shown in a respectable theater, Koster and Bial's Music Hall in New York. Soon vaudeville managers began to add a filmed "act" to the live performances they presented.

The audience for the new medium proved enormous. Live theater was expensive, and it relied on too many conventions for untutored audiences. There was also the language barrier. The early movies with their giant images and simple stories were especially appealing to urban working-class people. And the fact that they were silent broadened their audience to include the foreign-born. Once the medium's success was assured, Edison attempted to monopolize the runaway new industry by insisting on his patent rights and charging high fees to use his cameras and projectors. He did not succeed. Before long dozens of small picture makers, using equipment of their own make or imported from Europe, were shooting films in backyards and makeshift studios.

There soon was a similar proliferation of exhibitors. By 1900 hundreds of exhibitors were showing films in empty stores, town halls, school auditoriums—almost anyplace they could assemble some chairs in a darkened room. These early movie houses were often called "nickelodeons." They charged five cents for an eight-minute showing of a humorous, exciting, or exotic incident. Most of these primitive sketches were created on the spur of the moment by directors, camera operators, or other employees of the many small firms formed to provide material for the nickelodeons.

This impromptu approach to filmmaking soon gave way to more deliberate efforts. In 1903 Edwin Porter of the Edison company produced *The Great Train Robbery*, telling a story of some complexity,

By 1910 Americans had developed the movie habit. For urban newcomers, especially the hordes of immigrants, silent films offered cheap, accessible entertainment. Even children—as this view outside a New York city nickelodeon suggest—found movies irresistible.

in almost a full reel of film. Soon two other firms, Vitagraph and Biograph, were imitating Porter. Equipment became better, theaters more permanent and comfortable, and films more impressive artistically. By 1905 many of the classic film genres—western, comedy-romance, crime, travelogue, science fiction—had become established.

At first many of the film companies were located in the East, where most of the actors and technicians could be found. But the East had many drawbacks. Real estate for studios in the big eastern cities was expensive. When producers began to shoot outdoors, the cold and rainy eastern weather hindered them. The East was also close to the Edison "film trust," which pursued a policy of suing every company that did not pay a substantial fee for the privilege of making films. To escape the reach of the trust and to take advantage of cheap space and sunny weather, William Selig, a Chicago producer, moved his company to southern California in 1907. Soon Selig was joined by others. By 1912 the Los Angeles suburb of Hollywood had become the nation's filmmaking capital.

By this time, too, the audience for motion pictures had grown to between 10 and 20 million annually. Also fully developed was the star system, which relied on particular performers to pull the customers in each week. Among the earliest stars were Tom Mix, Mary Pickford, Charles Chaplin, "Bronco Billy" Anderson, William S. Hart, Mabel Normand, Buster Keaton, Pearl White, and Theda Bara. These performers commanded fabulous salaries, which added to their glamor and became a reason by itself for public adulation.

Eventually the motion picture audience grew more sophisticated and began to demand more than superficial glamor and excitement. Talented people were happy to meet the more exacting demand. In the years after 1910, D. W. Griffith worked for the Biograph studio and helped to make its films a superior product. Griffith was the first producer-director who truly understood the new medium and successfully exploited its unique potential. In 1915 he produced, for the then-immense figure of $100,000, *The Birth of a Nation*. Concerned with the tribulations of Reconstruction, the movie was blatantly racist and pro–Ku Klux Klan. It aroused fierce opposition among blacks and white liberals wherever it was shown, but it was an immense popular success. And from a purely artistic perspective, deservedly so. Twelve reels long, it employed the fade-out, the dissolve, crosscutting, the close-up, and the long-shot. In the special theaters where it was shown, orchestras accompanied the action with great effect. However deplorable ideologically,

The Birth of a Nation set a new standard of artistic and technical excellence for the entire film industry.

Education

In their various ways, then, the arts, both "high" and "low," responded to the transformation of America from a rural and agricultural society to one marked by cities and industry. The educational life of the nation between the Civil War and World War I revealed a similar shift. In the process it managed simultaneously to serve Amercians' quest for material gain, to become more democratic, and to create more stringent cultural and intellectual standards.

The Public Schools.   The greatest change in education in the half century following 1865 was its sheer expansion. In 1870 about 7 million pupils were enrolled in public day schools; by 1915 there were over 18 million, with another 1.5 million in private schools, mostly Catholic parochial institutions. Not only had the number increased; so had the proportion of the school-aged population attending school, so that by 1915 well over 80 percent of all young people were attending classes of some sort. School outlays rose even faster than enrollments, growing to $605 million, or $31 annually per pupil, in 1915.

Many factors helped produce the increasing costs and numbers. In 1860 few states in the South had systems of public education. By the end of Reconstruction, however, southern states had joined the rest of the country in accepting responsibility for supporting elementary schools. Meanwhile, in the large cities a parallel system of parochial schools sprang up, largely to serve the nation's growing Catholic population. More and more states also made school attendance compulsory. By 1881 nineteen states and territories in the North and West had compulsory attendance laws; by 1898 there were thirty-one. At the same time legislatures raised school-leaving ages and made the school year longer.

All these changes added substantially to the taxpayers' bills. But education seemed well worth the cost. As the nation's economy grew larger and more complex, not only was education easier to pay for, it was also more essential. With each passing year business needed more and more young men and women who could calculate receipts, add figures, write letters, and understand written instructions. With well-paying jobs requiring a high degree of literacy becoming more common, staying in school became attractive to the young.

As the need for managerial and clerical personnel expanded, so did the demand for public high schools. Before the Civil War, Massachusetts was the only state that had authorized a system of high schools supported by public funds. Secondary education elsewhere was the domain of the private "academy," which charged tuition to young women preparing for the teaching profession and young men preparing for college. After 1865 several states followed Massachusetts's lead. At first taxpayers resisted the new burden on the grounds that no state owed its citizens an education beyond the elementary level. In 1874, however, the Michigan Supreme Court upheld a state law allowing citizens of local school districts to tax themselves for the purpose of establishing public high schools. Thereafter, with the legal roadblocks eliminated, other states followed suit; by 1915 there were more than 11,000 public high schools in the United States with over 1.3 million pupils.

Initially the curricula of the public high schools emphasized the same liberal arts and classic languages that were dominant in the private academies. Before long, however, school administrators introduced commercial programs, including typing, bookkeeping, and accounting. Latin and Greek gave way to modern foreign languages. Even more "practically" oriented were the vocational classes that began to invade the high schools under the prodding of the National Society for the Promotion of Industrial Education. In 1917 Congress—recognizing the value of teaching "manual training," including carpentry, printing, home economics, mechanical drawing, and agriculture—passed the Smith-Hughes Act providing subsidies to the states to underwrite vocational and industrial skills courses for high school students.

Higher Education.   During these same years the United States became a world leader in college and university education. Before the Civil War the typical American college was a small church-related institution that prepared young men for the ministry or for the learned professions. Most had a few hundred students, a single classroom building, a museum containing stuffed and preserved animals, and a library of a few hundred books, mostly on religion, tucked into some corner. Faculties were small, and many of the professors were ministers who doubled in science and modern languages—if these subjects were taught at all.

After the Civil War change came swiftly. The Morrill Land Grant College Act (1862) provided funds for a new class of agricultural and technical colleges, many of which developed into major universities. At

The burgeoning high school system of the late nineteenth century was designed to produce office workers as well as better-educated citizens. Here we see the typing class in an 1899 Washington, D.C., high school.

the same time vast sums flowed from the swollen fortunes of post–Civil War tycoons to establish new colleges and universities and revive old, sleepy ones. Under the guidance of a new breed of college president, curricula altered rapidly to provide students with training in the sciences, modern languages, and the new social sciences, as well as vocational courses such as accounting. The boldest changes came when president Charles W. Eliot of Harvard developed the elective system, ending the requirement of tightly prescribed courses and allowing students to choose their own program within broad limits.

Another important change was the expansion of higher education for women. Before 1860 only a handful of institutions allowed women to take college degrees. After the Civil War these limits were quickly swept away as women's colleges proliferated and state universities opened their doors to men and women on an equal basis. In the older elite schools—the so-called Ivy League—women were admitted to sister institutions with separate faculties, courses, and buildings. In the state schools they sat in the same classrooms with men, though they used separate dormitories and were subject to stricter social rules.

In some ways the most important advance in higher education during this period was the appearance of the research university and the graduate school. Before the Civil War, though some professors occasionally performed experiments or engaged in scholarly pursuits, research was not considered a part of faculty duties. During the 1840s and 1850s, however, a number of Americans studied in Germany, where they encountered a different system. German universities were not just glorified academies. They were institutions where young men were trained in the techniques of discovering new knowledge and where faculty members were themselves engaged in pushing forward the frontiers of science and scholarship.

Americans trained in the German universities carried the new idea to their native land, and after the Civil War these seeds bore fruit in the modern American university. The first institution founded on the German model was Johns Hopkins, which opened in Baltimore in 1876. Hopkins was primarily a graduate school where the sciences, social sciences, and humanities were treated as scholarly disciplines. The new university employed the seminar system, wherein a prominent scholar and a small group of advanced students worked on a common set of problems. The result for the student was published research and the new degree of Ph.D., doctor of philosophy. In the process, it was hoped, the cutting edge of knowledge would be pushed forward a little.

Hopkins was soon widely imitated. Clark University, founded in 1887 at Worcester, Massachusetts, was also patterned after the German model. Meanwhile, other institutions—Harvard, Yale, Columbia, Chicago, Cornell, Michigan, Wisconsin, and Minnesota among them—set up graduate schools for training scholars and scientists. In 1900 some 240 Ph.D.s were conferred on American students, and the degree was well on its way to becoming the "union card" of college teachers.

Professional Education and Professionalism. The process by which college teaching was transformed from a field for amateurs to one dominated by trained and "credentialed" experts was paralleled in other professional areas. In part the trend was inspired by the sheer accumulation of knowledge, which forced each field to divide into ever narrower specializations. This trend was most apparent in the social sciences, where by the end of the century the old "moral philosophy" had been broken down into economics, sociology, psychology, and political science. Professionalization was also a consequence of efforts by occupational groups to raise their status and income by restricting entry into their field.

In law and medicine training through apprenticeship gave way in these years to formal education in law and medical schools. In medicine, at first, this led to an enormous proliferation of inferior schools, some mere diploma mills where students acquired M.D. degrees for a fee and perfunctory work. Doctors trained at these schools were seldom competent in the medical advances of the period, though no doubt some of them made adequate general practitioners. In 1910 a report by Abraham Flexner, supported by the Carnegie Foundation, exposed widespread abuses in medical education and led the American Medical Association to push for the closing of inferior schools and the upgrading of others. The effects were drastic. The number of medical graduates dropped from over 5,000 yearly between 1900 and 1906 to about half that number in 1922. Critics charged that the true purpose of the upgrading was to restrict the number of physicians in order to prevent overcompetition. Yet the changes did indeed improve the level of skills among doctors.

Legal training also improved, though the overall effect was less restrictive. During these years more and more universities established law schools with three-year courses of study. At first, students could begin legal training after high school. Gradually, however, the better law schools insisted on college preparation,

Women scientists were rare before our own day, but not unknown. Here is chemist Ellen Swallow Richards, sitting as part of a group portrait of the faculty of the Massachusetts Institute of Technology (MIT) around 1900. (First row, right.) The first woman to graduate from the institute, she was also the first to serve on its faculty.

and in the 1870s Harvard introduced the case method, a system of learning legal principles by studying actual cases decided by the courts. Lawyers also began to specialize. Increasingly, especially in the larger cities, university-trained lawyers joined corporate law firms where they spent most of their time preparing contracts and mergers and almost never appeared in court.

The process of professionalization soon spread to many other areas. The usual pattern was for some occupational group, feeling dissatisfied with their incomes, social status, and prevailing intellectual levels, to band together in a professional association. The association would then set new standards for education and training and often, in connection with the universities, establish a degree program to be required of all future entrants into the profession. Another step in many cases was to induce state governments to accept the new standards and require them of new entrants to the field. Finally, an examination administered by the state would be imposed on those seeking to practice the profession under state license. In this way such diverse groups as teachers, nurses, engineers, accountants, social workers, dentists, pharmacists, optometrists, and others raised themselves to professional status. As in the case of doctors, their professionalization improved the level of service for the public, but also increased the cost of those services. A final beneficiary of professionalization was the universities, which acquired crowds of students eager to gain professional degrees and the training needed to pass professional licensing exams.

Informal Education for the Masses.   Not all the educational progress and expansion of these years took place in formal schools. Adult Americans by the millions found self-education interesting and enjoyable and sought opportunities to acquire books and instruction outside the schools.

One of the most successful forms of adult education was the Chautauqua Assembly, an institution devoted to bringing learning and instruction to large numbers of people without formal requirements and degrees. Chautauqua began in 1874 when a Methodist clergyman, John H. Vincent, established a summer camp and school for Sunday school teachers in western New York. By the 1880s Chautauqua had left its religious focus behind and had become a sort of informal college where for ten summer weeks thousands of men and women gathered to hear learned and lively speakers such as economist Richard T. Ely; psychologist G. Stanley Hall, president of Clark University; philoso-

pher William James; and historian Herbert Baxter Adams. Chautauqua also offered courses more useful in daily life. Indiana author Edward Eggleston described the enormous range of Chautauqua's offerings:

> You can learn Greek, Latin, Hebrew, and for aught I know Choctaw here. You can learn . . . Penmanship and Pedagogy and Exegetics and Homiletics and History and Rowing and Piano Music and fancy bicycling and singing and athletics and how to read a hymn in public and the art of writing family and Business letters and everything else except dancing and whist.

Chautauqua had no formal ideology or philosophy; but as the century advanced, it tended to feature speakers who represented new ideas that challenged the intellectual pieties of the age. Many of the clergymen represented the new social gospel, which called on Christians to aid the weak and oppressed. Chautauqua economists like Ely rejected extreme laissez-faire doctrines and were friendlier to organized labor than their predecessors had been. Chautauqua speaks also favored women's suffrage, the peace movement, and even socialism. In fact, the Chautauqua Assembly of the 1890s and the first decade of the new century was a major dissemination center for the ideas that would be called "progressive." This effect was enhanced in 1904 when Chautauqua established summer seminars in small towns all over the country. These were held in communities for a week at a time and usually conducted in tents. In addition, the Chautauqua Assembly established more permanent summer camps, modeled after the New York original, in such places as Boulder, Colorado.

An even less formal disseminator of knowledge was the public library. Before the Civil War the few tax-supported free libraries had been concentrated in a handful of eastern cities. Elsewhere avid readers had either bought books or borrowed them from those who could afford private libraries. The few large libraries that existed had primitive system of classification that reduced their value to users. After the war, under the leadership of Melvil Dewey and W. F. Poole, the American Library Association (founded 1876) developed classification systems that would be an immense aid as libraries grew in size. The association also lobbied for tax support, and by 1898 eighteen states had authorized local communities to impose taxes to support public libraries. In 1881 Andrew Carnegie began his program of contributions to public libraries, which eventually dotted the nation with "Carnegie libraries" from the Atlantic to the Pacific. By 1900 there were over 9,000 free public libraries in the country, with nearly 50 million volumes.

Paralleling this development was the rise of the research library. By the end of the century, owing to generous gifts or legislative appropriations, institutions such as the Library of Congress, the New York Public Library, the Newberry Library in Chicago, and the Cleveland Public Library had become centers of scholarship in the humanities. College and university libraries, too, burgeoned as American institutions of higher learning moved into the forefront of scholarship and research. By the eve of World War I the largest American university libraries had surpassed in size those of European institutions founded many centuries earlier.

The New Journalism

Newspapers on the eve of the Civil War were very different from their counterparts today. They were much smaller, only sixteen to twenty pages long. In part this reflected the fact that they contained a fraction of the advertising they do today, but it also betokened far skimpier coverage of national and international events. News-gathering facilities were primitive. Foreign news, in the absence of the transatlantic cable (which was not successfully laid until 1866), took weeks to arrive. Domestic news was transmitted more quickly, but only a few of the very largest urban papers had reporters outside their home cities, and usually only in Washington and the state capitals. For coverage of any American community but their home towns, newspaper editors were forced to copy stories from other newspapers received in the mail.

The newspaper of 1860 was different from its modern version in other ways, too. It had no pictures, because it was not yet possible to print photographs on newsprint. There were a few illustrated weeklies, but they relied on woodcuts or copper engravings, which could not be prepared quickly enough for the daily press. There were no comic strips, syndicated news columnists, food columns, horoscopes, or advice to the lovelorn. Anyone reading an 1860 newspaper today would also be surprised by the relative sedateness of the news coverage. Editors reported crimes and disasters, but usually in a fairly sober, matter-of-fact way. Most of their space was filled with political news of Washington, the state capital, and the local board of aldermen. Such fare was reported in enormous detail that only a political historian can appreciate.

New Trends in Newspapers. By the early years of the twentieth century newspaper publishing had undergone a revolution. Part of the impetus for change came from the growing city population, which created a concentrated market. Part was the result of new ways of gathering news and packaging it. Technology transformed the collection and transmission of information, and the newspaper industry itself. At the end of the 1870s the modern typewriter, capable of printing both lower-case and capital letters, appeared. A decade later Ottmar Mergenthaler invented the linotype machine, which eliminated the need to set type by hand. Cheap pulp paper came into use about the same time, as did processes for fast reproduction of illustrations and photographs. The telephone, invented in the mid-1870s, was widely used by the 1890s and proved a useful tool for news gathering.

Meanwhile, promoters conceived the idea of an organization that would gather news from around the world and sell it to local editors. The first of these groups was the Associated Press, an organization that grew out of an antebellum pooling arrangement among New York newspapers. The United Press came in 1882. In 1884 S. S. McClure established "Newspaper Features," providing ready-made syndicated columns, stories, a "woman's page," and other features to subscribing newspapers.

Taking advantage of these changes was a group of aggressive editors. One of them, Joseph Pulitzer, was a man of broad social sympathies who retained his respect for journalism even while he appealed to popular taste. An Hungarian refugee who arrived in the United States in 1864 with hardly a penny, Pulitzer became active in St. Louis publishing and in 1878 acquired the St. Louis *Post-Dispatch*. He soon made the ailing paper a success and with the money he accumulated bought the *New York World*.

As editor of the *World*, Pulitzer helped create what critics would call "yellow journalism." His paper emphasized "human interest" stories—crime, corruption, disasters, strange reversals of the usual order of things, sudden luck, and the like. The *World* printed illustrations showing "X—where the Body Was Found." Its headlines ran to: "Baptized in Blood," and "Death Rides the Blast." Pulitzer also attracted readers by promotional schemes, such as dispatching the "girl reporter" Nellie Bly in a world-circling race to beat Jules Verne's fictional hero of *Around the World in Eighty Days*. He was also the first editor to print a comic strip, R. F. Outcault's "The Yellow Kid," printed in yellow ink, which provided the name for

The new yellow journalism of Hearst and Pulitzer was brash and readable. The city room of Pulitzer's *New York World*, with its shirtsleeved editors and reporters, captures some of the informality and hectic pace of the late-nineteenth-century urban newspaper.

Pulitzer's approach to the newspaper business.

Pulitzer's yellow journalism was enormously successful. When he acquired the *World*, its circulation was 15,000. By 1898 he was selling a million papers a day. He soon acquired a flock of imitators, including the Scripps brothers in Detroit, Cleveland, St. Louis, and Cincinnati and William Randolph Hearst in San Francisco. In 1895 Hearst came to New York, determined to outdo Pulitzer. He introduced his own comic strips, "The Katzenjammer Kids" and "Happy Hooligan," and then stole "The Yellow Kid" from Pulitzer. Before many months his *New York Journal* was engaged in a full-scale circulaton war with the *World*, with each editor attempting to outsensationalize the other. In later years Hearst acquired or established newspapers all over the nation and even set up his own press service. By the early years of the twentieth century he had become the nation's most powerful "press lord," using a formula of sensationalism plus human interest that usually lacked Pulitzer's saving grace of concern for the underdog.

Magazines. Magazines also responded to the new technology and new urban mass market for reading material. Most of the successful magazines before the Civil War had been highly literate small-circulation publications intended for the educated middle and upper class. In the 1880s a number of magazine publishers tried, like Pulitzer and Hearst, to take advantage of

new printing technology and city audiences. Dutch-born Edward W. Bok turned the recently established *Ladies' Home Journal* into a success by offering light fiction, pieces on interesting personalities, "Talks With Girls," and house plans, as well as articles on food, fashions, and house care—and all for 10 cents a copy. Samuel S. McClure took advantage of drastically reduced printing costs and growing advertising revenues to launch a mass-circulation magazine of general interest, *McClure's*. In 1893 the first copy, selling for 15 cents, appeared. Soon after Frank Munsey launched *Munsey's*, followed quickly by Hearst's *Cosmopolitan*, both priced at 10 cents. Until McClure hit on the muckraking formula in 1903 (described in Chapter 23), all three mass-circulation magazines relied on good illustrations and popular, skillful authors to attract enough readers to make a profit despite the low price. And they succeeded. By the end of the century magazine readership had expanded to over five times that of the 1870s.

New Modes of Thought

In the half century following the Civil War the way Americans thought about their world and about society underwent an enormous shift. Not all Americans were equally affected by the changes, of course. Inevitably, many continued to accept the received wisdom of their predecessors; some actively fought the new trends. But a substantial group of urban, educated men and women adjusted their thinking to a flood of new ideas, many of them derived ultimately from the theories of the English naturalist Charles Darwin.

We have already seen in Chapter 17 how the ideas of Darwin served as a prop for laissez-faire thinking. In this role Darwinian ideas played the conservative function of reinforcing accepted belief. Yet Darwinism had a profoundly disturbing tendency as well, unsettling old attitudes and ways of thinking about society.

American social thought at the end of the Civil War had been "formalistic." Attitudes tended to be rooted in some kind of received wisdom transmitted from the past. This wisdom, it was assumed by thinkers of the day, was based on universal characteristics or principles that changed little over time. To understand the world, to prescribe policies for society, one merely had to reason logically from these first principles. To a very large extent formalistic thinkers assumed a static, rather than dynamic, reality, and held tight to precedent and tradition when considering the lot of humankind.

The chief target of Darwin's revolutionary book, *The Origin of Species* (1859), was the traditional view that all the species of plants and animals in nature had been created at one moment of time and thereafter were fixed and changeless. Against this claim Darwin posited constant change through a fierce struggle for existence. Species with qualities that made for survival lived to pass along their attributes to their descendants; those ill equipped for the struggle died out, and their lines disappeared. Ultimately life forms once alike diverged into new species. In this way all living things had evolved over time from simpler to evermore complex and specialized ones. In *The Descent of Man* (1871) Darwin carried his analysis one step further: Humankind, too, he said, was not a product of special creation, but the result of evolution from other, lower species.

Reform Darwinism.   Darwinism worked a powerful effect in many realms of thought. As we have seen, in the form of social Darwinism, it was a conservative force buttressing laissez-faire social policies. But it could also reinforce the opposite view. Many social thinkers found it a force for progress. Darwin, they said, proved that all institutions were the products of change over time. They were not static; they evolved the way living species evolved. Indeed, this view said, society was more like an organism that went through cycles of changes as it matured than like a machine that conformed to fixed motions prescribed by the

nature of its design. Institutions, then, must be allowed to change. In fact, said these "reform Darwinists," they must be encouraged to change so as to maximize human welfare.

One man who found a progressive lesson in Darwinism was the sociologist Lester Ward. Ward believed that evolution implied cooperation as well as competition. Advance to higher forms and higher institutions did not necessarily emerge from a hands-off policy. A man who had spent many years as a federal civil servant, Ward did not fear government. Society's ultimate goal, he believed, should be "the scientific control of the social forces by the collective mind of society." Similarly, Richard T. Ely used Darwinism to support the idea that government should play a positive role in the economy. One of the founders of the American Economic Association (1885), Ely, unlike most contemporary academic economists, endorsed trade unions and believed the state was "an educational and ethical agency whose positive aid is an indispensable condition of human progress."

A still more radical break with the economic formalism of the past emerged from the fertile mind of the Norwegian-American Thorstein Veblen. Veblen rejected the economic "first principles" associated with the laissez-faire economists of England. These assumed that people made decisions based on rational self-interest and that people's efforts to maximize their material advantages explained how the economy operated. Nonsense! Veblen said. People behaved as illogically in the economic sphere as in others. They were more often impelled by inherited drives and historically transmitted cultural values than by the desire to maximize wealth or profit. In *The Theory of the Leisure Class* (1899) Veblen demonstrated to his own satisfaction that the great business magnates of the day were impelled as much by the primitive drives for status and emulation as by rational calculation. In later books he spoke about the "instinct of workmanship" as the wellspring of true economic progress. Veblen's major intellectual contribution, however, was to create a new school of "institutional" economics that substituted the study of economic practices evolving over time for model-making based on supposed first principles.

Legal thinking, too, felt the impact of the evolutionary revolt against formalism. Here the outstanding figure was Oliver Wendell Holmes, Jr., associate justice of the Supreme Court (1902–1932) and one of the great legal minds of his generation. Holmes attacked the idea that the law was unchanging, a static set of rules struck off by some great intellect in the past or the incontestable collective wisdom of the ages. Such

Social Darwinism

There were several ways that conservatives justified the inequalities of the social order in late-nineteenth-century America. One of the more popular was recourse to "social Darwinsim," a theory that held that in human society, as in the natural world, the struggle for survival was the only way that progress was achieved. The theory was drawn from the "evolutionary" ideas of Charles Darwin, the eminent English naturalist, as spread through the writings of the English philosopher Herbert Spencer. Among Spencer's disciples in the United States none was more forceful than William Graham Sumner, an Episcopal priest-turned-college professor, whose 1883 book, *What Social Classes Owe to Each Other*, is excerpted below.

"The humanitarians, philanthropists, and reformers, looking at the facts of life as they present themselves, find enough which is sad and unpromising in the condition of many members of society. They see wealth and poverty side by side. They note great inequality of social position and social chances. They eagerly set about the attempt to account for what they see, and to devise schemes for remedying what they do not like. In their eagerness to recommend the less fortunate classes to pity and consideration they forget all about the rights of other classes; they gloss over all the faults of the classes in question, and they exaggerate their misfortunes and their virtues. They invent new theories of property, distorting rights and perpetuating injustice. . . . When I have read certain of these discussions I have thought that it must be quite disreputable to be respectable, quite dishonest to own property, quite un-just to go one's own way and earn one's own living, and the only really admirable person was the good-for-nothing. The man who by his own effort raises himself above poverty appears, in these discussions, to be of no account. . . .

"We owe it to the other [person] to guarantee rights. Rights do not pertain to *results*, but only to *chances*. They pertain to the *conditions* of the struggle for existence, not to any of the results of it; to the *pursuit* of happiness, not to the possession of happiness. It cannot be said that each one has a right to have some property, because if one man had such a right some other man or men would be under a corresponding obligation to provide him with some property. . . .

"The only help which is generally expedient . . . is that which consists in helping a man to help himself. . . . Now, the aid which helps a man to help himself is not in the least akin to the aid which is given in charity. If alms are given, or if we 'make work' for a man, or 'give him employment,' or 'protect' him, we simply take a product from one and give it to another. If we help a man to help himself, by opening the chances around him, we put him in a position to add to the wealth of the community by putting new powers in operation to produce. . . .

". . . The class distinctions [in society] simply result from the different degrees of success with which men have availed themselves of the chances which were presented to them. Instead of endeavoring to redistribute the acquisitions which have been made between the existing classes, or aim should be to *increase, multiply, and extend the chances*. Such is the work of civilization. . . ."

a view, he stated in *The Common Law* (1881), was merely a convenient defense of the past. All law, even that embodied in revered documents like the federal Constitution, incorporated views that had evolved gradually in response to the needs of particular periods and groups: "the felt necessities of the time, the prevalent moral and political theories, institutions of public policy, avowed or unconscious, even the prejudices which judges share with their fellow men, have a good deal more to do than the syllogism in determining the rules by which men should be governed." When the law corresponded to existing circumstances and filled current needs, there was no reason to quarrel with it. But it must change, must evolve, with the times, said Holmes. When it lagged behind, when it was out of touch with modern conditions and needs, it merely served as a brake on progress. Holmes was seconded by Roscoe Pound, dean of Harvard Law School, whose "sociological jurisprudence" called for "putting the human factor in the central place and relegating logic to its true position as an instrument."

In the discipline of history we find the same critical spirit during the years following 1890. The scholars of the New History found Darwinism useful as a weapon against the prevailing tradition of their discipline. Amercian historical studies as promoted by Herbert Baxter Adams had emphasized the extent to which characteristic American institutions were planted as "germs" by northern European settlers. Thus the New England town meeting and ultimately the nation's democratic legislatures were survivals of ancient German assemblies. There was no sense in the work of Adams's students that the American environment had substantially altered those germs. Then in 1893 Frederick Jackson Turner delivered his famous address before the Chicago meeting of the American Historical Association and turned the study of American history on its head. "American democracy," Turner declared, "was born of no theorist's dream; it was not carried in the *Susan Constant* to Virginia, nor in the *Mayflower* to Plymouth. It came out of the American forest, and it gained new strength each time it touched a new frontier." Here, then, was an evolutionary view of American institutions, one that took seriously the three centuries of experience on American soil.

Turner eventually developed a theory of change that emphasized the molding effect of the physical environment. Charles Beard believed that class was more important. In his pioneering *An Economic Interpretation of the Constitution* (1913) Beard sought to demonstrate that the framers of the federal Constitution were not demigods free of class prejudices and interests and concerned only with dispassionate justice. Rather, he said, the Constitution was a document constructed by a coalition of merchants, speculators, and assorted businessmen to defend private property; it was based on the principles and interests of their class. By relating the Constitution to its time, Beard confirmed Holmes's view of the historical relativity of the law.

Pragmatism. The new spirit of dissent from static and excessively abstract ways of viewing social institutions also affected the most abstract area of thought, philosophy. The new approach was pragmatism, and its major examplars were John Dewey and William James.

Like many literate Americans of this era, the pragmatists were profoundly impressed by the success and prestige of the natural sciences and sought to make philosophy as useful as tool as physics, chemistry, or engineering. The old view, they noted, held that truth was an abstract, fixed reality. It assumed that there was some ultimate measuring rod to which statements or beliefs corresponded. But this was not so. Truth, in reality, was a quality that changed, evolved, as relationships were viewed from different perspectives or as an idea was employed for different purposes. To the pragmatists, most of the ideas about ultimate realities that had concerned philosophers and other thinkers simply had no real answers, except formal and inconse-

quential ones. What men and women needed to know was *what difference did it make* whether this was true or that was false. The value of an idea, then, was not in its truth or falsity in the traditional sense, but in what consequences flowed from believing it or applying it. Thus in *The Varieties of Relgious Experience* (1902) William James tackled the problem of the existence of God and the truth of traditional religion by asserting that belief or doubt could only be validated by showing whether it brought comfort and hope. Truth was related to consequences and could not be understood in any other way. In an unfortunate and misunderstood, but vivid, phrase, James declared that it was "the cash value" of an idea that counted.

Because true ideas were those that had desirable effects in the world around us, the purpose of thought was not to contemplate eternity but to solve problems and serve as a guide to some practical course of action. In John Dewey's version of pragmatism the model of all truth-seeking was the experimental method of the natural sciences. Social and political ideas could not be tested by rigorous experiments, perhaps, but social and political thinkers, like natural scientists, could ask about the consequences of choosing course *A* as opposed to course *B* and act accordingly.

The pragmatic approach was experimental, practical, relativistic, and evolutionary. To the pragmatists the world was not rigidly laid out and determined. It was, rather, incomplete, ongoing, open, diverse, and turbulent—very much like the urban-industrial America of the day—and the task of philosophers and other thinkers was to find solutions to the problems of real people in the real world.

As a whole, pragmatism was a method or approach rather than a fully rounded system with clear answers to problems. Yet in one area, education, Dewey sought to apply his ideas directly. He believed that the education of the day was excessively static, mechanical, and irrelevant to the new society he saw around him. Rather than memorizing by rote, he wanted students to be actively involved in learning. Dewey's disciples, the "progressive" educators, called this kind of teaching "learning by doing." He also believed that teachers should spend less time on books and more on showing students how to get along with one another so that they could ultimately make society less competitive and exploitative.

Besides a new pedagogical approach, pragmatic education demanded new subject matter suited to a new age. The traditional curriculum emphasized Latin and Greek, polite literature, ancient history, and formal mathematics as training for the mind. In the modern

A Historical Portrait

William James

Few men epitomize the American spirit at its best so well as William James, the philosopher and experimental psychologist. Optimistic, tolerant, generous, liberal, practical, and forward-looking, he transformed these attitudes into a major philosophical approach that we call *pragmatism*. Though at times expressed in the technical jargon of academic philosophy, pragmatism was a distillation of the American experience of subduing a continent and creating a people.

William James was the grandson of a Scotch-Irish immigrant, also named William, who arrived in America in 1789 and made a fortune in business in Albany, New York. His son, Henry, was afforded the leisure of a gentleman by his father's wealth, but he rejected his father's dour Presbyterian Calvinism. Henry devoted his life to literature, conversation, social reform, and the pursuit of spiritual fulfillment. The young William, his first child after his marriage to Mary Robertson Walsh, grew up in a household where Emerson, Thoreau, Bryant, Greeley, Tennyson, Carlyle, and Mill were frequent guests, and the great theories and ideas of the age were discussed more often than the price of eggs or the best way to remove a clothing stain.

William's father was physically as well as intellectually and spiritually restless. The family never seemed to settle down anyplace. The Jameses traveled often, and William and his younger siblings, including Henry Jr., the future novelist, lived for long periods in Albany, New York, Boston, London, Paris, Berlin, Geneva, Florence, and other places. The children attended schools of many different kinds, for their father had advanced ideas about the proper nurture of young people and was constantly trying out new schemes. It was an unusually cosmopolitan experience for a young American, but it never undermined William's quintessentially American values.

When William reached adulthood he was forced to consider a profession. His father preferred science; William preferred painting. For a time William studied under the artists William M. Hunt and John La Farge in Newport, but after a year concluded that he was not greatly gifted as a painter and in 1861 entered the Lawrence Scientific School at Harvard. Here he studied chemistry and physiology and in 1864 entered the Harvard Medical School. He did not earn his M.D. degree until 1869.

The delay was caused by indecisiveness and poor health. In 1865 William took nine months off to join an expedition to the Amazon region to collect plant and animal specimens. Back at Harvard, he met the young war veteran Oliver Wendell Holmes, Jr., then resuming his law studies after three years fighting the Confederates. James thought "Wendell" a "first rate article," but disagreed with his friend's overemphasis on thought. "Feeling counts," he retorted, thus announcing a principle that would remain fundamental to his philosophy throughout his life.

Another major delay in his formal education occurred soon after. James was attracted to the scientific side of medicine, but did not like the bedside visits with patients and daily hospital rounds. He found the work dull and tiring, and began to suffer severe back pains. He became deeply depressed and thought at times of suicide. In April 1867 he took another leave of absence from Harvard and sailed for Europe to "take the baths" at the German and Austrian spas and immerse himself in German science to rest his troubled spirit.

The year and a half abroad neither improved his health nor resolved his career uncertainties. He returned to Cambridge and obtained his medical degree, but found it impossible to settle down as a doctor. For almost three years James drifted, still depressed and beset by physical maladies. He also began to experience fierce attacks of dread and panic. He finally achieved a psychological breakthrough when he read an essay by the French philosopher Charles Renouvier, on the freedom of the will, that cut through his despair and made him feel it was possible to mold one's life as one wished; the human being was not simply a woodchip tossed about aimlessly by the currents of the world.

James's emotional recovery coincided with a renaissance at Harvard under its new president, Charles W. Eliot, one of James's old teachers. In 1872 Eliot appointed James to an instructorship in physiology at the college, and for the next ten years James taught comparative anatomy, hygiene, and physiology to Harvard undergraduates. But he did not teach his subjects in a conventional way. By this time he had become convinced that there was no easy way to separate body from mind. His own experience had taught him that thoughts and feelings had a profound influence on bodily functions. Out of this came a growing interest in psychology, then a new subject in the college curriculum. In 1875 he offered a course on the "Relations Between Physiology and Psychology." The course was soon transferred to the department of philosophy, and in 1880 James himself joined that department.

The 1870s and 1880s were decades of growing satisfaction for James personally and professionally. In 1878 he married Alice Howe Gibbens, an intelligent, competent, and interesting Boston schoolteacher, the daughter of a country doctor. The marriage was a rare success. They had five children, four of whom lived to maturity. Alice proved a supportive, though not infinitely tolerant, wife. She had saved him from hopeless neurasthnia, he later declared. William also took great pleasure in the literary success of his brother, Henry, who during this decade achieved celebrity as a novelist.

During the 1880s James's major intellectual preoccupation was a psychology text he had contracted for in 1878. He did not intend to supply a mere rehash of the accepted principles, though the publisher would have been content with that. Instead, he hoped to break new ground. Writing such a work, however, proved to be a gigantic task, and The Principles of Psychology did not appear until 1890, when it attracted wide acclaim as a new view of the way the mind worked.

James saw the mind as essentially a tool with which the individual dealt with his or her environment. It was not some mystical entity; it had a biological basis and, like all biological appurtenances, had evolved over time. In divorcing the idea of mind from older concepts, James went so far as to declare that what we perceive as emotions are really only the biological responses—rapid pulse, thumping heart, churning stomach, sweaty palms, and so forth—that are *associated* with emotions. Some of James's readers felt that he had reduced human beings to unfeeling ro-

bots, but that was never his intention. To the end of this life he refused to accept this sort of crude materialism because it seemed deterministic, suggesting a closed universe and the impossibility of human beings changing things or mastering their own fate.

During the decade following the publication of the *Principles* James made philosophy his field, with the issue of how we know his special interest. Here he encountered two competing philosophical schools. The first, *rationalism*, held that we know first principles instinctively because they are emanations from God. We then ultimately deduce from these all the other aspects of reality. The second, *empiricism*, rejected deduction from first principles and held instead that all knowledge comes from observation of discrete events and phenomena. James liked the empiricists' skepticism of grandiose systems that purported to explain everything, but he was impatient with their refusal ever to generalize. Empiricism's rejection of principles left the world a buzzing confusion and seemed both cold and arid. It was from a desire to preserve the best of both theories that James evolved his pragmatism. In the process he borrowed much from his Harvard colleague, the philosopher Charles Peirce, who had made "everything is to be tested by its practical results" his philosophical guide.

James's first big philosophic project was a book on religion. He could not accept traditional religious views as the exact truth. But he also found atheism and agonisticism unacceptable because they deprived the individual of the comfort of religion. In the essays collected in *The Will to Believe* in 1897, he asserted that individuals had the right to accept any view of the universe, whether "provable" or not, that provided the emotional support they needed. James himself followed this principle. How-

ever much the scientist, for example, he was a spiritualist who believed it possible to communicate through "mediums" with the dead.

At the end of the nineteenth century James found himself drawn into political controversy. He was a democrat who had enormous respect for the free and egalitarian institutions of his native land. He deplored the seizure of the Philippines after the Spanish-American War as a repudiation of American traditions of self-rule for all people. These views drew him into the anti-imperialist movement, which was dedicated to keeping the United States from joining the Western nations' race for empire.

James's major contribution to philosophy came in the last decade of his life, though it was foreshadowed many years earlier. In a series of lectures given in 1907 he elaborated the theory of pragmatism associated with his name. James expressed impatience at many of the age-old controversies about the "truth" of particular ideas or propositions. These would never be settled. But that was irrelevant, for what was important was not whether some concept was true in some supposedly final, ultimate way, but whether believing it *made a difference* and whether it was useful in human terms. As a Darwinian, James linked this view to the idea of an evolving universe, one that never reached a final, static form, but was perpetually open to change. Truths, then, were working hypotheses that we could use for our purposes. Critics charged that this reduced truth to personal opinion and made any view, any belief, as good as any other. James responded that it merely required that each person's view meet the test of workability, that it have "cash value." In the hands of a younger group of philosophers associated with John Dewey at the University of Chicago, pragmatism became a system called "instrumentalism," of subjecting social ideas to the scientific method.

James's last years were marked by both sunlight and shadow. His books and lectures were enormously popular and successful and he received international recognition. Frequent trips to Europe and to California, visiting professorships and lectureships, generous praise by much of the world's intellectual community, brought variety and satisfaction. Distinguished men and women from all over the Western world came to visit the Jameses in Cambridge or at their summer places in the Adirondacks and New Hampshire. His family life was happy. Alice, as always, was warm and supportive, and his children brought him pleasure. But for the last decade of his life James was afflicted with a severe heart condition; in 1909 he began to suffer serious chest pains. As a doctor, he knew how serious his condition was, but he could not relax or slow his pace. In early 1910 the Jameses sailed for Europe to visit Henry, now living permanently in England. William was sick during much of the time and the Jameses returned home in August, with William failing, and made their way to their New Hampshire summer house. On the evening of August 26th Alice recorded in her diary: "William died just before 2:30 in my arms. I was coming in with milk and saw the change. No pain at the last and no consicousness. . . . Poor Henry, poor children."

age, the pragmatists said, men and women must be trained for jobs, for solving personal problems, and for performing the civic duties of an industrial society. The history taught should be the past of the students' own society; geography, that of their own city and neighborhood. Dewey was also sympathetic to vocational education. Students should learn how to operate machines, cook and sew, and set type. Out of the new school would come new citizens who would know how their world worked, be prepared to perform the tasks it required, and be able to lead it along more humane paths.

Dewey first introduced these new attitudes and approaches into the experimental school at the University of Chicago during the 1890s. In 1904 he came to New York to join the faculty of Columbia University. At Teacher's College, a division of Columbia, Dewey profoundly influenced an entire generation of professors of education and through them hundreds of students. Eventually these young men and women fanned out across the nation, carrying the message of progressive education and spreading it to virtually every school system in the country.

Religion and Modernism.   Darwinian ideas were profoundly disturbing to many people. Not all scientists accepted them. Louis Agassiz, a distinguished Harvard zoologist, and James Dwight Dana, the nation's leading geologist, for example, both rejected Darwin's theory. Still more hostile were traditional Christians, both laypeople and ministers.

In 1865 religion played an immensely important role in the way Americans regarded the world. Of the nation's 36 million people, about 4 million were Catholic and perhaps a tenth that many were Jewish. The rest were nominally Protestant, although probably less than half were active church members. Christian, predominantly Protestant, ideas powerfully affected the way Americans thought about the world and their place in it.

Most Americans accepted the biblical account of Creation, in which the world and all its living creatures were created by God in six days. Most accepted the remainder of the Bible, both the Old and New Testaments, as God's revealed word, literally and exactly true. Darwinian ideas, however, challenged the Bible's authority by proposing evolutionary explanations for events that the Bible represents as occurring in one stroke. If Darwin was right, the Bible could not be literally true. Not only was this unthinkable, but it also undermined the crucial idea that all people were the children of God, made in God's image. How could human beings be regarded merely as higher forms of animals?

Traditional Protestant belief was also under attack from a different quarter, as scholars in England, France, and Germany began to examine the Bible as a historical document. Exponents of the so-called Higher Criticism saw the Scriptures as a work of men, compiled over generations and containing, not so much God's exact words, as the thoughts of inspired poets, chroniclers, philosophers, and prophets. Though the

Higher Criticism originated abroad, it quickly won disciples among the American Protestant clergy and laity.

Some clergymen—including popular Brooklyn preacher Henry Ward Beecher, Lyman Abbott, President James McCosh of Princeton University, and others—found it possible to accept both the essential truth of Christianity and the views of the Darwinians. Yet many Protestants, especially among the more evangelical denominations with rural roots, saw Darwin's ideas and the Higher Criticism as unproved theories that endangered true religion. To counter these forms of modernism the traditionalists insisted on certain basic principles as essential to Christian belief, and in 1910 they published a pamphlet, the *Fundamentals*, that enumerated five points as the foundation of true Christian faith: the infallibility of the Bible, Jesus' virgin birth, his resurrection, his atonement for humankind, and the inevitability of his second coming. In the following decades those who belonged to fundamentalist denominations that accepted the "Five Points" would wage an intense battle to halt the erosion of traditional Protestantism and the growth of the modernism they perceived as false and dangerous to society.

Religion and Social Justice. Another challenge to traditional Protestantism that arose during the 1870s and 1880s came from clergymen and laypeople who believed that Protestantism had retreated too far from the old Puritan zeal to make the world a better place and had lost contact with the urban poor. As a result, they felt, the United States was becoming a society of pagans who associated the church only with privilege.

One response to this perceived failure was the "social gospel" movement. To ministers such as Washington Gladden, William Bliss, and Walter Rauschenbusch, it appeared that Christianity had failed the poor by emphasizing the problem of personal salvation excessively. Religion to traditional Christians, Gladden explained, was "too much a matter between themselves and God." Yet true Christianity was social as much as individual. It required righteous dealings with other people, not merely concern for personal salvation. To the social gospel preachers it seemed essential that the churches take stands on social issues and defend the weak and oppressed from those who exploited them. As early as the 1880s Gladden endorsed trade unions and the right to strike. Bliss, an Episcopal minister influenced by the Christian socialists of England, organized an American society of Christian socialists in 1889. Rauschenbusch denounced the competitive economic system and supported one based on the cooperative ideal.

Social gospel ideas were especially powerful among the Unitarians, Episcopalians, Methodists, and Congregationalists—the denominations that were also most open to the Higher Criticism and new scientific ideas generally. In 1905 thirty-three social gospel–oriented denominations, representing millions of communications, banded together in the Federal Council of Churches of Christ in America. The Council endorsed the abolition of child labor, and the adoption of the six-day workweek, workers' compensation for injury, old-age insurance, a living wage for workers, and other social reforms.

Other Protestants responded to the poverty and demoralization of urban centers in more conservative ways. The Salvation Army, an evangelical body founded in England by William Booth and brought to America in 1880, sought to rescue drunkards, petty criminals, prostitutes, and other outcast men and women in the slums. At first the Army focused on the traditional evangelical methods of calling sinners to repentance and reform. To attract people to meetings, the Army deployed its forces on slum street corners and in city downtowns, armed with trombones and drums. After the sermon at the Army's "shelter,"

The now-familiar uniform of the Salvation Army was a welcome sight in the city slums of the late nineteenth and early twentieth centuries. As part of their evangelizing work, Army volunteers provided food, shelter, and other necessities to the homeless and destitute.

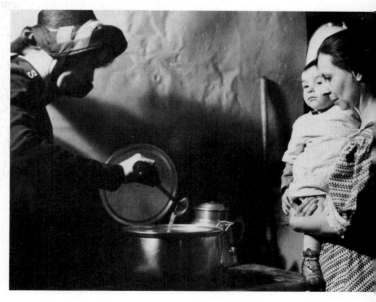

those who stayed could count on a free meal. By the 1890s the Army had begun to establish slum employment bureaus, provide cheap lodging for vagrants, and perform other social services.

The Young Men's Christian Association (YMCA) was a more middle-class organization. Founded in England, the "Y" was brought to the United States in 1851 and devoted its labors to preserving the Christian faith of young men newly arrived in the city. It provided reading rooms, religious classes, and clubs. It also offered gymnasiums and eventually established inexpensive hotels where young male newcomers to the city could stay until they found more permanent homes. In 1858 the Young Women's Christian Association (YWCA) was formed to provide the same mixture of nondenominational Protestantism and urban social services.

Conclusions

The cultural life of the United States underwent a colossal transformation in the half century following the Civil War. On every level, from the heights of academic philosophy to the everyday amusements of ordinary men and women, culture adapted to the new urbanism and to the changes in technology and in political and economic institutions that swept the nation.

The cultural effects of the new forces were both direct and roundabout. The movie industry was clearly a product of post–Civil War urbanization. It also depended on inventions possible only after years of technological advance. Other changes, however, were affected by the new forces in more oblique ways. Many of the ideas adapted to the emerging world of industry and cities derived from Darwinian evolution. Yet evolutionary theory itself was a product of scientific change and growing concern for the problems of a postagricultural society. It is significant that Darwin got his central idea of the struggle for survival from a book by the English economist-demographer Thomas Malthus, who was concerned about the population explosion that accompanied the English industrial revolution.

Were the cultural adaptations to the new forces cheap and vulgar? Did Gilded Age America become a "chromo civilization"? So many changes are involved that it would be difficult under any circumstances to answer these questions. The problem is made worse by the fact that we are seeking to evaluate ideas as well as artistic expression.

In the case of the arts, surely the changes of the period 1865–1915 were "progressive." In literature, for example, it is difficult not to applaud the eclipse of insipid gentility by a robust realism; in architecture it is difficult to defend the imitative old guard against the innovative Louis Sullivan and Frank Lloyd Wright. In these cases, as in many others, adaptations unleashed new creative energies. In the area of popular culture, too, the changes of the period were surely advances. Admittedly, the early movies, yellow journalism, and Tin Pan Alley music, to name a few examples, were generally naive, sensational, or lurid. Yet whatever their initial failings, in time the popular new media and forms of entertainment improved.

Changes in the realm of ideas, however, cannot be seen as a simple matter of progress. The struggle between the progressive thinkers and the formalists, for example, represents merely one round in a battle between competing views of the world, humanity, and God that has been fought in the Western world for hundreds of years. No irrefutable factual basis exists for deciding that one was right and the other wrong. If the formalists were rigid, their opponents could be such flexible relativists as to deny or undermine all moral and intellectual guideposts. Perhaps, for example, the law had to change to suit new circumstances, as Holmes and Roscoe Pound declared. But law that changed at every passing social whim or fad clearly had no claim to moral or intellectual respect. The uncertainty and ultimate subjectivity of conclusions about these approaches can be gauged by the continued existence today of arguments over these same issues.

Meanwhile, as the new century began, the reform impulse reflected in the social gospel, pragmatism, and reform Darwinism began to quicken. Before long the nation would embark on a new crusade informed and inspired by the ideas of James and Dewey, Holmes and Pound, Ward and Ely.

For Further Reading

Morton White. *Social Thought in America: The Revolt Against Formalism* (1957)
    This is not an easy book. Written by a Harvard philosopher who has made American thought his province, it is by far the best study of the changes in social thought as molded by Darwinism in these years.

Richard Hofstadter. *Social Darwinism in American Thought* (1944)

This work deals not only with the conservatives who used Darwin to defend the social and economic status quo, but also with those, like Lester Ward, who used evolutionary ideas to defend reform. Recently Hofstadter's linkage of Darwinism with Gilded Age businessmen has been challenged.

Lawrence Vesey. *The Emergence of the American University* (1965)

This is the best one-volume study of the new currents in graduate and professional training that arose during this period. There are also many goods histories of individual universities—such as Johns Hopkins, Cornell, Columbia, University of Chicago, Harvard, and Yale—that were in the forefront of the new trends.

Lawrence A. Cremin. *The Transformation of the School: Progressivism in American Education, 1876–1957* (1961)

Written by the outstanding historian of American education, this book examines the roots, the course, and the eventual transformation of the "progressive movement" in education that John Dewey helped to launch. Cremin ties changes in educational practice to changes in society and new ways of thinking.

Alfred Kazin. *On Native Grounds* (1942)

A brilliant interpretation of American literature from the 1890s onward. The first third of the volume deals with the "Search for Reality" during the years from 1890 to 1917.

Henry Steele Commager. *The American Mind: An Interpretation of American Thought and Character Since the 1880s* (1950)

An interpretive survey of American thought and the arts from about 1880 to about 1920. Covers an enormous range of topics, with a bias in favor of the new trends in each area discussed.

Arthur M. Schlesinger. *The Rise of the City, 1878–1898* (1933)

This older book is still one of the few good treatments of popular culture as a whole during the Gilded Age. It should be supplemented by the appropriate sections of Russel Nye's *The Unembarrassed Muse; The Popular Arts in America* (1970), which covers a much larger period.

Oliver W. Larkin. *Art and Life in America* (1949)

This work covers far more than the period of this chapter, and so can be consulted selectively by the student of the Gilded Age. Larkin seeks to tie the trends in the visual arts with social change in general. Well illustrated.

John Burchard and Albert Bush-Brown. *The Architecture of America: A Social and Cultural History* (1966)

What applies to Larkin's book also applies to this work.

Lewis Mumford. *The Brown Decades: A Study of the Arts in America, 1865–1895* (1931)

This still readable and useful book was a pathbreaking attack on Victorian architecture and a defense of the "modern" trend. Written by one of the deans of architectural history.

W. A. Swanberg. *Citizen Hearst* (1961)

A colorful, critical biography of William Randolph Hearst, one of the creators of yellow journalism, by an outstanding popular biographer.

Sidney Hook. *John Dewey* (1939)

An intellectual biography of Dewey by one of his most articulate disciples.

Burton Bledstein. *The Culture of Professionalism: The Middle Class and the Development of Higher Education in America* (1976)

Bledstein makes a linkage between the ambition of the mid-nineteenth-century American middle class, the development of the professions, and the rise of the university. The author rides his thesis too hard, but we do learn much about these interrelated events.

Justin Kaplan. *Mr. Clemens and Mark Twain* (1966)

An outstanding literary biography. As the title suggests, Kaplan sees Mark Twain as a deeply divided personality, a man who both wanted wealth and success and despised all that they represented.

Chapter 23

Progressivism

What Were Its Roots and What Were Its Accomplishments?

1874 Women's Christian Temperance Union established

1890 Jane Addam's Hull House opens in Chicago • National American Woman Suffrage Association is formed in a merger of two older groups

1892 Grover Cleveland elected president

1895 Booker T. Washington's Atlanta Compromise Address

1896 *Plessy* v. *Ferguson* legalizes segregation • William McKinley elected president

1899 The National Consumers' League is formed

1900–06 Governor La Follette of Wisconsin establishes state primaries and taxes railroads

1901 McKinley assassinated; Theodore Roosevelt becomes president

1902 Roosevelt's antitrust campaign begins

1903 Congress establishes the Department of Commerce and Labor and the Bureau of Corporations

1904 Roosevelt elected president

1905 W. E. B. DuBois launches the Niagara Movement

1905–07 Most states limit or outlaw child labor

1906 Congress passes Hepburn Act, Meat Inspection Act, and Pure Food and Drug Act

1908 William H. Taft elected president • Aldrich-Vreeland Emergency Currency Act

1909 Ballinger-Pinchot controversy • The Payne-Aldrich Tariff • National Association for the Advancement of Colored People (NAACP) founded

1910 The Mann-Elkins Act • The Mann Act

1911 *Standard Oil Co.* v. *United States*

1912 Woodrow Wilson elected president

1913 The Sixteenth and Seventeenth amendments follow a federal income tax and direct election of senators • The Federal Reserve Act • Underwood Tariff

1914 The Federal Trade Commission Act • The Clayton Antitrust Act • World War I begins in Europe

1916 Wilson sponsors the Federal Farm Loan Act, the Kern-McGillicuddy Act for federal employees, and the Keating-Owen Act limiting child labor

S lowly, as the new century began its first decade, wrote editor William Allen White from the vantage of 1946, "I saw the Great Light. Around me in that day scores of young leaders in American politics and public affairs were seeing what I saw, feeling what I felt. . . . All over the land in a score of states and more, young men in both parties were taking leadership by attacking things as they were in that day."

White's "Great Light" was the desire to change American society that historians have called the Progressive movement. In the years between the beginning of the new century and America's entrance into World War I, men and women of all national backgrounds and classes felt the urge to improve life for themselves and for their fellow citizens. They did not join any one organization; they had no single leader, no neat, well-defined set of goals. Their support of change was not always unselfish. Most groups—whether intellectual, professionals, wage earners, or farmers—understandably placed their own concerns first. Nevertheless, the social sympathies of many progressives would be extraordinarily broad, encompassing many groups besides themselves.

The new views first appeared in the cities during the 1890s. A little later they arrived at the statehouses. Finally, about 1904 or 1905, they came to Washington. When they did, they were given the name "progressivism" and helped transform the nation. How can we explain this sudden passion for reform? What made so many people conclude that things had to change? What did the reformers want and what did they accomplish?

Uncertainties

Fear of Bigness. If any single concern can be said to have united the forces of reform during the opening years of the twentieth century, it is the fear of big, uncontrolled private economic power. The feeling of being at the mercy of great aggregations of private power was not new; it was as old as the Republic. During the first years of the new American nation Jeffersonians had denounced the financial policies of the Hamiltonians as certain to confer too much power on bondholders and other creditors. Forty years later Jacksonians had attacked the Second Bank of the United States as the "monster bank." After the Civil War, dependence on the railroads, middlemen, and other business groups had provoked a strong agrarian reaction from farmers.

In each of these situations small producers—farmers, small manufacturers, and merchants—had found themselves pitted against "monopolists" who threatened to destroy their livelihoods. City people generally, however, had felt secure and had not supported nineteenth-century insurgent movements to reduce the influence of large corporations. Though labor unions fought for higher wages and better working conditions, on the whole they ignored the problem of bigness. This urban indifference, as we have seen, helps to explain the failure of the Populist party and Bryan's defeat in 1896. Then, in the decade following, the attitudes of city dwellers changed. One reason for this shift was the rapid business consolidation that occurred in the closing years of the nineteenth century; another, as we shall see, was the growing dependence of city dwellers on people who produced the goods and the services they needed.

The Growth of Trusts. In the generation following the Civil War the physical integration of the nation, begun in the antebellum years with the building of canals, was brought to swift completion by the railroads. As the cost of shipping goods declined, local markets evolved into regional markets and then into national markets. For a while business competition became sharper and prices dropped. Then, after the more efficient—or the more ruthlessly managed—firms undercut their adversaries and forced them out of business, they reestablished monopoly power over the expanded area. Where two or more competing firms remained, they often preferred to merge into one larger firm rather than engage in the cutthroat competition that did no one any good—except the consumer.

The merger process, as midwifed by J. P. Morgan and other investment bankers, came to a grand climax between 1898 and 1902. In those five years 2,500 big firms merged into giant ones. Every day, it seemed, formerly competing businesses were being consolidated into new, ever larger "trusts." In 1901 the process culminated with the formation of United States Steel, the world's first billion-dollar corporation.

Americans watched the consolidation process with apprehension. Trusts seemed to be everywhere. Not only were there monopolies in banking, railroads, and farm machinery—combinations that Grangers, Greenbackers, and Populists had been attacking for a generation—but in iron and steel, sugar refining, petroleum, meat-packing, can manufacturing, tobacco, public utilities, copper, and many other industries that directly affected city consumers. In 1904 financial analyst John Moody listed 318 trusts, with total capital of over $7.2 billion, "covering every line of productive industry in the United States."

The New Urban Consumers. Almost all Americans deplored the trend toward ever greater concentrations of private economic power. But to urbanites the trusts appeared particularly threatening. Many city people, of course, were producers who turned out manufactured goods in small or large shops. But many others were now white-collar workers—professionals, clerks, accountants, office workers—whose connections with a product were indirect at best. To an increasing extent urban Americans, especially those of the middle class,

viewed themselves more as consumers than producers.

The perception was a new one for Americans in 1900. Earlier most had been farmers. Even though American farmers had never been fully self-sufficient, they had been able to supply many of their own needs. They had slaughtered their own hogs and cattle, raised their own fruits and vegetables, and produced their own eggs and milk. Even urban folk had been less at the mercy of others in the simpler days before 1900. They had been closer to the country suppliers of their needs, and these needs had been less complicated. Through most of the nineteenth century average Americans had burned wood from their own woodlots in their stoves, read by candlelight or firelight, communicated with their friends face to face, gone to work on foot, and doctored themselves with nostrums from their own gardens or from a local medical practitioner. In all these matters they had relied on themselves or on someone they knew well.

For city dwellers in 1900 this self-reliance was a thing of the past. The economy had become more complex. The food they consumed, for instance, was now supplied by remote corporations—meat-packers, canners, millers, and other food processors. Formerly, they could avoid an unsanitary butcher and boycott a short-weighing grocer—if, indeed, they had to buy from them at all—for these were local people whose

Businessmen celebrate the merger of feuding steel companies into United States Steel in 1901. At its birth the company produced 65 percent of America's steel; by the eve of World War I, the company's gross income exceeded that of the U.S. Treasury.

practices were known. But now producers were giant corporations located hundreds of miles away that could not be held to account for their products. No doubt, the huge firms were efficient distributors and producers, but could they be trusted? Dishonest meat packers could and did doctor spoiled beef to make it appear fresh. Firms processed lard and suet as butter and packed turnips in syrup to be sold as canned peaches or pears.

Nor was this all. City dwellers now relied on public utilities to light their houses, fuel their stoves, and transport them from their homes to their offices and shops. But the gas and lighting companies had monopolies and could squeeze customers as they pleased. The traction companies that ran the streetcars and elevated railroads corrupted city officials to secure exclusive charters, and then provided poor and expensive service.

The dependence on others extended to personal health. When ill, city dwellers now counted on "patent medicines," bottled or packaged concoctions they saw advertised in the newspapers and magazines. Drug companies marketed useless and sometimes harmful potions fortified with alcohol or even opium for every disease known—and for several invented by the patent medicine purveyors themselves. In short, urban consumers were at the mercy of others and were exceptionally vulnerable to deception and exploitation.

Dependence and deception were bad enough, but consumers of this period also faced remorselessly rising prices. For a whole generation after 1897 the nation escaped major depressions such as those of the 1870s and 1890s. But the income gains that Americans made in these years were partly offset by the steady inflation that reversed the trend of the previous decades. Beginning about 1902, consumer prices started a steady rise that did not end until the 1930s. Deflation following the Civil War had hurt farmers and other producers; now inflation hurt consumers. Everyone who went to the corner grocery store or butcher or who paid a utility bill or brought a load of coal soon became painfully aware of the new trend. "All the host of men who are not engaged in the actual production or delivery of material things," lamented one observer of rising prices in 1903, "how will they fare?" In the opening years of the new century everyone wanted to know who was responsible for the "high cost of living." The answer seemed inescapable to many; the monopolies.

The new consumerism was a particularly effective political glue. As one journalist pointed out in 1913: "In America to-day the unifying . . . force is the com-mon interest of the citizen as a consumer of wealth. . . ." The producers were "highly differentiated," but "all men, women, and children who buy shoes (except only the shoe manufacturer) are interested in cheap, good shoes." Because consumers were "overwhelmingly superior in numbers than [sic] producers," consumer consciousness, this writer was certain, formed the basis for a political revolt of vast proportions that the politicians would not fail to note.

Besides their exposed position as consumers, urban people still confronted the special problems and hazards of the city environment. Large cities provided men and women with more opportunities to learn, grow, and amuse themselves. But for wage earners they were also places where crime, vice, loneliness, and poverty flourished. In the 1870s and 1880s, as we have seen, the city poor had often turned to the political machines to protect them against the hard edges of urban life; by the 1890s many had come to believe that urban reform might be in their interests. The urban middle class, meanwhile, saw city government as inefficient and wasteful. Why could it not be run like a business, though obviously one dedicated to the public interest rather than profit? Dissatisfaction with city government further fueled the desire for progressive reform.

Farmers, Blacks, and Women. The addition of urbanites to the ranks of uneasy and restless citizens may well have been the crucial trigger to progressivism. But city people would not be alone in their search for reform during the next few years. Although farmers would profit from the higher prices after 1900, they still faced many difficult problems. Railroad officials and farm machinery manufacturers remained arrogant and arbitrary; credit for farmers was still in short supply; country life continued to fall behind city life in its attractions, especially to young people. These persistent problems left rural Americans dissatisfied, and at times their voice would imbue progressivism with a strong agrarian tinge reminiscent of Populism.

We cannot categorize all the reform elements as rural and urban, producer and consumer. Groups defined in other ways were also part of the progressive coalition. In these years many women, especially of the middle class, found their lives limited in ways that no longer seemed acceptable. By now thousands of women were high school and college graduates, but there were few outlets for their talents and energies. Law, medicine, and teaching no longer barred women. But women lawyers and doctors labored under severe handicaps imposed by the men who dominated these

This 1889 cartoon caught the public's skeptical mood toward the United States Senate. Long before the Muckraking era, Americans were obviously concerned with the dangers of money in politics.

professions, and high-status jobs as college instructors and school administrators were virtually closed to women. Except in a few states women still could not vote or hold office. Many educated women with unused talents and energies joined women's clubs and spent their time discussing art, high culture, and great ideas. Women were active in church affairs. A few middle-class or wealthy women also did "charity work" among the poor. Yet as the new century opened, many talented women felt that society was not properly using their skills and brains, and they became receptive to major efforts for social and political change.

Black Americans, too, found much to complain of as the new century dawned. In the South blacks were often kept from voting either by intimidation or by ingenious legal devices. All through Dixie the system of legal segregation prevailed. There were separate public facilities for "white" and "colored," and invariably the "colored" bathrooms, schools, drinking fountains, waiting rooms, and hospital facilities were far inferior to the white ones. Worst of all was the brutal terror of lynchings. Each year scores of blacks accused of offenses were taken from local jails and hanged, burned, or maimed by white mobs unwilling to wait for the slow processes of law.

Blacks were better treated in the North. Few communities north of the Mason-Dixon line imposed legal segregation. But unofficial segregation, especially in housing, was common. Northern blacks also suffered from discrimination in jobs and colleges and professional education, and were often treated shabbily by whites in ordinary social relations. As the twentieth century began, a new generation of college-educated

black urban leaders appeared, determined to make white Americans grant black citizens their rights.

Some historians have seen progressivism as a predominantly middle-class movement. Yet is is clear that it embraced recent immigrants, factory workers, and slum dwellers as well. In fact, almost all Americans came to consider themselves progressives in some sense. Progressivism by about 1910 was definitely "in the air," a fact that helps to explain its complexity and its seeming inconsistencies. No coalition so large could have been all of a piece or possible to define in a sentence.

The Opinion Makers

The Progressive movement owed much to the intellectual and artistic currents that had appeared in the last decades of the nineteenth century. The revolt against formalistic thinking and against conservative social Darwinism in the 1880s and 1890s prepared the way for jurists, academics, politicians, and ultimately, ordinary literate citizens to demand social legislation designed to protect the weak and to control private economic power. Many of the new thinkers—including Oliver Wendell Holmes, Jr., John Dewey, and Charles Beard—were also reformers. But their evolutionary approach to thought and society did more to promote change than their political activities.

Artists and writers also contributed to the new political mood. Though the literary realists and naturalists often claimed that they were mere observers, their depictions of railroad abuses, big-business chicanery,

A Historical Portrait

Ida Tarbell

Ida Tarbell could never decide whether she was a muckraker or a historian. Today her contributions to history are largely forgotten; we remember her only as a muckraker. She may have been, in fact, the first of the muckrakers.

Tarbell belonged to that special breed of journalists and writers who shaped the way early twentieth-century Americans perceived their society. Their exposés of corrupt municipal governments, patent medicine deception, the revolting conditions in meat-packing plants, the unscrupulous business practices of trusts, the exploitation of child workers, and the venality of the American Senate, among other issues, produced the agenda for the reform movement we call progressivism.

Ida Tarbell was born during the financial crisis of 1857 in a log cabin in northwestern Pennsylvania. Her mother, Esther, a descendant of Sir Walter Raleigh, was a schoolteacher whose own mother insisted she give up her career when she got married. Her father, Franklin, was a farmer who, at the time of his first daughter's birth, was in Iowa looking for promising land on which to settle down with his family. The panic closed the bank where the Tarbell savings were deposited and compelled Franklin to return home on foot without buying the farm, teaching to earn money as he walked across Illinois, Indiana, and Ohio. By the time he arrived, Ida was already eighteen months old and greeted the father she had never seen by telling him, "Go away, bad man."

Franklin Tarbell still intended to move the family to Iowa, and for the next three years he saved his money. Then came the oil strikes in Erie County and all thought of moving ceased.

With "rock oil" gushing from the ground in vast amounts, storage space was in short supply. A skilled carpenter, Franklin created a new kind of wooden tank that could hold over a hundred barrels of oil without seepage. By the summer of 1860 he had established a profitable shop for building such tanks near the well that gave him his first order. He also built a house adjoining the shop, and it was there that Ida and her baby brother, Will, spent the next ten years. The log cabin where she had been born was near trees, streams, and flowers; the new house was encircled by oil pits and derricks and smelled of gas. Ida was often scolded and spanked for exploring her surroundings and climbing on the derricks in the front yard. After a few months she tried to run away, but could not find the road to her grandmother's farm. Her new home made her a rebel. "This revolt," she confessed in her autobiography, "was a natural and righteous protest against having the life and home I had known, and . . . loved, taken away without explanation and a new scene, a new set of rules which I did not like, suddenly imposed." This spirit of defiance remained with her throughout her life.

Her questing and independent personality was reinforced by her family environment. Her parents were ardent antislavery Republicans who followed the Civil War closely in *Harper's Weekly*, *Harper's Monthly*, and the *New York Tribune*. Her earliest memory of concern for things outside her own world, as well as her first "realization of tragedy," occurred when President Lincoln died. Her fa-ther and mother sobbed on hearing the news, shut up their house, and put black crepe on all the doors. Her parents also welcomed to their home reformers and crusaders, whether prohibitionists, women's suffragists, or independent oilmen fighting Rockefeller. Her mother, who had never reconciled herself to the loss of her own teaching career, was also deeply concerned with improving the lot of the poor and hungry, and for a while felt drawn to socialism. A further boost to Ida's doubting nature came in high school when she developed a strong scientific curiosity. She was then faced with the problem of trying to reconcile her religious beliefs with the contradictions she found in studying science. In an age when only a handful of women went to college, her father and mother encouraged her to get the higher education she needed to become a biology teacher.

In 1876 Ida went to Allegheny College in nearby Meadville, Pennsylvania. Although the institution was nominally coeducational, Ida was the only girl in the freshman class. The head of the natural science department was impressed with her dedication and allowed her to use the college microscope. He also permitted her to experiment with the electrical apparatus in the laboratory. When she graduated four years later, she found that there were few opportunities for women in science and took a teaching post at the Poland Union Seminary in Ohio. There she taught foreign languages as well as geology, botany, geometry, and trigonometry—on both high school and college levels. After two tiring years that left her no time to use her beloved microscope, she left teaching and went back to her parents' house.

Though she wanted to go on to further study, her father was now in financial trouble. Standard Oil, the biggest producer, had made an arrangement with the railroads. In exchange for all of Standard's enormous business, they would give the company a secret rebate on freight rates. This reduced Standard's overhead and allowed it to sell its oil at cut-rate prices. Standard's competitors, particularly the independents like Franklin Tarbell, could not market their oil because they could not obtain the cheap freight rates. Many oilmen simply gave in to the inevitable and sold out to the larger company. Ida's father resisted, but in 1882 he was forced out of business. "It was not the economic feature of the struggle in the Oil Region which deeply disturbed . . . me," Ida wrote many years later. "It was what it was doing to people themselves, . . . to my father and mother and their friends. It was the divided town, the suspicion and greed and bitterness and defeats and surrenders." At twenty-four, Ida was discouraged, feeling that she was faced with only two choices: marriage or becoming resident spinster in the family home. Neither appealed to her.

At this point her luck changed. Reverent T. L. Flood, publisher of a monthly magazine, offered her a job on his staff. *The Chatauquan* had a circulation of 40,000 and the right views on government, temperance, labor, monopoly, and feminism. Ida immediately accepted and moved back to Meadville, where the monthly was put out. Although she was hired on a temporary basis, she soon became a permanent staff member, doing everything from copy editing to advertising. Before long she was writing unsigned columns on current events as well. Her first byline appeared in 1886 under the title "The Arts and Industries of Cincinnati." Unfortu-

nately Flood wanted her to stick to editing, and Ida, by now tired of the circumscribed world of western Pennsylvania, decided to resign and move to Paris. When she told the publisher she was going to France to write, he told her rudely: "You're not a writer; you'll starve."

Undaunted, in 1891 Ida and two friends left for Paris, where they took inexpensive rooms in the Latin Quarter. She went to lectures at the Sorbonne, did research at the Bibliothèque Nationale on women's role in the French Revolution, began a biography of the revolutionary Madame Roland, and wrote columns for Pittsburgh, Chicago, and Cincinnati newspapers. She was thrilled when *Scribner's Magazine* bought one of her stories for $100. In the summer of 1892, S. S. McClure visited Paris and interviewed Tarbell. He immediately hired her to translate French newspaper articles into English and write her own stories when needed by his publishing syndicate and his new magazine. McClure was particularly interested in scientific discoveries, and Ida had a field day interviewing Pierre Janssen, the builder of the Mont Blanc observatory; Alphonse Bertillon, the inventor of a criminal identification system; and Louis Pasteur, the famous French bacteriologist. In 1893 McClure asked her to return to the United States and commissioned her to write a lengthy biography of Napoleon, to be serialized in his magazine. After her first installment appeared (the full-length biography was eventually reissued in book form), McClure assigned her to do a biography of Abraham Lincoln. By 1896 the popularity of Tarbell's series on Napoleon and Lincoln had helped raise the magazine's circulation and assure its success.

By the beginning of the century the magazine had acquired a permanent staff of young and talented reporters and writers. Reform was already in the air and McClure was

prepared to unleash them on the abuses that seemed to flourish everywhere. But he insisted that his staff be factual, accurate, and fluent. With the advantage of weekly, rather than daily, publication, there was no reason why journalists could not be held to high standards. McClure's reporters included Tarbell, Ray Stannard Baker, Lincoln Steffens, and William Allen White. This was the core of the influential group whom Theodore Roosevelt would soon dub the "muckrakers."

McClure knew that business monopoly was one of the problems that already troubled the American public. The huge business conglomerations frightened and confused people. The reporters thought it would be timely to pick out one industry to analyze—its origins, its growth, its strong-arm tactics, its combinations, "and so on, until it is finally absorbed into a great Trust." After a great deal of discussion the staff finally decided that they would choose the "greatest [trust] of them all—the Standard Oil Company." Tarbell was picked for the assignment, partly because of her family's experiences with Standard Oil, partly because she was such an assiduous collector of facts, and partly because Ray Baker declined the job.

In 1901 Tarbell started her research. The work was designed to be impartial, with material both favorable and critical, and Tarbell insisted that she had an open mind. "We were neither apologists nor critics," she wrote in her autobiography, "only journalists intent on discovering what had gone into the making of this most perfect of all monopolies." But as she got deeper into the project, important documents in the company's archives vanished, her father's former colleagues refused to speak to her, and she was physically threatened. One pamphlet that she tried to locate was *The Rise and Fall of the South Improvement Company*, pub-

A Historical Portrait (*continued*)

lished in 1873, that detailed how the company, under an earlier name, had conspired with railroads to get rebates, drawbacks, payments for each barrel of oil shipped by its competitors, and illicit information about shipments by its rivals. All the copies in circulation had abruptly disappeared. Finally Ida found one in the New York Public Library and learned how Rockefeller had actually bought the charter of the South Improvement Company to secure the enormous range of business powers granted it by the state of Pennsylvania. The only right he was not given was that of banking, and he soon rectified this by buying the National City Bank of New York. Tarbell's additional research included interviews with the Industrial Commission, the Interstate Commerce Commission, and Henry Rogers, a Standard Oil partner. She went to services at the Euclid Avenue Baptist Church in Cleveland to get a look at Rockefeller in person, and was amused to see that he wore a skullcap to cover his baldness. The project, which took five years to complete, was published in nineteen articles in *McClure's* and then as a two-volume history in 1904. Much of what Tarbell wrote has been confirmed by more recent scholarship.

By the time the Standard Oil series concluded, Ida Tarbell was famous and sought after. She was insulted, however, at being excluded from the Periodical Publishers' Din-

ner, an all-male affair that McClure, Baker, and Steffens, as well as other colleagues, attended. "It is the first time . . . ," she wrote, "that the fact of petticoats has stood in my way and I am half inclined to resent it." Although she researched and wrote about the status of women and chose a career over marriage, she never became a women's rights or suffrage activist. In fact, in two separate series on women she publicly opposed giving the vote to women on the grounds that suffrage would not cure all of society's ills, as the activists claimed, and that women did not pay enough attention to the values of home and family. When pressed by feminist critics, she finally confessed her position as "a kind of instinct. It is no logic or argument. . . ."

In 1906 Tarbell helped lead a staff revolution at *McClure's* over the founder's management policies, business practices, and philandering. The upshot was that she, Baker, Steffens, White, and Finley Peter Dunne left *McClure's* and bought a competitor, *The American Magazine*. It was for this latter publication that she wrote her series on tariff abuses. She also shifted from a negative to a positive attitude toward business after she visited Henry Ford's factories and was impressed by his mass-production techniques, his fair wages, and his benevolent treatment of his workers. In 1914 and 1915 she wrote a series in *The American Magazine* in favor of Frederick Taylor's scien-

tific management methods in industry. In the same year she published a series on women in *Women's Home Companion*, and this ended her full-time affiliation with *American Magazine*.

In 1916 Tarbell, dividing her time between her New York apartment and her Connecticut farm, became a free-lance writer, and continued this career until the end of her life. She served on the Women's Committee of the Council of National Defense in World War I, and as a member of President Wilson's Industrial Conference. In 1919 she covered the Paris Peace Conference and published her only novel. Throughout the 1920s she wrote on Lincoln and his family, and on Elbert H. Gary, the founder of United States Steel. She also visited Italy to observe Mussolini's regime. In 1930 she was elected the first woman member of the Authors' Club. She was a supporter of the New Deal, endorsing the National Recovery Administration and social security. She contributed a volume, *The Nationalizing of Business*, to the distinguished *History of American Life* series. In 1939 she published *All in the Day's Work: An Autobiography*. Five years later, at the age of eighty-seven, still in full possession of her mental faculties and working on *Life After Eighty*, she died of pneumonia. Ida Tarbell was buried in the Pennsylvania oil country in a cemetery in Titusville near her ancestors.

and the plight of the poor and of midwestern farmers also prepared the public for reform.

The Muckrakers.   The antiformalists, the pragmatist philosophers, the liberal Darwinians, and the new literary and artistic realists set the mood for the reform movement. But it was a group of talented editors, journalists, and essayists known as the muckrakers who

give a sharp focus to the public's fears and discontent.

The muckrakers aimed dazzling spotlights into every dark cranny of American political and social life to reveal the gross abuses that existed. They owed their name to Theodore Roosevelt, who often sympathized with their aims but considered their passion for uncovering wrongdoing excessive. TR likened them to a morose character in John Bunyan's *Pilgrim's Pro-*

gress who "continued to rake to himself the filth of the floor" even when offered a "celestial crown."

Exposé journalism was not an invention of the Progressive Era. Toward the end of the nineteenth century, newspapers, in their effort to help newcomers interpret the city environment, had increasingly resorted to exposing local political and business abuses. In 1894 Henry Demarest Lloyd had described in lurid detail the abuses of Standard Oil in his book *Wealth Against Commonwealth*. Yet it was not until after 1900—when lower printing costs, the new mass audience educated by the high schools, and the capacity to produce magazines in vast numbers all came together—that true exposé journalism appeared. Thereafter periodical publishers became more willing than ever to pay good prices for well-written and well-researched articles on controversial, disturbing, or sensational subjects that would arouse readers and keep them coming back for more.

Samuel S. McClure, a shrewd and ebullient Irishman, was the first publisher to take advantage of the new opportunity. His instinct for profitable journalism was sound, if at times disconcerting. He would have paid well, one wit observed, for a "snappy life of Christ." McClure did not intend to create a new kind of journalism; he wanted to sell magazines. But his practice of hiring talented writers and reporters to investigate various aspects of American life produced a journalistic revolution. In October 1902 *McClure's* carried an article by a young Californian, Lincoln Steffens, entitled "Tweed Days in St. Louis." It described the efforts of a young district attorney to prosecute the corrupt St. Louis Democratic machine. The November issue carried the first installment of a series by journalist Ida Tarbell exposing the monopolistic practices of the Standard Oil Company. Early in 1903 Ray Stannard Baker's article on unfair labor practices appeared. The public took notice of these articles, and McClure found himself selling more magazines than he had ever believed possible. Before long other publishers, observing their rival's success, rushed to hire men and women with a talent for uncovering wrongdoing and writing about it in a colorful and exciting way.

What followed was the greatest outpouring of exposé journalism in American history. Eventually the muckrakers probed into every national abuse: uncontrolled sale of patent medicines; the shady doings of stock market manipulators; the extent of businessmen's efforts to corrupt legislatures, city councils, and Congress; the harsh treatment of labor; the disgusting and unsanitary conditions in the meat-packing industry; the profiteering of the "beef trust"; the exploitation

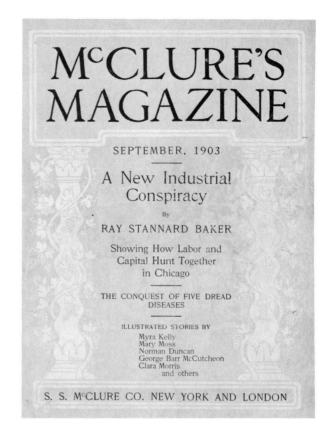

McClure's, Cosmopolitan, and many other turn-of-the-century magazines were the voices of muckraking reporters. Their sensational attacks on powerful institutions sold millions of copies, guaranteeing McClure and other publishers enormous profits.

of child workers; the savage treatment of defenseless young women by purveyors of vice; the behind-the-scenes effort of the "money trust" to manipulate the entire American economy. Some of the muckrakers' output does not stand up to careful rechecking. But it touched the public's exposed nerves, confirmed its uneasiness, and gave direction to its unfocused fears.

The New Republic Group. The muckrakers seldom saw far beneath the surface, nor did they generally offer profound solutions to the problems they uncovered. But there were also in these years more sophisticated thinkers who perceptively analyzed the nature of unrestrained private power and the vulnerability of the ordinary citizen, and suggested thoughtful remedies.

Three of these—Walter Lippmann, Herbert Croly, and Walter Weyl—expressed their views through a crusading new magazine, *The New Republic*. The older liberalism, the three precocious philosophers pointed out, assumed a social system of small producers, no one of whom could overawe and oppress the others. Although the Jeffersonians and their successors feared excessive private power, they had seldom actually faced it. In their day any group that attempted to gain excessive power was certain to find itself checked by others of equal strength and influence. If government had any role to play in maintaining a balance of forces in such a simple society, it was only as a disinterested policeman that would keep the various groups from hurting one another.

Now Americans lived in an age of giant corporations. Few people were small farmers or self-employed artisans. Although most still yearned for a past when people had done more or less as they pleased, that was no longer possible. Any effort to restore the past of small producers by breaking up the great corporations would fail and only make the economy less efficient. Instead, *The New Republic* writers said, liberals must accept bigness and insist that government be given a positive role in guiding the great corporations and regulating the economy for the general good. If all else failed, government must be allowed to take over, manage, and run the giant trusts. Croly called this approach the "New Nationalism." In effect, he declared, Hamiltonian, big-government means must be used to achieve Jeffersonian, egalitarian ends.

Progressivism Enters Politics

Muckraking journalists helped direct the attention of literate urban Americans to the ills of society and reinforced the uneasiness they felt at their exposed positions. What could they do to reduce their vulnerability? Answers began to appear as early as the 1890s.

The Cult of Efficiency in City Government. The first expressions of progressivism appeared at the local level. In the cities the "reform with a heart" that emerged in the 1890s (discussed in Chapter 18) was one aspect of the new reformist mood. A little later a group of city reformers emerged with somewhat different goals and a different clientele. Most of these people were professionals—engineers, lawyers, doctors, teachers, journalists—who believed that cities were much like large business firms and could be run effectively if subject to scientific management principles. Their motto, and their god, was efficiency.

In part, this "cult of efficiency" reflected the growing prestige of science and technology in these years. In industry, as we saw in Chapter 17, this same spirit was reflected in Taylorism—the meticulous examination and timing of industrial workers' motions in order to increase productivity. In part, too, the efficiency-oriented urban reform impulse was a throwback to the old economy-minded reform of the 1870s and 1880s. Like this earlier version, it seemed to ignore the urban wage earner class.

In the efficiency reformers' view there was no Democratic or Republican way to clean the streets or provide police protection or pure water. City government, accordingly, should be nonpartisan. Rather than elected mayors, cities should be headed by "managers" or "commissioners" who would run them on business principles designed to provide good value for the taxpayers' money. This may well have been desirable; all city people obviously benefited from inexpensive and efficient city services. But there is evidence that at times the new city government schemes, whatever their intentions, by making government nonpolitical, deprived the ethnic blocs and blue-collar workers of much of their former political influence.

In the 1890s the new city reformers organized the National Municipal Reform League and formulated a model city charter, which they hoped cities and state legislatures would adopt. Their first actual success came in 1901 when Galveston, Texas—following a catastrophic hurricane—adopted the commission plan. Under this scheme city government was turned over to a board of five commissioners chosen on a nonpartisan basis and at-large, rather than by wards, in order to eliminate old-fashioned politics from the selection process. The board combined the role of mayor and city council in one body. By merging functions and by eliminating party politics from consideration, the commissioners hoped to run city government like an efficient business. Still another idea was the city-manager scheme first adopted in Staunton, Virginia, in 1908. City managers were hired professionals who presumably knew how to run an urban community. They were hired by an elected city council and paid to manage the city much as a corporation might hire a president to run the firm. By the 1920s several dozen cities, usually small or middle-sized, had adopted one or the other of the new municipal government schemes.

The Social Progressives. The Progressive movement reached beyond city hall, down into the neighborhoods and slums. There men and women dedicated to changing the urban environment established a network of neighborhood voluntary associations designed to improve the lives of the poor. These "social" progressives formed the most militant wing of the Progressive movement. Many were inspired by the social gospel of Walter Rauschenbusch or the Christian socialism of Washington Gladden. They were for the most part idealistic young people who poured from the secondary schools and colleges in the last years of the nineteenth century. Particularly prominent among them were the new college women who sought to use their skills, education, and energies for something more fulfilling than the self-improvement of women's clubs. Many of these young people became voluntary charity workers or took up the new profession of social work. An especially dedicated contingent threw in their lot with the urban poor and went to live in settlement houses in the noisome slums that dominated the cities' centers.

Settlement houses were places where slum children could go for recreation and entertainment; where mothers could learn about nutrition, scientific child care, and household management; and where fathers could learn vocational skills, improve their English, prepare for citizenship, and meet other men to discuss city or community problems. Beginning with the Neighborhood Guild on New York's Lower East Side and Hull House in Chicago, settlements began to spring up during the 1890s in all the major cities. Hull House, under the leadership of Jane Addams, and New York's Henry Street Settlement, run by Lillian Wald, were the most prominent, but there were scores of others in every large city.

Most of the people who used the settlements were European immigrants and their children, but the settlement workers were also concerned with the problems of black city dwellers. Frances Kellor of New York's College Settlement helped organize the National League for the Protection of Negro Women after she discovered how young black farm women were lured to the cities by promises of good jobs and then harshly exploited by employers or forced into prostitution. Another white social worker, Mary White Ovington, established a settlement in a New York black slum. Mexican-Americans, too, benefited from the movement. The College Settlement in Los Angeles, located in a Mexican district, sought to provide the local poor with facilities for recreation and education and legal aid.

The settlements soon became springboards of social reform. Middle-class reformers living among the poor quickly learned that many of their problems could be solved only by legislation. In Chicago Jane Addams regularly supported city reformers who dared to challenge the city machine. Addams worked for tenement legislation as well as improved educational and recreational opportunities for the urban working class. She and her contemporaries in other communities regularly joined in citywide efforts to eliminate vice and reduce crime. Much of the support that the reform mayors of the 1890s and early twentieth century received came from the settlement workers.

As women's clubs caught the new reform spirit,

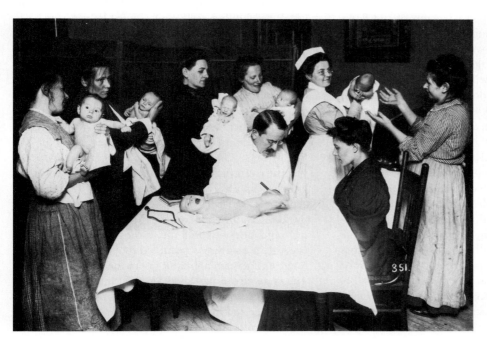

Settlement houses provided many services for the city poor. This settlement house in Chicago dispensed medical services for local infants. Such work may have contributed to the declining infant mortality rate of the early twentieth century.

they too became sources of reform in neighborhoods and cities. The clubs were especially active in the fight for honest city government, but middle-class women also battled for consumers and worked to help the urban poor. In 1899 a group of upper-middle-class women established the National Consumer's League, which threatened to boycott employers who did not adhere to fair employment practices. The league also labored to improve community health through licensing of food vendors and supported measures to protect urban consumers against retail fraud. Many local laws that now protect consumers are traceable to the efforts of these first consumer advocates three-quarters of a century ago.

Progressivism in the States.

Only so much could be accomplished on the neighborhood or city level, however, and in the end the reformers had to turn to the state legislatures to achieve their goals. Until the 1890s state governments all too often had been little more than junior partners of large business corporations. Despite the flurry of Granger laws in the 1870s, legislators and governors remained subservient to the great railroads, utility companies, and other corporations that exploited their constituents. Many were notoriously corrupt men who accepted money and other gifts from business people and did their bidding without concern for the public interest.

For years reformers had denounced the "unholy alliance" of state government and big business characteristic of the Gilded Age. Their voices went unheeded. Then the Panic of 1893 exposed many of the flaws in the country's economy and pointed up the dangers of unregulated economic power as never before. Public opinion soon began to change.

The revelation came with particular force to the people of Wisconsin, a state dominated by a Republican machine that had always worked hand in glove with the major corporations. The depression of 1893–1897 severely jolted Wisconsin's economy. By the winter of 1893/94 more than a third of the state's wage earners were unemployed. Meanwhile, the hard-pressed utility firms refused to pay their taxes and raised their rates to city consumers to offset declining revenue. To make matters worse, the distress of the unemployed and consumers were accompanied by revelations that a clique of bankers had been embezzling funds from depositors and stockholders. As the citizens of Wisconsin looked around them, they were shocked by the contrast between the continued affluence of a small group of men and women based on influence and corruption and the worsening plight of the average citizen.

The Wisconsinite who best understood the growing public outrage and disquiet was the ambitious young Republican lawyer Robert M. La Follette. The combative and eloquent La Follette had already run against the state machine for governor and failed. In 1897 he was seeking new issues and quickly saw that he could win wide public support by championing the citizenry against arrogant, irresponsible economic power. Defeated once more in 1898, he was finally swept into office two years later.

La Follette's victory was followed by a wave of legislation that made Wisconsin the pioneer in statewide reform and the "laboratory" for progressive lawmaking. First on the new governor's list of changes was a state primary system that permitted the voters to bypass the party bosses and nominate their own candidates for state office. His second measure was a railroad tax that shifted some of the burden of supporting government from farmers and wage earners to the previously untaxed railroad corporations and their stockholders. He later supported a state railroad commission to regulate the rates that the railroads could charge.

In 1902 La Follette ran for reelection. In his first successful campaign he had stressed his Republicanism. This time he appealed for nonpartisan support and got it. Virtually all Wisconsin citizens, not just Republicans, by now feared the power of the "interests." Vulnerability cut across ethnic lines, and many Catholic voters abandoned their earlier allegiance to the Democratic party to vote for the reformer. La Follette's resounding reelection victory helped supersede the old party politics of the Gilded Age.

In 1905 the young governor was elected to the United States Senate by the state legislature—still the normal procedure for election of senators. But Wisconsin continued to be a center of progressive reform. Under "Battle Bob's" successors, the state adopted two new instruments of "direct democracy" to reduce the power of the political boss–big-business alliance. The first of these, the *initiative*, was a procedure enabling voters to introduce legislation without waiting for legislators to do so. The *referendum* allowed voters to accept or reject, by a direct ballot, certain laws passed by the legislature. Progressives hoped that the two political innovations would allow the voters to bypass or overrule legislatures controlled by powerful economic interests and gain a greater say in the political process. The state also established a public utility commission to protect consumers against gouging by gas companies and power and light companies. Working closely with social scientists from the University of Wisconsin, successive state administrations enacted a workers' compensation act for injured or disabled wage earners and a state income tax to make wealthier citizens bear a larger part of the community's tax load. They established a board of public affairs to protect vital natural resources from corporate exploiters. The thrust of the whole reform wave was to ensure that ordinary citizens would be protected against the hazards of a vast, impersonal economy subject to the whim of private capital.

The "Wisconsin idea" captured the attention of millions of Americans. The muckrakers took notice of Battle Bob and transformed him into a figure of national importance. Other states soon adopted Wisconsin's program. In Oregon William S. U'Ren, who had in some ways anticipated La Follette, added other direct-democracy measures to the Wisconsin idea. U'Ren sponsored the *recall*, which enabled voters to remove corrupt or incompetent officials from office, and supported the secret ballot, to replace the prepared party-printed ballot that the voter was often forced to choose in full view of everyone, including the local party precinct captain.

Much of the new legislation was designed to protect citizens in general. A good deal of it was aimed specifically at weaker groups in society. Beginning with Illinois in 1899, for example, many states established special courts for juvenile offenders. Between 1905 and 1907 two-thirds of the states enacted laws limiting the hours of child labor or outlawing paid labor for young children. Working women, too, were increasingly surrounded by state regulations intended to prevent employer exploitation and abuse. The states also limited the working hours of men employed in exhausting or hazardous occupations like baking and mining. There was even some talk of health and unemployment insurance; but because the courts were sure to consider such measures beyond state powers, these advanced schemes did not get far.

Southern Progressivism. In 1912 La Follette remarked that he "did not know of any progressive sentiment or any progressive legislation in the South." The Wisconsin leader was only showing a common Yankee ignorance of Dixie. From many southern statehouses, beginning early in the century, progressive governors launched effective attacks against railroads, utility companies, insurance firms, and other business groups that seemed to be exploiting the region and its citizens. In Alabama there was Braxton Bragg Comer, a wealthy Birmingham manufacturer, banker, and farmer who joined the progressive fold when he discovered that the state's railroads, controlled by directors in Chicago

Robert La Follette (second from right) took his Progressive views to the people of Wisconsin in this special campaign train. It was successful, and La Follette went to the state house in Madison. His performance as governor promised him a successful national career.

or New York, were personally hurting him financially. What began as a private grievance soon grew into a public-spirited crusade. As governor, Comer expanded the authority of the state railroad commission and reduced passenger and freight rates. In Arkansas Attorney General Jeff Davis initiated scores of suits against insurance companies, tobacco firms, and oil companies, charging them with unfair, monopolistic practices and price-fixing.

Southern progressives were often openly anti-Yankee, aiming their sharpest barbs at "Wall Street" and "foreign"—that is, northeastern—corporations, which sucked profits out of the South and left nothing in return. At times skeptical southern progressives twitted their colleagues for reluctance to attack such homegrown abuses as child labor, when doing so might discourage the growth of local industry. But the South had its advanced social reformers, too. The Southern Sociological Congress—composed of ministers, urban humanitarians, and middle-class clubwomen—worked to improve the lot of children, the handicapped, consumers, and prisoners. The congress could claim credit for only a small amount of advanced social legislation, but it brought together men and women of like mind and helped to create the "southern liberal" type, whose efforts would help transform the region in later years.

Black Americans. The Sociological Congress worked to improve race relations, but by and large southern progressivism was "for whites only." A number of prominent southern politicians—James K. Vardaman and Theodore G. Bilbo of Mississippi, for example—managed to combine a desire to protect white yeomen farmers from the corporations with a violent antiblack rhetoric that poisoned the racial atmosphere. Even southern primary laws, widely adopted early in the century, did blacks little good. Southern progressives, arguing that the conservative southern Bourbons used the black vote to reinforce privilege, excluded blacks from the primaries. Thereafter black political influence in Dixie, much reduced already from Reconstruction times, declined almost to zero.

Meanwhile, as progressive laws poured from southern state legislatures, the "Jim Crow" system, which kept the races strictly segregated, expanded into every corner of the region's daily life. Blacks and a few white liberals tried to stop the process through legal action. But the Supreme Court ruled in the landmark *Plessy* v. *Ferguson* (1896) decision that segregation was legal as long as the facilities provided each race were equal in quality. Far worse, lynching continued and even grew as a savage weapon to keep blacks in "their place."

Militant egalitarians at times blamed the South's continued oppression of its black citizens on southern black acquiescence. Their villian was Booker T. Washington, who, well into the new century, wore the mantle of black leadership in Dixie.

Washington had risen to prominence in the nineties as a protege of southern whites. Born into slavery, he had been sent by charitable whites to Hampton Institute in Virginia, a glorified trade school, but one of the few existing all-black institutions of higher education. In 1881 whites chose him to head a school for black youths at Tuskegee, Alabama. Washington made Tuskegee into a flourishing institution emphasizing industrial education, modeled on the work-ethic, self-help principles of Hampton. In 1895 he achieved national prominence with an electrifying address at the Atlanta Cotton States Exposition. Speaking to a white audience, he proposed that blacks accept disfranchisement and racial segregation in exchange for the right to advance economically and be unmolested in their persons and property. This so-called Atlanta Compromise immediately impressed white southerners as a useful rationalization of existing practices. There-

after the white establishment made Washington the "spokesman" for his race and the quasi-official dispenser of white philanthropy and political patronage to blacks.

Washington's Atlanta Compromise surely acquiesced in segregation and appeared to encourage black passivity in the face of mistreatment. It undoubtedly reinforced the southern caste system. But Washington was by no means a complete "Uncle Tom." Although projecting a public image of meekness, he quietly fought segregation, lynching, and debt peonage. In 1900 he raised money to test southern laws disfranchising blacks in the federal courts. When President Theodore Roosevelt gave dishonorable discharges in 1906 to three companies of black soldiers

Throughout his long life (1868–1963), W. E. B. Du Bois's thinking anticipated developments in black positions on race. The first black to receive a Ph.D. from Harvard, he helped start the Niagara Movement and then the NAACP, advocated Pan-Africanism, lost faith in integration, became a Communist, supported Black Power, and finally moved to Africa.

for refusing to identify the leaders of a riot in Brownsville, Texas, Washington went to the White House to intercede for the wronged men, though without success.

Despite such efforts, to a new group of urban black intellectuals Washington seemed all too willing to surrender fundamental black rights and to consent to permanent second-class citizenship. Among this group were the Boston editor William Monroe Trotter, T. Thomas Fortune of the New York *Age*, the Jacksonville minister J. Milton Waldron, and, the most prominent member, W. E. B. Du Bois. The Massachusetts-born Du Bois was one of the first black men to receive a Ph.D. from an American university. An early advocate of black liberation from white economic and cultural domination, he insisted that black Americans must run their own businesses, provide their own professional services, write their own books, and create their own art. In 1903, in *The Souls of Black Folk*, he attacked Washington as a man who had "practically accepted the alleged inferiority of the Negro," and urged prominent black Americans to cease flattering the white South and to speak out on the race issue. Du Bois at this stage of his life was scarcely a democrat. A proud and sensitive man, he believed that black salvation rested with the "Talented Tenth" of liberally educated black men and women.

In 1905 Du Bois and Trotter convened a meeting at Fort Erie, Ontario, near Niagara Falls, to raise a militant voice against black oppression. The convention issued a manifesto demanding true manhood suffrage, the end of racial discrimination, the freedom of blacks to criticize American society, and free access for blacks to liberal education as well as to vocational training. Incorporated as the Niagara Movement, the group continued to meet annually for several years to defend black rights and demand that white America practice its professed principles of equality.

By 1908 Washington's counterattack and the growing divisions among the militants themselves had reduced the Niagara Movement's momentum. By this time, however, a group of white progressives had concluded that something must be done to end the brutality and injustice committed against black Americans. Among this group were Oswald Garrison Villard, grandson of the abolitionist William Lloyd Garrison; the social workers Jane Addams, Lillian Wald, and Mary White Ovington; lawyer Clarence Darrow; novelist William Dean Howells; and John Dewey, the Columbia philosopher. In 1909 these white progressives joined with the Niagara Movement militants to establish the National Association for the Advancement of Colored People (NAACP), which immediately sought to defend the legal and constitutional rights of blacks wherever they were threatened or denied. The modern movement for racial equality was now under way.

Female Progressives. Women were among the most active workers for social reform before and during the Progressive Era. They fought for improved labor laws, for consumer protection, for better race relations. One major cause that attracted many reform-minded women in these years was temperance. The battle to contain and perhaps end for all time the social and moral evil of drunkenness had engaged the attention of American women for many years. In 1874 female reformers had organized the Women's Christian Temperance Union (WCTU). After the turn of the century, in alliance with the predominantly male Anti-Saloon League, it propagandized in the schools and churches against alcohol and lobbied for state laws outlawing the production, sale, and consumption of beer, wine, and whiskey. In later years temperance advocates and prohibitionists would often uphold the social status quo; but in the early years of the twentieth century such temperance reformers as Frances Willard and Anna Shaw were strong advocates of child-labor laws and other progressive legislation.

No cause, however, engaged the energies of women reformers so completely as the suffrage issue. For decades women sufffragists had been struggling for the right to vote. Successes had been few. Most men and many women felt that enfranchising women would undermine their proper domestic role and weaken the family. Nothing concrete was achieved before the Civil War. Then, during Reconstruction, many women suffragists chose to defer their struggle until the fight for black civil rights was won.

The battle proved long and hard. In 1869 Susan B. Anthony and Elizabeth Cady Stanton, both pre–Civil War women's suffrage leaders, organized the National Woman Suffrage Association. This group scored some successes in the West. By 1896 Wyoming, Utah, Colorado, and Idaho had granted women the vote. Meanwhile, a more conservative group of women, including Lucy Stone and Julia Ward Howe, had formed the American Woman Suffrage Association. In 1890 the two organizations merged under the presidency of Stanton as the National American Woman Suffrage Association (NAWSA).

By the opening years of the twentieth century, new and more militant leaders had appeared, such as Carrie Chapman Catt and Anna Howard Shaw. These women introduced a greater degree of professionalism

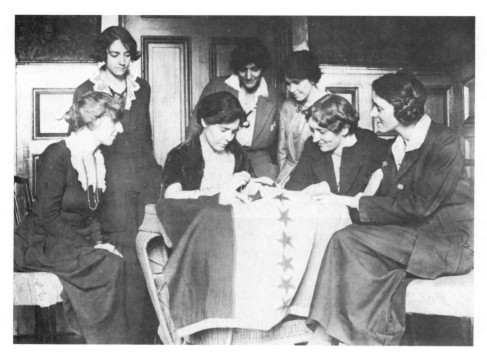

Women's rights leader Alice Paul sews the ratification star on the flag of the National Women's Party, celebrating the 1920 ratification of the Nineteenth Amendment, which gave women the vote. Paul also authored the Equal Rights Amendment, a source of great controversy over a half century later.

into the suffragists' work and streamlined NAWSA's operations. To NAWSA's left were a collection of women activists who combined suffrage with "social" demands designed to alter fundamentally the role of women in their relations with men, the economy, and the family. Charlotte Perkins Gilman, a leading social feminist, in *Women and Economics* (1898) argued that women's subordinate economic role had stunted their personalities and damaged their effectiveness as wives and mothers. Gilman demanded economic equality and proposed communal child-care centers to liberate women from economic dependence on men. Crystal Eastman, an active suffragist, also advocated sexual emancipation of women and free dissemination of birth-control information and devices. In 1914, Eastman and Alice Paul, a young Quaker activist, organized the Congressional Union to agitate for a suffrage amendment to the Constitution instead of a state-by-state approach. The new militants were not bound by the decorum of their elders, and they adopted the flamboyant tactics of English suffragists, which included mass marches, chaining themselves to lampposts, and prison fasts. In the elections of 1914 and 1916, Paul's group (organized as the National Women's Party in 1916), campaigned to punish the Democrats, the party in power, for failure to support a suffrage amendment. Resistance continued, however, and the suffrage victory would be delayed for four more years.

Progressivism Conquers the Nation

Progressivism was largely a local phenomenon at first. By the opening years of the new century, community halls, city council chambers, and state capitals were alive with people imbued with the new awareness of social problems and impatient with stand-pat institutions and leaders. But all was quiet along the Potomac. Then events moved quickly.

In 1899, a year after his much-publicized charge up San Juan Hill in the war with Spain, Theodore Roosevelt was elected governor of New York. Although he had been the candidate of Thomas C. Platt, the state's Republican boss, his administration brought little joy to the state machine. As governor, Roosevelt appointed honest people to office and supported bills to tax public utilities. Unhappy with his choice, and anxious to get him out of New York, Platt maneuvered Roosevelt into accepting second place on the 1900 Republican ticket with William McKinley. McKinley and Roosevelt won a landslide victory in 1900 over Bryan and Stevenson.

On September 6, 1901, while on a visit to the Pan-American Exposition in Buffalo, McKinley was shot by Leon Czolgosz, a demented anarchist. McKinley died a week later. Suddenly, at forty-two, Roosevelt found himself president, the youngest man yet to occupy the office.

The new president was a remarkable man. A graduate of elite Groton and Harvard, TR was a literate man whose histories, *The Naval War of 1812* and *Winning of the West*, can still be read with profit today. He was also a man of frenetic action who forced even the most distinguished guests at his country home, and at the White House itself, to join him on jogs about the countryside while he shouted his views of politics, art, and economics. Though capable of dashing off reviews, speeches, books, and articles, and holding his own with distinguished scholars, he also enjoyed living with the cowboys of western Dakota and spent long, happy months in the wilds of three continents hunting, exploring, and collecting zoological specimens. TR had a juvenile streak that often led him to snap judgments. One distinguished foreign observer remarked to an American friend: "You know your president is really six." An intense nationalist, Roosevelt identified the United States with virtue and tended to see other nations and other races besides the "Anglo-Saxon" as inherently inferior. Despite his failings—and perhaps partly because of them—Roosevelt charmed and delighted the American public, and his personal appeal would rub off on the programs he supported.

Roosevelt's First Term. The conservative Republican "old guard" did not trust Roosevelt. When Roosevelt was first proposed for vice president on the 1900 Republican ticket, Senator Marcus (Mark) Hanna warned that if he received the nomination, only one life would stand between the country and a "madman." Yet TR at first took a prudent and moderate course. His first annual message to Congress proved so conventional that the *New York Evening Post* declared that it might have been composed by "a man of sixty, trained in conservative habits." Yet there were some elements of the future progressive agenda in his recommendations for a cabinet-level department of commerce and labor to protect labor's rights and to publicize inflated corporate earnings, and for stronger measures to protect the country's forests and conserve its natural resources. Even closer to the emerging progressive program was his request for increased power for the feeble Interstate Commerce Commission to help guarantee fair treatment to shippers.

Congress eventually gave TR much of what he asked for. In 1902 it passed the Newlands Act, which set aside money from federal land sales in the arid West for dams and canals to irrigate the land (see Chapter 19). In 1903 it established the Department of Commerce and Labor with a Bureau of Corporations empowered to subpoena information from industry that could then be used for antitrust suits under the Sherman Antitrust Act. That same year Congress passed the Elkins Act outlawing rebates to favored shippers and giving the federal courts the power to issue injunctions ordering railroads to desist from practices that benefited some shippers at the expense of others.

Despite these successes, reform-minded observers considered Roosevelt's legislative performance disappointing and timid. In his executive capacity, however, he proved bolder and startled the nation in 1902 by ordering Attorney General Philander Knox to file suit against the Northern Securities Holding Company for violating the Sherman Antitrust Act.

Here was a new spirit indeed. The Northern Secu-

One reason for TR's success as a politician was that he enjoyed the political game. Clearly it would be hard to dislike anybody with such an infectious grin.

rities Company was a combination put together by J. P. Morgan, James J. Hill, E. H. Harriman, and the Rockefellers joining into one giant firm most of the railroads in the northwestern corner of the nation. If ever a business trust promised to "restrain trade" and impose a stranglehold on millions, this was it. Now, after twelve years, the Sherman Antitrust Act was finally to be used for its intended purpose. Soon afterward Knox also indicted Swift and Company, the Chicago meatpackers, for conspiring with its competitors to fix prices.

The liberal press and the growing contingent of reform-minded citizens hailed the antitrust suits with delight. Morgan, however, was dismayed by the Northern Securities indictment. How could the president act in such an arbitrary way? The uncrowned king of Wall Street did not see himself as a mere private citizen subject to ordinary law, and he told the president: "If we have done anything wrong send your man to my man to fix it up." Roosevelt was not swayed and the suit proceeded to a successful conclusion in 1904, when the Supreme Court ordered the dissolution of the Northern Securities Company.

The *Northern Securities* case, the Swift suit, and later suits against Standard Oil and the American Tobacco Company gave TR the reputation of being a trustbuster and an uncompromising foe of big business. Actually, Roosevelt distinguished between "good trusts" and "bad trusts." The first obeyed the law and did not use their power to squeeze the consuming public; the latter knew no such restraint. "Bad trusts" should be punished, but "good trusts" should be left alone because large firms were more efficient than small ones. Besides, TR felt, the country could as soon reverse the Mississippi spring flood as stop the processes of corporate growth. On the other hand, the nation need not allow the floods to surge unchecked. Instead, it could "regulate and control them by levees," preventing misuse of corporation power. In fact, though he rejected Morgan's overtures, TR was not adamantly opposed to negotiations with big business. In 1905, for example, he struck a bargain with Elbert Gary, board chairman of U.S. Steel. If Gary cooperated with an investigation of his company, then any wrongdoing detected would be reported to him to correct before the government prosecuted or commenced a suit.

Clearly TR was at most a qualified opponent of big business. He was an equally qualified friend of organized labor. Like many middle-class Americans of the day, the president feared socialism and at times confused it with trade union activity. As New York governor, he had sent state militia to put down disor-

ders that had followed a labor dispute. Yet far m[o] than most of his predecessors, TR believed that unio[n] had a legitimate place as agencies to protect wage earn-ers. By this time even conservative men such as Mark Hanna, the Cleveland industrialist and senator who had been a close adviser to McKinley, were willing to join such organizations as the National Civic Federa-tion, a body that brought together businesspeople, civic leaders, college presidents, and labor leaders for joint action to make the economy more efficient and promote good labor-capital relations.

Roosevelt demonstrated his sympathetic attitude toward organized labor early in his first term. In May 1902, after months of arguing with the coal-mine own-ers in eastern Pennsylvania over higher wages, union recognition, and an eight-hour day, the United Mine Workers, led by John Mitchell, walked off their jobs. The anthracite coal they produced was the major source of heating fuel along much of the Atlantic coast. if the strike dragged on through the summer and fall, there would be no coal for winter and millions of householders would suffer. Yet for months the mine owners arrogantly refused to negotiate. In reply to critics, George F. Baer, spokesman for the mine own-ers, haughtily declared that the "rights and interests of the laboring man will be protected and cared for not by labor agitators but by the Christian men to whom God has given control of the property rights of the country." When someone proposed that Arch-bishop John Ireland of St. Paul be brought in as mediator, Baer retorted that "anthracite mining is a business, and not a religious, sentimental, or academic proposition."

Roosevelt and a majority of the voters were of-fended by the owners' willingness to risk the public's welfare for their own gain. In early October, as winter approached, Roosevelt invited the union leaders and the mine operators to Washington to discuss a settle-ment. At an all-day conference Mitchell declared his willingness to negotiate with the owners directly or to abide by the decision of a presidential arbitration commission—if the owners also agreed to accept its decision. The owners refused to budge. Their spokes-man attacked Mitchell personally and demanded that the president use federal troops to end the strike.

Outraged by the stubbornness of the operators and their discourtesy toward Mitchell, Roosevelt threatened to seize the mines and run them as federal property. Faced with the president's determination, the mine owners finally yielded. At another White House conference representatives of the miners and the operators agreed to a settlement. The men would go back to work; and a five-man commission consisting of an army engineer, a mining engineer, a businessman, a federal judge, and an "eminent sociologist" would be appointed by the president to arbitrate differences. The eminent sociologist Roosevelt selected was a union leader: E. E. Clark of the Brotherhood of Railroad Conductors, a novel choice for the day. The commission granted the miners their wage increase and some reduction in hours, but not union recognition. It was at best a mixed result, but to many Americans it was, as TR described it, a "square deal." The settlement established an important new precedent: From now on, the national government would be a factor to reckon with in disputes between capital and labor that vitally affected consumer interests.

The New Nationalism. With a "Square Deal" for all Americans as his rallying cry, Roosevelt ran for reelection in 1904. Tired of two defeats in succession under Bryan's banner, the Democrats nominated the conservative New York judge Alton B. Parker. The change did not help. TR won an impressive victory with 56 percent of the popular vote.

Roosevelt soon moved significantly to the left, respnding to the changing mood of the American peo-ple, as well as to his growing political confidence now that he had been elected president in his own right. By this time a contingent of Republican progressives, including La Follette, Senators Albert Cummins of Iowa, Albert Beveridge of Indiana, Moses Clapp of Minnesota, Joseph Bristow of Kansas, and William E. Borah of Idaho, had arrived in Washington from the states where they had long been active in local reform movements. In later years they would be joined by other Republican progressives such as Hiram Johnson of California and George Norris of Nebraska. In addition, an increasing number of Democrats, caught up like their rivals in the surge of reform, were prepared to support legislation to protect the public against "the interests." The opposition promised to be formidable, however. The Republican stand-pat old guard—led by Senators Nelson W. Aldrich, Orville Platt, and John C. Spooner—were still powerful and would resist fiercely every attempt to alter the status quo.

Despite the stand-patters, during his second term Roosevelt was able to get some notable progressive legislation on the books. In 1906 he induced Congress to pass the Hepburn Act, for the first time giving a government agency—the Interstate Commerce Commission, in this case—the power to set rates for a private

T. R. viewed as a conquering hero in 1904 after his resounding election victory. Actually his great achievements still lay ahead.

business. The bill allowed the commission to inspect the books of interstate railroads before setting rates. It also outlawed the practice of issuing passes for free transportation, with which the railroads had bribed politicians. The bill was not a complete victory for the reformers. The railroads, through Aldrich, succeeded in inserting a provision giving the courts power to overturn commission-set rates. Nevertheless, the law was an important addition to the arsenal against business abuses.

Two other important regulatory measures passed in 1906 provided direct federal protection to consumers. For years reformers had attacked irresponsible meat-packers and food processors. In the government itself Dr. Harvey Wiley, chief of the Department of Agriculture's Bureau of Chemistry, had long warred against the patent medicine quacks and demanded that drug preparations be labeled to show their contents. Wiley supplied most of the data for "The Great American Fraud," a sensational muckraking article on the drug companies by Samuel Hopkins Adams, published in *Collier's* in 1905. An even more effective blow for consumer protection came in 1906, when the young socialist author Upton Sinclair published his lurid novel *The Jungle*. Sinclair's description of the filth of the Chicago meat-packing plants, of men falling into the lard vats and being rendered into cooking fat, and of packers injecting spoiled meat with chemicals and selling it to city saloons for their free lunch counters revolted the public and turned the stomach of the president himself.

After checking Sinclair's charges, TR threw his support behind a meat inspection bill then in Congress. Although the bad reputation of American beef had hurt their sales abroad, the meat-packers resisted the bill's passage strenuously. Only when the president warned them that he would publish the results of an official investigation of Sinclair's charges did they yield, though not without extracting concessions. The bill that Roosevelt signed into law as the Meat Inspection Act on June 30, 1906, provided for government supervision of sanitary practices in meat-packing plants, but the cost of the inspection would be borne by the treasury. On the same day, the years of agitation for drug regulation also bore fruit when TR approved the Pure Food and Drug Act requiring that the contents of food and drug preparations be described on their labels.

Conservation. Among the progressives' many contributions to the quality of American life none was so impressive as their efforts to conserve the nation's natural resources. Conservation appealed to a wide range of citizens. One group was composed of lovers of nature who gloried in the forests, mountains, and lakes and considered the unspoiled wilderness a delight in itself, one capable of renewing the soul and the spirit. Led by Scottish-born naturalist John Muir and groups such as the Sierra Club of California, these "preservationists" insisted that the country's natural heritage must be protected against any sort of defilement and preserved intact. Another group—the "conservationists"—was more pragmatic in its goals. Led by Chief Forester Gifford Pinchot, an upper-class Pennsylvanian trained in foresty and land management, these "conservationists" worshiped efficiency and sought the "best use" of resources. They had little patience with those who considered nature inviolable. Best-use conservationists of the Pinchot variety believed the natural endowment must be exploited, but exploited rationally, scientifically, so that it would remain available to future generations. They noted the destruction of the buffalo, the disappearance of the enormous Great Lakes forests, the erosion of the soil everywhere, and the neglect of usable resources, and called for scientific resource management. At times the preservationists and the conservationists fought one another, but they also cooperated to battle the great lumber and mining companies, which they accused of putting profit ahead of the nation's long-term interests. At times, too, they found themselves at odds with ranchers and other western groups that resented eastern attempts to interfere with the traditional free-wheeling way they exploited the land.

Both preservationists and conservationists reflected the growing realization, as the century came to an end, that the country's last frontier was rapidly filling in. The Forest Reserve Act of 1891 was a sign of changing attitudes. This measure restricted the transfer of federal lands to private parties and allowed the president to set aside forested portions of the public domain as reserves. Even earlier, in 1872, Congress had created Yellowstone National Park, beginning a regular policy of setting aside large tracts of scenic land in the West as permanent recreation areas.

As an authority on wildlife and a great lover of the outdoors, Roosevelt became an inevitable champion of the conservation movement. His approval of the 1902 Newlands Act expressed his conservationist views. In 1905 he transferred the supervision of the government's forest reserve from the Department of Interior to the Department of Agriculture, where Chief Forester Pinchot took charge. Two years later he and Pinchot snatched millions of acres of forest lands and several important power sites from western lumbering

The Panic of 1907, though short, was frustrating; it led Americans to rethink the country's banking and currency structure. This crowd—some looking worried, some unconcerned—is gathered outside New York's Trust Company of America in the early hours of the panic.

interests by putting them into forest reserves or designating them as ranger stations. In 1908 the president called a National Conservation Conference of forty-four governors and hundreds of experts to consider resource-management problems.

The Panic of 1907. Though good times generally prevailed during the Progressive Era, the country only narrowly averted a serious depression in 1907. During the years immediately preceding, the economy had expanded rapidly. Combined with the trust movement, this growth had absorbed enormous pools of savings. By the middle of 1907 credit was so tight that New York City could not borrow money from the public. Then, at the end of October, a major New York bank closed its doors, setting off a wave of panicky deposit withdrawals from other banks. If matters had taken their usual course, the panic would have spread to the stock market and then to the nation's other credit agencies. In the absence of a central bank, this in turn would have tripped off a major depression. Fortunately, the combined action of the treasury, which deposited $35 million of the government's surplus in various private banks, and large loans by J. P. Morgan and other private bankers to troubled financial institutions

stopped the panic in its tracks. A business downturn did follow, but it was both brief and shallow.

Morgan and the treasury had saved the day; but in the wake of the scare, many Americans began to ask what could be done to avoid future panics. In 1908 Congress passed the Aldrich-Vreeland Emergency Currency Act, making $500 million in new currency available to certain national banks that deposited bonds with the treasury and establishing a congressional commission to investigate the deficiencies in the country's banking system and to recommend changes.

Taft's Misfortunes. Roosevelt left the White House in March 1909 convinced that William Howard Taft, his hand-picked successor, would carry on in his progressive steps. He had reason to be confident. The ponderous but affable Taft—a former federal jurist, Philippine commissioner, and TR's secretary of war—had campaigned in 1908 on his predecessor's record. With the popular Teddy behind him, Taft defeated William Jennings Bryan, though he fell short of Roosevelt's vote in the West.

Taft was pledged to continue TR's progressive policies, but at heart he was a conservative with the temperament of an old-fashioned and rather indolent

T. R. chooses his successor. Carrying the mountainous William Howard Taft on his shoulder this way would have been quite a feat!

judge. He and his attorney general, George W. Wickersham, would be reasonably energetic in enforcing the Sherman Antitrust Act, for it was the law of the land. Indeed, Taft brought more suits against trusts than either Roosevelt or Wilson, Taft's progressive successor. But he was at best a timid reformer who refused to dramatize his policies or mobilize public opinion in their favor. When opposed by the party's stand-patters, he usually retreated.

Roosevelt had scarcely left office to go big-game hunting in Africa when the new president managed to alienate the progressives in his own party, turning them into fierce opponents. Taft's problems with the Republican "insurgents" began when, in fulfillment of a campaign pledge, he asked Congress to consider lowering tariffs. By 1909 tariff revision seemed long overdue. With brief and minor exceptions, taxes on foreign imports had risen steadily since the Civil War. Perhaps, as protectionists claimed, the ever-rising tariff had kept out foreign competition, enabling American industry to prosper. But, reformers charged, it had also been costly to the American consumer. The Dingley Tariff of 1897 had pushed import duties to their highest level in history and had inflated the price of everything the public wore, ate, and used. Indeed, some critics insisted that the Dingley Tariff explained the rising prices that Americans had been experiencing since the turn of the century. To make matters worse, they said, the high tariff was the "mother of trusts," encouraging the great industrial combinations that further gouged the public.

Prompted by the party's recent campaign pledge and the president's request, in 1909 the Republican House passed a tariff revision bill sponsored by Sereno E. Payne, cutting rates sharply. This bill ran afoul of Rhode Island's Nelson Aldrich when it came to the Senate. Aldrich, an industrialist himself as well as a stand-patter, transformed the House bill drastically by throwing out most of the lowered schedules. Taft was appalled by the Payne-Aldrich Bill, but he left the fight against it to the Senate Republican insurgents.

Day after day, during the hot Washington summer, La Follette, Albert Beveridge, Jonathan Dolliver, Moses Clapp, and other midwestern Republican progressives attacked the Payne-Aldrich Bill. Taking up each of the schedules in turn, they showed how the Senate version would raise costs to the consumer and benefit only the trusts. The Aldrich measure, La Follette declared, would assuredly continue the thrust of the previous tariff. That law had encouraged monopoly, and with competition gone there was now "shoddy in everything we wear and adulteration in everything we eat." The country, Beveridge admitted, had to protect wage earners and manufacturers, but it was "a high concern . . . to the prosperity of our people as a whole that a just and equal consideration . . . be shown the consuming public."

The progressives' fight was gallant but futile; the Aldrich rates prevailed. The results might have been different if the president had intervened, but Taft refused to use his influence to defeat the measure. When it came to his desk with the Aldrich changes intact, he signed it into law. Soon afterward he called it "the best tariff measure the Republican party has ever passed."

The president's response shocked progressives. The midwestern Republican insurgents considered Taft's performance a repudiation of TR's policies and the party's promises to the public. In short order the reformers found new cause for dismay in the president's handling of the Ballinger-Pinchot controversy.

Taft's secretary of the interior was Richard A. Ballinger, a Seattle attorney with close ties to western mining and lumbering interests. As secretary, Ballinger restored lands to commercial exploitation that Roosevelt had removed, interfered with the Reclamation Service, and canceled an agreement giving the Forest Service control over forest preserves on Indian lands. In each of these actions he clashed with Pinchot, who was still Chief Forester and who, somewhat self-righteously, considered himself the special guardian of the public against selfish business interests.

The argument between Ballinger and Pinchot came to a head when government-owned coal lands in Alaska were transferred to a Morgan-Gugenheim syndicate. Pinchot believed that this was a blatant giveaway of public resources, and he accused Ballinger of being in cahoots with the despoilers of the public domain. Rather than confining his criticism to memos to the president, Pinchot made public speeches all over the country attacking his department chief. He also leaked information to the newspapers pillorying Ballinger, and by inference condemning Taft himself. Eventually Pinchot clashed head-on with the president, who fired him while retaining Ballinger. Pinchot was now a progressive martyr, and his treatment another reason to distrust Taft.

The insurgent Republicans also clashed with Taft over congressional reorganization. They had long feuded with the Republican speaker of the House, the profane "Uncle Joe" Cannon, a man fiercely opposed to progressive legislation. Soon after Pinchot's dismissal, Cannon began to deprive the party rebels of committee chairmanships they had earned by seniority. The insurgent Republicans resolved to break his power and turned to the president for support. Taft disliked Cannon but declined to help the insurgents, claiming that the Speaker was too deeply entrenched to be ousted. The rebels refused to give up. At the opening of the March 1910 congressional session, led by George Norris, a young progressive Republican from Nebraska, they joined with anti-Cannon Democrats to strip the Speaker of his power to appoint members to the all-important House Rules Committee and deprived him of his own place on it. Some of the insurgents would have been happy if Cannon had also been deposed as Speaker, but they had to be content with limiting his ability to undercut progressive legislation.

By mid-1910, then, Taft had thoroughly alienated the progressive, largely midwestern wing of his party. In truth, the president's record on progressive measures was not all bad. He supported the Mann-Elkins Act (1910), which gave the Interstate Commerce Commission the power to suspend railroad-initiated rate changes if they seemed excessive and also authorized government supervision of telephone, wireless, and telegraph companies. That same year he endorsed a "postal savings" scheme to allow small savers, often victimized by private bank failures, to place their money in the safekeeping of the federal post office. He also threw his three hundred pounds behind the

Sixteenth Amendment to the constitution, which authorized a federal income tax, and signed the Mann Act (1910), which prohibited the interstate transportation of women for purposes of prostitution. Yet on most of these issues Taft so equivocated that he received little credit from the insurgents. Perhaps worst of all, in their eyes, the lethargic, ponderous, dull chief executive was not the dynamic, joyous, charismatic TR.

Republican Split. The progressive Republicans rapidly deserted Taft. In May 1910 Pinchot met with Roosevelt, who was touring Europe on his way back from Africa, and filled his ears with news of Taft's transgressions. By the time TR returned to the United States, his cordial feelings for his protégé had decidedly cooled. The last straw was the administration's revelation, in the course of an antitrust suit, that during the 1907 panic Roosevelt had allowed U.S. Steel to buy the Tennessee Coal and Iron Company without protest, though the purchase enhanced the firm's monopoly position in steel. Roosevelt believed that the move had been justified to restore business confidence, but the leak made him appear a tool of Morgan.

Besides his growing doubts about Taft's political wisdom and loyalty, TR simply could not abandon politics. In 1910 he was only fifty-two and still overflowing with energy. Permanent retirement seemed unthinkable. He had served only one elected term, even though he had been president for almost eight years, so tradition did not bar his reelection. Under the barrage of the anti-Taft insurgents, Roosevelt quickly warmed to the idea of opposing the president for the 1912 Republican nomination.

By this time TR had read Herbert Croly's *The Promise of American Life* (1909), which crystallized the activist view of the government's role that he had played with for some years. In a speech at Osawatomie, Kansas, in August 1910, TR used Croly's phrase, "the New Nationalism," to describe a federal government that, rather than forbidding combinations or attempting to break them up, would seek to "control them in the interest of the public." This New Nationalism would also place the well-being of the public ahead of property rights. "Every man," TR told his Kansas audience, "holds his property subject to the general right of the community to regulate its use to whatever degree the public welfare may require." Here was an endorsement of government paternalism and control beyond anything previously espoused by a major-party candidate. It distanced Roosevelt still further from the president.

Not all Republican progressives favored Roosevelt. Many, especially in the Midwest, preferred Wisconsin's La Follette. In January 1911 the midwesterners had organized the National Republican Progressive League to advance progressive ideas and promote La Follette's candidacy. Roosevelt refused to join. For a while the two men jockeyed for leadership of the party's progressive wing, but then, unable to compete with TR's broad national appeal, La Follette dropped out of the race.

Throughout the spring of 1912 Roosevelt and Taft battled for Republican convention delegates. TR won in the states, mainly western, that used presidential primaries to choose convention delegates. Taft swept the states in the South and East where tightly controlled conventions, dominated by party regulars, made the delegate choice. At the convention in Chicago the Republican National Committee, controlled by the Taft men, refused the Roosevelt forces' claim to a large block of disputed convention setas, giving almost all of them to Taft. The Roosevelt delegates walked out, leaving the convention firmly in the president's hands.

Roosevelt and his friends were not through. Early in August, 2,000 men and women, many of them distinguished social workers, settlement house leaders, and state and local reformers, assembled in Chicago to organize the Progressive party and nominate Roosevelt

Declaring himself "strong as a bull moose," Roosevelt made the 1912 election a three-way race. Ironically, all three candidates were progressives to one degree or another. Notice the moose biting the Republican elephant's rear end.

for president. The delegates selected Hiram W. Johnson of California as their vice presidential candidate. The platform of the Progressive party—or Bull Moose party, as it was called after TR's remark that he felt as energetic as a bull moose—was the most radical ever proposed by a major party, foreshadowing almost all of the modern American welfare state. Taking many of the emerging progressive ideas and carrying them several steps further, it endorsed direct popular election of United States senators; presidential primaries; the initiative, referendum, and recall in federal matters; women's suffrage; the recall (by citizens' petitions) of state court decisions; tariff reduction; a commission to regulate interstate industry, not just interstate commerce; a more stringent pure food and drug law; old age pensions; minimum wage and maximum hours laws; and the prohibition of child labor. The closing words of TR's acceptance speech conveyed the crusading mood of the new party. "Our cause," the candidate proclaimed, "is based on the eternal principles of righteousness, and even though we who now lead for the first time fail, in the end the cause itself will triumph. . . . . We stand at Armageddon and we battle for the Lord."

The Election of 1912.

Meanwhile, the Democrats had nominated Woodrow Wilson, former president of Princeton University and, most recently, progressive governor of New Jersey. The son of a Presbyterian minister from Virginia, Wilson was a slender, scholarly man who joined stubborn self-righteousness with an eloquence unequaled since Lincoln and a vision of human potential unmatched since Jefferson. In 1910 the New Jersey Democratic bosses had selected him as a figurehead candidate for governor, but he had gone on to repudiate his sponsors and make an impressive record as a strong, liberal leader who brought staunchly conservative New Jersey into the progressive era. At the 1912 Democratic convention in Baltimore, Wilson faced the formidable opposition of the progressive Speaker of the House, Missouri's Champ Clark. Wilson had Bryan's support, and his friends were able to win over the leaders of the big-city machines. The contest was close, however; it took forty-six ballots to reach a decision.

During the next few months the country experienced the liveliest presidential battle since 1896. The contest was really between Roosevelt and Wilson, with Taft lagging badly from the very beginning. During the weeks of campaigning the conflicting ideologies of the two front-runners were thrown into sharp relief. TR trumpeted the message of the new Nationalism:

Progressive Party Platform, 1912

In 1912 the progressive agenda at its most liberal was incorporated into the platform of the Bull Moose, or Progressive, party. The new party was made up of ambition and personal grievances as well as idealism; without the anger of Theodore Roosevelt at his protégé President Taft, there might not have been such an organization. Yet however derived, the party attracted all the most advanced progressives. Its 1912 platform is a summary of what these liberal men and women envisioned for the good society of the future. It is a remarkable foreshadowing of mid-twentieth-century liberalism.

"The conscience of the people, in a time of grave national problems, has called into being a new party, born of the nation's sense of justice. We of the Progressive party here dedicate ourselves to the fulfillment of duty laid upon us by our fathers to maintain the government of the people, by the people, for the people. . . .

The Rule of the People

. . . . In particular, the party declares for direct primaries for the nomination of State and National officers, for nation-wide preferential primaries for candidates for the presidency; for the direct election of United States Senators by the people . . . ; with responsibility to the people secured by the initiative, referendum and recall. . . .

Equal Suffrage

"The Progressive party, believing that no people can justly claim to be a true democracy which denies political rights on account of sex, pledges itself to the task of securing equal suffrage to men and women alike.

Corrupt Practices

"We pledge our party to legislation that will compel strict limitation of all campaign contributions, and expenditures, and detailed publicity of both before as well as after primaries and elections. . . .

The Courts

"The Progressive party demands such restriction of the power of the courts as shall leave to the people the ultimate authority to determine fundamental questions of social welfare and public policy. . . .

Administration of Justice

". . . We believe that the issuance of injunctions in cases arising out of labor disputes should be prohibited when such injunctions would not apply when no labor disputes existed. . . .

Social and Industrial Justice

"The supreme duty of the Nation is the conservation of human resources through an enlightened measure of social and industrial justice. We pledge ourselves to work unceasingly in State and Nation for:

"Effective legislation looking to the prevention of industrial accidents, occupational diseases, overwork, involuntary unemployment, and other injurious effects incident to modern industry;

"The fixing of minimum safety and health standards for the various occupations. . . ;

"The prohibition of child labor;

"Minimum wage standards for working women, to provide a 'living wage' in all industrial occupations;

"The general prohibition of night work for women and the establishment of an eight hour day for women and young persons;

"One day's rest in seven for all wage workers. . . ;

"The abolition of the convict contract labor system. . . ;

"Standards of compensation for death by industrial accident and injury and trade disease which will transfer the burden of lost earnings from the families of working people of the industry, and thus to the community;

"The protection of home life against the hazards of sickness, irregular employment and old age through the adoption of a system of social insurance adapted to American use. . . ;

"The establishment of industrial research laboratories to put the methods and discoveries of science to the service of American producers;

"We favor the organization of the workers, men and women, as a means of protecting their interests and of promoting their progress. . . .

Conservation

". . . We believe that the remaining forests, coal and oil lands, water power and other natural resources still in State or National control . . . are more likely to be wisely conserved and utilized for the general welfare if held in public hands.

"In order that consumers and producers, managers and workmen, now and hereafter, need not pay toll to private monopolies of power and raw material, we demand that such resources shall be retained by the State or Nation, and opened to immediate use under laws which will encourage development and make to the people a moderate return for benefits conferred. . . ."

Bigness as such was not bad; it only became bad when it injured the public and the national interest. Government could, and should, regulate private economic interests. Government also had a responsibility to protect citizens in many other aspects of daily life and reduce life's uncertainties and hazards. Wilson, a man from the Jeffersonian tradition of limited government, fought back with his New Freedom, much of it inspired by the liberal Boston lawyer Louis D. Brandeis. The New Nationalism was "big-brother government," Wilson charged. "You will find," he told a Buffalo audience of working men, "that the programme of the new party legalizes monopolies and systematically subordinates workingmen to them and to plans made by the Government. . . ." Like the Bull Moosers, Wilson believed that concentrated private economic power was a danger to the American public; he differed from them in holding that the way to salvation lay in breaking up these monopolies by vigorous antitrust action. TR's response to the new Freedom was blunt: It was "rural toryism," he declared, more suitable for a simpler age than for the twentieth-century world.

Wilson won the election by a plurality. The public loved Teddy, but many progressives were suspicious of his newfound radicalism, especially since he had allowed a Morgan partner, George Perkins, to play an important role in the campaign as fund-raiser and organizer. In the end TR received the votes largely of the Republican progressives; Taft, of the Republican stand-pat core. Wilson, on the other hand, won the votes of both Democratic progressives and traditional conservative Democrats. Eugene V. Debs took 900,000 votes for the Socialists. For the first time since 1897 a Democrat would occupy the White House, but only because a third party had split the opposition.

The New Freedom in Action. As president, Wilson proved to be a strong leader. Disregarding the precedent set by Jefferson in 1801, he appeared before Congress in person to read his annual message. His propos-

The election of 1912

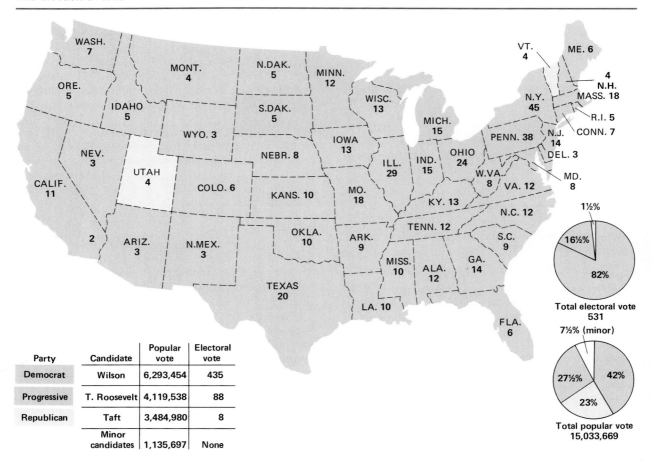

Party	Candidate	Popular vote	Electoral vote
Democrat	Wilson	6,293,454	435
Progressive	T. Roosevelt	4,119,538	88
Republican	Taft	3,484,980	8
Minor candidates		1,135,697	None

Total electoral vote 531

Total popular vote 15,033,669

als were less bold than his presentation. Wilson's first major concern was the tariff, which, he reminded Congress, had long fostered monopolies and exposed the consuming public to oppressive prices. The structure of "privilege" and "artificial advantage" must be destroyed and American businesses compelled to compete with their rivals in the rest of the world. Wilson was determined to do what Taft had failed at in 1909.

The fruit of the president's efforts was the 1913 Underwood Tariff. This measure substantially lowered the nation's tariff walls for the first time since the Civil War. To make up for the expected loss of federal revenue, Congress took advantage of the recently adopted Sixteenth Amendment and included a graduated income tax in the measure. Lobbyists for manufacturing and other special-interest groups resisted passage of the tariff bill, but Wilson fought back. Lashing out at the "industrious and insidious" lobbyists, he accused them of seeking to "create an artificial opinion and to overcome the interests of the public" for their own selfish ends. His counterattack jarred the Senate, and the bill passed.

Wilson's next important achievement was the Federal Reserve Act. The failings of the country's banking system had engaged the attention of the business community and farmers for fifty years. The national Banking Acts of the Civil War Era had failed to create a central bank to regulate the supply of money and credit and extend help to hard-pressed local commercial banks in time of crisis. Nor had the national banking system provided the flexible currency that could expand to meet the needs of the economy during peak periods like harvest time or the Christmas season, and then contract during quiet months. Farmers condemned the system for forbidding federally chartered banks to lend on mortgages, the only security for loans that they generally possessed. Yet agrarians feared a system that would be centralized in New York and tightly controlled by Wall Street.

As finally passed in 1913, the Federal Reserve Act was a compromise between the centralizers and agrarians, the supporters of government regulation and those who favored private control. It created twelve district banks, whose directors were chosen by both private bankers and the government. The whole system was placed under the weak overall supervision of a central Federal Reserve Board in Washington. The district banks would hold the reserves of member banks—the local commercial banks that did the day-to-day business of the nation. By lending money to member banks at low interest rates, or alternately by limiting such loans through high interest ("rediscount") rates,

the district banks could regulate credit and the money supply to suit the economy's seasonal needs and head off financial crises. The new system also allowed member banks to lend on farm mortgages. Despite the failings that time would reveal, the new system seemed a great improvement over the old.

The third major item on Wilson's first-term agenda was antitrust legislation to fulfill his campaign promise to break up the monopolies. Over the years the government's antitrust drive had been blunted by the federal courts. Most recently, in its 1911 "rule of reason" decision (*Standard Oil* v. *United States*), the Supreme Court had declared that only "unreasonable" restraints on interstate commerce were illegal; from now on a case of monopoly must be blatant to be subject to antitrust prosecution. But that was not all. For over a decade the federal courts had been treating labor unions as "combinations in restraint of trade," subject to antitrust prosecution. They had even issued injunctions (as in the 1894 Pullman strike) compelling unions to cease strikes and boycotts or face federal contempt-of-court charges. In the hands of the courts the Sherman Antitrust Act had become a union-busting weapon.

To protect organized labor's rights, help consumers, and get around the courts' limitations on antitrust actions, Wilson proposed two new measures. The first established the Federal Trade Commission (1914) to replace Roosevelt's Bureau of Corporations. The FTC was given powers to procure data from corporations and issue cease-and-desist orders against abuses like mislabeling, adulteration of products, trade boycotts, and combinations to fix wholesale prices. The new commission would be the public's watchdog against the trusts. The second measure, the Clayton Antitrust Act (1914), strengthened the Sherman Antitrust Act in several ways. It prohibited firms from charging one price to one customer and a different price to another when such discrimination tended to foster monopoly. It forbade contracts that required buyers not to do business with sellers' competitors. It also declared illegal most "interlocking directorates," a device by which one group of corporate directors headed several firms simultaneously. Similarly, a corporation was prohibited from acquiring stock in other corporations when the transaction threatened to reduce competition. A final provision—called by AFL president Samuel Gompers "labor's Magna Carta"—declared both labor unions and farmers' cooperatives exempt from the antitrust laws and limited the right of federal courts to issue injunctions in labor disputes.

Another important change during Wilson's first

months in office—one that was a general progressive initiative rather than Wilson's alone—was the adoption of the Seventeenth Amendment to the Constitution (1913): Henceforth all United States senators would be elected by direct vote of the people in each state rather than by the state legislators. No longer, the reformers felt, would the Senate be a bastion of conservatism that could ignore public opinion and protect the big corporations.

Wilson's Failings. Despite the president's successes, his first few years disappointed some of the most advanced progressives. He declined to support women's suffrage and at first refused to fight for a child-labor law. Nor was he as fierce an opponent of trusts as he had promised to be during the campaign. Like TR before him, he bargained with big corporations, agreeing not to prosecute them for combining to restrain trade if they would modify their behavior in some acceptable way.

But the most conspicuous defect of Wilson's first administration was its attitudes toward black Americans. The new president was a Virginian by birth and had lived much of his early life in the South. His party, moreover, was strongly southern in its makeup, and many of his closest advisers were white southerners. The new administration had few ties to the black community. Once in office, it abruptly cut off much of the political patronage that the Republicans had conferred on black supporters. In addition, one by one, federal departments and agencies began to segregate their remaining black workers, imposing on the federal government the Jim Crow system that permeated the South. Eventually, following loud protests from black leaders and their white progressive allies, the president tried to undo some of the damage. But it was too late. By the end of his administration the nation's capital had become a full-blown southern city in its racial practices.

Wilson Shifts Left. Wilson's first three years in office produced mixed results from the progressive perspective. And after passage of the Clayton Act of 1914, the president appeared to lose interest in pushing further progressive legislation. Then, as the 1916 election approached, his reformist enthusiasm revived.

The reason for the change was primarily political. Wilson had won in 1912 because the Republicans, who usually had been the majority party during these years, had been split between Taft and Roosevelt. By 1916 TR had returned to the GOP of his youth, virtually killing the Bull Moose party. To win, Wilson concluded, he would have to attract former Bull Moosers, and this meant moving to the left. Hitherto his brand of reform—the New Freedom—had emphasized the restoration of free competition as a way to protect the ordinary citizen against private power. He had avoided the social legislation that required expansion of federal control. Now Wilson shifted ground.

To aid farmers, who despite the Federal Reserve Act still had unmet credit needs, he supported the Federal Farm Loan Act of 1916. This measure established twelve Federal Farm Loan banks to lend money at low rates to farmers who joined certain farm loan associations. A bolder innovation was the Keating-Owen Act (1916), which discouraged child labor by prohibiting interstate traffic in goods manufactured by the labor of children under sixteen years of age. This prohibition, progressives believed, would virtually end child labor, for few manufacturers could afford to sell their products solely within their own state. Still other advanced progressive measures the president pushed were the Kern-McGillicuddy Compensation Act (1916) providing workers' compensation for injured federal employees, and the Adamson Act (1916) establishing an eight-hour day and time-and-a-half overtime pay for railroad workers. Though these new laws applied to only limited groups of employees, they represented a long step toward federal regulation of the labor market.

One additional move rounded out Wilson's shift to the left in 1916: the nomination of his friend Louis D. Brandeis as Supreme Court justice.

For years Brandeis had been one of the best-known labor lawyers in the country. His work in establishing arbitration procedures in the New York garment industry had been hailed as a model approach to labor-capital relations. In 1908, in the case *Muller* v. *Oregon*, his brief for the state against an employer challenging an Oregon law that limited the working hours of women had been called a progressive landmark. In the *Muller* case, Brandeis had not merely cited legal precedents to bolster his reasoning, but had also mustered arguments drawn from sociology to demonstrate that long work hours were detrimental to the health of women and seriously injured society as a whole. The "Brandeis brief" had saved the Oregon law and established an important precedent for defending future social legislation.

The Brandeis nomination raised a storm. The Supreme Court in 1916 had only one progressive member, Oliver Wendell Holmes, Jr., and the nation's liberals cheered the prospect of Brandeis joining him. But conservatives, including ex-president Taft and the

American Bar Association, fought the nomination with every ounce of their strength. Running through much of the opposition was a barely disguised streak of anti-Semitism. Despite the powerful opposition, Wilson fought hard for his friend and adviser, pulling all the strings he could. His success earned him additional gratitude from progressives of both parties.

By late summer of 1916 the Progressive movement had largely run its course. By now the public's attention had shifted from domestic issues to the question of war or peace. In a few months the country would embark on a crusade to make the whole world safe for the kind of liberal society that the progressives had been trying for a decade or more to construct at home. In the process the domestic reform impulse would lose its spark.

Conclusions

Between 1890 and 1917 more and more Americans became fearful of unrestrained private power. As the nation became ever more tightly knit together, giant corporations had become essential for providing the products people needed for a comfortable life. As growing numbers came to live in the cities, they became increasingly dependent on large firms for virtually everything they consumed. Seeking to protect themselves, urban Americans of all classes adopted a new political outlook, one that resembled views earlier held by rural reformers such as the Populists and the free-silver Democrats.

The progressives took much from Populism. Their primary enemy was similar—the trusts, the monopolies—and they borrowed the familiar rhetoric of an earlier rural age when they attacked "the interests." Especially in Wilson's New Freedom, we find echoes of Jefferson and Jackson in attitudes and ideas. Progressives also revived the Populist concern for direct democracy to bypass corrupt legislatures. Yet the addition of urban and middle-class people to the reform cause altered its quality. Progressivism was more sophisticated than Populism. Borrowing from the liberal social Darwinists and the new efficiency-oriented professionals, progressives abandoned monetary cure-alls and developed new ideas of direct government action to solve social ills. Inevitably they focused on city problems and on wage earners, though rural grievances were not ignored. Especially in its New Nationalism guise, progressivism pointed the way to future reform in a complex urban society.

Progressivism was not a complete success even

A portrait of President Woodrow Wilson in 1921, just before he left office, a sick and beaten man.

in its own terms. It did not end the dangers inherent in a society with large inequalities of wealth and power; it did not end the insecurity that afflicted many Americans. It would remain to a later generation to tackle these problems again, with somewhat greater success. The failure cannot be blamed solely on the progressives themselves. They were innovators and their support, while wide, was often thin. Americans were not yet accustomed to the idea of a strong, positive state that could override entrenched private rights if need be, a situation underlined by the frequency with which the federal courts overturned, and would continue to overturn, progressive regulatory legislation. In their battles to change society, progressives were often forced to accept half a loaf rather than none at all. Much progressive legislation proved inadequate, not because of a failure of the progressive vision, but because of insufficient progressive power.

Yet progressivism also had inherent limitations.

The prophets of efficiency clearly had a limited vision of a better society. Placing economic savings before human needs, they believed that reform consisted primarily in making political as well as economic machinery work better. Nor were progressives as a whole free of the prejudice that marked their predecessors. A few demanded that black Americans be included in the progressive agenda. But most, including the two progressive presidents, believed in the superiority of the white race, and within it the superiority of its North European branch. Clearly, not all those who called themselves progressive were in the forefront of their times. Many who were essentially conservative in na-

ture climbed aboard the progressive bandwagon once it started to roll. It seems that at times this charge can be applied to both Roosevelt and Wilson. Wilson's racial attitudes and failure to support women's suffrage, and TR's desertion of the Bull Moosers in 1916, surely point in this direction. And even at their most advanced their answers now seem naive. It is not, after all, as easy to end serious social and economic inequalities as they believed. Nevertheless, the progressives of 1900–1917 were the first generation to grapple with the new problems of an increasingly urbanized nation. For all their failings, they laid the foundation for much that would follow.

For Further Reading

Richard Hofstadter. *Age of Reform: From Bryan to F.D.R.* (1955)

> The middle portion of this interpretation of American reform movements deals with progressivism. Urban and middle-class in origin, according to Hofstadter, the movement failed to achieve real reform because its members distrusted organized labor and immigrants and were obsessed with threats to their own status from both the left and the right.

Lincoln Steffens. *Autobiography* (1931)

> The famous muckraker eventually became disillusioned with the liberal values that motivated progressivism, concluding that capitalism itself was responsible for political corruption and social oppression. Includes many anecdotes about business executives and political leaders of the Progressive Era.

James Harvey Young. *The Toadstool Millionaires: A Social History of Patent Medicines in America before Federal Regulation* (1962)

> Before the Pure Food and Drug Act of 1906, quacks and crooks sold pills, powders, and liquids in bottles shaped like pigs, Indian maidens, and Founding Fathers. This funny and tragic tale of the gullible public and the patent-medicine manufacturers will tell you something about modern advertising.

Allen F. Davis. *Spearheads for Reform: The Social Settlements and the Progressive Movement, 1890–1914* (1967)

> Concentrating on three cities—New York, Chicago, and Boston—Davis shows the frustration of settlement workers' efforts for social justice in the wards. He evaluates their success in citywide and national politics, especially their influence on education, housing, unions, and female and child labor.

David Thelen. *The New Citizenship: Origins of Progressivism in Wisconsin, 1885–1900* (1972)

> This well-written monograph on progressivism in Wisconsin emphasizes the role consumer anger and frustration played in launching the new reform movement. The depression of the 1890s, says Thelen, made the state's corporations squeeze consumers and awakened deep resentment of their power.

August Meier. *Negro Thought in America, 1880–1915* (1963)

> An analysis of the thought of Booker T. Washington, W. E. B. Du Bois, and other black leaders on politics, economics, migration, colonization, racial solidarity, and industrial and elitist education.

James Weldon Johnson. *Autobiography of an Ex-Coloured Man* (1912)

> This is a fictional composite autobiography of blacks before World War I by a black composer and lyricist, lawyer, founder of the NAACP, and chronicler of Harlem. Best known for its depiction of life on Manhattan's West Side and its appreciation of ragtime, this book was prophetic of the Harlem Renaissance in which Johnson took part.

Henry F. Pringle. *Theodore Roosevelt* (1931)

> Pringle's long and graceful biography follows the many TRs: sickly boy, university dude, reformer in New York City, Dakota rancher, Washington office seeker, Rough Rider in Cuba, president, Bull Mooser, and anti-Wilsonite.

Upton Sinclair. *The Jungle* (1906)

> Sinclair, a socialist, lived among the Chicago meatpackers during their strike in 1904. He intended this novel to arouse the nation's indignation about the packers' working conditions. Instead, his nauseatingly detailed descriptions of the meat prepared for public consumption turned the nation's stomach. The Meat Inspection Act of 1906 was the result.

Roy Lubove. *The Progressives and the Slums* (1962)

> Focusing on New York City, Lubove has written a fine study of how the progressives dealt with one

of the key social problems of the day—the slums. An important and interesting book.

William Harbaugh. *The Life and Times of Theodore Roosevelt* (1975)

Pringle's biography reads better than Harbaugh's, but the latter's is more up to date and more in tune with recent scholarship.

Samuel P. Hays. *Conservation and the Gospel of Efficiency: The Progressive Conservation Movement, 1890–1920* (1959)

This was a pathbreaking book when it appeared and is still important for the serious student of progressivism. Hays is one of those scholars who emphasize the progressive obsession with efficiency. His focus here is on the conservationist group within the larger environmental movement.

John D. Buenker. *Urban Liberalism and Progressive Reform* (1973)

Buenker believes that we must not ignore the interest in, and support of, progressivism by urban working people and their political spokespersons in Congress and the state legislatures. He shows that these leaders were as strongly in favor of the graduated income tax and direct election of senators, for example, as they were of legislation limiting working hours and regulating tenements.

George Mowry. *The California Progressives* (1951)

This study of progressivism in a banner progressive state helped introduce the thesis that the progressives were middle-class citizens suffering from acute social anxiety as a result of threats to their status. Hofstadter borrowed heavily from Mowry in his *Age of Reform*.

Arthur Link. *Woodrow Wilson and the Progressive Era* (1954)

Still the best study of the Wilsonian phase of progressivism. Link, who is completing a multivolume biography of Wilson, admires his subject, but he can also see his flaws.

Aileen Kraditor. *The Ideas of the Woman Suffrage Movement, 1890–1920* (1965)

A study of the thought of the women's suffrage movement leaders during the final drive that brought success. Contains an enlightening analysis of the way racism affected the goals of the white, middle-class women who led the women's suffrage movement.

William O'Neill. *Everyone Was Brave: A History of Feminism in America* (1971)

A lively, intelligent discussion of feminism with an especially good section on feminist politics in the Progressive Era.

Chapter 24

World War I

Idealism, National Interest, or Neutral Rights?

1914   American marines occupy Veracruz, Mexico • World War I begins in Europe; Wilson calls
for American neutrality

1915   Marines occupy Haiti • Germany declares a war zone around the British Isles • U-boats sink the
Falaba, the *Lusitania*, and the *Arabic*, all with loss of American lives • Wilson initiates the preparedness program
to enlarge the army and the navy

1916   Wilson orders General John Pershing and 6,000 troops to Mexico to capture Pancho Villa • Colonel
Edward House promises American intervention if deadlock on Western Front continues • U-boat sinks the
Sussex with resulting American injuries; Germany suspends submarine warfare • Wilson reelected on "He
kept us out of war" platform • Marines occupy the Dominican Republic

1917   Germany resumes submarine warfare and the United States severs diplomatic relations • British
intelligence intercepts the "Zimmermann telegram" • Wilson orders the arming of American merchant ships
• The Russian Revolution • Congress declares war on Germany; the War Industries Board, the War Labor
Board, and the Committee of Public Information manage the war effort at home • Congress passes the
Espionage Act

1918   The Sedition Act • Postmaster General Albert Burleson excludes publications critical of the war
from the mails • The Justice Department indicts socialist leaders Eugene Debs and Victor Berger on charges
of advocating draft evasion • Wilson announces his Fourteen Points • Germany collapses and armistice
ends the war

1919   Peace conference at Versailles; League of Nations incorporated into treaty

1919–20   Congress rejects the Versailles Treaty

1920   The states ratify the Nineteenth Amendment providing for women's suffrage • Warren G. Harding
elected president • Harding signs separate peace treaty with Germany in lieu of Versailles Treaty

A s Americans read their newspapers over morning coffee on June 29, 1914, many wondered: "Where is Sarajevo?" The day before, in that remote Balkan town in present-day Yugoslavia, a fanatical Serbian nationalist had shot and killed Archduke Francis Ferdinand, heir to the Austro-Hungarian throne. Few people could have anticipated how their lives and those of millions of others would be affected by the archduke's murder in that backward and unruly corner of eastern Europe.

Within six weeks the major European powers were at war. First, Austria demanded that Serbia suppress the nationalist movement it had allowed to flourish on its soil. The Serbs appealed for support to their Slavic big brother, Russia; the Austrians in turn asked Germany to come to their aid. Tied by a bewildering tangle of alliances and agreements, both public and secret, all the large nations of Europe were quickly drawn into the dispute, with France, Russia, and Great Britain (the Allies) on one side, and Germany and Austria-Hungary (the Central Powers) on the other. Before many months Japan and Italy had joined the Allies; and the Ottoman Empire (Turkey) and Bulgaria, the Central Powers. By the end of 1914 great armies were smashing at one another in Europe with the most lethal weapons that twentieth-century technology could devise, while on the high seas and in the air hostile navies and air fleets grappled in fierce and deadly combat.

President Wilson officially responded to the tragic events in Europe in mid-August. Americans, declared the president, must be "neutral in fact as well as in name during these days that are to try men's souls." We must, he pleaded, "be impartial in thought as well as in action, must put a curb on our sentiments as well as upon every transaction that might be construed as a preference of one party to the struggle before another." Thirty-one months later the same man would appear before a joint session of Congress to ask for a declaration of war against the Central Powers.

What had happened in those months to bring the peaceful and self-satisfied Republic into this "most terrible of wars"? Why did the United States and its people not heed the president's early advice and remain neutral both "in thought" and "in action"?

Wilson and the World Order

To understand American involvement in World War I, we must consider Wilson's view of the world and America's place in it. Progressive foreign policy came in two main varieties. Some progressives, like Theodore Roosevelt and Albert J. Beveridge, were aggressive internationalists who believed the United States must play a vigorous role in world affairs and serve as a force for international balance and morality. Others, like Senators Robert La Follette of Wisconsin and Hiram W. Johnson of California, were isolationists who feared that excessive United States involvement in concerns beyond its borders would interfere with reform at home. Both the progressive internationalists and the progressive isolationists believed that enlightened, liberal capitalism was the most benevolent social system in the world; all others fell short of the happy balance of individual freedom and equality.

Wilson's foreign policy views fluctuated between these poles. At times he seemed to believe progressive democracy was for domestic consumption only. On other occasions he acted as if it was for export as well. In addition, his attitudes were infused with an intense moralism derived from his Calvinist forebears and his father, a devout Presbyterian minister. To complicate matters further, like every national leader, he had to remember always his country's vital interests and defend them against any threatening power. To satisfy all these imperatives Wilson walked a tightrope, and his resulting unsteadiness and hesitation opened him to charges of inconsistency and even hypocrisy.

When he became president in 1913, Wilson's interest in domestic reform far outweighed his concern for international affairs. Yet he had misgivings. The world was at peace when he took office, but Europe, steeped in its age-old rivalries and tangled in its web of alliances, seemed poised on the edge of violence. Shortly before his inauguration the president-elect told a friend that it would be ironic if he had to spend most of his time as president attending to foreign affairs. His premonition proved sound.

Moral Diplomacy. Wilson chose William Jennings

Bryan as his first secretary of state. The long-time titular leader of the Democratic party was not a professional diplomat, but Wilson distrusted such men. Bryan was, rather, a fervent pacifist, a man who had worked long in the cause of peace and who shared Wilson's view that America must serve as the world's "moral inspiration." Bryan's first official exertions for world peace came in 1913 and 1914, when he negotiated conciliation treaties with twenty-one nations. The parties to these treaties agreed to submit all international disputes to permanent investigating commissions and to forgo armed force until the commission had completed its report.

A similar idealism infused other aspects of Wilson's early diplomacy. Both Bryan and his chief opposed using the American government to serve the interests of American businesses abroad. Under Taft, Wilson's predecessor, the government had supported the participation of American bankers in a multinational consortium to build railroads in China. Feeling that the arrangement might undermine China's fragile sovereignty, Bryan withdrew the government's support. The two foreign policy makers also induced Congress to repeal a 1912 law that had exempted American coastal vessels from paying tolls on the Panama Canal, a law that violated the Hay-Pauncefote Treaty and its promise of equal treatment for all nations.

But Wilson never forgot the country's "vital interests"; where they seemed to be involved, and where the risks appeared small, he was sometimes insensitive to moral considerations. In the Caribbean, which the United States considered an American lake, Wilson and his chief lieutenant proved as overbearing as Roosevelt. In 1914 Bryan negotiated a treaty with Nicaragua giving that small nation $3 million for exclusive American rights to construct a second Atlantic-Pacific canal. The agreement, not ratified until 1916, made the strategically located Central American republic a virtual satellite of the United States, with little control over its own foreign affairs or its international economic relations. In 1915 and 1916 the United States intervened militarily in Haiti and the Dominican Republic—in the first to put down disorder, in the second to prevent the European powers, especially Germany, from landing troops to protect their citizens and collect unpaid debts. In each of these cases Wilson believed that he was merely holding America's less scrupulous neighbors to universal standards of order and honesty. To outsiders it appeared that the United States was imposing its will on countries too weak to resist the American giant.

A minister's son and a historian, Wilson had been president of Princeton University. As president of the United States, he continued to lecture and preach. Here, symbolically, he instructs a rather skeptical Mexico in the principles of true democracy.

Mexico. In Mexico the United States managed to combine blatant self-interest and idealism in a particularly confusing way. For a generation following 1880 Mexico was ruled by dictator Porfirio Díaz. Díaz had encouraged foreign investment in Mexican mines, oil wells, and railroads; by 1913 American businesses had poured over a billion dollars into his country. Despite this infusion of capital, ordinary Mexicans remained as poor, illiterate, and oppressed as in Moctezuma's day.

In 1911 Díaz's enemies among the country's liberal intellectuals toppled him from power and made Francisco Madero president. Madero tried to effect sweeping democratic reforms and restore constitutional liberties denied by Díaz. His policies aroused the hostility of the Mexican landed aristocracy, the army, and the Catholic Church. Two years later Victoriano Huerta, Madero's chief military adviser, seized the government and had Madero murdered.

Great Britain, Germany, and France had already officially recognized Huerta when Wilson took office. Many Americans, including business people with investments in Mexico, advised Wilson to follow suit. He refused. The United States, like other nations, traditionally recognized established governments no matter how they gained power or what their internal policies were. In Wilson's eyes, however, Huerta was a "butcher" who did not represent the "eighty-five percent" of the Mexican people who were "struggling toward liberty." Instead of according diplomatic recognition to the Huerta government, Wilson proclaimed a new policy toward revolutionary regimes in Latin America: The United States would not recognize any new government unless it was "supported at every turn by . . . orderly processes . . . based upon law, not upon arbitrary or irregular force."

Wilson disclaimed any intention of intervening in Mexico, but he quietly sought to isolate the new Mexican tyrant by pressuring the British into withdrawing their recognition. He also stationed American naval vessels off Mexico's major ports to stop arms shipments to Huerta while allowing arms to go to his enemies. Eventually, he hoped, Huerta might be pushed out by some champion of liberal rule like Venustiano Carranza, an associate of Madero who had raised the banner of revolt in the northern part of the country.

Wilson's policies led to trouble. In April 1914 crewmen of an American naval vessel were arrested by an Huertista officer when they went ashore at Tampico. Although they were soon released, the American naval commander, Admiral Henry Mayo, demanded that the Mexican officer be punished and that the commander of the port give the American flag a twenty-one-gun salute as a sign of respect. The Mexican commandant apologized and promised disciplinary action against his subordinate, but refused the salute.

The incident now seems trivial, but Wilson made it a matter of principle. Appearing before Congress, he asked for authority to compel the Mexicans to show respect for American rights. At this point, a German vessel began to land arms for Huerta at Veracruz. To prevent this, Admiral Mayo shelled the city and ordered it occupied by marines. In the fighting that followed, over a hundred Mexicans lost their lives.

In explaining the Veracruz disaster, the president maintained that he meant only the best for the Mexican people and hoped to see them establish a new order based on "human liberty and human rights." Wilson then lectured the Mexicans on how they should arrange their affairs. Mexico would have to redistribute land to equalize the condition of rich and poor. The country would continue to need foreign capital, too, but foreign corporations should not be allowed to exert excessive power and influence in Mexican affairs. This prescription for Mexico's future, though worthy of the best sort of American progressive, revealed the progressives' limitations. Ignoring Mexico's legacy of deep class antagonism and bitter ideological conflict, Wilson had assumed that the fundamental social change required of an "underdeveloped" nation might be effected as peaceably and amicably as progressive legislative reform in the United States. Still more imperceptive was the president's conclusion that the United States had the right to prescribe for Mexico at all. The Veracruz incident was an excellent demonstration of how American intrusion, even in a good cause, could produce disastrous consequences for its intended beneficiaries.

Meanwhile, the Veracruz attack had outraged all patriotic Mexicans, raised Huerta's stock among his own people, and cast the United States in the role of a brutal aggressor. It looked as if the Wilson administration would now be forced into the folly of war with Mexico. The president was rescued from this fate when Argentina, Brazil, and Chile (the so-called ABC powers) offered to mediate. In May 1914 the United States, Mexico, and the ABC powers met at Niagara Falls, Canada, and thrashed out a compromise that averted war.

But war with Mexico soon threatened again. Unable to resist the growing pressure at home and abroad, Huerta finally resigned, and power in Mexico City passed to Carranza. Once in office, however, Carranza was faced by a revolt among his own followers led by Francisco ("Pancho") Villa. Hoping to goad the United States into some overt action against Mexico that would unite the Mexican people against the "gringos" and help his chances to seize the government, Villa ordered his men to attack American citizens both in Mexico and across the border.

American indignation quickly reached a new peak. Whatever they felt following the Tampico and Veracruz incidents, virtually all Americans now agreed that the United States must take strong action. In March 1916, after 35 Americans had been massacred by Villista soldiers, Wilson ordered General John J. Pershing to enter Mexico with 6,000 troops. The wily Villa eluded the American army, however, while drawing it deeper and deeper into Mexican territory.

Carranza, whose regime the Wilson administration had informally recognized in October 1915, had given the Americans permission to enter Mexico to capture Villa. But the Mexican president was appalled by the size of the expedition and the depth of the American penetration. Pershing, it appeared, was not pursuing a bandit; he was invading a friendly nation and violating its sovereignty. War was averted at the last minute only when Wilson, realizing that the United States had far more pressing concerns in Europe, ordered Pershing to return to Texas. The president then sent Ambassador Henry Fletcher to Mexico and formally recognized the Carranza administration.

With this move Wilson ended the threat of war with Mexico. Warned off by Pershing's military failure, he had resisted the temptation to make a popular war, although it probably would have guaranteed his reelection in 1916. Though his bungling caused anti-American feeling to run high in Mexico for years, his support for Carranza and his newfound determination to avoid war despite sharp provocations allowed the revolutionaries to establish control. The Mexican situation revealed the principal elements of the Wilson foreign policy: moralism, self-interest, missionary interventionism, and a deep reluctance to make war. These contradictory urges would also be apparent in the American approach to the war in Europe.

Pershing leads his troops across the Rio Grande into Mexico on a search for bandit Pancho Villa. Although Pershing's expedition failed, Wilson eventually promoted him to general and gave him command of the American Expeditionary Force in Europe.

Neutrality and Public Opinion

Wilson's call for neutrality in August 1914 had evoked a loud "amen" from the American public. Almost no one wanted to become directly involved in Europe's quarrel. Americans had a traditional distaste for the complicated alliances formed among the European nation-states. Moreover, America was now a nation of immigrants, and war would inflame conflicting sympathies with Old World countries, causing social tension and unrest. Finally, there were many pacifists who deplored all war regardless of the causes.

Americans Take Sides. Though most Americans wished to avoid war, they were not as emotionally removed from European concerns as they thought. And how could they be? Millions of citizens had been born in one or another of the belligerent nations and found they could not escape the ideological and emotional commitments of their heritage. Recent arrivals from England, Scotland, and Wales retained their affection for Britain and hoped to see it remain mistress of the seas. On the other side, the large German-American population still had strong attachments to the "fatherland" and cheered for the Central Powers. The picture was greatly complicated by the immigrants from Austria-Hungary and Russia. These sprawling empires contained millions of Poles, Czechs, South Slavs, Finns, Jews, and many other groups who suffered under repressive governments. Immigrants from the Hapsburg and czarist lands, despising the Austrian and Russian regimes, prayed for their defeat. The Irish further complicated this tangle of responses; many hated Britain as their centuries-long oppressor and hoped that England's troubles could be turned to Ireland's advantage.

Old-stock Americans looked askance at the continued attachment of newer arrivals to their native lands and accused them of putting European concerns ahead of American ones. Yet they, too, took sides. Aside from a small but prestigious group of intellectuals who respected German culture and scholarship or disliked the pervasive English influence on American life, most old-stock Americans were pro-Ally. Such people read the classics of English literature and admired English law and parliamentary instutions. Many of them tended to feel affection for France as well, remembering with gratitude French aid during the Revolution. The sophisticated set, which included many of the country's opinion makers, was fascinated with French fashions, food, and thought.

Partisanship for the Allies went beyond sentiment and aesthetic preference, however. England and France were democracies tied to the United States by a common bond of liberalism and egalitarianism. In an era of revitalized enthusiasm for liberal principles at home, Britain's and France's democratic insitutions seemed especially worthy of support. This natural sympathy of progressive Americans was to some extent offset by the revulsion they felt toward tyrannical and backward czarist Russia, but Russia was very remote and seemed, at most, a junior partner of the western allies.

Germany's conservatism, militarism, and arrogance confirmed American preferences. A nation dominated by Prussian discipline and obsession with order since its unification in 1871, Germany had allowed its imperial ambitions to swell to gigantic proportions under Kaiser Wilhelm II. Since 1898 American military and naval leaders had become increasingly worried about a German threat to the Western Hemisphere. As recently as 1910 the Navy General Board had estimated that Germany was probably America's most dangerous potential enemy. Opinion makers and the foreign policy elite shared the fear of German aggressiveness and power, and many other citizens could not help feeling that Germany's defeat would benefit America and democratic principles everywhere.

All told, a majority of Americans were pro-Ally from the outset. At no time would intervention to help Germany be conceivable. The best that the Central Powers could expect was American neutrality. From the beginning, however, the British and French had reason to hope that the United States could be turned into an active ally, willing to supply arms and even men to help them defeat their opponents.

The Propaganda War. Both sides sought to sway American opinion, the Allies for intervention, the Central Powers for neutrality. Before long they were waging a fierce propaganda battle in which truth often took a backseat. The *New York Times* would call the European conflict the "first press agents' war."

In the lively struggle for American minds the Germans labored under serious handicaps. The British and French controlled the transatlantic cables, which transmitted European news to the American press, leaving the Germans with only the still-primitive wireless for getting their message to the American public. The Central Powers were also inept. German war propaganda emphasized hate and destruction—an approach that often aroused more revulsion than sympathy. Some of the most effective Allied efforts to win American approval consisted of reprinting German hate propaganda against Britain and France.

More important in repelling American opinion than German words were German deeds. Germany opened its military campaign on the Western Front by invading Belgium, thereby violating an international agreement of long standing. The German chancellor then contemptuously referred to the treaty as a "scrap of paper." When patriotic Belgians challenged the occupiers, the German authorities retaliated by executing Belgian civilians—some 5,000 in the course of the war—and by burning the old university town of Louvain.

If the Germans were clumsy and brutal, the Allies were adroit and clever. The British in particular spoke the language of Americans, literally and figuratively. Instinctively, they knew how to arouse American sympathies. They were quick to blow up German atrocities to enormous proportions. In 1915 the British government issued an official report signed by James Bryce, a distinguished historian and respected former British ambassador to Washington, describing in gruesome detail the torture, multilation, and murder of Belgian civilians, especially women and children. The report concluded that under the German occupation "murder, lust, and pillage prevailed . . . on a scale unparalleled in any war between civilized nations in the last three centuries." Many of the atrocity stories were unfounded; others were grossly exaggerated. Nevertheless, the Bryce Report convinced many Americans that the Germans were savage "Huns" who deserved the condemnation of the entire civilized world.

The Administration's Partisanship. In some ways the Allies' strongest supporter in America was the president himself, despite his appeal for neutrality. Ever since his early manhood, when his admiration for British political institutions had led him to write *Congressional Government*, praising the English parliamentary system, Wilson had been an Anglophile. As president he felt close to the leaders of the Liberal party in England, whose program of social welfare in the years immediately preceding the war had closely paralleled his own.

The president tried to be neutral, but his true feelings often showed through his reserve. He once told the British ambassador that everything he loved most in the world depended on Allied victory. He remarked at another point to his private secretary that "England is fighting our fight. . . . I will not take any action to embarrass England when she is fighting for her life and the life of the world." In addition, Wilson and his closest advisers, Colonel Edward M. House and later Robert Lansing, took seriously the threat of German expansionism and looked to Britain and France to check the German emperor's ambitions. Ever since the Spanish-American War, when Britain alone among the European powers had supported the

United States, makers of American foreign policy had regarded England as a bulwark against the ambitions of expansionist Germany. This feeling remained a major, though unspoken, cornerstone of American foreign policy from the late 1890s onward. This informal alliance would influence American policymakers after August 1914.

Neutral Rights

Despite the pro-Ally bias of the American people and their government, American entrance into the war could have been avoided if it had not been for the issue of neutral rights. Although propaganda, admiration of the democracies, and fear of imperial Germany all worked to erode American determination to stay clear of the war, it was the issue of neutral rights that ultimately brought the United States in. Today, when warfare seems to have no rules, it is difficult to believe that Americans once took seriously the concept of neutral rights. But in 1914 they did.

In the early twentieth century, as during the Napoleonic Wars a hundred years before, the United States found itself the major neutral power in a world divided into two warring camps, each determined to defeat the other no matter what the cost to bystanders. The United States, however, expected European belligerents to observe the rights traditionally due neutral nations in wartime. Under these rules vessels owned by neutrals had the right to carry unmolested all goods except contraband. Contraband was strictly defined as arms and munitions, with commodities such as food, textiles, and naval stores explicitly exempt. Neutrals also had the right to trade freely with all belligerents, although they might be legitimately intercepted and turned back by an effective surface blockade maintained outside a belligerent port. If a neutral merchant or passenger ship was stopped by such a naval blockade, however, the blockading power was responsible for the safety of the passengers and crew of the detained vessel.

Wilson, in his characteristic way, gave the long-standing American policy of defending neutral rights a new moral emphasis. The right of neutral citizens to go wherever they pleased, sell whatever they pleased, to whomever they pleased, subject only to the recognized rules of war, he said, was more than a legal abstraction or a matter of profit. What was at stake was the fundamental structure of the international order. This structure must be based on well-defined inviolable rules, which in turn must be derived from the basic principles of respect for human life and fair treatment of all peoples and nations.

Still, no matter how pro-British or how determined he was to guarantee American rights, for many months following the outbreak of the war, Wilson saw no reason to intrude into European affairs. By remaining neutral, America might exert a strong moral force to end the fighting quickly and then help establish new relations among nations based on disarmament, arbitration, and international justice. A neutral America, Wilson declared, would be "fit and free to do what is honest and disinterested and truly serviceable for the peace of the world."

Allied Violations of American Rights. From the beginning of the war, both the British and the Germans disregarded what Americans considered their rights on the high seas and in international trade. The British severely limited American commerce with the Central Powers by extending the definition of contraband to include almost everything that might be useful to German survival. They stopped American vessels and forced them to go to British ports for thorough and time-consuming searches instead of allowing them to be examined at sea. They planted mines in the North Sea, endangering all neutral ships routed through the area. They set up blacklists of American firms suspected of trading with Germany through other neutral nations, and threatened these firms with the loss of English business.

As a supplier of goods and credit, the United States had the power to retaliate against the British and force them to relent. Soon after the war broke out, the British and the French had placed immense orders with American firms for arms, grain, cotton, and other supplies. In the beginning the Allies paid cash; but when cash ran low, they requested loans from American bankers. Secretary of State Bryan at first considered credits to the Allies a breach of neutrality and refused to sanction them. Gradually he retreated, and in October 1914 Wilson informed the National City Bank and the Morgan Company that he would not oppose bankers' credits to finance Allied war orders. By early 1917 Americans had lent Great Britain over $1 billion and France $300 million more. Had Wilson wished, he might have threatened to restrict loans or asked Congress to embargo munitions to belligerents unless the Allies complied with American demands. He justified his failure to use this powerful weapon of coercion—one employed by Thomas Jefferson in 1807—on the grounds that neutralizing the Allied advantage of control of the shipping lanes to Eu-

U.S.A.
1917

NORWAY
• Oslo

SWEDEN
Stockholm •

FINLAND
Indep. July, 1917

Lake Ladoga

Helsinki •
• Petrograd

ESTONIA
Indep.
Feb. 1918

NORTH SEA

LATVIA
Indep.
Nov, 1918
Riga •

RUSSIA
1914

Battle of Jutland
May-June, 1916

DENMARK

Riga offensive
Sept, 1917

Smolensk •

Edinburgh •

Copenhagen •

BALTIC SEA

Memel •

LITHUANIA
Indep. Feb, 1918

• Minsk

Kiel •

Konigsberg •

Vilna •

GREAT BRITAIN
1914

• Hamburg

Danzig •

Masurian Lakes
Sept, 1914

London •

NETH.
Amsterdam •

Berlin •

Tannenberg
Aug, 1914

Brussels •
BELG.
1914

• Cologne

GERMANY
1914

POLAND
Indep. Nov, 1918

• Pinsk

GERMAN INVASION
AUG-SEPT, 1914

Leipzig •

• Warsaw

Brest-Litovsk

• Kiev

Paris •

• Dresden

Prague •

• Lublin

Metz •

Mainz

Lemberg •

LUX.
• Strasbourg

Rhine R.

GALICIA

Cracow •

FRANCE
1914

BAVARIA

Danube R.

Vienna •

• Munich

Berne •
SWITZ.

Pressburg •

UKRAINE

Piave June, 1918

• Graz

Budapest •

Milan •

Vittorio-Veneto
Oct-Nov, 1918

AUSTRIA-HUNGARY
1914

• Odessa

Genoa •

Venice •
• Trieste

SPAIN

ITALY
1915

BOSNIA

Belgrade •

RUMANIA
1916

Bucharest •

Danube R.

BLACK SEA

Withdrew from
Triple Alliance 1914

Sarajevo •

CORSICA

• Rome

MONTENEGRO
1915

SERBIA
1914

BULGARIA
1915

Sofia •

Constantinople •

SARDINIA

Naples •

ALBANIA

OTTOMAN EMPIRE
1914

Salonika •

PORTUGAL
1916

GREECE
1916

Gallipoli •

Dardanelles campaign
1915-1916

• Smyrna

SICILY

Athens •

CRETE

1916 Date of entry into the war

⸻⸻ Maximum advance of the Central Powers

– – – – Maximum Russian advance

••••••• Line of the Brest-Litovsk Treaty Mar, 1918

⸻⸻ Armistice lines, eastern front Dec., 1917

0   500
Miles

Central Powers   Allied Powers   Neutral Powers

World War I

rope would be equivalent to helping the Central Powers. But it is difficult to avoid the conclusion that the president was less willing to enforce neutral rights against the Allies than against their enemies.

There were reasons beyond pro-Ally feelings for discriminating between British and German violations of American rights, however. Whatever they did, England avoided injuring too many American interests simultaneously lest an outcry from too many groups at once force retaliation. The English were also careful to blunt the edge of their actions. When placing cotton on the contraband list produced a loud protest from southern cotton growers, for example, the British agreed to buy enough cotton to make up for the lost German-Austrian market. On numerous occasions, moreover, they promised to compensate American businesses for losses after the war. But the most compelling reason for distinguishing between the Allies and the Central Powers was that Allied policies hurt only American pocketbooks; German policies took American lives.

Submarine Warfare. The chief German naval weapon was the U-boat (*Unterseeboot*), a tiny submarine armed with tropedoes and one small deck gun. U-boats could creep up on their targets unseen and sink them without warning. But because they were small and thin-skinned, they could not risk surfacing to warn of their intentions, to search for contraband, or to care for civilians aboard the vessels they sank. German U-boats could indeed strangle England—but only by attacking all shipping,

naval or merchant, enemy or neutral, engaged in trade with the British Isles, thereby endangering civilians and deeply offending international opinion.

Chancellor Theobald von Bethmann-Hollweg and a few other German leaders foresaw that a "shoot-on-sight" U-boat policy would lead to serious problems with the United States. Nevertheless, in February 1915 the German government announced that it would authorize its submarines to sink all ships found within a large war zone surrounding the British Isles.

The American State Department immediately denounced these "unprecedented" tactics and declared that the German government would be held to "a strict accountability" for any action that injured Americans or their property. The Berlin authorities remained unmoved. A month later a German submarine sank the British passenger liner *Falaba*, killing an American citizen. Bryan urged the president to forbid Americans to travel in the war zones, at least on belligerent ships; but Wilson refused on the grounds that to do so would surrender a valid American right. A far worse tragedy took place in May when the British luxury liner *Lusitania* was sunk off the Irish coast by a German submarine, with a loss of 1,198 lives, 128 of them American. Before the vessel left New York, the German authorities had advised Americans to avoid belligerent ships, but the actual attack had come totally without warning.

The sinking of an unarmed passenger liner, with such wholesale destruction of life, profoundly shocked Americans. "From the Department of State," the *New York Times* trumpeted, "there must go to the imperial

German U-boats were fragile vessels that could not be used effectively if forced to obey traditional rules of naval warfare. This reality placed Germany on a collision course with the neutral United States.

Americans thinking of embarking on the *Lusitania* were warned of the dangers, but the decision to brave them or stay out in safety was their own. Secretary of State Bryan argued that Wilson's insistence on the right of neutral citizens to travel anywhere would result in the loss of lives and, ultimately, in war.

U-boat warfare, the United States would go to war. A pacifist, he resigned in protest. Wilson replaced him with Robert Lansing, a man of a very different stripe, who believed that German success "would mean the overthrow of democracy . . . , the suppression of individual liberty, the setting up of evil ambitions . . . , and the turning back of the hands of human progress two centuries." Lansing's leadership of the State Department strengthened the pro-Ally groups and undoubtedly helped steer the country into war.

The conflict between the Central Powers and the United States remained unresolved when the Germans struck again in mid-August 1915, sinking the *Arabic*, another unarmed British passenger liner, and killing two Americans. The sinking brought to a climax the battle between the cautious Chancellor Bethmann-Hollweg and the German admirals, who wanted to continue unrestricted submarine warfare. This time the German emperor sided with the moderates and assured the State Department that his navy would stop attacking *passenger* ships without warning and in the future would provide for the safety of passengers and crews. The German government suspended submarine warfare against passenger vessels.

Government in Berlin a demand that the Germans shall no longer make war like savages drunk with blood." For days afterward editorials denounced the attack as "criminal," "bestial," "uncivilized," and "barbarous." "Condemnation of the act," the *Literary Digest* summarized, "seems to be limited only by the restrictions of the English language."

In the days immediately following, there was some loose talk of war with Germany. But the public was not ready to plunge into the European bloodbath, and before long most Americans concluded that strong words would be sufficient to check German atrocities. On May 13 Wilson dispatched a note to the German government demanding an apology for the brutal act. Germany must also renounce future attacks on merchant and passenger vessels and would be held responsible for any infringement of American rights on the high seas. The Germans expressed regret for the American dead, but defended the sinking as an act of "self-defense" because the *Lusitania* had carried arms that would have been used against German soldiers. In a second, stiffer note, Wilson insisted that the Germans give up submarine warfare entirely. A third note threatened to sever diplomatic relations if another passenger ship was attacked.

Bryan considered the second *Lusitania* note an ultimatum to Germany that if she did not abandon

The War Spirit Rises. The *Arabic* pledge prevented a break in diplomatic relations with Germany, but it did not fully comply with Wilson's demands. The German government had not agreed to exempt cargo vessels from attack and had not apologized for the *Lusitania* sinking. It also had not offered reparations for lost American lives.

While these grievances festered, Americans were treated to new demonstrations of what seemed outrageous German behavior. Shortly after the *Arabic* sinking, an American Secret Service agent picked up a briefcase carelessly left by a man on the Sixth Avenue elevated railroad in New York. The contents exposed its owner, Dr. Heinrich F. Albert, as head of a widespread German operation in the United States to influence American opinion and sabotage munitions factories and shipyards producing war matériel for the Allies. At almost the same time, the British released captured documents that disclosed German-Austrian plans to foment labor stoppages at American armament plants. Soon afterward the United States accused two German diplomatic attachés of spying and sent them home; another German agent was indicted for blowing up a bridge; and still others were held responsible for various unexplained explosions and accidents in American factories and war plants.

The sensational revelations of German undercover activities deeply antagonized the American public. Brutalities in Belgium and sinkings on the Atlantic were distant events that affected few citizens directly. Bombings and spying brought the terrible war to America's shores. By mid-1915 many citizens had begun to fear that the nation could not avoid entering the fight.

The changing public mood manifested itself in a "preparedness" movement to rearm the United States for any eventuality. Not all the preparedness advocates favored "intervention"; some professed to believe that if the country was strong militarily, it would not have to fight. But many were militant anti-Germans who thought war unavoidable, or even essential, and wanted to ensure that when it came, the country could fight effectively. The most militant leader of the preparedness-interventionist group was former president Theodore Roosevelt, who went around the country calling Wilson "yellow" for holding back on rearmament and for not taking a stronger line against the Germans. At one point, in his typically intemperate way, TR recommended that if war came, peace advocate Robert La Follette should be hanged forthwith.

A strong peace contingent confronted the preparedness movement. Besides the Quakers and members of other traditional "peace churches," the opponents of war included a fair proportion of the progressive community, who believed that domestic reform would be forgotten if the country became embroiled in a war. Women progressives were particularly prominent in the peace movement. War, asserted Harriot Stanton Blatch, represented the male principle of physical force and would be ended only when the "mother viewpoint" prevailed in international diplomacy. Socialists were even more strongly opposed to the preparedness campaign and intervention than progressives. The war in Europe, they held, was a battle between rival capitalist imperialists in which the world's working class had no vital interest.

At first Wilson himself was skeptical of the preparedness movement, but his growing anger at Germany and belief that preparedness was politically popular made him change his mind. In mid-summer 1915 the president finally asked his naval and military advisers to draw up plans for an enlarged army and navy. On the basis of these proposals, in November he recommended that Congress approve a $500 million naval building program and expand the army to 400,000 men.

Even as he readied the nation for the possibility of war, Wilson struggled to avoid it. In early 1915 he had sent Colonel House to Europe to try to bring the belligerents together around the peace table. House was ignored. In January 1916 Wilson sent the colonel back to Europe for the same purpose, determined this time that if either side refused to parley, the United States would use its "utmost moral force" to compel the reluctant party to accept compromise terms that would include disarmament and a world peacekeeping organization.

Once again, House accomplished little. The warring nations wanted no part of peace except on their own terms. Despite the stubbornness of both Allied and German leaders, House made some startling promises to Britain and France that exceeded the president's instructions. If the 1916 Allied effort to break the military deadlock on the Western Front failed, and if Germany appeared to be gaining, the United States, House told the British and French leaders, would intervene to prevent Allied defeat.

The Sussex Pledge. German-American relations took a turn for the better early in February 1916 when the German government finally expressed regret for the sinking of the *Lusitania* and offered to pay an indemnity. But the pendulum soon shifted once more when a U-boat torpedoed the unarmed French steamer *Sussex*, injuring a number of Americans.

Pushed by his advisers and by public indignation, Wilson shot off a note to the German government declaring that unless it ceased all attacks on cargo and passenger ships, the United States would immediately break off diplomatic relations. With Bethamnn-Hollweg and the moderates still in control, the German government gave the so-called *Sussex* pledge: It would abandon its practice of shooting on sight in all cases except those involving the enemy navy. The pledge was qualified, however. The Germans would honor it only if the United States compelled the Allies to abide by the rules of international law. Wilson accepted the *Sussex* pledge, knowing that it would be impossible to force the Allies to comply with Germany's conditions. But peace was preserved temporarily, and the president, still unprepared for American intervention, was grateful for the respite.

For some time following the *Sussex* pledge, the Germans acted in exemplary fashion. Meanwhile the British seemed determined to arouse the president's and the public's wrath. They seized American packages and parcels to look for contraband, opened and read letters to and from America, and refused to allow American shipowners to use British coaling facilities unless they submitted to British inspection. They also brutally suppressed the Easter Rebellion in Ireland. The execution of the Irish rebels against British rule appalled Americans and seriously damaged Britain's image as a defender of democracy. War talk ebbed as Americans had second thoughts about the Allied cause.

The Election of 1916. For the next few months public interest in foreign affairs was eclipsed by the excitement of a presidential election. In 1916 Wilson faced a Republican nominee, U.S. Supreme Court Justice Charles Evans Hughes, who did not have to split his vote with the Progressive party candidate as had Taft in 1912. Hughes was an attractive candidate. As counsel for the Armstrong Committee, he had established a solid reputation as a progressive crusader by helping to prosecute New York insurance companies for fraudulent practices. He had enhanced his reputation as a progressive during two terms as governor of New York. Then, in 1910, he had become an associate justice of the United States Supreme Court where he had upheld state power to regulate business.

Despite Hughes's appeal, Wilson was reelected. The president's success in part derived from his late turn to the left, as discussed in Chapter 23. But even more, the campaign outcome turned on the issue of war and peace.

Hughes had the difficult task of holding together a party deeply divided between a pro-Ally interventionist wing and a large number of German-American sup-

porters. A poor speaker, he seemed to waver on the issues to please every segment of the voting public. The Democrats were more forthright. "He kept us out of war" was their campaign slogan. A Democratic ad in the *New York Times* reminded voters:

> You are working;
> —*Not Fighting!*
> Alive and Happy;
> —*Not Cannon Fodder!*
> Wilson and Peace with Honor?
> or
> *Hughes with Roosevelt and War?*

The election was close. Hughes carried the Northeast and much of the Midwest. Wilson took the South, the mountain states, and most of the Pacific coast. Because of slow returns from California, not until Friday following the Tuesday balloting was President Wilson assured of four more years in the White House.

The Road to War. Wilson's reelection was a vote for peace. No doubt Americans as a whole were pro-Ally, despite Britain's recent blunders. Yet they still wanted very much to keep out of the war. In the wake of his victory Wilson decided to make one last effort to force both sides to hammer out a compromise settlement. Late in December 1916 he sent notes to the belligerents asking them to state their war aims and offering again to mediate. He warned both sides that only a "peace without victory" would last. Any other "would leave a sting, a resentment, a bitter memory upon which terms of peace would rest . . . only as upon quicksand." The president's words were prophetic, but neither side was willing to stop fighting and talk terms.

German-American relations now moved swiftly toward a final crisis. By the end of 1916 the military stalemate was becoming intolerable to the German leaders. Continued frustration weakened the moderates and strengthened the military. At a momentous conference in January 1917 the aggressive generals told Kaiser Wilhelm that the United States could never send enough men to Europe to break the stalemate. Because it was already providing the Allies with as much war matériel and financial aid as it could, America would make little difference if it formally joined the enemy. Moreover, Germany was now so well supplied with U-boats that if the submarine captains were not required to observe the rules imposed by concern for neutral opinion, they could deliver a knockout blow to the Allies in short order. The generals' analysis was convincing: Germany chose unlimited submarine warfare. This

This Wilson campaign truck carries most of the 1916 Democratic platform on its sides. Although his success in keeping the nation out of war was important to voters, Wilson was also running on his progressive domestic record.

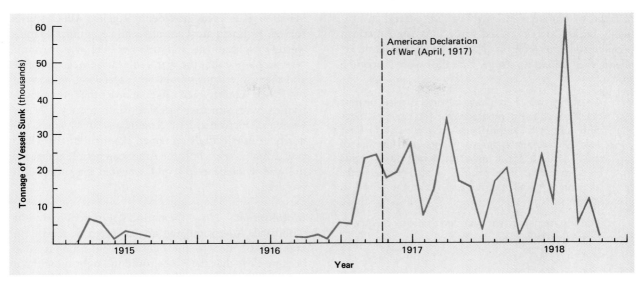

American losses to the German submarine campaign, 1915–1918
(*U.S. Navy Department*, American Ship Casualties of the World War, *1923*).

choice virtually guaranteed that American ships would be involved in incidents on the high seas and the American people would be drawn into the war.

On January 31, 1917, the German ambassador in Washington informed Secretary of State Lansing that Germany would direct its U-boats to sink without warning all ships, both neutral and enemy, found in the eastern Mediterranean and in the waters surrounding Great Britain, France, and Italy. The new German order totally repudiated the *Sussex* pledge. True to his promise, Wilson severed diplomatic relations with Germany. Most Americans, even many of Wilson's former critics, supported his decision. Volunteers began to show up at army enlistment centers.

Wilson still hoped to avoid hostilities and refused Lansing and House's advice to prepare for war. While he deliberated, rallies all over the country demanded American forbearance and further negotiations before taking the final step. Much of the president's and the public's remaining doubt was dispelled by the revelation of a secret note from the German foreign secretary, Arthur Zimmermann, to the German minister in Mexico proposing that if the United States and Germany came to blows, Mexico should ally itself with Germany and help persuade Japan to switch its allegiance to the Central Powers. In the event of victory, Mexico would be rewarded with its lost territory in Texas, New Mexico, and Arizona. Intercepted by British intelligence, the "Zimmermann telegram" pushed Wilson over the line. The day following the receipt of the incriminating document he asked Congress for authority to arm American merchant ships and employ "any

other instrumentalities or methods" to protect American interests on the high seas. When the isolationsists in the Senate, led by La Follette and George W. Norris of Nebraska, threatened to talk the measure to death, Wilson released the telegram to an astonished and furious public. Carried along by a wave of public indignation, the House gave Wilson the power he wanted. But the Senate isolationists blocked action despite Wilson's condemnation of them as a "little group of willful men, representing no opinion but their own."

Wilson refused to be stopped, and on March 9 he announced that he was arming American merchant vessels under his authority as commander in chief. Soon after, three American merchant vessels were sunk by submarines, with heavy loss of life. Public outrage now reached a new pitch, and even some prominent socialists demanded war. In the minds of many Americans, final doubts about the Allied cause evaporated when a liberal uprising in Russia overthrew the autocratic government of the czar. Now if the United States joined the Allies, it would be able in good conscience to claim it was fighting on the side of democracy.

Wilson's War Message. On the evening of April 2, 1917, the president appeared before a joint session of Congress to ask for a declaration of war. He could not escape the conviction, he said, that German contempt for American rights and American lives, displayed by the bestial, unrestricted U-boat war, left no other course. But he appealed to higher moral considerations than self-defense. The United States would be fighting for all people, he said, for the "vindication of right, of human right" against "autocratic governments backed by organized force." As the American people faced the months of "fiery trial and sacrifice" ahead, they would not forget that they were struggling for

the things which we have always carried nearest our hearts—for democracy, for the right of those who submit to authority to have a voice in their own Governments, for the rights and liberties of small nations, for a universal dominion of rights by a concert of free peoples as shall bring peace and safety to all nations and make the world at last free.

The Senate passed the war declaration on April 4. House approval followed on April 6.

The War

America was finally in! In London, Rome, and Paris crowds cheered the news and drank toasts to the United States and its great president. Sagging Allied spirits soared. At home most socialists and a number of midwestern isolationists still opposed the war. Senator Norris charged that the war's sole cause was economic and that Americans would be "sacrificing millions of . . . [their] countrymen's lives in order that other countrymen may coin their lifeblood into money." Many German-Americans, Irish-Americans, and a small minority of intellectuals remained skeptical of the Allied cause. But on the whole the American people embraced the war wholeheartedly and accepted the sacrifices it required.

Mobilization. Now, the nation's resources had to be mobilized. Americans had not expected to send large numbers of men to the fighting fronts, but it soon became clear that the Allies could not fight on without American troops. The liberal Russian Revolution of March 1917 had been followed by the Bolshevik Revolution of October 1917. The Bolsheviks soon opened peace negotiations with the Germans, freeing the Ger-

World War I: The western front

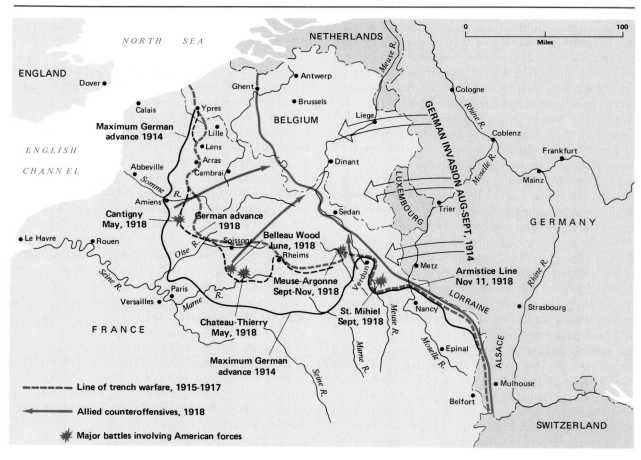

Line of trench warfare, 1915-1917

Allied counteroffensives, 1918

Major battles involving American forces

The Great War

Many months before President Woodrow Wilson, Robert Lansing, Bryan's successor as secretary of state, had come to the conclusion that imperial Germany was a menace to America and to democracy. Lansing was not shy about presenting his views. In the selection below he tells the president how he perceives Germany under the Kaiser and how the United States should respond. The date of the memo is July 11, 1915, almost twenty months before the American declaration of war.

"I have come to the conclusion that the German Government is utterly hostile to all nations with democratic institutions because those who compose it see in democracy a menace to absolutism and the defeat of German ambition for world domination. Everywhere German agents are plotting and intriguing to accomplish the supreme purpose of their government.

"Only recently has the conviction come to me that democracy throughout the world is threatened. Suspicions of the vaguest sort only a few months ago have been more and more confirmed. From many sources evidence has been coming until it would be folly to close one's eyes to it.

"German agents have undoubtedly been at work in Mexico arousing anti-American feeling and holding out false hopes of support. The proof is not conclusive but is sufficient to compel belief. Germans also appear to be operating in Haiti and San Domingo and are probably doing so in other Latin American Republics.

"I think that this is being done so that this nation will have troubles in America and be unable to take part in the European War if a repetition of such outrages as the *Lusitania* sinking should require us to act. It may even go further and have in mind the possibility of a future war with this Republic in case the Allies should be defeated.

"In these circumstances the policies we adopt are vital to the future of the United States and, I firmly believe, to the welfare of mankind, for I see in the perpetuation of democracy the only hope of universal peace and progress for the world. Today German absolutism is the great menace to democracy. . . .

"The remedy seems to me to be plain. It is that Germany must not be permitted to win this war or to break even, though to prevent it this country is forced to take an active part. This ultimate necessity must be constantly in our minds in all our controversies with the belligerents. American public opinion must be prepared for the time, which may come, when we will have to cast aside our neutrality and become one of the champions of democracy.

"We must in fact risk everything rather than leave the way open for a new combination of powers, stronger and more dangerous to liberty than the Central Allies are today."

man troops and equipment that had been fighting Russia to move to the Western Front. As this huge army was transferred to face the French and British, it became clear that only American forces could offset the surge in German strength.

The first military draft since the Civil War provided the needed manpower. It worked surprisingly well. Scrupulously administered by local civilian draft boards, it did not arouse the feeling of class discrimination that had appeared fifty years before. With its help the army grew from 200,000 to 4 million men. Draftees were sent to thirty-two training camps and were quickly transformed into soldiers.

Over 2 million American troops eventually went to France, and 1.4 million of them saw duty on the front lines. The lot of American "doughboys" on the Western Front was as miserable as that of their European equivalents. They faced mud, rain, cold, vermin, and constant fear of death. They huddled in the trenches while fierce artillery bombardments shook the earth for days at a time. They "went over the top" in savage assaults on the enemy's trenches, sacrificing their lives for a few yards of ground. About 50,000 died in combat; an equal number succumbed to disease.

The American navy, under Admiral William S. Sims, guarded troop and supply vessels to France and helped end the U-boat threat to Britian. For every American soldier it escorted safely to the fighting front, the navy had to guarantee the arrival of fifty pounds of supplies and equipment daily. Ultimately millions of tons of food, munitions, vehicles, medicines, clothing, guns, horses, and fuel were ferried from American ports to Le Havre, Bordeaux, Calais, Brest, and Boulogne, with minimal loss from U-boats.

The War Effort at Home. This enormous military and logistical effort was made possible by the effective mobilization of economic and emotional resources at home. The war cost the United States $33 billion, including $9 billion of loans to the Allies. About a quarter of this huge sum was raised by taxes. The war taxes were highly progressive, taking up to 75 percent of the largest incomes. Inheritance taxes of 25 percent, an excess-profits tax of 65 percent, and a variety of excise taxes also helped spread the burden throughout the population. The rest of the money came from banks and from campaigns to sell Liberty Bonds, which not only paid for the war but also helped whip up enthusiasm for the war effort.

The billions, however, had to be effectively deployed. For this purpose the Wilson administration borrowed a page from the New Nationalism progressives by setting up a collection of new federal war agencies. By the end of the war these administrative bodies were exerting many new powers and had unprecedented control over the economy. They also anticipated a number of governmental structures and mea-

sures of the New Deal and foreshadowed the mobilization effort of World War II.

Food production burgeoned under the direction of Food Administrator Herbert Hoover, who had supervised food relief to ravaged Belgium earlier in the war. Americans voluntarily observed "wheatless" and "meatless" days in a remarkably effective campaign to conserve food. The Food Administration guaranteed an attractive price for the entire 1917 wheat crop, causing a dramatic jump in the number of acres planted with wheat. Vegetable gardens appeared everywhere, and exotic meats such as horse and rabbit were introduced into the wartime diet. The Food Administration was a great success, and it played no small part in Hoover's popularity after the war.

The War Industries Board, headed by Wall Street broker Bernard Baruch, performed well after a slow start. American arms and clothing factories equipped the American doughboy better than any other soldier in the world. American shipyards struggled, not always successfully, with the crucial task of replacing Allied vessels sunk by U-boats. The board built new production facilities and converted existing ones for war purposes, developed new sources of raw materials, served as purchasing agent for the Allies, standardized thousands of items, and established strict economic priorities.

Meanwhile, the United States Railroad Administration took tight control of the country's rail transportation, now called on to carry millions more passengers and tons of freight than in peacetime. The administration combined railways into regional units, limited unnecessary passenger travel, standardized rates and schedules, and gave priority to munitions over nonessential goods.

Fuel Administrator Harry A. Garfield became a virtual dictator over the nation's fuel supply. When a coal shortage immobilized thirty-seven munitions ships in New York harbor during the bitterly cold winter of 1917/18, he closed down all civilian manufacturing plants to release their coal for the ships' use. The Fuel Administration also asked automobile owners to conserve gasoline for trucks carrying vital goods.

The war overstimulated the economy. Unemployment melted away, and men and women were soon working long hours at good pay. But despite high taxes and the Liberty and Victory Loans that drained off much excess purchasing power, prices rose sharply and offset many of the workers' gains. It soon became apparent that labor would have to be regulated, along with other sectors of the economy, to ensure uninterrupted work, prevent strikes for higher wages, and

Montgomery Flagg, a popular illustrator of the day, produced this saccharine poster urging boys and girls in 1917 to help the American war effort by saving money.

Drafting 4 million men into the armed forces opened up an employment gap on the home front. These women making cartridges at Bethlehem Steel were typical of thousands who joined the work force in 1917–18.

Even children were recruited to help in the war effort. This sentimental poster, put out by U.S. Food Administrator Herbert Hoover, was designed to encourage "victory gardens." With more Americans growing their own fruits and vegetables, more farm produce was available for shipment to troops and the Allies in Europe.

HELPING HOOVER IN OUR U.S. SCHOOL GARDEN

provide the highest priority for war industry. To attain these goals, Wilson created the War Labor Policies Board. By granting recognition to labor unions and establishing generally favorable working conditions for wage earners, the board imposed labor peace during the war. It prohibited strikes, but the board also forced management to negotiate with the unions. Under these policies the AFL and other unions expanded their membership to over 4 million, a 50 percent increase over 1914.

One firm principle of the War Labor Policies Board was that women should have equal pay for equal work in war industries. High wages, encouraged by wartime labor shortages and labor board policies, soon drew thousands of women into the labor force. Thousands of women went "over there" with the doughboys, working as ambulance drivers and nurses and representing organizations such as the Salvation Army and Red Cross. The war accustomed American women to working outside the home and accelerated their economic independence.

Blacks also made economic gains. With millions of men in the armed forces and European immigration at an all-time low, the American labor force fell drastically just the time when the economy needed labor most. To meet the shortage, employers were forced to lower their barriers to black workers. Thousands of black men and women were soon leaving southern farms for the high wages of the northern war plants.

One of the most important wartime agencies was the Committee on Public Information (CPI), established to "mobilize the mind of the world." To Wilson

An Historical Portrait

George Creel

World War II came abruptly with death from the sky over Pearl Harbor; the Civil War arrived with a bombardment of the United States fort in Charleston Harbor. Both attacks shocked the American people and united them at least temporarily behind the effort to defeat the enemy.

In 1917 war came only after two and a half years of debate that left a nation unsure of itself and its goals. Millions of Americans had little reason to love Britain or Russia, two of our chief allies; many others had strong reason to love Germany, their *Vaterland*, our chief enemy. Thousands of Americans opposed all wars; thousands, more opposed all "capitalist wars." Given these facts, many influential prowar Americans feared that the nation would be unable to mobilize itself for the hard struggle ahead. It was for this reason that on April 13, 1917, just a week after the war declaration, President Woodrow Wilson issued an executive order creating the Committee on Public Information (CPI) and appointed George Creel of Denver to head it.

Creel was a good choice, a man with the experience and the values that the task seemed to require. His father was a former Confederate officer who never got over the South's defeat and, while his wife supported the family by running a boarding-house, slowly drank himself to death. George Creel became a journalist as a teenager and for a while published a small crusading newspaper in Kansas City. In 1909 he moved to Denver to edit first the flamboyant *Denver Post*, and then the *Rocky Mountain News*.

Creel was a full-fledged progressive who used his journalism to advance the "people's cause" against the "interests." At one point he got into trouble by recommending that eleven Colorado state senators with close ties to exploitive business groups be lynched. Creel also had liberal social views. Elected police commissioner in 1912, he applied the legal theories of the famous Denver judge, Benjamin Lindsey, to the evil of urban prostitution. Rather than arrest the women or merely drive them from the city, he organized a rehabilitation center for them, headed by a sympathetic woman.

In 1916 Creel wrote a book, *Wilson and the Issues*, that became a major item in the president's reelection effort. The work depicted Wilson as nobly struggling to avoid war, yet always determined to protect the interests of the United States. It "mightily pleased" the president and he rewarded Creel with the appointment to head the CPI.

As director of the new agency, Creel tried to avoid encouraging hysteria or abandonment of America's liberal and humane values. In March 1918 he wrote to a progressive Democrat: "I shall support every necessary measure directed to the supreme end of defeating . . . the unholy combination of autocracy, militarism, and predatory capitalism that rules Germany and threatens

liberty and self-government everywhere. . . . (But) I ask and expect support only of those who believe that for the sake of political liberty and social progress, America must win this war while it consolidates at home every position won from the forces of reaction and political bigotry." Creel's hopes would be disappointed.

Even before the CPI began to beat the drums of patriotism, Americans had been gripped by a spasm of intolerance and irrational fear. During the period 1914–1916, when the United States had become a major supplier of munitions to the Allies, German agents had been active on this side of the Atlantic. Once the United States entered the war, among the unthinking, it was easy to equate the antiwar opposition of German-Americans, pacifists, and socialists with espionage. Some conservatives seized on the socialist issue to stigmatize all political views left of center, including progressivism, as anti-American. Congress encouraged the fearful mood by passing a series of repressive measures including the Espionage Act and the Trading-with-the-Enemy Act. These made aiding the enemy, obstructing military recruitment, or preaching disloyalty crimes punishable by stiff sentences. They established a Censorship Board to screen messages between United States citizens and citizens of foreign countries, and imposed severe penalities on anyone who uttered, wrote, or published

the fight for people's minds, the "conquest of their convictions," was just as urgent as the military effort. To lead the propaganda war he chose George Creel, a progressive journalist with a gift for storytelling and platform oratory. Creel mobilized thousands of people in the arts, advertising, and motion pictures to "advertise America." Under Creel's urging, some of the most talented artists in the country designed Liberty Loan

"disloyal, profane, scurrilous, or abusive language about the form of government of the United States, or the Constitution of the United States, or the military or naval forces of the United States, . . . or any language intended to bring the form of government of the United States . . . into contempt, scorn, contumely, or disrepute." One of Wilson's appointees to the Censorship Board was George Creel.

A chief function of the CPI was to distribute government releases. Officials saw this as a way of keeping the public well informed, but inevitably the CPI held back as much information about the war as it disseminated. Besides this indirect censorship, the CPI laid down prohibitive guidelines for news that should not be published under any circumstances and news of dubious propriety. Though the CPI had no power to punish, its rebuke to papers that violated its guidelines was inevitably coercive and a damper on the free flow of information to the American public. Creel's interference with the free operation of the press made him the target of countless attacks. Some of these he deserved, but often he was merely the scapegoat for administration opponents who feared to attack the president himself.

Far more important than censorship was the CPI's work as a propaganda agency. Creel hoped to clarify the nation's war goals and mobilize the public to achieve them. He solicited free space from newspaper and magazine publishers and filled it with patriotic articles, advertisements for Liberty Bonds, and attacks on the "Prussianism" that would sweep the world if the Kaiser was not stopped. The CPI created a Division of Pictorial Publicity with the illustrator Charles Dana Gibson in charge. Gibson and his recruits from the art world created hundreds of posters, cartoons, and magazine illustrations depicting heroic American soldiers and sailors, patriotic American housewives, and bestial-looking German "Huns."

One of Creel's most inspired schemes was the Four-Minute Men. These were 75,000 volunteers who delivered short rousing speeches urging such patriotic acts as bond purchases, food conservation, and donation of binoculars to the navy. They laid out American war aims, explained the workings of the draft, and told their audiences how to sustain morale. They often described German atrocities against civilians in Belgium. The volunteers spoke in school auditoriums, movie theaters, and opera houses, in every language current among the polyglot American population.

Two of the CPI's most powerful allies in molding public opinion were the movie industry and academe. Anxious to demonstrate their patriotism, the movie moguls quickly offered their services to the CPI. Creel was happy to take up the offer, and during the war the CPI and Hollywood collaborated on a series of documentaries and feature films. One of these was *Our Colored Fighters*, designed to appeal to black audiences. Another was *The Kaiser, the Beast of Berlin*, a no-holds-barred anti-German attack that attracted long lines to the theaters where it played. In addition, the CPI employed stars like Mary Pickford, Douglas Fairbanks, and Theda Bara to sell Liberty Bonds.

The nation's scholars and academics lent themselves to Creel's goals. The CPI's Division of Civic and Educational Cooperation, headed by Dean Guy Stanton Ford of the University of Minnesota Graduate School, employed some of the nation's most prominent historians and social scientists to churn out hundreds of pages of war propaganda in the guise of scholarship. Like almost all the wartime propaganda, this material glorified the American cause and disparaged imperial Germany, its values, and its institutions. The division's most widely circulated pamphlet was the German-language version of *American Loyalty by Citizens of German Descent*, a work that testified to the patriotism of the German-American population. Yet much of the CPI's effort to avert ethnic bigotry within the country failed. In the end the anti-German propaganda encouraged the intolerance that was sweeping the United States.

After the war Creel defended Wilsonian internationalism and the League of Nations. He moved to San Francisco in 1926 and became a member of the city's cultural elite. During the New Deal period he held posts with the WPA and other government agencies, but he broke with Roosevelt during World War II. The president and his colleagues, he believed, were too lenient toward the enemy. In his old age Creel became an intense anticommunist. For most of his life he had tried (though not always successfully) to avoid simplistic ways of thinking. But now he lost his sense of balance and came to exemplify the intolerance his enemies had, on the whole unfairly, ascribed to him many years before when he headed the Committee on Public Information.

and recruiting posters. An army of lecturers, called "Four-Minute Men," delivered pithy lectures all across the country on subjects like "Maintaining Morals and Morale," "Why We Are Fighting," and "The Meaning of America." "There was no part of the great war machinery that we did not touch," Creel wrote after the war, "no medium of appeal that we did not employ . . . to make our own people and all other peoples of the world understand the causes that compelled America to take up arms."

Civil Liberties During the War. Creel's campaign was immensely effective in whipping up enthusiasm for the war and Wilson's announced goal of making the world "safe for democracy." War fervor also unleashed a wave of intolerance against those who did not show the proper patriotic spirit or who harbored pacifist or socialist attitudes.

Quick to sense the new superpatriotic mood, Congress passed the Espionage Act and the Trading-with-the-Enemy Act in 1917. The Espionage Act imposed severe penalties on persons found guilty of obstructing recruitment, aiding the enemy, or encouraging anyone to be disloyal or insubordinate or to refuse duty in the armed forces. Under it the postmaster general could exclude from the mails any material he deemed treasonable or seditious. The Trading-with-the-Enemy Act authorized the government to confiscate and run German-owned businesses and to censor international communications and the foreign-language press. In 1918 Congress passed the Sedition Act, declaring "disloyal" or "seditious" all talk against the war and making "profane, scrurrilous, or abusive language" about the Constitution, the flag, or the armed forces a crime.

In the months before war was declared, Wilson had warned of the intolerance it might bring. After April 1917 his administration clamped down hard on dissenters. Postmaster General Albert S. Burleson excluded from the mails publications opposed to the war. In *Schenck* v. *U.S.* the Supreme Court upheld the conviction of a man for mailing circulars that urged draftees to refuse military induction. In war, said Justice Oliver Wendell Holmes, Jr., speaking for the majority of the Court, such material posed a "clear and present danger" to the nation and could by law be suppressed. In 1918 the Justice Department indicted and secured the convictions of Eugene V. Debs and Victor L. Berger, the Socialist party leaders, on the charge of encouraging draft evasion.

Local officials joined the repressive chorus and fined and imprisoned those who spoke out against the war. Meanwhile, vigilante groups and self-appointed guardians of the country intimidated "slackers" and supposed subversives.

One of the war's casualties was ethnic tolerance. With Creel's CPI portraying the German enemy as "Wolves of Kulture," "Prussian Curs," and "Beasts of Berlin," superpatriots, were encouraged to attack their German-American neighbors. Many schools and colleges suspended the teaching of German. To superpatriots sauerkraut became "liberty cabbage" and German measles "liberty measles."

The prevailing mood of intolerance found another easy target in the nation's black citizens. The influx of southern blacks into war plants created severe tensions in overcrowded northern cities. Despite their important contribution to the war effort, black Americans suffered acts of abuse and violence and economic exploitation. In East St. Louis in mid-1917 hatred exploded into a bloody race riot in which forty blacks were clubbed, beaten, stabbed, and hanged.

As if to counterbalance the decline in tolerance, the war gave a massive push to the women's suffrage movement. In 1916 Alice Paul converted her Congressional Union into the National Woman's Party (NWP) and during the presidential election she and NWP attacked Wilson and the Democrats for failure to act on the suffrage issue. Meanwhile, using gentler means, Carrie Catt of the National American Woman Suffrage Association managed to convert the president himself to the cause.

Still, Congress and much of the male public resisted. The suffragists appealed to the nation's conscience with slogans like "Democracy Begins at

The all-black 369th Regiment came under longer continuous fire than any other American army unit in World War I. However, they fought under French command: the American army would use black troops only as laborers and stevedores.

Progressive impulses survived on the home front through 1917, as when these women's suffragists marched in Washington, D.C. In fact, the women's rights movement found new unity during the war.

Home," and advertised the giant contributions women were making to the war effort. Alice Paul and her group used more aggressive tactics, including throwing picket lines around the White House. District of Columbia officials carted the picketers off to jail, but this only succeeded in making a flock of suffrage martyrs and arousing sympathy for their cause.

At last, in January 1918, the House of Representatives, anxious to further national unity during wartime, passed the women's suffrage amendment to the Constitution by precisely the two-thirds majority needed. The Senate took another year and a half to approve the amendment, and not until August 1920 was it ratified by three-fourths of the states. But without the impetus of war, women would have been forced to wait far longer for the right to vote.

Making the Peace

The American Expeditionary Force (AEF) under the command of General John J. Pershing began to arrive in France in July 1917, though it saw little fighting before early spring 1918. In March 1918 the Germans, strengthened by the armies brought west from Russia, attacked on a broad front, engaging the Americans in May and June around the town of Château-Thierry and at Belleau Wood, fifty miles from Paris. In September the American First Army, some 500,000 strong, pushed back a German salient at Saint-Mihiel. Between late September and the armistice on November 11,

1.2 million Americans were committed in the Meuse-Argonne campaign around Verdun, a thrust coordinated with major British and French attacks along the front. On November 1 the Americans broke the German line. Beaten on the battlefield and on the verge of collapse at home, the Germans began talking of peace.

Wilson's Hopes for the Future. The Central Powers' collapse was in part military. It also was the result of deteriorating morale.

The German will to resist had been undermined by expectations of a generous peace as laid out in Wilson's Fourteen Points. As announced in January 1918, this plan contained important specific provisions such as the evacuation of all German-occupied territory and the right of Europe's submerged nationalities to self-determination. Singled out for special mention were the Poles, a people long subjected to rule by Austria, Germany, and Russia, and denied nationhood.

The document also expressed Wilson's general principles for constructing a just peace and a new system of international security and international relations. The president wanted the nations of the world to settle their disagreements by "open covenants, openly arrived at"; the secret arrangements among governments that were negotiated without consulting the people must cease. Wilson also wanted freedom of the seas in both war and peace, general disarmament, and an end to trade barriers among nations. He wanted the conflicting claims of the colonial powers settled with proper regard for the wishes of the colonial peoples. Finally, as the capstone of the entire structure, Wilson proposed what he would later call the League of Nations—"a general association of nations . . . for the purpose of affording mutual guarantees of political independence and territorial integrity to great and small states alike."

These terms, and Wilson's pronouncements urging "peace without victory," promised a generous settlement that would preserve the German nation. When Wilson also demanded the ousting of the Kaiser, the war-weary Germans rose up against Wilhelm II and forced him to flee. An armistice was quickly arranged, and at 11 A.M. on November 11, 1918, the guns fell silent; World War I was over.

Versailles. On January 18, 1919, the Allied leaders met at Versailles, near Paris, to determine the shape of the peace. Wilson was there in person. Although he was widely criticized for his precedent-shattering decision to leave the United States while in office, the president insisted that only his physical presence could ensure that the victors would accept a just and secure peace.

Wilson was received like a savior in Europe. Wherever he went, enormous crowds greeted him. In Paris 2 million people lining the Champs-Elysées rained flowers and bouquets as he drove down the boulevard in his open automobile. The people of Europe were honoring not only the man. Wilson represented American idealism and the possibility of a more decent and democratic world system. Even the defeated Germans seemed willing to entrust their future to his hands.

But while the common people of Europe applauded the president, his chief Allied colleagues— Georges Clemenceau of France, David Lloyd George

On his way to Versailles, Wilson is showered with flowers. This warm reception suggested that Europeans would accept the League of Nations, the international manifestation of his ideas on constitutional government.

of Britain, and Vittorio Orlando of Italy—remained skeptical. To these unsentimental men Wilsonian idealism was all very well to shore up faltering Allied morale and weaken the German will to fight, but it seemed impractical as the basis for an international settlement. The major Allied powers wanted Germany condemned as a war criminal, totally disarmed, and forced to pay stiff indemnities that could be used to rebuild the devastated Allied economies. France, in particular, feared the might of a restored Germany and demanded guarantees that the attack of 1914 would not be repeated. The European Allies were also determined not to surrender any of their gains, including the German colonies that they had seized during the war. Finally, they were suspicious of the principle of self-determination. Could the patchwork of nationalities in eastern Europe really be sorted out into functioning nations? Reinforcing all anxieties and doubts, the specter of Russian Bolshevism hung over a continent devastated by war and shaken by the breakup of old empires. As the Allied leaders conferred amid the splendors of Louis XIV's palace at Versailles, it seemed necessary to move rapidly or face the prospect of Bolshevik-inspired "red" revolution in eastern central Europe.

Wilson soon discovered that he could not force the European powers to accept his Fourteen Points without drastic modification. The French were unwilling to place any other concern ahead of their paramount objective of secure borders. The British would not hear of the "freedom of the seas" clause. All the European Allies wanted a slice of the overseas German Empire, and they all wanted vengeance. The president

Wilson's Plan for a Lasting Peace

The Fourteen Points	Supplementary Points
From the Fourteen Points Address to Congress, January 8, 1918	From Speeches Delivered between February and September 1918
1. "Open covenants of peace, openly arrived at" and an end to secret diplomacy.	15. Base "each part of the final settlement . . . upon the essential justice of that particular case and upon such adjustments as are most likely to bring" a permanent peace.
2. Absolute freedom of navigation upon the seas . . . alike in peace and in war."	16. An end to bartering "peoples and provinces . . . as if they were mere chattels and pawns."
3. "The removal, so far as possible, of all economic barriers" to free trade.	17. Determine "every territorial settlement . . . in the interest and for the benefit of the populations concerned," and not as a compromise "amongst rival states."
4. Reduction of armaments "to the lowest point consistent with domestic safety."	18. Attempt to satisfy "all well-defined national aspirations."
5. An "absolutely impartial adjustment of all colonial claims" giving equal weight to the interests of the colonial populations and "the equitable claims" of the imperial governments.	19. "The destruction of every arbitrary power anywhere that can . . . disturb the peace of the world."
6. "The evacuation of all Russian territory" and cooperation to allow Russia "the independent determination of her own political development and national policy and assure her of a sincere welcome into the society of free nations under institutions of her own choosing."	20. Conduct of nations "to be governed . . . by the same principles of honor and of respect for the common law of civilized society that govern the individual citizens."
7. German evacuation of Belgium and restoration of full sovereignty.	21. Special interests "not consistent with the common interest of all" nationals cannot become the basis for any settlement.
8. "All French territory should be freed" and Alsace-Lorraine, taken by Prussia in 1871, should be returned to France.	22. No alliances or special understandings will be allowed within "the League of Nations."
9. "A readjustment of the frontiers of Italy . . . along clearly recognizable lines of nationality."	23. "There can be no special, selfish economic combinations" or economic boycotts except as used by the League of Nations for discipline.
10. Autonomy for the peoples of Austria-Hungary.	
11. Evacuation of Rumania, Montenegro, and Serbia; international guarantee of the political and economic independence of the Balkan states; and Serbian access to the sea.	
12. Autonomy for the subject nationalities within the Turkish Empire and free passage through the Dardanellas for ships of all nations.	
13. An independent Poland with "free and secure access to the sea."	
14. A general association of nations."	

was not happy with the changes his colleagues demanded, but he went along with most of them, convinced that the League of Nations would eventually right many of the injustices of the peace settlement.

The terms of the resulting treaty were a severe disappointment to idealists all over the world. The agreement allowed German-speaking peoples to be absorbed into the newly created nations of Poland and Czechoslovakia. Much of the Tyrol went to Italy, placing people who considered themselves Austrians under a foreign government. The German possessions in Africa and Asia were parceled out among the European Allies. And, disastrously, Germany was forced to accept complete responsibility for the war—"war guilt," it was called—and to pay overwhelming reparations of some $33 billion to the victors. Unmentioned in the treaty were Wilson's idealistic calls for disarmament, tariff reductions, and freedom of the seas.

Throughout the Versailles deliberations Wilson worked tirelessly for the point he considered the cornerstone of his peace proposals, the League of Nations. As finally hammered out, the League Covenant established two bodies: a general assembly composed of all member nations, and an executive council to consist of the United States, the British Empire, France, Italy, Japan, and four other countries to be elected by the assembly. These bodies would listen to disputes among member nations and dispense international justice. The League's decisions would be enforced first by world opinion; then by economic sanctions against the international wrongdoers; and finally, if necessary, by the use of military forces contributed by member nations. In addition, the League would help adjust minor disputes between citizens of different countries through a permanent International Court and seek to improve world social standards through an International Bureau of Labor.

As Wilson labored at Versailles during the winter of 1919, his support at home eroded. Before leaving for Europe he had put his prestige on the line by asking the American public to endorse the Democratic party in the 1918 congressional elections. When the voters gave the Republicans control of the Senate, his enemies claimed that they had repudiated the president's leadership. Wilson had further antagonized his political opponents by appointing only one Republican to the peace commission that accompanied him to Paris, although treaty ratification would require the support of both parties.

Now, as news of the emerging treaty's provisions filtered back to the United States, his opponents took sharp aim at its specific proposals. Irish-Americans were soon attacking the failure of the treaty to further the cause of Irish freedom from Britain. Italian-Americans complained because Italy had not been awarded the Adriatic city of Fiume (now Rijeka). German-Americans denounced the war-guilt clause that made their ancestral land a self-confessed criminal nation. Jingoes and superpatriots claimed that the treaty would compromise American sovereignty. Isolationists insisted that the League would commit the United States to an overly active role in world affairs.

After two months of hard negotiating at Versailles, Wilson returned briefly to the United States to discover that the still uncompleted treaty had come under withering fire. Thirty-seven senators, led by Henry Cabot Lodge of Massachusetts, had signed a "round robin" declaring that they would not vote for the treaty without amendment. The treaty had enough no votes to defeat it; clearly a bitter battle was in prospect.

Despite his disappointing reception at home, the president returned to Europe for further negotiations in an optimistic mood, certain that the American people—if not the Senate—shared his vision of a new world order. To accommodate his critics, however, he had the League Covenant modified to allow any member nation to withdraw from the organization and to refuse colonial trusteeships if it so wished. The League would also keep hands off member nations' domestic tariff and immigration policies and avoid intruding into regional arrangements like the Monroe Doctrine. The treaty, incorporating the revised League Covenant, was ratified by the delegates in the Hall of Mirrors at Versailles on June 28, 1919. Soon afterward Wilson departed for home to fight for its ratification.

The Battle for the League. The president found the opposition to the treaty and the League stronger and more determined than ever. Yet public opinion was by no means all negative. There were still some who shared Wilson's vision of a new progressive world order in which aggressive nations could be restrained by collective action. Scores of newspapers, labor leaders, and representatives of farm and women's organizations—much of the old progressive coalition—supported Wilson's League, fearing that the peace would otherwise prove fragile. Wilson counted on people like these to get the treaty through the balky Senate.

But by this time Senator Lodge had developed a clever strategy to defeat the League. He would not

Wilson found the Senate—whose three foremost isolationists are pictured here refusing to give "Peace" their seat—less willing to consider the League than the war-weary Europeans. The surge of sentiment against the League was in part a result of Wilson's inattention to political details, but it marked a more significant event: the reemergence of American isolationism.

vere stroke that partially paralyzed him. For months he was unable to work, and during this period his wife and the cabinet took over most of the duties of the presidential office. Though Wilson's strength gradually returned, he never fully recovered, and he remained irritable and quick to take offense. The illness exaggerated Wilson's stubbornness and heightened his belief in his cause.

Wilson's illness proved fatal for the treaty. By the time he returned to Washington, Senator Lodge had appended fourteen "reservations" to the Versailles agreement. These actually altered the document only in detail. But the obstinate president saw them as serious modifications that "emasculated" his work, and he insisted that his supporters vote against the modified treaty. They did. At the same time the isolationists refused to accept the original treaty. It looked as if the agreement hammered out at Versailles was finished.

The treaty and the League were not yet dead, however. Under public pressure the Senate was forced to reconsider its decision. In March 1920 the modified treaty was once more put to a vote. Wilson again proved rigid and unyielding. He insisted that the treaty with reservations be defeated. "Either," he declared, "we should enter the league fearlessly, accepting the responsibility and not fearing the role of leadership which we now enjoy, contributing our efforts towards establishing a just and permanent peace, or we should retire as gracefully as possibly from the great concert of powers by which the world was saved." Wilson's supporters were loyal to him again, but they did his cause a fatal disservice by defeating the treaty for the last time.

In the election of 1920 the Democrats endorsed the Versailles agreement; their presidential and vice presidential candidates, Governor James M. Cox of Ohio and the young Franklin Delano Roosevelt of New York, respectively, were League supporters. The Republican platform hedged on the League, and their candidate, Senator Warren G. Harding of Ohio, evaded the issue.

The ailing Wilson sought to make the election a referendum on the League. It was a wasted effort, for the public was tired of war and progressivism and great crusades. Campaigning for "normalcy," Harding won by a landslide of 16 million votes, enabling the isolationists to claim that the American people had repudiated internationalism. The new Harding administration eventually signed a separate peace treaty with Germany officially ending the hostilities, but the United States never entered the League of Nations.

oppose it directly but would demand a series of "reservations." (Reservations, unlike amendments, would not have to be approved by other League members.) Most of these would be moderate enough to attract support from a number of fence-sitting senators. But Lodge foresaw that Wilson and his supporters would reject them. If he managed the treaty-adoption process in the right way, Lodge believed, he might get its own supporters to defeat it.

First, Lodge played for time and called hearings that consumed many weeks. By the time the interested parties had finished their wordy testimony, the pro-treaty public had begun to lose interest. Wilson fought back. Although thoroughly exhausted by the arduous negotiations in France, he decided to take his case directly to the American people. For three weeks the aging president toured the country, speaking before large audiences in support of his work at Versailles. Soon after a speech at Pueblo, Colorado, Wilson collapsed and had to cancel the remainder of his trip. Following his return to Washington, he suffered a se-

Conclusions

The outcome of World War I was profoundly disillusioning to those Americans who shared Wilson's view of their country as a missionary nation ordained to carry the blessings of liberal democracy to every part of the world. Most citizens, however, were not deeply committed internationalists, and after 1918 were happy to return to the business of their daily lives. They might agree with Wilson that the world deserved a better international order, but far more than the idealist in the White House, they had supported the war as the only way to teach a lesson to the nation that had ridden roughshod over American "rights." Both the ordinary citizen's modest goal of fending off a brutal attacker who used barbarous U-boat warfare to gain his ends and the president's more exalted vision of a "new world" were needed to bring the United States into the great conflict. But the simple defeat of Germany was enough to satisfy the average American, and Wilson's hope remained unfulfilled. America, having entered the war from a position of self-proclaimed moral authority, was forced to recognize that there were limits to what could be accomplished with great wealth and missionary zeal. The unworkable settlement reached at Versailles, the failure of the League, and the resurgent American isolationism that followed World War I—all these contributed to the causes of World War II.

By 1919 progressivism, which had dominated the first two decades of the twentieth century, was in deep eclipse. The battle to defeat Germany had consumed the emotions that had helped fuel the crusade against trusts and unregulated private power. At home wartime intolerance had broken up the progressive coalition by pitting American against American. In the prewar decades the issues of trust control, more responsive government, and consumer protection had united Americans. Now the nation was about to enter an era when issues and prejudices would deeply divide them.

For Further Reading

N. Gordon Levin. *Woodrow Wilson and World Politics*: *America's Response to War and Revolution* (1968)

> Levin maintains that the "effort to construct a stable world order of liberal-capitalist internationalism"— safe from "imperialism of the Right" and "revolution of the Left"—was basic to Wilson's foreign policy and all subsequent American policy-making.

Robert E. Quirk. *An Affair of Honor*: *Woodrow Wilson and the Occupation of Veracruz* (1962)

> Quirk's treatment of the Tampico incident and the shelling and occupation of Veracruz by American marines is brief and well written.

Walter Millis. *Road to War: America, 1914–1917* (1935)

> Writing when most citizens believed that America's entry into World War I was a mistake, Millis blames Allied propaganda, American businessmen, and anti-German prejudice for dragging the nation into an unnecessary conflict. *Road to War* was a Book-of-the-Month Club selection in 1935 and helped create the isolationism that characterized the thirties.

Arthur S. Link. *Woodrow Wilson and the Progressive Era, 1910–1917* (1954)

> Half of this book is devoted to Wilson's foreign policy and the advent of war with the Central Powers. Link is far more sympathetic to Wilson than is Millis; he sees the president as motivated by idealism and a sincere desire to stop brutal aggression.

Randolph S. Bourne. *War and the Intellectuals*: *Collected Essays, 1915–1919*. Edited and introduced by Carl Resek (1964)

> A collection of essays by a man who opposed America's entry into World War I. Bourne, a brilliant political commentator, ridicules the tendency of many of his fellow intellectuals to justify American intervention in progressive and moral terms. Why did the United States fight? Because, Bourne says, "War is the health of the State."

John Dos Passos. *Three Soldiers* (1921)

> Three young men of very different temperaments and backgrounds meet in an army training camp and go to war. Dos passos traces their spiritual destruction in this novel.

Erich Maria Remarque. *All Quiet on the Western Front* (1929)

> The narrator and author of this novel was a German private serving in the trenches of the Western Front. Like Dos Passos, Remarque recounts the death of spirit and passion in living men under the extreme conditions of trench warfare.

Florette Henri. *Black Migration*: *Movement North, 1900–1920* (1975)

> This is a sympathetic survey of the migration of 1.25 million blacks from the South, the "hard-luck place," to northern cities, where wages were higher and jobs more plentiful. The author discusses

blacks' economic status, their leaders and goals, the development of ghettos, and the national progressives' neglect of black needs.

Ernest May. *The World War and American Isolation, 1914–1917* (1959)

A balanced study of American entrance into World War I. May has looked not only at American documents, but also at Allied and German ones. It is particularly fascinating to see what the German leaders were saying as Wilson was acting to stem unrestricted U-boat warfare.

Robert Ferrell. *Woodrow Wilson and World War I, 1917–1921* (1985)

The best one-volume study of Wilson and the war. Ferrell celebrates Wilson's soaring idealism but also criticizes his stubbornness and racial bigotry.

Chapter 25

The Twenties

Happy Adolescence or Decade of Stress?

1913 Henry Ford introduces the moving assembly line in his automobile plant

1916 Wilson is reelected president • The Federal Highways Act

1917 The Eighteenth Amendment provides for national Prohibition

1919 The Volstead Act enforces Prohibition • Steelworkers strike unsuccessfully for union recognition • Attorney General Palmer breaks miners' strike • Race riot in Chicago

1920 Palmer orders Department of Justice agents to jail 4,000 aliens suspected of radical activities • Warren Harding elected president • Pittsburgh station begins commercial radio broadcasting

1920–21 Postwar recession

1920–29 Unemployment and low profits beset the New England textile industry, coal mining, railroads, and agriculture; 1.2 million leave farms for cities

1921 The Sacco and Vanzetti trial • The American Plan is designed by the National Association of Manufacturers to resist unions • The Immigration Act establishes national quotas for first time

1921–23 Congress exempts farmers' cooperatives from antitrust laws and regulates middlemen's rates

1921–31 Treasury Secretary Andrew Mellon shifts the tax burden from the rich to the middle class

1922 The Fordney-McCumber Act raises tariff rates

1923 Harding dies; Calvin Coolidge becomes president • The Teapot Dome scandal

1924 Coolidge elected president • The Johnson-Reed Immigration Act establishes stricter immigration quotas

1925 Scopes trial • Ku Klux Klan membership reaches 3 million

1927 Sacco and Vanzetti executed • Charles Lindbergh makes first transatlantic solo flight • Marcus Garvey, black leader of "Back to Africa" movement, is deported

1928 Herbert Hoover elected president

1929 Southern mill owners defeat United Textile Workers' union drive • Automobile production reaches five times that of 1915 • National Origins Act further limits immigration

1930 Union membership falls to 3.6 million, down from a high of 5 million in 1920

To many of the men and women who reached adulthood soon after Versailles, the 1920s would seem a time of exuberance, vitality, nutty creativity, and bounding prosperity. Novelist F. Scott Fitzgerald called the twenties "an age of miracles, . . . an age of art," when world leadership "passed to America." It was "the greatest gaudiest spree in history." Joseph Wood Krutch, one of the decade's bright young men, later recalled that he and his fellow journalists and critics "were . . . fundamentally optimistic, . . . gay crusaders. . . . The future was bright and the present was good fun at least." Many of the serious scholars of the day also liked the new era. "We are approaching equality of prosperity more rapidly than most people realize," declared Harvard economist Thomas N. Carver in 1925.

Contemporary judgment was not one-sided, however. The novelist Sinclair Lewis considered the nation's heart hollow and sick in the 1920s. H. L. Mencken, a persistent critic of American life, thought only a tiny minority had escaped the sham and stupidity of daily life in America. After months spent in Muncie, Indiana, interviewing citizens and investigating social conditions, sociologists Robert and Helen Lynd concluded that "Middletown's" people had failed to adjust to rapidly changing technology. Change had produced serious "friction spots" that people tried to relieve with boosterism and police repression.

What were the 1920s really like? Was it an era of happy adolescence when Americans, released from puritanical restraints and blessed with newfound abundance, responded creatively and joyously to a new world? Or was it a period of friction, repression, and painful adjustment covered over with a glittering but thin veneer?

The Swing to the Right

One way to understand the twenties is to see it as a time when diversity replaced unity. During the Progressive Era Americans were in general harmony on the big issues. They shared a fear of big business and joined the crusade to check irresponsible power and protect the "common man." World War I extended this crusading mood to the rest of the world and reinforced the voluntary unity of the preceding decade and a half with overheated patriotism. But the war also exhausted the national zeal to right wrongs and opened ideological and cultural fissures. With the armistice the consensus came apart. Americans lost their sense of a common foe and abandoned their concern for social justice. In its place they substituted pursuit of the good life as each individual defined that term.

The Retreat to Privatism. The new mood of privatism and evasion affected politics first. By 1919 many progressive reformers were tired and disillusioned. Much of the great progressive crusade, it seemed, had ended in triviality. Walter Weyl of the *New Republic* despaired that the person "who aspired to overturn society, ends by fighting . . . for the inclusion of certain books" in a village library. Walter Lippmann, Weyl's progressive colleague, summed up the new attitudes, and expressed his own waning political faith: "The people are tired," he wrote, "tired of noise, tired of politics, tired of inconvenience, tired of greatness, and longing for a place where the world is quiet and where all trouble seems dead leaves, and spent waves riot in doubtful dreams of dreams." At times disillusionment with the liberal past was carried to extremes. During the 1920s, the crusading muckraker Lincoln Steffens became for a time a defender of the Italian fascist dictator Benito Mussolini.

Progressivism did not entirely disappear, however. Its legacy of concern for efficiency survived in Herbert Hoover's Commerce Department, which worked to eliminate wasteful practices in private industry and government. In New York Governor Alfred E. Smith successfully continued many progressive welfare programs. And the conservation ideal, well represented by Horace Albright, superintendent of Yellowstone National Park, remained before the public's mind. In Congress during the decade some fifty representatives and senators from the Midwest and South fought big-business domination of political life. Senators George Norris and Robert La Follette continued to demand that government protect the weak, whatever their occupation, from the rich and powerful. But most of this progressivism lacked a universal vision, and in the case of the farm bloc, all too often degenerated into a defense of narrow agricultural interests against urban ones. These survivals were at best a pitiful remnant of the once all-pervasive progressive impulse.

Isolationism, which had been in eclipse since the 1890s, once again became the dominant public sentiment in foreign policy. Not that the country cut all ties with the rest of the world. On the contrary, during the 1920s, under Harding, Coolidge, and Hoover, the government aggressively fostered outlets for American goods and capital abroad. But few Americans believed it necessary to become involved politically in the affairs of distant countries. The United States never joined the League of Nations, and after long dickering it failed to become a member of the League's Court of International Justice. The one foray into European concerns was a pact to "outlaw" war, the Kellogg-Briand Pact of 1928, jointly initiated by Aristide Briand of France and Secretary of State Frank Kellogg and eventually signed by sixty-two nations. The treaty provided no penalties for violators and was little more than a pious expression of hope.

During the 1920s American foreign policy makers ignored Europe while devoting their attention to the Western Hemisphere and the Far East. The major goal of the State Department was to promote international stability in the regions. At the beginning of the decade the United States still pursued the policies of Roosevelt and Wilson in the Caribbean, landing marines in several small Latin American countries to put down disorders and protect American lives and property. But gradually, under the leadership of secretaries of state Charles Evans Hughes and Frank Kellogg, the nation backed away from intervention in Latin America. The United States would continue to defend its Latin neighbors against Old World aggression, but it would no longer assert the right to intervene in their internal affairs.

Harding's Presidency. The swing in political mood was best expressed by Senator Warren G. Harding of Ohio. Speaking to a Boston audience early in 1920, the senator declared that the nation needed "not heroism, but healing, not nostrums but normalcy, not revolution, but restoration, not agitation but adjustment, not surgery but serenity, not the dramatic but the dispassionate, not experiment but equipoise, not submergence in international duty but sustainment in triumphant nationality." It is difficult to say precisely what Harding meant by these alliterative pairings, but the general drift was clear: The country was tired of all the excitement, commitment, and dedication of the previous decade and Americans wished to retreat to a quieter, less demanding, more private world.

And Harding was right about the public mood. Americans indeed wanted "normalcy." They particularly wanted to forget the Wilson administration, with its constant calls to virtue and international responsibility. By the end of his second term Wilson, his health broken, had lost control of his administration, and the public was treated to the gloomy sight of an embittered old man allowing affairs to drift.

Harding reflected the best and worst of postwar America. He was amiable, kind, and neighborly, as suited a small-town newspaper editor; but he was also provincial and morally flabby. The contrast between

This portrait catches Warren G. Harding in an unusually dignified mood. He was not an especially dignified man.

him and the well-educated, sternly upright, and inaccessible Woodrow Wilson suited the public mood. In 1920, when the Republican national convention stood deadlocked between General Leonard Wood and Governor Frank O. Lowden of Illinois, Harding carried off the nomination as the most "available" man. Against Democrats James Cox of Ohio and Franklin Roosevelt of New York, Harding and his running mate, Calvin Coolidge of Massachusetts, scored the most sweeping victory in a presidential election to that time.

Harding was an indifferent president. As he told a newspaper reporter, he could not hope to be the best president, but he would be happy if he were remembered as the best-liked. He did select for his cabinet talented men such as Charles Evans Hughes, the 1916 Republican presidential candidate, and Herbert Hoover, wartime food czar and administrator of Belgian war relief. Also to his credit was his generous release of Eugene V. Debs from prison where the Wilson administration had put him during the war. Harding successfully carried out the public mandate to reconcile government and business interests. During his administration, Washington became the friend and ally of business. The president himself supported the Fordney-McCumber Tariff (1922), which raised import duties far above those of the Underwood Tariff of 1913. He also pushed for a bill to subsidize the American merchant marine, which, now that the war was over, could not compete with the merchant fleets of other nations.

The Harding record had a prominent debit side as well. Though government-business reconciliation was probably unavoidable, the administration proved far too willing to give capital its way. The president allowed Secretary of the Treasury Andrew Mellon, a Pittsburgh industrialist and one of the world's richest men, to pursue "soak-the-poor" policies. Like most business people and many politicians of this era, Mellon believed that the nation's well-being depended on the proper climate for business investment and incentive. Convinced that the high corporate and personal income taxes imposed in 1917 and 1918 to finance the war were hampering enterprise, he persuaded Congress to eliminate the wartime excess-profits tax and to reduce income tax rates at the upper levels while leaving those at the bottom untouched. Between 1920 and 1929 Mellon won further victories for his drive to shift the tax burden onto the backs of the middle and wage-earning classes.

Except for Hoover and Hughes, and Agriculture Secretary Henry C. Wallace, most of Harding's appointments were deplorable. The president's criteria for selecting his advisers were those of a good-natured glad-hander: The appointee had to be a good fellow, cheerful, a regular guy. The results of this policy were predictable. As attorney general, his old friend Harry M. Daugherty distributed government favors with a free hand. The "Ohio gang" presided over by Daugherty's close friend Jesse Smith, dispensed Justice Department pardons and paroles, granted businessmen immunity from antitrust prosecution, and bestowed government appointments on any who would pay a price. To head the Veterans' Bureau, the president selected Charles R. Forbes, a man he had met on vacation and liked. Forbes sold supposedly surplus blankets, sheets, and medical supplies of veterans' hospitals for a song—and a kickback. Worst of all was Albert B. Fall, secretary of the interior. Soon after taking office, Fall got the secretary of the navy to turn over the government's naval oil reserves to the Interior Department. Then, disregarding the country's best interests, Fall promptly leased the Elk Hills (California) oil reserve to Edward L. Doheny of the Pan-American Petroleum Company and the Teapot Dome (Wyoming) reserves to Harry F. Sinclair. In exchange Doheny "lent" Fall $100,000 in cash, and Sinclair gave Fall's son-in-law $200,000 in government bonds.

Harding was probably unaware of the Teapot Dome frauds and the other unsavory doings of his subordinates. In subsequent months, Fall would be convicted of accepting bribes, and Forbes would be sent to prison. However, Harding would never learn about these events. In June 1923 he had set out on a speaking tour of the West Coast and Alaska. In San Francisco, on the way home, the president suffered a stroke and died in his hotel bed.

Coolidge Does Nothing. As inward and dour as Harding had been outgoing and friendly, Vice President Calvin Coolidge, who now succeeded Harding, was also an exceptionally indolent man. As governor of Massachusetts he had done little to attract attention outside the state and seemed merely another local politician. Then, in September 1919, when the Boston police went on strike, leaving the city exposed to unchecked crime and chaos, Governor Coolidge suddenly captured national notice by declaring that there was "no right to strike against the public safety by anybody, anywhere, anytime." These blunt words expressed the public's own growing impatience with labor unrest and won Coolidge the Republican vice presidential nomination the following year.

As president, Coolidge restored the public's faith in the honesty of the executive branch. He appointed

Calvin Coolidge was admired for his stubborn Yankee character, a relief from the shabby glad-handing of his predecessor. But he was also known for his tightfistedness: the title of this cartoon from the end of his presidency is "Mr. Coolidge refuses point-blank to leave the White House until his other rubber is found." He was also probably the laziest man ever to occupy the White House, sometimes sleeping as much as fourteen hours a day.

two outstanding attorneys as prosecutors of the government's case against the Teapot Dome culprits, thus bypassing Daugherty, the corrupt attorney general. He soon replaced Daugherty with the distinguished former dean of the Columbia University Law School, Harlan Fiske Stone. The White House itself, hitherto the scene of hard-drinking, poker-playing cronyism, became a more dignified place with Coolidge and his charming and cultivated wife, Grace, as its occupants.

Otherwise Coolidge slept away most of his five years in office. During his term the watchword of government was "do nothing." The administration avoided new programs, balanced its budgets, and reduced the national debt. This inaction pleased business, but it ignored the pressing social and physical needs of the country. The nation acquired a major new road system and hundreds of new schools, courthouses, and other public facilities; but the burden of constructing them was thrown largely on the states. Farmers found the new president a disappointment. Hoping for sub-

stantial assistance from the government to help them out of economic difficulties brought about by the contraction of war-inflated agricultural prices, they were dismayed when Coolidge twice vetoed congressional farm assistance plans.

Yet Coolidge suited the public mood. On balance, most Americans liked what they saw: dignity in the White House and a president who knew when to let well enough alone. When Coolidge ran for president in his own right in 1924, he won by a large majority over the combined votes for La Follette on the Progressive ticket and John W. Davis, a conservative corporation attorney from New York, on the Democratic ticket.

"New Era" Prosperity

Republican electoral success in the twenties was assured by the country's growing prosperity. By 1925 the economy was providing a flood of commodities beyond anyone's dreams, and most Americans could see little reason to challenge the party that stood watch over the affluent New Era.

The decade opened with a brief depression. Government spending during the war had produced a boom that poured money into the pockets of millions of Americans. For two years following the armistice, good times continued and eased the return of 4 million men to the civilian economy. The bubble burst in 1920. As Europe recovered and restored its devastated fields and factories, its reliance on American exports declined. At the same time American consumers, appalled by skyhigh prices, held off buying. Down came prices with a resounding crash, a collapse that particularly hurt farmers.

The depression was brief. By 1923 unemployment—which during our own day has hovered between 6 and 7 percent—was only about 3 percent of the labor force. Thereafter the economy surged. Even allowing for price changes, the income of the average American would be a third higher in 1929 than in the last prewar years. The gross national product reached heights never before attained. Total output in 1929 would rise to 75 percent above that of 1909.

The Consumer Durables Revolution. The great economic expansion of the middle and late 1920s was in part stimulated by readily available credit. Interest rates remained low through the decade. Thousands of citizens could and did borrow money to invest in factories and productive machinery, buy houses, and

Cities had known traffic jams in the age of the horse and wagon. But they got much worse—and spread to the suburbs as well—after the automobile became supreme in the 1920s.

acquire expensive goods "on the installment plan." Foreigners borrowed extensively from American bankers, and the borrowed dollars soon came back to pay for imported American automobiles, electrical equipment, petroleum, wheat, and corn.

More fundamental than cheap credit in explaining the boom was a major structural change in the economy. Between 1910 and 1920 average family income reached the point where many Americans had substantial amounts of discretionary income, that is, money left over after buying necessities, such as food and shelter. For the first time, a relatively large number of consumers could afford services and goods that had always been beyond their reach. Many middle- and working-class women could now buy silk, or at least rayon, stockings and pay for the services of beauty parlors and hairdressers. Middle-class families could "eat out" more often, go to the movies, and hire a maid. Most important, American consumers could now buy expensive "durables" like radios, vacuum cleaners, washing machines, electric irons, refrigerators, and, above all, automobiles. In 1929 automobile production

was five times greater than it had been fourteen years earlier, and there were over 23 million registered passenger cars. Theoretically, every American could be out taking a drive at the same moment, and on some summer Sundays it often seemed as if they all were. So extensive and important was this development that many scholars consider it an economic revolution, a "consumer durables revolution."

The total impact of these new markets was immense. Demand for consumer durables called forth billions of dollars of investment in new plants and factories, creating jobs and income for building contractors, architects, electricians, bricklayers, and a host of people directly involved in construction. The indirect effects, especially of the automobile, were also immense. Cars needed roads. Until the 1920s, despite some improvement to please the bicyclists of the 1890s, the typical American highway was a dirt track leading from the farm to the local railroad depot. Now the states, aided by matching federal outlays under the Federal Highway Act of 1916, poured billions into new, hard-surfaced, all-weather roads. At the end of the 1920s the nation had an unequaled network of 275,000 miles of asphalt and concrete intercity highways.

Investment in roads was only the beginning. To meet the demands of automobile manufacturers and users, investors directly financed steel, rubber, glass, and petroleum-producing facilities. The automobile also gave birth to a new generation of suburban communities now made accessible to city wage earners by the family car and the concrete highway. Within ten years new "automobile suburbs" grew up in a ring beyond the streetcar suburbs of an earlier period.

Growing industrial efficiency also fueled the economic boom. In 1913 Henry Ford had introduced the moving assembly line in his Detroit automobile plant. During the war the need for speed to supply the fighting fronts and offset a chronic labor shortage led to increasing acceptance of mass-production techniques using standardized, interchangeable parts. Meanwhile, the principles of Frederick W. Taylor, which reduced management to a precise "science," spread to more and more industrial concerns. All these elements combined increased labor productivity dramatically. By one estimate, the amount of labor time needed for a given output of industrial goods shrank 21 percent between 1920 and 1929.

Business and Labor.   Still another cause—as well as effect—of prosperity was the new public attitude toward private enterprise. Americans had far greater respect for business and business people during the 1920s than during the Progressive Era. At times their good opinion approached reverence. "The man who builds a factory builds a temple," intoned President Coolidge, and "the man who works there worships there." Henry Ford, the creator of the Model T and the person who perhaps did more than any other to bring about the consumer durables revolution, was listened to respectfully when he held forth on such matters as diet, world peace, and reincarnation. In a 1925/26 best-seller *The Man Nobody Knows*, an advertising executive could find no better way to communicate the glory of Jesus than by describing him as a first-rate businessman who "picked up twelve men from the bottom ranks of business and forged them into an organization that conquered the world." The ministry itself was saturated with business values. Typical sermon titles of the 1920s included "Christ: From Manger to Throne," "Public Worship Increases Your Efficiency," and "Business Success and Religion Go Together." Preachers were admonished by parishioners and church superiors to "preach the gospel and advertise."

The uncritical public support of business hurt organized labor. During the progressive years and the war, middle-class Americans had learned to accept organized labor and at times even supported it. Now the pendulum swung back. Without public support, the unions suffered a succession of defeats when they attempted to organize various sectors of industrial labor. In 1919, steelworkers lost a major strike to gain union recognition from the large steel firms. In 1929, mill owners defeated the efforts of the United Textile Workers to unionize southern cotton workers.

Antiunion American business leaders left nothing to chance. In 1921 a group of employers launched the American Plan to resist unions on every front. Business would use labor spies to ferret out and report on union activities. It would hire strikebreakers to defeat unions in labor disputes, and would spread propaganda among workers to overcome union-organizing drives. A major force behind the plan was the National Association of Manufacturers (NAM), an organization that during the 1920s would expend more of its funds and energy to defeat unions than to win congressional support for tariff legislation, its past priority.

Another element in organized labor's declining fortunes was the unfriendly role of government and

One of the fathers of modern advertising, Bruce Barton was also a glorifier of the 1920s business ethic. His bestseller *The Man Nobody Knows* made Jesus into a successful executive and so gave religious sanction to contemporary business practices.

the courts. The steel strikers lost in 1919 in part because Attorney General A. Mitchell Palmer dispatched federal troops to the United States Steel plant at Gary, Indiana, to protect strikebreakers. Shortly thereafter Palmer broke a mine workers' strike. In 1922 Attorney General Daugherty had a federal judge issue an injunction against idle railroad shopworkers, forcing them back to work. Under Chief Justice William Howard Taft, the former president, the Supreme Court gutted the provision of the Clayton Act exempting unions from antitrust prosecution and made it possible once again for employers to attack union activities as illegal restraints of trade. In these years Justice Louis D. Brandeis and Oliver Wendell Holmes, Jr., frequently upheld the unions, but their dissenting voices were seldom heeded.

In this atmosphere it is not surprising that labor unions languished. In 1920, as a result of wartime expansion, the number of organized workers had reached over 5 million; almost 20 percent of all nonagricultural workers belonged to labor unions. Soon, under the combined pressure of employers' attacks, public fear of radicalism, and an unfriendly government, union membership dropped to 3.6 million. For the remainder of the decade, it hovered around this figure, while the labor force grew rapidly. By 1930 scarcely 10 percent of nonfarm workers belonged to unions.

The Depressed Industries. The boom of 1923–1929—"Coolidge prosperity," the Republicans called it—was wide and deep enough to make Americans willing to accept the conservative, probusiness values of the day. But prosperity was by no means universal. Unemployment remained high and wages low in several chronically sick industries. Miners of soft coal experienced hard times throughout the decade. The railroad industry was depressed, and the railroad companies laid off workers. Cotton manufacturing also failed to benefit from prosperity. To survive in the face of stiff competition, many textile companies moved from New England to the southern piedmont region, where labor was cheap and where they could put up new mills with the latest and most efficient equipment. New England communities whose livelihood depended on the cotton mills were devastated. And the new opportunities for southern workers hardly offset New England's loss. The southern mill communities were often squalid places. Upton Sinclair reported that at Marion, South Carolina, most mill workers' homes lacked running water or toilets. Old newspapers served as wallpaper.

The most seriously depressed of all economic sectors was the most competitive one: agriculture. In 1925 there were still 6.5 million American farms, and growers of wheat and cotton faced millions of foreign competitors as well. During the war farmers had borrowed heavily to buy more land and upgrade their equipment to take advantage of high wartime prices. When farm prices dropped 40 percent at the end of 1920, farmers were still saddled with large interest payments but now had less income. Yet intense competition for the consumer's dollar forced them to continue buying machines like tractors, which reduced their production costs but put them further in debt.

Farmers responded to the agricultural depression in several ways. During the 1920s over 1.2 million people abandoned agriculture, most of them to go to the cities and their growing suburbs. The black migration out of the rural South became a flood, though many blacks were responding as much to new opportunities in northern manufacturing as to depressed conditions in the cotton fields. Farmers also turned to politics, as they had in the past. Except for La Follette's unsuccessful 1924 effort to create a farmer-labor alliance, however, they turned to pressure-group rather than third-party politics. The congressional farm bloc obtained legislation to ease agricultural credit, exempt farmers' cooperatives from antitrust prosecution, and regulate the rates various middlemen charged. The main difficulty, however, was low farm income. To remedy it the bloc proposed the McNary-Haugen plan. This scheme required the federal government to buy farm surpluses at prices that would guarantee growers a good income. The surpluses would then be sold abroad at the lower world price, with the loss made up from a small fee paid by each farmer. Twice the McNary-Haugen Farm Relief Bill was enacted by Congress, and twice Coolidge vetoed the measure on the grounds that it favored a special group of citizens and constituted undue interference with free markets. Though the scheme never became law, it familiarized Americans with the principle of farm price supports, which a more innovative decade would enact into law.

Old and New America

During the 1920s, then, the United States was not exempt from economic difficulties and class antagonisms. Yet relatively few Americans saw anything seriously wrong with the class or economic arrangements of their society. Support for the Socialist party, a useful barometer of American economic dissatisfaction in the early twentieth century, dwindled as working- and middle-class citizens lost interest in radical action. In 1928 Norman Thomas, the Socialist party's presidential candidate, received only 267,000 votes; William Z. Foster, of the new Communist party, only 49,000.

Still, the 1920s were scarcely harmonious. Americans fought bitterly over many issues, but they were primarily social and cultural ones. As in other periods of prosperity, the questions that set citizens apart involved religion, ethnicity, race, cultural values, and styles of life, rather than class or economic ideology.

Despite the confusion of voices debating the decade's problems, we can identify two general categories of opinion, separated by a deep cultural chasm. On one side were the forces of New America. New America was urban and professed to be urbane. It was also modernist and freethinking in religion and was apt to be liberal or, occasionally, radical in politics. It was also culturally liberal. At the level of ordinary people, this translated into "fun-loving" hedonism. Farther up the social ladder cultural liberalism was associated with avant-garde or modernist taste. New America accepted freer sexual standards and was "wet"—that is, it considered drinking alcohol a matter of private conscience. On the question of drinking, though not necessarily on the other issues, New America found itself allied with urban Catholics. Old America, on the opposite side of the chasm, was small town–rural and proud of its simplicity and homeyness. It was traditional Protestant, and at its most emphatic, fundamentalist. In political matters Old America tended to be conservative, and in matters of taste, traditionalist. It rejected the "looser" sexual practices of New America. As for drinking, Old America considered it either a social evil or a sin that must be restricted by the government or actually prohibited.

Not every person was clearly on one side of the line or the other, of course. Old America and New America were both loose coalitions that at no point had any formal embodiment in a single organization. And yet, to a surprising degree, these two sets of attitudes can be found consistently ranged against each other in the passionate cultural battle that raged throughout the 1920s.

Wets versus Drys. A major cultural battlefield of the twenties was Prohibition. The liquor questions had roiled American politics since before the Civil War. In the 1870s Frances Willard and a number of like-minded women had founded the Women's Christian Temperance Union (WCTU). Two decades later reformers interested in strengthening the family, business people anxious to upgrade the quality of the work

force, and citizens concerned about alcoholism as a health problem organized the Anti-Saloon League. By 1915 the league and the WCTU had induced fifteen states in the South, Midwest, and Far West to prohibit the production and sale of "demon rum."

Although the state-by-state campaigns had been modestly successful, much of the country, especially the Northeast, was unlikely ever to accept Prohibition; the big cities in the industrialized states were home to too many New Americans—Catholics, worldly sophisticates, and social liberals—to whom it seemed tyrannical for the state to dictate what a person could or could not drink. Also opposed were the brewers and distillers, loudly seconded by the saloonkeepers and proprietors of hotels and restaurants, who stood to lose business, if not their very livelihoods, if Americans were not permitted their beer, wine, and whiskey.

World War I helped the prohibitionists override their opponents and outlaw liquor nationally. Temperance organizations proclaimed that brewing and distilling consumed badly needed grain. They played on the public's concern for the morals of the young men drafted into the army and took advantage of the fact that many brewers were of German origin and hence in bad repute. In 1917 Congress passed the Eighteenth Amendment, outlawing the manufacture, sale, and transportation of intoxicating liquors one year after its adoption. In January 1920, after state confirmation, national Prohibition went into effect.

The Volstead Act of 1919 supplemented the Eighteenth Amendment by declaring any beverage containing more than 0.5 percent alcohol illegal and establishing a Prohibition Bureau for enforcing the law. But at no time during the Prohibition Era did Congress ever give the bureau enough money to do its job. Nor were city and state authorities particularly willing to spend money to enforce the federal law. Some states passed their own "baby Volstead acts," but their enforcement, too, was generally poorly funded and weak. Americans continued to drink.

Poor enforcement was as much a symptom as a cause of Americans' continuing homage to John Barleycorn. Many of those who supported Prohibition did so only for the sake of appearances or to guarantee someone else's good behavior. In a famous quip humorist Will Rogers remarked that the people of one thoroughly dry state would "hold faithful and steadfast to Prohibition as long as the voters [could] stagger to the polls." In fact, by adding an element of the forbidden to the usual attractions of drinking, Prohibition made the United States a nation not only of hypocrites but also of heavy drinkers. In former days the "better" people seldom consumed intoxicating beverages except a little wine at dinner. Now hard (distilled) liquor became a significant part of urban middle-class life. Before the decade was over, the cocktail party replaced the tea party as a social diversion—and indeed became the mark distinguishing the urban sophisticate from the puritanical, small-town "rube."

It has been argued that whenever a community forbids a practice that many people favor, it opens the door to other forms of lawbreaking. This formula held true in the Gilded Age, when laws against prostitution, gambling, and Sunday sports led to urban police corruption; it did so again in the 1920s. The United States might forbid the manufacture and sale of intoxicants, but the Canadians, Mexicans, and Europeans did not. Alcohol transported by truck across the borders or brought clandestinely into small American ports by boat produced huge profits for rumrunners. Once in the country, its distribution and sale were taken over by bootleggers, who were also happy to furnish customers with "moonshine," "white lightning," "bathtub gin," and other potent—and often dangerous—American concoctions.

Prohibition not only encouraged lawbreaking; together with the fast automobile and the Thompson submachine gun, it helped create organized crime. To accommodate the thousands of citizens who wanted alcohol and were willing to pay for it, enterprising and ruthless men organized liquor distribution networks that rivaled major legitimate business enterprises in their complexity and efficiency. Just as successful business people often diversified, successful bootleggers, organized into "families" under strong and ruthless leaders, extended their operations into prostitution, gambling, and the "protection" racket.

The mobs brought new violence to the cities. When one tried to invade another's territory, the result was gang warfare that left scores dead. In the 1929 St. Valentine's Day massacre, for example, six members of Bugs Moran's North Side gang were gunned down

Ben Shahn, a "message" artist in the 1930s, here tells of the evils of prohibition, including drunkenness and Al Capone. He also gets in a swipe at the rich.

Citizens and resident aliens suspected of having Communist sympathies board the Ellis Island Ferry. The "red scare" was closely linked with restrictions on immigration, and in California was justification for suppressing unions among Mexican and Oriental workers.

by unknown rivals in a Chicago garage while waiting for a shipment of bootleg liquor. Periodically, crusading district attorneys, goaded by newspapers or citizens' groups, tried to crack down on the gangsters, but indictments and convictions were hard to get. Members of rival gangs refused to testify against their opponents; victimized honest citizens were intimidated; officials and judges were bought off.

Eventually the connection between Prohibition and organized crime induced many Americans to change their minds about the Eighteenth Amendment. But throughout the 1920s millions of citizens continued to consider Prohibition a "noble experiment" that would advance national well-being and purify the country's morals. The "drys" agitated constantly to increase appropriations for Volstead Act enforcement; the Anti-Saloon League maintained lobbyists in Washington and the state capitals to ensure that lawmakers did not relax their vigilance. No group endorsed the noble experiment as vigorously as the Protestant clergy, especially those of the more evangelical denominations. In many communities the weekly Sunday sermon became the occasion for denouncing the wicked wets and defending the values of Old America against its enemies. Nevertheless, by the end of the decade the dry forces were losing ground, and each day more

and more people came to believe that the noble experiment had failed.

Immigration. During the war superpatriotism and suspicion of foreigners had run rampant in the United States. Tensions reached a new pitch after the armistice as Europeans sought to escape the devastation of their homelands by fleeing to the United States. European immigration soared, quadrupling between 1919 and 1920 and almost doubling again in 1921.

To Old America the new wave of foreigners seemed a serious threat. The immigrants were largely Catholic and Jewish and hence religiously alien. They were also certain to be "wet." Neither Catholics nor Jews considered drinking sinful, and judging by those who were already here, they would oppose Prohibition.

The new arrivals were also apt to be radicals— or so many Old Americans believed. Ever since the war and the Bolshevik Revolution of October 1917, many traditional Americans had become deeply concerned with radicals. Soon after the armistice a wave of bombings set by anarchists and other "reds" and an epidemic of strikes made the Bolshevik call for world revolution seem a real threat. Public fear was encouraged by Attorney General A. Mitchell Palmer, who blamed American violence and the labor troubles on

The "Red Scare"

More than once in our history Americans have been seized by a wave of hysteria over the danger of internal subversion. One such occasion was shortly after World War I, when the success of the Bolsheviks in Russia raised the specter of radical revolution in many Western countries.

The "red scare" of 1919/20 was fed by the chief legal officer of the United States government, Attorney General A. Mitchell Palmer. Under Palmer, the Justice Department imprisoned thousands of suspected radicals and began deportation proceedings against those who were not citizens. In the selection below Palmer justifies his actions in terms that appealed to the intolerant mood of the day.

"Like a prairie-fire, the blaze of revolution was sweeping over every American institution of law and order a year ago. It was eating its way into the homes of the American workman, its sharp tongues of revolutionary heat were licking the altars of the churches, leaping into the belfry of the school bell, crawling into the sacred corners of American homes, seeking to replace marriage vows with libertine laws, burning up the foundations of society.

"Robbery, not war, is the ideal of communism. This has been demonstrated in Russia, Germany, and America. As a foe, the anarchist is fearless of his own life, for his creed is a fanaticism that admits no respect of any other creed. . . .

"Upon these two basic certainties, first that the 'Reds' were criminal aliens, and secondly that the American Government must prevent crime, it was decided that there could be no nice distinctions drawn between the theoretical ideals of the radicals and their actual violations of our national laws. . . .

"My information showed that communism in this country was an organization of thousands of aliens, who were direct allies of [Leon] Trotsky [a leader of the Bolshevik Revolution]. Aliens of the same misshapen caste of mind and indecencies of character . . . were making the same glittering promises of lawlessness, of criminal autocracy to Americans that they had made to the Russian peasants. . . . How the Department of Justice discovered upwards of 60,000 of these organized agitators of the Trotsky doctrine in the United States, is the confidential information upon which the Government is now sweeping the nation clean of such alien filth. . . . In my testimony before the sub-committee of the Judiciary Committee of the Senate . . . I had fully outlined the conditions threatening internal revolution in the nation that confronted us. . . .

"One of the chief incentives for the present activity of the Department of Justice against the 'Reds' has been the hope that American citizens will, themselves, become voluntary agents for us, in a vast organization for mutual defense against the sinister agitation of men and women aliens, who appear to be either in the pay or under the criminal spell of Trotsky and Lenin. . . .

". . . [W]hat will become of the United States Government if these alien radicals are permitted to carry out the principles of the Communist Party as embodied in the so-called laws, aims and regulations? . . . There wouldn't be any such thing left. In place of the United States Government we should have the horror and terrorism of bolshevik tyranny such as is destroying Russia now. Every scrap of radical literature demands the overthrow of our existing government. All of it demands obedience to the instincts of criminal minds, that is, to the lower appetites, material and moral. The whole purpose of communism appears to be a mass formation of the criminals of the world to overthrow the decencies of private life, to usurp property that they have not earned, to disrupt the present order of life regardless of health, sex or religious rights. By a literature that promises the wildest dreams of such low aspirations, that can occur in only the criminal minds, communism distorts our social law. . . .

"These are the revolutionary tenets of Trotsky and the Communist Internationale. Their manifesto further embraces the various organizations in this country of men and women obsessed with discontent, having disorganized relations to American society. These include the I.W.W.s [Industrial Workers of the World, a radical trade union], the most radical socialists, the misguided anarchists, the agitators who oppose the limitations of unionism, the moral perverts and the hysterial neurasthenic women who abound in communism. The phraseology of their manifesto is practically the same wording as was used by the Bolsheviks for their International Communist Congress."

alien extremists. In January 1920 Department of Justice agents rounded up 6,000 men and women, mostly eastern European aliens on suspicion of radical activities, and threw them into unsanitary, overcrowded cells. There, in violation of their civil rights, they were kept for weeks without explicit charges being placed against them. Despite Palmer's assertion that a radical uprising was imminent, the police discovered no explosives and only three handguns among the hapless radicals. Eventually the courts released most of the prisoners.

By the end of Palmer's term of office in early 1921, the "red scare" had abated as the forces of common sense took hold. But through the entire decade fear of Bolshevism remained a central component of antiforeign feeling among traditional Americans.

No event threw this connection into more vivid relief than the agony of Nicola Sacco and Bartolomeo Vanzetti, two Italian-born anarchists who were convicted in 1921 of having robbed and murdered a shoe factory paymaster and his guard in South Braintree, Massachusetts. To this day no one is certain whether the two men were guilty of the crime. It is clear, however, that the judge who officiated at their trial and presided over a number of the review hearings was strongly prejudiced against foreigners and radicals; during their trial, Judge Webster Thayer privately called them "those anarchist bastards." And he was not alone. To many Old Americans the men were dangerous aliens, both in their "race" and views.

The liberal community rallied around the two Italian radicals. Led by Walter Lippmann and Felix Frankfurter, liberals and intellectuals turned the fate of Sacco and Vanzetti into a crusade for free speech and common justice. Meetings, petitions, lobbying, civil disobedience—all the accoutrements of modern political agitation—were deployed to drum up support for retrial or pardon of the two prisoners. The issue so deeply divided public opinion that one Sacco-Vanzetti supporter, the novelist John Dos Passos, described the opposing sides as "two nations." The liberals succeeded in getting the case reconsidered several times. But on August 22, 1927, after final appeals for clemency were rejected, both men were electrocuted. To many people of the political left, in both America and around the world, their execution seemed judicial murder.

It would be unfair to dismiss the arguments for restrictions on immigration as entirely unworthy. The United States could not have continued an open door policy on European immigration indefinitely. Yet clearly it was in part ethnic bigotry and political hyste-

ria that slammed shut the immigration door. In 1921 Congress limited for a one-year period the number of new arrivals of each nationality to 3 percent of that group present in the country in 1910. In 1924 it passed the Johnson-Reed Immigration Act. This law limited immigration to 154,000 persons annually, assigning national quotas that strongly favored northern and western over southern and eastern Europe. Great Britain and Ireland were to have almost 45 percent of the total immigration allotment, and Germany and Scandinavia much of the rest. Italy, Poland, and Rus-

Ben Shahn, a radical artist who supported Sacco and Vanzetti's battle for vindication, here in *The Passion of Sacco and Vanzetti* depicts their ultimate defeat. The man in the cap and gown is Harvard president A. Lawrence Lowell, who chaired a committee of investigation that supported the guilty decision of Judge Thayer's court.

sia—the major sources of recent immigrants—were left with ludicrously small quotas. The 1921 law and the Johnson-Reed Act ended the three centuries of free European immigration that had marked American history. It also enshrined into law the prejudices of native-born Old America against persons who, by their mere presence, seemed to be altering the customs, habits, and beliefs of the United States.

Black Pride. From the perspective of Old America, one of the most disturbing changes in postwar American society was the growing assertiveness of blacks. During the war thousands of black soldiers had served their country in France, where they had encountered a racially more liberal society than in their own country. When they returned home, southern segregation and bigotry only heightened their long-standing resentments. At times black veterans became targets of violence. In 1919 alone, ten were lynched in southern states, several while still in uniform. Thousands of southern blacks expressed their disgust by leaving for the North. By 1930 Chicago would have over 230,000 black residents; New York, over 327,000; Philadelphia, over 219,000; and Detroit, over 120,000.

Most blacks who came north found jobs, though seldom the best-paying or most attractive ones. The typical black worker in the North during the 1920s was an unskilled factory worker or day laborer. In increasing numbers black women replaced Irish and German women as domestics in middle-class urban homes.

The transplanting of thousands of southern rural families to northern slums caused painful social problems. Black families were placed under many of the same pressures as the immigrant families of the 1890–1914 period. Children, once physically close to parents, now lost touch as fathers and mothers went to work away from the home. Low income created further strains. Poverty in the city seemed worse, and often caused more discontent, than in the rural South.

The black migration to northern cities brought racial tensions in its wake. Many whites resented and feared the new arrivals and fought to exclude them from their neighborhoods. In Chicago racial antagonisms built during the summer of 1919 and exploded into a furious race riot in late July when a black teenager, swimming off a Lake Michigan beach that whites considered their preserve, was stoned and drowned. Within hours gangs of white and black youths were battling one another and beating innocent bystanders. For thirteen days the city was torn by riot, arson, and vandalism, with the authorities unable to stop the destruction. When the casualties were finally counted, the death toll stood at almost 40, with over 500 injured and thousands of dollars of property destroyed.

Despite the troubles and difficulties, a few blacks discovered opportunities for achievement and fame in northern cities. Sociologist and historian W. E. B. Du Bois, poet and critic James Weldon Johnson, and painter Henry Ossawa Tanner had already established themselves in American life. But the black achievements of the 1920s outshone anything that had preceded. Harlem, in upper Manhattan, became a black Athens where poets, writers, painters, musicians, and intellectuals gathered from all over the country and from other parts of the world. Among the Harlem Renaissance writers were Claude McKay, a Jamaican, who wrote eloquently and bitterly about the repression of blacks; Jean Toomer, an author of realistic stories about black life; and Countee Cullen, a master of delicate lyric poetry. Most impressive of all was Langston Hughes, a poet, novelist, and short-story writer of rare power who could employ humor as well as satire and argument to defend his race and express its hopes.

The 1920s was also an era when black musicians began to attract the attention of white Americans. Although they seldom gave it a second thought, whenever a white "flapper" and her "lounge lizard" boyfriend danced the Charleston or Black Bottom, they were celebrating the vitality of black musical creativity in the 1920s. Within the black community itself, great performing artists like the trumpeter Louis Armstrong, trombonist Kid Ory, and the powerful blues singer Bessie Smith were immensely popular. Their records sold millions of copies among the "cliff-dwellers" of Harlem, Chicago's South Side, and the other urban black neighborhoods. A small group of whites, mostly musicians, appreciated authentic jazz and even performed it with some success, but most white Americans took it in sugar-coated form in a Paul Whiteman or George Gershwin adaptation.

Among blacks the combination of renewed racial pride and the problems of adjusting to the new urban environment gave rise to a Back-to-Africa movement that resembled Jewish Zionism. The leader of the movement was Marcus Garvey, a native of Jamaica in the Caribbean who came to New York in 1916 to establish an American branch of his Universal Negro Improvement Association. Garvey's appeal was particularly strong among working-class urban blacks, who did not feel at home in the NAACP, the middle-class black defense organization. Like more recent black leaders, Garvey told blacks to be proud of their race. Everything

An outstanding figure of the Harlem Renaissance, Langston Hughes was deeply concerned about the ill treatment of black Americans by their white fellow citizens. Yet in his literature he avoided the angry voice of a later generation of black writers. "America never was America to me," he wrote in a poem whose title sums up his plea: "Let America Be America Again."

black was admirable and beautiful; and the blacker a man or woman, the better. Because America was unalterably white and racist, Garvey declared, blacks should return to Africa and there erect a new empire befitting their potential. The black middle class considered these ideas fantastic; but among the urban black masses straight from the rural South, Garvey's message was electrifying. They flocked to become knights of the Nile, dukes of the Niger and Uganda, and members of the Black Eagle Flying Corps or the Universal Black Cross Nurses, under the association's auspices.

Garvey was stopped by federal officials, who accused him of mail fraud in his effort to raise funds for a black shipping line. After being released from prison by President Coolidge, he was deported as an undesirable alien in 1927 and died in obscurity in 1940. Despite his failure, he had blazed a trail that other black leaders would follow over a generation later.

The Sexual Revolution. Sexual behavior was yet another issue that divided the two Americas. No matter how fiercely traditionalists might protest, the nation's sexual values were changing quickly, especially among the young.

Women were at the forefront of this change, yet while they were leading the revolt against traditional sexual taboos, they were losing their political punch. Once the battle for female suffrage was won, the women's rights movement began to retreat. The League of Women Voters succeeded the National American Woman Suffrage Association; but after arousing some initial enthusiasm for its program of enlarged economic rights for women, it lost support. Alice Paul's more aggressive National Woman's party, with an equal rights amendment to the Constitution as its major goal, survived into the 1920s; but with only 8,000 members, it had little influence. Observing the dismal turnouts of women at the polls, female political activists wryly asked themselves whether the struggle to get the vote had been worth the trouble.

The feminists should not have been so hard on their sisters. They had not abandoned their challenge to the status quo. Having won the right to vote, women activists and rebels turned their attention elsewhere and became the agents of fundamental change in the social realm. Young women, especially urban, middle-class women, began to demand in ever larger numbers that they be treated as adult individuals, not as overgrown children or fragile dolls. In the 1920s respectable wives, mothers, and daughters began to smoke, a habit that till then had been confined to men or to women of ill repute. They also began to drink as never before. The new cocktail party introduced a feminine element to social drinking, previously an all-male preserve.

Far more shocking was the new female sexual assertiveness. For women who reached their late teens or twenties between 1919 and 1929, sex was not so obviously linked to marriage and children as it had been for their mothers. Influenced by a popularized version of Sigmund Freud's theories concerning the primacy of the sexual instinct and the emotional dangers of sexual repression, many young women began to insist that they were as entitled as men to the pleasures of physical love and the free choice of sexual partners. The incidence of premarital sex increased sharply, especially among well-educated women. Adultery also became more common. Even when young women did not "go all the way," they were far more relaxed in their social relations with men than before. Young women of respectable families "petted"; they refused to be chaperoned; they danced cheek to cheek.

The "flapper," as the liberated young woman of the 1920s was called, also insisted on greater freedom in her dress and appearance. In contrast to the "womanly" long skirt, sweeping picture hat, rounded bosom, tight natural waist, and petticoats of the past, her skirt was cut off at the knee to reveal a long stretch of silk- or rayon-stockinged leg. Her waistline was high, her bosom flattened, her underclothes minimal, her cloche hat brimless. In 1913 a typical woman's outfit consumed nineteen and a half yards of cloth. In 1925 it required a scant seven. Hair, previously grown long and worn down the back or pinned up, was cut short and "bobbed" or "shingled." To offset the tomboy effect of her dress and reassert her femininity, the flapper painted herself as respectable women never had before. "Beautician" soon became a new professional category.

Older people, particularly those of traditional America, predictably deplored the new trends in dress and behavior among the female young. Smoking by women was the "beginning of the end," according to one male social critic. Dr. Francis Clark of the Christian Endeavor Society denounced modern dances as "impure, polluting, corrupting, debasing." One clergyman proclaimed: "We get our [dress] styles from New York, New York from Paris, and Paris from Hell." Legislators joined the disapproving chorus. In 1921 the Utah legislature considered a bill to fine or imprison any woman whose skirts were higher than three inches above the ankle.

The Media Assault the Small Town. In explaining the deterioration of the traditional sexual code, moralists often pointed to the debasing effects of the media. Novels like _Flaming Youth_ (1923) by Warner Fabian, _This Side of Paradise_ (1920) by F. Scott Fitzgerald, and _Moon-Calf_ (1920) by Floyd Dell glorified the wild pursuit of pleasure among the young. In the early part of the decade Hollywood studios put out a flood of films with such suggestive titles as _Up in Mabel's Room, A Shocking Night, Sinners in Silk_, and _Her Purchase Price_. One producer described his films as replete with "neckers, petters, white kisses, red kisses, pleasure-mad daughters, sensation-seeking mothers . . . the truth—bold, naked, sensational." Actually, compared with the explicit sexuality of recent "X-rated" films, these productions were almost prudish, but they brought down the wrath of the moralists and local censors. To avoid local legal repression, the movie industry in 1922 chose a "czar"—Harding's postmaster general, Will H. Hays—to lay down guidelines of taste and decorum. The Hays Office rules ended the rash of cheap exploitation movies. Critics charged that they also lowered the intellectual and artistic level of Hollywood films to that suitable for a sheltered child of twelve.

The moralists undoubtedly exaggerated the social impact of the movies. But they were not entirely wrong. Popular media helped undermine the values and culture of Old America even when they did not directly attack them. Good roads and the automobile had reduced the isolation of America's rural areas and small towns. Now the movies brought to the smallest communities an image of sophisticated urban life that appealed intensely to American youth. Young people learned what passed for romantic technique among worldly men and women. "It was directly through the movies that I learned to kiss a girl on her ears, neck, and cheeks, as well as her mouth," wrote one young man. After long exposure to the fantasies of Hollywood, one small-town girl told a social researcher that her "daydreams . . . consist of clothes, ideas on furnishings, and manners." Such young people were not easily induced to accept the sexual taboos, dress customs, and social values of their communities.

Radio, too, put small-town values under serious pressure. Radio was invented before World War I, but it did not come into its own until 1920, when

Checking the length of a bathing suit to be sure that a modicum of decency is maintained at the beach. The picture suggests the tension in the 1920s between traditional morality and the newer standards of sexual freedom, as exemplified by the liberated "flapper."

Rural Oregonians listening to the radio in July 1925. The new wonder exposed rural Americans to a big-city media invasion the likes of which it had never seen before.

Station KDKA in Pittsburgh began to broadcast commercially. By 1929 over 10 million American families owned receiving sets. Radio broadcasting might have been placed under government control, as in most of Europe. Instead, it became a private industry dependent on advertising for revenue. In 1927 the federal government did step in to assign station wavelengths to avoid chaos, but it did little to compel broadcasters to serve the public. Advertisers who paid the bills and naturally wished to attract the largest audiences were far more inclined to pay for "Roxy and His Gang" or "Amos 'n Andy" than for serious discussion or the Metropolitan Opera. Commercial broadcasting surrendered a great opportunity to elevate public taste, yet it exposed listeners to a high level of professionalism that did much to undermine the confidence and morale of village America. How could a community amateur hour outdo the "Ipana Troubadours"? How could the local high school dance band compete with Paul Whiteman, coming "live from New York"?

Rebel Artists.   Nor was the decade free from more direct assaults on traditional cultural values. The big cities, especially New York, were the havens of sophisticates who projected a barely disguised contempt for rural, small-town America. The bohemians of the shabby-chic apartments and refurbished town houses of Greenwich Village in lower Manhattan felt themselves escapees from small-town culture. They expressed their new freedom through hard-drinking, free sex lives, socialism, and devotion to the avant-garde in the arts and thought.

The bohemians of the twenties considered American culture hopelessly provincial. Europe, with its greater intellectual and artistic depth, seemed far more interesting. Many, including Hemingway, Fitzgerald, Edna St. Vincent Millay, and Gertrude Stein, felt so alienated that they left the country, most to go to Paris.

Some who stayed, as well as a few who left, wrote novels that ridiculed and condemned the life of the American small town. Sinclair Lewis's *Main Street* (1920) recounts the story of a young woman who moves to "Gopher Prairie," a typical small town. There she resolves to reform her neighbors' tastes, values, and politics, but is instead defeated by their ignorance and materialism. Sherwood Anderson's *Winesburg, Ohio* (1919) depicts the small-mindedness, hypocrisy, and secret vice that Anderson believed afflicted provincial Americans.

American writers and intellectuals ridiculed not only the small towns but also the entire culture of Old America. H. L. Mencken, the acid-tongued social critic of the *Baltimore Evening Sun*, took aim at almost everything in his native land and shocked traditional Americans by his irreverence, elitism, and attacks on established beliefs. Mencken reserved his sharpest barbs for the "booboisie," the absurdly crass and puritanical middle class he was convinced inhabited the country's heartland. Sinclair Lewis followed *Main Street* with *Babbitt* (1922), a novel about a businessman in a middle-sized midwestern city whose material success and irrepressible boosterism masked deep doubt about his own worth. *Babbitt* is a memorable

A Historical Portrait

Edna St. Vincent Millay

My candle burns at both ends;
It will not last the night;
But ah, my foes, and oh, my
   friends—
It gives a lovely light!

This quatrain became a rallying cry for the "flaming youth" of the 1920s, young men and women who experimented with new patterns of living, drinking, dressing, and sexual expression. Its author was Edna St. Vincent Millay, and her poem caught the essence of her own tempestuous life.

Edna St. Vincent Millay was born in Rockland on the Maine coast, on February 22, 1892. The poet's mother, Cora Buzzelle Millay, was an unconventional woman in her own right and set the stage for the drama of her daughter's life. A New Englander with literary and musical inclinations, she was determined that her three daughters, Edna, Norma, and Kathleen, be given the opportunity to fulfill themselves in a way that she was unable to. "My frustration," she declared, "was their chance." In 1900 she scorned custom by divorcing her husband, Henry, a school principal, and moved to Camden, Maine, a resort town on Penobscot Bay, where she supported her children by working as a district nurse.

When her daughters were little, Cora worked only at night so that she could be with them during the day. By the time Edna was twelve, her mother began to take on "live-in" cases, which meant she was away for days or weeks at a time. Edna was made responsible for all the household chores and her sisters' upbringing. She tried to prepare nutritious meals, but sometimes when there was no money, supper would consist of milk and the wild blueber-

ries they had just picked. The three girls washed the dishes singing Edna's composition, "I'm the Queen of the Dishpans." At night Edna would play the piano or tell her sisters stories she made up. The three girls depended on one another and were particularly affectionate and close-knit throughout their lives.

Though often absent, when she returned, Cora worked feverishly to get her house and children in order. She baked, cooked, preserved, gardened, made new clothes or mended old ones, and caught up on the girls' progress in school and music lessons. Edna remembered her childhood as extraordinarily happy. "Meseems it never rained in those days," she wrote later. The absence of a father, however, contributed to Edna's later distrust of men and made her doubt love's permanence, a motif that often appeared in her poetry.

At thirteen, having skipped eighth grade, Edna entered Camden High School and immediately joined the literary magazine, which published her autobiographical essay "The Newest Freshman," as well as her poems. In her senior year she became editor. When she graduated from high school she had no intention of going to college, partly because there was little money to pay for an education and partly because her mother disapproved of college for creative "genius." Instead, using her typing and shorthand skills, Edna worked part-time as a secretary for tourists and spent the rest of her time keeping house for her sisters.

In 1912 Edna entered a poem about nature and survival in a poetry contest. She came in fourth. The poem was published and many readers and critics wrote in claiming that Millay's work was the best in the

book. During the following summer she read it at a party at the Whitehall Inn, a large resort hotel in Camden. One of the listeners was Caroline Dow, head of the National Training School of the Young Women's Christain Association, who was so impressed that she convinced Edna to consider college and promised to obtain the necessary financial aid.

Edna spent the winter of 1913 in New York City, preparing for her entrance into Vassar College the following fall. Although she lived in the protected environment of the National Training School, she plunged into New York's cultural life. She attended the controversial Armory Show of avant-garde art, watched Sarah Bernhardt in *Camille*, and was invited to meetings, teas, and luncheons at the Poetry Society of America. She rode the double-decker buses with poet Sara Teasdale and explored the city with Salomon de la Selva, a young Nicaraguan poet teaching poetry at Columbia. "Recuerdo," written many years later, commemorates her trips on the Staten Island ferry and picnics on the island with de la Selva.

Millay entered Vassar in September 1913, four years older than most of the incoming students. Already acclaimed for her literary talents, and unusually independent and self-reliant as a result of her unsupervised childhood, she chafed at Vassar's strict rules of conduct for its young ladies. The college limited absences and cuts, required attendance at chapel, and prohibited smoking. It permitted young men on campus only on Sundays, and closely chaperoned them until they departed. "I hate this pink-and-gray college," Edna wrote to an older male friend. "They trust us with everything but men. . . . [A] man is forbidden as if he were an apple." A few months later, however, she wrote home that she was "crazy about the college." Although Edna made good use of her four years at Vassar, she broke every college rule she could. She cut classes regularly, came late to those she attended, missed chapel frequently, and smoked in a nearby cemetery. Just before her graduation she went for a car ride with some friends, and did not get back the same night. The faculty voted to suspend Millay indefinitely, forcing her to postpone her degree. This meant that she would have to miss graduation, though she had already composed the music and words for the Baccalaureate Hymn. Fortunately, the senior class circulated a petition on her behalf and the liberal president, Henry MacCracken, lifted the suspension, enabling her to graduate and attend the ceremonies.

With her B.A. in hand, Millay moved to New York in 1917, where she rented a tiny apartment in Greenwich Village. The Village had already become America's bohemia. Here lived the sculptors, the painters, the poets, the playwrights, the actors and actresses, the political radicals, and those who just wanted to escape conventional society. These people drew up their own codes of sexual and social mores. "We held the same views of literature and art," reminisced Floyd Dell, the popular Village novelist and playwright, "we agreed in hating capitalism and war. And, incidentally, of course, we agreed in disbelieving in marriage. We considered it a stupid relic of the barbaric past. . . ."

Edna was determined to find work as an actress to support her writing. She auditioned for Dell's play, The Angel Intrudes, then being rehearsed by the Provincetown Players, a theater group established to perform radical, controversial, and noncommercial plays. Dell was so charmed by the "slender little girl with red-gold hair" that he not only gave her

that part, but others in subsequent plays. He also became the first of her many lovers and, in spite of his declarations against marriage, wanted to make his relationship with her legal and permanent. Claiming she was "nobody's own," Millay refused on the grounds that marriage would tie her to one person. Women, she insisted, should have the right to love as freely and casually as men. She was also afraid that if she married and got involved with babies and domestic responsibilities, she would not have time for her poetry. The love affairs that came after Dell were similar in pattern. They started quickly and intensely and were followed by a period of idyllic companionship. The promising beginning ended, however, in bickering and fighting, possibly fueled by Edna's fear of being hemmed in. In this stage she cast around for a new flame, before the old had been entirely extinguished.

By 1920 every Villager knew Edna St. Vincent Millay, as the "beautiful young actress at the Provincetown" or "America's leading woman poet." She brought her popular and pretty sisters and her mother down to the Village to live with her. Not only did she continue acting, but the Provincetown Players produced her own poetic drama, Aria da Capo, with her sister, Norma, playing the lead. Most of her income, however, came from stories and poems that she published under the pseudonym Nancy Boyd. In 1920 she met Edmund Wilson, a rising young literary critic, who fell in love with her and got her work printed in the prestigious Vanity Fair. In the same year Millay published her first book of sonnets, twenty poems that expressed love from a woman's viewpoint, but without the sentimentality or romanticism that usually characterized female love poetry. A Few Figs from Thistles, with the "burning candle" quatrain, also appeared that year and established her as the spokesperson of the convention-flaunting postwar genera-

tion. During this period Millay was burning her own candle at both ends. She was working hard, eating irregularly, getting little sleep, drinking too much, and under emotional strain from pursuing and being pursued.

That same momentous year Edna and her family moved to Cape Cod for a summer of plain living, good eating, sea breezes, and sun. Edmund Wilson came to Truro to ask her to marry him. Edna, confessing that she was worried about money and the future, for a while considered it. In the end, however, she accepted an offer from Vanity Fair that took her to Europe. Millay sailed for Paris on the Rochambeau on January 21, 1921, forsaking, at least temporarily, her family, her theatrical career, and her importuning suitors. She joined the flood of young American literary expatriates—including Hemingway, Fitzgerald, Ezra Pound, and Gertrude Stein—who believed that Europe offered a kind of creative excitement and cultural freedom missing even from Greenwich Village.

Millay spent two years in Europe traveling and writing, but she could not escape the men who found her irresistible. Not only did she have to fend off a new flock of European lovers, but Wilson appeared in Paris to resume his marriage campaign. News reached her of both her sisters' weddings, and despite her many suitors, she felt unbearably lonely. In 1922 she received an advance for a novel and used it to bring her mother to Paris to keep her company. At this point, after years of eating poorly, Edna's stomach began to trouble her. Her mother took her to England to nurse her. There she worked on her novel, ate well, and exercised both on horseback and on foot. She still felt ill, and in the winter of 1923 she and her mother returned to the United States.

Millay was living in a small apartment in the Village when she won the Pulitzer Prize for poetry, based on Figs, eight new sonnets, and a long poem, "The Ballad of the Harp Weaver," on the impermanence of love. The prize made her America's foremost woman poet and she was soon a celebrity whose activities were followed at every step like a movie star's. Thousands of young Americans who read about her in the gossip columns quoted her and tried to imitate her. All this notoriety exhausted her and she continued to feel sick. With gratitude, Edna accepted the invitation of a friend to visit at her country house in Croton-on-the-Hudson.

Croton was then a sort of "suburb of Washington Square" where a group of political liberals and radicals had homes, including John Reed, Max Eastman, Stuart Chase, and Doris Stevens, a militant suffragist author. It was at a party at Stevens's that Edna was reintroduced to Eugen Boissevain, a Dutch coffee and sugar importer, whose former wife had been the beautiful Inez Milholland, a lawyer and suffragist. Boissevain, now a widower, loved the company of creative people and was himself a feminist.

He and Millay fell instantly in love, and Boissevain resolved to spend the rest of his life taking care of the poet and nurturing her creativity. "Anyone can buy and sell coffee," he declared, "but anyone cannot write poetry." At last Edna had met the right man. The newspapers had a field day with the decision of a

confirmed "free spirit of romance" to wed. "Has Happiness Come to Repay/Fair Edna St. Vincent Millay?" asked the title of a five-column article in the *Chicago Times*. It was subtitled "She Married As She Lived—On a Moment's Impulse." The moment's impulse lasted twenty-six years, until her husband died in 1949.

Eugen's first concern was Edna's health. He took her to doctors to diagnose her fatigue and illness. When they decided an operation was necessary, he insisted she marry him before going to the hospital. They were married by a justice of the peace in Croton and then drove to New York for Edna's operation. Before she went into surgery she declared: "If I die now, I shall be immortal." After she recuperated, Eugen and Edna moved into a narrow brick house at 75½ Bedford Street, in the heart of the West Village.

In November 1923 Millay appeared at a rally commemorating the seventy-fifth anniversary of the Senaca Falls Equal Rights Meeting. At the unveiling of a statue in honor of Mott, Anthony, and Stanton, she read "The Pioneer," a poem written for the occasion and dedicated to Inez Millholland. During the winter of 1924 Millay toured the United States, reading her poems to audiences who came to see what the "bohemian poetess" looked like and how many of her more scandalous

poems she would read. When the tour was over, she and Eugen visited the Orient and Hawaii, returning to Bedford Street early in 1925.

On Bedford Street they were constantly sought after by admirers and friends. On May 1, 1925, the Ashcan Cats, a group of students from Barnard, including future anthropologist Margaret Mead and poet Leonie Adams, brought Millay a May basket made up of moss, wild flowers, and twigs from Bronx Park. After they placed the basket on the doorstep, they shouted: "We want Edna!" and were delighted when she opened the door, dressed in a long bathrobe. She shook hands with each of them and asked their names, which she then diligently repeated. Much as she enjoyed this sort of attention and admiration, however, she began to feel that life in New York was too hectic for her to work.

In 1925 the Boissevains bought a farm in the Berkshire foothills at Austerlitz, New York, which they named "Steepletop." Here they planned to spend the rest of their lives, Millay writing and Eugen farming and landscaping as well as cooking, cleaning, and doing the laundry. The only problem was that Steepletop was not near the sea, which they both loved. To remedy this lack, in 1933 they bought Ragged Island in Casco Bay in Maine, and spent part of every year on their island. It is obvious that this woman who epit-

---

portrait of a troubled person in a shallowly optimistic society obsessed by gadgets and profits. Its hero's name gave a new word for conformity to the English language. Another powerful indictment of the nation's materialism was *An American Tragedy* (1925) by Theodore Dreiser, a tale of the corrupting effect of ambition for wealth and position on a weak young man.

F. Scott Fitzgerald was a more subtle denigrator of America's false values. A chisel-featured midwestern Irish-Catholic who had attended elite Princeton, Fitzgerald was alternately attracted and repelled by the life of the American upper bourgeoisie in the 1920s. He never lost his fascination for the rich and their doings, but in *The Great Gatsby* (1925) he brilliantly depicted the dry rot at the heart of America's business

omized the frenetic Jazz Age also had a deep yearning for tranquility.

At Steepletop Edna worked on the libretto for an opera commissioned by the Metropolitan Opera Company, with music by Deems Taylor. *The King's Henchman* premiered on February 17, 1927, before an audience glittering with celebrities from every field. Enthusiastic applause followed each act, and when the opera finally ended, the ovation lasted twenty minutes. "I thank you," responded Edna, "I love you all." Afterward critics called it "the best American opera we have ever heard," and one reviewer said she was the "young sovereign of the written word."

Later that year Edna went to Massachusetts to protest the impending execution of Sacco and Vanzetti, two Italian anarchists accused of robbery and murder. Like many other American intellectuals of the day, she believed that they were the victims of prejudice against both Italians and radicals. The execution was set for August 23, 1927, and Massachusetts Governor Alvan Fuller had earlier denied an appeal for clemency. On August 22 thousands of protesters began to gather on Boston Common. Millay and John Dos Passos led a demonstration of writers and poets. Millay was picked up by the police, thrown into a patrol wagon, and taken to a police station, where she was formally charged with "sauntering and loitering." Her husband arrived in time to bail her out. Later that day she made a personal appeal for clemency in an audience with Gover-

nor Fuller. At night she read a poem called "Justice Is Denied in Massachusetts" to a crowd in the shadow of Old North Church. Just before the execution at midnight, Millay wrote a letter to Fuller, which was hurriedly delivered to the statehouse. "There is need in Massachusetts of a great man tonight," she pleaded. "It is not yet too late for you to be that man." The electrocution took place as scheduled and the next day Edna was fined $10 for her part in the demonstration.

Over the next ten years Edna and Eugen spent most of their time at Steepletop or Ragged Island. Edna was in poor health and probably drinking too much, but she continued to write and publish her poetry. In 1929 she was elected to the prestigious National Institute of Arts and Letters; in 1931 she received a national prize for a collection of poems. Throughout the thirties she was active at her craft and also worked on a translation from the French of Baudelaire's decadent *Flowers of Evil*. By the middle of the decade her feverish life had truly begun to catch up with her and she felt ill much of the time. In addition, although her poetry continued to sell and receive critical acclaim, reviewers began to criticize her work and her popularity diminished. In 1936 a manuscript of a play she had written was destroyed in a hotel fire on Sanibel Island. During the summer she injured the nerves of her back in an automobile accident. Her last years were full of unwelcome drama and worries. Both

Edna and Eugen drank too heavily and their friends became very concerned for them.

During World War II Edna wrote nothing but propaganda poetry. She was no mere apologist for America, however, and warned that when the soldiers returned, they must beware of "the very monster which they sallied forth to conquer and quell." During the summer of 1944, weakened by years of frail health and worried about money because of her husband's financial setbacks, she had a nervous breakdown. She was confined to Doctors Hospital for a long time and could not write for two years. In August 1949 her husband died after a stroke following an operation for lung cancer. Millay started drinking relentlessly after the funeral and once again suffered a nervous collapse, spending many more months in the hospital. On her release, she resumed her writing, but she had little time left. In October 1950 she collapsed of a heart attack at Steepletop. A friend found her there the next afternoon, halfway up the stairs, a glass of wine and a page of poetry nearby. Her epitaph might have been her own beautiful lines:

Down, down, down into the darkness
   of the grave
Gently they go, the beautiful, the
   tender, the kind;
Quietly they go, the intelligent, the
   witty, the brave.
I know. But I do not approve. And I
   am not resigned.

civilization in the person of Jay Gatsby, a man who destroys himself in pursuit of wealth and glamor.

Another critic of American civilization was Ernest Hemingway, a quintessential young man of the "Lost Generation," who had fought in World War I and had returned to find "all Gods dead, all wars fought, all faiths shaken." In *The Sun Also Rises* (1926) he portrays a group of young Americans wandering

through Europe seeking a substitute for the ideals of the past that now seemed hollow and insincere. In this first book and such later works as *A Farewell to Arms* (1929), in stark, unadorned prose, Hemingway depicts characters struggling against the hypocrisies of the world and forced to find heroism and authenticity in their private lives.

Drama also became a vehicle of protest against

Sinclair Lewis's knowledge of small-town midwestern life came from his own childhood in Sauk Centre, Minnesota, and was deepened by a long car trip he and his wife took through the heartland on the way to San Francisco in 1916.

the conventionality of the decade. In Eugene O'Neill, the most important figure of the "little theater" movement, the United States produced its first playwright of international distinction. O'Neill and the stage designers, producers, and other writers connected with the Provincetown Players (at that time performing in Greenwich Village) sought to convert the American theater from mere commercial entertainment into a vehicle for expressing serious ideas. With such productions as Elmer Rice's *The Adding Machine* (1923), satirizing the emptiness of modern commercial life, and O'Neill's *Desire under the Elms* (1924), debunking American puritanism, the little theater groups looked critically at American life.

Not all men and women of talent and genius in this decade were so negative about their world. There were those who dealt with timeless human themes, wrote hymns of praise to nature, or celebrated regional virtues. In Robert Frost, America found a poet who expressed profound love for the beauties of rural New Hampshire. Willa Cather wrote moving novels and stories about the lives of passionate, vibrant, and decent men and women living in preindustrial America. Edith Wharton, a descendant of the early Dutch settlers of the Hudson Valley, composed novels about upper-class New York that were both sensitive and satiric. Ellen Glasgow did the same for her native Virginia.

Among the best-selling authors of the twenties the mood, as in the past, was upbeat and unruffled. To the purveyors of popular romances, historical melodramas, and comic entertainments, the world seemed bright and wholesome—or else thrillingly, if shallowly, wicked. Nevertheless, the more characteristic literary voice of the decade disapproved of the prevailing folkways of America, and the most original thinkers and artists were generally sharp critics of their nation.

Confrontation

Old America watched the influx of immigrants, the new assertiveness of blacks, the frivolous and "immoral" behavior of the young, the rise of organized crime, and the ridicule and naysaying of the novelists with pain, frustration, and anger. America, it seemed to them, was being taken over by people with nothing but contempt for the values and beliefs that had made the nation great. The "intellectuals and liberals," declared one defender of the old ways, had "betrayed Americanism" and created "confusion in thought and opinion, a groping and hesitancy about national affairs and private life alike." Old America seized on every sign that all was not lost. The successful solo flight of Charles Lindbergh to Paris in 1927 touched off a wave of hero worship unequaled since Washington's day. "Lindy," the clean-cut, blond young American from the Midwest, demonstrated that something survived of the noble past. His achievement, noted one social critic, showed "that we are *not* rotten at the core, but morally sound and sweet and good!" Old America also set off a series of confrontations that alternately disturbed and fascinated the nation.

The Klan Reborn. At its most disruptive and aggressive, Old America's counterattack took the form of a revived Ku Klux Klan. The Klan of Reconstruction days had not long survived the federal government's attack during the 1870s. But it lived on in the South's collective memory as the heroic savior of white culture and the enemy of "ignorant" blacks and their "rascally" carpetbagger allies. This view of the Klan was reinforced and widely disseminated when it was incorporated into a popular historical novel, *The Clansman* (1905), by Thomas Dixon. In 1915 the novel became the basis for D. W. Griffith's spectacular film *The Birth of a Nation*.

The movie profoundly moved William Simmons, an Atlanta Methodist preacher, sometime salesman, and professional organizer of fraternal orders. Soon after he saw it in Atlanta, he set about establishing a new "high class order for men of intelligence and character," which he named after its Reconstruction predecessor. The war's superpatriotism and intolerance helped swell the Klan's ranks to several thousand, all dedicated to defending white Protestant America against blacks, "aliens," and dissenters. After 1918, with the help of Edward Young Clarke and Elizabeth Tyler, two skilled publicists, Simmons capitalized on the anxiety that widespread social change had aroused in many native Americans to recruit members for his new organization.

The Klan represented the most extreme fringe of fundamentalist Protestant, traditional, white, native-born America. Utterly devoted to white supremacy, it held Catholics and Jews to be aliens, under obligation in one case to the pope and in the other to an international conspiracy. The Klan also considered itself a defender of traditional public morals. It endorsed Prohibition and denounced the liquor traffic; it attacked prostitution and sexual laxity; it warned wife beaters and criminals to cease their nefarious doings; it stood for "100 percent Americanism" and opposed all forms of radical ideology.

During the 1920s the Klan became a political force in the rural parts of the nation, especially in the South, Midwest, and Far West. It even penetrated the big cities, where it appealed to white Protestants recently arrived from rural areas, who felt lost amid the social and ethnic diversity that surrounded them. The Invisible Empire entered politics in many states and cities. At one time it virtually controlled the governments of Indiana and Oregon. Denver and Dallas fell under its sway; in Denver it succeeded

in defeating the reelection bid of the famous liberal judge Ben Lindsey.

For a while it looked as if the Klan could not be stopped. By 1925 there were 3 million Klansmen, and their presence was felt everywhere. Daytime Klan parades of sheeted, robed men and nighttime gatherings under immense fiery crosses became common in many American communities. Some Klansmen were well-meaning but misguided men who sincerely believed that they were upholding decency and traditional values. Yet many lawless people hid behind Klan regalia and secrecy to lynch blacks, tar and feather supposed radicals, and wreck the businesses of Catholic and Jewish merchants.

Outraged by Klan atrocities, various Catholic, Jewish, black, and liberal groups fought back. Many big-city newspapers, led by the *New York World*, denounced it. Even many conservative Protestants, frightened by its divisive influence on the nation, detested the Klan.

This counterassault was aided by the hypocrisy of Klan leaders. Thousands of dollars poured into Klan coffers, but much of the money stuck to the fingers of Klan officials. Even more damaging were instances of sexual laxity by several prominent Klan leaders. For an organization that denounced the ethical slackness of the times and appointed itself the guardian of community morals, the financial and carnal weaknesses of its leaders were damaging blows.

By 1925 or 1926 the Klan was in retreat; by 1930 it was practically dead. But it had established a precedent, and in later years, when social tensions once more intensified, it would again become a vehicle for hate, intolerance, and mindless superpatriotism.

Night riders, in Virginia, out for a daytime drive with their ladies, 1921. This second incarnation of the Klan had a larger political base than the first.

The Klan fight was only one of many battles pitting Old and New American against each other. Two others were the Scopes trial in Dayton, Tennessee, in 1925 and the presidential election of 1928.

The Scopes Trial. The Scopes trial brought to a boil the simmering dispute between the liberal Protestantism and secularism of the big cities and the fundamentalism of Old America. Fundamentalism was not a new force in American life. Ever since the Gilded Age, conservative Protestants, as we saw in Chapter 22, had fought againt Darwin's teachings and against attacks on orthodox Christian views, hoping to stop what they saw as the erosion of old-fashioned Bible religion and the growth of atheism.

Education became a major battleground between the conservative fundamentalists and the liberal modernists. Conservatives held that the schools had to be kept from purveying skepticism and irreligion; modernists held that teachers had to be free to teach the latest theories of science, wherever they led. Inevitably, Darwinism and evolution became the focus of a furious battle over the schools between the Old and the New America.

The confrontation came to a head in 1925 when the Tennessee legislature passed the Butler Law, which made the teaching of Darwin's theory of evolution illegal in the state's public schools. Many Tennesseans had had misgivings about the measure but had been afraid to oppose its passage. In the small town of Dayton, however, a young high school biology teacher named John Scopes proved more courageous. When a group of his friends suggested casually over lemon phosphates at Robinson's Drug Store that he challenge the law, Scopes agreed. Several days later he lectured to his class on evolution and was arrested.

The response of outsiders to Scopes's arrest was startling. The venerable William Jennings Bryan volunteered to help the prosecutor protect traditional America from the theory that humanity had evolved from lower forms of life. The American Civil Liberties Union (ACLU), an organization dedicated to free speech, joined the prominent liberal lawyer Clarence Darrow in helping the defense. All the major wire services set up shop in sleepy Dayton. Reporters representing the major newspapers poured into the town. So did many curiosity seekers and hundreds of local farmers. The square in front of Dayton's courthouse became a county fair with hawkers of soft drinks, souvenirs, fans, books, and religious tracts everywhere.

Scopes's guilt was never in question; he had violated the letter of the law. But Darrow and the ACLU

Bryan (left) was an attorney for the prosecution at the Scopes trial, but Darrow had him called as a defense witness to try to poke holes in his literal interpretation of the Bible. The Scopes trial was the last political battle of Bryan's long and frustrated career; he died shortly afterward.

were far more interested in striking a blow against what they belived to be the irrationality and ignorance of traditional America than in establishing their client's innocence. At one point Darrow declared that his purpose was to "show up Fundamentalism . . . to prevent bigots and ignoramuses from controlling the educational system of the United States." Enraged, Bryan responded that his purpose was to "protect the word of God against the greatest atheist and agnostic in the United States."

Neither side came off well in the encounter. Bryan was revealed as grossly misinformed about modern science; Darrow showed himself to be a cocky smart aleck. The trial accomplished nothing. The jury found Scopes guilty and fined him $100, but the state supreme court later threw out the verdict on a technicality. The law remained on the books, and its violator went free. Still, though the results were anticlimactic, the Scopes trial provided a window into the forces contending for America's cultural soul.

The Election of 1928. Equally dramatic and more momentous for the country was the 1928 presidential election. The contestants were Secretary of Commerce Herbert Hoover and Alfred E. Smith, the progressive Democratic governor of New York.

The two men seemed complete opposites. Smith was an extrovert who loved clubhouse politics and enjoyed the company of men and women from all walks of life. Hoover was a painfully shy man who seldom evoked warm personal affection. Smith was a natty dresser who made his trademark the striped suit and the brown derby that had been high fashion in his youth. Hoover's clothes were almost always conservative, well cut, and black. Smith's formal education was slight, Hoover was a mining engineer, a graduate of Stanford University, and a world traveler. Most important of all, Smith's origins were urban, Irish-Catholic, and wet. Hoover was a Quaker from the tiny hamlet of West Branch, Iowa, of mixed English-German stock, who believed Prohibition was "a great social and economic experiment, noble in motive and far-reaching in purpose."

Traditional Americans distrusted Al Smith and what he stood for. And some of their reservations—to Smith's Tammany Hall affiliations, to his dislike of Prohibition—were clearly valid by any usual political measure. There was also nothing wrong with rural voters questioning his knowledge of, and concern for, the farm problem. Hoover, the wartime food administrator from Iowa, obviously was better informed and more concerned. But traditional voters often displayed an ugly bigotry toward the Democratic candidate's religion as well. At the lowest level there was the Klan's blind, unthinking prejudice against Catholicism as a perversion of Gospel Christianity and an evil international force.

More sophisticated critics charged that Catholics did not accept American traditions such as the separation of church and state and secular public education. One Vermonter expressed the essentials of the anti-Smith position succinctly when he prayed that "the good Lord and the Southland [might] keep us safe from the rule of the Wet, Tammany, Roman Catholic Booze Gang."

No Democrat could have won in 1928. However divided over short skirts, the pope, jazz, the Eighteenth Amendment, and the foreign-born, most Americans agreed that the country had never been so prosperous. During the campaign, while some Republicans attacked Smith's religion and his personal social preferences, others, including the Republican nominee himself, played up the blessings of good times. "Given a chance to go forward with the policies of the last eight years," Hoover intoned in his acceptance speech to the Republican convention, "we shall soon with the help of God be in sight of the day when poverty will be banished from this nation." Elect the great engineer, the Republi-

can campaign slogans declared, and there would be a "chicken in every pot and two cars in every garage." Good times, added to the fear of Catholicism, made the Republican ticket unbeatable in November 1928.

Nevertheless, the Democratic candidate did exceptionally well in the cities. If thousands in the South and the rural West and North voted against him because of his Catholicism, thousands of others in the northern cities voted for him for the same reason. Catholic women, especially, who had not voted in large numbers in the two previous presidential elections, came to the polls in record numbers in 1928 and voted Democratic. In some Irish and Italian election districts in New York City, Smith received 97 or 98 percent of the total vote! Viewing the campaign in the context of American party history from the Civil War to the

Al Smith waves to his supporters during a 1928 rally. Although he lost the election, his party would win the next five with the support of the coalition Smith assembled. Voter turnout was 30 percent higher in 1928 than in 1924.

present, Smith's candidacy marks a point where the urban immigrant vote, which had been loosened from its nineteenth-century Democratic moorings by World War I and Republican New Era prosperity, became more strongly fastened to the Democrats than ever before. Hoover carried 40 of the 48 states, with 444 electoral votes and over 21 million popular votes, to Smith's 87 electoral votes and 15 million popular ones. For the first time since Reconstruction, Texas, Florida, North Carolina, Tennessee, and Virginia went Republican. On the face of it, it was a Democratic disaster. In reality, it was the beginning of a great resurgence that would soon make the Democrats the party of the normal American majority.

Conclusions

Herbert Hoover took the oath of office in March 1929. In his inaugural address he told the American people that he had "no fears for the future of the country." The years ahead were "bright with hope." However wrong he proved to be, Hoover was expressing the optimism that many Americans felt, and he and they had good reason for their sunny expectations.

The decade was a period of unusual achievement. For the middle class and upper levels of American wage earners, it was a breakthrough into a new affluence. It was also a time of expanding freedom for women, young people, and intellectuals, and it was a creative age generally in the arts.

But the decade had a darker side. It was a time of contraction for farmers and of severe material limits for the semiskilled and unskilled. It was also a decade of bitter cultural and social strife. Between 1919 and 1929 an older, rural, traditional, native, fundamentalist America collided with a newer, urban, modernist, foreign-born, non-Protestant America. The Klan, immigration restriction, Prohibition, political intolerance, and organized crime were all ugly manifestations of that cultural clash.

And now a new force was about to intrude into the cultural battleground. Eight months into Hoover's term the stock market collapsed, altering the lives of millions of Americans and the course of the nation's history.

For Further Reading

Frederick Lewis Allen. *Only Yesterday: An Informal History of the 1920s* (1931)

> This 1932 bestseller vividly sketches the politics, morals, fashions, heroes, business, and arts of the "bally-hoo" twenties. Allen popularized the theory that the collapse of Wilsonian idealism left Americans disillusioned and discontented, prey to Mah-Jongg, Freudianism, marathon dances, and real estate speculation in Florida.

Irving Bernstein. *The Lean Years* (1960)

> A history of the American worker from 1920 to 1933. Bernstein describes the very different responses of organized and unorganized workers to change, the role played by employer associations, and the courts' use of injunctions to break strikes.

Ray Ginger. *Six Days or Forever? Tennessee* v. *John Thomas Scopes* (1958)

> Ginger analyzes the cultural and political background of the Tennessee law and the subsequent "monkey trial." His sharp, witty portraits of Darrow and Bryan are entertaining, and quotations from the court proceedings make this book valuable for research as well as good general reading.

William E. Leuchtenburg. *The Perils of Prosperity, 1914–1932* (1958)

> Brief and beautifully written. Leuchtenburg treats the cultural conflicts of the 1920s, industrial development, labor, morals, and the nature and limits of the decade's prosperity. He emphasizes the confrontation of the city and the small town, believing it to be the key to understanding America in these years.

Robert S. Lynd and Helen M. Lynd. *Middletown: A Study in Modern American Culture* (1929)

> In this classic sociological study of Muncie, Indiana, during the 1920s, the Lynds examine the effects of mass production, the car, electricity, and advertising on attitudes toward work, leisure, eduction, the family, and the community.

Robert K. Murray. *Red Scare: A Study in National Hysteria, 1919–1920* (1955)

> A fine study of the post–World War I Palmer raids. Murray is highly critical of the attorney general's brutal disregard of civil liberties.

William Manchester. *Disturber of the Peace: The Life of H. L. Mencken* (1951)

> A state legislature once prayed for his soul. College presidents blamed him for undergraduate suicides. Mencken retorted that America needed a wave of suicides among college presidents. Superpatriots,

public officials, intellectuals, reformers, and "homo boobiens"—none were safe from Mencken's gibes.

Roderick Nash. *The Nervous Generation*: *American Thought, 1917–1930* (1970)

Nash writes of the uncertainty and contradiction in American thinking about war, democracy, the nation, aesthetics, nature, humanity, and ethics during the 1920s. He also examines the heroes, popular literature, moral and social crusades, and religious life of the period.

Andrew Sinclair. *Prohibition*: *Era of Excess* (1962)

Sinclair explores the social and psychological forces behind the enactment and repeal of Prohibition. Considering the events of those thirteen dry years, he judges Americans to be born extremists with strong compulsions to make and break laws.

Paula Fass. *The Damned and the Beautiful*: *American Youth in the 1920s* (1977)

The title is misleading; this is really a book about college youth in the twenties. But on that subject it is the last word. If you think some of your own peers are not serious enough about their education, be assured that they are dedicated scholars compared with "Betty Coed" and "Joe College" of the 1920s.

Geoffrey Perrett. *America in the Twenties*: *A History* (1982)

A brilliant account of a period that has often inspired brilliant writing. One of Perrett's major themes is the contrast between the Old and New America that characterized the era.

Chapter 26

The New Deal

Too Far or Not Far Enough?

1929　Depression begins with financial panic on Wall Street • President Hoover increases federal spending on current projects but avoids deficit spending

1930　4 million Americans are unemployed • Hawley-Smoot Tariff

1932–35　Drought makes Great Plains a "dust bowl"

1932　Congress establishes the Reconstruction Finance Corporation (RFC) • Dispersal of the Bonus Army • Franklin D. Roosevelt elected president

1933–35　First New Deal

1933　Roosevelt orders a four-day "bank holiday" • New Deal legislation and agencies: Emergency Banking Act, Agricultural Adjustment Act (AAA), National Industrial Recovery Act (NIRA), Public Works Administration (PWA), National Recovery Administration (NRA), Home Owners Loan Corporation (HOLC), Federal Emergency Relief Act, Civilian Conservation Corps (CCC), Federal Deposit Insurance Corporation (FDIC), Tennessee Valley Authority (TVA), Civil Works Administration (CWA)

1934　Securities and Exchange Commission established • Conservative Democrats and wealthy Republicans form the anti-Roosevelt Liberty League

1935–38　Second New Deal

1935　Legislation: Emergency Relief Act, National Labor Relations (Wagner) Act, Social Security Act, Public Uility Holding Company Act, Revenue (Wealth Tax) Act, Banking Act, Frazier-Lemke Farm Mortgage Moratorium Act, Resettlement Administration Act, Rural Electrification Act • The Supreme Court strikes down the NIRA • Committee on Industrial Organizations (CIO) formed • The Supreme Court invalidates the AAA • Huey Long is assassinated • Benny Goodman organizes his own orchestra

1936　Roosevelt reelected president • Soil Conservation and Domestic Allotment Act

1937　Roosevelt's attempt to "pack" the Supreme Court • General Motors Corporation and United States Steel recognize unions as the bargaining agents for their employees • Chicago police kill ten while breaking up a strike against Republic Steel • The Farm Security Administration established • Wagner-Steagall Housing Act

1938　Agricultural Adjustment Act • Food, Drug, and Cosmetic Act • Fair Labor Standards Act

The New Deal, that wide-ranging movement to end the Great Depression, ease the country's massive social problems, and alter the structure of the freewheeling 1920s American economy, has always been controversial. Contemporaries on the right called it "socialistic" and believed it had destroyed fundamental American liberties. On the left, critics past and present have condemned it for preserving America's capitalist institutions and the inequalities of wealth and power that went with them. According to Barton J. Bernstein, "The liberal reformers of the New Deal did not transform the American system; they conserved the protected American corporate capitalism. . . . There was no significant redistribution of power in American society, only limited recognition of other organized groups, seldom of unorganized peoples." Other recent historians and political scientists have blamed the New Deal for initiating an enormous expansion of federal and presidential influence that has impoverished local governments reduced individual freedom, and permitted serious abuses of executive power.

Was the New Deal's role in American life positive or negative? Did the New Deal fall short of the goals it set for itself? Were its goals too limited? Did it really create as many problems for our society as it solved? To answer these questions we must look at the difficulties the nation faced during the Great Depression, and for this purpose we must turn back to the closing months of the New Era.

Boom and Bust

Nineteen twenty-nine was a dazzling year for American capitalism. By almost every measure the economy had never performed so well. Automobile production reached almost 4.5 million units, 800,000 more than in 1928; steel production climbed to 5 million tons above the year before. Manufacturing output as a whole reached an all-time peak. Late in the summer the stock market soared to a historic high, with shares in American corporations selling for prices never before attained. When economists got around to figuring out the gross national product for 1929, they would put it at over $104 billion, or $857 for every man, woman, and child—25 percent higher than a decade before.

Life for millions of Americans seemed good as the 1920s drew to a close. Over 20 million of the nation's 30 million families had automobiles. Radios were prized possessions in over 10 million households; many people were beginning to acquire electric washing machines and refrigerators. Almost half of all American families owned their own homes, and over two-thirds had electric power—twice the proportion of a decade previously. Never before had so many enjoyed so much. Despite some persistent dark spots, few Americans doubted that 1929 was a charmed year.

Abruptly, the spell broke. In the weeks following Labor Day the stock market, which had been rising at an unprecedented rate for three years, dropped and dropped again. On Thursday, October 24, a record-breaking 13 million shares changed hands at prices so sharply deflated that $9 billion in investments were wiped out in that single day. Thousands of investors and speculators scrambled to sell rapidly falling stocks for whatever they could get. The New York banking houses, led by J. P. Morgan, Jr., tried to stem the tide as Morgan's father had done in the Panic of 1907, but this time the effort failed. On October 29, 16 million shares were sold, with prices down an average of 40 points.

For the next two and half years the 1920s "bull market" deflated. At times there were rallies, but they were short-lived. By July 1932 stock prices had reached bottom at a fraction of their former value and would recover only very slowly. During the long slide over $70 billion of investments and paper wealth were wiped out, $616 for every person in the country!

Causes of the Depression. Americans often blamed the stock market crash for their plight. The blame was not entirely misplaced. The Crash impaired for years the ability of American business and industry to raise money by borrowing from banks or selling stock. If the blind optimism of stock market investors during the New Era had helped cause the Crash, the equally blind pessimism following the Crash helped prolong the Great Depression.

The stock market crash, however, was only the

most visible cause of economic collapse. The 1920s had been a time of economic growth, but that growth had depended on an unstable balance of factors. New markets for automobiles, radios, refrigerators, and other durables had induced business people to invest vast sums to expand production. In addition, governments had poured more billions into roads, bridges, and other capital improvements, while private citizens, now able to rely on the family automobile for quick transportation to city jobs, bought homes in the burgeoning suburbs. Pushed by the consumer durables revolution, construction, steel, cement, petroleum, rubber, and scores of other industries boomed, creating jobs and income for millions of urban Americans. Most people came to see the new affluence as normal and to assume that it would never end. President Hoover shared the prevailing confidence that somehow America had discovered the formula for permanent growth and prosperity.

Both the president and the people were wrong. Few contemporaries discerned that the boom was sustained by the special circumstances of the consumer durables revolution and could not outlast it. And the end of the revolution was inevitable. With 50 percent of the nation's income going to only 20 percent of its families, the market for expensive consumer durables, though wider than in the past, was strictly limited. When all those who could afford the new car or the new radio had satisfied their needs, demand had to decline. By 1927 or 1928 these effects were already being felt and manufacturers were beginning to cut production and lay off workers. A spiral was now set in motion: Fewer new orders for goods led to fewer jobs; the unemployed in turn could not buy what the factories produced and so orders further declined.

This pattern was soon evident in many enterprises. Building starts, the most sensitive barometer of economic conditions, leveled off in 1926 and dropped sharply in 1929. Expansion in the public sector also reached its limits: The new road network was largely complete, and the need for new highways became less urgent. State highway departments were soon investing less and hiring fewer people. Over all, the massive push to invest, which had fed the economy since World War I, had lost its momentum.

The international economy also contributed to the decline. The burdens of war debts and tariff barriers were becoming harder and harder to bear as the decade neared its end. England and France had emerged from World War I owing enormous debts to America. Their foreign investments drastically reduced, they no longer received the dividends that had formerly enabled them

to buy American goods. Lower American tariff barriers might have permitted them to sell more in the United States, in turn allowing them to buy American commodities and pay their American debts. But, as we have seen, the United States raised tariffs during the 1920s, a policy that made it increasingly difficult for the British, French, and other Europeans to sell their goods in America, buy American exports, and pay their American creditors.

Britain and France saw German reparations as the way out of their dilemma. If the Germans could be compelled to pay the $33 billion indemnity set by the postwar Reparations Commission, all would be well: German reparations could then be used to buy American coal, wheat, steel, and automobiles. The sum was unrealistic. The Germans could not pay it, and in two successive stages (the Dawes Plan, 1924, and the Young Plan, 1929) the payments were pared down and stretched out. For a while large-scale lending by American banks took up the slack, enabling the former Allies to buy American goods on credit. By 1928, however, the bankers were beginning to have second

October 29, 1929, the Day of Judgment—or so it seemed. The financial structure that had supported the New Era's prosperity collapsed, generating a tidal wave of misfortune that affected every American.

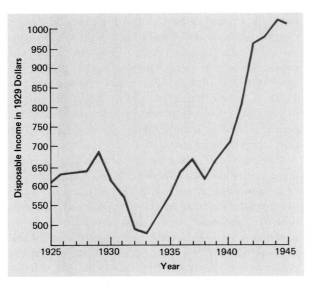

Per capita disposable income, 1925–1945

Source: Historical Statistics of the United States, Colonial Times to 1970.

thoughts about foreign loans. The whole shaky structure of foreign trade was now in jeopardy.

Finally, the Wall Street bull market was itself a cause of serious instability in the 1920s economy. During the early 1920s many corporation stocks sold at low prices relative to the dividends they yielded; that is, whatever the price of the stock, each dollar invested repaid healthy dividends. A few years of good returns brought a flood of investors into the market, and the

Unemployment, 1929–1945

Source: Historical Statistics of the United States, Colonial Times to 1970.

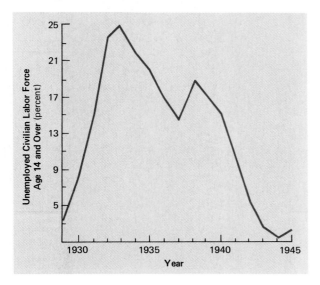

huge sums of money they invested helped finance spectacular industrial growth. After 1926, however, many investments were on paper only; that is, many of the investors were speculators gambling heavily with borrowed money. Under the rules of the day, stock could be bought with as little as 10 percent down, a practice known as buying "on margin." The rest of the money needed to make up the purchase price could be borrowed from a broker, who in turn would borrow it from a banker. This system put billions of borrowed money into the market and drove up stock prices, producing a glut of paper wealth. Speculators paid outrageous prices and borrowed beyond their ability to repay on the blithe assumption that prices would keep going up and rescue them. If stock prices fell, however, all the players in the system—speculators, brokers, and bankers—would be locked together and fall together. The speculators, unable to pay back the loans from the brokers, would default. When enough speculators defaulted, brokers would be unable to pay off the bank loans, and would also default. When enough brokers defaulted, the banks would go bankrupt. The chain of failures would depress stock prices even more, further reducing the value of holdings and the ability to avoid default all along the chain.

The Great Depression. The collapse of the stock market when business was already weakened by declining consumer demand and a shaky international economy brought the entire structure down with a resounding crash. Credit became tight, and interest rates soared. The Federal Reserve Board, which could have eased the situation by lowering the interest rate charged to member banks, took no action to shore up the banking system. To save themselves, banks cut off credit to businesses and foreign borrowers. All trade slowed, but foreign commerce, which had been sustained largely by constant infusions of American credit, was hit especially hard.

The collapse of the world's principal source of financing upset the entire international system. The trading nations had used a currency exchange system pegged to the price of gold, which now collapsed. As the gold standard fell apart, values of goods and currencies fluctuated wildly, making people millionaires one minute and paupers the next. To protect their economies from the chaos in exchange rates, nations resorted to strict trade barriers and tariffs. Under the double blow of trade restrictions and collapse of the currency exchange system, international trade declined to a trickle. By mid-1930 the Depression had been exported from America and was virtually worldwide.

Now came the turn of the banks. Frightened depositors rushed to withdraw their savings. Bank after bank failed as the "runs" forced even solvent institutions into bankruptcy. In November 1930, 256 banks with deposits of $180 million closed their doors. Most severely affected were the financial institutions of the farm areas where bank failures had been numerous even in the 1920s.

The shock to general investor confidence overshadowed all other effects. The Crash badly frightened the people who made the economy's major decisions to invest. By 1932 gross private domestic investment had sunk to one-ninth the 1929 amount.

Consumers, too, turned timid after the Crash and ceased to make their indispensable contribution to the economy. By wiping out billions of dollars in assets, the Crash instantly reduced the expenditures of the thousands of upper-income families headed by men and women who had bought stock. Though not numerous enough to make a difference to farmers or to manufacturers of soap, shoes, and hairpins, their belt tightening cut sharply into the sale of luxury automobiles, golf clubs, and expensive restaurant dinners. The Crash also had a disastrous effect on ordinary consumers. Few were directly hit by the market collapse, but their confidence in the economy rapidly waned. Here the nation's very affluence hurt it. In former times cosumers had had little choice about whether to spend or not because almost all of their income went for necessities. But in this rich era of mass markets for expensive durables and other former luxuries, they could cut expenditures—and did. People put off vacation trips and decided not to buy new radios, cars, or refrigerators; all consumer durables sales plummeted. The most durable of all durable goods—houses—could be deferred the longest, and new housing sales dropped off disastrously.

The economic retreat quickly became a rout. Deferring purchases and investment at first was largely voluntary, but it soon became inescapable. As unsold inventories built up in stores and showrooms, retailers reduced their orders to manufacturers and suppliers. They in turn lowered their investment goals, cut back on production, slashed wages, and fired employees. Unemployment shot up. By the end of 1930 over 4 million men and women were out of work. Many more were working part-time or for sharply reduced wages. Families whose breadwinners lost their jobs cut their budgets to the bone. Total demand now declined still further, establishing a vicious downward spiral of economic deflation.

If commodity prices had fallen as far and as fast as consumer income, goods might have continued to move, and workers might have kept their jobs. Prices did fall in certain areas of the economy. Where there were many competitive producers, most notably in agriculture, prices plummeted. Between 1929 and 1933 agricultural prices declined 56 percent, but the output of farm products and the number of farmers and farm laborers remained almost the same. The drop in the price of produce was unfortunate for farmers, but it kept farm production and farm employment high and prevented widespread hunger. In segments of the economy where there were relatively few producers and competition was limited, however, prices stayed high. Automobiles remained expensive—about $600 for the average vehicle both in 1929 and in 1932. Because most people could not buy cars, production—and employment—fell. By 1932 automobile output had dropped to 25 percent of the 1929 figure, and the number of automobile workers had declined to a fraction of the 1929 total.

The Great Crash and ensuing Great Depression spared neither working-class nor middle-class people, though clearly the former suffered more absolute deprivation. The Depression's near universality made it an exceptionally potent political force.

Many American artists of the 1930s found the Depression a fascinating subject. Here, in *Shoeshine*, George Grosz sums up the era's economic misery in the person of a huddled shoeshine boy.

The Human Toll.   The Great Depression was a human disaster of colossal proportions. Despair spread through every part of the country and penetrated every walk of life. By the winter of 1932/33 a quarter of those Americans who wanted work were without jobs. The situation of blue-collar wage earners, who had few resources to cushion them against adversity, was the worst. Millions of factory hands and construction workers tramped the streets looking for work or waited in lines to apply for handouts from charity organizations. But hard times did not respect class lines. Small business people went bankrupt as their customers dwindled. Lawyers had fewer clients, and the clients they retained could not afford to pay high fees. Doctors and dentists discovered that most of their patients put eating before health care. The sharp decline in building and construction left architects without clients.

Private agencies were not equipped to handle the thousands of destitute families who applied for help. Nor could state and local governments provide relief. During the Depression three states and hundreds of municipalities went bankrupt trying to cope with widespread want at a time when tax revenues were declining. Few, if any, Americans died of starvation. But many went hungry, and doctors saw thousands of cases of malnutrition.

What did the unemployed and their families do to survive? Most of them had little to fall back on. When a family's savings had been exhausted, day-to-day survival became precarious. Men and women borrowed money from pawnbrokers, from friends, or against insurance policies, until all sources dried up. In past times Americans had often dealt with their problems by abandoning them. And so it was again. Many young men and women took to the road, traveling from hobo jungle to hobo jungle by freight train, dodging railroad police, begging, or working at ill-paying odd jobs. So many were riding the rails by 1933 that railroad officials decided to accept the inevitable and told their guards to look the other way. Some of the unemployed tried setting up small undercapitalized stores. Other sold apples on the streets. These pathetic efforts became symbols of pluck and determination, but they seldom succeeded.

One of the most urgent problems of the unemployed and their families was housing. Without income, a family could not pay the rent or the mortgage. A common sight on city streets was the dispossessed family sitting disconsolately on their streetside furniture, not knowing where to go. (A joke that made the rounds in 1933 was a version of an old classic. Bill asks Mike: "Who was that lady I saw you with last night at the sidewalk café?" Mike replies: "That was no lady; that was my wife. And that was no sidewalk café; that was my apartment furniture.") Thousands of Americans moved in with friends or relatives. On the outskirts of every large city the unemployed and their families moved into squatters' settlements thrown together from loose boards, packing crates, sheet tin, and cardboard. In Oakland, California, jobless men set up housekeeping in surplus sewer pipes. In western Pennsylvania unemployed steelworkers kept warm by sleeping in the big coke ovens of the idle steel plants. For the first time migration from the country to the city was reversed as young men and women returned in droves to the rural homestead.

Among the most unfortunate victims of the Great Depression were many of the nation's 12.5 million blacks. In the North, where black Americans had only

Private charities tried to relieve the effects of poverty and unemployment during the 1930s, but were overwhelmed by conditions. Here black children in Harlem line up to receive food from a Catholic agency.

recently found a toehold in industry, they were often the first to lose their jobs when employers cut back their work force. Besides, construction, bituminous coal mining, and domestic service, which provided employment for large numbers of blacks, were among the occupations that were particularly depressed. In April 1931, 35 percent of the black workers in Philadelphia were unemployed, compared with 24 percent of white wage earners.

In the South the lot of the black population was even bleaker. The economic crisis provided a new basis for white bigotry. In Houston black and Mexican-American relief applicants were regularly turned down by officials. In Atlanta, in 1930, a group of Klanlike "Black Shirts" paraded downtown carrying banners inscribed "Niggers, back to the cotton fields—city jobs are for white folks." Things were no better in the cotton fields. In 1931 the price of cotton slumped to 4.6 cents a pound, the lowest since 1894. Producers of cotton, farmers and sharecroppers, black and white alike, suffered severely. Early that year a Red Cross worker in a rural cotton-growing area of Arkansas found that more than half the homes he visited did not have enough food to last forty-eight hours.

Life Goes On. Despite hard times a majority of Americans continued to work and to provide their families with the necessities of life. They even managed to enjoy themselves. During the winter of 1929/30 a craze for miniature golf took hold, and by the summer of 1930 thousands of Americans were tapping golf balls through drainpipes and over little bridges. By 1930 radio had produced its first superstars: Freeman F. Gosden and Charles J. Correll, both whites, who amused listeners with their comic stereotypes of the ignorant but cunning black characters Amos 'n Andy. The theater flourished as well. In the fall of 1931 the big Broadway hit was *Of Thee I Sing*, a musical spoof of American politics. Equally popular that season was George White's *Scandals*, featuring Rudy Vallee singing "Life Is Just a Bowl of Cherries."

Through the worst years of the Depression, Hollywood continued to prosper. During the 1930s, 85 million Americans went to the nation's 17,000 movie houses each week. While the country lived on short rations, movie moguls like Louis B. Mayer and Sam Goldwyn and stars like Carole Lombard, Greta Garbo, Clark Gable, Joan Crawford, and James Cagney earned thousands of dollars a week. The public did not seem to mind Hollywood's affluence. The movies provided an escape from the drabness and worries of their lives, and they were grateful.

Reading was another form of escape during the Great Depression. Publishers were equal to the challenge of hard times. Using the high-speed presses employed by magazines, along with glued bindings and paper covers, they reduced the price of reprints to as little as a quarter. Before long the public was buying millions of "pocketbooks" and other paperbound volumes by such entertaining writers as Hervey Allen (*Anthony Adverse*, 1933), Pearl S. Buck (*The Good Earth*, 1931), Edna Ferber (*Show Boat*, 1936), James Hilton (*Lost Horizon*, 1933, and *Goodbye, Mr. Chips*, 1934), and the biggest best-seller of all, Margaret Mitchell, whose "moonlight and magnolias" epic of the Old South, *Gone with the Wind* (1936), sold 8 million copies by the time of her death. Paralleling the paperback revolution was the picture magazine revolution ushered in by *Life* magazine in 1936. Mixing brilliant photography with the breezy verbal style developed by Henry Luce and his *Time* editors, *Life* and its imitators provided the American public with light-hearted glimpses of culture, customs, and costume, as well as grimmer "photo-essays" of the world in distress.

Popular music, too, helped people, especially the young, get through the bleak days. New Orleans–type jazz had gone into eclipse with the end of good times, though here and there black, and a few white, musicians continued to play Dixieland or Chicago-style jazz in small ensembles. By the early 1930s black arrangers, including Edward ("Duke") Ellington, Fletcher Henderson, and Sy Oliver, had adapted jazz to the big-band format. Then, in 1935, clarinetist Benny Goodman created a sensation with a new sort of big-band dance music, "swing." Thousands were soon dancing the Lindy Hop, the Suzie-Q, and the Big Apple to the arrangements of Tommy Dorsey, Glenn Miller, and Count Basie, as well as the King of Swing himself. In 1938, swing became a part of "culture" when the Goodman band gave a sensational concert at New York's Carnegie Hall.

Hoover and the Depression

Though a few Americans prospered and others managed to squeeze some pleasure from life, the vast majority found their lives contracting with each passing day.

As we view the era from the present, the reaction of the federal government seems limited and slow. But we must recognize that it took months before anyone could assess how serious the damage had been and, in any case, there was a very strong presumption that self-righting forces would soon assert themselves. Besides, orthodox economic doctrine held that govenment could only play a limited role in financial crises.

Federal Inaction. President Herbert Hoover was one of the more ardent believers in the necessity for business to regulate itself. His rigid adherence to the ideas of

The movie business suffered less from the Depression than many others. Americans needed diversion, and 25 cents for admission to a musical bought them two hours of escape from harsh realities.

rugged individualism was perhaps appropriate to the 1920s, but it now proved disastrous. Republican orthodoxy held that periodic depressions were natural and inevitable, a sort of purging of the poisonous from the economy. Andrew W. Mellon, the secretary of the treasury, proposed that the adminstration do nothing whatever and allow the downturn to find its own level. Though Hoover was a confident and energetic man, willing to take decisive action, he, too, was reluctant to use the power of government to impede the business cycle.

But the president was not in total agreement with his secretary of the treasury. In November 1929 he called a series of conferences of business and labor leaders and local government officials to consider the economic crisis. At his urging they pledged to maintain wages, desist from strikes, and continue the existing level of investment and local public works spending. Simultaneously, because he was convinced that the collapse of confidence was an important component of the slump, Hoover went to great pains to exude optimism. The "fundamental business of the country," he told the public several days after the Crash, "is on a sound and prosperous basis." What the country needed, he later declared, was a "big laugh" or a "great poem" to make people "forget their troubles and the Depression." The collapse was certain to be short-lived if everyone retained faith in the system and resolved to buy and invest as in the past.

As the dreary months passed, each worse than the preceding, voluntary efforts to maintain spending, employment, and investment levels became inadequate. The obvious solution was a public works program to get the unemployed back on the job and put money into the hands of consumers and investors. Hoover did increase the federal government's planned outlays for public projects, and because federal tax revenues had plummeted, he could not avoid a deficit in doing so. But he steadfastly refused to allow the govenment to adopt a deliberate policy of borrowing money to finance massive public works. In his view, such a procedure would force it into competition with weakened private industry for limited investment funds and injure the economy further. Actually, by 1930 or 1931 business confidence was so thoroughly riddled that virtually no business people wanted to borrow; there was no need for the president to worry about the government outbidding private industry for limited capital.

Hoover was not alone in his failure to perceive the appropriate policies for a time of mass unemployment and underused capital equipment. Few people during the Depression understood that the only cure

for the collapse of private business expectations was for the federal government to stimulate the economy by deficit spending—spending beyond what it took in in taxes. The rigid belief in a balanced budget, shared by Republicans and Democrats alike, had to die a bitter death before the government would use deficit spending to aid economic recovery.

Hoover's limited fiscal understanding was coupled with a reluctance to use federal funds to relieve human misery. The president argued that it was dangerous to make people dependent on federal handouts. Yet for a man whose early public reputation was earned as relief administrator for Europe during and immediately following World War I, Hoover seemed strangely insensitive to his fellow citizens' misfortunes. Aid to the unemployed, he believed, must come from voluntary organizations and local governments, not from Washington. Hoover's view disregarded realities. Private religious and charitable organizations could not come close to meeting the needs of the vast army of the unemployed; cities, counties, and states found themselves overwhelmed by demands on their resources. Only the federal government could deal with a disaster that deprived millions of the nation's families of their fundamental means of support.

Hoover's Programs. The president never endorsed direct federal outlays for relief, but gradually he came to see that something more than private talks with business and labor leaders, sprinkled with public smiles, was necessary to check the economic decline. As he pondered the causes of the nation's plight, Hoover concluded that they originated abroad. To help restore the international economy, in 1931 he proposed a one-year moratorium on German reparations and the intergovernmental debts of the former Allies.

This effort to restore international trade was a wise, if limited, move. But Hoover was inconsistent. The previous year, against the advice of the country's best economists, he had accepted a traditional Republican solution to economic difficulties and signed the Hawley-Smoot Tariff Act, which raised the already high American protective wall and further weakened international trade.

By late 1931 Hoover finally recognized that the federal government must intervene directly in the domestic economy to get the country moving again. In his State of the Union message to Congress, he proposed establishing a Reconstruction Finance Corporation (RFC) to lend federal funds to business on the theory that the loans would check the economic slide, restore confidence, and increase employment. Congress set up the RFC in 1932 and gave it a $500 million appropriation with authority to raise $1.5 billion more by borrowing. These funds it could lend to faltering banks, railroads, savings and loan associations, and industrial firms. In addition, the president signed into law measures providing new capital to federal land banks, liberalizing the credit-granting powers of the Federal Reserve System, and establishing home loan banks to refinance home mortgages.

Hoover's liberal opponents labeled his progam, particularly the RFC, a "breadline for big business" that only indirectly touched the plight of ordinary men and women. To be fair to Hoover, his moves—though tardy and insufficient—were steps in the right direction. But Hoover got little credit from the public for his vigorous actions in the last two years of his administration. He lacked the popular touch and appeared far too stiff and formal. Characteristically, through the worst years of his term, he continued to wear formal clothes when dining at the White House, even when he and his wife were alone. As the economic clouds became ever darker, the president's popularity plummeted. Soon people were referring to empty pockets turned inside out as "Hoover flags," shantytowns on the outskirts of cities as "Hoovervilles," and newspapers wrapped around the body for warmth as "Hoover blankets."

The Bonus Expeditionary Force. Most difficult to forgive, in the public's estimate, was the president's treatment of the Bonus Army. World War I veterans were among the "forgotten men" of the Depression. In 1924 Congress had authorized a "delayed bonus" for veterans, to be paid in 1945. In 1931, over Hoover's veto, Congress liberalized the law to allow veterans to borrow immediately up to 50 percent of the amount ultimately due them. This money was gratefully accepted but quickly spent, and veterans, like most Americans, continued to suffer from the winding down of the economy. "Why wait until 1945 for the rest of the bonus?" veterans wondered. In June 1932 several thousand former doughboys, calling themselves the Bonus Expeditionary Force (BEF), arrived in Washington, D.C., to demand the remainder of the bonus immediately.

Most of the veterans camped out in tents and shacks at Anacostia Flats, a vacant area on the edge of the city. They asked to see the president, but he refused to have anything to do with them. When Congress rejected a new bonus bill, 15,000 veterans resolved to "stay till 1945." The men, many of whom had brought their wives and children, were orderly and sober. There were a few radicals and troublemak-

ers, but most were prepared to wait patiently for Congress to act. As the congressional session drew to a close, however, tensions mounted. Hoover was reluctant to involve the federal government in what he considered a local police problem; but when the District commissioners asked for federal help, the president called in the army.

The troops evicted the veterans from some abandoned buildings in the city and then, despite Hoover's orders not to cross the Anacostia River to the main BEF encampment, General Douglas MacArthur ordered his men onto Anacostia Flats. Firing tear gas in every direction, the soldiers put the tents and the shanties to the torch and drove the BEF out of the camp with bayonets and sabers. Over a hundred people were injured in the melee, and two infants died of tear gas inhalation.

The scene at Anacostia shocked many Americans. Men who had served their nation well had been treated like dangerous revolutionaries. Hoover's standing, already low, dropped still further. The president was not responsible for ordering the attack; but he had refused to see the BEF leaders and he shared the blame for the outcome.

Hoover Defeated. The Bonus Army was not the only episode of social confrontation during the first years of the Depression. Desperate midwestern farmers organized a "farm holiday" movement during mid-1932 that stopped shipments of food to cities, halted the forced sale of farms whose impoverished owners had fallen behind in tax payments, and dumped underpriced milk into gutters. In parts of the country hungry men looted stores and food delivery trucks. Early 1932 saw 3,000 unemployed men march on Henry Ford's River Rouge plant to demand jobs. Police used tear gas to stop them, and then opened fire with revolvers and a machine gun, killing four.

Still more ominous to convervatives was rising public interest in socialism as a solution to the crisis. Big business, which had claimed so much credit for good times, now bore the brunt of the public's wrath when times turned bad, and angry voices began to denounce capitalism as a cruel fraud against humanity. In September 1932 the Marxist journal *New Masses* published a symposium in which prominent intellectuals Edmund Wilson, Clifton Fadiman, Sherwood Anderson, Upton Sinclair and others declared that socialism alone could save the country. Two months later the Socialist party candidate for the presidency, Norman Thomas, received 880,000 votes, the largest Socialist vote since 1920.

Before New Deal programs began to operate, private charities were almost the sole sources of relief for the jobless. Louis Ribak in *Home Relief Station* shows how often they were sources of humiliation to the poor.

There is no way of telling how far the disenchantment with capitalism might have carried the American people if the nation had been forced to endure four more years of Hoover. Despair might have pushed Americans into communism or into a right-wing dictatorship such as emerged in central Europe in response to similar pressures. But, through the two-party system, Americans had an orderly and constitutional way to express their anguish, and they used it.

During the last two years of Hoover's administration the Democrats made steady political gains. In the congressional elections of 1930 they won control of both the House and Senate. The Democratic candidates did not offer drastic alternatives to the Republicans. In fact, many of them held political and economic views as conservative as Hoover's. Yet they could not be considered responsible for the debacle, and that in itself was enough to lure voters into the Democratic camp.

In the end the public got more than it expected. By early 1931 the Democratic presidential front-runner was Franklin D. Roosevelt, the governor of New York. FDR had achieved a commendable record in Albany by continuing the progressive policies of Al Smith. An only child born to comfort at Hyde Park, New York, Roosevelt had developed the confidence and poise that came with an assured position in society and the love of a doting mother. Though from an upper-class, old "Knickerbocker" family, he was a Democrat. In 1912 he supported Wilson for president and in 1913 went to Washington as assistant secretary of the navy. As a Wilson supporter, Roosevelt received the vice presidential nomination of his party in 1920. During the 1920s he contracted polio and for the rest of his life was confined to a wheelchair. The experience confirmed FDR's sense that any obstacle could be overcome with enough determination. Encouraged by his strong-willed wife, Eleanor, he refused to give up politics. In 1924 he ran for governor of New York and was elected, although Smith, the party's chief, went down to defeat in the presidential race. In 1930 Roosevelt was reelected governor in a landslide. Surrounded by astute political managers, a proven vote-getter in the nation's most populous state, FDR won the 1932 Democratic presidential nomination handily.

Hoover had little difficulty securing renomination. Though many Republicans had misgivings about the president, they could not deny their leader the chance for a second term. In a lackluster convention the president and vice president were renominated without opposition.

The campaign that followed was not an inspiring one. Neither party platform was especially bold or innovative. Nevertheless, Roosevelt promised increased aid to the unemployed and endorsed government involvement in electric power generation, national planning, and federal regulation of utilities and the stock market. The Democrats also favored the repeal of Prohibition. Hoover warned that Roosevelt's election would worsen the country's economic plight; but everywhere he went, he was greeted with hoots, catcalls, and hostile demonstrators accusing him of killing veterans or of personally causing the country's economic catastrophe. He soon became his party's worst liability, a man exuding gloom from every pore. On election day, as expected, Roosevelt and the Democrats were swept in with 23 million votes to Hoover's 16 million. FDR captured 282 counties that had never gone Democratic before.

FDR's New Deal

In the four months between the election and Roosevelt's inauguration, the economy plunged to a new low. During the early weeks of 1933 virtually every bank in the country stopped paying its depositors or tottered on the verge of doing so. To stave off legal bankruptcy, by March 4 the governors of thirty-eight states had been forced to declare bank holidays, allowing the banks to close their doors rather than acknowledge insolvency. By the eve of the inauguration.* it seemed that the whole financial structure on which American capitalism rested was about to crumble.

* Until the 20th Amendment to the Constitution was adopted in 1933, the president was inaugurated in early March.

During these dismal weeks President Hoover tried to enlist Roosevelt's cooperation on emergency measures. But even at this early point FDR favored more vigorous action to revive the economy and more humane measures than Hoover believed necessary and proper. The president-elect listened to Hoover's suggestions, but, unwilling to tie his hands, he refused to commit himself and his administration to anything.

The First Hundred Days. Roosevelt's inaugural speech set the tone for the early months of what would be called the New Deal. He proposed federal public works, measures to redistribute population from the cities to the country, to force up the prices of agricultural produce, to end home and farm foreclosure, to cut costs at all levels of government, to improve and make more efficient relief measures, and finally, to tighten federal regulation of banking and stock speculation. His specific proposals were less important than his tone and manner, however. The president told the American people that "fear itself" was the chief danger and that they must regain their confidence and self-esteem. If they worked hard, pulled together, and submitted to sacrifice and discipline, all would be well. He hoped that the normal balance of authority between Congress and the executive could be maintained in the days to come, but the crisis might call for expanded presidential authority. If necessary, he declared, he was prepared to ask for broad emergency powers similar to those he would need if the nation were facing a foreign invasion.

The response to the inaugural address was remarkable. In the succeeding days the White House received a half-million letters and telegrams from people who were deeply moved and cheered by the president's words. "It was the finest thing this side of heaven," wrote one citizen. "It seemed to give the people, as well as myself, a new hold on life," exclaimed another. Actually, Roosevelt had not moved much beyond what he had proposed during the campaign, but he had conveyed to the public some of his own jaunty confidence and had given people the feeling that there was now a strong hand at the helm.

Despite his generalities and brave words, Roosevelt had few specific remedies in mind. He was not a brilliant economist or a man with a clear-cut set of principles to guide him. At times these deficiencies would create confusion and lead to serious mistakes. But FDR had some impressive assets, notably his open-mindedness and willingness to experiment. "Take a method and try it," he advised. "If it fails, admit it frankly and try another." And he had gathered around

A naive depiction by Mexican artist Miguel Covarrubias of the pomp surrounding FDR's inauguration in 1933. But also notice the angels of hope with their trumpets over his head.

him a talented array of advisers, a so-called Brain Trust—drawn from the universities, from law, and from the social work profession—who could supply him with the ideas he himself lacked.

The new president's first move, on March 5, was to order the nation's banking system closed. The four-day bank holiday was accompanied by an order that, in effect, took the country off the gold standard. Four days later, acting with the enthusiasm it had never shown Hoover, Congress passed the Emergency Banking Act, confirming the bank closings and providing for an orderly reopening of those that proved sound. The administration's bold action reassured the American people, who expressed their confidence in the president when the banks reopened by redepositing the cash they had earlier withdrawn in panic.

The bank holiday was the first shot of a whirl-wind hundred-day war on defeatism, despair, and decline such as Americans had never witnessed before. The assault was marked by confusion and contradiction and did not end the Depression. But it did check the decline and restore a sense of forward motion to the American people.

The president's major goal during the First Hundred Days was to turn the economy around. To do so he proposed two key measures, the Agricultural Adjustment Act (AAA) and the National Industrial Recovery Act (NIRA). The AAA (1933) was the New Deal's major effort to deal with the acute farm crisis.

Based on the ideas of Secretary of Agriculture Henry A. Wallace and others, it sought to raise farm prices by creating scarcity. The measure provided that farmers who agreed to reduce their output of seven basic commodities would be compensated for their sacrifice from the proceeds of a special tax levied on food processors (millers, meatpackers, canners, and so on). Because prices normally rise when the supply of a product shrinks, the administration expected the reduction in farm output to check the price slide and ultimately raise farm income.

The NIRA (1933) was intended to restore industrial prosperity by ending deflationary price-cutting and by achieving balance among sectors of the economy that had supposedly been disturbed in the years preceding the great crisis. Like the AAA, the NIRA was a retreat from the idea of free competition and accepted limited output as the key to restoring prosperity. The bill established the National Recovery Administration (NRA) with power to draw up codes of "fair competition" in consultation with representatives of industry. Fair competition was actually a disguise for allowing businesses to divide up the market, reduce output, and raise prices. Business people were to be exempt from the antitrust laws. To placate organized labor, which feared it might be crushed by organized management, the codes were to contain a provision for collective bargaining between employers and employees (Section 7a). Tacked on to the NIRA measure was Title II, establishing a Public Works Administration (PWA) with a $3.3 billion budget to undertake large-scale public construction projects.

The two major recovery measures fell far short of their goals. By the time the AAA went into effect in the spring of 1933, southern farmers and sharecroppers had already planted many acres of cotton, and in the corn belt millions of sows had produced their annual litters. To keep this supply of fiber and food from coming to market and further weakening prices, the Department of Agriculture had to persuade cotton growers to uproot a quarter of their crop. In September 1933 it induced farmers to destroy 6 million pigs. Some of the pork was given to people on relief. Nevertheless, the wholesale destruction of commodities at a time when people were hungry and ill clothed seemed irrational to many Americans.

More serious were the long-term social effects of the AAA. Reducing cotton production squeezed sharecroppers off the land. Those who remained, both black and white, were often deprived by landlords of the federal cash due them.

Despite the AAA's failings, during the two years following its passage farm income more than doubled. Some of the gains consisted of direct payments to farmers for cutting production; some came from the higher prices that the cuts produced. But the AAA was responsible for only a part of the advance. Higher wheat prices, for example, owed as much to the great drought that parched the Great Plains between 1932 and 1935 as to government programs. The drought turned a vast area stretching from Texas to the Dakotas into a "dust bowl," where the skies were obscured by blowing topsoil and crops withered. Thousands of tenant farmers in Oklahoma and Arkansas were uprooted. Imprecisely called Okies, many became "gasoline gypsies" and set off in jalopies for the warmth, jobs, and presumed easy living of southern California. The sharp

The Dust Bowl, an ecological disaster created by years of bad land management plus bad weather, was a major problem of the Depression era. It displaced thousands of Plains' farmers, but it also helped raise depressed farm prices.

drop in wheat production added substantially to the impact of the AAA wheat program. When the federal judiciary declared the tax on food processors unconstitutional, the AAA's major crop-reduction features were reincorporated into a new law, the Soil Conservation and Domestic Allotment Act (1936).

Unlike the AAA, the NIRA was almost a complete failure. The flamboyant NRA administrator, General Hugh S. Johnson, had hoped to use the Public Works Administration (PWA) established by the NIRA to beef up demand by putting people to work. But Roosevelt handed over the PWA to Secretary of the Interior Harold Ickes, depriving Johnson of one of his tools. Working with what he had, Johnson succeeded in bullying the nation's largest industries into writing codes of fair practices. These agreements contained some progressive labor features, including mandatory collective bargaining for employees and limitations on child labor. In return for these, however, the NRA authorized price-fixing and output limitations and allowed big business to adopt policies that discriminated against small firms.

But the greatest disappointment of the NRA was that it failed to stimulate industry. The government gave its program a symbol—a blue eagle—and a slogan—We Do Out Part. Blue eagle parades wound through the downtowns of a score of cities; blue eagle stickers were plastered over store and factory windows. For a time the ballyhoo boosted investor confidence and consumer morale and kept the Depression from worsening. But the agency established no effective machinery by which to restart silent mills and factories, and industrial production remained stalled. When in May 1935 the Supreme Court struck down the code-making sections of the NIRA as unconstitutional, few people, even in the administration, mourned its passing.

Fiscal Stimulus. It is easy to see today why the two major recovery measures failed. In addition to their unfortunate side effects, they did little to increase investment rates or consumer spending. Only by spending large sums of money in excess of its receipts could the government have given the economy the stimulus it needed.

The treasury under Roosevelt did spend more money than it took in. Under the New Deal the RFC funneled money into business. The Home Owners Loan Corporation (HOLC) dispensed billions of dollars to savings and loan associations to refinance mortgages. The PWA, which survived the Supreme Court's invalidation of the NIRA, poured millions into major federal works projects. Between 1933 and 1939 the agency built 70 percent of the new schools and 65 percent of the new city halls, sewage plants, and courthouses constructed. It was responsible for more than a third of all the nation's new hospitals. It funded university libraries, the Lincoln Tunnel connecting New York and New Jersey, the causeway linking the Florida Keys to the mainland, and many other outstanding construction projects.

Whatever his critics charged, however, Roosevelt was never a deliberate "spender." He believed that a little "pump priming" by government could be useful, but he worried about running the treasury consistently in the red. "I doubt if any of his reform legislation," a Roosevelt adviser wrote in 1936, "would give him as much satisfaction as the actual balancing of the budget." Federal spending exceeded federal income in every year of the New Deal, but the deficits were always incidental to relief; they were never part of a deliberate program. Nor were they ever large enough to spark a complete recovery. At their maximum, in

Rural poverty, especially in the South and southern Plains, drove many people to seek a better life in California. "Okies," as they were called by contemptuous observers, loaded their meager belongings onto rattletrap vehicles and headed west, many ultimately to become prosperous citizens of their adopted state.

1936, treasury deficits totaled a scant $4.4 billion, scarcely enough to make up for weak investment by the private sector or even to offset the simultaneous spending cutbacks of impoverished city and state governments. Few in the Roosevelt administration had read the apostle of deliberate deficit spending—John Maynard Keynes—though Marriner Eccles, a Utah banker who headed the Federal Reserve Board, was an instinctive Keynesian.

Relief. By far the largest outpouring of federal funds throughout the New Deal Era went to jobs and relief for the unemployed. Although conservative in fiscal matters, FDR—unlike Hoover—put the welfare of ordinary men and women before a balanced budget.

As part of the First Hundred Days, Congress established the Civilian Conservation Corps (CCC). The corps took 2.5 million idle young men on relief rolls and put them to work on public lands at $30 a month planting trees, building forest ranger stations, clearing branches, and restoring historic battlefields. Congress also passed the Federal Emergency Relief Act, creating the Federal Emergency Relief Administration (FERA) and appropriating $500 million for local and state relief agencies to distribute to the unemployed. Administering the program was a fast-talking,

poker-playing young social worker, Harry L. Hopkins, who believed that jobs, rather than outright charity, were needed to restore individual morale and self-respect. In late 1933 Hopkins persuaded Roosevelt to establish the Civil Works Administration (CWA) with funds drawn from FERA and the PWA to put the unemployed directly on the federal payroll. By mid-January 1934 the CWA was providing 4 million men and women with a steady paycheck averaging $15 a week.

Needless to say, CWA was popular with the unemployed. It was also popular with local storekeepers and other small business people, who quickly felt the stimulating effect of new paying customers. But the president worried that it was too expensive and would create a permanent class of government dependents. By summer Roosevelt had shut down the program and returned relief to the local governments.

It did not remain there. In January 1935 Roosevelt asked Congress for $5 billion to support other work relief programs. The men would be employed on various government projects at wages higher than the straight dole under FERA, but lower than the amount paid by CWA. Congress responded to the president's request and made the largest single appropriation in the nation's history. The questions now were

The WPA under Harry Hopkins sought to rescue people in the arts, as well as other Americans, from idleness during the Depression. Moses Soyer here, in *Artists on WPA*, depicts a room full of WPA painters using their skills and earning some money in the process.

With the WPA, the New Deal extended relief to professionals, writers, performers, and artists. Shown here is William Gropper's mural "Construction of the Dam."

who would spend this great sum, and how? Secretary Ickes wanted it devoted to long-term projects under his PWA. Hopkins wanted it for short-term projects like those of his CWA. The two men fought like spoiled children. In the end Roosevelt recognized that quick relief was the need of the hour and allotted most of the funds to a new agency, the Works Progress Administration (WPA), under Hopkins's direction.

For the remainder of the Depression, the WPA was the major distributor of government funds to the unemployed and an important stimulant to the economy. Government spending, however incidental, pushed up the GNP and cut into unemployment. By 1935 the number of jobless had declined from almost 13 million, or 24.9 percent of the labor force, to 10.6 million, a little over 20 percent of those seeking work.

The relief programs cannot be measured solely by their statistical consequences. True, much of the WPA outlay went to make-work projects. But Hopkins was an imaginative man with broad cultural and human sympathies who saw that artists, writers, intellectuals and performers were also victims of the collapse. Under his direction the WPA sponsored programs to put these people to work enriching community life, while preserving their own skills. Hundreds of musicians were paid to perform in school auditoriums and community halls. Artists were hired to paint murals for the new federal courthouses and post offices built with PWA funds. Writers were set to work compiling state guidebooks. Many talented men and women—including Saul Bellow, Ralph Ellison, Richard Wright, and Arthur Miller—owed their starts to the Federal Writers Project or the Federal Theater Project under the WPA. The WPA also established a National Youth Administration to give part-time work to college and high school students to enable them to complete their studies.

Reform and Innovation.   Much of the first two years of the New Deal was devoted to emergency legislation to revive the economy and relieve public distress. But the president had promised reform and innovation, too, and he came through on his promises. A series of New Deal measures sought to end stock market abuses by placing the management of Wall Street under the new Securities and Exchange Commission (SEC). The banking system was made more secure and stable by creation of the Federal Deposit Insurance Corporation (FDIC) to ensure depositors' accounts and prevent the sort of panic withdrawals that had almost destroyed the banking system following the Crash.

The most important innovation of the First Hundred Days was the Tennessee Valley Authority (TVA). In the tradition of the old progressives, Roosevelt was a conservationist who placed an almost Jeffersonian value on nature and rural life. In his inaugural address he had proposed the more effective use of the nation's land and natural resources. In May 1933 he secured congressional approval of the TVA, a resource-management project long advocated by Senator George Norris of Nebraska and other conservationists who were dismayed at the physical and social deterioration of the potentially rich Tennessee River valley and the waste of its precious water resources.

The TVA was given the authority to build dams, manufacture fertilizer, undertake soil conservation and reforestation measures, and join with local authorities within the seven-state valley in various social improvement projects. Between 1933 and 1944 the TVA built nine major dams, which not only brought low-cost light and power to valley homes and farms but also provided new recreational facilities. Cheap power attracted large industries to the region, especially during World War II. Together with reforestation and soil conservation, inexpensive electricity helped reverse the valley's long decline, turning it into one of the most prosperous parts of the South.

Friends and Enemies

The early months of the New Deal were a hectic time. The public wavered between fear and hope, still stunned by the economic catastrophe but encouraged by the new surge of energy in Washington. Congress gave Roosevelt almost everything he wanted without looking too closely at the cost or questioning the wisdom of his proposals. As the months passed, however, opposition mounted at both ends of the political spectrum, and by 1935 Roosevelt and the New Deal were surrounded by critics and enemies.

Thunder on the Right. Despite the new legislation to regulate the banks and Wall Street, FDR was not a foe of business. Many of his advisers, particularly Professor Raymond Moley of Columbia, were conservative men who endorsed the kind of business-government cooperation that had been incorporated into the NIRA. Unfortunately for FDR, once the worst of the economic crisis had passed and business people

The Tennessee Valley Authority

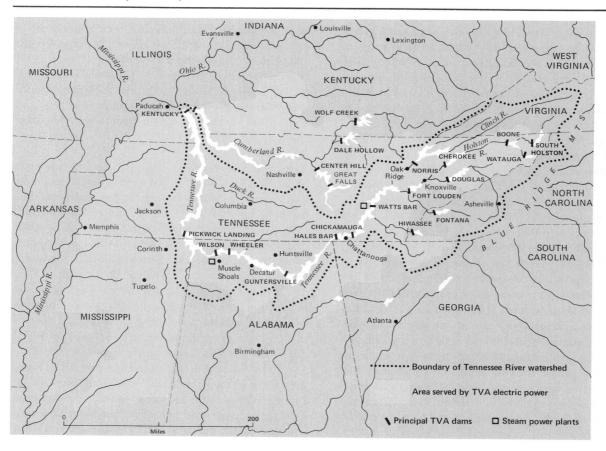

lost their fear of total collapse, many began to accuse the New Dealers of unwarranted interference with the economy, fiscal irresponsibility, and socialist leanings. In August 1934 a group of conservative Democrats and executives of Du Pont, General Motors, and other large corporations organized the Liberty League to fight the New Deal and prevent the "further aggrandizement of an ever spreading governmental bureaucracy."

At the same time a more formidable conservative challenge came from the Supreme Court. Composed of men whose average age was over seventy, the Court was dominated by some of the most tradition-bound conservatives in the American bar. On May 27, 1935, in the Schechter case, it struck down the NIRA on the grounds that it unconstitutionally conferred legislative power on the executive branch. Shortly thereafter, in *United States* v. *Butler*, the Court invalidated the AAA on the grounds that the processing tax that provided the fund to pay farmers was not a true tax but a means to regulate production. The AAA, the Court's conservative majority declared, granted the government powers far beyond any that the Constitution intended. If the principle of the AAA were allowed to stand, federal taxing power could be used to regulate industry throughout the United States.

The Attack of the Left. The conservative challenge to the New Deal was only half the story. By 1935 Roosevelt was also under attack by the extreme left. Neither the Socialist nor the Communist party had had many supporters during the 1920s, but the Depression gave both—especially the Communists—a new lease on life. Most Americans continued to believe in the fundamental soundness of private property and a market economy; but many artists, intellectuals, journalists, and students were won over to the view that capitalism was doomed and the only hope lay in a government takeover of the means of production. To these people the vivid contrast between the reeling capitalist United States and the growing and apparently prosperous Soviet Union was undeniable proof that communism, with its "dictatorship of the proletariat," was the hope of the future.

Encouraged by capitalism's apparent plight, the left mounted a direct attack on the New Deal. The Socialist party leader, Norman Thomas, at first was friendly to Roosevelt. By 1935, however, he and his fellow Socialists were denouncing the New Deal as "the greatest fraud among all the utopias." Earl Browder, leader of the American Communist party, echoed whatever Moscow's current attitude toward the Western democracies happened to be. In 1934 Browder called the New Deal "a program of hunger, fascization, and imperialist war." But after 1935, when the Soviet Union began to feel threatened by the increasing militancy of Nazi Germany and sought the support of the Western democratic countries, the American Communists considerably softened their criticism.

The Socialists and Communists were only an annoyance. The real political challenge to Roosevelt from the left came from a collection of neopopulists in the dissenting tradition of the West and South. Closest to the Populist heritage was Senator Huey Long, the Louisiana Kingfish. An earthy man who wore pink suits, called fellow officeholders "dime-a-dozen punks," and conducted public business in pajamas and a silk bathrobe, Long was also a shrewd politician who knew that the times cried out for a savior. As governor of Louisiana he had forced the state's corporations to pay a larger share of taxes than they had before and had used the money to build bridges, hospitals, mental institutions, and schools. To carry out his program, Long had employed any weapon at hand, including physical intimidation, political blackmail, and kidnapping.

In 1932 Long came to Washington as a Democratic senator. At first he supported the president, but he soon concluded that the New Deal was too friendly to big business. In part the argument between Long and Roosevelt was a clash between two strong and ambitious men. But they also disagreed ideologically. The Kingfish professed to be a radical egalitarian. He wanted to "share the wealth" by taxing away all large incomes and fortunes and giving every citizen $5,000 and a guaranteed income of $2,000 a year. Many Americans dismissed the Share Our Wealth program as an unworkable scheme that was more likely to produce chaos than solve the nation's problems. Nevertheless, Long's proposals to make "every man a king" appealed to millions of ordinary people. Roosevelt considered Long a demagogue and one of the most dangerous men in America, and by the beginning of 1933 Long and the administration were at war.

Another outspoken critic of the New Deal was Father Charles E. Coughlin, a Catholic priest of Royal Oak, Michigan. Coughlin's radio broadcasts of sermons and commentary had begun in the late 1920s, and by 1933 the golden-voiced Coughlin had an audience of millions. Like Long, he first supported the New Deal but turned against FDR when the president refused to endorse inflationary measures to end the Depression. In late 1934 Coughlin formed the National Union for Social Justice, a pressure group advocating

Father Coughlin, the "radio priest," gathered an enormous following with his weekly "Golden House of the Little Flower" broadcasts. Every week he received more mail than Roosevelt himself.

silver inflation and the nationalization of power, oil, light, and natural gas companies, and ultimately the seizure of the banks as well. At various times he was denounced by Catholic prelates for his rhetorical excesses, especially his anti-Semitism; but secure in the support of his own bishop, he continued to attack Roosevelt and those he called the "money-lenders."

A third Populist challenge came from an aging California physician, Francis E. Townsend. Townsend was a generous man with a tender heart. Outraged by the lack of public concern for the elderly victims of the Depression, he proposed that all persons over sixty be given pensions of $200 a month on the condition that they retire and "spend the money as they get it." The scheme, he declared, would simultaneously remove thousands of older workers from the overcrowded job market and inject millions of dollars of fresh purchasing power into the economy.

The Townsend Plan quickly won a following among older people and was incorporated into a bill introduced in Congress in early 1935. Critics attacked the measure as unworkable and unfair to the great majority of Americans under sixty. Many of its opponents were conservatives who saw the plan as socialistic, but the secretary of labor also derided the scheme as crackpot. The *Townsend Weekly*, the doctor's edito-

rial voice, soon responded with an angry attack on the administration.

The Roosevelt Coalition. Fortunately for FDR, although he had made many enemies, he had also won hordes of friends. By 1935 millions of Americans had reason to thank the New Deal and the Democratic party for their compassion and help. Creative men and women were grateful for the opportunity under the WPA to do productive work and maintain their skills and talents. Young people were grateful for the dole from the National Youth Administration that allowed them to stay in school and prepare for careers; they were glad to be taken off the city streets by the CCC and given the chance to earn some money working in the forests and national parks. Thousands of middle-class homeowners sang Roosevelt's praises for sparing them the humiliation of eviction from their homes through a timely HOLC loan. Unemployed factory workers could thank the president for the relief that kept them from hunger.

Black Americans were especially grateful to Roosevelt and his party. Not that the administration's policies were ideal. AAA programs, as administered, had hurt black sharecroppers. Roosevelt, who needed southern votes in Congress, was unwilling to attack the racial caste system of the South. He endorsed a federal antilynching bill, but then refused to fight for it and allowed it to be filibustered to death in the Senate. Nevertheless, not since Reconstruction had black Americans received as good a shake from their government. Blacks shared in WPA programs; the National Youth Administration helped many hundreds of young black men and women. When the New Deal adopted a slum-clearance program, blacks would become prominent beneficiaries of the new public housing. New Dealers, moreover, were often solicitous of black pride. Eleanor Roosevelt and Secretary Harold Ickes, particularly, accorded recognition to talented black men and women, supported black aspirations, and sought to further the cause of civil rights. When the Daughters of the American Revolution refused to allow the distinguished black contralto Marian Anderson to sing at Washington's Constitution Hall, Secretary Ickes invited her to use the steps of the Lincoln Memorial for an open-air concert. Black Americans appreciated the benefits of the New Deal and ignored its deficiencies. By 1935 they had broken their traditional Republican ties and shifted their votes to the Democratic column.

By late 1935 organized labor had also joined the Roosevelt camp. During the 1920s the unions had

Hoover Hits Back

Roosevelt and the New Dealers succeeded in creating a political coalition that included broad segments of the American people. They did not convince all Americans that they had found the correct formulas for national health, however. One of the outspoken dissenters was former president Herbert Hoover. Here, speaking on the eve of the Roosevelt landslide of 1936, Hoover attacks the New Deal and his opponent of four years before, and expounds the Republican philosophy of "freedom" against what he portrays as the New Deal doctrines of centralized power and "personal government."

"Through four years of experience this New Deal attack upon free institutions has emerged as the transcendent issue in America. All the men who are seeking for mastery in the world today are using the same weapons. They sing the same songs. They all promise the joys of Elysium without effort.

"But their philosophy is founded on the coercion and compulsory organization of men. True liberal government is founded on the emancipation of men. This is the same issue upon which men are imprisoned and dying in Europe right now. . . .

"I gave the warning against this philosophy of government four years ago from a heart heavy with anxiety for the future of our country. It was born from many years' experience of the forces moving in the world which would weaken the vitality of American freedom. It grew in the four years of battle as President to uphold the banner of free men.

"And that warning was based on sure ground from my knowledge of the ideas that Mr. Roosevelt and his bosom colleagues had covertly embraced despite the Democratic platform.

"Those ideas were not new. Most of them had been urged on me. . . .

"I rejected the notion of great trade monopolies and price-fixing through codes. That could only stifle the little business man by regimenting him under the big brother. That idea was born of certain American Big Businesses and grew up to be the NRA.

"I rejected the scheme of 'economic planning' to regiment and coerce the farmer. That was born of a Roman despot 1,400 years ago and grew up into the AAA.

"I refused national plans to put the government into business in competition with its citizens. That was born of Karl Marx.

"I vetoed the idea of recovery through stupendous spending to prime the pump. That was born of a British professor.

"I threw out attempts to centralize relief in Washington for politics and social experimentation. I defeated other plans to invade States' rights, to centralize power in Washington. Those ideas were born of American radicals. . . .

"I rejected all these things not only because they would not only delay recovery but because I knew that in the end they would shackle free men. . . .

"It was not until after the [1932] election that the people began to awake. Then the realization of intended tinkering with the currency drove bank depositors into the panic that greeted Mr. Roosevelt's inauguration.

"Recovery was set back for two years, and hysteria was used as the bridge to reach the goal of personal government. . . .

"The people knew now the aims of the New Deal philosophy of government.

"We propose instead leadership and authority in government within the moral and economic framework of the American system.

"We propose to hold to the Constitutional safeguards of free men.

"We propose to relieve men from fear, coercion, and spite that are inevitable in personal government.

"We propose to demobilize and decentralize all this spending upon which vast personal power is being built. We propose to amend the tax laws so as not to defeat free man and free enterprise.

"We propose to turn the whole direction of the country toward liberty, not away from it. . . .

". . . [D]o not mistake. Free government is the most difficult of all government. But it is everlastingly true that the plain people will make fewer mistakes than any group of men no matter how powerful. But free government implies vigilant thinking and courageous living and self-reliance in a people.

"Let me say to you that any measure which breaks our dikes of freedom will flood the land with misery."

declined in power and numbers. After 1924 leadership of the labor movement rested in the conservative hands of William Green, Samuel Gompers's successor as head of the AFL. Green did little to counteract the decline in union membership and influence that had begun in the 1920s; nor did he do anything to bring the millions of new industrial wage earners into organized labor's house. There were a few industrial unions in the nation. Among them were the feeble United Mine Workers under the unpredictable John L. Lewis and two unions of garment workers, predominantly Jewish and Italian, under Sidney Hillman and David Dubinsky. Both these leaders and their unions were exceptional. Most factory and mine workers were unorganized.

The Depression further weakened organized labor. Membership dropped as union workers lost their jobs. Desperate men and women turned to unauthorized, or "wildcat," strikes in hope of stemming the erosion of their wages and preserving their jobs. But with millions unemployed and the economy steadily worsening, the position of labor was pitifully weak, and these efforts invariably failed.

Then came the NIRA and its Section 7a, authorizing collective bargaining in industries that adopted NIRA fair-practice codes. Roosevelt was at first indifferent to organized labor. But many prominent New Dealers, particularly Senator Robert F. Wagner of New York and Secretary of Labor Frances Perkins (the first female cabinet member), were strongly prounion. The administration established to enforce the NIRA labor provision pursued a vigorous policy of encouraging labor unions and collective bargaining. Before long

thousands of workers, spurred on by labor organizers' claim that "the president wants you to unionize," were flocking into both old and new labor organizations, glad to oblige the president and certain that he wished them well.

The Welfare State

Roosevelt did not respond to attacks from both ends of the political spectrum by moving toward the middle, as we might expect. The assault from the right annoyed him, but he expected it. The criticism of the left was more wounding. FDR considered himself left of center, and when challenged by the neopopulists, he worried about his liberal credentials and feared he might lose his popular support.

The first New Deal had been devoted largely to recovery and relief. Of the two goals, only the second had met with any large measure of success. In 1935 growing opposition and the sense that the New Deal had stalled caused Roosevelt and his advisers to veer left with a new program to weaken the power of big business, equalize opportunity, and increase economic

Eleanor Roosevelt was an ardent champion of the nation's poor, causing wealthy conservatives to label her, like her husband, a traitor to her class. Here she encourages a group of farmers about to begin new lives under a program of the Resettlement Administration, one of the boldest experiments of the New Deal.

security. In a burst of energy known as the Second Hundred Days, or the Second New Deal, they transformed the nation by creating the modern welfare state.

The stimulus for the new tack may have been immediate problems, but the inspiration was derived from the reform impulse of the early twentieth century. Many of its authors were old progressives or their later disciples. Justice Brandeis, one of the key figures of the Second New Deal, had been Woodrow Wilson's mentor, and Brandeis's protégé, Felix Frankfurter, was a prominent figure in the new drive. Other people in the Roosevelt administration were also old progressives. The feisty "old curmudgeon" with the sharp tongue, Harold Ickes, was a former Bull Mooser. Frances Perkins had been a settlement house social worker and social justice reformer before World War I. In local government, where the New Deal relied on friendly administrators to carry out its wishes and create grassroots support for its programs, there were many former progressives in high office. The mayor of New York City between 1933 and 1945 was the bouncy, exuberant Fiorello La Guardia, a former progressive Republican congressman who helped deliver New York City's votes for Roosevelt each time he ran for president. Congress was full of surviving progressives, many of them midwestern Republicans, who supported New Deal reform measures despite their Democratic inspiration. Some of these progressives personally disliked Roosevelt, but they could not stop the New Deal from appropriating many of their ideas.

The Second New Deal elevated the progressive social welfare programs that had been largely confined to the states before 1917 to the national level. Now the federal government would not only complete the job of taming the "vested interests" but also make Washington the guardian of the weak and unfortunate and the source of security for all Americans.

In June 1935 the president sent Congress a list of "must" legislation consisting of four crucial items: a social security bill, a measure to replace the collective bargaining provision of the defunct NIRA, a banking regulation proposal, and a new progressive income tax with rates that rose sharply as income increased. In addition, he demanded that Congress pass several important secondary measures to expand social and economic benefits for various segments of the nation.

Labor's New Charter.   Over the next few months FDR got almost all that he asked for. In July Congress passed the first of the major measures, the National Labor Relations Act, also called the Wagner Act, after its chief congressional sponsor, Senator Robert Wagner

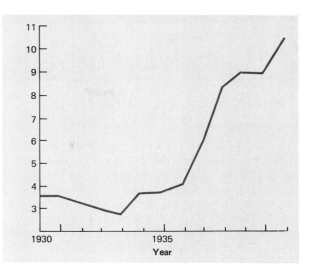

Membership in labor unions, 1929–1941
Source: Historical Statistics of the United States, Colonial Times to 1970.

of New York. It became the charter of the modern American labor movement.

The new law established a permanent National Labor Relations Board with the authority to supervise elections to determine whether workers in an industry wanted union representation. Their union, if approved, would become the legal collective bargaining agent for its members, whether employers liked it or not.

The Wagner Act would prove a powerful weapon in the struggle to organize the nation's miners and factory workers. But obstacles remained. For years American industrialists had bitterly and successfully opposed unions. Using labor spies, strikebreakers, strong-arm methods, and legal injunctions, they had checked efforts of their employees to win collective bargaining rights. They were now certain to fight back.

Nor could the industrial unionists expect much help from the AFL. William Green and the heads of the powerful craft unions that made up the AFL considered the growth of industrial unionism a threat to their own power. They were also contemptuous of the semiskilled workers of predominantly southern and eastern European stock who labored in the factories and mines. At the 1935 annual AFL convention Green and his friends refused to support the principle of organizing industrial workers. In response, dissenters Sidney Hillman, David Dubinsky, and John L. Lewis set up the Committee for Industrial Organization. Until 1938, when it became the Congress of Industrial Organizations, the CIO remained within the AFL. It received little support from Green and his lieutenants.

The steel industry was the first target of CIO

A Historical Portrait

Fiorello H. La Guardia

The New Deal was a political upheaval that resounded through the whole of America, affecting the politics of cities and states as well as the nation's. In New York, the country's largest metropolis, it was personified not by the patrician Democrat in the White House, but by a Republican of Italian-American ancestry, Fiorello H. La Guardia.

The Little Flower (his first name in Italian) was, as one of his biographers says, Brotherhood Week all by himself. His father, Achille, was a lapsed Catholic from Foggia in southern Italy; his mother, Irene Luzatto Coen, was a moderately observant Jew from Trieste on the Adriatic. Fiorello was born in New York's Greenwich Village in 1882, two years after his parents arrived in the United States. He grew up in western military posts, where his father served as army bandmaster. He always considered Arizona his native state, and throughout his career as a New York political leader wore western string ties and a high-crowned Stetson hat.

The young La Guardia imbibed his democratic political principles from an improbable source: the pages of Joseph Pulitzer's *World*. Though the paper arrived in Prescott, Arizona, almost a week late, young Fiorello avidly read its socially conscious columns and editorials and absorbed Pulitzer's sincere concern for the underdog. His years in the West were formative for La Guardia, but they ended in 1898 when Sergeant Achille La Guardia set off to fight the Spaniards, only to be struck down by the "embalmed beef" that the Quartermaster Corps served the troops. Discharged from the army as unfit for service, Achille took his family to Trieste, where they moved in with Irene's widowed mother. There, in the Italian-speaking part of Austria-Hungary, and later in Budapest, Fiorello got a job as a U.S. consular representative and learned seven languages.

La Guardia returned to the United States in 1906 and for a while worked as an interpreter for the immigration service at Ellis Island. He went to night law school and opened a law office in New York. The experience did not enhance his views of lawyers or judges. The ones he met were invariably associated with Tammany Hall, the New York Democratic machine, and as invariably dishonest, ignorant, or stupid. La Guardia himself stayed free of the machine and its corrupting patronage by establishing ties with the Italian-Jewish garment worker unions. In 1909/10 he helped to settle a major garment industry strike and received much favorable attention.

In 1914 Fiorello, a Republican out of hatred for Tammany, received his party's nomination for Congress. The choice meant little; no Republican had ever won in the 14th District, and the weak Republican organization gave him no help. He lost, but his impressive showing won him appointment as deputy state attorney general by the Republican governor. Two years later he won the same congressional seat, largely through the votes of Italian-Americans who resented the Irish-dominated Democratic machine and wanted to see one of their own in office.

The first Italian-American ever to sit in Congress, La Guardia arrived in Washington in time to vote for war against Germany and Austria-Hungary. During the war the young congressman took a leave and joined the air corps. He was sent to Italy to learn to fly and to establish liaison with America's Italian ally. La Guardia never became a very good pilot, but he utterly charmed the Italians with his American bumptiousness and exuberance. He returned home a decorated hero in 1918, in time to win reelection for a second term, but then resigned to run successfully for president of the New York Board of Alderman. In 1921 he sought the Republican nomination for mayor but was defeated. The following year, however, he was returned to Congress from a new Manhattan district, and then reelected to three more terms.

La Guardia was a political maverick in every way. At a time when the country as a whole had become conservative, he retained his skepticism of big business and joined with Senator George Norris of Nebraska to prevent sale of the Muscle Shoals waterpower site to private utility companies. When the country turned isolationist, he fought for the League of Nations. When most Americans were still convinced that Prohibition was a "noble experiment," he sought to have the Volstead Act rescinded. La Guardia was considered a troublemaker by his colleagues. The practice of the day allowed congressmen to introduce bills on Wednesdays to benefit constituents under "unanimous consent." It was understood that these would not be challenged. La Guardia had no patience with such boondoggles at the taxpayers' expense and regularly raised objections, thereby forcing a vote. He did not endear himself to his fellow representatives.

During the boom years of the 1920s men like Norris, Robert La Follette, and La Guardia were ignored. Though he served seven terms in Congress, La Guardia never received coveted committee chairmanships, and never was entirely happy with his job in Washington. In 1929 he ran for mayor of New York against the Democratic incumbent, Jimmy Walker. Walker spent more time in nightclubs than in his City Hall office. He was a heavy drinker and a womanizer who had left his wife for a showgirl mistress. He was also politically corrupt. But he suited the devil-may-care spirit of the Jazz Age, and he swamped the gadfly little congressman by almost half a million votes.

The Crash and the Depression abruptly changed the fortunes of the country's political insurgents. In the liberal Congress elected in 1930 La Guardia joined with western progressives to push through important legislation. He jointly sponsored the Norris–La Guardia Anti-Injunction Act outlawing "yellow-dog" contracts (agreements by employees, signed as conditions of employment, not to join unions) and forbidding federal court injunctions in labor disputes except when they threatened to become violent. The new law eliminated a major weapon that management had for years wielded against organized labor.

The Depression irreparably tarnished the luster of "Beau James," the playboy mayor of New York. In 1931 a commission under the patrician judge Samuel Seabury revealed Mayor Walker as an unvarnished crook who had taken thousands from people doing business with the city. The mayor had stored $1 million of his illegal gains in a safety deposit box. When the Seabury investigation finished its work, Walker abruptly resigned and sailed off to Europe.

Walker was gone, but Tammany remained. To challenge the machine, the good-government forces, composed primarily of upper-middle-class professionals and business leaders, organized a Fusion party. Their natural candidate was Seabury himself, but the judge, anxious to preserve the objectivity of his continuing investigation, refused to run. Seabury instead endorsed La Guardia, who also received the support of the New York City Republicans and of the president, Franklin Roosevelt. Though a Democrat, Roosevelt liked La Guardia and despised Tammany.

La Guardia won with a 250,000-vote majority. On January 1, 1934, in the oak-paneled study of Judge Seabury's Upper East Side townhouse, the Little Flower took the oath as ninety-ninth mayor of New York.

His first task was to save the city from bankruptcy. New York, like almost all American cities in this the fifth year of the Great Depression, confronted intolerable burdens with drastically reduced means. A million unemployed people depended on the city Department of Public Welfare for food and shelter, but the city was broke. Five hundred million dollars of short-term city obligations were past due, and the bankers would not lend New York another dime. As the new mayor began his term, over 140,000 city teachers, firefighters, police, and sanitation workers faced the prospect of payless paydays.

La Guardia got the state legislature to grant the city fiscal autonomy and allow it to consolidate departments to cut expenses. The arrangement reassured the bankers, and New York was able to borrow again at reasonable rates. The mayor's friendship with FDR also paid off. Federal money soon began to flow into the city's coffers.

With the financial crisis past, La Guardia could devote his energies to reform. The Little Flower was the best mayor the city ever had. He was compassionate, dynamic, honest, candid, amusing, and effective. He made it clear right off who was boss.

"In this administration," he told the Tammany-dominated Board of Aldermen, "I am the majority." He rejected all patronage appointments, even of Fusionists who had worked for his election. Merit alone counted. There was not, he said, "a Republican or a Democratic way to collect garbage." His appointees to high city office were almost invariably the top people in their field, and he never let them relax their vigilance. On one occasion he telephoned his sanitation commissioner at 3 A.M. to find out if he had a snow-alarm plan in place. "Sure," the startled official replied. "I'm called as soon as the first flake falls." "Wonderful," the mayor responded. "Stick your head out of the window." The commissioner did; there was a raging blizzard under way. Like other officials who committed boners, the commissioner got a polished sheep shank as a trophy.

La Guardia was a ruthless antivice and anticrime crusader. He cracked down on illegal gambling and, to the dismay of some, drove burlesque from the city. He imprisoned hoodlums who preyed on legitimate business people, and he supported the efforts of New York's crusading district attorney, Thomas Dewey, to break the power of racketeers. He told the city police at one point: "I want you to put so much fear into the heart of every crook in New York that when he sees a cop he'll tip his hat."

The mayor carried into his office the same sensitive social conscience he had shown as a congressman.

La Guardia procured millions of dollars of federal money for public housing to replace the most squalid of New York's slums. During the bitterly cold winter of 1934 he opened the city's armories to the homeless and heatless. He established a large covered market in the city for the hundreds of pushcart peddlers who had to face inclement weather and

A Historical Portrait (*continued*)

police harassment. He was also a master builder. He and his parks commissioner, Robert Moses, often with federal aid, built dozens of bridges, scores of schools, hundreds of playgrounds and parks, and the city's two major airports.

The mayor was a newspaper reporter's delight. He was funny. When, in 1945, New York newspaper deliverers went on strike, the mayor turned up at the city's municipal radio station to read the comics over the air to the city's children. It was a memorable performance. "Ahh! what do we have here? The gardener! Stabbed! . . . But Dick Tracy is on the trail!" When the city was legally forced to allow the pro-Nazi German-American Bund to stage a rally in Madison Square Garden, the mayor assigned only Jewish policemen to maintain order. When Commissioner Moses had tried the tactic of resigning to force concessions from him once too often, the mayor had a pad of forms printed reading: "I, Robert Moses, do hereby resign as ____, effective ____." The next time Moses swept into his office with a resignation threat, La Guardia handed him the pad and said: "Here, just fill in the blanks." La Guardia was theatrical. He was always at the scene of the crime, the fire, or the disaster—often wearing the hat of the city service in charge.

La Guardia's three terms as mayor (1934–1946) coincided almost exactly with FDR's reign. The two political leaders worked closely together. La Guardia seldom came back from Washington without some tribute for the city in his pocket. Roosevelt could always count on Fiorello to use his popularity to win him votes in Congress and every four years at the polls. FDR was also grateful for the mayor's effective neutralizing of Tammany, always an embarrassment to him. In many ways, what La Guardia accomplished in New York was a little New Deal that helped to bind the city's voters to the new Democratic coalition.

By the time his third term ended, La Guardia had lost interest in the mayor's office. After FDR died in 1945, his successor, Harry Truman, appointed La Guardia head of the United Nations Relief and Rehabilitation Administration, the agency for rescuing and resettling the millions of Europeans made homeless by the war. The work was not congenial, and he soon resigned. Though only sixty-three, his health was now poor. In the spring of 1947 his severe back pain was diagnosed as cancer of the pancreas, a virtually incurable disease.

On September 20 Fiorello La Guardia died. When they opened his safety deposit box, they found $8,000 in war bonds. The only other asset he could pass along to his wife, Marie, and their two adopted children was a heavily mortgaged modest house in the Bronx. The Little Flower had lived the exemplary life he preached after all!

---

organizers. The smaller companies resisted, and on Memorial Day, 1937, outside Republic Steel, strikers and the police clashed violently, leaving several strikers dead and many injured. The giant of the industry, United States Steel, however, quickly capitulated, signing an agreement with the steelworkers recognizing the union as their bargaining agent in March 1937. The automobile industry was tougher, but it, too, yielded. In February 1937, after a series of dramatic sit-down strikes in which workers refused to leave the plants until their demands were met, General Motors surrendered and recognized the United Automobile Workers. Ford Motor Company, under the fiercely individualistic Henry Ford, held out for many more months, using toughs and spies to break the union drive. Despite Ford's resistance, by the eve of World War II the entire auto industry had been unionized.

By 1941, as a result of the Wagner Act and the doggedness of Lewis, Hillman, and other leaders of industrial labor, the number of men and women belonging to unions had swelled to a record 8.4 million—23 percent of the nonfarm labor force. It would not be easy for the politicians to ignore labor representatives again. The successful organizing of industrial labor was a power shift as dramatic as any that had taken place since the Civil War.

Social Security. The next piece of "must" legislation passed during the Second Hundred Days, the Social Security Act (1935), had consequences for American life that were even more far-reaching than those of the Wagner Act. From the beginning of the century, advanced progressives had advocated a system of social security for the unemployed, the handicapped, and the aged. Other nations had adopted such schemes, but in the United States the burdens of job, health, and old-age uncertainties were placed on the individual. Besides creating personal insecurity, the lack of social insurance guaranteed that even a small economic setback would produce a sharp drop in consumer demand. Workers who lost their jobs had little to fall back on and quickly ceased buying. The economy then weakened still further.

The Social Security Act established a system of unemployment insurance under the joint administration of the states and the federal government, financed by a payroll tax levied on employers. It also set up a pension scheme for retired people over sixty-five and their survivors to be paid for by a tax levied on both employers and employees. Finally, it provided federal funds to the states to aid them in caring for the destitute blind and for delinquent, crippled, and homeless children; and in setting up public health programs, maternity care, and vocational rehabilitation services.

The United States had finally joined the ranks of the other advanced industrial nations in providing reasonable security for its citizens.

Additional "Must" Legislation. Other legislation of the Second Hundred Days also fulfilled or reinforced old progressive promises. The Public Utility Holding Company Act gave the federal government control over interstate transmission of electricity and gas. It also conferred on the new SEC power over monopolistic corporate holding companies. To help equalize income

the Wealth Tax Act increased estate and gift tax rates and imposed stiffer levies on high-income recipients. The final "must" law was the Banking Act of 1935, which strengthened the federal government's control over the Federal Reserve System and gave the hitherto weak Federal Reserve Board a stronger voice in the management of the country's monetary affairs.

Several measures of the Second New Deal were designed to improve the qualify of rural life. In May 1935 Congress established a Rural Electrification Administration (REA). In a few years this agency brought electricity to millions of the nation's farms, created large new markets for electrical appliances, and dramatically changed the lives of farm families. The Soil Conservation and Domestic Allotment Act of 1936 rescued the crop-limitation features of the AAA by paying farmers not to grow "soil-depleting" crops. The Frazier-Lemke Farm Mortgage Moratorium Act extended farm mortgages for three years to save farmers from foreclosures.

Although conservative critics often accused the New Dealers of being "planners" and "socialists," the nearest thing to social planning, aside from TVA, was the Resettlement Administration Act, establishing an agency with authority to transfer farmers from poor lands to better ones. There they would use new equipment purchased by low-interest government loans and

Though America never came close to revolution during the Depression, it did not escape disorder. Here we see a riot on Union Square in New York in 1930 growing out of a labor protest organized by radicals.

would be advised by government experts. The Resettlement Administration (RA) was also given the responsibility for moving unemployed city people to "greenbelt" towns, where they could escape the poverty and other presumed evils of big cities. Under Rexford G. Tugwell the agency established three such towns, but accomplished little else because of lack of funds. The RA's successor was the Farm Security Administration (FSA), set up under the Bankhead-Jones Farm Tenant Act of 1937. The FSA took over the functions of the Resettlement Administration and had the added task of converting tenant farmers into farm owners. It, too, was underfunded and failed to reshape the social basis of American rural life. Despite their modest results, both measures demonstrated a potential for social experimentation by government rarely encountered in American history.

End of the New Deal

By the end of the Second Hundred Days the 1936 presidential race was well under way. Roosevelt easily won his party's renomination. The Republicans turned to Governor Alfred M. Landon of Kansas, a modest, likable man with progressive leanings. To the left of the Democrats—or to the right, some insisted—was the Union party, whose nominee, William Lemke of North Dakota, was a farmer-laborite in the Populist tradition. In all likelihood Huey Long would have headed the third-party ticket had he not been assassinated by one of his many Louisiana enemies in September 1935.

The campaign outcome was never really in doubt. By now a new political coalition had formed around Roosevelt, composed not only of the Democratic party's traditional southern, Catholic, and European ethnic voters but also of blacks, Mexican-Americans, intellectuals, and organized labor. Many of these people were the beneficiaries of New Deal programs. They also admired FDR as a man and a leader. Millions listened to his "fireside chats" on the radio and felt that their government cared.

Conservatives charged that Roosevelt was a dictator who had gathered to the presidential office unheard-of powers over every aspect of American life. They denounced the "bloated" federal bureaucracy and warned that "big government" would soon overawe every other institution. They were not entirely wrong. No American administration had ever achieved such dominion over the economy and over so many people's lives. The combination of big government and a vigorous leader who had a rare rapport with the people focused more attention on Washington than ever before.

Whatever drawbacks time would disclose in this arrangement, in 1936 relatively few Americans took the conservatives' warnings seriously. In November they turned out in record numbers and expressed their enthusiastic support of the Democrats. Roosevelt carried every state except rock-ribbed Republican Maine and Vermont and won the most impressive popular mandate in American political history: almost 28 million votes to Landon's 17 million. In the congressional contest the results were equally decisive. When the new Congress convened, the Democratic side of the House was so crowded that many of the new Democrats were forced to sit with the opposition.

In his second inaugural address Roosevelt promised to extend New Deal social and economic programs to meet the needs of the "one-third of a nation" that was "ill-housed, ill-clad, ill-nourished." He secured a part of what he wanted. In September 1937 the National Housing Act (Wagner-Steagall Act) launched a generation of federal slum clearance and public housing projects for the urban poor. The Agricultural Adjustment Act of 1938, without the unconstitutional processing tax, restored the crop-limitation provisions of the first AAA and made farm price supports a permanent feature of the American economy. The Food, Drug, and Cosmetic Act of June 1938 strengthened the consumer-protection features of the progressives' Pure Food and Drug Act of 1906. The Fair Labor Standards Act established for the first time a minimum hourly wage and a maximum workweek for millions of workers in occupations involved in interstate commerce. But the Fair Labor Standards Act was the last important piece of New Deal legislation. Thereafter New Deal legislative initiatives ceased. The effort to reform America and promote recovery had run out of steam.

Given Roosevelt's overwhelming mandate in 1936 and the top-heavy Democratic majority in Congress in 1937 and 1938, this outcome is startling. Yet we can understand its sources by considering where the nation was at this point. Despite every New Deal effort, the economy had failed to make a complete recovery. During 1937 the nation's output forged ahead, but unemployment remained at 7.7 million, some 14.3 percent of the labor force. The gains made, moreover, had been accompanied by sharp price rises. Fearing inflation, Roosevelt cut back sharply on federal spending and threw the economy into an unexpected tailspin. By the following year unemployment was back to 10.4 million, 19 percent of the work force. Roosevelt

Many Americans were disturbed by Roosevelt's plan to "pack" the Supreme Court, and some enemies of the New Deal believed he was planning to impose one-man-rule on the nation. His attempt might have succeeded had not the Court reversed its stands on several issues. Said one wit: "A switch in time saved nine."

quickly increased relief and other spending, and checked the descent, but by this time it had become clear to everyone that the country had not solved its chronic unemployment problem.

The persistence of a depressed economy undoubtedly damaged New Deal zest and morale. Nothing seemed to work—or work well—and the administration seemed to have no new ideas. FDR's inability to get the economy going again injured his prestige within his own party. Divisions between northern liberals and southern conservatives, which had been papered over by the mutual concern for recovery, now broke through. Within months of the November electoral victory, the Democrats were in disarray, squabbling with one another and uncertain which way to turn.

At this point Roosevelt launched an ill-advised attack on the Supreme Court. FDR saw the Court as a bastion of judicial conservatism. It had struck down the AAA and the NIRA, and no matter how imperfect these measures had been, he resented the Court's actions. It had also declared unconstitutional the Frazier-Lemke Act and several other New Deal measures. What it would do with the major social legislation of 1935/36 no one knew, but the president feared the worst.

The justices were almost all elderly men, and Roosevelt could have allowed resignations and deaths to change the Court's complexion. Instead, in February 1937 he asked Congress for the power to name up to six new judges, one for each incumbent who refused to resign after reaching seventy years of age. This scheme to "pack the Court" with more liberal judges stirred up a storm. Predictably, conservatives saw it as an attempt to subvert the Constitution. Even many liberals, including Justice Brandeis, balked at the proposal. When the Court, perhaps intimidated by the president's stand, unexpectedly sustained several crucial pieces of New Deal legislation and several liberal state laws, the Court-packing bill's congressional support melted away. In late July the Senate sent the bill back to the Judiciary Committee, where it quietly died. The president had suffered a major legislative defeat, almost his first, and the blow to his prestige was damaging. Thereafter, as confidence in Roosevelt's leadership waned, southern Democrats would increasingly side with conservative Republicans against their own party leader.

The loss of support was also expressed by the public at the polls. In the 1938 congressional elections, hoping to restore his liberal majority in Congress, Roosevelt urged the voters to defeat conservative Democrats in the congressional primaries. Many voters resented the interference in local politics and ignored the president's wishes. In the elections themselves the Democrats lost eighty-one seats in the House and eight in the Senate. Such losses by the party in power in midterm national elections are not unusual, and in any case the Democratic majority of 1936 was too lopsided to last. Nevertheless, the election suggested that many citizens had lost confidence in the man and the party they had turned to to save them and the country. In the turbulent years that followed, Roosevelt continued to be admired as the country's savior; but for all intents and purposes the New Deal was dead.

Conclusions

The New Deal did not create a revolution. The United States remained a capitalist nation after 1938. But it would be capitalist with a difference. In the words of John Maynard Keynes, Roosevelt had made himself "the trustee" for all those who sought "to mend the evil of our condition by reasoned experiment within the framework of the existing social system." Never again would Americans be completely exposed to the uncertainties of a freewheeling economy modified only in favor of powerful business groups. The government's ability to restore full employment by massive deficit spending was still unproved. But after 1939 it would be difficult for any president to insist that the business cycle had to work itself out no matter what the human consequences.

Even more important, the New Deal created permanent safeguards against another collapse and against private insecurity with unemployment insurance, old-age pensions, a strengthened Federal Reserve System, price supports for farmers, and the minimum wage. Perhaps Roosevelt could have done more to reduce the inequalities of wealth and power. A more rigorous system of progressive taxation—without loopholes—and a better-funded and more sustained welfare program might have created a more egalitarian society. But that he could have achieved a socialist society, as later critics have implied—even assuming that this goal was desirable—is doubtful. Public fear in 1933 did give FDR a broad mandate for change and experiment. Yet few Americans would have supported anything so much against national tradition as federal ownership of industry and the banks. And if, in panic, they had supported such measures, they certainly would have regretted and reversed their action once they had regained their confidence.

In reality, only a small minority of Roosevelt's aides were radicals, and in the end Roosevelt's New Deal saved capitalism. It did so by reviving hope, providing the nation with a sense of forward motion, and preventing mass starvation. In retrospect, it is easy to see that the New Deal was precisely what the majority of Americans wanted.

In the process of creating the modern welfare state, there were losses as well as gains. Federal power and executive authority were both greatly expanded. Few, except the hidebound conservatives who opposed virtually every New Deal measure, could see the dangers in this change as the 1930s came to an end. Only time would reveal to what extent FDR had encouraged an "imperial presidency." But there can be no doubt that by his programs and his awesome charisma he had helped expand federal and presidential power to the detriment of local and congressional autonomy. Meanwhile, as the 1940s loomed, the country began to turn away from domestic concerns and direct its attention to the threatening events taking place beyond its shores.

For Further Reading

John Kenneth Galbraith. *The Great Crash, 1929* (1955)
    This account of the great Wall Street panic of 1929 explains its causes and effects without resorting to technical jargon. Galbraith discusses the weaknesses of the banking structure, the spirit of speculation, and the dishonesty of highly placed men.

Peter Temin. *Did Monetary Forces Cause the Great Depression?* (1976)
    Temin tackles the question raised by the economic school that emphasizes the importance of the money supply in major economic cycles: Was it money mismanagement that produced the Depression? He concludes that the answer is essentially no, and he accepts the Keynesian view that weak investment was the culprit.

William E. Leuchtenburg. *Franklin D. Roosevelt and the New Deal, 1932–1940* (1963)
    In this excellent short history of Roosevelt and the New Deal, Leuchtenburg maintains that Roosevelt assumed "that a just society could be secured by imposing a welfare state on a capitalist foundation."

Richard H. Pells. *Radical Visions and American Dreams: Culture and Social Thought in the Depression Years* (1973)
    Confronted by the devastation of the early Depression, intellectuals and artists sought radical alterna-

tives to the beliefs and values of the 1920s. In an extraordinarily well-written analysis of articles, books, novels, plays, and films of the 1930s, Pells seeks to demonstrate an underlying conservatism in the thought of the intellectual elite.

Studs Terkel. *Hard Times*: *An Oral History of the Great Depression* (1970)

Here Terkel records his interviews with miners, farmers, migrant farm workers, corporation presidents, a "Share Our Wealth" organizer, hobos, and teachers. The unavoidable poverty of the Depression created feelings of confusion, shame, and guilt in many of these people.

Robert S. and Helen M. Lynd. *Middletown in Transition*: *A Study in Cultural Conflict* (1937)

The Lynds returned to Muncie, Indiana, to study its experience of the Depression. (See Chapter 25's reading suggestions.) They found that its citizens believed the Depression to be a temporary problem that did not require radical changes in the economic system.

James Agee and Walker Evans. *Let Us Now Praise Famous Men* (1941)

Evans's photography complements Agee's sensitive, compassionate record of the daily lives of three white tenant cotton farmers in Alabama during the hard years of the 1930s.

Theodore Rosengarten. *All God's Dangers*: *The Life of Nate Shaw* (1974)

An aged black Alabama cotton farmer tells of his years as a sharecropper in a world dominated by white landlords, bankers, fertilizer agents, gin operators, sheriffs, and judges. Central to his story is his participation in the Alabama Sharecroppers Union during the Depression, for which he was shot by white lawmen and jailed for twelve years.

Tom Kromer. *Waiting for Nothing* (1935)

An estimated 2 million Americans were homeless wanderers during the Depression, and Kromer was one of them. This autobiographical novel describes the constant degradation of down-and-outers: Panhandling, soup lines, job hunting, imprisonment for vagrancy, and the sermons and lice-ridden bunks of the "missions" were their lot.

Robert E. Sherwood. *Roosevelt and Hopkins*: *An Intimate History* (1948)

Only about a third of this dual biography concerns the New Deal years. But that third is one of the best brief histories of political leadership during the Depression. Written by a well-known playwright who was also a speechwriter for FDR.

James M. Burns. *Roosevelt*: *The Lion and the Fox* (1956)

The best discussion of Roosevelt as a domestic leader. Also works as a biography. Burns describes FDR's early life and his preparation for ultimate greatness.

Paul Conkin. *The New Deal* (1967)

A strong attack on the New Deal from the vantage of the political left. Conkin sees it as an instance of missed opportunities to equalize wealth and power in the United States.

John Steinbeck. *The Grapes of Wrath* (1939)

The best novel of the Great Depression. Recounts the story of midwestern farmers fleeing the Depression by heading west to California, and their reception there. Strongly pro–New Deal.

Chapter 27

World War II

Blunder, or Decision in the National Interest?

1904 Japan defeats Russia, takes control of Korea and Manchuria

1908 Root-Takahira Agreement

1921–22 Washington Conference • Benito Mussolini rises to power in Italy, imposing Fascist regime

1928 Kellogg-Briand Pact

1931–32 Japan reoccupies Manchuria

1932 Franklin D. Roosevelt elected president

1933 Adolf Hitler ends Weimar Republic and becomes German chancellor, imposing Nazi rule

1936 Hitler occupies the Rhineland • FDR reelected

1937–38 Japan invades China

1938 Hitler annexes Austria • Munich Pact cedes Czechoslovakia's Sudetenland to Germany

1939 Germany occupies the remainder of Czechoslovakia • The Soviet Union and Germany sign a nonaggression pact • Germany invades Poland; Great Britain and France declare war on Germany

1940 Germany conquers Norway, Denmark, Belgium, Luxembourg, Holland, and France • Japan, Italy, and Germany sign a military and economic agreement forming the Axis alliance • FDR reelected

1941 Lend-Lease Act • Germany invades the Soviet Union • Roosevelt and Churchill issue Atlantic Charter • Japan bombs Pearl Harbor; U.S. declares war on Japan; Germany and Italy declare war on U.S. • Manhattan Project begins • Fair Employment Practices Act • Hitler begins extermination of Jews

1942 Roosevelt orders the War Department to confine Japanese-Americans on West Coast • Battle of Midway checks Japanese Pacific advance • Women's Army and Navy corps (WACS, WAVES) established

1943 Allies defeat the German Afrika Korps, invade Sicily; Soviets stop Germans at Stalingrad • "Big Three" in Teheran • MacArthur and Nimitz close in on Pacific islands • California and Detroit race riots

1944 Normandy invasion • Japanese launch first kamikaze attacks • FDR reelected

1945 Yalta Conference • MacArthur recaptures Philippines • Germany defeated • FDR dies; Harry S. Truman becomes president • Atomic bombing of Hiroshima and Nagasaki • Soviets declare war on Japan • Japan surrenders

D ecember 7, 1941 dawned partly cloudy over the Hawaiian island of Oahu, 2,200 miles southwest of San Francisco. At Pearl Harbor, base of the United States Pacific Fleet, eight battleships, nine cruisers, twenty destroyers and forty-nine other American naval vessels lay in their berths or were at dry dock. It was Sunday, and many of the crew members were on weekend liberty. Elsewhere on the island Army Air Corps planes sat idle. Not one was in the air. Crews were away or asleep in the barracks. Some were attending religious services.

Suddenly at 7:55 A.M. Pearl Harbor burst into flames as Japanese torpedo planes and bombers unleashed tons of explosives onto the American ships tied up in Battleship Row. At the military airfields American planes were sitting ducks for the attackers. Only forty American pursuit planes took to the air to challenge the enemy. Meanwhile, several Japanese midget submarines, having sneaked through the harbor net, were launching torpedoes at every target in sight. Two hours later, when the attack ended, much of America's Pacific naval power had been destroyed.

In that brief, hellish interval 2,400 American sailors, marines, soldiers, airmen, and civilians died; 8 battleships were sunk or badly damaged; and 183 planes were lost. If the aircraft carrier force had been berthed rather than at sea, the destruction would have been almost total. Still, it was the worst naval disaster in American history.

A few minutes after news of the raid reached Washington, Japanese Ambassador Kichisaburo Nomura and special envoy Saburo Kurusu met with Secretary of State Cordell Hull. They had been instructed to inform Hull just prior to the attack that their government had broken off negotiation of the serious differences then existing between the United States and Japan. Tokyo did not want to alert American forces, but hoped to avoid the charge of having struck without warning. Unfortunately, the diplomats' instructions arrived late.

On December 8, at a little after noon, President Roosevelt appeared before a tense joint session of Congress to ask for a declaration of war against Japan. The country, he declared, would never forget that the Japanese had attacked while their emissaries were talking peace. December 7 was a date that would "live in infamy." With only one dissenting vote, Congress declared war against Japan. On December 11 Germany, Japan's ally, declared war against the United States; Italy, the third Axis power, immediately followed. The crowded and tragic events of four days had finally brought the United States into the greatest war in history.

How did the country arrive at this unhappy point? In early December 1941 few Americans doubted that the United States had been treacherously attacked and had no choice but to defend itself. The war stilled the discordant voices that for three years or more had debated war or peace. After 1945 Americans resumed the argument. A majority continued to believe that the nation had been placed in mortal danger by the Axis powers; the attack on December 7, 1941, they insisted, was merely the culmination of Axis plans to enslave all free peoples. A minority denied the danger from Germany, Italy, and Japan and concluded that the United States had blundered into the war or had even been pushed into it by scheming men. Who was right? Was American entrance into the war a mistake that might have, and should have, been avoided? Or was it the only way the United States could have protected itself and its vital interests against a pack of dangerous aggressors intent on destroying democracy and freedom?

Seeds of Conflict

The tragedy of Pearl Harbor had roots that extended back to the beginning of Japanese-American relations and were entangled with historical developments on at least three continents—Asia, America, and Europe. The Japanese attack, and the great war that followed, were the culmination of events that began as much as a century earlier and involved the relations of one half of the industrialized world with the other.

Friction with Japan. American interests in the Far East dated from early in the nineteenth century. At first these had focused on China, a United States trading partner and an object of American philanthropic and missionary concern. American-Japanese relations began in the 1850s when Captain Matthew Perry of the United States Navy forced the Japanese to abandon their traditional isolation and open trade relations with the West. Perry's visit thrust Japan into the modern world. The Japanese were soon imitating not only the West's parliamentary institutions, universal education, and industrialization but also its aggressive nationalism and imperialism. In 1895 Japan wrenched Korea from China. In 1904 it went to war against czarist Russia over China's loosely attached northern provinces and defeated the Russian colossus in a brief and bloody confrontation.

American-Japanese relations in the early twentieth century deteriorated. The United States supported the Japanese against the Russians in 1904/05. But when, at Portsmouth, New Hampshire, President Theodore Roosevelt helped bring the Russo-Japanese War to an end by compromise, the Japanese blamed the United States for losing the gains they considered their due. Matters worsened two years later when the San Francisco Board of Education placed Japanese students in segregated schools. The Japanese were outraged. Theodore Roosevelt patched things up with the so-called Gentlemen's Agreement: The school board would cancel its order, and the Japanese government would not issue any more passports to would-be immigrants to the United States. The issue was superficially settled, but by this time feelings between the two nations had been rubbed raw. In succeeding years there would be talk, particularly in the Hearst press, of the "yellow peril" in the Far East.

In the next few years Japanese and American interests would frequently clash in Asia. In the 1908 Root-Takahira Agreement, the Japanese agreed to accept the American view that China must remain independent and retain its territorial integrity. But to the Japanese it seemed that the United States and the other Western powers—"have" nations with abundant resources either at home or within their own empires—were trying to keep them—a "have-not" nation—from becoming a great power. Densely populated and confined to a small, resource-poor island chain, Japan felt it must have the resources of China and Southeast Asia or remain weak. For this vigorous nation to be confined to a small group of islands while other powers seized control of the rest of the non-Western world would be not only demeaning but also detrimental to Japan's vital interests.

During World War I the Japanese took advantage of Europe's preoccupation and presented China with the so-called Twenty-one Demands (1915), which

America's Pacific Fleet was decimated in the Pearl Harbor attack. The jumbled mass of wreckage in the foreground is the remains of two destroyers. Behind it rests the *Pennsylvania*, one of the few capital ships in the harbor to escape heavy damage.

would have reduced China to a Japanese protectorate. American protest forced the Japanese to back off. The Washington Armament Conference of 1921/22 further restricted Japan. Called by Secretary Hughes to help stabilize international relations in the Far East, the conference resulted in the Four Power Treaty by which France, the United States, England, and Japan pledged to respect one another's possessions in the Pacific. A Nine Power Treaty concluded among the same four, along with four smaller European nations plus China, promised to respect Chinese territorial integrity and the Open Door principle.

For a while Japanese ambitions diminished, and relations with the United States improved. At the end of the 1920s, however, Japanese military leaders gained control over their country's internal affairs and launched a more aggressive policy toward China. In 1931/32 the militarists provoked an "incident" with China and seized its rich northern province of Manchuria, converting it into a puppet state, renamed Manchukuo. The United States viewed Japan's aggression against its weaker neighbor as a violation of Japan's agreements. But distracted by the Depression and unwilling to take action stronger than the American public would then support, the government limited itself to diplomatic protests. In January 1932 Secretary of State Henry L. Stimson, reasserting John Hay's Open Door policy of a generation before, announced that the United States would not recognize any act that impaired the "territorial and administrative integrity of the Republic of China."

The Stimson Doctrine put Japan on notice that the United States opposed its China policy, but it did not deter the Japanese military leaders. Early in 1932 Japanese army units clashed with Chinese troops in Shanghai, and during the fighting thousands of Chinese civilians were killed. In 1937, following a shooting incident at the Marco Polo Bridge near Peking, the Japanese began a piecemeal occupation of the Chinese Republic. Before long their armies had seized major Chinese cities and torn vast chunks of the republic from the control of Chiang Kai-shek, leader of the Kuomintang, China's ruling party. In 1938 the Japanese announced a "new order" in the Far East based on thinly disguised Japanese domination of East Asia.

World War II: Japanese advances, 1941–1942

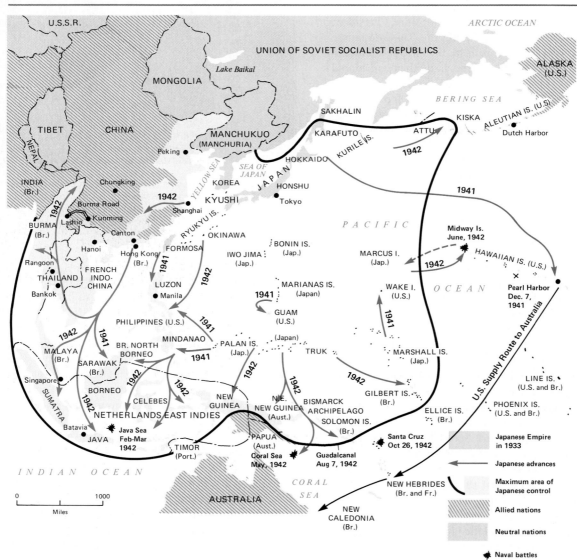

Map legend:
- Axis nations
- Annexed by Axis nations

NORWAY
FINLAND
Oslo • SWEDEN
Helsinki • • Leningrad
Stockholm •
ESTONIA
Moscow •
NORTH SEA
IRELAND
DENMARK
Copenhagen
LATVIA
LITH.
MEMEL (1939)
UNITED KINGDOM
London •
NETH.
GERMANY
Berlin •
EAST PRUSSIA
U.S.S.R.
ATLANTIC OCEAN
BELG.
RHINELAND (Remilitarized, 1936)
SUDETENLAND (1938)
• Warsaw
POLAND (Invaded Sept. 1, 1939)
Paris •
LUX.
CZECHOSLOVAKIA (1939)
FRANCE
SWITZ.
AUSTRIA (1938)
HUNGARY
PORTUGAL
Lisbon •
• Madrid
SPAIN
Corsica
Balearic Is.
Sardinia
ITALY
• Rome
YUGOSLAVIA
RUMANIA
BLACK SEA
BULGARIA
ALB. (1939)
SP. MOROCCO
MEDITERRANEAN SEA
Sicily
GREECE
TURKEY
MOROCCO
ALGERIA
TUNISIA

Fascist expansion in Europe, 1935–1939

The Rise of Fascism in Europe.

Meanwhile, an even more dangerous group of aggressors had appeared in Europe. In Italy, where bitter conflict between Communists and conservatives had undermined the parliamentary system, Benito Mussolini seized power in 1922 in the name of law and order. "Il Duce" and his Fascists before long brutally eliminated their opponents, established a centralized totalitarian regime, and revealed their aggressive foreign policy. In 1935 Fascist Italy attacked Ethiopia, one of the few still independent African nations, and conquered it. The moving plea of Ethiopia's emperor, the eloquent Haile Selassie, to the League of Nations brought economic sanctions against Italy. However, these were weakly supported by member nations and did not deter Mussolini.

Authoritarian governments resembling Fascist Italy's spread through eastern and southern Europe following the collapse of the international economy in the early 1930s. Clearly, Versailles and the various secondary treaties that had ended World War I had not stabilized the Continent. The boundaries drawn by Wilson and his colleagues had created several small nations out of the ruins of Austria-Hungary and the czarist empire; few of these had democratic traditions or the social institutions to support parliamentary government. By the early 1930s Hungary, Poland, Yugoslavia, and the Baltic states all had authoritarian regimes. Many of the new states were not viable economically or politically, and their weaknesses would be a permanent temptation to their greedy, more powerful neighbors.

Most dangerous of all, the postwar settlement failed to create a stable German democracy. By blaming Germany for the war, imposing vast indemnities on the German economy, and forcing the German nation to disarm, the Versailles treaty left a legacy of intense bitterness. German nationalists held the Weimar Republic, successor to Kaiser Wilhelm II's regime, responsible for the degrading treaty and never became reconciled to it. The Weimar leaders in turn never developed much confidence in the republic's parliamentary institutions or in their ability to govern a people without a democratic tradition.

Despite these problems, for a few years in the late 1920s the German people experienced a period of prosperity and cultural creativity under their new government. When the bottom fell out of the world economy in 1929, however, the inability of the Weimar government to stop Germany's downward economic spiral destroyed the public's fragile confidence. Right-wing and Communist groups quickly took advantage of the situation to attack democracy. By 1930 Weimar's enemies, on both the extreme left and the extreme right, were engaged in a life-or-death struggle to see who could destroy the democratic republic first and impose its own system on the German nation.

The victor in the competition was Adolf Hitler, a fanatical right-wing German nationalist whose National Socialist (Nazi) party proclaimed its intention to repudiate Versailles and the galling military restraints and financial burdens it had imposed on Germany. The new Third Reich would restore German pride and German might. Like Italy's Fascists, the Nazis glorified the state and expressed contempt for democracy and parliamentary institutions.

Indeed, Hitler's hatred of liberal values went beyond even Mussolini's. The Nazis were rabid racists who carried ideas of Nordic supremacy to a chilling conclusion: All other peoples were inferior beings who must ultimately bow to the *Herrenvolk*, the superrace of northern Europe. In Hitler's view the Jews, especially, were inferior beings who were responsible for all of Germany's calamities. Blaming the Jews for Germany's defeat in 1918, Hitler promised the German people that he would punish the Jews and make Germany a great nation once more.

Few Americans had paid much attention to events in Germany before 1933, but Hitler and the Nazis could not be ignored. Once head of the German state, the new chancellor renounced the armaments limitations of the Versailles treaty and began to rearm Germany. He swept away parliamentary government and either assassinated his democratic and leftist opponents or threw them into concentration camps. Finally, he instituted a reign of terror against Germany's Jewish population that sent thousands of the nation's most talented scientists, writers, musicians, doctors, and scholars fleeing to western Europe and the United States.

From the start Hitler's lust for territory and dominance was scarcely concealed. In 1936 he reoccupied the Rhineland, which had been demilitarized by the Versailles treaty. That same year he and Mussolini concluded an alliance of mutual support (the Rome-Berlin Axis). In 1937 the two dictators intervened in the civil war in Spain, siding with the fascist strongman Francisco Franco against the coalition of liberals, socialists, Communists, and anarchists (the Loyalists) who supported the Spanish Republic. In 1938 Hitler began his campaign to reincorporate all German-speaking territories in Europe into "Greater Germany" by annexing Austria. Hitler's next target was Czechoslovakia, a democratic republic formed in 1918 from parts of the Austro-Hungarian Empire that contained several million Germans in its Sudetenland region.

Americans watched Hitler's course with dismay. Not all saw fascism-nazism as a serious danger. Some Catholic Americans and conservatives preferred Hitler's client, Franco, to the Spanish Loyalists. A small number of Italian-Americans and German-Americans endorsed the dictators of their respective mother countries. There was even a very small contingent of old-stock Americans who believed that nazism represented the "wave of the future." Yet it is safe to say that the great majority of Americans deplored and feared what they saw taking place in central and southern Europe.

Hitler's progress disturbed his European neighbors even more. Under the Nazis Germany once more was becoming an expansionist nation that threatened the balance of power in Europe. But England and France, traumatized by their enormous losses in World War I and deeply troubled by the domestic repercussions of the worldwide Depression, were reluctant to take a strong stand against the German threat. When Hitler demanded that Czechoslovakia turn over the Sudetenland to Germany, the Czechs asked the Western democracies for aid. British Prime Minister Neville Chamberlain and French Premier Édouard Daladier refused. Believing they could successfully appease the Germans, they agreed at a conference with the German dictator at Munich in September 1938 to support Hitler's demands on the Czechs. Unable to confront Germany alone, the Czechs were forced to surrender the Sudetenland.

Chamberlain returned home from Munich convinced that appeasement would work and that the Munich Pact would bring "peace in our time." It did not. In March 1939 German forces occupied the now defenseless Czechoslovakia and set up a puppet regime. Hitler soon made territorial demands on his eastern neighbor, Poland. By this time only the near-blind could believe that Hitler and Mussolini did not pose a serious threat to the peace and stability of Europe.

Adolf Hitler in 1938, at a major Nazi party conference at Nurnberg. He was about to provoke the greatest war in history.

Roosevelt and the Interventionists. Though most Americans deplored the rise of the dictators and the European retreat from democracy, they did not agree on their implications for the United States. Liberals and leftists saw a rising tide of authoritarianism about to submerge free government everywhere. Even many conservative Americans feared that German, Italian, and Japanese expansionism would upset the delicate international balance of power long maintained by Britain and France, throwing the world into turmoil. The Nazis seemed particularly dangerous. When Hitler violated the Munich Pact, Americans were forced to confront the possibility that he could be stopped only by force. Would the British and French have the will or the strength to oppose him, or would they continue to appease him? And if they yielded, would he and his allies eventually become a direct threat to the United States?

Yet few Americans wished, in the mid- to late-1930s, to see the United States become directly involved. By this time American isolationism had hardened into an ideology that deplored all foreign wars and all foreign entanglements. The American people had no vital interests in these transoceanic conflicts, isolationists believed, and in the past they had been duped into them by munitions manufacturers, bankers, and other cunning, self-serving manipulators.

Between 1934 and 1936 isolationist views were reinforced by the Senate Munitions Investigating Committee hearings probing the origins of World War I. The committee, chaired by Senator Gerald P. Nye, advanced the view that those who profited from munitions manufacture had encouraged United States involvement in the war. In the wake of the Nye Committee hearings, Congress passed a series of Neutrality Acts requiring the president in the event of war to prohibit arms shipments to belligerents, forbid American citizens to sail on belligerent ships, and deny bankers the right to extend credit to warring powers. By 1937, according to an opinion poll, 94 percent of the American people favored nonintervention abroad regardless of who the combatants were or how just their cause.

President Roosevelt from the outset was more

interventionist than most Americans. A disciple of Admiral Alfred Thayer Mahan and Woodrow Wilson, FDR believed in America's responsibility as a great power and, later, in international cooperation to achieve a stable world order. During the 1920s he moved with the drift of American public opinion to isolationism, but the rise of the dictators quickly revived his internationalist convictions. At what moment Roosevelt and his advisers concluded that the dictators must be stopped is unclear. As early as 1933 he tried to induce Congress to prohibit the sale of arms to aggressor nations. In 1935, in the interest of world security, he tried to get the United States admitted to the World Court. Congress, dominated by isolationists, rejected both schemes.

Frustrated in Europe, Roosevelt worked to strengthen the United States against "the aggressors" by establishing closer ties with Latin America. His Good Neighbor policy, built on the efforts of his Republican predecessors, was designed to create "hemispheric solidarity." During his first term of office FDR renounced the Platt Amendment, which had allowed the United States to intervene in Cuban affairs. At two Latin American conferences in 1933 and 1936, the United States reinforced the pledge (given in the 1928 Clark Memorandum) to cease intervening in the affairs of Central and South America. Before long the United States had ended its remaining occupations of Caribbean nations. The Good Neighbor policy would pay dividends: When war came, almost all the Latin American countries would support the United States against its enemies.

During his second term, as the international situation darkened, the president turned to face the aggressors directly. In 1937, following Japan's attack on China, he denounced "international lawlessness" and suggested that nations contributing to "international anarchy" be "quarantined"—isolated and walled off by the rest of the world. By this time the president clearly considered Germany, Italy, and Japan potentially dangerous adversaries; in private conversations he referred to them as the "three bandit nations."

Ideology affected Roosevelt's views. The totalitarian and militaristic regimes of Germany, Italy, and Japan represented everything a liberal democrat despised: repression, racism, and brutality. The president, moreover, was surrounded by advisers who saw Hitler as Antichrist, embodying every primitive, irrational, reactionary current in Western society. But there were also more self-interested motives at play. Ever since the late nineteenth century the United States had relied on the Western European nations, especially Britain,

to impose stability in the world outside the Americas. With England and France threatened by Germany, and the Japanese on the rampage in the western Pacific, the president feared for the safety of the United States. What would happen if Britain and France would not, or could not, check Hitler? A triumphant Germany to the east, allied with a triumphant Japan to the west, would leave the United States a besieged outpost in the middle of a hostile and dangerous world.

Many, perhaps most, Americans shared FDR's opinion of the dictators. A Gallup poll in mid-1939 showed that 65 percent of Americans endorsed a boycott of Germany and Italy, and 55 percent wanted the Neutrality Acts revised to aid the democracies. Few citizens favored their nation's direct involvement, however. There seemed little need. If war were to erupt, Britain and France would surely win. But even if they did not, the American fortress could hold out indefinitely against the victorious dictators, safe behind its ocean moats, patrolled by its powerful navy.

The Erosion of American Neutrality

In the fall of 1939 American complacency would be put to the test. On September 1, after signing a nonaggression pact with Russia's Joseph Stalin, his former archenemy, Hitler attacked Poland. Two days later Britain and France, having pledged their support to Poland, declared war on Germany.

On September 3, Roosevelt delivered a fireside chat to the American people. Like Wilson in 1914, he promised to expend "every effort" to avoid war. Consciously diverging from his predecessor, however, he refused to ask Americans to "remain neutral in thought as well." As required by the neutrality legislation, he forbade the export of arms to the belligerents. But on September 21 the president called a special session of Congress to ask for repeal of the arms embargo.

Roosevelt's tactics when Congress met typified his cautious behavior in dealing with his isolationist opponents. The president knew they would use anti–New Deal feelings to win support for their position and he kept out of sight while others carried the burden of getting repeal through Congress. Meanwhile, behind the scenes he used his patronage to bring fellow Democrats into line. The strategy worked. On October 27, by a vote of 63 to 30, the Senate replaced the embargo with a "cash-and-carry" provision that permitted the British and French to buy war matériel as long as they paid cash and transported their purchases in their own ships. A week later the House accepted the revision, 243 to 181.

Hitler Conquers Europe.

Had the war against Hitler gone well for the Allies, the United States could have preserved its neutrality. It did not. Poland fell to the German invaders in five weeks. For several months thereafter an ominous quiet hung over Europe. During the "phony war," as the isolationists contemptuously called it, nothing happened to indicate that the major European powers were locked in a life-or-death struggle. Then on April 9, 1940, the German army struck at Norway and Denmark. Denmark fell virtually without a shot. Norway, with the aid of British and French troops and naval units, fought bravely against the invader but was quickly subdued. On May 10 German armored units smashed across the borders into Belgium, Luxembourg, and Holland. In a week German armored columns were sweeping across France toward Paris.

The British and French fought back, but their armies were overwhelmed by the fast-moving German tank columns supported by terrifying Stuka dive bombers. The German *Blitzkrieg* destroyed French military resistance in a few weeks. By the end of May the British forces in France were pinned against the English Channel near Dunkirk by a tightening ring of German tanks and artillery. The British army was able to hold the German tanks at bay long enough for an armada of small ships to rescue its troops from the flaming beaches, but most of their equipment had to be left behind. On June 10 Paris surrendered, and Italy entered the war as Germany's ally. On June 22, with more than half their country in German hands, the French, now led by Marshal Henri Philippe Pétain, an arch conservative, signed an armistice with the Germans that allowed the invaders to occupy the whole northern half of the country and the Atlantic coast. Some Frenchmen refused to surrender, however, and rallied around the free French leader, Charles de Gaulle, who established a London-based government-in-exile. Before long the Free French and the Pétain government located at Vichy were battling for control over the French overseas empire.

In a little over three months Hitler had conquered Norway, Denmark, Luxembourg, France, Belgium, and Holland, and had almost destroyed the military power of mighty Britain. He had done what his imperial predecessor, Wilhelm II, had been unable to accomplish in four years of war. Americans were stunned by the rush of catastrophic events. *Time* magazine in its issue of May 20, 1940, reported American opinion as appalled but determined. Among the crowds that gathered on Boston's Washington Street to read the fast-breaking news bulletins, the talk was: "We'll be in it if it keeps up six months." In California "many . . . talked of U.S. naval participation in the war; and a feeling of inevitability was widespread." Even in Omaha, in the heart of the strongly isolationist Midwest, the magazine reported people saying: "It looks like we can't keep out."

Roosevelt's reaction was swift: He asked Congress for vast sums for rearmament, including funds for 50,000 planes a year and a "two-ocean navy." By October Congress had appropriated $17 billion to strengthen the nation's weak defenses. In September it had authorized peacetime compulsory military service for the first time in American history. On October 16, 1940, 6.5 million young men registered for the draft and prepared to go to training camps.

Meanwhile, the Germans had launched the Battle of Britain, an all-out air attack designed to soften England up for invasion. German aircraft bombarded the British Isles by day until the losses exacted by the gallant but badly stretched Royal Air Force made these raids too costly. In early September the Luftwaffe began night raids that set London and other English cities ablaze. The British people suffered grievously but held on. Sustaining them were the words of their eloquent prime minister, Winston Churchill, who had succeeded Chamberlain after the defeat in Norway. A master of English prose, Churchill declared that if the British Empire lasted a thousand years, men would say: " 'This was their finest hour.' " He promised victory though the cost would be "blood, toil, tears, and sweat."

Britain's brave struggle aroused the admiration of virtually all Americans. News from Europe for the first time was relayed immediately to the United States by short-wave radio, creating a sense of participation impossible in an earlier day. From London Americans heard Edward R. Murrow and other American correspondents describe the Nazi air attacks while sounds of air-raid sirens and bombs filled the background. They also heard the defiant and moving words of Churchill. As they listened to the broadcasts, most Americans found it impossible not to feel that they themselves were cowering with the British under the rain of German bombs.

Roosevelt's Third Term.

By mid-1940 few Americans doubted that Britain's plight was desperate, and most believed that their country was next on Hitler's list after he had gobbled up and digested his enemies in

After France's fall, American admiration and support for Britain was reinforced by the fortitude the British showed in the face of the German blitz. Pictures like this one, showing Londoners bedding down in the city's subway to escape the Nazis' bombs, created an outpouring of sympathy in the United States.

Europe. In the spring supporters of England, New Deal liberals, and what would later be called the eastern intellectual establishment organized the Committee to Defend America by Aiding the Allies. Its chairman was the Kansas newspaper editor William Allen White. That fall a Gallup poll showed that half the voters were willing to help England "even at the risk of getting into war." Yet the isolationist voice remained powerful and insistent. In early September of 1940 a group of isolationists organized the America First Committee, composed of philosophical isolationists and conservatives with a fringe of Anglophobes, Roosevelt haters, and pro-Nazi anti-Semites. For the next year the two groups waged a bitter war for the minds of the American people.

Meanwhile, the country found itself in the middle of another presidential campaign. After keeping everyone guessing for months, FDR concluded that the survival of liberal policies and the nation's safety during the international crisis required his strong hand at the helm. Having effectively eliminated all potential party rivals, Roosevelt left the Democrats with no choice but to break with the two-term tradition and nominate him for a third time.

The Republican nominee was Wendell Willkie, a utility magnate from Indiana whose sincerity and boyish charm appealed to younger, less conservative Republicans. Fortunately for the country's unity,

Willkie proved to be as much of an internationalist as Roosevelt. He denounced the president's gift of fifty overage destroyers to England in exchange for bases in British North American possessions (September 3) as "the most dictatorial and arbitrary act of any President in the history of the United States." But on the whole, the two candidates were careful to avoid arguing over foreign policy.

Toward the end of the campaign, however, Roosevelt uttered some words that would later make his friends wince. In a speech in late October he promised his audience that American men would not go overseas to fight. "I have said this before," he declared, "but I shall say it again and again and again: Our boys are not going to be sent into any foreign wars." FDR would have been elected in any case; in the midst of the grave world crisis Americans were not inclined to exchange the veteran leader for a novice. But the promise helped. On election day Roosevelt carried 38 states to Willkie's 10 and won a popular majority of 27.2 million votes to his opponent's 22.3 million.

Lend-Lease. During the next full year of peace Roosevelt deliberately moved the country ever closer to war, certain that the United States could not avoid confronting the dictators. A month following the election Churchill wrote to FDR, laying out Britain's plight in stark outline. The desperate prime minister warned that the well-being of the American people was "bound up with the survival and independence of the British Commonwealth of Nations." British sea power protected the United States against its enemies. But it was spread very thin and might collapse entirely if the Pétain government at Vichy turned over the French navy to the Nazis. Furthermore, if the Nazis gained control of the French fleet, they could then threaten Latin America. Nor was this all. In the Far East Japan was taking advantage of French, Dutch, and British weakness and inability to protect their Asian possessions by expanding its power and influence. Britain did not need American manpower, said Churchill, but it did need to guarantee that American supplies could get through the tightening German submarine blockade. Churchill pleaded for American naval assistance and for an end to the cash-and-carry aid. Britain was running short of money. Cash-and-carry was a great improvement over the embargo, but more direct help was needed if Britain was to continue to serve as a bulwark against the Nazi scourge.

Churchill's letter was a masterly plea that played effectively on Roosevelt's deepest fears. The president quickly responded. On December 17 he called a press conference and, after puckishly informing the assembled reporters that there was no particular news that day, he proceeded to tell them a parable. Suppose, he said, my neighbor's home catches on fire and he needs my garden hose to put it out. Do I bargain with him over the cost of the hose? Obviously not. I give it to him and then say: "I want my garden hose back after the fire is over." If it is damaged, you replace it "in kind."

Soon afterward in a fireside chat, Roosevelt prepared the ground for his new aid scheme by warning the public of the critical danger to civilization posed by the Axis powers and explaining the need for the United States to become the "arsenal of democracy." In January 1941 he submitted the "lend-lease" bill to Congress. The measure broke sharply with the country's isolationist past. It authorized the president to "lend" military equipment to any country "whose defense the President deems vital to the defense of the United States" and provided $7 billion for the purpose, the largest single appropriation in the nation's history. Most Americans apparently favored the measure, but the great power it seemed to confer on the chief executive made them uneasy. The bill immediately came under withering attack. Senator Burton K. Wheeler of Montana called lend-lease the "New Deal's Triple A foreign policy" that would "plow under every fourth American boy." The isolationist *Chicago Tribune*

called it "a bill for the destruction of the American Republic . . . [and] a brief for an unlimited dictatorship . . . with power to make war and alliances forever." Administration officials retorted that Britain faced invasion within three months and without such aid would be defeated. If the British navy were destroyed or seized, the United States would be in serious danger.

Both sides had a point. Wheeler was being grossly unfair, and the *Tribune*'s attack was as much anti-Roosevelt, anti–New Deal as a legitimate defense of the Constitution. But in later years many Americans would come to regret the erosion of congressional control over foreign policy that began under FDR. Yet the president was not consciously attempting to usurp power; he and his advisers were expressing their honest fears. And most informed citizens supported them. After a furious battle the congressional isolationists were defeated. On March 11 Roosevelt signed the lend-lease bill into law. In a few weeks the $7 billion of war matériel that Congress had authorized began to flow to Britain.

English ordinance personnel unpack American revolvers delivered under the terms of lend-lease, the program for supplying the Allies with desperately needed weapons. If American equipment made its way to the fighting fronts, could American soldiers be far behind?

United States Aid Increases. The additional aid provided by lend-lease had little immediate effect. During the spring of 1941 Americans held their breath as Germany and Italy smashed the Yugoslavs and the Greeks and forced the British to retreat almost to the Nile in North Africa. Meanwhile, Britain was losing the Battle of the Atlantic, as German submarines sent vast quantities of American munitions and guns to the bottom of the ocean. Could nothing be done to stop the Axis?

In Washington, Roosevelt was uncertain what course to take and moved cautiously. On April 9 he concluded an agreement putting Greenland, a Danish colony, under United States protection, thereby extending American naval patrols partway to Britain. His advisers urged him to use the United States Navy to convoy arms all the way to Britain, but the president held back. On May 13 he agreed to shift part of the Pacific Fleet to the Altantic. In mid-May he told Secretary of the Treasury Henry Morgenthau, Jr.:"I am waiting to be pushed into the situation."

On May 27 Roosevelt proclaimed an unlimited national emergency giving him expanded powers over the economy. He followed this move in June by an executive order freezing Axis assets in the United States and placing German and Italian ships in American ports under federal control. Each action brought the nation a trifle closer to outright belligerency, but still the president was reluctant to throw the country's full weight behind Britain. He believed war must come; but fearing the wrath of the isolationists, he felt unable to start it himself. Instead, he waited impatiently for the Germans to move offensively against the United States.

Hitler carefully avoided a showdown with America. However outraged at United States aid to Britain, he looked the other way, for he had other things in mind. Four thousand miles from Washington, on the plains of eastern Europe, German and Soviet troops faced one another along a common border that ran through what had once been the independent republic of Poland. For almost two years the two countries had maintained an uneasy marriage of convenience. Then, on June 22, 1941, in fulfillment of his long-cherished ambition to destroy communism and expand German power eastward, the Nazi dictator sent his tanks, aircraft, and troops hurtling across the border toward the heart of the Soviet Union.

In London and Washington the Nazi attack provoked a quick response. The British and Americans could have ignored Russia's plight. The Soviet Union, after all, was the seat of international communism, and many people in both countries considered it no better than Nazi Germany. These anti-Soviet feelings had been reinforced by the 1939 Nazi-Soviet pact and by the brutal Soviet invasion of small, democratic Finland in the winter of 1939/40. Yet neither the British nor the American governments hesitated very long to offer help to the Russians. Two days after the German attack Roosevelt promised aid to the Soviet Union. In the fall a British-American mission traveled to Moscow to determine Soviet war needs. Soon afterward the United States pledged $1 billion in lend-lease matériel to the embattled Russians; by the end of the war American aid had grown to $11 billion in value.

Although he welcomed Russia as a new ally against Hitler, Roosevelt could not lose sight of Britain and the Atlantic. In July he sent troops to occupy Iceland and announced that the American navy would escort British-bound supplies as far east as that strategic island. The following month the president met Churchill on a ship off Newfoundland. Out of that meeting came the Atlantic Charter. This document affirmed and expanded upon the Wilsonian ideals of self-determination for all people, freer international trade, cooperative efforts for world prosperity, freedom of the seas, disarmament, and "freedom from fear and want." The charter was a moving declaration of liberal principles, but its real significance was its linkage of America and Great Britain in a common set of world goals.

Bit by bit, Roosevelt was pushing the United States toward a direct confrontation with Germany. He did not confide his goals to the American people, and that lack of candor has troubled even his firmest admirers. Yet the president was not seeking power or glory. FDR was certain that the fate of civilization depended on Hitler's defeat, and he felt he must do whatever was necessary to guarantee that defeat. Yet he feared taking a divided people into war and was still convinced that the enemy must act first.

Events seemed to be moving the way FDR hoped in the fall of 1941. Soon after his return from Newfoundland, a German U-boat commander off the coast of Iceland, believing his vessel to be under British attack, launched two torpedoes at the United States destroyer *Greer*, which had been tracking the submarine and radioing its location to the British. The *Greer* returned the fire. Roosevelt (neglecting to mention that the *Greer* had not been engaged in neutral activities) called the incident an act of "piracy legally and morally," adding that from now on American naval vessels would "shoot on sight" at any German submarine found between Iceland and North America. On October 9, 1941, he asked Congress to modify the Neutrality Acts further to permit the arming of American merchant vessels. Early in November, after the Germans had torpedoed the destroyer *Kearney* and sunk the U.S.S. *Reuben James* with heavy loss of life, Congress authorized the arming of American merchant vessels and removed restrictions on their carrying cargoes to belligerent ports.

By mid-November the United States was in an actual naval war with the Germans. Yet a substantial minority of the American people still hoped to avoid full-scale military intervention. As recently as August the House had voted to extend the draft period an additional eighteen months by a margin of a single vote. Isolationist sentiment in Congress was powerful enough to prevent easy passage of the modifications of the Neutrality Acts. In the Senate the president's majority was only 50 to 37; in the House, 212 to 194.

The continuing isolationism troubled Roosevelt. What if the Germans avoided further serious incidents? How could Americans be brought, united, to the point of war? The problem stumped the president. As his friend and biographer Robert Sherwood later wrote: "He had no tricks left. . . . The bag from which he had pulled so many rabbits was empty." Fate—and the Japanese—would soon solve the problem for the president and the undecided nation.

Miscalculations in the East.

Roosevelt and his advisers misunderstood and underestimated the Japanese. Japan had a deep emotional involvement in its East Asian expansionist policies. It also feared that without the resources of Manchuria, China, and the East Indies, it could not survive as a great power. It would not be easy to get the Japanese to back down in China, or the Far East generally, without running a serious risk of military confrontation. In addition to underestimating Japan's commitment to expansionism, the American government did not take Japan seriously as a military opponent. Americans knew that Japanese industry was capable of producing the shoddy trinkets and gewgaws that flooded the five-and-dime stores of the day. But could it produce modern weapons?

Although it underestimated the Japanese, the American government, believing Hitler the more dangerous threat, at first sought to appease Japan. Having neither the steel nor the petroleum to maintain a modern war machine, the Japanese had to rely on imports. Until the fall of France, the United States, over the protest of China's many American friends, supplied much of them. When the Japanese began to pressure the Vichy French for bases in Indochina and threatened the Dutch in the oil-rich East Indies, however, the American government imposed licensing requirements on the export of American oil and scrap metal and forbade the export of aviation gasoline.

These moves goaded the Japanese into seeking allies elsewhere. In September 1940 Japan signed an agreement with Italy and Germany, converting the Rome-Berlin Axis into the Rome-Berlin-Tokyo Axis. The agreement pledged the three nations to support one another's plans to establish a "new order" in Europe and a "Greater East Asia" in the Far East. If any one of them was attacked by a fourth power— with which it was not then already at war—the others would go to its aid. The Soviet Union, which the Japanese feared, was specifically exempted from this provision, making it clear that it was aimed at the United States. In effect, if the United States attacked either Japan or one of the European Axis nations, it would find itself with a two-ocean war. The American government responded to this threat by prohibiting the export of scrap iron and steel outside the Western Hemisphere.

As yet, neither the Americans nor the Japanese were prepared for a showdown. In March 1941 the moderate government of Prince Fumimaro Konoye opened conversations with Secretary of State Hull in Washington to prevent an irreparable break between the two countries. The Japanese were willing to make minor concessions but not, as Hull demanded, to evacuate China. As the talks dragged on, the Japanese, who already controlled northern Indochina, moved to seize the rest of the French colony. In July 1941 Japan forced the Vichy government to grant it bases in southern Indochina, close to the East Indies and British Malaya. Shortly thereafter, Roosevelt ordered all Japanese assets in the United States frozen, virtually ending trade between the two nations. This move was quickly followed by the order of the Dutch governor of the East Indies embargoing Dutch oil to Japan.

By showing Japan how dependent it was on foreign sources of raw material, the Americans and Dutch hoped to give the Japanese government pause. Their moves had the opposite effect. During the remaining months of peace two groups of Japanese leaders—the military chiefs on one hand and the royal family on the other—battled over what policy to pursue toward the United States. Among the military leaders, the army generals were most confident and militant. The admirals, though convinced that Japan had little chance to win a war with America, favored a massive surprise blow that would so damage American military power that the United States would be forced to give Japan a free hand in East Asia. The American refusal to supply Japan with oil would soon cripple the Japanese war machine, the admirals said. Why not seize the oil wells in the Dutch East Indies and the vital rubber and tin of Malaya? Because such a move would certainly bring an American declaration of war, it would be advisable to open with a surprise knockout punch against the American navy. Prince Konoye and Emperor Hirohito opposed this aggressive course except as a last resort.

In August, Konoye proposed a meeting with President Roosevelt to iron out Japanese-American differences. Secretary Hull distrusted the Japanese, however, and the meeting was never held. But the American government was not anxious for a showdown, and for a while strung Prince Konoye along. In October, his credibility with his own people damaged by American delays, Konoye resigned in favor of the more militant war minister, Hideki Tojo.

Tojo was determined to break the deadlock between the two nations or attack. On November 5 the Japanese government resolved to adopt the admirals' policy unless the United States and Great Britain halted their aid to the Chinese and allowed Japan access to oil and other vital raw materials from America and Southeast Asia. In return, Japan would agree to withdraw its troops from the French possessions when the war with China was over and would eventually leave China itself. On November 25 Admiral Isoroku Yama-

moto ordered the navy strike force to put to sea, subject to last-minute recall.

The United States refused to accept the final Japanese terms. America could not, Hull believed, end its aid to Chiang Kai-shek; we were too firmly committed to a stable Chinese republic to desert him. Moreover, the Japanese could not be trusted to evacuate China.

The American government had broken the top-secret Japanese "purple cipher" by this time and knew from intercepted messages that unless a settlement with the United States was soon reached, Japan would launch an attack against American or British-Dutch forces somewhere in the Pacific. The American government assumed that the blow would land in Southeast Asia and alerted the United States military commanders in Hawaii and the Philippines. On the morning of December 7, Washington time, Army Chief of Staff General George C. Marshall sent radiograms to San Francisco, the Canal Zone, Hawaii, and the Philippines, warning of an imminent attack. Electrical interference delayed the radio message to Hawaii, and it had to be sent by cable. By the time it arrived at the Western Union office in Honolulu, the bombs were falling over Pearl Harbor. On December 8 the United States declared war on Japan. Three days later the Germans and Italians ended American uncertainty regarding the European conflict by declaring war on

Americans were horrified—and suddenly unified—by Japan's surprise attack on Pearl Harbor. But the Japanese were unified too, and certain they were in the right. A Japanese pilot aboard Admiral Yamamoto's carrier strike force made this prophetic sketch before he and his fellow pilots set out to attack Pearl Harbor.

the United States. The titanic struggle over intervention was finally over: A united American people were now heart and soul in the crusade to stop Hitler and the other aggressors.

Mobilization and Social Change

World War II was the most costly war in American history. Between December 1941 and the Japanese surrender in the fall of 1945, almost $300 billion was poured into the war effort. Sixteen million men and women served in the armed forces. Of these, almost 300,000 died in combat; another 700,000 were wounded.

The government, as we saw, had begun raising a military force before Pearl Harbor. Late in 1940 the first peacetime draftees were inducted into service. Most found the process of becoming a soldier exciting but painful. After induction the new GI—so called because of his "government issue" gear—was shipped off to a training camp for eight weeks or more of "basic training," followed by either advanced infantry training or, if he was qualified, for instruction in some specialty. The voluntary branches of the service—Navy, Marine Corps, Coast Guard, and Army Air Corps—conducted similar training operations.

Most young Americans found it difficult to adjust to the armed forces. They were fed well, and the transformation of many once-skinny adolescents into well-muscled young men amazed their families and friends when they returned home on their first leave. But they did not like military discipline and despised the hard, dirty jobs of obstacle-course running, calisthenics, bivouacking, and marching—not to speak of KP (kitchen police) and guard duty. The War and Navy departments tried to make the hardships acceptable by providing libraries, movies, and religious services. Church and volunteer organizations sponsored camp dances to which young women were invited. Yet complaints about the military's stupidities and foul-ups became the mark of the wartime citizen-soldier; SNAFU, an acronym usually politely interpreted as *situation normal, all fouled up*, was added to the American vocabulary. Nevertheless, as time would show, American youths would make fine soldiers when well led. They would go through the hell of war griping all the way, and yet fight bravely when they had to.

Racism on the Home Front. Pearl Harbor was a tremendous shock to American confidence. For days after the frightening news from Hawaii, Americans peered anxiously at the skies, expecting to see bombers overhead with Japan's rising-sun emblem on their wings. In the early weeks following December 7 there were air-raid scares in several cities.

The fears were aggravated by an unbroken string of Japanese victories that followed the initial Pearl Harbor attack. On the West Coast something close to panic seized Americans in these early months. Jittery citizens, certain that the Japanese population was a potential "fifth column," demanded their removal from the exposed Pacific coast. Fear was reinforced by racism and greed. Long the targets of white bigotry, the Japanese were envied for their economic success. Many whites coveted their property, much of it rich farmland.

For a time Washington officials resisted the pressure for relocation by West Coast congressmen and state officials, including the zealous California attorney general, Earl Warren. But they soon yielded. On February 19, 1942, Roosevelt signed an executive order allowing the War Department to "prescribe military areas . . . from which any or all persons may be excluded." Within weeks thousands of Issei (immigrant Japanese) and Nisei (American-born Japanese) were forced to sell their homes, businesses, and farms, often at a fraction of their true value, and move to detention centers in isolated areas of inland states such as Utah, Arizona, and Arkansas.

Though these centers were a far cry from the concentration camps of Nazi Europe, they were a disgrace to American democratic principles. Fortunately most of the imprisoned people survived the war; remarkably, many of them retained their loyalty toward the United States.

By comparison, the government treated other enemy nationals generously. Italians and Germans, even those not citizens, were left alone. Leaders of the pro-Nazi German-American Bund, along with a handful of native-born Fascists, were indicted under the antisubversive Smith Act of 1940, which imposed tighter controls over aliens and made it a crime for any person or group to teach the overthrow of the government by violent means. But the extreme anti-Germanism that characterized World War I did not surface. Nor was there very much of the superpatriotism that abounded during the earlier war. Antiradical sentiment declined sharply. The Communist party, which had denounced Roosevelt as a warmonger during 1940 and early 1941, hailed him as a hero after the Soviet Union was attacked by Hitler. Thereafter, the American Communists threw themselves into the war effort with great fervor. Impressed by the patriotic enthusiasm of the Communists and deeply moved by the heroic

Some 110,000 people of Japanese descent—many of them American-born and citizens—were rounded up in California, Washington, Oregon, and Arizona, and sent to "relocation camps" following the Pearl Harbor attack. The move, spurred by panic and bigotry, was without precedent in American history, and was a blot on an otherwise good record on civil liberties during the war.

struggle of the Russian people against Hitler, Americans avoided most of their antiradical excesses of 1917/18.

Of course, the war did not turn the country into a democratic paradise. Besides the hostility toward the Japanese, antagonism surfaced toward Mexican-Americans. In June 1943 some young Mexican-Americans attacked U.S. sailors on liberty in Los Angeles. The Chicano youths had been wearing "zoot suits"—flashy outfits with broad-shouldered jackets, tightly pegged trousers, and wide-brimmed flat hats. The sailors retaliated by beating up every zoot-suiter they could find. It was, *Time* magazine said, "the ugliest brand of mob action" in California "since the coolie riots of the 1870s." Hundreds were injured before the violence ended.

Blacks, too, fell victim to wartime social stresses. War brought a mixture of good and bad to black Americans, much as it had in 1917/18. During peacetime rearmament defense contractors had resisted hiring black workers. When A. Philip Randolph, president of the all-black Brotherhood of Sleeping Car Porters, threatened in May 1941 to organize a mass march on Washington to protest this exclusion, Roosevelt established the Fair Employment Practices Committee (FEPC). Thereafter, the FEPC and the pressure of urgent war orders forced open the employment doors to black Americans. Black men and women by the

thousands soon found jobs in the tank factories of Detroit, the steel mills of Pittsburgh, the shipyards of Puget Sound, and the aircraft factories of southern California, Texas, and Kansas.

Economic improvement for blacks during the war was not matched by major gains elsewhere, however. More black Americans than ever before became commissioned officers, and for the first time blacks were admitted to the Marine Corps and to the navy at ranks higher than mess boy. But through most of the war they were kept in segregated military units. Their obvious second-class status injured black military morale. In the South and at army camps in the North, serious tensions existed between black servicemen and neighboring white civilians. In Detroit, where thousands of blacks and newly arrived southern whites lived and worked side by side, racial friction set off a bloody race riot in mid-1943 that left 30 people dead, 800 injured, and over $2 million in property destroyed.

Despite their mistreatment, black Americans were loyal and patriotic. Hitler's virulent racism, of course, was particularly repulsive to black Americans; but many of them might have been attracted to the Japanese if only because they were nonwhites fighting the white Western nations. A tiny minority did find the Japanese cause appealing; the overwhelming majority, however, supported the war effort. Like other Americans, black citizens bought bonds, worked in war plants, and collected scrap metal and rubber. Thousands of black troops fought in Europe and the Pacific. In Italy the all-black Ninety-ninth Fighter Squadron achieved a distinguished record in air combat against the German Luftwaffe.

Yet many black Americans remained skeptical of the great war to make the world safe for freedom, and black leaders put the nation on notice that it could not continue to treat black people as badly as it had in the past. Rather than opposing the war effort, however, they called for the "Double V"—"victory over our enemies at home and victory over our enemies on the battlefields abroad." Ultimately, black people would have to fight for their own civil rights, black leaders declared. As Walter White, head of the NAACP, noted, the majority of black soldiers would "return home convinced that whatever betterment of their lot is achieved must come largely from their own efforts. They will return determined to use these efforts to the utmost."

Pressures on the Family. The war was hard on families. Married men had been exempted from the peacetime draft; but in 1943, when the need for manpower reached its peak, even fathers were inducted. The wartime industrial boom also strained family relations. Much war industry was located in the South, the Southwest, and the Pacific Coast states. Whole families from the Northeast and Midwest moved to remote parts of the nation to work in war plants, but sometimes male workers left their wives and children behind to move in with parents or other relations. Between 1940 and 1945 the number of families headed by a married woman with her husband absent rose from 770,000 to almost 3 million.

Young wives and mothers made the best of a bad situation, but the best was often not very good. Women were lonely and sought out one another's company. Some inevitably found other male companionship, and marriages broke up. More than a few GIs received "Dear John" letters telling them that other men had taken their place.

Many young women found the war an opportunity. In 1942 Congress authorized the Women's Auxiliary Army Corps (the WACS, after *auxiliary* was dropped from the title), and later established the WAVES, the navy equivalent. In all, a quarter of a million young women donned military uniforms and served as clerk-typists, technicians, jeep drivers, or nurses at home and behind the front lines.

Many women went to work to keep busy, to supplement their incomes, or to help the war effort.

Black Americans fought in segregated units in World War II, just as they had in World War I. Here the Army Air Force's all-black 99th Fighter Group assembles at the beachhead of Anzio, Italy.

Woman war workers made up for the manpower shortage during World War II.

"Rosie the Riveter" in overalls and cap became a familiar figure in every American industrial community. The nation admired her type, but working mothers compounded the problems caused by absent fathers. Children often did not get proper care. Agnes Meyer, wife of the *Washington Post* publisher, observed their plight in California:

> In the San Fernando Valley . . . where several war plants are located, a social worker counted 45 infants locked in cars of a single parking [lot]. In Vallejo the children sit in movies, seeing the same film over and over again until mother comes off the swing shift and picks them up. Some children of working parents are locked in their homes, others are locked out.

During the war juvenile delinquency soared. Crime as a whole dropped, but juvenile arrests increased 20 percent in 1943. In San Diego, a major aircraft-manufacturing center and naval base, 55 percent more boys were charged with crimes in 1945 than in the previous year; the arrest rate for girls climbed 355 percent.

The pressures on families were particularly severe where there was an especially heavy concentration of war industry. In such areas housing was in short supply, and families had to live in trailers or Quonset huts. Classroom space was often limited, and schools were forced to hold double sessions. The government provided money for "war-impacted" areas, but it was not enough to improve conditions created by the influx of new people.

To a degree, all civilians paid a price for the war. After Pearl Harbor the government clamped down on automobile production and housing construction. It soon began to ration rubber tires and later restricted gasoline consumption. Racetracks, motels, and vacation resorts lost business; but passenger railroad service boomed. Metals, deflected into war production, disappeared from many familiar items, and consumers had to accept familiar commodities made of wood or plastic. Rationing of meat, sugar, coffee, butter, and cooking fats—all needed by the armed forces or requiring essential shipping to import—began in 1942. Rationing of clothing began at about the same time. The housing, gasoline, and rubber shortages produced hardships, but the food and clothing rationing were relatively easy to accept. Meat was often hard to get, but once people stopped hoarding things they thought would become scarce, they generally discovered that they had ration "points" for more items than they either needed or could afford. Compared with the experiences of besieged Britain or Russia, life in wartime America remained easy.

Economic Prosperity. The war's most important effect on the home front was the boost it gave the economy. By 1941 lend-lease and defense spending had reduced unemployment to less than 10 percent of the civilian labor force, the lowest figure since 1930. By 1943 it was down to a nominal 1.9 percent. The gross national product leaped, and by 1943 the country enjoyed a per capita GNP some 70 percent higher than in the "miracle" year 1929. Even when purely military items are subtracted, Americans were better off economically by the middle of the war than in the most prosperous peacetime era. In essence, by forcing the government to forsake a balanced budget, the war made up for lagging private consumption and investment.

Everyone welcomed the return of prosperity, but a new danger, inflation, soon appeared. The public had billions of extra dollars to spend; but because

On the home front speedy production was essential to victory. This ship was completed in ten days, a remarkable feat that brought FDR (in the foreground, left) to the Portland, Oregon, shipyard where it was accomplished.

Price Controls

The first economic effect of the outbreak of war in December 1941 was to put everyone back to work. Before long, however, the flood of federal war spending began to produce enormous pressures on prices. By mid-1942 prices and wages were being closely regulated by the government through the Office of Price Administration to prevent runaway inflation.

Not every American accepted the regimentation that this system entailed. One of the objectors was John L. Lewis, president of the powerful United Mine Workers' Union. Lewis believed that his men's wages had been fixed *after* prices had already risen, thus depriving them of considerable income. On the other hand, he charged, nothing was being done to limit business profits. Roosevelt responded to Lewis's attempt to scuttle price-and-wage controls by the Executive Order below, issued in early April 1943. [His proposal, at the end of the order, to increase taxes, was never adopted by Congress.]

"The Executive order I have signed today is a hold-the-line order.

"To hold the line we cannot tolerate further increases in prices affecting the cost of living or further increases in general wage or salary rates except where clearly necessary to correct substandard living conditions. The only way to hold the line is to stop trying to find justifications for not holding it here or not holding it there. . . .

"All items affecting the cost of living are to be brought under control. No further price increases are to be sanctioned unless imperatively required by law, . . . any further inducements to maintain or increase production must not be allowed to disturb the present price levels; such further inducements, whether they take the form of support prices or subsidies, must not be allowed to increase prices to consumers. . . .

"On the wage front the directions in the order are equally clear and specific.

"There are to be no further increases in wage rates or salary scales beyond the Little Steel formula [a 15 percent increase authorized in 1942], except where clearly necessary to correct substandards of living. Reclassifications and promotions must not be permitted to affect the general level of production costs or to justify price increases or to forestall price reductions. . . .

"Some groups have been urging increased prices for farmers on the ground that wage earners have unduly profited. Other groups have been urging increased wages on the ground that farmers have unduly profited. A continuance of this conflict will not only cause inflation but will breed disunity at a time when unity is essential. . . .

"We cannot stop inflation solely by wage and price ceilings. We cannot stop it solely by rationing. To complete the job Congress must act to hold in check the excess purchasing power. We must be prepared to tax ourselves more—to spend less and save more. The details of new fiscal legislation must be worked out by the appropriate committees of the House and of the Senate. The executive department stands ready to submit suggestions whenever the committees desire."

much industrial capacity was diverted to military needs, there was relatively little to spend it on. The absence of expensive consumer durables such as automobiles, household appliances, and new homes put great added pressure on the prices of those goods that were available.

To deal with this imbalance of commodities and cash, the government raised taxes drastically. Beginning with the first "defense" budgets in 1940, Congress lowered the personal income tax exemption, raised tax rates sharply, and established the excess-profits tax for business firms. In June 1943 the treasury began withholding income taxes from paychecks. Forty-four percent of the cost of the war was paid with tax money; for the first time most working Americans paid income taxes.

To further reduce the danger of inflation, the government once again issued war bonds. As in World War I, bond sales also whipped up support for the war effort and nurtured civilian morale. In September 1942 the treasury launched its first war-bond drive with a massive advertising campaign in print and on radio. Prominent athletes, politicians, and literary figures contributed their names and services to the enterprise. The most effective support for these drives came from Hollywood stars, who were credited with selling bonds worth $834 million in the first drive alone.

Neither taxes nor bond sales were sufficient to skim off all the excess purchasing power, and prices soon began to rise. The largest increases, of over 30 percent, occurred between 1940 and 1942. Then in 1942 Congress established the Office of Price Administration (OPA) and the War Production Board, with the power to ration scarce raw materials, set wage rates, and fix wholesale and retail commodity prices, rents, and other charges. From April 1943 to August 1945 retail prices rose only 4.2 percent, a figure that seems remarkably small today.

Admittedly, the public paid a hidden cost for price stability. The amount of regimentation and paperwork was enormous. Labor was forced to accept wage regulations that deprived it of the advantages that a tight labor market would otherwise have conferred. Profits, too, were closely controlled, but—many liberals complained—not tightly enough. The government essentially paid war contractors what they asked without looking too closely at costs.

Yet the scheme got the job done. Under a succession of "dollar-a-year" men called in from private industry to run various superagencies, war production burgeoned despite bottlenecks, labor and raw material shortages, strikes, and union disputes. Between 1940 and 1945 United States factories turned out 300,000 aircraft, 5,425 merchant ships, 72,000 naval vessels, 87,000 tanks, 2.5 million trucks, 372,000 artillery pieces, and 44 billion rounds of small-arms ammunition. The country truly became, as Roosevelt had promised, the arsenal of democracy.

The Fighting Fronts

The months immediately following Pearl Harbor were a time of disastrous American and Allied retreat. In quick succession, the Japanese invaded and captured Singapore, Hong Kong, the Dutch East Indies, and Burma. In May 1942, after a long siege of the Bataan Peninsula and Corregidor Island, near Manila, they compelled the surrender of a combined force of Americans and Filipinos. Before the final collapse, however, the American commander, General Douglas MacArthur, was rescued and brought to Australia to lead the defense and reconquest of the South Pacific. Despite these critical losses, Roosevelt and his advisers, believing Hitler the more dangerous enemy, accepted the British commitment to Europe first. The war against Japan would be a holding operation until American factories and training camps had provided enough arms and men to deal with Hitler and the Japanese simultaneously.

Unlike the British, who favored an indirect attack on Germany, either through Africa or against Europe's "soft underbelly" along the Mediterranean, Roosevelt and Chief of Staff Marshall wanted a major buildup of Anglo-American strength in Britain, followed by a direct thrust into the heart of German-occupied Europe across the English Channel. In the end British and American strategies were combined, but the decision probably spread Allied strength too thinly and lengthened the war.

Early in 1942 the first American GIs arrived in Northern Ireland. They were the vanguard of millions of American soldiers and airmen who poured into the United Kingdom to prepare for the cross-Channel attack. At the end of the year the United States and Britain undertook Operation Torch, an invasion of North Africa that pitted Allied troops against combined German and Italian forces commanded by General Erwin Rommel.

Meanwhile, the Allies were winning a vital battle in the Atlantic. By the use of destroyers, aircraft, and new submarine-detection equipment, and by the sheer productivity of American shipyards, losses to the U-boats were either cut drastically or made up, though not before millions of tons of Allied shipping went to the bottom.

The year 1942 was the darkest of the war, but it also brought the turning of the tide. At the Battle of the Coral Sea (May 7–8) American carrier planes stopped the Japanese advance southward toward Australia. A month later (June 3–6) they inflicted an even greater defeat on the Imperial Navy at the Battle of Midway, sinking 4 Japanese carriers and shooting down 275 enemy aircraft. Midway shifted the balance of naval strength in the Pacific permanently to the United States. Soon afterward, American marines, soldiers, and naval forces attacked the Japanese base on Guadalcanal island, opening a three-year "island-hopping" counteroffensive against the Pacific enemy.

In Europe, however, Hitler held on tenaciously. He had subjugated millions of Europeans, from France in the west to European Russia in the east. His treatment of these people, especially the Slavs of eastern Europe and the millions of Jews who had fallen into Nazi hands in Poland, occupied western and central Europe, and the Soviet Union, was savage. Hitler considered the Slavs and Jews subhuman, and he treated them like animals. He forced many into slave-labor camps where they were worked to death. Far worse, in late 1941 the Nazi SS (*Schutzstaffel*, an elite military corps) began the "final solution to the Jewish problem": the mass extermination of Jews—men, women, and children. By the time the war ended, almost 6 million Jews—along with hundreds of thousands of Russians, Poles, Gypsies, and other "inferior beings"— had been shot, starved or gassed to death in such con-

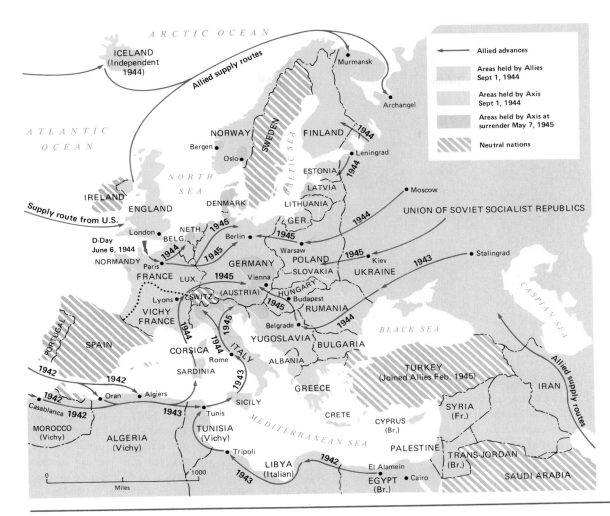

World War II: closing the ring, 1942–1945

centration camps as Auschwitz, Treblinka, and Majda-nek. This event—the Holocaust—is one of the darkest pages in human history.

Wartime Diplomacy. The war effort required complex interactions among nations allied as much by necessity as by affection and sentiment. Relations among the Western Allies were relatively good. Roosevelt did not get along with the touchy Free French leader de Gaulle, but Britain and the Commonwealth countries (Canada, South Africa, Australia, and New Zealand) cooperated closely with the United States. Roosevelt and the half-American Churchill, both extroverts, got along famously. With its vast manpower and industrial output, America was clearly the senior partner. If the British resented that seniority, they recognized its inevitability.

Wherever the Nazis conquered, they murdered and destroyed. Here soldiers of the German occupation army in Warsaw round up Jewish civilians for deportation to the concentration camps and eventual execution.

It is not difficult to guess who is winning this game of World War II dominoes. Note the benign figure of "Uncle Joe" Stalin to the right. His image would soon become much more sinister in the perception of Americans.

Generally speaking, relations with China were good, too. Roosevelt believed that under Chiang Kai-shek China had the makings of a great power, once freed of the Japanese yoke. In 1942 he and Churchill agreed to abandon the remaining special privileges their nations held in China. In November 1943, at Cairo, the two Western allies and China agreed to exact "unconditional surrender" peace terms from Japan if the Allies won the war, and resolved to return to the Chinese territories like Manchuria, Formosa (Taiwan), and the Pescadores, which Japan had wrenched from her in past years.

Relations between the Western partners and the Soviet Union were not so cordial. In 1943 the Russians dissolved the Comintern, the central body of the international Communist movement, as a gesture of cooperation with the West. Nevertheless, Stalin remained suspicious of Britain and the United States, and they of him. The mutual distrust dated from the years of the Russian Revolution (1917–19), when Britain, France, and the United States, along with Japan, had sent troops to support the enemies of the Bolsheviks in order to keep Russia in the war against imperial Germany. Thereafter, suspicion had been kept alive by continued competition between capitalists and Communists in the world arena.

Though Hitler's invasion of Russia temporarily eclipsed East-West differences, the war itself created grounds for mutual distrust. Stalin suspected that Roosevelt and Churchill would be content to see the Soviet Union and Nazi Germany destroy each other on the Eastern Front. Starting in late 1941, he repeatedly demanded that Britain and America open a second front in Western Europe, to relieve the pressure on Soviet troops. That the Allies delayed the opening of that second front until the invasion of Normandy in June 1944 was a chronic sore point with the Soviet Union.

Still, suspicion did not prevent cooperation. In October 1943 Secretary of State Hull, British Foreign Secretary Sir Anthony Eden, and Vyacheslav M. Molotov, the Soviet foreign minister, met in Moscow to discuss wartime problems and consider postwar reconstruction. The ministers agreed to establish a European Advisory Commission to formulate policy for Germany after victory and to set up a world organization to maintain international peace. One knotty problem that they could not solve was the postwar fate of Poland. Britain and the United States were committed to returning the Polish government-in-exile, then in London, to power when the war ended. The Soviet Union preferred a government friendlier to itself. The issue was not settled at Moscow and continued to rankle; but as a token of good faith, Stalin promised to join the war against Japan as soon as Germany was defeated. At Teheran, Iran, a month later, Churchill, Roosevelt, and Stalin met personally to confirm the results at Moscow and plan joint military operations against the common foe.

The Defeat of Germany. By the time of the Teheran meeting, Soviet fortunes had begun to improve. The initial German offensive against Russia had carried Hitler's armies to the gates of Moscow by September 1941. In the course of their eastward drive they had killed, captured, or wounded some 2.5 million Soviet troops, virtually wiped out the Soviet air force and tank corps, destroyed enormous quantities of war matériel, and laid waste to hundreds of Russian cities.

But during the winter of 1941/42 the Soviets counterattacked, forcing the Germans to retreat at some points. In the spring the German offensive resumed, and by fall Hitler's armies had penetrated to Stalingrad, on the Volga River, and Maikop, in the Caucasus. During this critical period vast Allied air fleets based in England dropped tons of bombs on Germany and German-occupied territories. These raids devastated the civilian population of Germany but did little to relieve pressure on the Russians or impair the German war effort.

The war on the Eastern Front turned in February 1943 when the Russians forced the German forces at Stalingrad to surrender. In August the annual German summer offensive was stopped dead by the Soviet armies and then reversed. In the spring of 1943, in North Africa, the combined British and American forces led by generals George S. Patton and Bernard Montgomery, under the overall command of General Dwight D. Eisenhower, dealt the final blow to Rommel's Afrika Korps. Rommel was rescued to fight again, but on May 13 some 250,000 Axis troops surrendered to the British and Americans. In early July the Allies invaded Sicily. The King of Italy soon announced the resignation of Mussolini and negotiated the surrender of Italy. Mussolini was rescued by German troops and placed at the head of a puppet Italian regime. Meanwhile, British and American troops had invaded the Italian boot, only to encounter fierce and effective opposition from the entrenched Germans.

The following year, 1944, was the beginning of Nazi Germany's end. In January, in the east, the Russians freed Leningrad from a devastating two-and-a-half-year siege and began their major westward drive. By February they had crossed the 1939 Polish-Russian frontier. In Italy the stalled Allied advance resumed, and on June 4 the American Fifth Army liberated

The beachhead in Normandy, June 1944, shortly after D-Day. This was the largest military operation in history, and the immense power of the Western Allies is apparent. In England, 3 million troops, 4,000 landing craft, 600 warships, and 11,000 planes gathered for the assault.

A Historical Portrait

George S. Patton

General George S. Patton once wrote: "War is very simple, direct and ruthless. It takes a simple, direct and ruthless man to wage war." Everyone who knew Patton recognized that he was describing himself.

Patton was destined to be a soldier. One of his ancestors had been a Revolutionary War general; his grandfather, the first George Patton, had commanded a regiment of Virginia infantry during the Civil War and had died of battle wounds in 1864. His father attended the Virginia Military Institute (VMI), though he became a California lawyer and politician rather than a regular army officer. As a child, George was fascinated by military history and military heroes and read about them voraciously while growing up on his father's ranch near Pasadena. He eventually developed the strange sense that he had been a soldier in many previous incarnations—with Caesar in Gaul, with the English at Crécy and with Napoleon at Jena and Austerlitz.

The young Patton spent his childhood riding horses and learning the classics by heart. In 1904 he entered West Point. Though bright—even intellectual—he was poor in mathematics and took five years to graduate, and then only in the middle of the class. Fortunately, he had money, both through his own family and through his wife, Beatrice Ayer, a New England heiress, and this would help the young second lieutenant's army career despite his undistinguished record at "the Point." While other young officers in the peacetime army were forced to get ahead on their merits, Lieutenant Patton entertained lavishly and often provided his superiors with mounts from his stable of thoroughbreds.

But Patton had more than generous hospitality to offer. He was well-read, literate, and charming. He was also colorful and impetuous. In 1916 he served as aide to John ("Black Jack") Pershing, commander of the army expedition sent into northern Mexico to capture Pancho Villa, and attracted wide attention by killing three of Villa's bodyguards in a Wild West–type shootout.

Patton liked to dress the part of military hero. Tall and erect, he wore high, shiny cavalry boots, starched cavalry breeches, a well-tailored khaki wool shirt, and a tie neatly tucked into his shirt between the second and third buttons. Strapped to his hips in open holsters, he carried two pearl-handled revolvers.

In 1917 Patton fought with the American Expeditionary Force in France in a new military branch, the tank corps. He won several medals, and was promoted to the rank of colonel, but was severely wounded before the final drive against the Germans. He returned to the boredom of peacetime army service in 1919, and during the next twenty years occupied himself largely with polo, riding, writing articles on the art of war for military journals, and attending every army school available. During the late 1930s he attracted the attention of George C. Marshall, the army deputy chief of staff.

Marshall regarded Patton as hot-tempered and insubordinate, but also as brave and aggressive. When America began to rearm to meet the growing German and Japanese threats, he saved Patton from oblivion by assigning him a prominent role in the revival of the army's tank force.

When war broke Marshall gave Patton command of the First Armored Corps, and in October 1942 he and his men landed in North Africa to wrest the region from the Vichy French and their German masters. Patton's own men, though green and half-trained, fought well. But other American troops, pitted against the veterans of Erwin Rommel's Afrika Korps, were whipped badly at Kasserine Pass in Tunisia. Hoping to restore morale, General Dwight Eisenhower, in overall command of the British-American forces, sent Patton to the Tunisian front. He performed as expected. Taking command from his beaten predecessor, he clamped down on the lax practices previously allowed. Because too many officers were reporting late to duty each morning, he closed the officers' mess at 7:30 A.M. He also insisted that all personnel under his command, including the nurses, wear their steel helmets at all times. Patton did not leave compliance to chance. He personally gathered up violators and, after chewing them out en masse, told them they could either pay a $25 fine or be court-martialed. It was even rumored that he peeked into unit latrines to see if men answering the call of nature did so with their helmets firmly on their heads. Patton's tactics were not always appreciated, but they were effective in restoring morale and infusing fighting spirit into the Tunisian front troops.

In July 1943 Patton led the American forces in the invasion of Sicily from North Africa. His superior in the campaign was British Field Marshal Bernard Montgomery, a cautious man whose indecisiveness angered and frustrated the American. Patton's pent-up rage boiled over in August when, on a series of visits to Sicilian military hospitals, he slapped and kicked several American soldiers awaiting evacuation for what he considered malingering and cowardice. Eisenhower forced Patton to apologize when he got wind of these incidents, but he tried to keep them from the American people. In November, however, the story was leaked by the radio commentator Drew Pearson and produced a storm of public outrage. Americans who felt that citizen-soldiers of a democracy should not be abused by their officers demanded that Patton be relieved of command. Eisenhower thought Patton too good a soldier and refused, but he also denied Patton the coveted command of the great cross-Channel invasion of France being prepared for 1944.

In March 1944 Patton was assigned to command the U.S. Third Army in England as a subordinate of Omar Bradley, the American general in charge of the invasion. He and his men did not land on the beaches of Normandy on D-Day, June 6, 1944, but arrived weeks later, when the Anglo-American forces were penned up in the Cotentin Peninsula, unable to break out of the pocket and sweep south and east to destroy the Nazis and liberate Europe. On August 1 Patton's tanks punched through the German line at Avranches and burst out into open country. The Third Army rolled up the enemy into Brittany to the west and simultaneously sliced through the German lines to the south and east. The triple-pronged tactic was probably a mistake. Though made worse by the caution and tardiness of the British and Canadians on the eastern end of the Normandy front, the thrust into Brittany slowed the American advance eastward and prevented the encirclement at Falaise of most of the German army in France.

By mid-September Patton's army had dashed to the east as far as the Franco-German border, but then ground to a halt for lack of supplies and gasoline, much of which had been commandeered by Montgomery for *his* drive eastward. Patton was forced to mark time while the Germans themselves prepared a counterblow. At this point—if the supplies had been available and if Bradley and Eisenhower had given him the go-ahead signal—the war could probably have been quickly won. Instead, just before Christmas, having squeezed every available man, gun, tank, and plane, from their depleted resources, the Germans attacked the Americans in the Ardennes Forest.

The Battle of the Bulge was Germany's last gasp on the Western Front, but it produced a near disaster for the American army. The blow fell on General Courtney Hodges's First Army, which reeled back fifty miles and threatened to crack. At Bastogne 18,000 Americans were surrounded by the German forces. They refused to surrender, though greatly outnumbered. Eisenhower called on Patton for help, scarcely believing he could turn his Third Army, oriented eastward toward Germany, northward in time to aid Hodges and save the besieged Americans troops. But Patton shifted direction in a few days and launched a powerful counterattack against the Germans from the south that lifted the Bastogne siege and broke the Wehrmacht's offensive.

This was the last major military effort the Germans were capable of. They were now too exhausted by five years of war against half the world to make more than a token fight. By March 1945 Patton and his colleagues had driven to the Rhine. Soon after, the Anglo-American troops were slicing through Germany virtually without opposition, while the Russians, coming from the opposite direction, were steamrolling over the few ill-equipped troops the Germans could still muster. Patton was one of those American officers who hoped that American troops could drive on to Czechoslovakia and exclude the Russians. But on April 16 he was ordered to turn south to prevent the Nazis from retreating to a supposed "redoubt" in the mountains, where, it was feared, they would hold out to the bitter end. In the end the Soviets liberated the Czechs from Nazi control and ultimately made the country into a Soviet satellite.

The Third Army's last day of fighting was May 6, 1945. It was also George Patton's. Following the German surrender Patton was placed in charge of the program in Bavaria to uncover and punish the ex-Nazi leaders, but he was now convinced that the Russians were a greater danger to America and urged a German-American alliance to drive the Russians back across the Soviet border. It is not surprising that the Bavarian denazification program was a conspicuous failure. Patton was soon at the eye of a storm over his seemingly pro-Nazi position, and shortly after was removed from his command and placed in charge of a largely paper army as punishment.

In December, scarcely six months after the war's end, Patton suffered a broken neck in an automobile accident. Twelve days later, at the army hospital at Heidelberg, he died of a blood clot on the lungs. He was buried at the big American military cemetery at Hamm in Luxembourg, alongside 6,000 other men of the Third Army that had done so much to destroy the power of Hitler's savage empire.

Rome; then in August the British marched into Florence.

By this time Eisenhower had launched Operation Overlord, the long-awaited second front in France. The cross-Channel attack began before dawn on the morning of June 6, when a colossal armada of Allied warships, transports, landing craft, and concrete caissons that could be converted into artificial ports approached the French coast in Normandy. After several days of ferocious fighting, the beachheads were secured. For six weeks the Germans were able to contain the Allies. Then, at the end of July, the Third Army under Patton broke out and began the drive east toward Germany. On August 15 the United States Seventh Army landed on the French Mediterranean coast and began moving north to attack the Germans from behind. On August 25 the Free French Second Armored Division liberated Paris.

The end of Hitler's empire was in sight. In October American troops crossed onto German soil. The Germans rallied briefly at the Battle of the Bulge, but in March American armies leaped the Rhine in force and dashed eastward. Meanwhile, the Russians, too, had crossed into Germany. On April 22, 1945, they reached Berlin. Rather than face defeat, Hitler committed suicide in his underground Berlin bunker. On April 25 American and Russian troops met at Torgau on the Elbe. On May 7 the German military commander accepted unconditional surrender at Allied headquarters. The war in Europe was over.

Yalta. In February 1945, as Germany's collapse neared, Stalin, Churchill, and Roosevelt met once again, this time at Yalta in the Soviet Crimea. Out of their deliberations emerged a set of important agreements that helped mold the postwar world. The three

"The Big Three" meet for the last time at Yalta in February 1945. There they discussed the partition of Germany, boundaries and political arrangements in eastern Europe, and the United Nations. Two months later, Roosevelt died.

powers stated their intention to set up four occupation zones in Germany, one for each of the three major powers plus France, to remain under military control until a final peace settlement with Germany. They agreed to meet at San Francisco in April 1945 to draw up the charter for a "United Nations" that would replace the old Wilsonian League. In the nations liberated from the Nazi yoke, there would be established, they said, provisional governments composed of all "democratic" elements to be chosen by free elections. The future Polish government, the published report declared, must be made up largely of the pro-Soviet provisional government established at Lublin, rather than the London-based, pro-Western government in exile. Finally, Poland's postwar boundaries would be shifted westward at the expense of Germany. In addition to these publicly announced provisions, the conferees secretly agreed that "two or three months after Germany . . . surrendered," the Soviets would enter the war against Japan. As reward for its aid, it would receive the Kurile Islands and the southern half of Sakhalin, be given the right to establish an occupation zone in the northern half of Korea, and be allowed special privileges in Manchuria and Outer Mongolia.

Roosevelt's generous terms to Russia at Yalta have since been sharply criticized. Eventually the Soviet Union would establish puppet regimes in Poland and eastern Europe generally, and strengthen its position in the Far East. But the Yalta Conference was not to blame for this outcome. By the time of Yalta, Soviet troops had swept across Poland and were already entering Germany in great force. Nothing could have kept the Soviet Union from imposing its will on Poland or the Balkan and Danube regions. As for the concessions in the Far East, the American atomic bomb had not been successfully tested and no one could foresee that by the time Germany surrendered, Japan would be on its knees and Soviet aid not needed. In February 1945 Roosevelt faced the prospect of having to launch a huge amphibious invasion of the Japanese islands, and he believed that Soviet help would be vital to that campaign. Roosevelt knew that the Russians had driven a hard bargain at Yalta, but he did not see how it could have been avoided. As he told a close adviser shortly after the conference: "I didn't say it was good. . . . I said it was the best I could do."

The Last Days of the Pacific War.
Meanwhile, there was still a war to win in the Pacific. From 1943 to 1945 the United States mounted a score of bloody and expensive amphibious operations. Moving from the east under the command of Admiral Chester Nim-

itz, American naval task forces thrust deep into Japanese-controlled areas. Under cover of carrier bombers and fighters and the big guns and rockets of the battleships and cruisers, waves of marines and army troops landed on the island beaches and smashed Japanese resistance. After Midway the Japanese navy no longer controlled the open seas, but it continued to be effective against the landings, especially as American forces neared Japan itself. On October 25, 1944, the Japanese launched their first kamikaze attacks—suicide missions of untrained pilots willing to fly their bomb-loaded planes directly into American invasion ships. Meanwhile, MacArthur's forces, coming from their bases in Australia to the south, made a series of brilliant end runs around Japanese-controlled islands, leaving large pockets of imperial troops behind to be mopped up at leisure.

The Japanese fought desperately for every scrap of coral reef. Even when overwhelmingly outnumbered and at the end of their strength, they refused to surrender. Whole Japanese garrisons went to their deaths in suicide charges against the Americans. Where the terrain permitted, Japanese troops retreated to interior caves and mountains and fought to the last man. The Pacific fighting was always on a smaller scale than in Europe or North Africa, but it was more vicious and proportionately more costly. At Iwo Jima, 775 miles from the main Japanese island of Honshu, over 4,500 Americans lost their lives early in 1945. Japanese casualties were even greater: over 21,000 of the emperor's finest troops died defending the small dot of land.

In late February 1945 MacArthur's troops marched into the wrecked Philippine capital, Manila. Soon marines and army units invaded Okinawa, 360 miles from the Japanese main islands. This attack was the largest amphibious operation of the Pacific war and also one of the costliest. Kamikaze planes sank or badly damaged 30 American vessels, and Japanese ground troops inflicted almost 40,000 casualties, including 7,300 deaths, on the invaders before the Americans could take the island.

Once in American hands, Okinawa was converted into a powerful air base in preparation for the invasion of the Japanese home islands. By now Japan was in desperate straits. Many Japanese cities were in ruins, the Imperial Navy rested on the bottom of the Pacific, and the surviving parts of the empire that had supplied Japan with vital raw materials were either in American hands or inaccessible because of American submarine attack on vital shipping lanes. Yet the Japanese still had the will and the means to fight. On the main islands 2 million troops and 8,000 kamikaze planes awaited the final attack. If the experience of Okinawa, Iwo Jima, Guadalcanal, and the other islands was an accurate foretaste of Japanese determination to resist, the Americans could expect hundreds of thousands of casualties in any invasion attempt. MacArthur worried that his men would face a fanatical enemy prepared to sacrifice every Japanese subject rather than surrender.

The First Nuclear Attack. After the capture of Saipan in July 1944, American B-29 superfortresses began the systematic bombing of Japanese cities that culminated in the nuclear destruction of Hiroshima and Nagasaki on the Japanese main islands of Honshu and Kyushu. The long course that led to these atomic attacks began quietly in 1939, when a group of scientist-exiles from Hitler's Germany informed Roosevelt that the Nazis were preparing to construct a new bomb of unimaginable destructiveness, based on the newly discovered process of uranium fission. The United States, they declared, must undertake a program to develop an atomic bomb before Germany could succeed. In mid-1940 Roosevelt turned the proposal over to a newly formed National Defense Research Committee.

After Pearl Harbor the government launched the so-called Manhattan District Project. At three major centers hundreds of scientists and technicians, headed by J. Robert Oppenheimer, searched for ways to build an atom bomb. The cost ran to almost $2 billion, but the engineering problems were gradually solved.

As the war approached its end in 1945, Niels Bohr, Albert Einstein, and several other scientists concluded that the bomb would not be needed and, fearing a postwar international atomic weapons rivalry, they sought unsuccessfully to stop the Manhattan Project. By the time the first atomic bomb was exploded experimentally at Alamogordo, New Mexico (July 16, 1945), the decision to use the bomb against Japan had been the subject of much heated debate in high government circles and among atomic scientists. Opponents of the bomb argued that the Japanese were on their last legs and would sue for peace shortly with or without the atomic bomb, especially if the Allies allowed the emperor to remain on the throne. In any case, why not demonstrate the bomb's power on some dummy target and so spare many lives? Proponents of dropping the bomb noted that the United States had warned the Japanese in late July that unless they accepted Allied "unconditional surrender" peace terms, they would suffer "prompt and utter destruction." The warning had been spurned as "unworthy of public notice."

As for providing a demonstration of the bomb's potential, only two bombs were available, and no one knew for sure that they could be used under combat conditions. If a demonstration were arranged and the bomb failed to go off, the Japanese would become more firmly committed than ever to fighting to the end. And if the casualties had been so high in the outlying islands, what would they be like when American troops landed on the sacred home islands?

The decision to use the bomb would not be made by FDR. In 1944 Roosevelt had been elected to a fourth term. His running mate was Senator Harry S. Truman of Missouri, who had achieved prominence as Senate investigator of abuses in war production. Roosevelt barely survived two months of his new term. In early April 1945 he died of a cerebral hemorrhage in Warm Springs, Georgia, worn out by twelve years of office during some of the nation's most trying and momentous times.

Truman did not even know the atomic bomb existed when he took the oath of office. Once he learned of the bomb's power, he was determined to use it, convinced that invading the Japanese home islands could be a colossal bloodbath. The new president had no doubt that the atomic bomb represented the fastest way to end the war with the fewest American casualties.

Early on the morning of August 6, 1945, the B-29 Superfortress *Enola Gay* left Tinian Island for Japan. The plane and its two escorts arrived over southern Honshu at dawn. At 9:15 the bomb was released over Hiroshima. Sixty seconds later the *Enola Gay* crew watched in disbelief as an immense fireball rose over the city and slowly turned into a mushroom cloud.

For the bustling city of Hiroshima it was a moment of unspeakable horror. Hundreds of people simply vanished from the face of the earth, incinerated by the intense heat. Others were torn to pieces. Thousands, unshielded from the flash, were severely burned. All told, over 60,000 people died in the first few minutes of the attack. Others, exposed to high radiation, sickened and died later. The entire center of the city was flattened except for a few concrete structures.

Now the war moved swiftly toward a conclusion. Two days after the Hiroshima attack, the Soviet Union declared war on Japan and sent troops across the Manchurian frontier. On August 9 another atomic bomb was exploded over Nagasaki, killing another 35,000 Japanese. By this time the Japanese leaders were meeting to consider surrender. The military advised fighting to the bitter end, but the emperor vetoed the idea. Assured at the last minute that Hirohito would not

World War II: assault on Japan, 1942–1945

be forced to abdicate, the Japanese accepted Allied surrender terms. On September 2, aboard the battleship *Missouri* anchored in Tokyo Bay, the Japanese signed the capitulation that ended the most devastating war in history.

Conclusions

During the two days of official jubilation that marked VJ (Victory-Japan) Day, few people asked themselves why the nation had gone to war. Thereafter, speculation ballooned as many of those who had at first opposed the war sought to justify their positions or to take intellectual revenge on their opponents.

Those critics asserted that the United States had no vital reason to join the anti-Axis coalition. Only Roosevelt's need to escape the political and economic impasse confronting the New Deal or, alternately, his unwarranted and grossly exaggerated fear of Hitler's designs, led him to favor American involvement. Nor was the president honest in his actions, they said. While denying that he wanted war, he was actively turning the United States into the anti-Axis arsenal and maneuvering the Japanese into a position where they had to attack the United States or surrender their vital

One month after its destruction by an atomic bomb, the heart of Nagasaki was nothing but a mass of debris. Sixty-five thousand people were killed or wounded in the surprise attack.

interests. Some suggested that Pearl Harbor was the result of a conspiracy by the administration to turn public opinion in favor of war: By ignoring the intercepted Japanese messages, these critics said, the government made the American navy a sitting duck for Japanese bombs.

As we have seen, these charges are, at best, half-truths. By 1941 the president undoubtedly believed that war was unavoidable. But he wanted to fight Hitler, not Tojo; the Japanese could be attended to eventually after Germany's defeat. The Pacific war *was* a blunder, but only in the sense that Roosevelt preferred to contain the Japanese while taking care of the Nazis first, and Pearl Harbor forced the United States to fight both simultaneously.

Nor was the president seeking primarily to evade a political impasse. Roosevelt's fear of the dictators predated the New Deal's political and economic difficulties. FDR was a Wilsonian who believed in collective security and detested authoritarian regimes long before the problems of his second term stopped the New Deal in its tracks. It was Hitler's astounding and alarming successes that awakened his concern after 1937, not

political frustration. The president was indeed less than candid in his tactics. While denying that he favored war, he was goading the Nazis into attacking American ships. But however mistaken he was in not taking the voters into his confidence, his purpose was governed by his concern for free American institutions.

And still another qualification is in order. Roosevelt's view of the Axis danger was not his alone; it was shared by a majority of Americans. The president was more eager than many of his fellow citizens to intervene, but the public was treading closely on his heels. Every move FDR made to aid Britain—cash-and-carry, the destroyer deal, lend-lease—was strongly endorsed by the American public. By the late summer of 1941 Hitler had either frightened or antagonized an overwhelming majority of the American people. They were not yet ready to take the final plunge, but they did not have very far to go. In the end it was Germany's brutality, contempt for humanity, and apparent threat to every nation's independence, not Roosevelt's duplicity, that was responsible for America's intervention in World War II.

For Further Reading

William Langer and S. Everett Gleason. *Challenge to Isolation, 1937–40* (1952); and *Undeclared War, 1940–41* (1953)

These weighty studies support the view that war between Germany and the United States was inevitable. They are defenses of the Roosevelt foreign policy, and critics have claimed that they are in effect "official histories," that is, treatments that express the official United States government view.

James M. Burns. *Roosevelt: The Soldier of Freedom* (1970)

Sees foreign policy before and during the war through Roosevelt's eyes. Burns believes that FDR foresaw the danger Hitler posed to America and validly sought to stop him.

Rober Dallek. *Franklin D. Roosevelt and American Foreign Policy, 1932–1945* (1979)

A monumental study (540 pages) covering all of Roosevelt's foreign policy. Complete and exhaustive. Fine for the serious student.

Charles A. Beard. *President Roosevelt and the Coming of the War, 1941* (1948)

Written by the dean of American progressive historians just before his death, this book indicts Roosevelt for bringing on an unnecessary war in 1941 to revive the flagging fortunes of his party and the New Deal. A book both fiercely criticized and fiercely defended.

Samuel Eliot Morison. *The Two-Ocean War: A Short History of the United States Navy in the Second World War* (1963)

A condensation of the multivolume history Morison wrote for the navy. Morison had the good fortune to witness much actual sea action in both the Atlantic and Pacific, so this well-written account is often based on firthand knowledge.

Barbara Tuchman. *Stilwell and the American Experience in China, 1911–1945* (1971)

General "Vinegar Joe" Stilwell brilliantly commanded American forces in China until 1944, when Chiang Kai-shek had him recalled for advocating increased aid to Chinese Communist forces. This book illuminates the little-known war in the Far East and helps to explain why the Chiang government eventually collapsed.

Dwight D. Eisenhower. *Crusade in Europe* (1948)

An account in Eisenhower's own words of the American war effort in Europe that led to the final defeat of the Germans.

John Morton Blum. *V Was for Victory: Politics and American Culture During World War II* (1976)

Shows the greed, bigotry, dishonesty, and stupidity as well as the selflessness, goodwill, patriotism, and intelligence of Americans "back home" during the war.

Richard Lingeman. *Don't You Know There's a War On? The American Home Front, 1941–45* (1970)

Lingeman's book is lighter fare than Blum's and better at catching the flavor of American civilian life during the war.

Audrie Gardner and Anne Loftis. *The Great Betrayal: The Evacuation of the Japanese-Americans During World War II* (1969)

A critical account of an event that weakened the moral position of the United States in a war against the enemies of freedom.

James P. Baxter. *Scientists Against Time* (1946)

In few wars did scientific research play so decisive a role as in World War II. This popular history of the Office of Scientific Research and Development tells how industrial and university scientists worked with the military to develop improved radar, antisubmarine devices, rockets, blood substitutes, and medicines.

John Hersey. *Hiroshima* (1946)

Hiroshima has become a classic. It is a factual account of how the first atomic bombing affected six survivors: a clerk, two doctors, a poor widow with three children, a German missionary priest, and the pastor of a Japanese Methodist church.

John Toland. *The Rising Sun: The Decline and Fall of the Japanese Empire, 1936–1945* (1970)

An American journalist-scholar tells the story of Japan's tragic try for world greatness. A gripping account by one with intimate knowledge of what was happening in Tokyo. Sympathetic to Japan.

Chapter 28

Postwar America

Why So Security Conscious?

1944   Bretton Woods Conference • Congress passes the GI Bill of Rights

1945   United Nations charter approved • Potsdam Conference • Roosevelt dies; Truman becomes president

1946   Winston Churchill's "Iron Curtain" speech • The Chinese civil war resumes • U.S. gives $3.75 billion in aid to Britain and $11 billion to the United Nations Relief and Rehabilitation Administration

1947   Truman orders the FBI to locate "bad security risks" in government • Congress endorses the Truman Doctrine, voting $400 million in military and economic aid to Greece and Turkey • Taft-Hartley Act • Congress creates the Central Intelligence Agency (CIA) • Cold War begins

1948   Congress approves the Marshall Plan • Berlin Airlift supports West Berlin against Soviet takeover • Executive order desegregates the armed forces • Truman elected president

1949   North Atlantic Treaty Organization (NATO) organized • The Soviet Union explodes its first atomic bomb • People's Republic of China established under Mao Tse-tung; Nationalists retreat to Taiwan

1950   GNP rises above its wartime peak • Alger Hiss convicted of perjury • Senator Joe McCarthy begins campaign against alleged American Communists • McCarran Internal Security Act passed over Truman's veto

1950–53   The Korean War

1952, 1953   The United States and the Soviet Union explode hydrogen bombs

1952   Dwight D. Eisenhower elected president

1954   *Brown* v. *Board of Education* • Army-McCarthy hearings; Senate condemns McCarthy

1954–59   Housing Acts free credit for home buying, accelerating the middle-class move to the suburbs

1955   Montgomery bus boycott; Martin Luther King, Jr., rises to national prominence

1956   Interstate Highway System construction begins • Eisenhower reelected

1957   Federal troops enforce desegregation of Little Rock, Arkansas, Central High School

1960   John F. Kennedy elected president

ometimes a book expresses the essence of a time so well that it captures the imagination of a wide public. One such work was *The Lonely Crowd: A Study of the Changing American Character*, by David Riesman, Reuel Denney, and Nathan Glazer, published in 1950.

According to Riesman and his associates, Americans had once been "inner-directed" people, guided through life by values learned in their youth. But most Americans were now "other-directed." They were no longer sure of themselves. What they did and said depended on what their peers were doing and saying; they were anxious to fit in, to conform to a group average. Using the technical imagery of the new postwar era, Riesman described the change as the shift from people with internal gyroscopes to those with internal radar sets.

Riesman was not contrasting individuality with a new conformity, but that is how *The Lonely Crowd* was understood, for that was what the public saw on every side. The spirit of adventure seemed to have gone out of American life in the 1950s, and safety appeared the only sensible course. Even young people, social observers said, were now sedate, at least in matters that counted. They were committed to security. Theirs was the "silent generation," aspiring to little more than a secure job, a new car in the garage, and a house with two smiling and obedient children in the backyard. Moralists of the generation that had experienced the Depression and the war, finding almost none of the usual irresponsibility and callowness of youth to complain about, lamented that young people seemed crushed and dispirited. As the literary critic Leslie Fiedler observed: "The young, who should be fatuously but profitably attacking us, instead discreetly explain, analyze and dissect us. How dull they are!"

Fiedler's barb implies the survival of an older group of intellectual naysayers. And there were such people. Fiedler obviously was one. Yet most of the thinkers of the "fifties," as we may conveniently refer to the decade and a half following VJ Day, were celebrators. American writers and intellectuals of the 1920s and 1930s had been critics of their society. Some had been Marxists as well. But during the postwar decade and a half this skeptical mood changed drastically.

In religious thought beliefs emphasizing humanity's limitations and the inevitability of imperfection and injustice in this world became more common. In political thought the ideological battles of the 1930s waned, and pragmatism—once a liberating approach—became narrowly practical and a force for rejecting change and reform. In history, sociology, and political science American scholars ceased to be adversaries and began to praise their society, sometimes uncritically. When Daniel Bell published *The End of Ideology* (1960), he coined an epitaph for the intellectual life of the period.

Why had Americans become so timid? Why had they lost their taste for political change and social reform? Why did they reject achievement and fear self-expression? What made this the decade of the safe thought, the safe course, the safe life?

The Politics of Dead Center

Timidity and fear of change clearly permeated political life from 1945 to 1960. Regardless of who was president, governing seemed little more than a holding operation. Reformers would find the fifties disappointing. The public was cautious and divided. Every step toward reducing inequalities of income and status and expanding the safeguards against life's mischances would be hard-fought. And in some areas the nation would actually retreat from the gains of the 1930s.

Liberalism did not die, however. The major trade unions, with more members than ever before, remained an important liberal force. The CIO's Political Action Committee continued to fight for higher minimum wages, expanded social security, federal health insurance, and racial justice. A liberal press, although a minority voice, survived from the previous decade. And the universities continued to be bastions of liberalism, though some of the more stylish campus intellectuals became neoconservatives.

Liberalism did not lack capable leaders after 1945. Philip Murray of the CIO and Walter Reuther of the United Automobile Workers continued to battle for greater social and economic equality and more effective security. So did Eleanor Roosevelt; after her husband's death she became the figure around whom many surviving New Dealers rallied. In 1947 she joined with economist John Kenneth Galbraith, historian Arthur Schlesinger, Jr., Minneapolis mayor Hubert H. Humphrey, labor leaders Reuther and David Dubinsky, and others to organize Americans for Democratic Action (ADA), a group dedicated to greater social justice and an expanded welfare state.

The Man from Missouri.
Harry S. Truman, who inherited Roosevelt's job, was himself a throwback to an earlier, more liberal era. The temper of the times, however, frustrated his New Dealism and severely diminished what he could accomplish.

Truman was an interesting though limited man. Though a protégé of Thomas J. Pendergast, boss of the Kansas City, Missouri, Democratic machine, his record as a county judge was a good one, and in 1934 he was elected to the United States Senate. As a freshman senator, Truman identified himself with the New Deal wing of his party. During his second term he achieved national stature by uncovering several sensational cases of waste and corruption in defense procurement, and in 1944 he replaced the erratic and visionary Henry Wallace as FDR's running mate.

Truman was unprepared for his abrupt elevation to the presidency in 1945. He had not been admitted to the inner war councils of the administration, and FDR's death, he later declared, hit him so hard it felt as if "the moon, the stars, and the planets" had landed on his head. Despite his dismay, the new president moved quickly to take up the reins of domestic policy. Days after the Japanese surrender he submitted to Congress a legislative program that contained the essential features of what he would later call the Fair Deal, in imitation of Roosevelt's New Deal. Among his proposals were an extension of unemployment benefits to ward off a depression; continued support of the U.S. Employment Service to help returning veterans get jobs; a permanent Fair Employment Practices law to ensure equal job rights to minorities; retention of price and wage controls to prevent runaway inflation; an increase in the minimum wage from 40 cents to 65 cents an hour to maintain consumers' purchasing power; a large public works program to build roads, hospitals, and airports in order to provide jobs; "broad and comprehensive housing legislation" to give returning GIs places to live; government aid for small business; continued agricultural price supports for farmers; an expanded social security system; a bill to guarantee full employment; and, eventually, a national health insurance program.

Liberals applauded Truman's agenda. It seemed to contain something for everyone in the liberal coalition: minorities, wage earners, old people, farmers, consumers, and small business people. But they soon discovered that Truman was quick to propose but bewildered by the task of pushing his program through Congress. At the same time he seemed suspicious of Roosevelt's New Deal advisers, people with good liberal credentials, and turned instead to old cronies from his Kansas City days, men who seemed to one liberal editor "a lot of second-rate guys trying to function in an atom bomb world."

A crucial test of the president's liberalism came with the battle over what eventually became the Employment Act of 1946. Fighting for the bill was a flock of liberal journalists, lawyers, and economists who believed that wartime experience had confirmed John Maynard Keynes's theories that unemployment could be ended by massive government deficits. Conservatives, opposed to unbalanced budgets and big govern-

Here Ben Shahn depicts Truman and Dewey in 1948: They did *not* make beautiful music together.

ment, succeeded in getting the administration's proposal to guarantee full employment, by large federal outlays if needed, bottled up in the House. Liberals called on Truman to appeal to the public over the heads of congressional conservatives and to use his influence in Congress. The president complied, but without apparent conviction, and the measure that finally passed was a weak one. It established a Council of Economic Advisors to help maintain full employment and it set up a Joint Economic Committee of Congress. It also declared that the government was committed to the maintenance of *maximum* employment. Absent from the bill were a commitment to *full* employment and the explicit authorization of deficit spending when needed that liberals desired. As the liberal magazine *The New Republic* wrote: "Alas for Truman, there is no bugle note in his voice."

Liberals were disappointed again during the president's fight for price controls. They had hoped that wartime price regulations would be retained to protect middle- and lower-income consumers against serious postwar inflation. Conservatives opposed price controls, claiming that they merely fostered government bureaucracy and meddling and encouraged producers and retailers to keep goods off the market, thus guaranteeing shortages. When Congress passed a weak price-control bill, the president vetoed it, leaving the country without any price regulation at all. Prices of still-scarce civilian commodities, especially beef, quickly soared, rising faster in a few weeks than they had during the four years of war. The frightened Congress now became more receptive to a stronger bill, but Truman failed to fight effectively for one and signed a measure not much better than the first one. To make matters worse, the president used the powers granted him by the bill inconsistently. When his control board ordered a rollback of beef prices, ranchers refused to ship cattle, creating a beef famine that had the public up in arms. Truman held out for a few weeks, then ordered the end of price controls on beef. Meat reappeared in stores, but at prices that shocked consumers. Once more the president seemed exposed as an ineffectual, confused, and inexperienced man.

The steady and rapid rise in prices in the postwar months injured all consumers, but few could make their discontent felt as effectively as organized labor. In January 1946 the steelworkers, under Philip Murray, demanded a wage increase and threatened to strike if they did not get it. The following April John L. Lewis of the United Mine Workers led 400,000 coal miners out of the mines to force the coal operators to meet his wage demands. Truman ordered the government to take over the mines and then met the union's demands. Soon afterward the president barely averted a strike of railroad workers by threatening to seize the roads and have the army run them. The labor troubles left a bad taste in everyone's mouth: Labor leaders felt Truman had been too tough; the middle class felt he had not been tough enough.

The voting public was probably less concerned than ardent liberals by Truman's failure to round out the New Deal. But many Americans were dismayed by his feeble leadership, inconsistency, and apparent lack of direction. They also resented his public profanity and his tendency to shoot verbally from the hip. In the 1946 congressional elections the Republicans made "Had Enough?" the party's slogan. The voters responded with a resounding "yes," electing a Republican Congress for the first time since 1928.

Election: 1948. They quickly discovered that they had gotten more than they bargained for. The public mood was more conservative than during the Great Depression, but it was not reactionary. Yet the Eightieth Congress seemed intent on dismantling the New Deal and in short order made fierce enemies among important blocs of voters.

In June 1947, Congress sought to reverse some of organized labor's New Deal advances by passing the Taft-Hartley Act. This measure made the "closed shop" illegal: Labor unions could no longer force employers to hire none but union members. Further, the Taft-Hartley Act allowed the government to impose an eighty-day cooling-off period on strikers in key industries, ended the practice whereby employers collected dues for unions, required unions to disclose their financial practices, and imposed an anti-Communist loyalty oath on union officials. Congress also refused to abolish racial segregation in the armed forces and rejected efforts to pass a federal fair employment practices act.

Truman helped reestablish his liberal credentials by vetoing the Taft-Hartley measure, though Congress overrode him. He also accomplished by executive order the armed forces desegregation and the fair federal hiring practices that Congress had refused to legislate.

Truman capitalized on the backward-looking record of the Eightieth Congress in his campaign for a full term in 1948. His major opponent was the moderate Republican governor of New York, Thomas E. Dewey. But he also faced challenges from both extremes of the political spectrum. To his right was Senator J. Strom Thurmond of South Carolina, candidate of the States' Rights Democratic party (Dixiecrats), a

Truman

Democratic gains from election of 1944

Dewey

Republican gains from election of 1944

Thurmond

The election of 1948

new group of rebellious southern Democrats strongly opposed to Truman's racial liberalism. To his left was the former vice president, Henry Wallace, running on the Progressive party ticket supported by left-liberals, Soviet sympathizers, and those who feared that Truman's foreign policies would lead to war. In the end neither Thurmond nor Wallace proved formidable, but from the outset Dewey appeared impossible to beat. Fortunately for Truman, Dewey was a stiff, overcontrolled man who reminded one observer of the little spun-sugar groom on the top of a wedding cake. The Republican candidate's chief difficulty, however, was the negative record of the Republican Eightieth Congress.

Through the late summer and into the fall, Truman traveled 22,000 miles by train and spoke 271 times, often to small audiences in villages and whistle stops from the back of his observation car. The president attacked the "do-nothing Congress" and warned that those who had benefited from the New Deal—farmers, wage earners, ethnic Americans, and blacks—would lose all their gains if Dewey and his party won.

The public took heed of his words and came to admire his pluck. Across the country the crowds began to shout "Give 'em hell, Harry!" at the game little man with the awkward gestures and rough syntax. The result was the greatest upset in American political history. All the polls had predicted that Truman would lose; but he beat Dewey by a popular plurality of 2 million votes.

The Fair Deal. The American people had announced that they did not want to return to the "bad old days" of Herbert Hoover. It soon became clear that they did not want to go forward very far or very fast, either. The next four years disappointed those who looked for further liberal change. In his State of the Union message soon after the election, the president unveiled his program for domestic reform. His Fair Deal, foreshadowed by his 1945 proposals to Congress, aimed merely at rounding out the limited welfare state inaugurated by Roosevelt. But Congress, dominated by a coalition of conservative northern Republicans and Dixiecrat Democrats, refused to give him what he wanted.

Little of the Fair Deal passed. Congress defeated Truman's farm program (the Brannan Plan), the administration's effort to add health insurance to the Social Security system, and its scheme to provide federal aid for education. The only concessions that Truman could extract were a higher minimum wage, an extension of social security coverage to an additional 9 million citizens, and a Housing Act (1949) for slum clearance and low-cost federal housing. All chance of significant domestic change evaporated when high administration officials, including the president's aide, Harry Vaughan, St. Louis Collector of Internal Revenue James Finnegan, and Assistant Attorney General T. Lamar Caudle, were accused of selling their influence to people who wanted government favors. Truman himself was innocent of these misdeeds, but in the midterm elections of 1950 the Republicans picked up many additional seats in Congress.

The Republican Decade Begins. In March 1952 Truman announced that he would not be a candidate for reelection. This decision threw the Democratic nomination wide open for the first time since 1932, and it went to the one-term governor of Illinois, articulate, witty, and patrician Adlai E. Stevenson, the man favored by the party's liberal northern wing.

At the Republican convention the party regulars and conservatives supported Senator Robert A. Taft of Ohio, son of the twenty-seventh president and a man of rare intelligence but little personal warmth. The liberal wing and those who prized victory over ideological purity wanted Dwight D. Eisenhower, the hero of the great crusade in Europe. Ike was an attractive figure. Benevolent in mien, bland but reassuring in speech, he seemed to be everyone's kindly if slightly bumbling father. The general had no known politics; but he was clearly a patriot and a moderate, and he seemed certain to prove an irresistible candidate. After adopting a conservative platform, the Republican convention turned to Eisenhower. As its vice presidential candidate it chose a young senator from California, Richard M. Nixon, whose reputation as an aggressive campaigner and hard-line anti-Communist had recently brought him to prominence.

The race that followed had more than its share of uncertainties. When it was disclosed that Nixon was the beneficiary of a businessmen's fund to help pay his political expenses, it looked as if the Democrats had a winning issue. But Nixon maneuvered out of the tight spot. Appearing on nationwide television, he explained that he had not received any personal benefit from the fund. He was not a rich man, he

told his viewers. His wife, Pat, unlike the mink-coated wives of men in the Truman administration, wore a "Republican cloth coat." He had accepted one gift while in office: a black-and-white cocker spaniel, which one of his two young daughters had named Checkers. No matter what anyone said about that transaction, he was not going to give Checkers back!

The response to the "Checkers Speech" was overwhelming and positive. Most voters liked the homey, sentimental quality of the talk, and the public clamor guaranteed that Nixon would not be dropped from the ticket. In fact, the entire Republican campaign sounded a note of wholesome domesticity and traditionalism that the public found congenial. By contrast, Stevenson seemed too smart, too irreverent. He was amusing, no doubt, but could a witty man—and a divorced one at that—be trusted? By the end of the campaign the Republicans were making the Democratic candidate and the men around him seem vaguely un-American. They were "longhairs," "highbrows," and—a new term tailored to fit the baldpated Stevenson—"eggheads." The clincher came in October, when Eisenhower promised that if elected he would go to the Far East to help end the Korean War. Stevenson, in his characteristic way, quipped that if elected, *he* would go to the White House. In the end the Eisenhower-Nixon ticket won with a 7-million-vote margin.

"I Like Ike." In domestic matters Eisenhower was an indifferent, even lazy leader. Ike allowed his staff, headed by Sherman Adams, former governor of New Hampshire, to conduct most day-to-day business while he spent many happy hours on the golf links, especially after his heart attack in 1955. In later years the president declared that he had intended to "create an atmosphere of greater serenity and mutual confidence," and he accomplished his end. His opponents attacked him for his indolence, but most voters found it soothing.

Ideologically, Ike was a moderate conservative. He opposed deficit spending as "fiscal irresponsibility" and considered New Deal–Fair Deal social programs "creeping socialism." His cabinet was heavily weighted with businessmen, one of whom, Defense Secretary Charles E. Wilson of General Motors, offended many liberals by his remark that "what is good for the country is good for General Motors, and what's good for General Motors is good for the country." *The New Republic*, taking account of Labor Secretary Martin Durkin, an official of the Plumbers and Steamfitters Union, dubbed Ike's cabinet "eight millionaires and a plumber."

Eisenhower's policies tended to favor business

Here "Ike" is about to make his acceptance speech to the Republican National Convention in 1952. The slogan was platform enough for victory in November.

and the growing suburban middle class over wage earners and city dwellers. Between 1954 and 1959 a series of housing acts made credit for home buying more readily available, accelerating the middle-class flight to the suburbs. In 1956 Congress passed the Highway Act, which authorized $32 billion for an immense interstate highway system financed by a federal gasoline tax. The measure, whatever its intent, further drained the central cities. Moreover, by destroying the passenger traffic of the railroads, it made suburbanites still more dependent on the wasteful, polluting private automobile. In later years many Americans would come to regret these changes, but at the time they clearly suited the fast-growing suburban middle class.

In 1956 the general ran for reelection with Stevenson his opponent once more. The team of Eisenhower and Nixon won an even greater victory than in 1952, despite the misgivings many Americans had about Ike's health. During his second term the president spent more time than ever on the golf course. Yet at times Ike could rise above his indolence and natural conservatism. In his parting words to his fellow citizens, he warned against the "military-industrial complex." This close alliance of defense industry and government was in some ways unavoidable, he noted; it was also a potential danger to the country's liberties. It was a

strange conclusion for a military man, but his warning would be remembered and often praised by dissenting citizens in later years.

The Guard Changes.   Prevented by the new Twenty-second Amendment (1951) from renominating Ike, the Republicans turned to Richard Nixon as their candidate in 1960. The Democratic front-runner as the campaign for the nomination began was Senator Hubert H. Humphrey of Minnesota. Opposing Humphrey was the young Democratic senator from Massachusetts, John F. Kennedy. Like Al Smith, Kennedy was a Catholic. But as a Harvard graduate, naval hero, and son of a rich and conservative businessman, he was poles apart from the poor boy from New York's Lower East Side. Kennedy's effective young staff was generously supplied with Kennedy family money and conducted a brilliant campaign. After overcoming party fears that voters would reject a Catholic candidate as they had in 1928, Kennedy won the Democratic nomination.

The presidential race itself was close. Nixon was the more experienced man. Liberals considered him too conservative, and even many middle-of-the-road voters judged him unprincipled. They remembered his devious smear tactics against past opponents and called him "Tricky Dick." But his long years in office, his close association with the beloved Ike, and his proven anticommunism gave him an early edge. By contrast, for all his glamor, Kennedy seemed too young and unproven. Moreover, although anti-Catholicism had declined, it still remained a potent force in the South and Midwest.

In the end the race became a popularity contest. Some of Nixon's initial advantage faded after a series of joint television debates established that the younger, handsomer man was also more adept at parrying difficult questions. Kennedy, moreover, was able to defuse the issue of his Catholicism by discussing his religion frankly and making it clear that he supported the separation of church and state. Strongly backed by blacks, Catholics, Jews, and the big-city machines, and aided by a recession that had begun in 1960, Kennedy squeaked into office by a wafer-thin 100,000-vote margin over Nixon.

Even in politics, then, the fifties were a time when the public avoided activism and change. The period was bracketed by two moderately liberal presidents. But the first, Truman, had won election in his own right by the narrowest of margins, although he had the tremendous advantage of incumbency; the second, Kennedy, almost certainly would have lost without overwhelming Catholic support. The voters did not want to turn back the clock, but neither did they want unsettling change. Except on the racial front, where the New Dealer–dominated Supreme Court acted without direct public sanction, political activism declined and unresolved problems piled up.

The Good Life

Prosperity was a major ingredient of 1950s conservatism. And its impact was all the greater for being unexpected and hard-won.

Between 1941 and 1945, for many long, often grim months, 12 million GIs had yearned for the day when they could return to normal lives. Their dreams and goals were understandably domestic. After the pain and danger, they craved the tranquillity and pleasant pursuits of family, home, and successful careers. Women, too, after many months working the swing shift and living with parents and in-laws in temporary accommodations, looked forward to starting families and enjoying domestic routines in their own homes.

This vision of private satisfaction, so appealing and powerful to ex-soldiers and their wives or girlfriends, left a deep impression on the values of the postwar generation. After 1945 the average age for marriage dropped sharply, birthrates soared, and family sizes swelled. In 1945 the country had 37.5 million households; by 1960 there were almost 53 million. In 1954 *McCall's* magazine would coin the word *togetherness* to describe the new commitment to a close family life revolving about children, one-family suburban houses, and home entertainment.

The year of victory itself was a time of difficult new beginnings, of course. Children long fatherless and wives long without husbands had to adjust to an important new figure in the house; men had to get used to the company of women and children once more. Former GIs had to wind down and come to grips with—or forget—their war experiences. Yet most were able to make the difficult emotional adjustment to peace.

Avoiding a New Depression. They were also able to make a successful economic adjustment. During the final stages of the war Americans had begun to worry about what the defeat of Germany and Japan would mean for the economy. Knowledgeable observers forecast disaster once the stimulus of gigantic government spending ceased. Economist Leo Cherne envisioned hungry veterans roaming the streets in packs, fomenting strikes and rioting. Ordinary Americans, remembering the days of Depression breadlines, shuddered.

To prevent disaster, in 1944 Congress passed a measure popularly known as the GI Bill of Rights. This law extended to all honorably discharged veterans several benefits, including generous monthly allowances for education; loans to purchase farms, businesses, or homes; and unemployment compensation of $20 a week for a maximum of fifty-two weeks. Millions of veterans became members of the "fifty-two, twenty club" until they were able to find jobs. Thousands of others started small businesses financed by government loans. Every ex-GI who entered college or a recognized trade school was entitled to $500 a year for tuition and $75 a month for personal support while attending school. Millions of veterans poured into the nation's colleges and universities. The GI Bill of Rights ultimately cost the government billions of dollars; but it eased the problem of postwar readjustment and, more significantly, created a giant pool of educated, trained people that would serve the economy well in the years to come.

The Rage to Consume. Luck also played a part in preventing economic catastrophe. During the war high wages and acute shortages of new homes and consumer durables had forced a high rate of saving. By the end of 1945 the American people had piled up $134 billion in bank accounts and government bonds. The public might have held on to this money, but the postwar mood was anything but frugal. Having gone without the good things of life for so long through the Depression and the war, Americans now seemed unwilling to deny themselves anything. In the closing months of the war advertisers reminded their customers that civilian products would shortly become available. "There's a Ford in your future," announced the car manufacturer. A month before Japan's surrender General Electric advertised its "all electric kitchen-of-the-future." The breathless advertising copy noted that the dishwasher "washes *automatically* in less than 10 minutes. And the Disposall disposes of food *electrically*—completely eliminates garbage."

The immense pent-up demand ensured that there would be no repetition of 1929–1933. After an initial period of scarce consumer goods and tremendous price increases, industry completed its conversion to peacetime production and caught up with demand. During the first full year of peace only a little more than 2 million cars were produced—fewer than in 1934. In two years that output almost doubled. Americans soon came to consider many new items essential for the good life. General Electric's prophecy came true: By the end of the decade the public was buying 225,000 automatic dishwashers and 750,000 electric disposals a year. In 1946 the first electric clothes dryers appeared, and housewives began to order them enthusiastically.

One electronic gadget not foreseen by GE would be even more momentous. In 1939 the Radio Corporation of America had tentatively offered for sale the first home television sets. The war stopped further growth in the industry, but after Japan's surrender the market took off. In 1948 RCA and other domestic manufacturers turned out a million sets; in 1956, almost 7.5 million. By 1960 almost half of all American homes had one or more television sets.

The new industry not only created jobs but also had a powerful social and cultural impact. Hollywood shuddered as families gave up their Saturday nights at the movies to watch "sitcoms" or variety shows. Television proved to be more than an entertainment medium. It was capable of providing instruction, though parents complained that its reliance on dramas steeped in violence was dangerous to young children, and educators were certain that young TV viewers were losing their capacity to read. Local, as well as major national and international, events came "live" into the living rooms of millions of viewers. Television affected how the public perceived politicians. It made a difference in the 1960 election and also helped bring down Senator Joseph McCarthy, as we shall see.

The drastic increase in the number of families made new housing the nation's most pressing postwar need. At first private industry responded to this demand ineptly. For months following VJ Day thousands of returned veterans and their families lived in army surplus Quonset huts or moved in with their parents. Then came William J. Levitt and his imitators. Levitt used standardized components and automatic equipment to create "tracts" or "developments" on a gigantic scale. His houses were virtually all the same, but they had the indispensable modern comforts and a price of $10,000, payable in thirty years on an FHA or GI home mortgage. They sold briskly. Levitt's two largest developments were on Long Island and in eastern Pennsylvania, but his methods quickly caught on. Before long there were "Levittowns" in every part of the country, each boasting the same rows of houses with picture windows, small front lawns, and tree-bordered streets full of playing children.

And so the postwar depression did not come. Despite several brief recessions, GNP grew at an annual rate of 3.2 percent between 1950 and 1960, higher than for many years past. Prices rose, but after 1950

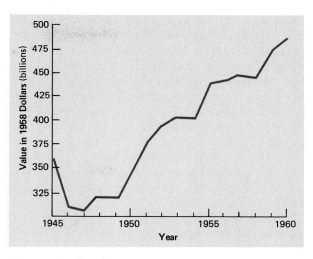

Gross national product, 1945–1960
Source: Historical Statistics of the United States, Colonial Times to 1970.

at less than 2 percent a year for the remainder of the decade. The vast improvement in the economy's performance owed little to government policy, though federal aid to education and science and highways no doubt played a part. Far more important was the enormous pent-up domestic demand, cheap international raw materials, including fuel, and America's unique position after 1945 as the only great industrial power capable of meeting the needs of war-ravaged Europe. Whatever the reasons, prosperity helped convince Americans that there was little need to tamper with existing political arrangements.

Suburbia Triumphant. The postwar economy slowed slightly during the late 1950s, but it did not stop. Economic expansion dramatically altered the quality of American life. As the economy grew, its structure changed. By 1960, occupations like farming, mining, and manufacturing had sharply declined; more and more Americans worked at service jobs like advertising, technical and clerical services, publishing, accounting, and teaching. Particularly dramatic was the drop in farm workers: from 9 million to 5.2 million between 1940 and 1960. Increasing numbers of Americans ceased to wear overalls and uniforms on the job; more and more went to work in skirts, white shirts, and gray flannel suits. By 1960, for the first time in history, there were more white-collar than blue-collar Americans.

The new white-collar class developed a characteristic lifestyle centered around suburban living. The pattern was home- and child-oriented. Wives became experts in house decoration, gardening, and meal planning. Husbands took up handicraft hobbies like carpentry and boat building. A "do-it-yourself" craze swept the suburbs as much to accommodate the new domestic interests of men as to help keep down the high cost of home repairs. The doings and problems of children became major new concerns of suburban parents. They worried about their offspring more than in the recent past when simple economic survival overshadowed difficulties about schools, dating patterns, orthodontics, and "cultural advantages." With so many children in the house and some money to spare, parents discovered the babysitter problem for the first time.

The suburban pattern of life was not confined to white-collar people; it was shared by better-paid skilled workers. For both groups it was often a heavy financial burden. Many married women went to work to help out, especially after 1950. Between 1950 and 1970 the percentage of married women who worked went from 23.8 to 40.8 percent. During the 1950s, at least, few of these working wives were looking for personal fulfillment; caring for home and children remained their ideal. But a job to supplement the family income until husbands completed school on the GI Bill or received a promotion seemed unavoidable if the precious new lifestyle was to be maintained.

"Levittown," wherever located, was geared to the family. This picture was certainly staged, but it does capture the daytime demographics of the new suburbs of the 1950s— women and babies. The only men around are the "diaper service" truck drivers.

The Other Half

The shift of population from central city to suburb was one of the dramatic social developments of the 1950s. Yet millions of people remained in the central cities; many rural or semirural folk moved into the urban neighborhoods emptied by the lure of the suburbs.

Urban Poverty. Some of the newcomers were, as in the past, Europeans—refugees from postwar poverty and disorder. During the decade Congress passed a number of measures that admitted GI "war brides" and several hundred thousand displaced persons. (Not until 1968 did the country fully elmininate the national quotas that discriminated in favor of northern Europeans.)

Most of the arrivals in the central cities, however, were blacks from the South and people of Hispanic background. Their experiences in some ways repeated those of earlier newcomers to American cities. Largely unskilled, they, too, took the lowest-paying jobs; they, too, moved into housing rejected by the middle class; they, too, were victims of prejudice and discrimination. Like their predecessors, they found themselves caught in a web of poverty, crime, and family disruption and were blamed for their afflictions.

Many Americans assumed that the latest arrivals—like the Irish, Germans, Jews, Italians, Poles, and other groups of the past—would move up in society as they acquired skills. But first they needed unskilled or semiskilled jobs, and mid-twentieth-century America did not offer as many of these as in the past. A construction worker now had to know how to operate a bulldozer; he could no longer merely wield a pick and shovel. The few unskilled jobs that did exist paid so little that they were unsuited to people with families to support. Thousands of Puerto Rican, Mexican, and black women found jobs as domestics, waitresses, and hospital attendants; but their husbands, brothers, and sons often looked vainly for decent-paying work. And even when newcomers had some skill, they often found that their way up was blocked by unions whose members were hostile to them or wanted to save the declining number of skilled blue-collar jobs for their relatives.

Civil Rights. Despite the continuing poverty of many minorities, the 1950s did see major advances in civil rights. The war had made a considerable difference for America's racial and religious minorities. By pointing up in ghastly relief the fruits of Nazi racism, it shamed many Americans into reconsidering their own

Braceros were Mexican farm hands brought into Texas and the Southwest to help solve the acute shortage of labor in agriculture. Though supposedly only temporary residents of the United States, many stayed permanently. They were followed by thousands of other Mexican immigrants to the Southwest, both legal and illegal.

behavior and attitudes. Hostility toward Japanese-Americans, whose spectacular fighting record in Italy was widely acclaimed, rapidly dissipated. Jews, the Nazis' chief victims, also experienced a new kind of acceptance. And the wartime mingling of Americans of all kinds in a common struggle reduced traditional anti-Catholic prejudice.

Black Americans benefited least by the wartime changes. In the South segregation imposed by state and local laws continued. Hospitals, theaters, buses, trains, playgrounds, parks, and other public accommodations maintained separate facilities for blacks and whites, mandated by local and state ordinances. Prodded by a new generation of liberal federal judges, southern states by the 1950s were making an effort to upgrade black schools so that they could meet the "separate-but-equal" test of *Plessy* v. *Ferguson*. But almost everywhere they remained both separate and inferior. Worst of all, lynching and other kinds of racial violence survived in the South.

The situation for blacks in the North was better. The movement of thousands of black Americans out of the South, where they had been effectively disfranchised, to northern cities, where they could vote, enormously increased their political influence. In most northern communities there was no legal bar to the schools that black citizens could attend or theaters, hotels, restaurants, or sports events they could patronize. On the other hand, many white northerners continued to believe that blacks were inherently inferior. Their prejudice informally accomplished many of the same ends that laws did in the South. Whites excluded blacks from private social clubs; restaurant and hotel managers refused to accept black patrons. Landlords' prejudice forced blacks to accept inferior housing even when they could afford better. Few blacks, no matter how well qualified, could find skilled work. The AFL craft unions, making up the building trades, excluded

During the early 1950s segregation was legal in much of the South. Defending themselves against the charge that segregation denied blacks their constitutional rights, segregationists theorized that "separate but equal" treatment was consistent with American ideals. Too often, though, blacks were forced to accept separate and unequal status.

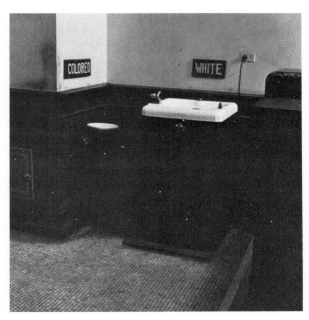

black workers. Only a few industrial unions, like Walter Reuther's United Automobile Workers, did not discriminate against black members. Although black talent was often recognized in the arts and in sports, even there bigotry persisted. In baseball, presumably the "national sport," there were no black players in the major leagues until 1947. In that year Branch Rickey, the courageous owner of the Brooklyn Dodgers, signed Jackie Robinson to play second base, finally breaking the major leagues' color bar.

The struggle for black civil rights engaged many white liberals, but most of the burden was carried by blacks themselves. During the 1940s Walter F. White, secretary of the NAACP, and A. Phillip Randolph, president of the Brotherhood of Sleeping Car Porters, fought for legislation that would benefit blacks. Among their goals were a federal antilynching bill, an end to poll taxes in federal elections, and the outlawing of discrimination in work under government contract. The NAACP instituted a succession of suits aimed at breaking down segregation sanctioned by southern state and local laws.

By 1950 black citizens were growing ever more discontented as they watched the snaillike pace of change in race matters. The political system, however well it responded to the wishes of the white middle class, seemed incapable of meeting blacks' needs. Congress was paralyzed by the resistance of the well-organized southern Democratic bloc to any change in the racial order. The Republicans owed little to black voters and seemed indifferent to their problems.

The Warren Court. Into this void stepped the branch of government traditionally the least democratic and the least responsive to public pressures: the federal courts. Beginning in 1953, the Supreme Court was led by Chief Justice Earl Warren, an Eisenhower appointee. Most of the other justices were holdovers from the New Deal and stood for an earlier liberalism. Composed of judicial activists who were willing to extend the Court's power into areas hitherto considered legislative concerns or beyond the reach of law, the Warren Court broke through the legal barriers to racial change.

Even before Warren's appointment, the Court, under NAACP goading, had begun to restrict segregation in housing and in graduate and professional education. Then, in 1954, came its momentous decision in the case of *Brown* v. *Board of Education of Topeka*, ably argued for the NAACP by black attorney Thurgood Marshall. Resting its decision on the findings of sociologists and psychologists that separate schooling inevitably stigmatized black children, the Warren Court declared that segregation in the public schools was a denial of the Fourteenth Amendment's requirement that the states accord to every person "equal protection of the laws." "We conclude," the chief justice wrote, "that in the field of public education the doctrine of 'separate but equal' has no place. Separate educational facilities are inherently unequal." The Court had spoken, and in the next decade it would speak many times again until the system of legal segregation had been totally dismantled in every part of national life.

The road to equality would be long and difficult, however. In the border states of the upper South compliance with the *Brown* decision was generally good. School segregation in practice remained, but it was based on deeply embedded patterns of residential segregation and no longer had the sanction of law. In the lower South the decision produced a storm. The more respectable conservatives organized white citizens' councils—"uptown Ku Klux Klans," their critics called them—to defeat the Court's order by boycotts and other economic weapons against both black and white supporters of desegregation. The Klan itself revived and used violence and threats of violence to prevent compliance with the *Brown* decision. At Little Rock, Arkansas, in 1957 the Klan supported Arkansas governor Orval Faubus when he defied a court order that black students be admitted to Central High School. Eisenhower could not allow such blatant disregard of the law of the land and used federal troops to guarantee admission of the black children.

Yet the president was not a civil rights enthusiast. He was willing to march with the times, but he did not care to lead the parade. He would later call his appointment of Earl Warren as chief justice "the biggest damnfool mistake" he had ever made.

Grassroots Protest. Besides legal action through such groups as the NAACP, black Americans resorted to personal defiance of segregation ordinances. In December 1955 Rosa Parks, a black seamstress in Montgomery, Alabama, weary from her day's work, refused to give up her seat on a local bus to a white man. For this violation of a city segregation law, she was arrested and fined $10. The outraged local black community quickly organized a boycott of the city buses, declaring that black riders would sooner walk than accept segregation. The city struck back by indicting the boycott leaders, starting with the Reverend Martin Luther King, Jr., a Georgia-born, northern-educated Baptist minister. King was convicted and jailed but appealed the decision. Meanwhile, the black communities of other

The Supreme Court's decision in *Brown* v. *Board of Education* in 1954 was a triumph for civil rights and for the NAACP, which fought the legal battle for desegregation. Lawyers for the NAACP (chief attorney and future United States Supreme Court Justice Thurgood Marshall is in the center) express their feelings at the news of the Court's decision.

southern cities, including Tallahassee, Florida, and Birmingham, Alabama, followed the Montgomery example. In November 1956 the federal courts freed King and ordered the end of segregation on the Montgomery bus system.

The grassroots self-help that marked the Montgomery boycott established an important precedent in the emerging civil rights struggle. Equally important, the events in Montgomery marked the rise to national leadership of the most magnetic and respected leader the postwar civil rights movement would produce, Martin Luther King, Jr.

Progress was also being made on other racial fronts. Besides fighting segregation, black Americans and their white allies launched a major attack on the long-standing disfranchisement of black citizens in the South. In September 1957, after beating back a filibus-

ter by Senator J. Strom Thurmond, Congress passed the first of several measures designed to restore voting rights to black southerners. The Civil Rights Act of 1957, the first such legislation since Reconstruction, set up a six-member Civil Rights Commission and a Civil Rights Division of the Department of Justice. The commission was to investigate complaints that voting rights had been denied. The Civil Rights Division could then prosecute authorities who were found responsible. The 1960 Civil Rights Act strengthened the 1957 law by requiring voting registrars to retain their records for some months following an election so that they could be examined by federal officials. Both laws provided the government with weapons to end black disfranchisement. But as the 1960s began, the slow and painful process of restoring rights guaranteed by the Fourteenth and Fifteenth amendments almost a century before had just begun.

The Cold War

The fifties retreat of white Americans to private satisfactions can be explained in part by the "payoff" of an affluent society that fulfilled people's hopes beyond their fondest expectations. Yet there was something else that contributed to conformity. As millions of Americans surrendered to the pleasures of a consumer society, a great anxiety remained: the threat of nuclear holocaust. This fear would reinforce the inward turning of the American people and encourage a political and social philosophy that avoided all criticism of the nation and its dominant capitalist, middle-class values. Cold War fears, when superimposed on the more positive values of togetherness and career building, made Americans yea-sayers and self-celebrators to a degree almost unique in their history.

The United Nations. Few Americans after 1945 expected their nation to withdraw from world affairs as it had following Versailles. To avoid this possibility, leading internationalists had labored during the war years to commit the country to various forms of world cooperation. In 1944, at Bretton Woods, New Hampshire, American and other anti-Axis diplomats signed agreements for an international bank and a world monetary fund to stablize international currencies and rebuild war-torn economies. In November 1945 the Senate endorsed "an international authority to preserve peace," an act, the *New York Times* noted, that undid "a twenty-four-year-old mistake."

The work of the internationalists was realized

in the conference at San Francisco, April–June 1945, called for at Yalta. There, 282 delegates representing the 50 nations arrayed against the Axis powers organized the United Nations, modeled after the League of Nations. The UN charter established a General Assembly composed of all member nations, which would be the ultimate UN policy-making body. It also set up an eleven-nation Security Council, consisting of five permanent members—the United States, Great Britain, the Soviet Union, France, and China—and six others elected by the General Assembly for two-year terms. Each permanent member was given the power to veto Security Council decisions. The Security Council would meet in continuous session and would be the chief agency for settling disputes among member nations.

The creation of the UN was a triumph for the old Wilsonian ideal of international cooperation to preserve world peace. But it could not disguise the discord that had long been growing between the Soviet Union and the West or settle all the conflicts brewing in the troubled postwar world.

An Unsettled World. Clearly the international balance following VJ Day was very different from the past. Western Europe, long the world's power center, emerged after 1945 profoundly enfeebled and shaken. France was demoralized and faced with the serious problem of reestablishing national unity and a political consensus. Germany and Italy were shattered societies where children begged on the streets and women sold themselves to American GIs or Soviet soldiers for packs of cigarettes and chocolate bars. Most disturbing of all, victorious Britain was impoverished and incapable of holding its vast empire together. All over the Continent misery prevailed. Millions of displaced persons wandered across Europe looking for a place to live and ways to reconstruct their lives. The physical scars of war marked every city and town. Hunger and disease afflicted populations weakened by wartime deprivations and continuing shortages. Winston Churchill scarcely exaggerated when he described Europe in 1945 as "a rubble heap, a charnel house, a breeding ground of pestilence and hate."

In Eastern Europe, too, the prewar balance had been upset. The Nazi invasion of Poland and the Soviet Union had been devastating. Millions of Russians, Jews, and Poles had died either in combat or in concentration camps. Cities had been totally destroyed by the warring armies. The political equilibrium had also been profoundly altered. Before 1939 a group of independent nations, including the Baltic states (Lithuania, Latvia, and Estonia), Finland, Poland, and Rumania, had walled the Soviet Union off from the rest of Europe. The regimes in these countries, as well as the next tier to the west, were generally unfriendly to the USSR.

Forlorn residents of Nuremberg, in 1945, wait for something to happen. The United States responded with the Marshall Plan, which helped rebuild the shattered heart of Western culture. On the twentieth anniversary of the plan, the German government initiated the German Marshall Fund to support cultural exchange between the United States and Europe.

The benevolent-looking Chiang Kai-shek, leader of Nationalist China both during and after the war. His critics called him a devious, tyrranical man who condoned corruption and brooked no opposition.

After 1945 the picture was transformed. During the last year of the war Soviet forces had swept as far west as central Germany. They had defeated the Finns and occupied Poland, the Baltic states, Rumania, most of the Balkans, as well as part of Austria. When the war ended, the Soviets shared occupied zones in Germany and Austria with the Western Allies; had established pro-Soviet "satellite" regimes in Poland, Hungary, Rumania, Bulgaria, Albania, and Yugoslavia; had incorporated the Baltic states into the Soviet Union; and had extended the USSR's official borders westward by annexing eastern Poland and compensating the Poles with territory in eastern Germany. Finland and Czechoslovakia remained independent, but the former did so only at the price of avoiding policies that offended the Soviet Union, while the latter's autonomy would be short-lived.

Meanwhile, the decline of Western Europe had created a power vacuum in Asia and Africa. In the Far East the Japanese military successes of 1941–1943 had stripped away the myth of white superiority and had wakened dormant nationalist feelings in Indonesia, Ceylon (Sri Lanka), Indochina, Burma, India, and Malaysia. In the Middle East and North Africa, Arab nationalism, long held in check by France and Britain, began to seethe. In sub-Saharan black Africa, too, by 1945 Western-educated intellectuals were demanding an end to European colonial rule.

The most troubled nation of all in the Orient was China. During the war the United States, Great Britain, and even the Soviet Union had supported the Kuomintang, the Nationalist government under Chiang Kai-shek. Though Chiang's regime still had the support of many liberal, Western-educated Chinese in 1945, increasingly it had come under the domination of corrupt bureaucrats, privileged landlords, and big merchants. It had failed to win the support of the Chinese peasantry and seemed unable to deal with China's industrial backwardness and social inequalities.

For many years Chiang had opposed the Chinese Communists led by Mao Tse-tung. In the portion of north China they controlled, the Chinese Communists had given land to the peasants and established an honest, though authoritarian, administration. They had also been far more effective than the Kuomintang in fighting the Japanese. Hoping to combine the best of both regimes, president Truman sent General George C. Marshall to China in December 1945 to end the Nationalist-Communist rift. Although Marshall succeeded briefly in bringing Chiang and Mao together, by mid-1946 their arrangement broke down, and China was soon in the midst of a devastating civil war.

Sources of the Cold War. The postwar instability in Europe, Asia, and Africa set the stage for competition between the only two large nations still strong—the United States and the Soviet Union. Eventually all three continents became arenas for conflict between the two superpowers. After 1947 *Cold War* became the common label for the chronic rivalry between the Soviet Union and the United States and their respective allies. Eventually it became a worldwide struggle waged by diplomacy, propaganda, economic pressure, and military intimidation. Occasionally the Cold War would entail physical combat, though, fortunately for humanity, only through surrogates, never directly between the two superpowers.

The causes of the Cold War were complex, and both the Soviet Union and the United States contributed to them. Both nations were certain that they, and they alone, were struggling for international justice and a better life for all humanity. Both were certain their systems alone must ultimately prevail. Viewed objectively, however, the Cold War was the attempt of two superpowers to ensure their safety and protect what they perceived as their vital interests in the new, dramatically transformed international environment after 1945.

The conflict began well before the end of World War II, but during the war itself the Russians and the Western powers had maintained an outward show of friendship and cooperation that papered over serious political disagreements. Then, as Russian troops pushed the Nazi invaders westward into Poland, the Baltic states, and the Balkans, questions of postwar boundaries, spheres of influence, and relations between the Soviet Union and its immediate neighbors became urgent.

By the time of the Big Three's Potsdam Conference in July 1945, the postwar world was already taking shape. Churchill, defeated by the British voters before Japan surrendered, was replaced at the conference by Clement Attlee. President Harry Truman came in place of the fallen Roosevelt. During the conference he received word that the United States had successfully tested an atomic bomb. Roosevelt had believed he could charm Stalin. Truman, influenced perhaps by the sense of America's new strength, took a more skeptical approach toward the Soviet dictator. The conferees agreed to little of consequence and most pending issues remained unsettled.

Determined to eliminate all hostile regimes from his western border, Stalin moved rapidly toward political domination of Eastern Europe and permanent division of conquered Germany. With the Red Army holding the territory Stalin coveted, his allies had to concede the Soviet gains or make war on the USSR. The American people, led by Roosevelt to believe that he could handle Stalin, were severely disappointed when Eastern Europe was "lost" to the Communists under Truman. Britain, which had entered the war in response to Hitler's attack on Poland, was particularly anguished over Stalin's refusal to restore free institutions in Russia's western Slavic neighbor.

Most Western Europeans and Americans, except those who openly sympathized with Communist ideology, were alarmed by this westward shift of Soviet power, seeing it as a direct threat to their own nations. The Soviets, and their supporters in the West, argued that they could not allow the Soviet Union to be surrounded by hostile states as in the past. And, in any event, they said, the new Communist regimes within the Soviet orbit expressed the will of the local people

far better than the aristocratic and semifascist ones that had existed in 1939. The United States generally avoided direct challenges to Soviet actions in Eastern Europe. But as changes occurred elsewhere, particularly in the Third World, it would watch with a wary eye, and often respond.

The Third World presented both opportunities and dangers to both superpowers. With France, Britain, Holland, and Japan too weakened to maintain empires, who would benefit from the political changes bound to come in their former colonies? The United States had never been a major colonial power like France or Britain, and during the post-1945 occupation of Japan it had demonstrated an attractive zeal for encouraging free, liberal institutions abroad. Could it now capitalize on the goodwill it possessed to win the emerging Third World nations over to Western-style liberal capitalism? But the Soviet Union also had advantages. It, too, had taken little part in the earlier race for overseas colonies, and so could claim to be free of imperialist taint. The people in almost all these emerging societies were desperately poor, and would be attracted by drastic schemes to redistribute land and end the privileged status of local elites. The Soviet Union sought to identify itself with these changes. Many Third World intellectuals, moreover, were strongly influenced by Marxist ideas, which promised quick modernization without the complexities and inconveniences of democratic institutions. Moreover, the middle class—the traditional backbone of liberal democracy that might have offset these groups—was tiny and weak.

In any struggle over the "nonaligned" world, then, it was not clear who would win. Some Americans, and perhaps some Soviet leaders, did not see the world as a simple polar division of "East" versus "West." But clearly during the immediate postwar period most Americans and Soviets found it difficult to imagine that nations could be permanently nonaligned or that there might be "blocs" of nations both non-Soviet and non-Western. Either "they were for us, or against us," opinion leaders on both sides seemed to believe. It was a certain formula for confrontation.

Inexperience, too, helped bring on the Cold War. Both antagonists found themselves the only great powers left in a world otherwise composed of has-beens and would-bes, and neither was equipped by history or tradition to handle this situation well. Soviet foreign policy in the fifties bore a marked resemblance to the czars' traditional quest for warm-water ports on the Mediterranean and Pacific and for secure western borders. U.S. policymakers continued to believe that all people craved democracy and private property as much as Americans did.

Ideology deepened the mutual distrust. Marxist doctrine told the Soviet leaders that Russia, the "socialist motherland," had a mission to destroy capitalism and Western colonialism and to unite under one banner the proletariat of the world. This mission required it to support Communist movements among the Western working class and to offer aid to "wars of national liberation" in the Third World. Though professedly idealistic, these attitudes often led to cynical, self-seeking Soviet exploitation of working-class and peasant aspirations for a better life. Americans took an opposite but at times equally self-seeking view. The world must be kept safe for free institutions, inlcuding private property rights. Americans perceived themselves as defending freedom against tyranny and protecting the world against "godless communism." Though often sincere, their attitudes at times served to prop up authoritarian pro-Western regimes that Third World peoples detested.

So an objective view of the Cold War must recognize that both East and West fueled tensions. But an additional fact must be acknowledged: The USSR, especially under Stalin, was a brutal police state where the press was an extension of the government and all private dissent was muzzled. Before, during, and after the war, Stalin's secret police arrested hundreds of thousands of men and women who were accused, often on the flimsiest evidence, of being enemies of the state and were sent to grim prison camps or simply executed. During his last years Stalin became a half-mad recluse who locked himself in the Kremlin and imagined terrible plots against his rule. As the Cold War evolved, he acted the absolute tyrant whose every word was a command that made strong men and women tremble. Even after his death in 1953, his successors, though never as bad, continued to impose harshly repressive and authoritarian regimes on their own people and the peoples of the satellite states.

At first pro-Soviet Westerners denied the charges against the Soviet regime, calling them capitalist propaganda. Eventually, especially during the brief thaw following Stalin's death in 1953, many recognized their mistake and ceased to support the Soviet Union. Yet others remained opposed to American Cold War policies on the grounds that they sacrificed the interests of former colonial peoples to those of Aemrican capitalism.

Containment. The end of World War II brought rapid international change. The Soviet Union moved not only in Eastern Europe, securing its western borders, but also in southern Europe, seeking access to warm-water ports. In 1945 it demanded that neighboring Turkey cede several frontier districts and allow Soviet control

The Cold War, 1955

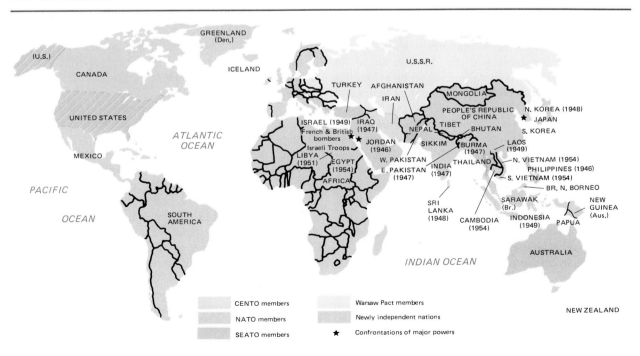

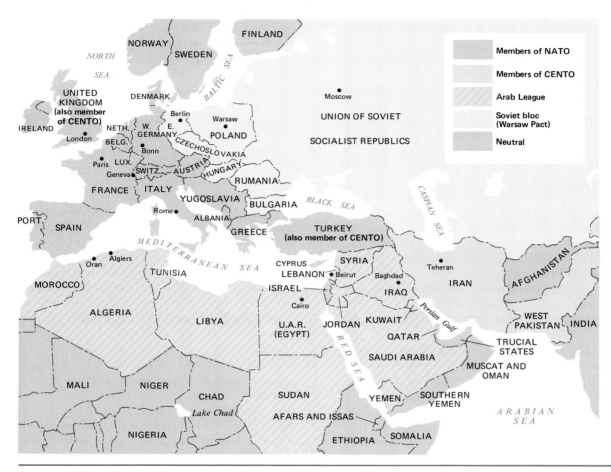

Postwar alliances in Europe and the Middle East

over the Dardanelles, the all-important strait connecting its Black Sea ports with the Mediterranean. In the following year Greece was torn apart by a Communist-led revolt sustained by supplies sent by Stalin and Marshal Josip Broz Tito, the leader of the Yugoslav Communists. Meanwhile, after 1945 the French confronted a strong nationalist movement in Indochina under Ho Chi Minh, the founder of the Indochina Communist party. In 1947, nationalists, inspired by Mohandas Gandhi, ousted the British from the Indian subcontinent and established the new republics of India and Pakistan. In 1949, the Dutch were forced to recognize the independence of the United States of Indonesia formed out of their East Indies colony.

The Soviets seemed likely to make major inroads into war-damaged, demoralized Western Europe too. Yet at first the United States was slow to recognize Europe's plight. In 1946 Congress authorized a $3.75 billion loan to Great Britain and contributed to the United Nations Relief and Rehabilitation Administra-

tion (UNRRA), which funneled money and supplies to starving Europeans. This generous effort was not enough, however, and by 1947 Europe seemed on the verge of chaos.

Americans were sincerely concerned with the suffering of Europe's people. They were also worried that poverty and social disruption were playing into the hands of the Communists. Americans deplored the Soviet domination of Poland, the Balkans, and Eastern Europe. They perceived the creation in 1947 of the Cominform, the Moscow-based association of world Communist parties, as a revival of Communist agitation and subversion outside Soviet borders. Soviet policy probably did not call for direct control of France, Italy, or Great Britain. Nevertheless, Moscow was certain to take advantage of Western Europe's weakness to win support for pro-Soviet parties and to reduce the influence of America's friends. Even a neutral Europe would be an enormous defeat for the United States.

During the first two years of peace a growing chorus of Western leaders warned that something must be done to stop Soviet expansion. In March 1946 Winston Churchill told an audience at Fulton, Missouri, that an "iron curtain" had "descended across the continent of Europe" behind which Communist tyranny reigned supreme. Elsewhere "Communist fifth columns" were threatening Christian civilization. A little over a year later George F. Kennan, a senior American diplomat, asserted that the Soviet Union was committed to an "aggressive intransigence with respect to the outside world." American policy, he advised, must be one of "long-term, patient, but firm and vigilant containment of Russian expansive tendencies."

The first significant move to implement containment and wall in the spreading "red tide" came during the cruel winter of 1946/47 when Europe seemed about to sink into the abyss. In February 1947 the British government told George Marshall, now Truman's secretary of state, that the situation was becoming desperate in Greece and Turkey. Britain itself was laboring under austerity measures as severe as those of wartime and could no longer continue its traditionally active role in the eastern Mediterranean. On March 12 Truman asked Congress for $400 million in aid for the two beleaguered nations. Under the leadership of Republican Senator Arthur H. Vandenberg of Michigan, Congress endorsed the Truman Doctrine of containment of Soviet expansion and Communist influence and made the appropriation. Massive aid to Greece and Turkey, combined with the break in 1948 between Tito and the Soviet Union, which blocked Russian aid to the Greek guerrillas, soon ended the Communist threat in both countries. The Truman Doctrine established a precedent that would inspire American foreign policy for the next forty years.

The Marshall Plan. With the Soviet Union contained in Greece and Turkey, there still remained the threat of subversion in Western Europe. This danger Americans met with an economic recovery program first broached by Secretary of State Marshall in June 1947. To restore "the confidence of the European people in the economic future of their own country and of Europe as a whole," Marshall proposed a gigantic joint economic recovery effort by Europe and the United States. The European response was enthusiastic. In July an all-European conference convened in Paris, formed the Committee for European Economic Cooperation, and agreed on a recovery program financed jointly by the United States and the European nations. The American call for a cooperative effort included the Soviet Union,

although the prospect of Soviet participation made American officials uneasy. The Soviets, suspicious and wanting no part in any program that would strengthen Western capitalism, came to the conference; but when Molotov discovered he could not disrupt the meeting, he walked out.

In the United States some conservatives deplored the Marshall Plan as a subsidy of Europe. On the left, Henry Wallace, the former vice president, considered it warlike and called it the Martial Plan. Anti-Communist public opinion, reinforced by the interest of farmers and manufacturers in enlarged export markets, endorsed the administration proposal. In March 1948 Congress passed the European Recovery Program—the Marshall Plan's official title—and in a few weeks vessels were steaming for Europe with cargoes of grain and manufactured goods.

In all, the United States contributed $12.5 billion to European recovery. It was not pure generosity. By shoring up Western Europe, the United States was protecting its strategic interests and helping to bolster its own economy. However motivated, the plan's results were spectacular. By 1950 Europe's economic output had outstripped that of 1939, the last prewar year,

American Marshall Plan money helped rebuild a badly damaged Europe brick by brick and, in doing so, cemented an alliance that dominates the international policy of the West to this day.

by 25 percent. The European Continent was beginning a dramatic economic surge that would carry living standards far beyond anything dreamed of before the war. The political effects were invaluable, too. As poverty receded, so did communism. By 1950 the fast-recovering nations were confident once again, and the growth of the Western European Communist parties had been effectively checked.

The Marshall Plan was accompanied by other moves to stiffen European resistance to Soviet and internal Communist pressures. Britain, France, and the United States were determined to restore an independent German state. In 1948 they stabilized the German currency and created out of their occupation zones a West German Federal Republic with its capital at Bonn. Threatened in their hopes of further westward expansion and fearful of a revived and militant Germany, the Russians reacted strongly. In June 1948 they imposed a blockade on all traffic into the western sector of Berlin, a city deep inside Soviet-occupied eastern Germany. To save Berlin and prevent its complete takeover by the Soviet East German satellite, the United States sent vital supplies into the city by plane. The Berlin Airlift lasted for more than ten months, until the Russians withdrew their barricades and allowed the city to be supplied once more by railroads and highways.

Moves and Countermoves. During these critical postwar years the two superpowers played a deadly game across the board of Europe. In February 1948 a Communist coup d'état in Prague, Czechoslovakia, turned the only Eastern European country with a democratic regime into another Soviet satellite. In September 1949 the USSR exploded its first atomic bomb. Knowledge that the Soviets were capable of waging atomic war sent shock waves through the Western nations.

The Prague coup and the Berlin blockade goaded the Western powers into a defensive response. In April 1949 Belgium, Canada, Denmark, France, Great Britain, Iceland, Italy, Luxembourg, the Netherlands, Norway, Portugal, and the United States formed the North Atlantic Treaty Organization (NATO). Each NATO member pledged to go to war if any other member were attacked. Conservative Republican senators fought the NATO treaty, but with the support of Senator Vandenburg, the leading Republican internationalist, it passed. For the first time the United States had committed itself to an international alliance in time of peace.

The Soviets did not take what they considered Western provocation lying down. Especially fearful

of NATO moves to include West Germany in the Western alliance, in 1955 they organized the Warsaw Pact, a military alliance of Albania, Bulgaria, Czechoslovakia, East Germany, Hungary, Poland, and Rumania with the USSR.

Despite these moves and countermoves, the West and East moved slowly toward a mutual accommodation in Europe. Crises continued, however. Until 1971 Berlin would remain a Western hostage in Soviet–East German hands, periodically triggering dangerous confrontations. Americans were slow to accept Soviet domination in Eastern Europe. In January 1953 Secretary of State John Foster Dulles declared in a television broadcast that people in the Soviet satellite nations could "count on" the United States. Soon afterward he had his supporters in Congress introduce the "captive peoples" resolution; it implied that America would aid anti-Soviet forces in Eastern Europe. When anti-Soviet Hungarians rose up in revolt in 1956, however, and demanded the departure of Soviet troops and an end to Soviet control, the United States refused military aid and allowed the Hungarian "freedom fighters" to be crushed brutally by Soviet might. The tragic failure of the Hungarian uprising clarified the limits of American commitment: The United States would fight for NATO and West Germany; it would not go to war to liberate the "captive peoples" of the East.

The Arms Race. Adding to the uncertainties of balance-of-power politics, and coloring almost every international event, was the threat of a direct armed clash between the two superpowers and the possibility of nuclear cataclysm. Although Stalin had professed indifference to the American atomic bomb when he officially learned of it, the Soviets were actually frightened by their adversary's new weapon. They quickly put their best technical brains to work and imported German scientists to help overtake the West. When the United States proposed international control of atomic weapons in 1946, the USSR rejected it on the grounds that it would freeze the weapons regime while the Americans were still ahead. The Soviet atom bomb project was helped by extensive Soviet wartime espionage in Britain, Canada, and the United States that had revealed the techniques needed to produce uranium-235 and the mechanisms to set it off. The Russians would have acquired a working bomb under any circumstances. Still, in September 1949, when President Truman announced that the Soviet Union had exploded its first atomic weapon, many Americans were certain that spying had greatly speeded the Soviet drive for nuclear parity.

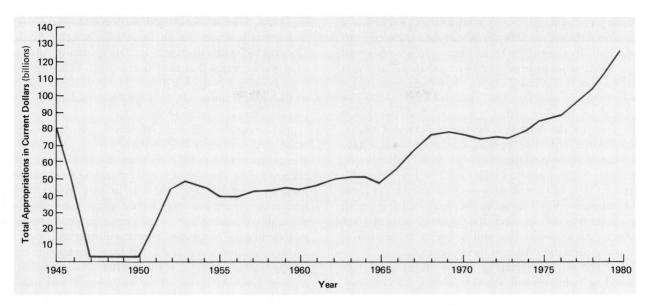

National defense outlays, 1945–1980. (*Source: Historical Statistics of the United States, Colonial Times to 1970 and Statistical Abstract of the United States 1980*).

The Soviet race for the bomb was only the first phase of the great superpower struggle to achieve arms supremacy by every means possible. At first each side sought bigger and better bombs. In 1950, over the protests of Robert Oppenheimer and other prominent scientists, the American government ordered the Atomic Energy Commission to develop the far more destructive hydrogen bomb. On November 1, 1952, the first H-bomb was exploded at Eniwetok, an atoll in the Marshall Islands. Within ten months the Soviet Union exploded its own hydrogen bomb, thus ending America's brief nuclear advantage.

Over the next few years both sides set off dozens of H-bombs to test their effectiveness and improve their capacity. It soon became obvious that the H-bomb was indeed a "hell" bomb that made it theoretically possible to destroy the world. Each test explosion, moreover, released large amounts of radioactive Strontium-90 into the atmosphere, threatening to cause thousands of cases of cancer in future generations. So serious was the outcry against testing that both sides were forced to acknowledge the protests. In 1963 the Soviet Union and the United States signed a treaty enjoining atomspheric testing of nuclear weapons. Nevertheless, both continued to stockpile nuclear weapons, so that by the mid-1960s each could destroy every one of its rival's cities many times over.

Once both superpowers had acquired weapons of unimagined power, the arms race shifted to delivery and detection systems. During the early 1950s the United States maintained a 270,000-person Strategic

Air Command, which kept a constant patrol of B-29 bombers in the air, each one carrying H-bombs. The Russians did not try to compete with SAC but sought to outflank the United States by developing guided missiles. Soviet engineers succeeded in producing unmanned, radar-guided rockets that could travel great distances and hit their targets within an error of a few miles. To counteract the Russian intercontinental ballistic missiles (ICBMs), the United States established a chain of radar stations, the DEW (distant early warning) line across northern Canada. At the same time American scientists worked furiously to close the "missile gap." They succeeded in late 1958, when an American Atlas rocket traveled from Florida to hit its target on Ascension Island 6,325 miles away.

Missiles and H-bombs did not preclude heavy investment in conventional weapons. American budget outlays for planes, tanks, artillery, atomic submarines, and other "defense" items went from $13 billion in 1950, when it was about one-third of the total federal budget, to $46 billion in 1960, when it was half. Added to the actual arms expenses were other Cold War costs. In July 1947 Congress passed the National Security Act unifying the army, navy, and air force under a single Defense Department and establishing the Central Intelligence Agency (CIA). Over the next three decades the CIA's budget for information-gathering and undercover operations around the world grew to billions of dollars, most of it hidden from the eyes of all but a handful of American officials.

A vocal minority of Americans protested against

these expenditures. Some conservative Republicans deplored the unbearable burden on the taxpayer. During the Eisenhower years Secretary Dulles supported the military doctrine of "massive retaliation" as a way of keeping down costs. Rather than seeking to match the Russians gun for gun, tank for tank, plane for plane, ship for ship, and man for man, Dulles proposed that we use the much less expensive "massive retaliatory power" of atom bombs. Critics of the secretary of state's massive retaliation policy noted that it would turn every confrontation with the USSR into a possible atomic war. Because Dulles enjoyed playing the game of brinkmanship—bringing the country to the edge of war in order to force the Soviet Union to back down—his emphasis on atomic weapons seemed to many a prescription for world holocaust.

The most determined critics of the arms race could be found on the liberal to radical left. Pacifists, women's civic groups, SANE (Committee for a Sane Nuclear Policy), supporters of unilateral disarmament, and liberal-to-left college professors denounced the massive armaments outlays: They were certain to lead to war, for all arms races in the end did. What was more, they said, the arms race drained off money that could better be used to restore the nation's crumbling cities, improve its schools, provide social services to the poor, and make the United States a more attractive nation.

Despite the protests, most citizens, heeding the cry that the country was in danger and the Soviet Union must be stopped, endorsed the enormous outlays. Before long, as Eisenhower had anticipated, many people, and whole communities, acquired a vital stake in continued defense spending: It provided jobs for local wage earners and business and tax revenues for local communities.

Containment in Asia. In Asia, meanwhile, the United States found itself facing a new danger. Since the end of the war it had sent $2 billion in aid to Chiang in China with little result. Much of the war matériel meant for Chiang's Kuomintang was sold off by corrupt nationalist officials and ended up in the hands of either profiteers or the Chinese Communists. The Kuomintang soon lost the confidence of the Chinese people. Although the United States had done its diplomatic best, and even though the Soviet Union, fearing a rival in Mao, had supported Chiang, by 1948 Mao's Communist forces were sweeping all before them. In December 1949 Chiang, his entourage, and his remaining troops fled the mainland to reestablish the Republic of China on Taiwan (Formosa), off the south coast of China. Now unchallenged on the mainland, Mao and his supporters set up the People's Republic of China (PRC) with its capital at Beijing. Many Americans were certain that the "free world" had suffered a grievous and avoidable defeat. Hundreds of millions of Chinese, it appeared, had now been added to the Communist side of the scales.

During the Chinese civil war a few Americans associated with the "China lobby," had supported direct military intervention to prevent the Communist takeover. The Truman administration had rejected the idea, convinced that a land war in Asia would be a bottomless quagmire that would drain the nation's strength and could not be won. Even after the Communist victory the American government sought to avoid a direct military role in East Asia as a strategically insupportable position. We could defend Europe but, it seemed, not Asia, too, where we had no strong allies and where the appeal of communism to the impoverished masses was exceptionally powerful. In January 1950 Secretary of State Dean Acheson declared that the United States did not consider Taiwan, mainland Southeast Asia, or South Korea essential to American security. If any of these places were invaded, the "initial resistance" would have to come from those attacked.

Acheson did not intend to give the Communists the green light for further expansion, but that was the effect of his pronouncement. Since shortly after World War II, Korea, for years a Japanese possession, had been divided into Soviet and American zones at the thirty-eighth parallel, pending its eventual reunification. By 1948 there were two governments in Korea: a Republic of Korea (ROK) in the South led by Syngman Rhee, elected president under UN supervision, and a People's Republic in the North, closely allied with the Soviet Union. In 1949 the United States withdrew its last remaining troops from the South, leaving the ROK unprotected.

Soon after Acheson's statement the North Koreans—apparently with Stalin's approval—concluded that it was time to reunite Korea under their own auspices. On June 25, 1950, 95,000 Soviet-armed North Korean troops crossed the thirty-eighth parallel in a massive invasion of the Republic of Korea, which was still formally under United Nations control. Reversing his administration's previous position, Truman acted decisively to stop what he considered a blatant act of aggression. The United States immediately called an emergency session of the Security Council, from which the USSR had temporarily withdrawn its representive. On June 27, unimpeded by a Soviet veto, the Council asked all members of the United Nations to contribute "such assistance to the Republic of Korea as may be necessary to repel the armed attack and restore international peace and security in the area." By this time President Truman had already instructed General Douglas MacArthur, Supreme Allied Commander in Japan, to send military assistance to the ROK defenders. Yet the UN resolution was invaluable. Because of it, the United States would be fighting a "police action" in Korea as agent of the UN. Not only would it receive valuable material aid from other UN members, but outside the Communist bloc no nation would accuse it of imperialist motives.

The initial North Korean attack quickly overran most of the South, pushing ROK and American forces into a tight pocket around the port of Pusan. There they held on desperately until reinforcements began to arrive from Japan and the continental United States. On September 15, 1950, MacArthur made an end run by sea around the North Koreans and began to sweep the enemy northward. By October he had reached the

Harry Truman and Douglas MacArthur did not like one another, but at least at this meeting at Wake Island in October 1950 they could smile together for the cameras.

The Korean War

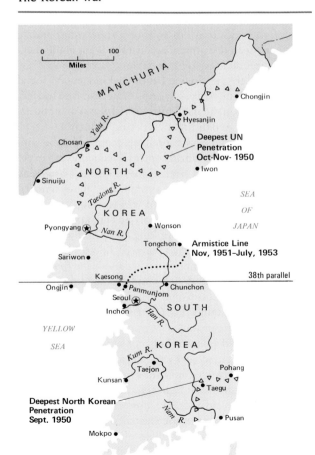

thirty-eighth parallel. Here he might have paused; but convinced that America could defeat the Chinese if they should intervene and prodded by Truman, the UN, and America's European allies, he drove past the old border all the way to the Chinese-Korean boundary at the Yalu River.

Mao had threatened to support the North Koreans if they appeared certain to lose, and by October MacArthur's troops began to encounter Chinese military units. Despite these signs of Chinese intentions, in November 1950 MacArthur launched a final offensive to crush all remaining North Korean resistance. He drove his men into a gigantic Chinese trap. Masses of Chinese troops overwhelmed the ROK and American forces and for a while threatened to capture thousands. MacArthur succeeded in extricating the bulk of his army but was forced to retreat to the thirty-eighth parallel. There the two armies settled down to a cruel and costly static trench warfare that resembled the Western Front during World War I.

Month after dreary month passed with daily casualties but no movement. Americans found the military stalemate exasperating. Unused to such total frustration, some on the far political right demanded that the country use atomic weapons. Others, led by MacArthur, insisted that UN forces be allowed to attack the Chinese at home, where their real strength lay. This might require "unleashing" Chiang and his Taiwan armies to assault the Chinese mainland. Or it might be necessary to bomb Chinese bases in Manchuria. If either of these acts brought the Soviet Union into the war, so be it. Truman and his advisers, however, backed by many moderates and liberals, feared an expanded war and decided that the only reasonable conclusion was a negotiated peace. On several occasions the president warned MacArthur that he must stop making warlike pronouncements and provocative declarations. MacArthur considered the administration's "no-win" policy disgraceful and tried to scuttle pending overtures to the Chinese for a diplomatic settlement. Truman finally concluded that the general had allowed his years as benevolent tyrant in Japan to go to his head, and in April 1951 relieved him of his command.

MacArthur's demotion shocked many conservatives, who saw it as weakness in the face of the great international Communist threat. When the general returned home, he was welcomed as a great hero; conservative Republicans talked about nominating him for president in 1952.

MacArthur's firing cleared the air. In July 1951, at Kaesŏng, the United Nations and the North Koreans opened negotiations for an armistice. The discussions dragged on for two years and became another source of frustration; but finally, in June 1953, the two sides signed a truce ending the fighting.

Nothing much had been accomplished. A generation later Korea remained divided along a line within a few miles of the June 1950 border between South and North. Meanwhile, the American people had paid dearly for the Korean War. At home the country had returned to a war footing. Congress had revived the draft and expanded the armed forces to more than 3 million men. The decision to restore a conventional military force proved expensive and pushed the military budget to over $50 billion by 1952. The economy, which had been in the doldrums in 1949, quickly revived and then began to overheat. By 1951 prices had risen about 12 percent despite the government's efforts to hold them down by price controls like those in World War II. The total cost in lives and wealth was immense for a struggle that had accomplished so little. The United States had suffered 135,000 casualties (including 33,000 killed) and spent an estimated $54 billion.

A Second Red Scare

The Cold War and the Korean conflict profoundly affected the national mood. It had been the proudest boast of patriots before 1945 that America had never lost a war. With the advent of nuclear weapons, however, final victories seemed impossible. Nuclear war promised mass slaughter, if not the total destruction of all life on the planet. There were a few "tough-minded" people who, under the banner "Better dead than red," advocated a nuclear "first strike" against the Soviet Union. At the other extreme were those who reversed the slogan to "Better red than dead" and favored "unilateral"—that is, one-sided—disarmament. Few Americans cared to accept either devastating nuclear war or certain surrender to the Soviet Union, and the unresolvable world crisis tried the patience of millions of citizens.

Heightening this frustration was the feeling that the new enemy was maddeningly elusive. Hitler, Mussolini, and Tojo had been straightforward military aggressors, and the danger they posed had been clear for all to see. These and other past enemies had challenged the United States frontally, and Americans had marshaled their energies and finished them off. But the Cold War was fought through surrogates and by subversion and propaganda. Few Americans knew much about the emerging Third World of former colonial states, and did not recognize that their lack of democratic traditions, absence of a substantial middle class, and deep resentment against the West made them unlikely candidates for U.S.-style governments. They tended to see the Soviet Union behind every social upheaval in Asia, Africa, or Latin America. And indeed, the Soviet Union did use Third World wars of "national liberation" to expand its power and influence.

The Communists, moreover, appeared to be winning the struggle for world control. Disinclined to make distinctions among Chinese Communists, Yugoslav Communists, and Soviet Communists, many Americans thought the whole world was turning "red." Because communism was obviously an evil, atheistic, brutal force that all right-thinking people must abhor, how could its success be explained? Besides the visible enemy there must be another, disguised one that operated internally in the West to undermine anti-Communist resistance. Confusing the democratic socialism espoused by Britain's Labour party and the various social democratic groups of Western Europe with communism, it could seem to many conservative Americans that dangerous ideologies were expanding and the West was being undermined and subverted. The enemy was an invisible presence, it appeared, hiding behind familiar institutions and secretly supported by respectable people in high places in the United States and Europe. However simplistic this analysis of the Cold War, during the 1950s it gained wide currency.

The Enemy Within. Frustration, suspicion, and fear tripped off a repressive reaction. The public mood during the 1950s was clearly overwrought, but it was also true that the Soviet Union supported extensive espionage operations in the United States. In 1950 the British uncovered the doings of Klaus Fuchs, a German refugee atomic physicist who had been employed at Los Alamos during the war and had transmitted atomic secrets to the Soviet Union. The trail of Fuchs's betrayal soon led to David Greenglass, an enlisted man at the Los Alamos Atomic energy center. Greenglass accused his brother-in-law and sister, Julius and Ethel Rosenberg, of passing secrets to the Russians. Although many people believed them innocent, the Rosenbergs were eventually convicted of espionage and executed in what became an international *cause célèbre*. In March 1950 Judith Coplon and her Soviet agent-lover, Valentin Gubitchev, were convicted of spying. Gubitchev was deported and Coplon sentenced to jail.

Most disturbing of all was the apparent betrayal of the country by a prominent public servant, Alger Hiss, president of the Carnegie Endowment for International Peace. During the 1930s Hiss had been a New Dealer who had served in the State Department, been a delegate to the UN, and had accompanied Roosevelt to Yalta. In 1948 Whittaker Chambers, an admitted former Communist, told the House Committee on Un-American Activities (HUAC) that during the 1930s he and Hiss had been members of a Soviet spy ring in Washington and that Hiss had given secret government documents to the Russians. Summoned before the committee, Hiss was subjected to close questioning by Congressman Richard Nixon and others, but he denied that he had ever known Chambers or stolen official secrets. Because of the statute of limitations, Hiss could no longer be indicted for espionage. He sued Chambers for libel, however, and in the libel suit Chambers produced new evidence that Hiss had been a spy. The federal government now tried Hiss for perjury, and in the second of two trials he was found guilty and sentenced to five years in prison.

The Hiss-Chambers case was one of the pivotal political events of the early postwar period. Many Americans were deeply disturbed that a man so generously honored by his nation should, apparently, have betrayed it. Conservatives would use the Hiss case to attack their foes to the left. Hiss's actions, they said, were symptomatic of the whole New Deal. Alien to the American way, it had represented "twenty years of treason." Nor had the betrayal ceased. The Democrats were still protecting traitors. The Truman administration, charged Congressman Nixon, "was ex-

tremely anxious that nothing happen to Mr. Hiss." On the pro-Hiss side feelings were equally impassioned. The far left considered Hiss an innocent martyr to Cold War hysteria, and at times even moderate liberals reacted to the charges of Chambers and others as if no one had ever engaged in espionage against the United States or that such spying had ever posed a threat to the nation.

McCarthyism. But in addition to the valid fear of spying, there was a parallel, less legitimate, fear of subversion. Often the public confused the two, with many people failing to distinguish between stealing military secrets and merely advocating ideas that were, or seemed to be, pro-Communist or pro-Soviet or simply "un-American." Before long the country was in the grip of a full-scale panic that endangered the civil liberties of many Americans.

The Truman administration was in part responsible for the hysteria. Fearful of being attacked by conservative opponents as too lenient with Communists, Truman in 1947 ordered the FBI to flush from government service those who were bad security risks, whether because of their dubious politics or because of some personal or sexual trait. In 1948 Truman's attorney general indicted eleven top officials of the American Communist party on charges of violating the Smith Act of 1940 by advocating overthrow of the government by force. After a tumultuous trial, all were convicted and sentenced to prison.

The president did not want the antisubversive drive to go too far, however. In 1950 he vetoed the McCarran Internal Security Act requiring registration of Communist and Communist-front organizations, excluding from the country would-be immigrants who belonged to a totalitarian party, forbidding the employment of Communists in defense work, and providing for the internment of radicals during national emergencies. "In a free country," Truman declared in his veto message, "we punish men for the crimes they commit, but never for the opinions they have." These were stirring words, but Congress overrode his veto. Whether he acted out of conviction or from fear, Truman cannot escape blame for having stimulated, through his earlier "anti-Communist" moves, the excessive reaction to internal subversion that marked the decade. Nor was the president the only liberal who, through timidity or miscalculation, piled fuel on the anti-Communist blaze. At one point Senator Hubert Humphrey, for example, proposed a bill to outlaw the Communist party. Other liberals, while refusing explicitly to support the intolerant mood, declined to

Joe McCarthy

The career of Senator Joseph R. McCarthy of Wisconsin was a Cold War artifact. McCarthy was an undistinguished member of the upper house faced with a stiff fight for reelection when he happened on the anti-Communist issue in 1950. Thereafter, he became a power in the land, winning reelection handily in 1952, and striking fear into the hearts of his political enemies by his grip on the imaginations and loyalties of millions of Americans. The following is the heart of McCarthy's famous Wheeling Lincoln Day speech of February 1950 wherein he first broached the issue of "treason" in high places.

"Six years ago, at the time of the first conference to map out the peace—Dumbarton Oaks—there was within the Soviet orbit 180,000,000 people. Lined up on the antitotalitarian side there were in the world at that time roughly 1,625,000,000 people. Today, only 6 years later, there are 800,000,000 people under the absolute domination of Soviet Russia—an increase of over 400 percent. On our side, the figure has shrunk to around 500,000,000. In other words, in less than 6 years the odds have changed from 9 to 1 in our favor to 8 to 5 against us. This indicates the swiftness of the tempo of Communist victories and American defeats in the cold war. As one of our outstanding figures once said, 'When a great democracy is destroyed, it will not be because of enemies from without, but rather because of enemies from within.'

"The truth of the statement is becoming terrifyingly clear as we see the country losing each day on every front. . . .

"The reason why we find ourselves in a position of impotency is not because our only powerful potential enemy has sent men to invade our shores, but rather because of the traitorous actions of those who have been so well treated by this Nation. It has not been the less fortunate or members of minority groups who have been selling this Nation out, but rather those who have had all the benefits that the wealthiest nation on earth has had to offer—the finest homes, the finest college education, and the finest jobs in Government we can give.

"This is glaringly true in the State Department. There the bright young men who are born with silver spoons in their mouths are the ones who have been worst. . . .

"When Chiang Kai-shek was fighting our war, the State Department had in China a young man named John S. Service. His task, obviously, was not to work for the communization of China. Strangely, however, he sent official reports back to the State Department urging that we torpedo our ally Chiang Kai-shek and stating, in effect, that communism was the best hope of China.

"Later, this man—John Service—was picked up by the Federal Bureau of Investigation for turning over to the Communists secret State Department information. Strangely, however, he was never prosecuted. However, Joseph Grew, the Under Secretary of State, who insisted on his prosecution, was forced to resign. Two days after Grew's successor, Dean Acheson, took over as Under Secretary of State, this man—John Service . . . was not only reinstated . . . but promoted . . .

"Then there was a Mrs. Mary Jane Kenny, from the Board of Economic Warfare . . . , who was named in an FBI report and in a House committee report as a courier for the Communist Party while working for the Government. And where do you think Mrs. Kenny is—she is now an editor in the United Nations Document Bureau.

"This, ladies and gentlemen, gives you somewhat of a picture of the type of individuals who have been helping to shape our foreign policy. In my opinion the State Department . . . is thoroughly infested with Communists.

"I have in my hand 57 cases of individuals who would appear to be either card-carrying members or certainly loyal to the Communist Party, but who nevertheless are still helping to shape our foreign policy. . . .

"As you know, very recently the Secretary of State proclaimed his loyalty to a man [Alger Hiss] guilty of what has always been considered the most abominable of all crimes—of being a traitor to the people who gave him a position of great trust. The Secretary of State in attempting to justify his continued devotion to the man who sold out the Christian world to the atheistic world, referred to Christ's Sermon on the Mount as a justification and reason therefore, and the reaction of the American people to this would have made the heart of Abraham Lincoln happy.

"When this pompous diplomat in striped pants, with a phony British accent, proclaimed to the American people that Christ on the Mount endorsed communism, high treason, and betrayal of a sacred trust, the blasphemy was so great that it awakened the indignation of the American people.

"He has lighted the spark which is resulting in a moral uprising and will end only when the whole sorry mess of twisted, warped thinkers are swept from the national scene so that we may have a new birth of national honesty and decency in Government."

attack it publicly, thereby lending it their tacit support.

It was perhaps inevitable that a demagogue would appear to exploit Americans' fears and suspicions for his own purposes. The man was Joseph R. McCarthy, the Republican junior senator from the once proudly progressive state of Wisconsin. Like many demagogues, McCarthy had his attractive side. He genuinely liked people and could never understand why they despised him. Though he was a scrappy man, willing to take on anyone, he did not make his political foes into personal enemies. But he was also a liar, a petty tyrant, a crude opportunist, and an insensitive boor who could not comprehend that a democratic society required a modicum of civility and political decency.

At the beginning of 1950 McCarthy was in political trouble. Sent to the Senate in the Republican sweep of 1946, he could not rely on reelection by Wisconsin's normally liberal voters. He needed exposure and a good press to survive, so he assumed the pose of public protector against the Communist menace at home. In Wheeling, West Virginia, before the local Republican women's club, McCarthy opened his campaign by charging that the United States found itself "in a position of impotency" in international affairs because of "the traitorous actions" of men in high government posts. The State Department, especially, was "thoroughly infested with Communists," bright young men from the privileged class who had betrayed their country. He could, he said, name 205 members of the State Department whom the secretary of state knew to be members of the Communist party.

McCarthy could do nothing of the sort. But the press began to take notice of his sensational charges, and the country was soon in an excited mood. President Truman and Secretary of State Acheson angrily denied the senator's claims. On Capitol Hill McCarthy's Senate colleagues asked him for proof. In response he carried out the feeble charade of reading some unconvincing documents that at many points completely exonerated the supposed culprits. The presentation was so shoddy that even the Republican leaders, who had at first welcomed his charges as likely to discomfit the Democrats, were embarrassed. Soon afterward,

Senator Joseph McCarthy makes reckless charges as a dejected Joseph Welch turns away.

An Historical Portrait

Jack Kerouac

Jean-Louis ("Jack") Kerouac would be a hero to young rebels trying to escape the stifling conformity of the 1950s. He was also a "mamma's boy" who invariably returned from his misadventures to the safety and comfort of Gabrielle Lévesque Kerouac ("Mémère").

Jack Kerouac always believed that his ancestors were noble Celts from Cornwall who later settled in France. The truth is more prosaic. Jack's parents, Leo and Gabrielle, were both born in Quebec of peasant stock and emigrated with their families to New England as small children. They were part of the flood of French Canadians who crossed the U.S. border seeking better livelihoods than afforded by the thin soils of the St. Lawrence Valley. When Jack was born in 1922 his parents were living in the old mill town of Lowell, Massachusetts, where Leo ran a print shop.

The three formative influences of Jack's childhood and youth were the death of his older brother, Gerard, when Jack was four, his discovery of the novels of Thomas Wolfe when he was fifteen, and football at Lowell High School. Gerard's tender, long-suffering character left his little brother with an image of saintly purity that would always be one pole of his personality. Wolfe's sprawling, disorderly style would be Jack's literary inspiration. Varsity football at Lowell High School in his teens would be his ticket of escape from the narrow world of immigrant Lowell.

In 1939 Columbia University offered Kerouac a football scholarship, and he arrived in New York in the fall to attend Horace Mann, a Columbia-affiliated prep school, to make up deficient academic credits and put on some weight. Kerouac's college football career was short-lived. In 1940 he played for the Columbia freshman squad but broke his leg and spent the rest of the year on campus in a cast. When he returned to school the following September he played briefly for the varsity, but quit the team when Coach Lou Little relegated him to a line position. Meanwhile, the United States had entered World War II, and Kerouac joined the merchant marine as a cook's galley helper and went on one trip to Greenland. He returned for a brief stint at Columbia and then quit for good. In early 1943 he was inducted into the navy but was discharged for psychiatric reasons: He could not obey orders.

Kerouac learned little from Columbia, but New York would become a major focus of his life. In 1943 the elder Kerouacs moved to New York, where Leo and Mémère both got jobs. Jack divided his time between their apartment in Queens and that of Edie Parker, an attractive art student from Michigan, who lived in the Columbia neighborhood. At Edie's he met a crowd of young bohemians, including Lucian Carr, a Columbia freshman from St. Louis, and his friend, Allen Ginsberg, another Columbia student from Paterson, New Jersey. Through Carr, Kerouac also met an older man, William Burroughs, who, like Ginsberg, was physically attracted to Carr.

His new friends were different from anyone Kerouac had encountered before. They were cultural rebels with a streak of surrealism in their nature. On a visit to Burrough's Greenwich Village apartment, Carr, imitating André Gide's *acte gratuit*, chewed up a beer glass. To continue the game, host Burroughs served his guests a plateful of razor blades. Burroughs also introduced Kerouac to Oswald Spengler's celebration of Western civilization's decay, *The Decline of the West*. Nineteen forty-five was also the year that Jack married Edie (the marriage was brief and unhappy); started to take Benzedrine, a powerful stimulant; and discovered Bop, the new, "cool" form of jazz that black musicians such as Dizzy Gillespie, Charlie Parker, Miles Davis, and Thelonious Monk were beginning to play in New York. It was from the "hipster" fans of Bop—young people who despised the "square world" of postwar America—that Kerouac and their friends borrowed the term "beat" to describe their cultural stance.

Toward the end of that momentous year Leo Kerouac was diagnosed as having stomach cancer. Jack came back to Queens to help his mother nurse him. His father's death in May 1946 plunged Jack into gloom, but shortly after he began to write *The Town and the City*, his first novel. An even more important event of the first full postwar year was Jack's meeting with Neal Cassady, a young man who came to represent heroic freedom and inspired the book that made Kerouac famous.

Cassady was essentially a juvenile delinquent. He had been raised by a wino father in a Denver flophouse. He began to steal cars at fourteen, and by the time he reached twenty had stolen over 500. After reform school in New Mexico he decided that he wanted to write and came to New York in the fall of 1946, determined to enter Columbia.

To Kerouac, Cassady represented the vital life force and liberation from conventional morality. Jack admired his friend's sexual freedom, his western openness, his physical fearlessness. He seemed a "mad genius of jails and raw power." The two planned a car trip west together, but then, in March, Cassady suddenly returned to Denver with his sixteen-year-old wife and a stolen typewriter. That summer both Kerouac and Ginsberg turned up in Denver. The visit with Cassady was not a success, and Kerouac went on to San Francisco after a few weeks for his first stay of many in that lively, creative city. In July he returned to Mémère in Queens, finished his 1,100-page novel, and met John Clellon Holmes, another aspiring writer. The two young men got along well and it was in a discussion of their generation that Kerouac would remark, "I guess you can call us a beat generation," one weary "with all the forms, all the conventions." Holmes later wrote a novel about Kerouac and "the Beats" called Go.

While The Town and the City made the rounds of the publishers, Kerouac took courses in literature at the New School and began a novel about a long-distance car trip. In October Cassady turned up in New York with a brand-new silver-colored Hudson Hornet, and he and Kerouac set off on a marathon drive that took them south to visit Burroughs in Louisiana, across Texas to Tucson, and on to San Francisco. The two young men hurtled across the landscape of fifties America, exhilarated by the sheer joy of moving fast. The impressions collected on this trip, when merged with the earlier car manuscript, became the building blocks of Kerouac's most famous novel, On the Road.

By the mid-1950s, in isolated pockets across America, young men and women were declaring their independence of their society's conventionality and timidity. Few of them were "creative." Most were merely consumers of culture, but this culture was intensely antagonistic to middle-class fifties values. "Beatniks" sought a particular personal style. They assumed a "natural" look. They dressed in working-class style: jeans, open-necked plaid shirts, workshoes. They led freer sex lives; they often smoked marijuana; they listened to Bop; they struck poses of personal "coolness"—uninvolvement—including indifference to politics.

There were also more creative Beats. In New York, Los Angeles, and especially San Francisco, small clusters of young, cool poets and novelists gathered together to provide mutual support for their writing. In San Francisco, a refuge for mavericks and bohemians ever since Gold Rush days, the Beat poets reached a critical mass under the aegis of a former Chicagoan, Kenneth Rexroth, and Lawrence Ferlinghetti, a San Francisco poet who ran a combined bookstore–publishing house called City Lights that became a haven for the city's Beats. Both Kerouac and Ginsberg were in the Bay Area in October 1955, just in time to be included in a Rexroth-sponsored poetry reading at the Six Gallery in an old San Francisco garage. Jack himself was only a spectator, but it was here that Ginsberg first read his long poem "Howl," a work that became the anthem of the cultural left for a generation and made Ginsberg famous.

Jack was soon to make his own very large literary splash. In September 1957 Viking Press published On the Road to rave reviews in The New York Times and other leading newspapers and magazines. Written on a continuous roll of typewriter paper in a twenty-day burst of creative energy fueled by oceans of coffee, the novel recounted the adventures of "Dean Moriarity" and "Sal Paradise" as they rolled frenetically across the continent in Moriarity's tail-finned behemoth, drinking in the essence of American vitality. Soon after, following articles on them in Harper's Bazaar, The New York Times, Evergreen Review, the Nation, and other publications, the Beats became culture heroes to the rebellious young and curiosities to their conventional elders of fifties America.

Kerouac spent much of the remaining 1950s as a restless wanderer shuttling among New York, San Francisco, North Carolina, Mexico, Florida, Long Island, and Tangier in Morocco. He was often in the company of Cassady, Ginsberg, Burroughs, or one of the new Beat poets. At least half the time he stayed with Mémère in several different places. Kerouac became a devotee of Zen Buddhism and wrote about his Zen friend Gary Snyder in The Dharma Bums, a book finished in ten mammoth typing sessions. He wrote a flock of other works in the 1950s and early 1960s, but few were taken seriously by the critics.

As Kerouac's stock fell, Ginsberg's rose. Ginsberg became a prophet who, as the sixties unfolded, adapted to the new political rebelliousness of the young. Unlike Kerouac, who grew more conservative and misanthropic as he got older, Ginsberg moved politically left and became a gentle, nonviolent guru-radical. He also became an apostle of the new "psychedelic" drug culture, while Kerouac's mind-bender of choice remained alcohol—and ever larger quantities of it. In 1967 Kerouac moved with his mother and third wife back to Lowell, and then to St. Petersburg, Florida. In 1968 Neal Cassady collapsed and died in Mexico after overindulging in liquor and drugs. By now Kerouac's own health had deteriorated. The former varsity football player had become, at forty-six, a bloated, seedy alcoholic. On October 20, 1969, as he sat in front of his TV set with a can of tuna fish and a small bottle of whiskey, Jack suffered a massive intestinal hemorrhage. Eighteen hours later he died in surgery.

When they heard the news, reporters rushed to interview Allen Ginsberg at his upstate New York farm. Ginsberg started to quote William Blake's lines, "The days of my youth rise fresh in my mind," but he was too choked to finish. When the journalists left, he inscribed on a tree with a hunting knife: "Jack Kerouac, 1922–1969."

---

while testifying before a Senate subcommittee, McCarthy announced dramatically that the "top Soviet espionage agent" in the United States was Owen Lattimore, a professor of Far Eastern affairs at John Hopkins University, who had been a State Department adviser on China policy. The testimony of witnesses failed to support McCarthy's claims, but many Americans, deeply chagrined at the recent "loss" of China, were willing to believe that Lattimore and men like him had betrayed the nation. For days the senator made the headlines. In a few short months the word *McCarthyism* had been added to the language as a term for irresponsible mudslinging and defamation.

Civil libertarians notwithstanding, McCarthy and his cause were genuinely popular. Opinion polls in 1950 showed that the senator had the approval of 50 percent of the American people. Thereafter his popularity grew. McCarthy's views appealed strongly to many Catholics, whose anticommunism went very deep. He also drew considerable working-class support by playing on class resentments, choosing as his favorite targets people of elite background like Hiss, Acheson, and Lattimore. McCarthy's strong political base was confirmed when, in the 1950 congressional election, he came to Maryland and helped defeat Democratic Senator Millard Tydings, one of his severest critics. His strength with the voters made McCarthyism an effective weapon for conservative Republicans to use against liberals and Democrats. As such it was sanctioned by many GOP leaders, including Mr. Republican himself, Robert Taft. So pervasive was McCarthy's popularity that even liberal Democrats had to reckon with it. In the early 1950s the young Massachusetts congressman John F. Kennedy noted that "Joe . . . may have something."

McCarthyism became a mood and an attitude that penetrated many layers of American life, with malign consequences. Besides McCarthy's own probes, the House Committee on Un-American Activities and the Senate Internal Security Subcommittee regularly investigated Communist infiltration of the universities, the churches, private industry, and the media. HUAC's well-publicized hearings usually focused on very visible fields such as the movies, the universities, and the unions. It forced men and women under subpoena to answer charges, often anonymous, that they had been members of "subversive" organizations. These groups were not necessarily formally Communist; they might be "Communist fronts" included on the attorney general's "list" of several hundred suspect organizations. HUAC did not punish offenders directly, but many of those called before the committee lost their jobs and their reputations.

Private organizations and local officials quickly joined the antisubversive chorus. The broadcasting industry refused to hire anyone for radio or television work who was listed in *Red Channels*, a volume compiled by three former FBI agents that purported to identify all entertainers and media writers with past or existing radical affiliations. In Hollywood there were unofficial blacklists of performers, screenwriters, and directors whom no studio would touch. The theater, too, was rife with accusers and lists of "disloyal" people. Universities imposed loyalty oaths on faculty; states and local governments, on clerks, typists, laborers, and officials.

The prevailing hysteria over communist and subversion cast a dark shadow over American life. Among performers, artists, and intellectuals, some of whom had been attracted to radical politics during the 1930s, the fear of attack and the possible consequences for their careers and personal lives squelched creativity.

Many former leftists convinced themselves that they had been wrong about socialism—or even liberalism—and retreated to conservatism or became profoundly apolitical. With the whole left end of political and social ideology either silenced or converted, the tenor of the country shifted to the right. The witch-hunts destroyed many artistic and intellectual careers, but even ordinary citizens were deeply affected. When vigilantes were attacking every dissenting view and every dissenter as Communist, it seemed wise to keep silent and repress any opinion that could be considered irreverent. Fear of attack as a dangerous subversive, then, reinforced the 1950s tendency to focus on domestic joys and confirmed the American retreat into privatism.

After Eisenhower's victory and McCarthy's re-election in 1952, observers expected the senator to quiet down. The Republicans were now in office, and attacks on government officials would hurt his own party. But he refused to stop. In February 1953 he accused officials of the United States Information Agency, the information arm of the State Department, of attempting to undermine the American propaganda war against the Soviet Union. Panicked, Secretary of State John Foster Dulles ordered hundreds of books by such authors of "doubtful loyalty" as Theodore H. White and Dashiell Hammett removed from the agency's shelves.

McCarthy's Downfall. With his popularity at its peak, the Wisconsin senator launched an attack on the army. His initial target was Secretary of the Army Robert T. Stevens, whom he accused of condoning the promotion of Irving Peress, an army dentist who had once been a member of the radical American Labor party. The promotion was actually a routine reranking of all drafted medical personnel, but in the next few weeks McCarthy made the cry "Who promoted Peress?" as famous for a while as "Remember the *Maine.*" The army responded by accusing McCarthy of using his influence to gain preferential treatment at Fort Monmouth for G. David Schine, a draftee who had been a member of the senator's staff and a protégé of Roy Cohn, his committee counsel.

Eventually Congress voted to hold an investigation before McCarthy's own committee with Republican Senator Karl Mundt of South Dakota presiding. On April 22, 1954, the hearings commenced, and when they were over eight weeks later, McCarthy had to all intents and purposes run his course. Before the glaring lights of the television cameras, the senator seemed like a scowling Hollywood villain. He badgered witnesses and insulted them; he constantly interrupted the proceedings with points of order and irrelevancies.

The army's special counsel—a puckish, deceptively mild-mannered Boston lawyer named Joseph N. Welch—proved to be the senator's undoing. To weaken Welch's credibility, McCarthy chose to attack one of Welch's young Boston associates for his membership, years before, in the National Lawyer's Guild, a communist-front organization. The young man had been dropped from Welch's hearing staff because of this association, but Welch had forgiven him his youthful indiscretion and retained him in his law firm. He saw no reason to bring the attorney's past to the attention of the public. When McCarthy broached the subject, Welch turned on him furiously: "Let us not assassinate this lad further, Senator. You have done enough. Have you no sense of decency, sir, at long last? Have you no sense of decency?" When he had finished his impassioned denunciation, the audience in the hearing room cheered. Even more important, television viewers in the living rooms and the neighborhood bars also cheered.

McCarthy's stock quickly plummeted. On December 2, 1954, the Senate passed a resolution condemning him for bringing the Senate into disrepute. From that day on, his colleagues shunned him, and when he rose to speak, they left the Senate chamber. Worst of all, the media began to ignore him. No matter what he said, he could no longer make the headlines. On May 2, 1957, he died, unlamented by most Americans.

McCarthy's Legacy. McCarthy himself was dead, but in various guises the feelings he fed on and the movement he helped launch survived. In 1958 a Massachusetts candy manufacturer named Robert Welch founded the John Birch Society, a far-right anti-Communist organization. Welch and his followers insisted that the entire nation was riddled with secret Communists. From 60 to 80 percent of the world had already fallen to the Communists, they said, and the United States, having rejected Christian orthodoxy, rugged individualism, and free enterprise, was virtually lost as well. According to Birch Society members, everything since Herbert Hoover represented a conspiratorial effort to undermine Christian American civilization, and even the Eisenhower administration was actively aiding the forces of communism.

Despite attacks by public officials, journalists, scholars, and aroused citizens, the Birch Society flourished. Well supplied with money from southwestern oil, cattle, and electronics magnates, it attracted intolerant fundamentalists, people obsessed with the Communist danger, and, seemingly, every opponent of change or novelty. Local chapters of the society fought against the fluoridation of drinking water, instigated recall elections against liberal school board members, attacked "subversive" college professors, demanded the impeachment of Chief Justice Earl Warren, and resisted efforts to impose gun controls. Allied with the society were the Christian Anti-Communism Crusade, let by Australian preacher Fred Schwarz, and the Christian Crusade, led by another Protestant minister, Billy James Hargis. Neither Welch nor the others were Nazis, but some active anti-Communists also belonged to George Lincoln Rockwell's American Nazi party or some similar hate group. Others joined semisecret paramilitary organizations like the Minute Men, which collected arms and held drills in expectation of an imminent Soviet invasion or internal Communist takeover.

McCarthyism also affected American foreign policy. Fear of attack by professional anti-Communists at times forced policymakers to pursue a hard line against communism even when it did not best serve American interests. America's refusal to accord diplomatic recognition to Communist China, for example, was in part a response to pressure from the McCarthyite witch-hunters. Even more serious, perhaps, fear of being attacked for "losing Indochina," as Truman had "lost China," would, as we shall see, help lure Lyndon Johnson into one of the most unfortunate military escapades in American history.

Conclusions

Well into the 1960s Americans remained a timid, insecure people. Having suffered through the nation's worse depression and its most agonizing war, they could not help regarding the postwar era as an improvement. With all its flaws, prosperity was real, and they turned from politics to revel in the pleasures of growing abundance and domesticity. The pursuit of private goals and satisfactions and the avoidance of controversy after 1945 was to some extent, then, a predictable consequence of the surprising success of the postwar economy.

It was also the result of fear. The Soviet Union seemed like a colossus astride half the planet. Moreover, for the first time since the Ottoman threat to Christendom in the seventeenth century, the West had to reckon with the competition of non-Europeans with values and cultures different from its own. And there was no way Americans could deal with these challenges militarily. America's only effective weapon was the atom bomb, but its use was ruled out by the instincts both of humanity and of self-preservation.

The only valid response to this impasse was patient diplomatic and intellectual struggle. But Americans are not a patient people, and the resulting frustration and anxiety brought out their worst side. McCarthyism was the major expression of that frustration. McCarthyism in turn engendered further fear. Why, most would-be dissenters asked, stick one's neck out? People who spoke up would be labeled Communists, and once so labeled, their lives and careers would be blighted. Intimidated by public events that seemed to threaten their safety, and exposed to the pleasures of consumerism as never before, Americans turned inward and sought private, safe satisfactions.

Despite the appeal of privatism and prudence, by the mid-1950s acute observers could detect signs of change. In 1956 a popular sociologist, John Keats, wrote *The Crack in the Picture Window*, attacking suburbia as deadening to the mind and spirit. By the end of the decade a new cultural bohemia composed of "Beat" poets and novelists had begun to appear in San Francisco and New York. For bohemians, the Beats were unusually apolitical and "cool," but they took drugs, wore sandals, and were sexually promiscuous. Clearly, times were beginning to change.

For Further Reading

Dean Acheson. *Present at the Creation* (1969)
> This is Secretary of State Acheson's own account of his State Department experiences from 1941 to 1953. It is, not surprisingly, a strong defense of the Truman Doctrine, the Marshall Plan, NATO, and the Korean intervention.

Walter LaFeber, *America, Russia, and the Cold War* (1975); and David Horowitz, editor, *Containment and Revolution* (1967)

These two books are "revisionist" studies of the Cold War that strongly endorse the view that American policy was the predominant, and avoidable, cause of the confrontation with the Soviet Union. The Horowitz work is an anthology of New Left—and some Old Left—writings on aspects of American foreign policy from 1917 to the mid-1960s. It treats the United States as a counterrevolutionary force in the world during that period.

Daniel Yergin. *Shattered Peace: The Origins of the Cold War and the National Security State* (1977)

American policy toward the Soviet Union since the 1940s was governed by two distinct views, says Yergin. One, identified with FDR, saw the possibility of U.S.-Soviet accommodation. The other, the view of certain groups within the State Department, saw no possibility of compromising with an aggressive, expansionist power. The United States after 1945 vacillated between these two positions.

Alonzo Hamby. *Beyond the New Deal: Harry S. Truman and American Liberalism* (1973)

This solid volume is a defense of Truman and Truman liberalism. Hamby sees the latter as a valid adaptation of the New Deal.

Charles C. Alexander. *Holding the Line: The Eisenhower Era, 1952–1959* (1975)

A good summary of domestic and foreign policy in the Eisenhower years. The title suggests the author's view of the Eisenhower administration.

Douglas T. Miller and Marion Nowak. *The Fifties: The Way We Really Were* (1977)

The authors have little patience with those who would romanticize the 1950s. They see it as a time of real but neglected problems. In their eagerness to restore the critical balance they probably are too harsh on Americans during that decade.

David Riesman, Reuel Denney, and Nathan Glazer. *The Lonely Crowd: A Study of the Changing American Character* (1950)

The influential study that made Americans worry about the loss of "inner direction." An important cultural document.

Scott Donaldson. *The Suburban Myth* (1969)

Most intellectuals and social observers despised the post–World War II suburbs. Donaldson examines this phenomenon. He also disagrees with his colleagues. Suburbs, he believes, were the most realistic solution of the mid-twentieth-century housing problem.

Richard O. Davies. *The Age of Asphalt: The Automobile, the Freeway, and the Condition of Metropolitan America* (1975)

We Americans are so dependent on cars and highways because we love to move about and because, in 1956, Congress decided to build a gigantic interstate highway system. Davis describes the reason for the Highway Act and discusses the neglected alternatives that might have eased our energy and urban crises.

Richard Rovere. *Senator Joe McCarthy* (1959)

Like most political reporters, Rovere is fascinated by McCarthy's career. This is the standard liberal account of McCarthy by the late political correspondent of *The New Yorker* magazine. For a conservative treatment, far more favorable to the Wisconsin senator, see William F. Buckley, Jr., and L. B. Bozell, *McCarthy and His Enemies* (1954).

Richard Kluger. *Simple Justice: The History of Brown v. Board of Education and Black America's Struggle for Equality* (1975)

The best single volume on the civil rights movement in the 1950s. Focuses on the famous 1954 school desegregation decision of the Supreme Court.

Bruce Cook. *The Beat Generation* (1971)

Cook's thesis is that the Beat movement of the 1950s anticipated much of the cultural and political radicalism of the 1960s. In the poems and novels of Jack Kerouac, Allen Ginsberg, Gergory Corso, and others, the author finds the disdain for authority, the antimilitarism, and the taste for mysticism, sensuality, and drugs that also characterized the later "Age of Aquarius."

Jack Kerouac. *On the Road* (1957)

Experience was everything to the Beats, and this attitude explains their constant need to move, to be on the road. A novel of characters frantically moving across the American landscape of the 1950s.

Ralph Ellison. *Invisible Man* (1952)

A beautifully written, convincing, and often amusing novel of the coming of age of a young black man who is caught up in—and then dumped by—the Communist party. He learns that he will have to "stay in the dark" as an invisible man.

Max Hastings. *The Korean War* (1987)

An English military historian seeks to rescue the Korean War from what he considers recent neglect. This lively review of the Korean "police action"—based on interviews as well as documents—depicts the conflict as a dress rehearsal for Vietnam, with many of the same frustrations and confusions. Yet at the same time Hastings does not condemn those who insisted that the United States had to intervene to save the South Koreans from the invaders from the North. With all its faults, he says, the present South Korean regime is better than the one that would have replaced it if the Communists had won.

J. Ronald Oakley. *God's Country: America in the Fifties* (1986)

A very readable survey of America in the flush 1950s when the United States was an economic colossus. Oakley shows that all was not necessarily well in the Garden of Eden, what with racism, the Cold War, and Joe McCarthy.

Chapter 29

The Dissenting Sixties

Why Protest in the "Great Society"?

1954   French defeated at Dien Bien Phu; Geneva Accords

1957   Russians launch Sputnik into orbit • Martin Luther King, Jr., founds the Southern Christian Leadership Conference (SCLC)

1959   Castro overthrows Batista regime in Cuba • U-2 incident

1960   Student Nonviolent Coordinating Committee (SNCC) founded • Birth-control pill introduced • John F. Kennedy elected president

1961   Peace Corps founded; Kennedy announces the Alliance for Progress • CIA and anti-Castro Cubans launch the Bay of Pigs invasion of Cuba • Berlin Wall built • Kennedy sends American troops to Vietnam

1962   Cuban Missile Crisis

1962, 1963   Attorney General Robert Kennedy enforces integration of state universities in Mississippi and Alabama

1963   Civil rights demonstrators numbering 250,000 march on Washington • Kennedy assassinated; Lyndon Johnson becomes president

1964   Johnson launches the "War on Poverty" • China explodes its first atom bomb • Congress passes the Civil Rights Act • Tonkin Gulf Resolution

1964–65   Berkeley Free Speech Movement sets precedent for major campus revolts

1965   Johnson orders the bombing of North Vietnam • Great Society Legislation and agencies: Elementary and Secondary Education Act, Medicare, Department of Housing and Urban Development (HUD), Omnibus Housing Act, Voting Rights Act, National Foundations of the Arts and Humanities, Higher Education Act, Metropolitan Area Redevelopment Act, Truth in Lending Act

1965–67   Black riots in Los Angeles, Detroit, Newark

1966   Highway Safety Act • Betty Friedan organizes the National Organization for Women (NOW)

1968   My Lai Massacre • Martin Luther King and Robert Kennedy assassinated • Street riots at Democratic national convention in Chicago • Richard Nixon elected president

1969   American Indian activists occupy Alcatraz Island • Woodstock and Altamont rock festivals • Americans land on the moon

In April 1968 a group of young actors appeared in a new musical at the Biltmore Theater in New York. The play, *Hair*, glorified every rebellious, nonconformist theme of the decade. *Hair* announced that the Age of Aquarius was at hand, that "harmony and understanding" and "crystal revelation" would soon prevail. A song called "Sodomy" described the delights of oral sex and masturbation; "Air" detailed the horrors of air pollution; and "Walking in Space" was simultaneously about the space program and "tripping" on drugs. The musical theme of "Hare Krishna" was borrowed from a Hindu sect whose adherents could be seen ringing bells and chanting on the streets of large American cities. The high point of the performance came at the end of the first act, when members of the biracial cast removed all their clothes while singing "Beads, Flowers, Freedom and Happiness."

To a Rip Van Winkle of 1948 awakening twenty years later, *Hair* would have been a profound shock. Radical in politics, "liberated" in social vision, ecstatic and orgiastic in cultural texture, it was almost the antithesis of the values Americans had accepted in the years between 1945 and 1960. Then, only in the darkest corners of American life had there been a hint that such things existed. But in 1968 the members of the *Hair* cast became culture heroes who, according to theater critic Clive Barnes of the *New York Times*, expressed "the authentic voice of today."

How did this startling turnabout come to pass? Was it merely the inexorable swing of the cultural and political pendulum? Having moved so far to the right, could it move only left? Why had radicalism and dissent replaced timidity and conformity, and where was America going?

Politics in Camelot

The freedom and experimentation of the 1960s owed much to the political environment of the decade. The thousand days of the Kennedy presidency have been likened to Camelot, the mythical court of King Arthur, where all was bright and shining. The advisers the dashing new president brought to Washington in early 1961 were like John F. Kennedy himself—young, charming, and full of confidence that there were new answers to old problems. They worked hard and they played hard, and the public enjoyed watching them do both. We now know that the young president was not the personal paragon of the Camelot legend, but for the first time since FDR the White House became a lively and interesting place, and the public delighted in the change.

Kennedy appealed especially to the idealism of young people. In his inaugural address he noted that a "torch" had "been passed to a new generation of Americans, born in this century," who would not "permit the slow undoing of those human rights to which this nation has always been committed." One of his first moves was to propose a Peace Corps of young men and women who would invest their skills and part of their lives in working abroad among the sick and poor of Third World nations. Soon afterward he announced the Alliance for Progress, a foreign aid proposal to pump $20 billion into Latin America to raise economic output and redistribute it among the hemisphere's poor and oppressed.

Kennedy Foreign Policy. However idealistic in tone, Kennedy's Alliance for Progress did not fundamentally alter "containment" as the dominant American foreign policy. The Alliance, after all, was intended as much to prevent Communist-led revolutions in the Americas as to improve the lot of the Latin American peoples. Yet Kennedy and his advisers also brought new ideas to American foreign policy.

In his 1960 campaign Kennedy had warned that his Republican predecessor had allowed the Soviet Union to build more missiles than the United States. This "missile gap" threatened the nation's security. After taking office he found that the gap did not exist. But the new president had more substantial objections to Eisenhower's weapons policy as well. The Eisenhower administration, he claimed, had relied far too much on nuclear weapons. Rather than spend the money for conventional arms, the Republican president and his chief foreign-policy adviser, John Foster Dulles, had built up stockpiles of hydrogen bombs. This meant that in the event of international crisis. America's only possible response was threat of nuclear retaliation. Such a threat might be used to deter the Soviet Union from, say, a major attack on NATO, but what about other, lesser, Soviet advances? Around the world—in Berlin, Cuba, the Middle East, and Asia—were areas where United States and Soviet interests clashed. We clearly could not use "massive deterrence" to discourage Soviet aggression at such pressure points, for the risks of nuclear holocaust were simply too great for the gains that could be expected. In effect, then, the lack of conventional military forces left the United States without any practical way to deal with the sort of small Soviet actions that the future would bring. Such shortsightedness only guaranteed successful Soviet subversion all over the world.

To avoid the unacceptable alternatives of holocaust or surrender, Kennedy and Secretary of Defense Robert McNamara urged a "flexible response." The United States must build up its conventional forces and prepare itself to use counterinsurgency tactics so it could tailor its response to the extent of the threat. To implement the new policy, the Kennedy administration expanded the army from eleven to sixteen combat divisions and began retraining troops for jungle and guerrilla fighting. This was expensive, and during the Kennedy years the defense budget increased about 25 percent.

Early Tests. The first attempt at counterinsurgency was a fiasco. Carrying out an operation planned by the Eisenhower administration, in April 1961 the president authorized a tiny amphibious group of anti-Castro Cuban refugees to land in Cuba at the Bay of Pigs. The CIA had persuaded Kennedy that a small invading force would trigger a general uprising that would easily topple Fidel Castro, the leader who had overthrown the Cuban dictator Batista in 1959 and installed an anti-American revolutionary regime in Havana. But the uprising did not materialize, and the invaders were quickly pinned down on the beach. Not wishing to involve the country more deeply in an embarrassing enterprise, the president refused to provide American air and military support to rescue them. In a matter of days they were all killed or captured, and the United States found itself condemned before the world as an ineffectual bully.

Kennedy's first direct contact with the Soviets was not much happier in its consequences. Soviet Premier Nikita S. Khrushchev was a blunt, outspoken man who favored a settlement of outstanding differences with the United States but did not intend to surrender what he believed to be his country's vital

If any American president ever was charismatic, John Fitzgerald Kennedy was. Intelligent, youthful, handsome, and articulate, he possessed all the equipment for successful leadership except maturity. Those who hoped that this would come in time were to be tragically disappointed.

interests. A summit meeting between Khrushchev and Eisenhower had been canceled in 1960 after an American U-2 plane spying on the Soviet Union had been shot down and Eisenhower had refused to apologize for the incident. Now Khrushchev had another opportunity to put the United States on the defensive. From the Bay of Pigs fiasco, he assumed that the young president was indecisive and could be pushed around, and he resolved to take a tough line. In June 1961 Khrushchev and Kennedy met at Vienna to see if they could iron out differences over Berlin. That city, divided between East and West, was a Communist sore point. An enclave of Western freedom and prosperity set deep inside Communist territory, it was a magnet for East Germans. Hundreds escaped daily to the Western zone, and each person who left the German Democratic Republic advertised the superiority of the Western over the Communist way of life.

At Vienna the Soviet leader was abrupt, even insulting. The Allied and West German presence in Berlin must be removed, he told Kennedy. If it was not, the Soviet Union would sign a treaty with the Communist German Democratic Republic and would place its military might behind that country's claim to all of the divided city. When Khrushchev returned to Moscow he delivered a set of warlike speeches and increased the Soviet military budget.

Though shaken by Khrushchev's threats, Kennedy refused to be intimidated. Back at home, he asked Congress for an additional $3.5 billion for defense, announced the call-up of army reserves and National Guard units, and urged Americans to build bomb shelters.

Meanwhile, in Berlin the stream of refugees to the West became a flood. To stanch this hemorrhage, East German authorities on August 13, 1961, abruptly blocked all traffic between the city's zones and the next day began to erect a high wall of brick, concrete blocks, and barbed wire. For the next quarter century the Berlin Wall would testify to the barriers separating the two Cold War antagonists.

For a while longer the tension over Berlin continued. In early September the Soviets resumed nuclear testing on a massive scale, releasing enormous quantities of radioactive matter into the atmosphere. In retaliation Kennedy authorized the resumption of American nuclear testing, though only underground. Then Khrushchev backed down. At the end of the month in Moscow he told a visiting diplomat from NATO Belgium: "I'm not trying to put you in an impossible situation; I know very well that you can't let yourself be stepped on." In mid-October he told the Communist Party Congress that the Western Powers appeared conciliatory and he, accordingly, would defer a peace treaty with East Germany. The second Berlin crisis was over.

The Cuban Missile Crisis. Khrushchev forced one more major confrontation in his war of nerves against the United States and its young president. Following the Bay of Pigs invasion he sent Soviet troops and technicians to Cuba and, more important, installed on the island medium- and long-range ballistics missiles pointed at the United States. Such missiles, if launched from the Soviet Union, would allow the United States a full fifteen minutes warning time. If launched from Cuba, the warning would be reduced to about two minutes, seriously reducing American power to retaliate. In one bold stroke, as Khrushchev later noted in his memoirs, "our missiles would have equalized the balance of power."

Suddenly the world stood at the brink of nuclear disaster. From the moment American intelligence revealed the presence of the missiles in mid-October, the National Security Council met in continuous session to debate what course to take. Air Force General Curtis LeMay favored an immediate attack on Cuba. Defense Secretary McNamara and the president's brother, Attorney General Robert F. Kennedy, favored a blockade of the island to prevent the missiles still on their way by ship from being landed. The president rejected the aggressive LeMay course. On the evening of October 22, 1962, he appeared on national television to tell the American people about the Soviet missiles and explain that the government had decided to "quarantine" Cuba to prevent delivery of more missiles. If the Soviets tried to run the blockade, the American navy would shoot.

The announcement startled the nation and the world. Never before had the two superpowers found themselves on such a collision course. A wrong move by either might thrust the world into nuclear war. Americans generally supported the president's course, but outside the United States many people blamed Kennedy for gambling with the very existence of humanity.

What would the Soviets do when their missile-carrying ships, fast approaching Cuba, encountered the American blockade? For four days the world waited apprehensively. In Cuba, Soviet technicians worked feverishly to complete the missile launch pads, and began to assemble crated Soviet bombers. Washington kept NATO leaders informed of minute-by-minute developments. The world held its breath. Then the break came. On October 26 Khrushchev sent a long message to the American government acknowledging for the first time that Soviet missiles were being installed in Cuba. The Soviet Union, Khrushchev stated, would send no more missiles if the United States agreed not to attack Cuba. At the same time he released publicly an offer to remove the missiles from Cuba if the United States would remove its missile bases from Turkey. Ignoring the issue of Turkish bases, Kennedy agreed not to attack Cuba if the Soviet missiles were taken out. Khrushchev did not insist on his terms. The crisis was over.

A wave of relief swept the country; Kennedy's popularity, which had suffered from the Bay of Pigs blunder, rebounded strongly. The Soviets removed the missiles, but their technicians lingered, and Castro rejected on-site inspection of the former bases. Though Kennedy and Khrushchev had averted global destruction, Cuba, as a Soviet ally just ninety miles off the coast of Florida, would remain a sore point for Ameri-

This Department of Defense photo shows a missile base in Cuba. President Kennedy used such photos on television to explain the crisis to the nation, and Ambassador Adlai Stevenson displayed them on the floor of the United Nations.

can policymakers. In later years the Cubans would be accused of trying to export revolution to other parts of Latin America and of endangering American interests in the Western Hemisphere and in Africa.

Vietnam Intervention Begins. Even as these encounters were absorbing American and world interests, a larger confrontation was developing in Southeast Asia. Vietnam might have remained just another Cold War pressure point but for Kennedy and McNamara's new "flexible response" policy. This policy tempted the United States into a prolonged military involvement in Southeast Asia that would prove disastrous.

The setting for the American debacle was Vietnam, Cambodia, and Laos, nations carved out of French Indochina in the years following the Japanese surrender in 1945 and made "associated states" of the French Union—that is, French protectorates. In the northern part of Vietnam, however, Ho Chi Minh, a Communist nationalist, refused to accept French rule. Ho established a "Democratic Republic" ruled from Hanoi and claimed to speak for all Vietnamese, including those in the south. The French fought Ho, but in 1954 they were defeated by Ho's insurgent forces at Dien Bien Phu. Soon after, they agreed to a division of Vietnam along the seventeenth parallel, pending a 1956 election that would decide the future government for a united country. This decision was ratified by a

meeting of the major powers at Geneva, but the election was never held. Fearing that a free ballot might topple his anti-Communist regime, South Vietnamese Premier Ngo Dinh Diem dithered and delayed and, when the Eisenhower administration failed to exert pressure to coerce him, postponed the election indefinitely.

In the next few years under President Eisenhower the United States gave military and economic aid to pro-Western or neutral regimes in Laos, Cambodia, and South Vietnam in the hope that they might resist Communist efforts, led by the Ho regime in the North, to gain control. The policy failed. In Laos the Pathet Lao, a Communist nationalist movement, grew more powerful and threatened to overthrow the neutral government. In South Vietnam Diem's regime proved corrupt and unpopular with the Buddhists and peasantry. Before long a Communist insurgent force, the Vietcong (called by its friends the National Liberation Front), supplied with arms from North Vietnam and ultimately from the Soviet Union, gained support and established control in many places especially in the South Vietnamese rural countryside.

Kennedy, believing that Soviet power must be "contained" in East Asia as well as in Europe, felt compelled to intervene. In May 1961 he sent 400 Special Forces troops, trained in counterinsurgency tactics, to South Vietnam to aid the Diem regime. Soon after, however, he rejected the urging of General Maxwell

The 1963 March on Washington was for civil rights, but as several of these signs show, it was also a demonstration for jobs.

D. Taylor and presidential adviser Walt W. Rostow that he send 10,000 American combat troops to help defeat the Vietcong.

Within the inner circle of Kennedy's advisers, George Ball, Averell Harriman, Robert Kennedy, and others were appalled by the growing military commitment. The president himself believed that the South Vietnamese needed only limited American help to win. But by October 1962 over 16,000 Americans were in South Vietnam advising and assisting the South Vietnamese, and the number of American casualties had risen to almost 600.

The New Frontier. Kennedy's domestic program, the New Frontier, was no more an unqualified success than his foreign policy. Like Truman, his Democratic predecessor, Kennedy was unable to overcome the resistance of congressional Republicans and conservative Democrats to his moderately liberal legislative program.

Civil Rights was one area of conflict. Whatever his personal views, Kennedy had received the margin of victory in 1960 from blacks in the North, and he could not afford to alienate black voters. Kennedy's Justice Department, under his brother's aegis, enforced voting provisions of the 1957 and 1960 Civil Rights Acts and helped thousands of black southerners get on the voting rolls. Robert Kennedy also forced Governors Ross Barnett of Mississippi and George C. Wallace of Alabama to permit integration of their state universities in 1962 and 1963.

Meanwhile, black southerners were pushing the administration into still more vigorous action against racial discrimination. On February 1, 1960, four black students at the North Carolina Agricultural and Technical College took seats at the lunch counter of Woolworth's in Greensboro. In the segregated South this act was illegal and the store's serving people ignored them. The next day the students returned with friends and continued their sit-in all day. Day after day they continued their protest despite the catcalls and jeers of unfriendly whites. In a few days the press took notice and the movement to sit in quickly spread all over the South. The brave action of the southern black students inspired other civil rights activists. In the summer of 1963 more than 200,000 demonstrators marched to the Lincoln Memorial in Washington to hear Martin Luther King's "I Have a Dream" address. The speech and the demonstration pushed the Kennedy administration into bolder action. In its wake the president proposed the most sweeping civil rights legislation ever to come before Congress; it would be passed, however, only after his death.

Kennedy's New Frontier made progress on other fronts as well. He succeeded in pushing through Congress an extension of the number of workers covered by the minimum wage, increases in minimum wage and Social Security payments, and the Housing Act of 1961, which pumped nearly $5 billion over four years into preserving urban open spaces, developing mass transit, and building middle-income housing. He also got Congress to raise unemployment compensation benefits and aid to economically depressed areas. In a bold anti-inflationary move Kennedy "jawboned" the steel companies out of a sudden price increase.

Yet much of the New Frontier program failed to pass. Congress defeated his bill to provide funds for school construction and scholarship aid for college students. It also defeated a health insurance plan for the aged and measures to help unemployed youth, migrant workers, and commuters. The most important Kennedy initiative in domestic affairs was a tax cut designed to stimulate the economy by putting more money into the hands of consumers. Many liberals, led by economist John Kenneth Galbraith, felt that an increase in government spending for schools, hospitals, better housing, and social welfare programs was the best way to attack the recession inherited from the Eisenhower period. But the administration chose a cut in government income instead, the line of least resistance. As usual in the case of Kennedy's domestic proposals, the measure moved slowly. A year after its introduction the tax cut was still wending its way through Congress.

It would be hard to give the Kennedy administration the highest grades for its handling of domestic and foreign affairs. Yet despite his mixed record, Kennedy's popularity grew. The public remembered his successes and forgot his failures or blamed them on Congress. Young Americans identified with him and his wife. In 1963 Camelot was still untarnished.

The president was not universally loved and admired, however. The far right, particularly strong in the South and Southwest, despised him. The reemerging left saw him as a conservative and a cold warrior. When, in November 1963, the president and his wife set off on a political peacemaking trip to Texas, he was warned that he might encounter trouble. Shortly before, Adlai Stevenson, then ambassador to the United Nations, had been verbally abused and spat on in Dallas.

The president ignored the advice and went to Texas. In Dallas, while his motorcade traveled through downtown streets lined with surprisingly friendly crowds, the president was shot by a sniper. He was rushed to the hospital, where he was pronounced dead a half hour later. His apparent killer, Lee Harvey Oswald, was an unstable leftist who had spent some years in the Soviet Union and had been active in the pro-Castro Fair Play for Cuba organization. Oswald had admitted nothing when, two days later, before the eyes of millions of horrified television viewers, he was shot by Jack Ruby, a shady Dallas nightclub owner who apparently saw himself as an avenging angel.

Few events in what would be an extraordinarily catastrophic decade so shocked the American people. The assassination in Dallas had not only killed an American president but it had also struck down a young hero whose career had come to symbolize all that was best and most worthy in American life. To the young, especially, his death seemed a bitter tragedy. In the somber hours between the murder and the burial at Arlington National Cemetery, television's coverage of the events helped draw the nation together as a family united by a shared grief.

Just before the tragedy. The President and the First Lady in Texas on November 22, 1963. Vice President Lyndon Johnson is beaming in the background.

In the months that followed, dismay gave way to uneasiness and frustration. President Lyndon Johnson, hoping to allay remaining public doubts about the assassination, appointed an investigative commission headed by Chief Justice Earl Warren. In September 1964 the commission reported that Oswald was indisputably the culprit and had acted alone. Many Americans accepted the Warren Report, but a large minority suspected that it was incomplete or even a cover-up. Many young people found it difficult to believe that the deed had not involved some right-wing conspiracy. There were too many loose ends, they insisted; too many questions unanswered. In the next few years, as the toll of assassinated leaders grew, more and more Americans would find it hard not to believe that there was a deep plot to kill off the nation's great popular champions.

The Affluent Society

Though a decade of turmoil both at home and abroad, the 1960s were also a time of growing affluence and rising economic expectations. During these years the country enjoyed the longest sustained economic boom in its history, with the Gross National Product increasing at the rate of 4 percent annually, well above that for the preceding fifteen-year period. By 1970 the GNP, measured in 1958 dollars, had risen from $488 billion to $722.5 billion, an increase of 48 percent in average per capita real income. Unemployment did persist, and toward the end of the decade prices began to rise at a fast clip. Yet through most of the 1960s, the public's sense of economic well-being surpassed even that of the 1950s.

The 1960s was the decade when the promise of a mass consumer society finally seeped down to a majority of the American people. In every objective index of comfort the nation forged ahead. Dishwashers, freezers, clothes dryers, garbage disposals, color television—all luxuries in the 1950s—became almost universal possessions among middle-class Americans by 1970.

International Trade.   One of the essential components of 1960s prosperity was burgeoning international trade. Under the General Agreement on Tariffs and Trade (GATT) of 1947, international trade barriers progressively declined. At the same time, the United States dollar served as gold had served in the past to stabilize international exchange rates. Under the influence of GATT and a stable exchange medium, world commerce grew enormously. During the 1960s German cars, Japanese cameras and electronic equipment, Italian shoes and typewriters, and French wines and perfumes flooded the American market, while American computers, jet passenger aircraft, machinery, wheat, and soybeans flowed back the other way. Simultaneously, petroleum and the other raw materials necessary for industrial production moved at low prices to the developed nations from the Third World, helping to guarantee cheap production of industrial goods.

The Knowledge Industries.   The enormously accelerated accumulation and diffusion of knowledge also helped to fuel the decade's economic surge. In some ways this knowledge explosion was the payoff from years of previous scientific advances. It also owed much to the great postwar outlays for research and higher education. In 1950 Congress had established the National Science Foundation to encourage research, especially in areas related to national defense. By 1957 outlays for research and development (R&D) by public and private organizations had reached almost $10 billion annually. Meanwhile, the country's higher education system grew astronomically. In 1940, the last full peacetime year, there were 1.5 million college students; by 1950 there were 2.6 million.

From the mid-1950s on, the country's support of what would later be called the "knowledge industries" was dazzling by any previous standard. A few Americans complained that the public schools were not teaching children to read or to calculate and blamed it on John Dewey's disciples, the "progressive educators." But most citizens were proud of the job the nation was doing. Their complacency was suddenly shattered when, in October 1957, the Russians put a hollow steel ball called Sputnik into orbit around the earth. Having long considered themselves the world's most scientifically and technologically advanced people, Americans were dismayed to discover that they had been abruptly pushed off their pinnacle by their chief international rival.

For the next few years Americans subjected themselves to one of their periodic agonizing reappraisals of education. A dozen books were soon echoing the complaints of earlier critics about American educational failings. Articles appeared in all the popular magazines informing readers that Russian high school students did not waste their time taking courses in marriage and the family, driver education, or social dancing, but spent long hours at chemistry, biology, physics, and mathematics. The dismay produced quick results. By 1970 federal appropriations for research had almost tripled, and federal funding of higher education was four times as high as it had been ten years earlier. Industrial firms, universities, and foundations also invested billions in basic scientific research and the development of new products. With research and industry booming, a college education became even more valuable than in the past. By 1970, 7 million young men and women were enrolled in colleges and universities, an increase of nearly 500 percent in little more than a generation.

The Impact of Science and Technology. The scientific and technological advances that flowed from the laboratories were often dramatic. Linus Pauling, James Watson, H. Gobind Khorana, and others discovered how the gene, the basic unit of heredity, was constructed. Besides solving one of the great mysteries of life, genetics bore fruit—literally—in great increases in the output per acre of rice, corn, and wheat, producing in the Third World what was called the Green Revolution. The electronic computer became a powerful tool for solving mathematical and scientific problems and controlling production processes. Soon computers were being used to do everything from building H-bombs to guiding automated factories, recording checks, and helping libraries keep track of their books and universities of their students. And there was much more. The textile industry adopted new high-speed looms and developed new synthetic fibers. A long list of thermoplastics filled needs hitherto met at higher cost by natural materials. The subsonic passenger jet, first introduced in the early 1950s, replaced the propeller plane in the 1960s and shrank the world to half its former size. Meanwhile, the space program, begun under the auspices of the National Aeronautics and Space Administration (NASA) to challenge the Soviet Union, yielded unexpected scientific dividends. Communications satellites were launched, and new metals and alloys and miniaturized computer elements developed to solve the problems of space travel found surprisingly down-to-earth commercial and technical uses.

Medicine, too, made giant strides in these years. An arsenal of new antibiotic drugs, X-ray techniques, isotope tracers, computerized studies of environmental factors in disease, and other applications of the new science markedly improved the nation's and the world's health. In the 1950s researchers developed vaccines to fight polio. In 1963 they introduced a measles vaccine. Heart disease and cancer remained major killers, and indeed lung-cancer deaths from smoking soared, but the death rate from infectious diseases plummeted.

These medical advances, combined with better

One of the greatest feats of modern technology was the landing of men on the moon in July 1969. This picture of astronaut Edwin "Buzz" Aldrin was taken by fellow moon-walker Neil Armstrong, whose reflection is visible in the visor of Aldrin's helmet.

nutrition, produced a healthier, longer-lived population than ever before. Life expectancy for a newborn baby rose from 68.2 years in 1950 to 70.9 years in 1970. At the later date it was considerably higher for women (74.8) than for men (67.1) and for whites (71.7) than for blacks (65.3). Still, the improvement was substantial for every part of the population.

The rapid expansion of the economy and the great surge in technology had costs. American life became increasingly bureaucratized as the federal government expanded its power and size and as private business concentrated itself into giant corporations. Much of the new technology was damaging to land, water supplies, and the air people breathed. By the end of the decade these environmental drawbacks had produced a powerful impulse to protect the public that came to be called the ecology movement.

The Rise of Dissent

A majority of Americans in the 1960s, then, were living better, longer, and fuller lives than at any time in the past. Through the entire decade, the polls would show, most citizens continued to consider their country the most decent and benevolent in the world. But the great gains of the 1960s clearly left many Americans behind and failed to impress others. Before the decade was out, the country would experience a full-scale insurgent movement by blacks, students, women, American Indians, and many other groups.

The Sources of Dissent. The sources of a revolt were complex. In the political realm it was fueled by the decline of repressive McCarthyism and the emergence of a new generation less certain than their elders that the Cold War was inevitable. These young people had been raised in the affluence of postwar suburbia, and never doubted that at its best America was capable of providing all its people with the means to lead fulfilling and interesting lives. Yet as they looked around them they perceived racism, inequality, repression, and international belligerence that seemed to belie the nation's professed values. Less aware than their parents of the fragility of postwar prosperity, they rejected the self-congratulation of the 1950s and demanded change. With so many of these idealistic young people going to college, the nation's campuses became potential political bombs.

Socially and culturally, too, the nation was ripe for dissent by the mid-1960s. A new, more permissive attitude toward sex was foreshadowed by the investigations in the late 1940s and early 1950s of Dr. Alfred C. Kinsey and his associates, which showed Americans as far less traditional in their sexual behavior than the conventional wisdom taught. Even more important was the advent of oral contraceptives in 1960. Besides reducing the birthrate, "the pill" reduced the chances of unwanted pregnancies, and so encouraged sex outside marriage. More permissive sexual values were also encouraged by the declining power of communities to censor books, movies, and magazines. Beginning with a 1952 decision holding that films were covered by the First Amendment's guarantee of free speech, the Supreme Court extended the principle so that a book, play, or motion picture had to be "utterly without redeeming social value" to be regarded as obscene. Soon long-banned classics were available at bookstores, and before long it became clear that even works with social values no one could detect could be legally published and sold. In 1968, in recognition of the new situation, Hollywood dropped its old, self-imposed censorship code and adopted a rating system that placed films in categories ranging from *G* for family movies to *X* for out-and-out pornography.

The ground for the changes of the mid-1960s was also prepared by a new mood among the nation's artists, writers, and thinkers. During the immediate postwar period the nation's intellectual and cultural leaders had been conservative and conformist. By the end of the 1950s this began to change. One sign of the shift was the appearance of "Beat" bohemias in San Francisco, Los Angeles, and New York. To the Beat poets and writers—Allen Ginsberg, Lawrence Ferlinghetti, Jack Kerouac, and William Burroughs—the life of "square" America seemed deadening and oppressive, and they demanded in their works, and exemplified in their actions, freer, less inhibited lives.

Another sign was the advent of radical social thinkers, such as the sociologist C. Wright Mills, the social psychologist Paul Goodman, and the neo-Marxist philosopher Herbert Marcuse. In their various ways, each of these men condemned existing society as oppressive, repressive, and rife with inequalities of wealth and power. In 1960 Mills gave general currency to the term "New Left" to describe a new radical mood among the young that he detected emerging in the United States and around the world.

Popular culture, too, especially music, both expressed and stimulated the new dissent. In the 1950s singers such as Woody Guthrie and Pete Seeger continued the 1930s connection between folk music and the political left. Rock-and-roll, a merger of black rhythm and blues and electronics, burst on the scene in the mid-1950s with Bill Haley's "Rock Around the Clock." Soon after, Elvis Presley, a white southerner, gave rock a strong sexual cast.

Rock was the music of the rebellious young. The most successful rock group of the sixties, the Beatles, wore the long hair and mod clothes of angry English working-class adolescents. The Rolling Stones, also an English group, and Jefferson Airplane, the Grateful Dead, Country Joe and the Fish, and other whimsically named American groups wore the "love beads," Indian headbands, and gaudy jeans that soon became trademarks of youthful cultural revolt. Eventually some rock groups began to dabble directly in political matters. When the Rolling Stones came out with "Street-Fighting Man" in 1968, the more moderate Beatles responded with "Revolution." Folk singers like Joan Baez and Bob Dylan became increasingly political. Dylan's "The Times They Are A-Changin' " would become an anthem of youth rebellion.

Four young men who helped create the 1960s cultural revolution. The Beatles in a satiric mood.

Civil Rights and Black Power.

During the 1960s dissenters of every race and persuasion would draw inspiration from the black civil rights movement. Through the first half of the decade the tactics of passive resistance, as preached by Reverend Martin Luther King, Jr., dominated the civil rights movement. King's own Southern Christian Leadership Conference (SCLC) employed it effectively. So did the Student Nonviolent Coordinating Committee (SNCC), which King helped organize in 1960. Even the older NAACP adopted civil disobedience, although it continued to devote most of its energies to civil rights legal work.

Nonviolent disobedience was a powerful weapon in the desegregation drive. It prodded Congress to pass legislation to end segregation and guarantee civil rights. It moved southern towns to admit blacks to previously segregated lunch counters, bus terminals, swimming pools, and other public facilities. It forced the South's leading colleges and professional schools to begin to admit black students.

Changes came in part because the nonviolent protests stirred the consciences of whites, in part because of pressure from the federal government, in part because of a desire to avoid worse conflict, and in part because of changes within white southern society. Ever since World War II northern industries had been moving to the South, attracted by its cheap, nonunion labor, mild climate, resources, and low taxes. The new industries brought together thousands of well-educated technicians and executives, both home-grown and imported from the North. These people would constitute a large middle class such as the South had never before possessed. Their politics and racial attitudes, of course, varied. But many wanted to overcome the South's reputation as the land of racial violence and oppression. The economic changes in the South thus strengthened the forces for "moderation" in southern racial policies.

But the desegregation drive was not enough. It could not produce jobs or economic equality, nor could it end the informal segregation in housing and the private social discrimination that prevailed throughout American society, North as well as South. Something more drastic seemed necessary. Especially among younger black Americans, increasing frustration and the surviving inequalities of American society produced a militancy and an aggressive defiance after 1964 that alarmed many whites, older blacks, and white liberals as well as conservatives.

Riots began in the Los Angeles suburb of Watts in 1965, and reappeared in other cities—Newark, Detroit, Cleveland, New York, Washington—every summer for the next three years. During these eruptions the inner-city black slums were overrun by mobs of black rioters, who overturned cars, broke into stores, and burned houses and office buildings. When the police or National Guard arrived, shooting began, with blacks usually suffering the heaviest casualties. "Responsible" black leaders did not condone the violence and looting. But by 1965 these leaders, including King, had lost much of their hold over the young. In the South SNCC was taken over by Stokely Carmichael, who attacked nonviolence in a violence-prone society. H. Rap Brown, who succeeded him in 1967, called violence "as American as cherry pie." In the North, novelist James Baldwin spoke out in anger against whites. In his book *The Fire Next Time* he concluded reluctantly that whites faced destruction if they did not take black demands seriously. Most militant of all was the paramilitary Black Panther movement organized by Bobby Seale and Huey P. Newton in the black ghetto of Oakland, California, in 1966 as a response to police attacks on ghetto dwellers.

Separatism was another new feature of the civil

An Historical Portrait

Martin Luther King, Jr.

The birthdays of only three Americans have become national legal holidays. One is that of George Washington, father of his country; another that of Abraham Lincoln, preserver of the Union. The last is the birthday of a black American, Martin Luther King, Jr., the most powerful and effective leader of the post–World War II civil rights revolution.

King was born in Atlanta, Georgia, in 1929 at a time and in a place not favorable for a young black male. Racism and its legal reflection, segregation, permeated every corner of southern life. Martin escaped almost all of this. The Kings belonged to the small black elite of Atlanta. Martin's father, Martin Luther King, Sr., was a respected, influential Baptist minister, the pastor of one of Atlanta's richest and most prestigious black churches, Ebenezer Baptist. Martin's family lived in a large house provided with all the most modern amenities. He and his small circle of equally prosperous friends—the children of doctors, lawyers, academics, morticians, and small business people—attended the best black schools in the city, and many, including Martin, went on to Morehouse College, the liberal arts school affiliated with the black community's greatest symbol of achievement, Atlanta University.

Yet even such a sheltered life could not spare King or his parents the cruel snubs, insults, and penalties of being black in racist, segregated Atlanta. When Martin was eleven a white woman walked up to him in a local department store and, without warning, slapped his face. "The little nigger stepped on my foot," she later explained. It was a small incident but it revealed the depth of white contempt for blacks in the 1940s South.

"Daddy" King wanted Martin to enter the ministry and become co-pastor at the Ebenezer Church and eventually succeed him. But Martin demurred. He wanted to expand his intellectual horizons before settling down comfortably as head of a large and prosperous southern congregation. In 1948 he went to Crozier Theological Seminary in Pennsylvania and earned his Bachelor of Divinity degree, graduating first in his class. In 1955 he earned his Ph.D. at Boston University with a dissertation comparing the concepts of God in the thinking of two contemporary Protestant theologians. In Boston Martin met and married the beautiful Coretta Scott, a young Alabama woman then training as a singer at the New England Conservatory of Music.

Before getting his doctorate, Martin accepted a parish. The Kings moved to Montgomery, Alabama, where Martin became pastor of the Dexter Avenue Baptist Church. He and Coretta had been in the Alabama capital only a year when they found themselves thrust into the middle of a momentous struggle over segregation that would make Dr. King the most famous and powerful civil rights leader in America.

Like all southern cities, Montgomery was thoroughly segregated along racial lines. All public facilities had white and black sections. Almost without exception the facilities available to blacks were inferior to those provided whites. Any black person who refused to obey the city ordinances prescribing the racial divisions was committing a misdemeanor and subject to fine and imprisonment.

Then, on Thursday afternoon, December 1, 1955, Rosa Parks, a dignified black woman, boarded a Montgomery city bus to return home after a day's work as a seamstress in a downtown department store. She took her seat, as prescribed, in the black section at the rear. But when more whites got on, the blacks in the front row of their section were asked to surrender their seats, as prescribed by law, to the new white passengers. Rosa Parks refused to move. The bus driver called the police and Mrs. Parks was arrested and fingerprinted.

The arrest triggered a strong reaction among Montgomery's black leaders. Ever since the *Brown* school desegregation decision in 1954 they had determined to challenge the city's Jim Crow system. The arrest of Mrs. Parks, a respectable middle-aged lady, promised to make an excellent case. In a matter of hours Montgomery's civil rights activists had decided on a boycott of the bus company until all black bus riders were treated as the equals of whites. Though King was a newcomer to Montgomery and just settling into his new duties and responsibilities, he was elected chairman of the Montgomery Improvement Association, the group formed to run the boycott, with the Reverend Ralph Abernathy of the First Baptist Church as his chief lieutenant.

Planned for a single day, the boycott lasted for almost thirteen months. Black passengers, the chief users of the buses, walked to work or made do with the Improvement Association's car pools. The bus company and the city authorities fought back. They procured injunctions; they harassed King and the other boycott leaders with minor traffic violation charges and threw them into jail; they invoked an ordinance to prevent black taxi drivers from transporting passengers at the same low rates charged by the bus company. At the end of January someone bombed King's home, and Mrs. King and the children barely escaped death. Despite the provocation, the young minister admonished blacks not to resort to violence. "We want to love our enemies," he told a black audience. "We must love our white brothers no matter what they do to us." Though inspired primarily by the Christian concept of charity, these words contained a trace of Mohandas Gandhi's nonviolent civil disobedience philosophy, *Satyagraha*, that King had encountered at Crozier Seminary.

Victory at Montgomery was ultimately won by the courage and sacrifices of the city's black citizens. But it was also helped immeasurably by the Supreme Court decision of November 1955 declaring that Alabama's state and local laws upholding segregation in transportation were unconstitutional. On Friday, December 21, the Montgomery city buses were officially desegregated. The long battle was over.

The Montgomery victory made Martin Luther King a national leader. He was soon in demand wherever black activists needed his eloquence, his leadership, and his ability to attract media attention to their plight. A literate man, he wrote widely for the national press on the goals of the civil rights movement and, despite a killing schedule of speaking engagements and personal appearances, authored several eloquent books. In 1957 he helped to found the Southern Christian Leadership Conference (SCLC), and for the remainder of his life this organization, located in Atlanta, was his chief base of operations. In 1959 King's Gandhian convictions were

powerfully reinforced by a trip to the places in India where the saintly Mahatma had actually practiced his nonviolent precepts.

Montgomery proved to be only one of a hundred battles to dismantle the huge edifice of segregation that loomed over the South. During the 1960s the civil rights movement that King helped lead could count on wide liberal support in the North and in Washington. John F. Kennedy owed black voters a debt for his hairline election victory in 1960. Yet relations between the Kennedy administration and King were at best, touchy. During 1961/62 King and the SCLC sponsored a series of "Freedom Rides" in conjunction with the militant Congress of Racial Equality (CORE) and the equally militant Student Nonviolent Coordinating Committe (SNCC) to test the compliance of southern towns with court rulings desegregating bus terminals. Once beyond the border states, the Freedom Riders were met by angry white mobs who burned the buses and beat many of them mercilessly. King and the other civil rights leaders demanded that federal marshals intervene to ensure the Freedom Riders' safety, and were deeply disappointed when the attorney general, the president's brother, Robert, was slow to respond.

King had his share of failures. In Albany, Georgia, the authorities were able to blunt the drive he led to end segregation and improve the job opportunities of black workers by a policy that combined evasion and careful avoidance of police brutality. By the time King left the small city little had changed. King and his colleagues had greater success in Birmingham, the New South's industrial showcase. Here the city's safety commissioner, T. Eugene ("Bull") Connor, was a hothead racist who used brutal tactics against the protest marchers organized by King and his colleagues to dramatize the discrimination prac-

ticed against the city's black population. Connor's police attacked marchers and demonstrators with nightsticks, cattle prods, vicious dogs, and high-pressure hoses. The most shocking attack was directed against a thousand black children marching from the Sixteenth Street Baptist Church to downtown. Public outrage forced the active intervention of the Kennedy administration and much of the business community. Powerful men in Washington and in New York corporate offices contacted friends and associates in Birmingham and demanded that the scandal be stopped. On May 10 the city capitulated and signed an agreement with the civil rights leaders desegregating department stores, promising accelerated hiring of black workers, establishing a biracial committee to plan additional desegregation, and dropping charges against all those arrested in the demonstrations.

The Birmingham victory was capped by the mass march on Washington of August 1963. Organized by CORE, SCLC, SNCC, and the National Urban League, and cosponsored by white liberal organizations, the march was the biggest civil rights demonstration of all time. Over a quarter of a million people, white and black, came to the nation's capital for the purpose of supporting a major civil rights bill pending in Congress. The high point of the enormous rally was King's ringing "I Have a Dream" address at the Lincoln Memorial, which lifted the hearts of everyone present with its vision of a democratic society where "all God's children, black men and white men, Jews and Gentiles, Protestants and Catholics," would "be able to join hands and sing in the words of that old Negro spiritual, 'Free at last! Free at last! Thank God almighty, we are free at last!' "

Though he would achieve international recognition when he was awarded the Nobel Peace Prize in

A Historical Portrait (*continued*)

1964, never again would Martin Luther King come so close to personifying black America's aspirations. By this time rifts had appeared within the civil rights movement. To King's right were the conservative NAACP, which emphasized lawsuits to end discrimination, and the Urban League, which favored education and persuasion. Both believed that street demonstrations and marches were dangerous and unproductive. To King's left was SNCC, which had accepted nonviolence as a tactic, but not as a principle. Blacks, the young SNCC workers believed, could not be expected to turn the other cheek when brutalized by white supremicists. Still further left were the Black Muslims, who demanded complete withdrawal from any association with "white devils," and proclaimed the superiority of blacks over whites. King also had little appeal for the unorganized militants in the northern cities, who saw nothing to recommend in a Christian nonviolent approach to the frustrations of ghetto life. Besides ideological differences, many in the civil rights movement resented King's eminence and believed that he and his associates encouraged the view that Martin Luther King, Jr., *was* the civil rights movement. Some of these people called King "de Lawd" behind his back.

After 1963 King and SCLC began to slip in influence. SCLC played only a secondary role in the voter registration drives and freedom schools organized by SNCC and CORE in the Deep South during the summer of 1964. It recouped somewhat when King helped lead the voter registration drive at Selma, Alabama, in early 1965. King's adversary this time was Sheriff Jim Clark, a man as hot-tempered as Birmingham's Bull Connor. He wore a big badge on his lapel with the word "Never." Clark's men shocked the nation when they used tear gas and clubs against 500 blacks crossing the Pettus bridge on their way to the Alabama state capital to present their grievances to Governor George Wallace. Seventeen of the marchers were seriously hurt and forty were hospitalized. The violence at Selma brought a wave of white liberals to the city for a second march in defiance of a court order. This time, faced with state troopers, King stopped the marchers just after they crossed the bridge. For this he was criticized by many militants. But the Selma Campaign had done its work. In its wake President Johnson announced that he was sending a tough, new voting rights bill to Congress.

After Selma SCLC ran into increasing difficulties. In the summer of 1965, beginning with Watts in Los Angeles, the northern black ghettoes began to explode. King deplored the violence but could neither prevent it nor repudiate the rioters. He also found it difficult to deal with the growing separatism of black militants who rejected the integrated society he envisioned and, under the banner of "black power," repudiated the nonviolence he preached. Finally, there was the Vietnam War. King was appalled by the war, but felt that to join SNCC and other leftists civil rights groups in demanding that the United States leave Vietnam would risk destroying his ties with the Johnson administration. Ultimately, he took the principled course and in 1967 proclaimed the folly and injustice of Vietnam.

When the end came, King was shifting his focus from segregation and voting rights—issues primarily relevant to the South—to poverty, job discrimination, and substandard housing—issues primarily of concern to the northern urban ghettoes. In 1966 and 1967 SCLC launched a campaign to force the city of Chicago to improve the housing of the city's black poor. In early 1968 King and his colleagues drew up plans for a march on Washington to demand a $12 billion "economic bill of rights" from Congress. But before the Poor People's Campaign could be launched, King was induced to come to Memphis to lend support to a sanitation workers' strike against the city.

King visited the city several times during the early spring of 1968 to help the predominantly black garbage collectors. On the evening of April 4, as he prepared to go to dinner, he stepped out on the balcony of his motel. A shot rang out and King fell dead. The killer was a white escaped convict whose motives have never been fully explained.

Martin Luther King was buried under a marble tombstone inscribed: "Free at Last, Free at Last, Thank God Almighty, I'm Free at Last."

rights movement. During the early 1960s the Black Muslims, a religious group professing a freely adapted version of Muhammadanism, had strongly endorsed separation of blacks from white society. In 1965 the young Muslim militant Malcolm X was assassinated by members of another faction of this intensely anti-white organization. But it was not until 1966 that Carmichael first used the cry "black power" to describe the new attitude. The expression had been coined by SNCC member Willie Ricks, and Carmichael defined it as "move over or we'll move on over you." Martin Luther King insisted that it was only "an appeal to racial pride, an appeal to the Negro not to be ashamed of being black." But whites were not reassured. Increasingly, white liberals found themselves thrust out of civil rights leadership positions and attacked for being white or insufficiently militant. Some accepted the new arrangement and considered it a sign of black maturity. But many others felt hurt at the rejection. Particularly dismaying to white liberals was the resurgence of segregation in the guise of demands for exclusive black control of schools, college dormitories, and college programs. Black nationalism, a hidden theme of earlier black dissent, was now a force to reckon with.

Student Activists. Many white students admired the militancy and bravery of black civil rights workers who risked their lives for their ideals. Some went to Mississippi and other southern states to help blacks register to vote and to teach black children at "freedom schools." The black student sit-ins inspired white students on northern college campuses to picket local branches of national chain stores that accepted segregation in the South. The experience was radicalizing, and when, after 1965, black militants rejected white participation in the civil rights movement, many northern students were ready to embark on their own course of political activism.

Another critical element in the rise of student radicalism was the accelerating war in Vietnam. By the middle of the decade American involvement had become massive and manpower needs could only be filled by a draft. At first young men were exempt from the draft merely for attending college. Then it became necessary for them to pass a test and maintain good grades. Besides this intense academic pressure, there was the guilt that exempted students felt for escaping danger while nonstudents, both black and white, were sent off to Southeast Asia to fight and die. The cast of *Hair* proclaimed the injustice of this arrangement when they sang: "War is white people sending black people to make war on yellow people to defend the land they stole from red people." Some students tried to avoid the war by seeking conscientious objector status. Others left for Canada. Many, however, channeled their personal dilemma into an angry political movement to get the United States out of the Vietnam conflict in any way possible.

Also contributing to student militancy was the physical setting in which students found themselves in these years. The baby boom following World War II altered the age structure of the country so that by

Beginning in 1965 with Watts in Los Angeles, each summer for five years saw violent riots in the black ghettoes of American cities. Young black men, especially, vented their anger against the oppression of the larger society. These angry blacks are confronting a National Guardsman in Newark, New Jersey, in 1967.

the mid-1960s a majority of Americans were under thirty. This demographic change, combined with the expansion of opportunities in business and science, guaranteed that campuses would be jammed. Strained by the huge enrollments, they inevitably became more impersonal and bureaucratic. Students soon felt that they were only numbers rather than human beings. Joined with the other radicalizing cultural and political forces, this alienation produced an explosive combination on many college campuses.

The first blowup occurred at the University of California at Berkeley, where a mixture of bohemia, drugs, pacifism, leftist politics, and overcrowding existed earlier than in most places. There, in the fall of 1964, the university administration withdrew the right of students to use an off-campus area as a free-speech enclave and a staging ground for civil rights forays into the surrounding community. Many white Berkeley students had been active participants in the civil rights movement both in the South and the Bay Area. Confronted with the ban, they exploded. On December 2 a thousand students singing "We Shall Overcome," the civil rights hymn, took over the administration building and refused to leave until the university agreed to cancel its order. The authorities called in the police, who arrested hundreds of protestors. For the next three months the campus remained in an uproar while the

Port Huron Statement

The major organized expression of the radical student movement during the 1960s was SDS, Students for a Democratic Society. Formed in 1959 as the student auxiliary of the old socialist League for Industrial Democracy, it eventually broke away from the staid parent organization and eventually became a byword for campus radicalism. By the end of the sixties it had evolved into the urban guerrilla group called the Weathermen.

In 1962, long before its final violent stage, SDS issued a manifesto expressing the new mood of dissent among young college students. The document, composed largely by Tom Hayden, a recent University of Michigan graduate, was adopted at an SDS convention at Port Huron, Michigan. It catches the spirit of SDS when it was still young and more strongly influenced by Jefferson than by Marx. The selection below is the Port Huron Statement's preamble.

"We are people of this generation, bred at least in modest comfort, housed now in universities, looking uncomfortably to the world we inherit.

"When we were kids the United States was the wealthiest and strongest country in the world; the only one with the atom bomb, the least scarred by modern war, an initiator of the United Nations that we thought would distribute Western influence throughout the world. Freedom and equality for each individual, government of, by, and for the people—these American values we found good, principles by which we could live as men. Many of us began maturing in complacency.

"As we grew, however, our comfort was penetrated by events too troubling to dismiss. First, the permeating and victimizing fact of human degradation symbolized by the Southern struggle against racial bigotry, compelled most of us from silence to activism. Second, the enclosing fact of the Cold War, symbolized by the presence of the Bomb, brought awareness that we ourselves . . . might die at any time. We might deliberately ignore, or avoid, or fail to feel all other human problems, but not these two, for these were too immediate and crushing in their impact, too challenging in the demand that we as individuals take the responsibility for encounter and resolution.

"While these and other problems either directly oppressed us or rankled our consciences and became our own subjective concerns, we began to see complicated and disturbing paradoxes in our surrounding America. The declaration 'all men are created equal . . .' rang hollow before the facts of Negro life in the South and the big cities of the North. The proclaimed peaceful intentions of the United States contradicted its economic and military investments in the Cold War status quo.

"We witnessed, and continue to witness, other paradoxes. With nuclear energy whole cities can easily be powered, yet the dominant nation-states seem more likely to unleash destruction greater than that incurred in all wars in human history. Although our own technology is destroying old and creating new forms of social organization, men still tolerate meaningless work and idleness. While two-thirds of mankind suffers under-nourishment, our own upper classes revel amidst superfluous abundance. Although the world population is expected to double in forty years, the nations still tolerate anarchy

leaders of the Free Speech Movement and the administration fought over free expression and an ever-wider range of issues including university government, classroom overcrowding, and restrictions on students' private lives.

Berkeley became the precedent for a rash of student upheavals that spread across campuses from coast to coast. Many students saw university administrations as oppressive agencies that were a prototype of all governments—except those few in the Third World that, they believed, truly represented the people. The War in Vietnam and the supposed complicity of universities in the war effort soon became principal campus targets.

Organized opposition to the war began with the "teach-ins" on college campuses in 1965. Teach-ins were followed by "peace marches" in many cities, which brought together thousands of pacifists, antiwar liberals, student radicals, and other concerned citizens. Radical students burned draft cards and mobbed recruiters from the armed forces and companies engaged in war production when they came to interview students on college campuses. They also denounced their universities' role in war planning and weapons research.

After 1966 many of the campus upheavals were led by the Students for a Democratic Society (SDS). Formed in 1959, SDS, at the onset, avoided dogmatic

as a major principle of international conduct and uncontrolled exploitation governs the sapping of the earth's physical resources. Although mankind desperately needs revolutionary leadership, America rests in national stalemate, its goals ambiguous and tradition-bound instead of informed and clear, its democratic system apathetic and manipulated rather than 'of, by, and for the people.'

"Not only did tarnish appear on our image of American virtue, not only did disillusion occur when the hypocrisy of American ideals was discovered, but we began to sense that what we had originally seen as the American Golden Age was actually the decline of our era. The worldwide outbreak of revolution against colonialism and imperialism, the intrenchment of totalitarian states, the menace of war, overpopulation, international disorder, supertechnology—these trends were testing the tenacity of our own commitment to democracy and freedom and our abilities to visualize their application to a world in upheaval.

"Our work is guided by the sense that we may be the last generation in the experiment with living. But we are a minority—the vast majority of our people regard the temporary equilibriums of our society and world as eternally functional parts. In this is perhaps the outstanding paradox: we ourselves are imbued with urgency, yet the message of our society is that there is no viable alternative to the present. Beneath the reassuring tunes of the politicians, beneath the common opinion that America will 'muddle through,' beneath the stagnation of those who have closed their minds to the future, is the pervading feeling that there simply are no alternatives, that our times have witnessed the exhaustion not only of Utopias, but of any new departures as well. Feeling the press of complexity upon the emptiness of life,

people are fearful of the thought that at any moment things might be thrust out of control. They fear change itself, since change might smash whatever visible framework seems to hold back chaos for them now. For most Americans, all crusades are suspect, threatening. The fact that each individual sees apathy in his fellows perpetuates the common reluctance to organize for change. The dominant institutions are complex enough to blunt the minds of their potential critics, and entrenched enough to swiftly dissipate or entirely repel the energies of protest and reform, thus limiting human expectancies. Then, too, we are a materially improved society, and by our own improvements we seem to have weakened the case for further change.

"Some would have us believe that Americans feel contentment amidst prosperity—but might it not better be called a glaze above deeply-felt anxieties about their role in the new world? And if these anxieties produce a developed indifference to human affairs, do they not as well produce a yearning to believe that there is an alternative to the present, that something *can* be done to change circumstances in the schools, the workplaces, the bureaucracies, the government? It is to this latter yearning, at once the spark and engine of change, that we direct our present appeal. The search for truly democratic alternatives to the present, and a commitment to social experimentation with them, is a worthy and fulfilling human enterprise, one which moves us and, we hope, others today. On such a basis do we offer this document of our convictions and analysis: as an effort in understanding and changing the conditions of humanity in the late twentieth century, an effort rooted in the ancient, still unfulfilled conception of man attaining determining influence over his circumstances of life."

theories. The SDS members proclaimed the need for personal freedom and individual autonomy and condemned both capitalism and Soviet-style communism for depriving people of their liberty. They usually avoided violence. When police came to remove students occupying buildings at Berkeley, Columbia, and elsewhere, the students, following the precepts of the civil rights movement, went limp and allowed themselves to be dragged off to jail.

Beginning in 1966–67, SDS, by now the major organizational expression of the New Left, became increasingly militant. It organized strikes against recruiters from Dow Chemical, manufacturer of the napalm used in Vietnam, and ROTC (Reserve Officers'

Training Corps); demanded student participation in university decisions; and attacked university policies as racist or sexist. (Ironically, feminists would soon attack SDS itself as sexist.) In general, SDS sought to radicalize the student body in the belief that students were the leaders of the future and would eventually move on to radicalize the society at large. In 1968, between January 1 and June 15, SDS and other radical groups organized 221 major student demonstrations on 101 campuses involving 40,000 students.

The Counterculture. SDS and the New Left sought political change primarily, but simultaneously American middle-class youth were in revolt against bourgeois behavior, dress, and expression. Middle class conventions, they announced, were brutally repressive tools by which a frightened society dominated by the middle-aged controlled people's dangerous instincts and in the process reduced human potential. Unlike the New Left, the counterculture lacked an organizational center, though at different times the Yippies, the Mayday Tribe, and other colorfully named groups would claim to speak for it.

The countercultures' chief practitioners were called "hippies," from hip, a jazz musician's expression meaning knowledgeable or "with it." Hippies displayed their contempt for middle-class values by wearing tattered jeans, sandals, and beads; displaying an abundance of hair; and cultivating a casual way of speaking. Hippies adopted an aesthetic outlook that emphasized natural things. They wore flowers in their hair and around their necks and referred to themselves as "flower children." They considered material possessions fetishes of the "straight culture," and furnished their own "pads" with a few castoffs.

As we have seen, old sexual values, a major target of the counterculture, were already changing when the hippies appeared on the scene. But as the 1960s wore on, and as the counterculture influenced the mainstream, practices that seldom had been talked about and had been relegated to the sexual underground were now celebrated and placed on display. In Tom O'Horgan's play *Futz* one character had sexual intercourse with a pig. "X-rated" movies brought the depiction of oral sex acts to every large city's downtown theaters. Homosexuality, too, ceased to be a shameful aberration in the eyes of many Americans. Toward the end of the 1960s more and more homosexuals and lesbians began to "come out of the closet" and acknowledge their sexual preferences.

The counterculture seized on these tendencies and magnified them. Hippies believed in freer sex lives and an end to sexual taboos. Gatherings of counterculture people at times included displays of mass nudity and even public sexual intercourse, as at the rock-and-roll festival near Woodstock, New York, in August 1969. Hippies refused to be "uptight" about homosexuality and lesbianism. They also experimented with communes where everything, including sexual partners, was shared, and accepted cohabitation without marriage as normal.

Like sex, drugs offered a new way for young men and women to flaunt their disdain of middle-class life. For the first time in American history large numbers of middle-class white youths began to experiment with substances that had only been used in the ghetto or

in bohemia before. Marijuana became a staple among the hippies, replacing alcohol, a substance identified with "square" culture. As marijuana use spread, it became difficult to impose severe criminal penalties on users and eventually in many communities possession or use of "grass" ceased to be treated as more than a misdemeanor. In the early 1960s two Harvard psychology instructors, Timothy Leary and Richard Alpert, had experimented with a new chemical substance, lysergic acid diethylamide (LSD), which they believed capable of "expanding" human consciousness and enabling people to conquer their "inner space." Soon LSD and other consciousness-altering drugs were incorporated into the hippie revolt against bourgeois society.

Though the hippie phenomenon was short-lived, it left a residue of social permissiveness that would characterize the following decade. The hippie enclaves in San Francisco, New York's East Village, and elsewhere, after the 1967 "summer of love," deteriorated into squalid youth slums where mental disturbance induced by "speed" and LSD marked personal relationships. The hippie style—of talk, dress, and behavior—also became commercialized and hence tainted in the eyes of counterculture purists. Meanwhile, the great rock festivals degenerated into saturnalias of drugs and violence. The commune movement for a while became the refuge for the more idealistic counterculture people, but then it, too, deflated. The cause was often practical. As one former commune member described his experience: "We were together at the level of peace and freedom and love. We fell apart over who would cook and wash the dishes and pay the bills."

Liberation. The student political left soon followed the counterculture in a downward spiral. Toward the end of the decade SDS was infiltrated with Marxist ideology, some borrowed from Maoist China, some from the guerrilla movements of Latin America and other parts of the Third World. Frustrated by the continuation of the Vietnam War and its failure to expand its base of support, in 1969 SDS surrendered its vision of participatory democracy and adopted the notion of a vanguard party of the political elect who alone could see the social needs of the people. In June, at its annual convention in Chicago, SDS split in two over abstract issues of who would make the hypothetical revolution. One faction, the Weathermen, led by Mark Rudd, Bernadine Dohrn, and Bill Ayers, fought with the Chicago police during the Days of Rage in October 1969. Thereafter its members became underground terrorists determined to attack "imperialist

Amerika" from within. Over the next few years the Weathermen would be responsible for dozens of bombings of government facilities and corporate offices. In February 1970 a Weathermen bomb factory in a Greenwich Village townhouse erupted when someone connected a wrong wire, killing three Weathermen leaders. The resort to violence, the declining economy, and a recognition that revolution was still a long way off combined to finish off what remained of the New Left.

Though both the counterculture and the New Left were largely defunct by the opening years of the new decade, they left behind important traces. The protests of white and black radicals and hippies broke through the perceived limits of the "system" and created among many outsiders in America a new sense of the possible. Among ethnic minorities, the example of the black civil rights movement inspired Mexican-Americans, Puerto Rican–Americans, and Indian-Americans (Native Americans) to organize movements to fight for political recognition and an end to discrimination.

Mexican-Americans, or Chicanos, were the largest of these groups, numbering over 6 million in California, the Southwest, and the Chicago area. A few were descended from the original Spanish-speaking population of the 1840s Mexican Cession. Most, however, were recent immigrants from Mexico. Chicanos occupied the same low social and economic position in the Southwest that blacks did in the South. They worked as domestics and took unskilled factory jobs. As migrant farm laborers, they picked lettuce, tomatoes, fruit, and other crops in California's fertile valleys.

Beginning in the 1960s, a new generation of Chicano leaders began to demand better treatment for their people. In New Mexico, Reies Tijerina's *Alianza* organization insisted that lands in the Southwest that originally had belonged to Mexican-Americans be returned to them. Tijerina accomplished little, but César Chavez was more effective. As leader of the California grape pickers, he forced the grape growers to accept unionization of their largely Chicano work force. Chavez then moved on to organize the lettuce pickers. In both endeavors he was helped by consumer boycotts of nonunion grapes and lettuce by sympathetic liberals and radicals.

The 1960s was also a decade of revived self-awareness for American Indians. For some time their lot had been improving. During the 1920s a group of white reformers led by John Collier perceived that assimilation as exemplified by the Dawes Severalty Act degraded the heritage of the Indians and took away their culture without providing a truly satisfactory alternative. When Collier became commissioner of Indian affairs in 1933, he promptly set about changing Indian policy. The chief legislative embodiment of his work was the Wheeler-Howard Act of 1934, which repealed the allotment policy of the Dawes Act, recognized the right of Indians to organize "for the purpose of local self-government and economic enterprise," and stated that the future goal of Indian education should be to "promote the study of Indian civilization, arts, crafts, skills, and traditions."

Yet even after the passage of this measure, Indians continued to be poor; infant mortality rates on the reservations remained appalling; Indians continued to

United Farm Workers union leader César Chavez was an important voice in the swelling chorus of Mexican-American protest. The union's strikes against California grape and lettuce growers received the support of many non-Hispanic liberals, who participated in boycotts of the growers' products.

be treated as second-class citizens; white culture continued to erode traditional Indian values. After World War II the federal government sought to improve conditions on the reservations. In 1946 Congress established the Indian Claims Commission to settle outstanding Indian claims against the United States from the very beginning of the federal government. In 1953, by a joint resolution, it authorized "termination" of all federal benefits and controls over the tribes. Over the next six or seven years both aspects of federal-Indian relations were reduced drastically. Though the ostensible purpose of termination was to end federal paternalism and accord the Indians equality with other citizens, the process was often harmful. Before long the National Congress of American Indians was protesting that termination had become primarily a way of lowering federal costs rather than of benefiting the Indians. The process was soon slowed, but not before it had raised up a new class of Indian leaders more militant than any in the recent past.

On the reservations these leaders were primarily concerned with health conditions, poverty, poor education, religious autonomy, and resource development. Many had been working to improve the lot of their tribes since the end of World War II. In the cities, to which many Indians had been drawn during the 1950s and after, the leaders were often young activists inspired by the civil rights movement of blacks and Chicanos. These young people resorted to propaganda and demonstrations to convince white America that it had treated Indians unjustly in the past and must make restitution. F. David Edmunds and Vine Deloria, Jr., wrote Indian history from an Indian viewpoint, siding with Sitting Bull against Custer and with the Apaches against the cavalry. In 1969 a group of young activists occupied the abandoned federal prison on Alcatraz in San Francisco Bay and demanded that it be converted into an Indian cultural center. In 1970 the American Indian Movement (AIM) emerged as the center of the young urban activists.

Potentially the most powerful of all the liberation movements that appeared during the 1960s was the new feminism. From a feminist perspective, the immediate postwar period had been depressing. As we have seen, at the end of World War II many Americans had turned toward domesticity and togetherness. For middle-class women this meant devoting more attention than ever to the responsibilities of suburban homemaking. From 1945 onward, moreover, large families confined women to the home for a longer time than at any period since before World War I.

Economically, working women were better off during the 1950s, but they seldom worked at personally rewarding or well-paying jobs. In part this was a matter of skill: On the whole, women did not have the training or work experience of men. But it was partly a result of what would later be called sexism: Even when women were qualified, they were not given the pay or the promotions they deserved.

The discrimination, feminists would note later, was often indirect and subtle. Society in the 1950s had treated girls and women as second-class human beings. Female children, they said, were "programmed" from the earliest age to assume that they were emotionally and mentally weaker than men. So successful was this process that women themselves believed, consciously or not, that they were inferior and professed to find total satisfaction in nonassertiveness and the traditional roles of wife and mother.

As the 1950s drew to a close, the situation began to change. By 1960 millions of women had gone through college. There they had been exposed to psychological, anthropological, and sociological concepts and evidence that many supposedly feminine characteristics were merely the result of upbringing. Educated women were confronted with the contrast between their training and the routine lives they led, either as housewives or as "gal Fridays" to some male executive. By this time, too, the precedent of black liberation had illuminated the path that the nation's largest "minority" could take.

The intellectual breakthrough for the new feminism came in 1963, when Betty Friedan published *The Feminine Mystique*, an eloquent and angry attack on the silken bondage imposed on women. Like most feminist activists of the past, Friedan spoke mostly for middle-class college women, but among this group her message rang a very loud bell. In June 1966 aroused feminists organized NOW, the National Organization for Women, with Friedan as its first president.

NOW was only part of the women's liberation movement. It was a moderate body composed largely of college and professional women that sought to end sex discrimination in education and jobs and to liberalize abortion laws. It worked through the courts and legislatures. To the left of NOW were more radical groups. Led by militant activists, these groups employed "guerrilla" theater—outdoor dramas dealing with controversial issues—and such attention-getting tactics as disruption of the "sexist" Miss America Pageant. They also developed the technique of "consciousness raising," small-group sessions in which women expressed their deepest frustrations with their male "oppressors" and tried to free themselves from the stultifying sense of inferiority that they perceived had been instilled in them as children.

Radical liberationists agreed with most of the moderates' demands, but they went beyond them in rhetoric and program. The militants wanted all sex differences eliminated, even if that meant radically altering the structure of the family. Their antimale tone was far more emphatic. Many seemed to consider men, by their very nature, enemies and—turning the usual stereotype upside down—inferior to women. At times their antimale bias was so strong that critics of radical feminism charged it was dominated by lesbians. Like the other "entitlement" movements (organized by groups seeking what they considered to be their rights), women's liberation in fact was an amalgam of moderate and radical sentiment.

Another late manifestation of the new liberation mood was the gay rights movement. Homosexuality had always existed in American society, of course, but gay men and lesbian women had carefully hidden their sexual preferences in the face of "straight" society's stern disapproval and laws that made many homosexual practices criminal offenses. In many large cities homosexuals congregated in their own neighborhoods and developed their own cultural and social institutions where they could be comfortable. Gays often led double lives: one at home, where they felt free; and one at work, where they felt compelled to conform to the straight world's expectations. This enforced concealment, added to the legal hazards, created a deep sense of resentment and the feeling among homosexuals that they, too, constituted an oppressed minority.

By the mid-sixties male and female homosexuals had formed defense organizations of various kinds for mutual support. Then in 1969 came a crucial event in the response of homosexuals to their circumstances. In June, the police raided the Stonewall Inn, a homosexual bar in New York's Greenwich Village. Gays, who usually accepted such raids as a normal part of existence, this time fought back. A riot broke out that lasted far into the night and continued the next day. This battle marked the end of homosexual acquiescence and the beginning of the Gay Liberation movement. In its wake militant gays began to "come out of the closet" and demand that the laws against free sexual expression and practice and those denying gays employment and other rights be removed from the statute books.

An Adversary Culture. The tensions, pressures, and ideologies of the 1960s helped create an adversary response among the nation's artists and intellectuals.

Freed from the political fears of the 1950s and inspired by the militancy of students, blacks, ethnics, and women, American writers, painters, and intellectuals began once again to question, ridicule, and satirize their society and its values.

American movies in these years reached a new level of intellectual maturity as the function of providing escapist entertainment was taken over increasingly by TV. In movies such as *Who's Afraid of Virginia Woolf?* (1965) and *The Graduate* (1967), director Mike Nichols poked fun at widely accepted assumptions—that fulfillment could be found in work, that men and women should behave as their age and status prescribed, that marriage made people happy. Stanley Kubrick turned a similar critical and disillusioned eye on the American political and military establishment in *Dr. Strangelove*. Released in 1964, following the Cuban missile crisis and an upwelling of anxiety over nuclear testing, the movie depicted in broad, gallows-humor strokes the triggering of World War III by a demented right-wing general who believed that "they" (the Communists) were destroying his "precious bodily fluids." The kind of violence depicted in the nightly TV reportage of Vietnam became an integral part of film during these years. *Bonnie and Clyde* (1967), directed by Arthur Penn, made heroes of two 1930s bank robbers and showed in full color the gory effects of a rifle bullet hitting a woman's head. *Easy Rider* (1969) was a counterculture epic about two young men who set out to cross the country by motorcycle to peddle heroin. Along the way they visit a New Mexico commune and have sexual adventures in New Orleans. On the way back to California, while in the Deep South, they are killed by malicious "rednecks," who spot them as intruders into their America. Toward the end of the decade the science-fiction movie came into its own. But unlike the "space operas" of the 1970s, the sixties films were skeptical of the brave new world in store for humanity. Kubrick's *2001: A Space Odyssey* (1968) showed not only the grandeur of the new scientific world that was evolving but also its chilling dehumanization as computers seize control.

And even TV, though reserved for the mass "family" audience, began to develop some bite. In 1961 Newton Minow, Federal Communications Commission chairman, referred to television as a "vast wasteland." Dominated by quiz shows and "sitcoms," the medium did nothing to challenge its audience. The typical sitcom of the 1950s, such as *Father Knows Best*, portrayed the orderly world of a middle-class white family where problems were confined to solving disputes among siblings and what dress daughter should wear to the prom. By the late sixties there were signs of change. *Rowan and Martin's Laugh-in* hit the top of the ratings with sophisticated sexual humor. The Smothers Brothers' comedy show contained political satire. Prime-time dramas, too, moved a small distance from the bland, upbeat material of the past.

But TV had its chief impact on the era in its reportorial role. During the decade the TV screen brought shocking real events into people's living rooms: the murder of Lee Harvey Oswald, the assassination of President Kennedy; executions of Vietcong sympathizers; the rioting at the 1968 Democratic convention in Chicago. One could flip from the news to conventional TV drama without changing one's seat in a way that blurred the distinction between truth and fiction. The breakdown of this distinction worried educators. Would the next generation be able to tell the difference between image and reality?

Writing also began to merge fact and fiction in a disconcerting way. During the decade three major authors, Truman Capote, Norman Mailer, and Tom Wolfe, began to practice a literary form that fused the factual and the fictional. Capote's *In Cold Blood* (1965) described the murders of a Kansas family and the pursuit, capture, conviction, and execution of the killers. Capote, like the other practitioners of this genre, seemed to know everything that went on in the heads of his characters, even ones he never met. In *Armies of the Night* (1968) Mailer imposed a novelistic form on an account of the antiwar Pentagon march of October 1967. Tom Wolfe's *Electric Kool-Aid Acid Test* (1968) depicted the evolution of the drug culture on the West Coast through invented dialogue and scenes that Wolfe re-created from second-hand reports. Science-fiction, too, at times became a vehicle for interweaving fact and fiction. Kurt Vonnegut's *Slaughterhouse 5* (1969) portrayed a man who "comes unstuck in time" and experiences the mass slaughter in 1945 of German civilians by the RAF in Dresden.

Distinctions among art forms eroded as well. In the visual arts traditionally separate forms like comics and advertising were merged to create Pop Art. The work of the two major Pop artists, Andy Warhol and Roy Lichtenstein, protested against the materialism and shallowness of American culture while at the same time seeming to celebrate it. Claes Oldenburg's huge paintings of hamburgers, when hung in the same museum with Rembrandts and French Impressionists, mocked the pretensions of the museums themselves.

Theater experimented with new forms and new subject matter. The Theater of the Absurd sought to break down the boundaries between audience and players by having actors circulate through the auditorium and by inviting viewers to join the actors on stage. The new experimental companies, such as the San Franciso Mime Troupe, the Living Theater group, and the Open Theater, also used pantomime, ritual, masks, and other nontraditional devices to communicate their message. The message itself was often radical. Barbara Garson's *MacBird* (1966) was an updating of Shakespeare's *MacBeth* with Lyndon Johnson cast in the role of the bloody king of Scotland. Arthur Kopit's *Indians* (1969) bitterly assailed white treatment of Native Americans. *The Connection* (1959), by Jack Gelber, depicted the anguished world of junkies and criminals. Nudity became a staple of some of the new plays. *Hair* had a nude scene. Richard Schechner's Performance Group production of *Dionysius in '69* invited the audience to suggest sexual acts that it would like to see the actors carry out on stage.

The cultural mood, then was experimental, critical, and hostile to traditional forms and conventions. But the arts were influenced not only by the dissenting political and social mood of the 1960s but also by the decade's affluence. During the 1960s the high arts began for the first time to develop something like a mass audience. Foreign travel, widespread college education, and higher incomes created a new audience for classical music, the dance, museum-going. Government agencies such as the National Endowment for the Arts helped disseminate high culture beyond the normal orbit of a half dozen major cities through subsidies for local orchestras, dance companies, and museums.

The Johnson Years

Many Americans were appalled, even frightened, by the sudden upsurge of political and cultural radicalism during the 1960s though the dissenters were never more than a small minority. Yet when Lyndon Johnson took office, in 1963, most citizens were positively inclined toward change in two areas: race and economic inequality. The bombing of black churches in the South, Police Commissioner T. Eugene ("Bull") Connor's use of police dogs and fire hoses against black demonstrators in Birmingham, the persistence of widespread national poverty as revealed by Michael Harrington in his startling book *The Other America* (1963)—these things made many middle-class citizens ashamed and receptive to a major legislative effort to end them.

The Johnson years saw enactment of a flood of legislation that promised to bring American life in line with the new insistence on social justice.

The Great Society. Lyndon B. Johnson was in many ways the antithesis of his predecessor. Middle-aged, homely, coarse, and self-made rather than young, handsome, elegant, and patrician, Johnson's image was unattractive to many Americans and impaired his ability to lead the nation.

Yet he was incomparable as a legislative leader. His long years as Senate minority and then majority leader had honed to a fine edge his talent for getting laws enacted. As president his skills were put to good use. A congressman who resisted the president's legislative demands got the "Johnson treatment." The legislator was marched into Johnson's office, seated next to the towering Texan, and subjected to a powerful verbal assault of jokes, promises, threats, cajolery, and ego stroking, along with thumps, squeezes, and pokes. Few men could hold out against the treatment for very long, and in the course of his five years as president, Johnson initiated more important reform legislation than any chief executive since Franklin D. Roosevelt.

Johnson's program was an updating of the New Deal. The president was a long-time admirer of Roosevelt, and he hoped to complete and round out the welfare state that FDR had launched between 1933 and 1938. Invoking the memory of his martyred predecessor, the new president got Congress to enact many of the measures that were pending when Kennedy died. In January 1964, following through on a Kennedy initiative, Congress passed the Economic Opportunity Act. The law established an Office of Economic Opportunity (OEO), and under Sargent Shriver, JFK's brother-in-law, the OEO launched a "War on Poverty" designed to reduce illiteracy, end unemployment among inner-city youths, improve depressed conditions in the Appalachian area, sharpen skills among the poor, and provide capital to minority businesses. One provision of the new measure authorized the OEO to set up community-action groups that would give local-area people a hand in designing and running new antipoverty programs. Such participation, the theory held, would instill in the poor a new sense of confidence and ultimately help them help themselves.

Johnson also convinced Congress to enact the tax reduction that Kennedy had asked for, a measure that gave the economy a much-needed jolt. In the summer of 1964 Congress passed a strong civil rights act giving the federal government new authority to protect the voting rights of black citizens and to bar discrimination in employment, housing, schools, and public accommodations.

The president quickly made his mark as an effective domestic leader and was rewarded with his party's 1964 nomination, with Hubert H. Humphrey, Minnesota's liberal senator, as his running mate. The Republicans chose Senator Barry Goldwater of Arizona along with an obscure New York congressman, William Miller. Goldwater was a likable and handsome man, but he represented the extreme right wing of his party. His supporters claimed that by nominating him they were offering the country "a choice, not an echo." The choice, it seemed to many voters, was to dismantle the Social Security system, sell the New Deal's Tennessee Valley Authority to private interests, and return to Hooverism. Given the Republican candidate's bellicose foreign-policy statements and his affection for uniforms and air force bombers, his election also promised an enlarged Vietnam involvement that few Americans wanted. Goldwater made matters worse by his inept public statements. When many moderate Americans were still worried about the John Birch Society and extremists in general, Goldwater told them, "extremism in the defense of liberty is no vice! And . . . moderation in the pursuit of justice in no virtue!"

The Democrats did not play fair. At the very time Johnson was considering escalating the American commitment in Vietnam, he was denouncing Goldwater as a warmonger. Johnson won with 61 percent of the popular vote. A year later a bitter joke would make the rounds: "I was told if I voted for Goldwater we would be at war in six months. I did—and we were!"

With his landslide victory Johnson embarked on one of the most ambitious legislative programs in history, the Great Society. This program, he said, would end poverty, equalize opportunities for all Americans, restore the decaying central cities, guarantee the voting rights of every American, provide access to college for virtually every young man and woman, protect the health of older people, raise the cultural level of the nation, and restore the safety of the highways, and the pristine purity of the nation's air, streams, and lakes.

During the following months the administration made a remarkable effort to fulfill its promises. In the spring of 1965 Congress appropriated $1.3 billion for the country's poorer elementary and high school districts. In July it enacted Medicare, a federal health insurance program for the retired. One month later the Omnibus Housing Act set up a rent supplement

LBJ visits a farm family, 1964. The fourth "accidental" president of the century inherited power at a time when the nation's mood was changing from confident to self-critical and distrustful. Johnson's War on Poverty eventually failed when commitment to its goals evaporated.

program for low-income families. In recognition of the cities' needs, Congress established the Department of Housing and Urban Development (HUD). Johnson promptly appointed as its head Robert C. Weaver, the nation's first black cabinet member. Later, in September, the president signed a bill to set up the National Foundations of the Arts and the Humanities to subsidize artists, writers, composers, painters, and scholars and provide aid to local cultural institutions. Clean air and clean water acts to improve the environment followed soon afterward, as did a Higher Education Act providing the first federal scholarships for college students, the Highway Safety Act, the Model Cities Demonstration and Metropolitan Area Redevelopment Act to revive and reconstruct decaying city centers, and a measure to subsidize noncommercial educational television and radio broadcasting. Still more Great Society legislation included the Truth in Lending Act to protect consumers in credit transactions, and the Voting Rights Act of 1965. This last measure suspended literacy tests for voters, which were aimed against blacks and implemented in ways that discriminated

against them, and gave the federal government supervision of voter registration in southern states.

Some of these measures were hastily drawn and ultimately proved unworkable. Some offered opportunities for "ripoffs" of the government; others were merely underfunded. Most controversial of all were a number of community-action programs. Many local officials disliked them because they bypassed city hall. Other critics claimed that white radicals and black militants used them to encourage social upheaval. Although the fastest-growing items in the federal budgets were for meeting long-neglected social needs, the programs were often not ambitious enough to solve the problems they addressed. But the record was not all bad. Many programs proved immensely valuable. The nation's cultural institutions were revitalized by government subsidies, low- and moderate-income students were helped through college, cities acquired new civic and commercial centers, automobiles were made safer, and many thousands of southern blacks were registered as voters for the first time.

Kennedy had set the goal of beating the Soviet Union to the moon, but it was under Johnson that most of the program was carried out. The space competition was attacked by the left, which believed its immense cost starved needed social programs here on earth. Black Americans often considered it a white man's enterprise, and many did not seem interested. Many experts claimed that the scientific community could have learned as much about the solar system by using far cheaper unmanned rockets. Still, most of the public found it fascinating, and the television audiences for the Apollo launchings ran into the millions. By the end of Johnson's full term, Frank Borman, James Lovell, Jr., and William Anders in Apollo 8 had orbited the moon ten times. On Christmas Eve, 1968, they transmitted greetings by television to the earth from seventy miles above the moon's rugged and forbidding surface. It was now only a matter of time before the first human beings would place their feet on some part of the universe besides Mother Earth.

Quagmire in Vietnam. If not for Vietnam, Johnson's policies would have entitled him to be considered one of the greatest American presidents. For all his personal failings and his inability to win the affection of the American people, LBJ was a man of imagination and deep human sympathies. Although he was capable of crude manipulation and harsh partisanship, he was also clearly in the great popular tradition of Wilson and the two Roosevelts.

But Vietnam brought out the worst in the president. In foreign affairs Johnson was naive. He believed his close advisers, military and civilian, when they told him, as they constantly did, that great progress was being made in defeating the Vietcong and only a few more divisions of soldiers and a little more money would do the trick. He was also a captive of the past. Like many of his generation, he viewed Vietnam in terms of the "lessons" learned from Hitler in the 1930s. If you did not stand up to the enemy, if you appeased him, as Chamberlain had appeased Hitler at Munich, he would consider you weak and take advantage of you. Applied to Vietnam, this analogy meant that if the Communist forces were allowed to conquer South Vietnam, their victory would produce a "domino effect": One by one the other nonaligned or pro-Western nations of Southeast Asia would fall to Communist control. This logic was faulty. Ho Chi Minh was not ruler of a powerful militarized nation such as 1938 Germany. Ho's ally, the Soviet Union, might have expansionist tendencies of uncertain dimensions, but there was no evidence that Ho himself had designs on any part of Asia beyond former Indochina. Yet the domino effect was a convincing notion to the president and to many other Americans as well. Truman had been charged with "losing" China; Johnson was determined that similar charges not be leveled at him. "I don't want it said of me that I was the president who lost Vietnam," he remarked.

Early in 1965, following a Vietcong attack on a U.S. airbase at Pleiku, the administration decided to bomb North Vietnam to induce the Ho Chi Minh government to withdraw support from the Vietcong forces in the South. Its legal sanction for what was an act of war was the Tonkin Gulf Resolution, passed by Congress in 1964 in response to a supposed attack on American naval forces off the Vietnamese coast. When this move proved ineffective in stopping the North Vietnamese, he increased the number of United States advisers and soon after dispatched the first American ground combat troops.

All through 1965 and 1966 Johnson increased the pressure on the Vietcong and North Vietnamese in hopes of forcing a settlement that would preserve South Vietnam as an anti-Communist bastion under the pro-American leaders Nguyen Van Thieu and Nguyen Cao Ky. In April 1966 the United States sent B-52s to bomb Hanoi, the North Vietnamese capital, and Haiphong, the major North Vietnamese port of entry for supplies from the Soviet Union. Meanwhile, on the ground, United States marines and army units fought a guerrilla war in the jungles and rice paddies. The fighting was dirty work in every sense of the term.

The American military used body counts to chart their progress. The Vietcong, refusing to meet the Americans head-on, chose to hit and run, slipping away into the jungle when confronted by superior forces. South Vietnamese villagers were often caught in the middle and were attacked by both sides. American guerrilla-warfare experts tried to establish secure areas free of "the Cong," but the villages seldom remained secure for very long. Too many villagers considered the guerrillas less dangerous than the Americans or the corrupt officials of the Thieu government, or simply could not resist Vietcong threats.

There were atrocities on both sides. The Vietcong set off bombs on the streets of Saigon that killed inno-

The Vietnam War

* Major battles

△ U.S. bases

✖ Areas of guerrilla activity

Communist countries

Allied with U.S.

Neutral countries

Many Americans realized that the Vietnam War was far from won when the Vietcong were able to mount a major offensive during Tet, the celebration of the Vietnamese Lunar New Year, in 1968. The attackers almost succeeded in penetrating the heavily protected United States embassy in Saigon, actually managing to blow a hole in the outer wall.

cent civilians. They tortured and murdered South Vietnamese villagers, policemen, teachers, and Catholics who opposed them. Americans also committed atrocities. In March 1968 an American army unit under Lieutenant William L. Calley, Jr., attacked My Lai, a village of 600 people suspected of harboring Vietcong, and massacred virtually every inhabitant. The Defense Department attempted to cover up this crime, but it became known when a former member of Calley's unit informed several high government officials. Calley was eventually tried, but received a light sentence.

By 1968 the United States had sunk into a dirty, divisive, expensive war. As in the Korean conflict, there seemed to be no way to conclude the fighting. Bland, reassuring government statements were undercut daily by television broadcasts from the battlefields that showed no cause for optimism.

As the war dragged on month after month, it began to blight the economy. Johnson was at first afraid to ask Americans to pay for the war directly, lest any economic sacrifice make it even less popular than it

was. Yet by 1967 it was costing the country $25 billion a year. This sum, on top of Great Society domestic programs, produced what then seemed gigantic budget deficits: $8.7 billion in 1967 and $25.2 billion in 1968. Finally, the president asked for higher taxes to siphon off excess purchasing power, but by then the damage was done. Until 1966 yearly consumer price increases had remained below 2 percent. In 1966 they rose to 3.4 percent and in 1968 to 4.7 percent. Good times continued, measured by employment and output, but the dollar was becoming one of the war's casualties.

Organized protests against the war, as we have seen, were begun by college students in 1965. In early 1966, J. William Fulbright of Arkansas, chairman of the Senate Foreign Relations Committee, conducted televised hearings on the war during which he grilled Secretary of State Dean Rusk remorselessly and exposed many of the weaknesses of the prowar "hawk" position. Before long, liberal and radical clergy began to demand an end to the Vietnam slaughter. In early 1967 Martin Luther King, Jr., made a "Declaration of Independence" from the war, declaring that it was "time to break silence." Soon after this he led the New York Spring Mobilization parade, and he and black militant Stokely Carmichael denounced the war before an audience of cheering antiwar protesters. In 1967 Father Daniel Berrigan and his brother, Philip, priests who carried the new Catholic liberalism further than most, organized the Catholic Ultra-Resistance.

Most Americans continued to support the war. Many were angered by the protesters and considered them traitors. Bumper stickers reading "America: Love it or leave it" began to appear on the highways. The American Legion, the Veterans of Foreign Wars, and the conservative Young Americans for Freedom organized rallies where the crowds carried signs: "Bomb Hanoi," "We Love America," "My Country—Right or Wrong." Even many anti-Communist liberals continued to believe that abandoning South Vietnam would destroy the credibility of American foreign policy and play into Soviet hands.

After 1967, however, support for the president's policies eroded rapidly. Even those Americans who favored the containment policy began to conclude that the war was becoming far too costly economically and morally, and probably could not be won.

The greatest blow to hawk confidence came in early 1968 when, during the Vietnamese Lunar New Year (Tet), the Vietcong and North Vietnamese launched a major offensive against Saigon and other South Vietnamese cities. After fierce and bloody fighting, the attack was stopped, but Tet made a mockery of the administrations' confident propaganda. Until this point many Americans had found it possible to believe that the war, however protracted, was being won. Tet seemed to show that the enemy was, if anything, growing in strength.

Soon after Tet, even Johnson began to have doubts. He now saw that the war was getting out of hand and must, if continued, rip the country apart. The presidential election of 1968 was at hand, and Johnson, his credibility and popular support seriously eroded, faced a formidable challenge within his own party.

The 1968 Election. The president's challengers for the Democratic nomination were Eugene J. McCarthy of Minnesota and Robert F. Kennedy of New York. Both were United States senators, liberals, and Irish Catholics. Both opposed the Vietnam War. In most other ways, however, they were different. McCarthy, a former Catholic seminarian, was a philosopher and poet. A witty and learned man, he was also aloof and

cerebral. To the Minnesota senator, the war was a moral evil that must be fought as one fought sin. Kennedy, the former president's younger brother, was a man of action. He, too, detested the war—but as much for what it was doing to the nation's morale and self-respect as for its conflict with moral law. McCarthy attracted many students and academics who appreciated his ethical stance. Kennedy could communicate more readily with blue-collar workers and blacks. Wearing the still-shining mantle of Camelot, he projected a warmer image as friend of the masses.

McCarthy was first in the field against Johnson. When Kennedy refused to be enticed into running, the Minnesota senator reluctantly announced his candidacy. Few expected that he could make much headway against an incumbent president, but in the New Hampshire Democratic primary in March thousands of students turned out to ring doorbells, make phone calls, and stuff envelopes for him. The results were startling: The challenger received only a few hundred votes less than the president. Having concluded that Johnson was beatable, Kennedy now also entered the race.

By early 1968 Johnson had decided to renounce another full term. In late 1967 he had replaced Secretary of Defense Robert McNamara, a Kennedy holdover, with the debonair Clark Clifford. Clifford, and the informal group of foreign-policy advisers known as the "Wise Men," had told him after the Tet offensive that the war was unwinnable. They advised reducing the American military commitment. Reluctantly accepting their position, Johnson refused to grant the request of General William Westmoreland for an additional 200,000 troops. He also realized that he could encourage a negotiated peace if he ceased the bombing campaign and himself withdrew from public life. In any event, if he continued in the reelection campaign, he decided, he would only suffer a humiliating defeat in the primaries. On the evening of March 31, in an address to the nation announcing a bombing halt and a peace initiative, he concluded with the words: "I shall not seek, and will not accept, the nomination of my party for another term as your president." The two Democratic antiwar candidates now began the long struggle through the state primaries to secure the nomination.

Before the campaign's end two tragedies intervened. The first took place in Memphis, where Martin Luther King, Jr., had gone to support a local strike of the predominantly black city garbage collectors. King's nonviolence was under attack by black-power militants, but he was about to open a new phase of his career by leading a poor people's campaign. He never did. On April 4, 1968, he was shot and killed by James Earl Ray, an escaped white convict. Black ghettoes around the country exploded in rage and despair. Twenty blocks of Chicago's West Madison Street went up in flames. Black neighborhoods in Detroit, Cincinnati, and Minneapolis erupted. From their offices on Capitol Hill congressmen could see the flames and smoke from Washington's burning ghettoes.

The second tragedy came on June 6. Following a successful battle against McCarthy in the California primary, Kennedy was shot by a confused Arab national named Sirhan Bishara Sirhan during his victory celebration in Los Angeles. The senseless violence of these two events encouraged the view that something had to be done to extricate the nation from the contaminating brutality of Vietnam. The United States seemed to many to be at the edge of anarchy.

The forces that converged on Chicago for the Democratic convention in late August represented an explosive mixture. Now that Johnson was gone, the hawks had gathered around Vice President Humphrey, who, however much he disliked the war, had become Johnson's heir apparent, tied to his policies by loyalty and dependence. On the other side were the combined antiwar groups representing McCarthy and the delegates who had supported Kennedy. In the city's streets and parks were the Yippies (Youth International Party), politicized counterculture people led by Jerry Rubin and Abbie Hoffman, along with New Left radicals, antiwar students, and pacifists. Some young people, as Jerry Rubin would later admit, were intent on rioting to show up the "politics of death" represented by the traditional party system. In response, Chicago's Mayor Richard Daley warned that "as long as I am mayor, there will be law and order."

Within the convention hall itself the Humphrey forces triumphed. Supported by the remaining hawks, union leaders, party regulars, and big-city power brokers, Humphrey defeated McCarthy and the insurgent peace forces and was nominated on the first ballot. In the streets of Chicago Mayor Daley's police and the antiwar activists collided in battle before the eyes of the delegates and the shocked public, who watched the gassing, the clubbings, the trashings, and the stone-throwing on television. To many viewers the contrast between political business as usual in the convention hall and burly policemen propelling young people through plateglass windows was final evidence that America was divided by forces that were out of control. In great numbers the voters blamed the chaos on the Democrats and on Hubert Humphrey; his campaign was in deep trouble from the start.

Meanwhile, in Miami, in a convention as bland as the Democrats' was violent, the Republicans nominated Richard M. Nixon. The nomination was a spectacular comeback. In 1962 Nixon had run for governor of California and had been beaten by the incumbent, Edmund Brown. After his defeat, in an intemperate outburst accusing the press of "kicking him around" during the campaign, he had said he would never run for office again. Soon after, Nixon joined a New York law firm to spend his remaining days making money and enjoying the pleasures of private life. He could not stay out of politics, however, and soon started the comeback campaign that finally brought him victory at the Miami convention.

The 1968 presidential contest was a close one. Many observers felt that the Democrats had destroyed themselves on Chicago by their bitter, divisive in-fighting and the rioting in the streets. The Republicans, on the other hand, worried about defection on the right to Governor George Wallace of Alabama, running as the American Independent party candidate on a platform of law and order, pushing the war until victory, and repressing dissenters and civil rights activists. To avoid losing the South and the conservatives to Wallace, Nixon promised Senator Strom Thurmond of South Carolina that if elected he would keep the nation strong militarily, work for a less activist Supreme Court, and slow the pace of desegregation. It was with Thurmond's approval that Nixon selected Spiro T. Agnew, the little-known governor of Maryland, as his running mate.

At the start of the campaign the Republicans were well in the lead. But as November approached, the traditional Democratic coalition of ethnics, blacks, eastern liberals, and union members began to rally around Humphrey. Had the campaign gone on for just a few days longer, the ticket of Humphrey and Senator Edmund S. Muskie of Maine might have pulled ahead. But the surge came too late. On November 5 Nixon won by 31.7 million votes (301 electoral) to Humphrey's 31.2 million (191 electoral) and Wallace's 9.9 million (46 electoral). Richard Nixon would be the thirty-seventh president of the United States.

Conclusions

During the 1960s the United States attained a level of material well-being beyond anything dreamed of in the past. Affluence altered the dominant public mood. Among minorities, already mobilized to secure

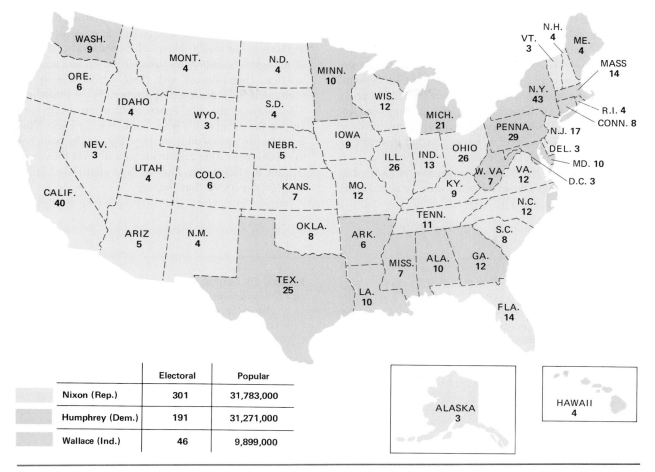

	Electoral	Popular
Nixon (Rep.)	301	31,783,000
Humphrey (Dem.)	191	31,271,000
Wallace (Ind.)	46	9,899,000

The election of 1968

Even Richard Nixon could inspire enthusiasm, at least before Watergate. Here he is seen campaigning for president in 1968. He won, but it was close.

their long-denied basic civil rights, it aroused a sense of fury and hurt at exclusion from the benefits of abundance. Among members of the middle class it encouraged a spirit of generosity. If there was plenty to go around, then why not distribute some of its benefits to those who could not make it by themselves? Generosity, reinforced perhaps by guilt, and underscored by the sweeping 1964 victory of Lyndon Johnson over Barry Goldwater, set off a wave of social reform not equalled since the New Deal.

Yet despite the nation's prosperity, or rather because of it, the decade witnessed a wave of social criticism. Especially among the privileged young, the America of bounding wealth and conspicuous consumption seemed an unlovely place of bureaucratic rigidity, meaningless relationships, manipulation, and aesthetic squalor. Their disgust with their society was in turn reinforced by a distant and apparently pointless war. Thus, some of the chief beneficiaries of prosperity were among the very people who despised it the most. Their excesses in turn would outrage those who still held to traditional values and attitudes and force the dissenters on the defensive. The election of Richard Nixon in 1968 expressed that outrage.

For Further Reading

William O'Neill. *Coming Apart: An Informal History of America in the 1960s* (1971)
A witty, highly readable, and opinionated overview of the mores, politics, culture, and thought of the 1960s. Both entertaining and informative.

Irwin Unger and Debi Unger. *1968: Turning Point* (1988)
A panorama of the 1960s from the perspective of its culminating year. Strongly recommended.

Morris Dickstein. *Gates of Eden: American Culture in the Sixties* (1977)
This work demonstrates what a bright scholar can do with the popular culture of the 1960s. Written by a professor of literature who is young enough to have been at the center of things himself during the 1968 student uprising at Columbia University.

Theodore Roszak. *The Making of a Counter Culture: Reflections on the Technocratic Society and Its Youthful Opposition* (1969)
Both a description of the 1960s counterculture phenomenon and an influential part of it. Roszak's attitude is very positive toward the 1960s cultural left.

Arthur M. Schlesinger, Jr. *A Thousand Days: John F. Kennedy* (1965)
A highly sympathetic portrait of the Kennedy presidency by a professorial participant in it. Written with grace and verve.

Doris Kearns. *Lyndon Johnson and the American Dream* (1976)
A fascinating combination of psychological study, biography, and memoir, written by a scholar who enjoyed Johnson's trust and confidence from 1967 to his death in 1973. Kearns quotes the private man at length and demonstrates how his personal behavior affected the course of the Great Society and American policy in Vietnam.

Frances FitzGerald. *Fire in the Lake: The Vietnamese and the Americans in Vietnam* (1972)
American policy in Vietnam was based in part on ignorance of Vietnamese history and society. FitzGerald discusses the Vietnamese people and their history with great sympathy. A complex and rather difficult book.

David Halberstam. *The Best and the Brightest* (1972)
A sharply critical account of the foreign policy "establishment" under Kennedy and Johnson and how its members entangled the United States in the Vietnam War.

Michael Harrington. *The Other America: Poverty in the United States* (1962)
This short book is said to have influenced Kennedy's thinking and led him to propose a federal program anticipating Johnson's War on Poverty. Harrington rediscovered poverty in America after the other experts had said it no longer existed.

Betty Friedan. *The Feminine Mystique* (1963)
This is the feminist "Declaration of Independence" of the 1960s. In this book Friedan, a leader of the women's movement, devastatingly attacked the 1950s cult of female domesticity and left it a shambles among most intellectuals and a large proportion of college-educated women.

Lyndon B. Johnson. *The Vantage Point: Perspectives of the Presidency, 1963–69* (1971)
Johnson defends his administration's policies—not only the Great Society programs, but also the continued intervention in Vietnam.

Norman Podhoretz. *Why We Were in Vietnam* (1982)
The author, a leading neoconservative intellectual, makes the best case possible for American involvement in Vietnam.

George Herring. *America's Longest War: The United States and Vietnam, 1950–1975* (1986)

A scholarly treatment of the Vietnam War. Herring is a dove who believes that America's containment policy, as displayed in Vietnam, was "fundamentally flawed in its assumptions."

Allen Matusow. *The Unraveling of America: A History of Liberalism in the 1960s* (1984)

A critical examination of 1960s political liberalism as seen from the left. Matusow views the Kennedy-Johnson New Frontier–Great Society era as seriously damaged by exaggerated rhetoric and limited commitment to the goals of equality.

Nancy Zaroulis and Gerald Sullivan. *Who Spoke Up? American Protest Against the War In Vietnam, 1963–1975* (1984)

A blow-by-blow account of the anti–Vietnam War movement. Encyclopedic.

Chapter 30

The Uncertain Seventies

Why Did the Right Fail?

1960   Organization of Petroleum Exporting Countries (OPEC) is formed

1969   Paris peace talks on Vietnam begin • Nixon orders the secret bombing of Cambodia • Strategic Arms Limitation Talks (SALT) begin in Helsinki • Americans land on the moon • Nuclear Nonproliferation Treaty

1970   United States invades Cambodia • Four students killed by National Guard in antiwar demonstration at Kent State University in Ohio • Congress repeals the Gulf of Tonkin Resolution

1971   The *New York Times* publishes the Pentagon Papers • Nixon imposes wage-and-price controls • Berlin Accord

1972   Nixon visits China • Congress passes the Federal Election Campaign Act • Nixon visits Moscow; The U.S. and the Soviet Union ratify arms limitation treaties • Watergate break-in • Nixon reelected in landslide

1973   Truce in Vietnam • Senate Select Committee holds public hearing on Watergate; House Judiciary Committee begins hearings on impeachment resolutions • Vice President Agnew resigns in disgrace; Gerald Ford becomes vice president • Israel and Egypt go to war, touching off Arab oil embargo • Abortion legalized by Supreme Court in *Roe* v. *Wade*

1974   Arab oil embargo ends, but OPEC raises oil prices drastically • House Judiciary Committee recommends impeachment of Nixon; Nixon resigns; Ford becomes president; Ford pardons Nixon

1975   North and South Vietnam are reunited

1976   Bicentennial celebrations • Jimmy Carter elected president

1977   SALT II talks collapse • Carter launches "moral equivalent of war" on United States dependency on foreign oil • Camp David Accords

1978   Panama Canal Treaties

1979   SALT II agreement • Three Mile Island nuclear power plant disaster • Shah of Iran exiled • 66 American hostages taken by Khomeini's followers in Iran • Russia invades Afghanistan

1980   Ronald Reagan elected president

The Uncertain Seventies: Why Did The Right Fail?

In January 1969 a new conservative administration came to power in Washington seemingly dedicated to dismantling the Great Society, slowing the pace of social change, and pushing back the tide of world communism. Between that date and the end of the 1970s American public opinion would, by and large, support such a conservative agenda. Yet very little of it would be achieved. Indeed, by the opening of the 1980s the United States, in the eyes of many committed conservatives, had retrogressed. By then the welfare state seemed more deeply entrenched than ever, the courts were upholding new principles of racial equality, and the United States had recognized Red China and achieved at least a superficial détente with its arch-enemy, the Soviet Union.

How had such results come about? How had Richard Nixon, the man who epitomized conservative anticommunism, managed to perpetuate the welfare state that he and his followers despised and to replace the hardline anticommunism of recent American policy with a more flexible approach?

The Nixon Presidency

Richard Nixon was one of the most puzzling and inconsistent men to occupy the White House. Some of Nixon's personal qualities could be explained by his difficult childhood. The second of five sons, he saw two of his brothers die of tuberculosis. His father was a hot-tempered man and a financial failure. His mother, a Quaker and a woman with an especially sweet nature, could not save him from his father's frequent anger. The contrasting personalities of his parents helped mold the extremes of Nixon's own character: one side self-pitying and vindictive, particularly in the face of frustration; the other kindly, even idealistic.

Both sides of Nixon's nature could be detected in his approach to public issues. He could support welfare reform, environmental protection laws, and reconciliation with Red China and the Soviet Union, for example. But he could also seek to weaken civil rights protection, allow the illegal political acts we call Watergate, and attempt to cover them up to protect his administration. His enemies, remembering his aggressive partisan style, seldom found it in their hearts to forgive him for anything. Adlai Stevenson would describe "Nixonland" as a place of "slander and scare, of sly innuendo, of a poison pen, the anonymous phone call, and hustling, pushing, shoving—the land of smash and grab and anything to win."

Nixon's initial appointments deserve mixed reviews. His tough, partisan side was reflected in his choice of John Mitchell, his former New York law associate, as attorney general. His inner White House circle was dominated by people who placed loyalty to their chief above all other considerations. White House chief of staff, H. R. Haldeman, was a rigid right-winger. A powerful force in the Nixon administration, he guarded his chief from all contact with people who disagreed with administration policy. Chief White House adviser on domestic affairs was John Ehrlichman, a former Seattle lawyer. Both men agreed with Nixon that in politics anything goes; that winning was all that counted. They also shared with their boss a deep suspicion of the "eastern establishment," a vaguely defined circle of elite liberal leaders who, they believed, dominated the press, the universities, and the upper reaches of the professions and American business.

Among Nixon's advisers there was also another side, however. Daniel Moynihan, assistant for urban affairs, was one of the more imaginative men in American political life. Henry Kissinger, Nixon's national security adviser and later secretary of state, though he harbored a streak of deviousness, was an unusually adept diplomat with a vision influenced by his deep knowledge of history. Other competent men whom Nixon would appoint to high office included treasury secretary John Connolly and Secretary of Defense Melvin Laird. Unfortunately, the inner circle of White House aides under Haldeman and Ehrlichman—men without wide experience of elective office and government—often exerted disproportionate influence on administration policy.

Détente. Nixon was far more interested in foreign policy than in domestic affairs; it was as an international statesman that he hoped to make his mark in history. Foremost, he and Kissinger sought to stabilize relations with the Soviet Union by a policy called *détente*. Unfortunately, détente had no precise limits, and many Americans, eager to end the anxieties of the Cold War, were quick to believe that superpower rivalry might be ended once and for all.

However commendable their goals, the Nixon–Kissinger diplomatic style disturbed many observers. Kissinger believed in secret "back channel" negotiations with foreign representatives that bypassed the State Department. Although he was at first only the president's national security adviser, Kissinger, rather than Secretary of State William Rogers, was the chief foreign-policy maker. All too often the State Department head, the cabinet officer officially responsible for directing foreign affairs, was treated as little more than a high-level bureaucrat capable only of shuffling diplomatic papers. This awkward situation was rectified in 1973 when the German-born Kissinger became Rogers' successor.

However ill-defined, the Nixon–Kissinger policy made substantial progress toward reducing superpower tensions. During the summer of 1969 American prestige had soared when astronaut Neil A. Armstrong took the first step on the moon while millions around the world watched the momentous event on television. Soon after, Nixon visited the Soviet Balkan satellite, Rumania. As he rode through the streets of Bucharest, the American president was wildly cheered by large crowds. In November 1969 Nixon and Soviet president Nikolai Podgorny signed the Nuclear Nonproliferation Treaty with sixty other nations. Those countries possessing nuclear weapons pledged not to transfer them to other nations. The nonnuclear nations promised to refrain from developing such weapons. In 1971 and 1972 the perennial problems of Berlin and the two Germanies was finally settled by the Berlin Accord: Britain, France, the United States, and the Soviet Union agreed to cease threatening communications between Berlin and West Germany. They also formally recognized the existence of two separate German nations, the Federal Republic (West Germany) and the Democratic People's Republic (East Germany).

Another major step in the détente process came in May 1972, when Nixon visited the Soviet Union, the first American president ever to do so. The visit produced a series of agreements pledging the two nations to improve commercial relations and cooperate in science, medical, and environmental pursuits. It also led to the signing of the SALT I (Strategic Arms Limitation Treaty), negotiated over several years by the two powers. SALT I limited defensive antiballistic missile systems and the number of offensive missiles each country might deploy. The world was still a long way from nuclear disarmament; all that the superpowers had accepted was a slowing down of the arms race. But millions around the world applauded when SALT I was ratified by the U.S. Senate in 1972 with relatively little opposition.

The People's Republic of China. Even more remarkable than détente with the Soviet Union was the breakthrough in relations with the People's Republic of China. Until Nixon became president, the United States had treated Communist China as an outcast. It had refused to recognize the Chinese mainland regime and had vetoed every attempt to admit it to the United Nations. As far as the United States was concerned, China was the Republic of China on Taiwan where Chiang Kai-shek's Nationalists had fled after the Communist mainland victory in 1949 and created a prosperous if authoritarian regime. American troops were sta-

Nixon, John Erlichman, and Arthur Burns, the president's economic advisor, shown in a rather glum moment.

tioned on Taiwan to provide military support if the Chinese Communists should ever attempt to invade the island of Taiwan.

The situation was peculiar. Good reason existed to dislike the regime in Beijing. Communist methods were often brutal. Following the civil war against the Nationalists, the Communists had killed thousands as class enemies and, during the so-called Cultural Revolution of the 1960s, had let loose a reign of anarchy intended to purge the nation of all non-Communist elements. The new regime, on the other hand, had also freed China of the worst of the economic misery of the past and had forged a functioning, if repressive, social order on the mainland. China, with its 800 million people, was clearly a major power, and its existence could not be wished away.

Not only was America's China Policy unrealistic; it was also harmful to this country's interests. Although his enemies accused him of being a crude anti-Communist ideologue, Nixon recognized that world Communist unity was a myth. China and the Soviet Union, though once closely allied, were now, since Stalin's death, adversaries. Each nation was suspicious of the other, and periodically Soviet and Chinese military forces clashed along their long common border in Asia. It seemed foolish not to take advantage of the Sino-Soviet rift and use one Communist nation to check the goals and ambitions of the other. Indeed, an opening to China seemed an essential ingredient of achieving stable relations with the Soviet Union.

Soon after the 1968 presidential elections, the Red Chinese indicated to Nixon their desire to smooth over Sino-American differences. Before long both countries were holding secret meetings in Warsaw. Early in 1971 the Chinese invited an American Ping-Pong team visiting Japan to tour the country and play Chinese teams. In July 1971, Nixon startled the world by announcing that he had been invited to visit the People's Republic of China and would go there sometime in the early part of the following year. In October, the United States for the first time abstained from vetoing the admission of Red China to the United Nations. The Beijing government was promptly seated and the Taiwan regime's representatives expelled.

Not all Americans liked what was taking place. To the far right the reconciliation with Red China and abandonment of Taiwan seemed a surrender to communism. Most Americans, however, accepted the move as sensible and long overdue. Many of Nixon's liberal critics noted ruefully that it could only have been carried off by a conservative with a reputation as a militant anti-Communist.

On February 21, 1972 Nixon, his wife, and a large presidential entourage arrived in Beijing by plane. Scores of American reporters and the TV media were present, and millions of viewers in the United States watched the American president shake hands with Premier Chou En-lai. The discussions that followed with Chou and Communist party chairman Mao Tse-tung, China's aging top leader, were largely exploratory; little of a concrete nature was accomplished except for an agreement to withdraw American troops from Taiwan. Much of the Nixons' time was spent in sightseeing and banqueting. But the meeting was momentous symbolically. Television pictures of Nixon toasting Chou, quoting chairman Mao, and strolling along the Great Wall made clear to the American people that the policy of ignoring the world's most populous nation was finally ended.

Richard Nixon never did have laugh lines around his mouth. Even an occasion such as this toast with Chou En-lai during his 1972 trip to China did not seem to cheer him up.

"Peace With Honor." The worst of the foreign policy past, however, still held on in Vietnam. Nixon came into office when the war appeared to be winding down. In March 1968 Johnson had vetoed any further American troops for Vietnam. The next month, following his decision to stop the bombing of North Vietnam, peace talks between North Vietnam and the United States opened in Paris. Months of controversy over

In May 1970 Ohio National guardsmen who had been called in to quell disorder on the campus of Ohio State University fired on protesting students. Four students died, and the university became a byword among those who opposed the Vietnam War.

seating the Vietcong followed, and not until January 1969, just days before Johnson left office, did serious peace talks begin. The war continued, however. The North Vietnamese had no intention of abandoning their goal of reuniting Vietnam under their firm control and pursued the policy of "fighting while negotiating."

The new American administration had no interest in continuing the war. Nixon at one point declared: "I'm not going to end up like LBJ, holed up in the White House afraid to show my face on the street. I'm going to stop that war. Fast." But, like his predecessor, the president also wanted to avoid the charge that he had "lost" South Vietnam to the Communists. America must somehow disengage, but it must preserve an independent South Vietnam to keep its reputation and pride intact. Nixon called this "peace with honor;" his critics called it foolish, among other things.

Nixon resolved to use every means to force the North Vietnamese to accept a compromise position. At one point, to intimidate the Hanoi government, he spread the view that he was a Communist-obsessed nuclear madman capable of blowing up the world if he did not get his way. In March 1969, he secretly ordered the massive bombing of Cambodia—a suppos-

edly neutral nation—to hamper Communist operations in South Vietnam. At the same time, however, he announced that the United States would adopt the policy of "Vietnamization": It would gradually shift military responsibility to the South Vietnamese, and begin to withdraw American combat troops.

The militant antiwar forces at home refused to believe that Nixon intended to withdraw. The president talked peace, they said, but the fighting and dying continued. America should leave immediately. "Out Now" was the only valid policy. Then, in late April 1970, the president sent American forces on a sweep through Cambodia to attack bases, which, he claimed, were refuges for Vietcong guerrillas. This apparent escalation of the fighting electrified the antiwar movement. In response, protest demonstrations erupted on scores of college campuses. At one of these, Kent State University in Ohio, national guardsmen fired live ammunition at student antiwar demonstrators killing four and wounding eleven. This attack seemed to confirm every radical charge of government repression and brutality. Hundreds of American campuses shut down to protest the Kent State killings and to allow students to mobilize against the detested war. In June, Congress itself reacted to the new antiwar surge by repealing the 1964 Gulf of Tonkin resolution that Johnson had used as a legal equivalent of a declaration of war.

By now even many of the government's Cold War experts were convinced that the war was evil. In June 1971, Daniel Ellsberg, a former Pentagon official, made public a collection of stolen classified documents describing the slow steps to American entrapment in the Vietnam morass and the deception of the public that accompanied the escalation. The Justice Department indicted Ellsberg and tried to get publication of the "Pentagon Papers" in *The New York Times* legally stopped. The move failed. A still worse sign of growing discontent was the deteriorating morale of American soldiers in the field. While Vietnamization steadily reduced the number of fighting men, it damaged the spirits of those who remained. What was the point of risking one's life in a war that was winding down? More and more combat troops sought to avoid risks. They disobeyed orders or "fragged" officers by rolling live hand grenades into their tents while they slept. Others turned to drugs to make the time till their tour of duty ended pass more quickly. Even supporters of American Vietnam policy began to fear that the war was destroying the American military.

In 1972, with only a few thousand American combat troops remaining in South Vietnam, the Communists launched a major offensive to destroy the Saigon government led by Nguyen Van Thieu. Unwilling to allow them a military victory, Nixon ordered the resumption of massive bombing of North Vietnam and the mining of Haiphong harbor, the port of entry for most of the arms and supplies from the Soviet Union. It looked as if the escalation pattern of the past would be repeated once more. Fortunately, by this time, both the Chinese and the Russians were more anxious for better relations with the United States than for North Vietnamese good will, and they told Hanoi that it must act more reasonably. Meanwhile, the Saigon government, reassured by a billion dollar gift of American military hardware to help it defend itself against a Communist takeover, also proved more amenable to negotiation.

These events finally broke the Paris peace talks logjam. In January 1973 the United States, South Vietnam, and the Vietcong–North Vietnamese signed an agreement to end the fighting. The document provided for the release of all American prisoners of war, a cease-fire between Hanoi and Saigon, the withdrawal of all remaining U.S. military personnel, massive American economic aid to South Vietnam, and a flock of complicated arrangements intended to reconcile the South Vietnamese government and the Vietcong. Nixon and Kissinger claimed that this agreement would preserve the separate existence of South Vietnam. Whether they believed this is not clear, but in any case it did not. By April 1975, Communist forces had overwhelmed the Saigon government and occupied all of Vietnam, forcibly uniting the North and South under their control—their goal for thirty years.

The war was over, but at immense cost to all participants. Vietnam was devastated—physically, economically, socially. Millions of Vietnamese had died; over 46,000 American soldiers had lost their lives. At home the war had left a bad taste in everyone's mouth. At first those who had opposed the war could boast that their efforts had helped end the killing and destruction and replaced a repressive government with a more popular one. It soon became clear, however, that the Hanoi government was as benighted as its enemies had long charged and that the people of South Vietnam would be worse off than before. The North Vietnamese conquerors rounded up thousands of the Saigon regime's friends and sent them to forced labor or "reeducation" camps. Over 1.4 million refugees fled the country, many in small boats. Thousands settled in the United States. In early 1978 the Vietnamese attacked Cambodia, precipitating an inconclusive war with China. Today Vietnam remains one of the poorest, most backward nations in all of East Asia, an embarrassment to all who supported its struggle to win control over the south.

Those people who had cheered the American cause in Vietnam could extract little more satisfaction from the result. The war seemed to demonstrate the nation's impotence: It was the first war that America had lost, and it undermined the nation's confidence in itself.

Finally, the war's ambiguous outcome would also color the debate over future American foreign policy. Some citizens would see Vietnam as a lesson in limits: The United States could not expect to police events everywhere; it must confine its role to matters that affected its vital interests closer to home. Others would view it as an instance of how defeat would inevitably follow loss of nerve and confidence. For a time the first group would predominate, and during the mid-1970s American foreign policy would enter a phase that observers called neo-isolationist.

Courting the Backlash Vote. In domestic affairs Nixon looked two ways. In part, he acted as the agent for reversing the social and political trends of the 1960s. His 1968 election campaign had been based on the idea that there was a "silent majority," mostly composed of nominal Democrats who were fed up with many of the social trends of the day. If the Republicans emphasized the social issues over the bread-and-butter ones, the silent majority's disgust could be used to forge a new and unbeatable Republican majority.

The theory was politically sound. Since the late sixties a backlash—a powerful negative reaction—to that decade's social and political liberalism had been emerging. Angry backlash voters, generally middle-aged and white, felt that traditional institutions and values were being destroyed. Many were "ethnics," the children and grandchildren of the immigrants of the 1880–1920 period, who believed that the government was showing the sort of favoritism toward blacks that their own forebears had never experienced. Others were old stock white Protestants, particularly well represented in the South and West, who feared the collapse of traditional Christian morality under the assault of the counterculture, drug abusers, and sexual outsiders. Backlash voters were dismayed by rock music, long hair, "pot," and sexual permissiveness. They were usually committed patriots who suspected the antiwar forces of disloyalty, and they considered student activists spoiled brats who deserved to be spanked. They feared the street violence of the cities and were appalled by the "porn shops" and X-rated movies that had sprung up in urban areas. They were skeptical of the new, assertive feminism that seemed to deny gender differences and to blame men for all of women's misfortunes. Backlash voters were incensed, too, by Supreme Court decisions to protect the rights of accused criminals (*Miranda* v. *Arizona*), to forbid school prayer (*Engel* v. *Vitale*), to bus school children for "racial balance" (*Swann* v. *Charlotte-Mecklenburg Board*), and to permit abortion during the first trimester of pregnancy (*Roe* v. *Wade*). All these seemed major assaults on their values and way of life.

Nixon and his advisers found many backlash views personally congenial. Administration officials wore American flag pins on their lapels and cultivated a reverent attitude toward traditional American values. The backlash also promised to be political gold, and in 1969 the Nixon people set out to woo all "middle Americans," whether Democrats or Republicans. The president and vice president made themselves spokesmen for backlash views. Campus radicals, Nixon declared, were "bums." As for crime and disorder, ordinary citizens, he said—raising his hand to his neck—"have had it up to here." Vice President Spiro Agnew ranged the nation denouncing "rad-libs," the "nattering nabobs of negativism," and "troglodytic leftists."

Not everyone loved Vice President Spiro Agnew. But "hard hats," blue collar workers who resented antiwar and civil rights activists and campus militants, made him their hero.

"The disease of our time," he said, "is an artificial and masochistic sophistication—the vague uneasiness that our values are false, and there is something wrong with being patriotic, honest, moral and hard-working."

The campaign to restore pre-sixties values was more than rhetorical. Following the president's lead, federal officials eased up on the enforcement of desegregation processes in the South. In March 1971 Nixon asked Congress to halt "forced busing" of children from neighborhood schools to more distant ones to achieve racial balance. In April he directed veterans' hospitals to cease abortions for ex-service women. The president frequently called for "law and order" and sponsored numerous bills and measures to strengthen the hand of judges and the police. Nixon and his advisers believed, as had Johnson, that antiwar and New Left dissenters were encouraging the Vietcong and the North Vietnamese to continue their fight. They cracked down hard. During a May 1970 antiwar march on Washington, Attorney General Mitchell threw thousands of demonstrators into jail and detention compounds. The Justice Department indicted scores of pacifists and student activists for crimes of conspiracy to commit crimes. The defendants won most of these cases, but the legal defenses depleted the energies and financial resources of the antiwar movement.

Unlike Republicans in the past, Nixon looked for support to the white, formerly solid Democratic South. During the 1968 Republican convention he had promised conservative Dixie leaders to defer to traditional white southern feelings and wishes in regard to appointments, and after the election he tried to keep his word. In early 1969 he nominated Judge Clement F. Haynsworth, Jr., of South Carolina to the U.S. Supreme Court. The Democratically controlled Senate was anxious to preserve recent civil rights gains. When it discovered that Haynsworth had officiated in cases in which he had a personal financial interest, it used this as the basis for rejecting his nomination. Nixon then sent forward the name of Florida federal judge G. Harrold Carswell. Antilabor and racially conservative, the new nominee was a man whose decisions had frequently been reversed by higher courts. The Senate rejected this appointment too. Nixon eventually succeeded in getting confirmed another conservative, Harry Blackmun. Blackmun was a northerner, but the president's efforts on behalf of southerners Haynsworth and Carswell were appreciated by conservative white voters in Dixie.

Nixon helped to slow the movement for social change. The student revolt subsided; the hippies gradually disappeared; antiwar protest did not last much beyond 1973. Still, the results did not satisfy backlash voters. Drug abuse reached into the high schools of suburban America, teenage pregnancies soared, crime and disorder spread, and movies and books continued to deal with sexually explicit themes. Backlash voters would remain dissatisfied, and would continue to search for ways to restore the nation to old-fashioned virtue.

Yet Nixon did not send the American ship of state into full reverse. Those who had hoped that a Republican president would decrease the size and power of the federal government were disappointed. The president was also not as much a rigid small-government fiscal conservative as his opponents believed. In 1970 he signed into law the Water Quality Improvement Act, the Occupational Safety Act, and the Clean Air Act. He also endorsed the welfare reform proposals of Daniel Moynihan to provide a $1,600-a-year minimum income to each poor family. Many Great Society programs continued and, in fact, achieved higher funding levels than before. In 1968, federal social welfare expenditures totaled $142 billion; in 1974 they reached $229 billion. Nixon was also willing to intervene forcefully into the economy when it suited his purposes. To deal with soaring prices in 1971–72, on the eve of the presidential election campaign, he imposed tight federal wage and price controls.

The 1972 Election. Whatever the reservations of the far right, it was clear as the 1972 election approached that the Nixon-Agnew team would get its mandate renewed handily for another four years. As he and his advisers had hoped, the president had succeeded in aligning most of the nation's social and political conservatives with the GOP. The Democrats, on the other hand, seemed still to be captives of the "new politics" forces that had arisen in the 1960s. Their candidate for president was Senator George McGovern of South Dakota, a leader representing the party's most liberal wing. McGovern won the nomination under new convention rules requiring each state delegation to reflect separate voter blocs—youth, women, minorities, as well as white males—in approximate proportion to their numbers in the general populace. The Democratic delegates at Miami were a far better cross section of the country's citizens than in past conventions, but many traditional Democrats—white southerners, blue-collar Catholics, older people, trade unionists—felt left out. It soon appeared that many of them either would not vote or would vote Republican.

A more effective campaigner than McGovern might have reunited his party after the convention, but the senator proved to be inept. He selected Senator Thomas Eagleton of Missouri as his running mate without a careful background check. When Eagleton admitted that he had been hospitalized for mental illness, McGovern first rallied to Eagleton's side and then dropped him for former Peace Corps director Sargent Shriver. The Democratic candidate also stumbled over his welfare reform plan, revealing his own uncertain grasp of a guaranteed annual income scheme that many found extravagant. By early fall the polls were pointing to a Democratic disaster.

With the Democrats obviously fumbling away the election, Nixon could avoid the political rough-and-tumble and act "presidential." By fall the economy was firmly in hand under phase one of Nixon's wage and price control program. The GNP was up; unemployment and inflation were down. The results were predictable. Nixon won 60.8 percent of the popular vote, a tiny fraction below Lyndon Johnson's 1964 landslide, and all the nation's electoral votes except those of the District of Columbia and Massachusetts.

Watergate

The mandate was one of the most stunning on record, and it appeared that Nixon was set for four more years of impressive achievement. It was not to be. On June 17, 1972, almost six months before the election, five men had been arrested at the Washington, D.C., headquarters of the Democratic National Committee in the Watergate housing–office complex; two other accomplices were caught outside. All seven, it was revealed, had been attempting to spy electronically on the Democrats.

Although one of the accused was James W. McCord, Jr., a security consultant to the Committee to Reelect the President (CRP), and two others had White House connections, no information damaging to the administration came to light before the election. When questioned by reporters in mid-June, White House press secretary Ron Ziegler called the Watergate break-in a "third-rate burglary" that had nothing to do with the administration. McGovern struggled to make a campaign issue of Watergate, but in the end he could prove little. The public and the press ignored his charges, and Watergate did not affect the outcome. Then, by the time of Nixon's second inauguration, the story behind the break-in began to emerge. As the media revealed the facts, the president's reputation and the fate of his administration sank like a stone.

In January 1973 the seven accused Watergate burglars faced federal District Court Judge John Sirica. Though a lifelong Republican and a Nixon supporter, Sirica aggressively grilled the defendants himself. If they cooperated with Senator Sam Ervin Jr.'s Senate Select Committee, recently appointed to investigate the Watergate affair, he would consider leniency. Under this pressure McCord soon revealed to the Ervin committee investigators that the president's counsel, John Dean, and Jeb Magruder, of the CRP staff, were both involved in Watergate. Before long the rush to secure immunity by confessing to the United States attorney threatened to become a stampede.

Early in April both Dean and Magruder began to tell the federal prosecutors all they knew, disclosing that Haldeman, Ehrlichman, and Mitchell had tried to hide the administration's role in the break-in. In effect, three of Nixon's closest associates were seeking to obstruct justice, a clearly indictable crime. On April 30, the president learned that Dean intended to accuse him of attempting to hide the administration's responsibility for Watergate. At this point Nixon announced that he had accepted the resignations of Haldeman, Ehrlichman, and Attorney General Richard Kleindienst, and had fired Dean. He also directed the new attorney general, Elliot Richardson, to appoint a special prosecutor to probe Watergate. Richardson named Archibald Cox of the Harvard Law School to fill the post.

John Dean, on the far right, with his blonde wife just behind him, spills the beans to the Ervin Committee. The president, he said, had been party to a cover-up for eight months.

Early Disclosures. When the Ervin committee opened its televised hearings in May 1973, viewers watched a steady parade of witnesses who revealed the administration's disreputable efforts, through CRP (called CREEP by the unfriendly media), to crush its political opponents and illegally hide its acts. Other judicial agencies and the press, led by the *Washington Post* reporters Bob Woodward and Carl Bernstein, exposed other horrendous misdeeds.

The list of actions eventually uncovered—actions that violated civil liberties, broke the laws governing political financing, and undermined respect for the law and the political process—was a long one. Watergate began as part of a "plumbers" operation financed by CRP to "plug" information leaks perceived as damaging to the administration. But it soon ballooned far beyond this.

> Administration operatives had broken into the office of Daniel Ellsberg's psychiatrist, looking for evidence to use against him in his trial for leaking the classified Pentagon Papers.
>
> Ehrlichman had sought to influence the presiding judge in the Ellsberg case by hinting to him that he might be appointed FBI director. (The White House effort backfired; when the attempt to suborn the judge came out, charges against Ellsberg were dismissed.)
>
> White House representatives had paid large sums of cash to the Watergate burglars after they were arrested to keep them silent on the connection between the break-in and CRP.
>
> Acting director of the FBI, L. Patrick Gray, had destroyed evidence in the Watergate case. The FBI had also shared information from its Watergate investigation with White House counsel Dean, though the White House itself was clearly the target of the investigation.
>
> The Nixon reelection committee had engaged in "dirty tricks" to disrupt the campaigns of several Democratic candidates during the 1972 primaries.
>
> CRP had collected large sums of cash from corporations with promises of favors, or threats of retaliation, in violation of federal law, and had then tried to conceal it.
>
> The White House had drawn up an "enemies list" of administration adversaries in the media, the universities, and the entertainment world. These people were to be harassed by Internal Revenue Service audits and by other means.
>
> One of the Watergate burglars, E. Howard Hunt, had forged State Department messages to implicate the late President John F. Kennedy in the assassination of Vietnamese leader Ngo Dinh Diem. This

was designed to besmirch the reputation of President Kennedy's brother, Ted, a potential Nixon presidential rival.

> The administration, in its suspicious way, had engaged in illegal wiretapping, even of its own officials, to ferret out national security and political leaks.
>
> The president himself had taken dubious tax breaks for contributing his personal papers to the Library of Congress and had used federal funds to make improvements on his personal homes in Florida and California.

The most telling testimony before the Ervin committee came from John Dean, who claimed that the president had known of the illegal break-in for eight months and had tried to cover it up, even offering executive clemency to the burglars if they would keep quiet. But Dean's testimony could not be corroborated. Then, on July 16, Alexander Butterfield, a former presidential assistant, revealed that since 1971 all conversations in the president's Oval Office and in the Executive Office Building had been taped, and all the president's phones had been linked to recording devices. Now, everything that John Dean and others had disclosed in their testimony could be checked against the actual record.

The president immediately tried to block access to the tapes. For a full year, until the Supreme Court announced its crucial decision against him on July 24, 1974, his lawyers asserted that "executive privilege," needed to preserve the president's freedom of action, permitted him to keep the tapes of vital White House conversations confidential.

When the Ervin committee hearings concluded, the burden of uncovering the remaining truth of the break-in and alleged coverup shifted to special prosecutor Archibald Cox. In July, Cox subpoenaed nine tapes. Nixon refused to surrender them, and Cox went before Judge Sirica to demand that they be produced. In late August, Sirica ordered Nixon to comply. The president's lawyers promptly appealed to the District of Columbia Circuit Court, which upheld Sirica's order.

Nixon Fights Back. On October 20, 1973, Nixon ordered Attorney General Richardson to fire Cox. Richardson refused, as did his deputy, and both resigned. Solicitor General Robert Bork, now acting attorney general, finally performed the deed.

This "Saturday Night Massacre" produced a storm of criticism. The White House was deluged with telegrams denouncing the president and his actions. *Time* magazine, a conservative journal, in the first formal editorial in its fifty-year history declared "the President should resign." Even prominent Republicans began to wonder out loud whether Nixon would not have to go. On October 30 the House Judiciary Committee began to consider impeachment charges against him.

Taken aback by this ferocious reaction, Nixon retreated. On October 23 he agreed to obey Sirica's order to deliver the tapes. On November 1 he appointed a new special prosecutor, Leon Jaworski, a conservative Texas attorney. But then the president's lawyers revealed that two of the tapes requested did not exist and that another, of a crucial June conversation with Dean, contained an 18-minute gap as the result of an "accidental" erasure. By this time few Americans believed anything the president said, and most doubted that the erasure had been an accident.

Meanwhile, Vice President Agnew was having his own troubles with the law. Accused of income tax evasion and of accepting payoffs for favors to contractors when he was governor of Maryland, he resigned from office on October 10, 1973. Immediately after, under terms of the recently adopted 25th Amendment to the Constitution, Nixon nominated House Minority Leader Gerald Ford of Michigan as his successor. Ford took the oath of office on December 6, 1973, as the new vice president. Now, if Watergate did force Nixon out, the country would at least have an honest man as his successor.

Impeachment. Other bombshells soon went off. In late April 1974, in response to a subpoena from the House Judiciary Committee, Nixon released 1,200 pages of edited transcripts of White House tapes. This was the public's first glimpse of what the president and his advisers had actually been saying and doing about Watergate. The view was appalling. The transcripts revealed Nixon as a profane, confused, and bilious man, willing to use any tack against his enemies and prone to mean-spirited and bigoted remarks. Worse than this, several conversations seemed to confirm his role in abetting a coverup.

On May 1 the House Judiciary Committee denied that the release of the edited transcripts constituted full compliance with its subpoena. Jaworski's office had also subpoenaed tapes, and on May 20 Judge Sirica ordered Nixon once more to comply. The president's counsel appealed his decision to the Supreme Court.

That summer matters came to a head. First, the Supreme Court unanimously ruled that Nixon must release all the tapes asked for by Jaworski. For reasons that would soon become clear, Nixon resisted the

Court's order, but then relented. The process of transcribing the tapes began. On July 24 the Judiciary Committee began televised debates on articles of impeachment. A few days later it voted to recommend to the full House of Representatives three articles of impeachment: (1) that Nixon had obstructed justice by his role in the Watergate coverup; (2) that he had misused federal agencies in violation of the rights of American citizens; and (3) that he had withheld information subpoenaed by the House Judiciary Committee. On August 5, 1974, Nixon released transcripts of three talks between him and Haldeman recorded on June 4, 1972, a scant week after the break-in. The tapes showed that the president clearly had conspired to obstruct justice. Here was the "smoking gun" that could not be explained away, and Nixon's remaining congressional supporters, including Senator Barry Goldwater, now abandoned him. Facing almost certain impeachment by the full House, he resigned as president on August 8 effective at noon the next day. On August 9, 1974, Gerald Ford took the oath of office as the new president.

Causes and Effects. The Watergate crisis had its roots in a complex set of circumstances. To Nixon's combative and suspicious personality must be added the growth of presidential power since the New Deal. Nixon twisted executive powers granted FDR and his successors to deal with the Great Depression, World War II, and the Cold War, and used them crudely against his political enemies. These powers, visibly manifested in the squads of planes, helicopters, limousines, and other trappings of "an imperial presidency," increased the influence and power of the executive at the expense of the other branches of government. The administration, moreover, confused itself with the American government itself. This position made it possible to see its political opponents as national traitors entitled to no consideration. Nixon and his advisers were also victims of the paranoid Cold War mentality that at times excused unacceptable activities if done for the sake of "national security." By the early 1970s, for example, the FBI and CIA had grown into semiautonomous fiefdoms that collected vast files on private citizens considered disloyal, opened private mail, and engaged in dirty tricks operations of its own against suspected subversives. In such an atmosphere it is no wonder that the White House itself should adopt a no-holds-barred attitude toward its opponents.

The postmortems on Watergate would vary widely. Some Americans saw reasons for optimism in the outcome of Watergate. The "system had worked," they said; the villains had been caught and punished, and honest, constitutional government had been restored. Others were not so sure. Nixon had, after all, been reelected in a landslide and might easily have gotten away with it all if a very few lucky events had happened differently. Many Americans could not avoid feeling more cynical than ever about the honesty of politicians and more skeptical about the effectiveness of the nation's political system.

One thing that is clear is that Watergate ended whatever hope remained that Nixon would turn back the clock politically. Those voters who had believed that Nixon would lead the country back to traditional values felt bitterly betrayed. Liberals felt joy that "Tricky Dick" had got his comeuppance.

The Ford Interlude. America's only nonelected president, Gerald Ford, assumed office at a time when the nation desperately craved an end to distrust and uncertainty. Ford seemed the right man to start the healing process. A stolid legislator who had served in the House of Representatives for many years without special distinction, he was nevertheless an open, decent, and generous man who most Americans quickly got to like.

The public's respect for Ford the man was not, however, matched by its view of Ford the president. Physically awkward and a wooden speaker, Ford squandered much of the public's trust at the start of his presidency by granting a pardon to Nixon, thereby cutting off any further legal action against the ex-president. Though in his remarks announcing the pardon Ford emphasized personal compassion toward Nixon and his determination to end the controversy and distrust caused by Watergate, many people suspected that there had been an agreement made between the two men at the time of Nixon's resignation and that the pardon was part of the deal.

In foreign affairs, the area where his predecessor had achieved the most, Ford continued the initiatives of the recent past, retaining Kissinger as secretary of state and continuing to push détente. Gradually, however, high hopes for mutually advantageous arrangements with the Soviet Union dissipated. Soviet-American cultural exchanges helped dispel Cold War views that Russians personally were ogres, but Soviet violations of its own citizens' rights and mistreatment of its Jewish population offset such gains. Besides, the Soviet Union seemed determined to pursue its expansionist ends through surrogates. When, for example, the African nation of Angola, newly independent from Portugal, collapsed into civil war, Soviet-armed Cuban troops supported the Angolan Marxist's drive to take control.

In domestic affairs Ford was even less successful. In response to a serious business recession following the spectacular hike in oil prices that accompanied the fourth Arab-Israeli war in 1973, he endorsed a tax cut and sought lower interest rates. By the fall of 1975 national output began once more to rise, but large pockets of unemployment remained.

In his early months as president, Ford had shown little interest in running for a full term. But as he settled into the job, he changed his mind and announced his candidacy for the 1976 election. By the bicentennial year the economy was recovering and he could count on good economic news to help his campaign.

The 1976 Election. Ford supporters in 1976 believed the president deserved a vote of confidence for having restored Americans' faith in their government. But the bad smell of Watergate lingered on with many Americans convinced that Washington was tightly controlled by wheeler-dealers and politicians on the take. Even the president, though personally liked, seemed tainted by the supposed "deal" with his predecessor.

The public's disgust with the "mess in Washington" helped the nomination campaigns of two outsiders, Ronald Reagan of California and Jimmy Carter of Georgia. Reagan, a former Hollywood actor turned conservative politician, had been an effective governor of California. He had placed his conservatism aside when necessary and compromised with his opponents to get things done. Carter was an Annapolis graduate who, after a stint in the navy, had grown peanuts in Georgia and served a single term as his state's governor. A "born-again" Baptist, his record marked him as a fair-minded man who, unlike many southern politicians of the past, hoped to end the South's racial conflicts and reduce discrimination against blacks. Neither candidate had served in Congress or the executive branch of the federal government nor had they any significant experience in foreign affairs. Both, accordingly, could claim to be untouched by the dirt that besmirched Washington insiders.

Despite the Reagan challenge, Ford got the Republican nomination at Kansas City and selected Senator Robert Dole of Kansas as his running mate. Carter won the Democratic nomination on the first ballot in New York and balanced his ticket by choosing as his partner Senator Walter Mondale of Minnesota, a liberal and a close former associate of Hubert Humphrey.

In November, the support of black voters and white southerners, along with traditional Catholic and Jewish voters, helped carry the Carter-Mondale ticket to victory. At the time many observers saw the Carter-Mondale vote as a reassembly of the old New Deal coalition, and a return of the voters to a more liberal outlook. It now seems clear that it was a special case of post-Watergate disgust with the Republicans added to a temporary revival of the "solid South," which was determined to elect the only southerner since before the Civil War to win a major party nomination (if we except Lyndon Johnson, a Texan).

Seventies' Discontents

Carter had his work cut out for him. The nation he would lead was one buffeted by cross-currents, uncertainties, and uncomfortable challenges to its self-confidence and its leading position in the free world.

The celebration of the two-hundredth anniversary of American independence on July 4, 1976, was symbolic of the public's insecurities and hesitations. There had been much talk as the date approached of a major international exposition at Philadelphia or some other large city to proclaim, as a century before,

America's achievements to all the world. It proved impossible to bring off such a celebration. The America of 1976 was far richer than in 1876, but many people lacked the easy confidence in the political and economic future that prevailed a century earlier. The bitterness of Vietnam lingered, and thousands of antiwar movement veterans doubted that America had much to boast about. Spokespersons for blacks, Indians, and other minorities insisted that they, the perennial outsiders, had scant reason to celebrate 200 years of nationhood. The country, of course, did not let the day go unmarked. In New York City a fleet of sailing ships from all over the world drew throngs of spectators to the harbor and banks of the Hudson River. Millions more watched "the tall ships" on television. In San Antonio a longhorn cattle drive, commemorating the days of the Texas cattle trails, was the celebration centerpiece. In Washington, D.C., half a million people watched a parade down Pennsylvania Avenue. Other communities had their own moving ways of commemorating the great event. But all told, it seemed primarily a party by the white middle class mainstream, with millions of others standing on the sidelines.

Blacks and Hispanics. As the 1970s began their downward slope, the predominant mood among black

New York City, of course, was not the only community to celebrate the bicentennial of independence. But as the nation's biggest city and its media center, its "tall ships" got the most attention.

Americans was one of disappointment. The previous decade had promised so much and, in truth, some of it had been achieved. Legal segregation was dead. Nowhere could the law be used to bolster exclusion of blacks from public places or services or to enforce separation of the races. Even in the South blacks voted without restraint and were becoming a force to be reckoned with in southern politics. By the early eighties, in many big cities—Cleveland, Chicago, Washington, D.C., Los Angeles, Philadelphia, and Atlanta—the mayors would be black.

There had also been sweeping economic and social advances for black Americans. The number of black college students, for example, had risen from 141,000 in 1960 to 718,000 in 1980, a shift from about 6 percent of enrollments to almost 10 percent. Black median family income had grown from $3230 in 1960 to $12,674 in 1980. Yet the picture was at best mixed. The gains since 1960 had not ended black poverty; nor had they eliminated the differences between black and white family incomes. At the end of the 1970s the average black family was still only 60 percent as rich as its average white counterpart.

A new disturbing feature of the racial picture was the appearance of a two-tier black social structure. By 1980 there was a new black middle class of professionals, government workers, skilled white-collar employees, and business managers. But at the same time there was an expanding "underclass" of ghetto-dwellers who seemed stuck in the groove of poverty, welfare, drug dependence, and—at times—crime.

Many sociologists believed that family structure was the key causative factor in producing this result. The black middle class derived from intact, two-parent families, they said; the black underclass was composed of mothers without husbands—many of them mere teenagers—and their young children. Since the 1960s single-parent, female-headed families had grown disproportionately. Teenage illegitimacy was rampant in the United States generally. But the phenomenon was more extreme among blacks than any other group. In such families the processes of nurture and social conditioning necessary for producing self-confident and competent young people were apparently absent, and these circumstances fostered successive generations of citizens who were unable to cope with jobs or their own lives and who were chronically dependent on social welfare services.

Unfortunately, no one knew for certain why the black underclass had grown. Some observers blamed it on the welfare system. It encouraged dependency, they said. Some blamed it on the breakdown of family values. That was why presumably so many young women were willing to engage in premarital relations and why they became pregnant. Others attributed it to black underclass cultural values that accepted illegitimacy and welfare dependency without serious qualms. Some pointed the finger at the disappearance of unskilled and semiskilled work that consigned many young black men to unemployment and made them unwilling or unable to support the families they created. Whatever the reasons, by the 1980s single-parent families had become the chief locus of poverty for all families, but especially for black ones.

Hispanic Americans, by and large, improved their lot during the 1970s, though they too remained behind in most measures of well-being and progress. During the decade their numbers increased enormously, both absolutely and proportionally. By 1980 over 14.5 million Americans identified themselves as of "Hispanic" origins, an increase of 61 percent for the decade. The states with the largest number were California, Texas, New York, Florida, New Jersey, and New Mexico.

Many Hispanics, including all Puerto Ricans, were American citizens by birth. Others were naturalized citizens. But there was also a very large group of "undocumented" immigrants without visas or immigration clearances who were fleeing the poverty of Mexico, Central America, or South America to find jobs and a better life in the United States. Many undocumented Hispanics were employed in low-paying service jobs in hospitals, restaurants, or offices, and in unskilled construction and factory work. In fact, many of these industries could not survive without them.

Though most Hispanic Americans were poor, there were pockets of notable Latin economic success. In the Miami area, for example, Cuban exiles from Castro's Marxist regime—most middle-class people with skills and capital—had reestablished themselves comfortably in their new American homes and were respected if not always liked by their "Anglo" neighbors.

Another racial group, Asians, hitherto small in numbers, had increased spectacularly during the 1970s. By 1980 there were 800,000 Chinese, 700,000 Japanese, 774,000 Filipinos, 350,000 Koreans, and 260,000 Vietnamese in the United States. The Asians had done extraordinarily well in their new homeland. Like some white groups before them, strong family ties and an intense desire for education had brought many Asian families into the middle class in a single generation. Asian students studied hard and gained admission in significant numbers to the country's best

"Little Havana," the Cuban enclave in Miami, was refuge to thousands of middle class people fleeing Fidel Castro's Caribbean tyranny.

colleges and universities. By the mid-1980s admissions officers at Ivy League colleges would talk privately of establishing de facto quotas for Asian-Americans to give everyone else a chance.

As in past eras, the newcomers to America in the sixties and seventies were not integrated into American society without friction. On the Texas Gulf Coast, "Anglo" and Vietnamese fishermen clashed in a series of violent incidents. Some middle-class people resented the academic success of Chinese and Japanese students. Hispanics too aroused rancor. In Miami, for example, blacks felt bitter about the success of the Cubans. In the Southwest and California some whites feared that Anglo ways would be submerged under a wave of illegal Hispanic immigration. In many communities in the Northeast and Southwest the use of Spanish as a language of instruction in the public schools became a divisive issue. Whites feared the displacement of English. Hispanic-Americans, on the other hand, worried about the loss of Spanish and with it their cultural heritage.

The concern over illegal immigration went beyond mere bigotry. Cheap imported labor promised to depress American wage standards; the immigrants, some said, would overburden welfare services. In fact, there was evidence that the undocumented immigrants paid more in taxes to federal and local governments than they received in benefits. And besides, in most cases they performed the unskilled, often dirty jobs, that native-born Americans would not take.

Yet it seemed clear that the nation could not tolerate borders that anyone could cross at will, and some controls had to be extended over immigration. In 1986 Congress passed the Simpson-Rodino Act imposing fines on employers who hired undocumented immigrants, but at the same time granting a general amnesty to all illegal immigrants who had arrived in the United States before January 1, 1982. The law required that newcomers apply for amnesty, but by 1988 compliance had been slow, and it was not clear whether the measure would end the frustration many Americans felt about unregulated immigration.

Women. In some ways the most important social issues of the 1970s concerned women. In the 1960s feminists had argued that women should be free to choose roles other than that of "homemaker." In the 1970s thousands did by entering the labor market in record numbers. In 1965, 37 percent of all women over sixteen were employed; by 1978 the figure was 50 percent. Single women had worked in substantial numbers for many years. The new working woman contingent for the first time, however, included thousands of married women with children. Only 19 percent of women with children under age six had worked in 1960; by 1980 the figure had reached 45 percent.

Many of these jobs represented serious careers. Women in record numbers flooded into law, medicine, science, college teaching, computer programming, and other professional fields. They also flocked to the graduate business schools and joined large firms as executive trainees. By the mid-1980s, the list of women who had attained prominent positions in business, professional life, and government service had grown long indeed: Jeanne Kirkpatrick, Ambassador to the United Nations; Governor Ella Grasso of Connecticut; Mayor Jayne Byrne of Chicago; Sandra Day O'Connor, associate justice of the U.S. Supreme Court; Geraldine Ferraro, Democratic vice presidential candidate in 1984; Hannah Gray, president of the University of Chicago; Sherry Lansing, executive of Twentieth-Century-Fox. Even the military service academies at West Point, Annapolis, and Colorado Springs opened their doors to women, as did the armed services in all their branches, except a few involving direct combat.

Yet women had not reached equality with men in the job market. Women's salaries were lower, and relatively few women were found in top-executive positions. Women activists charged that the major cause of this shortfall was "sexism"—sex discrimination. And clearly there was some of this, especially in subtle forms. But others pointed to women's delayed educa-

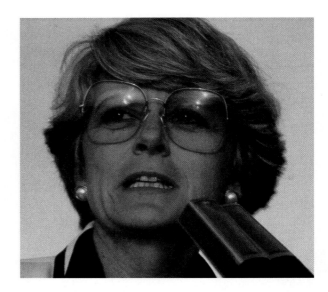

Congresswoman Geraldine Ferraro was the first woman ever to receive a major party vice presidential nomination. The time was not yet ripe.

tions, greater job instability, and overall lower expectations as important factors in slowing their advance.

The flood of women into the labor market inevitably imposed strains on society as a whole. Increasingly, the "typical" American family no longer consisted of dependent children, a working father, and a mother at home to do the family cooking and cleaning. By the late 1970s only one in five families followed this pattern, and many conservative observers wondered what the change would do to child-rearing practices and the shape of family dynamics. Feminists and liberals demanded better and cheaper child-care facilities so that mothers could work without fear that their children's development would suffer.

Marriage patterns changed too. During the 1970s marriage seemed to be going out of style. In 1960, there were 148 marriages for every 1,000 women between the ages of fifteen and forty-four. By 1980 there were only 108. To some extent this change reflected the replacement of the legal spouse with the "live-in" partner with no net loss of stability. In many cases, however, it represented a decline in real commitment by young people to permanent relationships. And even among the legally married, commitment was down. In 1960 the divorce rate had been 2.2 percent per thousand people. By 1970 it reached 3.5 percent, and by 1980 had climbed to 5.2 percent. In 1980 there was almost one divorce for every two marriages, twice the proportion of twenty years earlier.

Families were not only less stable; they were also

During the 1970s women even made it to West Point, the U.S. Military Academy, where the nation trains its professional soldiers.

smaller. The baby boom of the 1950s and 1960s was over. In 1960 there had been almost 24 births per thousand Americans. In 1970 this figure was down to 18.4. In 1976 it had further fallen to 14.8. Social observers speculated on the reasons for the birth rate decline. Some emphasized the selfishness of many young adults, especially the "Yuppies," young, upwardly mobile professionals. Children cost money and interfered with career goals, especially of female Yuppies. Others saw it as an inevitable product of a rich, advanced urban society. It was part of a long-term trend, they said, only briefly interrupted by the post–World War II baby boom, and it was worse in other advanced industrial nations like West Germany and Japan than in the United States.

The "birth dearth" disturbed thoughtful Americans. Added to improving health technology for older people, it was producing a steadily aging society. In 1970 the median age for Americans had been twenty-eight; by 1980 it was thirty and rising each year. This meant there would be an ever-growing burden on health services, as older people needed more medical care; it threatened economic progress, for an older society was probably a less creative and productive one; it endangered America's relative standing in the world because it reduced the pool of potential military personnel. It also disturbed the comity between the generations. Young people would be forced to pay an ever larger portion of their income to support their seniors, with no promise that there would be enough young people following them to provide support in turn. The Social Security system, many experts predicted, would be in serious trouble once the baby-boomers of the fifties and sixties had reached retirement age about the year 2020. By the early 1980s some social observers were talking about a demographic and social time bomb ticking away in the heart of American society.

Affirmative Action. Despite the efforts of the "disadvantaged" to achieve equality, then, racial minorities and women continued to occupy positions below white males on the economic ladder. Ending discrimination by itself was not enough, argued some activists and social critics. Minorities and women had suffered so much from past handicaps, that even if overt discrimination were totally eliminated these groups would not be able to catch up in the foreseeable future. What was needed was not merely *equal opportunity*, but *equal results*. This required, at least as a temporary measure, "affirmative action,"—that is, giving preferential treatment to minorities and women in job hiring, promotions, and admissions to training, apprenticeship, and professional programs.

Opponents of affirmative action called it reverse discrimination: It disregarded "merit," they said, and hurt those who by accident of birth did not belong to officially recognized disadvantaged groups. It was also, they claimed, inherently sexist and racist because it assumed that the present disadvantaged groups could not make it on their own in America as other outsiders had done in the past. Some people saw it as the return of a "quota" system that had hurt their groups in past eras.

Despite the opposition, affirmative action was applied increasingly by private employers and government agencies. Opponents challenged the principle in court with mixed results. In the *Bakke* decision of 1978 the Supreme Court struck down a University of California Medical School rule that denied admission to a white applicant—Allan Bakke—while accepting less qualified nonwhites. Yet the Court did not declare affirmative action invalid, only that the university's method of achieving it—through a rigid quota system—was illegal. The following year, in the *Weber* case, the Court ruled that private employers could adopt voluntary affirmative action plans to eliminate "manifest racial imbalance."

Women's groups, often the chief beneficiary of affirmative action, in the 1980s developed another weapon, the principle of "comparable worth," to improve women's relative economic standing. Claiming that many traditional women's jobs—secretarial, teaching, and so forth—paid less than many jobs traditionally held by men—truck driving, plumbing, construction work, for example—though requiring no less training, skill, or general competence, they demanded that employers be required by law to equalize pay scales. Critics said comparable worth was a purely subjective concept fraught with difficulties. It would be expensive, hurt men, and applying it, moreover, would amount to imposing administered wages on the nation. Yet by the mid-1980s several state governments had adopted the scheme for their employees over the protest of many taxpayers.

ERA and Abortion. The two most controversial social issues of the day were the Equal Rights Amendment (ERA) and abortion. Both would attract fierce partisans and arouse equally fierce opponents.

The ERA stated simply that "equality of rights under the law shall not be denied or abridged by the United States or any State on account of sex." First officially proposed by Alice Paul's National Woman's

Roe v. Wade

In 1973 the United States Supreme Court issued a momentous decision striking down a Texas statute making abortion a crime. A pregnant unmarried woman, given the name Jane Roe to protect her identity, who wanted an abortion had sued the Dallas district attorney in 1970, claiming that the Texas antiabortion law was a violation of her right to privacy under the federal Constitution. The case was finally decided in the Supreme Court by an opinion written by Associate Justice Harry Blackmun.

Justice Blackmun not only struck down the Texas law but all others with similar provisions, arguing that they were medically out of date, that they no longer expressed the common view of the community, and that they did indeed violate the constitutional rights of pregnant women. Though the decision did not make all abortions legal, it did open the door to widespread use of abortion to limit births and thereby created a major social controversy that still roils the nation.

"In view of all this, we do not agree that, by adopting one theory of life, Texas may override the rights of the pregnant woman that are at stake. We repeat, however, that the State does have an important and legitimate interest in preserving and protecting the health of the pregnant woman, whether she be a resident of the State or a nonresident who seeks medical consultation and treatment there, and that it has still *another* important and legitimate interest in protecting the potentiality of human life. These interests are separate and distinct. Each grows in substantiality as the woman approaches term and, at a point during pregnancy, each becomes 'compelling.'

"With respect to the State's important and legitimate interest in the health of the mother, the 'compelling' point, in the light of present medical knowledge, is at approximately the end of the first trimester. This is so because of the now-established medical fact, referred to above . . . , that until the end of the first trimester mortality in abortion may be less than mortality in normal childbirth. It follows that, from and after this point, a State may regulate the abortion procedure to the extent that the regulation reasonably relates to the preservation and protection of maternal health. Examples of permissible state regulation in this area are requirements as to the qualifications of the person who is to perform the abortion; as to the licensure of that person; as to the facility in which the procedure is to be performed, that is, whether it must be a hospital or may be a clinic or some other place of less-than-hospital status; as to the licensing of the facility; and the like.

"This means, on the other hand, that, for the period of pregnancy prior to this 'compelling' point, the attending physician, in consultation with his patient, is free to determine, without regulation by the State, that, in his medical judgment, the patient's pregnancy should be terminated. If that decision is reached, the judgment may be effectuated by an abortion free of interference by the State.

"With respect to the State's important and legitimate interest in potential life, the 'compelling' point is at viability. This is so because the fetus then presumably has the capability of meaningful life outside the mother's womb. State regulation protective of fetal life after viability thus has both logical and biological justifications. If the State is interested in protecting fetal life after viability, it may go so far as to proscribe abortion during that period, except when it is necessary to preserve the life or health of the mother.

"Measured against these standards, Art. 1196 of the Texas Penal Code, in restricting legal abortions to those 'procured or attempted by medical advice for the purpose of saving the life of the mother,' sweeps too broadly. The statute makes no distinction between abortions performed early in pregnancy and those performed later, and it limits to a single reason, 'saving' the mother's life, the legal justification for the procedure. The statute, therefore, cannot survive the constitutional attack made upon it here."

Party in the early 1920s, it had been introduced into every session of Congress from 1923 on. In March 1972 Congress finally approved it by the constitutionally required two-thirds vote and sent it along to the state legislatures for ratification.

At first the amendment moved swiftly through the states, with thirty-two of the needed thirty-eight ratifying it in a little over a year. Then the forces opposing the amendment began to rally. In early 1973, Phyllis Schlafly, an Illinois lawyer and mother of six, organized a "Stop ERA" campaign. The Schlaflyites touched a deep pool of antifeminist feeling in women as well as men. Studies would show that traditional women were often nonworking wives and mothers, or women who worked only to supplement their husbands' income. They viewed feminists not only as enemies of the things

Not all women liked the new feminism. Phyllis Schlafly, herself a successful lawyer, was one who objected to most of the feminist agenda.

that gave their lives worth but also as potential disrupters of important personal relationships. In the end, it was feelings like these that halted the ERA ratification process and killed the amendment for the foreseeable future.

The abortion issue provoked still stronger reactions. On one side were those who applauded the 1973 Supreme Court decision, *Roe* v. *Wade*, legalizing abortion during the first three months of pregnancy. The pro-abortion forces—a coalition of feminists and liberals—considered the decision a validation of an individual woman's right "to control her own body." They called their position "pro-choice." Opponents of legal abortion—traditional Catholics, evangelical Protestants, Orthodox Jews, and political conservatives—called abortion murder. They identified themselves as "pro-life." There were many positions in-between these extremes, and most Americans probably belonged somewhere in the middle, accepting abortion as desirable under many circumstances, but deploring its necessity.

From 1973 on, antiabortionists sought to limit women's access to abortion in several ways: by requiring that minors obtain prior parental consent to the procedure; by denying welfare recipients the right to federally subsidized abortions; by trying to limit conditions under which abortions could be legally obtained to cases where the pregnancy resulted from rape or incest, or where the birth threatened the life of the mother. The focus of much of the pro-life effort by 1980 was on passage of what was called the Human Life Amendment, a measure designed to prohibit abortion and place it beyond the jurisdiction of the courts and also to forbid some forms of birth control.

In the 1980 elections the bitter abortion debate would turn several local and state campaigns into single-issue battles. Interest groups devoted solely to the antiabortion position would spend large sums to convince voters to support selected candidates on the basis of their abortion stands. Later in the decade there would be a rash of abortion clinic bombings instigated by fanatical pro-life militants frustrated by their inability to stop by legal means what they considered a "slaughter of the innocents."

Many American considered legal abortion murder. Here anti-abortion advocates—"right-to-lifers"—bring their message to Washington.

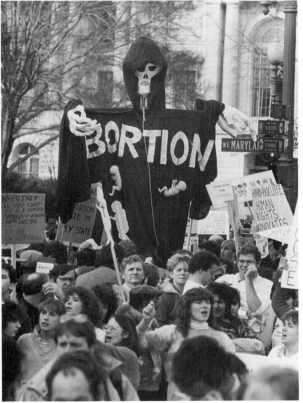

The "Me" Generation.   While some Americans continued to do battle over major social and political issues, many others turned inward away from public concerns and issues. Some retreat was probably inevitable given the intense social activism of the 1960s, but it was also encouraged by the unusual difficulty of the problems of the seventies and early eighties. Unable to find easy formulas to inform their responses to pressing public issues, many people simply turned to cultivating their personal gardens. The journalist Tom Wolfe called the mid-seventies the era of the "me generation," a period when people placed personal fulfillment and pleasure before other considerations. Historian Christopher Lasch called the phenomenon the "new narcissism," a mood, he said, that suited the new "age of diminishing expectations." Lasch was obviously wrong in his diagnosis, for in the form of the Yuppie the selfish mood would afflict young men and women even in the prosperous mid-1980s.

One sign of the new narcissism was the extraordinary new interest in physical culture. Americans had long allowed their health to suffer through lack of exercise and poor eating habits, and no doubt reformation was long overdue. By itself, however, this did not explain the remarkable interest in "natural" diets, "working out," and jogging that appeared in the late 1970s. Another cause of the health-exercise craze was the new obsession with self. Still another manifestation of this "me" mood was the growth of a multitude of new psychological mental health therapies. Affluent young urbanites flocked to teachers of "primal scream," EST, Rolfing, and other therapeutic programs that promised mental comfort or personal fulfillment. Others sought satisfaction in one of the host of new religious cults such as Sun Myung Moon's Unification Church, L. Ron Hubbard's Scientology, Baghwan Shree Ravneesh's Oregon commune, or Jim Jones' People's Temple. Cults provided many young men and women with a sense of purpose and community. They also lent themselves to fraud, manipulation, and charlatanism. Americans would be deeply shocked when, in November 1979, over 900 of Jones' American followers committed mass suicide in their settlement in Guyana at the behest of their unbalanced leader.

Sun Belt versus Snow Belt.   One of the most important social trends of the seventies and early eighties was the shift of population, wealth, and leadership from the long-dominant northeastern quarter of the country—the so-called Snow Belt—to the South and West—the Sun Belt.

For a century or more the region stretching from southern New England through the Middle Atlantic states and on through the Old Northwest had been the richest, most populous, and culturally creative part of the United States. It had harbored the nation's most productive industries—clothing, steel, automobiles, electronics, rubber. Its largest cities had been the centers of the nation's cultural life, sheltering its major museums, universities, publishing houses, symphony orchestras, theater, and dance companies.

The balance began to shift during the 1960s and accelerated thereafter. As more and more Americans retired to live on pensions, they chose to leave behind the cold winters of the Northeast and Midwest. Immense retirement communities sprang up in California, Florida, and Arizona. Industry, too, particularly light industry and industry connected with defense, found the warmer climate, abundant land, cheaper nonunionized labor, and lower taxes of the South and West an advantage. Under four presidents from the region—Lyndon Johnson of Texas, Richard Nixon and Ronald Reagan of California, and Jimmy Carter of Georgia—government seemed to favor the Sun Belt through tax and defense-contract policies. Texas, Louisiana, and California, for a time, would also profit from the energy crisis of the late 1970s. With their large reserves of oil and natural gas, these states could offer cheap energy to business and individuals alike. Congress magnified this advantage when it decontrolled most natural gas and petroleum prices in 1978. Though the avowed purpose of the decontrol measure was to encourage greater energy exploration and production, one effect promised to be an enormous transfer of income from consumers in the Snow Belt to producers in the South and West.

All this was anticipated by economists as early as the 1960s, but the message was driven home by the figures provided by the twentieth census. The preliminary results, announced on the last day of 1980, showed small increases, or even declines, in the populations of the northeastern and midwestern states during the previous decade. By contrast, already massive California grew by 17.7 percent; Nevada by almost 64 percent; Texas by 26.4 percent; Arizona by almost 53 percent, and Florida by more than 41 percent. While the population of many older Snow Belt cities declined, Phoenix, Albuquerque, Tucson, Houston, Dallas, San Antonio, Miami, Tampa, San Diego, and San Jose leaped ahead.

The statistics both confirmed previous trends and foreshadowed new ones. Political power would clearly shift with population. When Congress was reapportioned, New York, Illinois, Ohio, and Pennsylvania would lose seats in the House of Representatives, and Texas, California, Florida, and Arizona would gain several seats each. Because the newer regions were more conservative politically than the older Snow Belt, this obviously meant a rightward trend in the nation's political climate. Besides politics, the nation's cultural life was certain to be affected. Already the Snow Belt's near-monopoly of high culture—painting, music, dance, and theater—had been loosened, partly through the National Endowment for the Arts and its counterpart in scholarship and literature, the National Endowment for the Humanities. Since their founding in 1965 as part of Lyndon Johnson's Great Society, these two federally funded bodies had pumped large sums of money into universities, theatrical and dance companies, and orchestras located outside the old Snow Belt cultural centers. Their efforts had been effective. By the early 1980s, universities in the Mountain states, Texas, and the Far West were matching the prestige and creativity of those of the East, while local culture in the Sun Belt was flourishing as never before.

The Energy Crisis and the Seventies' Economic Malaise

The growth of the Sun Belt and decline of the Snow Belt were tied to profound problems facing the United States in the 1970s. The country was perturbed not only by the Vietnam defeat, Watergate, and social strife, but also by an acute energy crisis.

Oil and the American Way of Life. For Americans, the "pursuit of happiness" has traditionally meant the quest for increasing material abundance based on advanced technology and industrial preeminence. In the 1970s, however, the world's industrialized nations confronted the problem of growing resource dearth. Such crucial metals as platinum, silver, tin, copper, and nickel—all needed in modern industrial products and processes—seemed to grow scarcer. Most serious was the oil shortage. To many Americans in the late 1970s the mile-long lines to buy scarce gasoline at prices soaring into the stratosphere seemed to foretell the end of an affluence they had come to accept as part of their national heritage.

The energy problem had evolved over several decades. By the post-World War II era energy had become synonymous with oil, and by the 1950s much of the world's supply came from the Middle East. The oil wells were located primarily in Saudi Arabia, Kuwait, Iran, and Iraq, but their contents were extracted, refined, and marketed by seven giant Western oil companies, five of them American. These companies had helped finance and develop the oil fields and for many years took the lion's share of the revenues they yielded.

After World War II the collapse of Western hegemony and the growing militancy of Arab nationalism led the Middle Eastern rulers to reconsider their agreements with the Western oil companies. This impulse toward economic self-assertion was influenced by the Arab confrontation with Israel, viewed by Arab nationalists as a Western neo-colonial intrusion into Islam.

This spectacular city-scape (Houston, Texas) suggests how scarce oil in the 1970s benefited the oil-rich Sun Belt region.

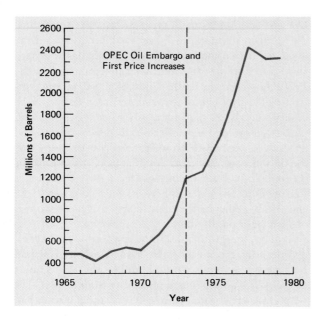

American oil imports, 1966–1979 (*Source: Statistical Abstract of the United States 1980*).

At first the Middle Eastern rulers demanded and got an increase in the royalties they received from the Western oil companies. Then, in 1960, the major oil-producing nations, led by the Middle Eastern countries, organized a cartel, the Organization of Petroleum Exporting Countries (OPEC), for the purpose of setting world petroleum prices and greatly increasing the profit for themselves.

In the early 1970s political and economic events aided OPEC's monopoly pricing effort. The Western nations, including the United States, increased their oil consumption, becoming ever more dependent on imported energy sources. In the years between 1971 and 1973 alone, America quadrupled its oil imports, mostly from the Middle East. The flood of American demand would help create a world seller's market.

Then, in October 1973, two Arab nations, Egypt and Syria, suddenly attacked Israel. The OPEC nations were meeting in Vienna during the October War, and when the United States backed Israel the OPEC countries responded furiously by boosting the price of oil from $3 to $5 a barrel and announcing an oil embargo against the United States and other nations supporting Israel. Suddenly the United States faced its first peacetime oil shortage since the discovery of petroleum more than a century before.

The uncomfortable winter of 1973/74, with its cold homes and long gas lines, passed. But the embargo made it clear that America had become dependent for energy on the Arab world. The October War itself had other effects on America's energy situation. After heavy casualties on both sides the conflict ended with a United Nations-supervised cease-fire but no decrease in the hostility between Arabs and Israelis and no prospect for a long-term peace settlement. Though the Egyptians and Syrians had not won the war, their limited success had increased Arab unity and buoyed Arab self-confidence. In the years that followed, the OPEC nations would be far more effective than in the past in acting in concert to control the oil market. Their dominance of a resource vital to the West and their hostility toward an American ally—Israel—raised the ominous prospect that they would someday be able to hold American foreign policy hostage. Soon after the October War, President Nixon announced that the United States would begin working toward energy independence.

Energy Alternatives. For a time the energy crisis forced Americans to consider their future as a people of plenty. Some concluded that we must accept "lim-

Such signs plagued American motorists in the summer 1979. The 1979 gas famine, caused in part by the overthrow of the shah in revolutionary Iran, pointed up the long-term energy crisis the nation faced.

its." The United States, they said, had been living beyond its resource means for many years. The age of abundance was over and the wastefulness must stop. The most extreme members of this school anticipated a "no-growth economy" and predicted that the country would face years of rising social tensions as groups fought over how to distribute a diminished economic pie.

At the other extreme were those who refused to face the facts of change. Some of these people believed that the oil companies had contrived the energy shortage to increase their profits. Others blamed the continuing dearth on the environmentalists who, they said, resisted every attempt to find new energy sources in the name of safety or ecological balance.

Whatever their conclusions, the energy crisis reinforced Americans' sense of malaise brought on by the Vietnam defeat and Watergate. Besides impotence abroad and corruption at home, it seemed we now had to face for the first time the possibility of long-term material limits. America appeared to have passed its prime; it could no longer achieve all the goals it set for itself.

In its actual energy policies the government pursued a middle course. Congress clamped a fifty-five-mile-per-hour speed limit on drivers and prescribed minimum gas mileage requirements for car manufacturers. It offered tax credits to homeowners who insulated their houses to conserve fuel. It also passed measures to encourage the development of alternative energy sources, such as geothermal, wind, and solar power. In July 1979, President Jimmy Carter would ask Congress to fund a synthetic fuels program to free Americans from dependence on foreign energy sources.

Americans also conducted a major debate over nuclear power. Lauded by some as the complete solution to America's energy problems, nuclear power came under increasing fire on environmental and safety grounds as the seventies advanced. The critics' arguments were given frightening relevance by an accident at Three Mile Island nuclear power plant near Harrisburg, Pennsylvania, in March 1979, which for a time threatened to produce a "meltdown" of the nuclear core. Had that occurred, thousands of lives might have been lost and property in the billions contaminated for decades.

The near disaster intensified the nuclear power debate. Supporters of nuclear energy pointed out that the overall safety record of the industry had been good. Opponents insisted that the accident confirmed the unsuitability of the nuclear solution of the energy prob-

An air view of the Three Mile Island nuclear reactor in Pennsylvania a few days after it misfunctioned and scared the wits out of millions of Americans.

lem. Moreover, power from the atom raised difficult issues of nuclear waste disposal. During the next few years the environmentalists, organized in various "alliances," conducted a crusade against nuclear power that helped delay construction of new plants and imposed stricter safety standards on old ones. The assault raised the costs of construction so that by the early 1980s the building of new nuclear power plants stopped, and several, almost completed plants, had to be abandoned.

Turmoil in the Economy. The public's disquiet over energy and environmental problems was enormously magnified by the relentless rise in general consumer prices. By mid-1979 the average American family had to earn almost double its 1970 dollar income to achieve the same standard of living. In effect, the value of the dollar had fallen to half its worth from a decade before.

By the end of the decade inflation had become

A Historical Portrait

Henry Cisneros

In April 1981, a tall, slender Mexican-American was elected mayor of San Antonio, Texas, with 62 percent of the vote. Henry Cisneros' election victory marked the triumph of a talented young man. It also marked the abrupt arrival on the political scene of the millions of Mexican-Americans who, until Cisneros' victory, had failed to make a major impression on American public life.

Henry Cisneros' career is the epitome of one sort of immigrant success story. His way was eased by education, by strong family standards and values, and by elite patronage. He was never confrontational. Cisneros learned that in San Antonio in the 1970s and 1980s the way to get results was by hard bargaining and compromise, not by intimidation and angry attack.

Cisneros was born in June 1947 into a middle-class Mexican-American home. His mother was the daughter of Jose Romulo Munguia—a supporter of the Mexican democratic leader Venustiano Carranza—who left his homeland for the United States in 1924 with 18 cents in his pocket and established a successful print shop on San Antonio's West Side. His father's family had roots in the original Spanish settlers of New Mexico. Though his paternal grandfather was poor and worked as a farm laborer, George Cisneros, Henry's father, managed to wrest an education for himself. After college he worked for the government as a civil servant and, following World War II military service, remained in the Army reserve, rising to the rank of full colonel.

Henry grew up in San Antonio's Prospect Hill. Four blocks away began the *barrio*, the delapidated slums where most of the city's thousands of Chicanos lived in poverty. The Cisneros' neighborhood was an attractive area of tree-lined streets and substantial frame houses, many formerly occupied by San Antonio's large German population. Clearly Henry would not have to start from the lowest rung of the ladder.

The Cisneros-Munguia clan provided an ideal climate for achievement. Grandfather Munguia was a self-taught intellectual who had accumulated a large library on Mexican history and culture. He introduced his grandchildren to the pleasures of reading and encouraged them to respect their ancestral heritage. Henry's parents, George and Elvira, were ambitious for their four children, but reinforced their wishes by both precept and example. Each of the Cisneros children had prescribed household chores to perform. The family also dined together regularly and George and Elvira made the dinner table a forum for the exchange of ideas. The Cisneros dinner table debates often went on for hours after the dishes were cleared.

Henry and the other children attended good Catholic parochial schools. At Central Catholic High Henry was spotted as a bright lad and taken under the wing of Brother Martin McMurtrey, the school's outstanding teacher of English and literature. This sort of patronage would be repeated more than once in later years, and it would be an invaluable boost to Henry's career.

Drawing on his father's example, Henry at first considered a military career. When he failed to get into the Air Force Academy, however, he settled for Texas A & M, at College Station, Texas. There, his lively intelligence, his good humor, and his capacity for friendship made him a big man on campus. At the close of his sophomore year he was selected sergeant-major of the Texas "Aggie" band. Success at Texas A & M by itself was a useful accomplishment for any ambitious Texan. But equally important was the patronage of Wayne Stark, director of the Aggie Memorial Student Union. Stark sought out talented young people, especially from the minority communities, and encouraged them to use their potential. With wide connections around the state, he was able to gain entry for the tall, skinny Mexican-American to the Houston and Dallas business community.

Henry's life changed when he was sent to a student conference on United States affairs held at West Point. The meeting was an eye-opener. For the first time Henry met undergraduates from the elite colleges and discovered how far behind he was. "I was totally outclassed," he later said. "We sat around a conference table and I never opened my mouth." After this trip east Henry surrendered all thought of a military career and decided to become an urban planner.

In January 1969, after graduation, Henry, just twenty-one, became assistant director of the Model Cities Program for San Antonio. Before the Model Cities era, San Antonio politics had been dominated by the Good Government League (GGL), a coalition of civic-minded business people and good-government reformers. The GGL represented the "Anglo" establishment, though it generally received much Mexican-American support. Model Cities, by raising Mexican-American ethnic pride, split many Mexican-Americans away from the GGL. In 1969 Pete Torres ran against the GGL slate as an independent and won election to the City Council.

The Model Cities experience was a wonderful training ground for Henry Cisneros. "Everything I know about citizen participation and the mechanics of making government work, I learned during the Model Cities years," he later declared. Model Cities also convinced him that he needed more training in administration and finance and in 1970 he, and his young bride, Mary Alice, left for Washington, D.C., where Henry enrolled in George Washington University's doctoral program in urban administration.

While pursuing his studies, Cisneros worked for the National League of Cities (NLC), a lobbying agency for American cities seeking federal grants. At the NLC offices he met a flock of big-city mayors who had come to Washington to beg Congress and the administration for favors. Before completing his degree at George Washington University, Cisneros applied and was accepted as a White House Fellow, a highly competitive internship program established by Lyndon Johnson to introduce bright young people to the problems and challenges of government.

Cisneros was assigned to Elliot Richardson, Nixon's Secretary of Health, Education, and Welfare, as a general assistant. He was singularly fortunate. Richardson was a blue-blood Bostonian with high principles. He would later become the Nixon administration's "Mr. Clean," one of the few Nixon associates not tainted by Watergate. Richardson took the young couple from San Antonio under his wing and not only provided Henry with valuable political training, but also exposed him and Mary Alice to the cultural life of Washington and taught Henry how to dress. Richardson also helped Cisneros get

financial support for two years at the Kennedy School of Government at Harvard. In 1973, Harvard granted him a master's degree in public administration.

In August 1974 Henry and his wife returned to San Antonio where Henry had a job waiting as assistant professor of environmental studies at the local branch of the University of Texas. By the time the couple returned home, the Good Government League was in a shambles, having the previous year failed to get its candidate elected mayor for the first time in twenty years. Despite its disarray, and although many Mexican-Americans no longer supported the GGL, Henry accepted the league's nomination for city councilman. Mounting a highly personal campaign, he won in a landslide and, at twenty-seven, became the youngest councilman in the city's history.

The young council member came to office at an auspicious time. The San Antonio Anglo leadership was divided between an older group of businessmen belonging to the downtown Greater Chamber of Commerce and a younger element, with roots in the suburbs, that belonged to the Northside Chamber of Commerce. The first represented the remnants of GGL power in the city; the second had little use for the decrepit GGL. The two groups also disagreed over the city's future economic growth. The Greater Chamber people were essentially contented. They did not oppose growth, but neither did they push for it very hard. Their adversaries were aggressive promoters of new shopping malls, industrial parks, and housing developments, but mostly on the city's suburban outskirts where land was cheap.

Cisneros was pro-development and pro-business, unlike Ernie Cortes, head of Communities Organized for Public Service (COPS), a grassroots organization inspired by Saul Alinsky's Chicago-based Indus-

trial Areas Foundation. Alinsky was the father of a community organized by neighborhood people to force concessions out of "the establishment," and COPS adopted an angry confrontational approach to the business community. As a city councilman, Cisneros often cooperated with COPS, but he believed their style was counterproductive. The Southwest "Sun Belt" was undergoing an explosive period of growth, and San Antonio, he believed, must grab some of it for itself. But the growth must not be confined to the new suburban areas and solely benefit the white middle class. Rather, business people who sought favors and concessions of San Antonio must promise to build their factories, stores, and offices close to minority neighborhoods so that jobs, contracts, and other boons would come to the city's black and Mexican-American population as well as the Anglo middle class.

Cisneros served three terms on the San Antonio City Council and became in those six years the hero of the city's Mexican-American population by fighting for protection of the city's water supply and for lower natural gas rates. In 1980 he decided to run for mayor when Lila Cockrell, the well-liked Anglo lady and the first woman mayor of a large American city, decided to return to private life.

His opponent was John Thomas Steen, a rich insurance executive and a member of the city's old business establishment, though himself a self-made man. Steen's supporters included the old GGL people and the downtown business community. Cisneros, of course, had his own Mexican-Americans on his side. He also won over a segment of the new suburban developers, at odds with the city's traditional business establishment. These business people were willing to accept Cisneros' vision of a community-benefits oriented development and contributed generously to his campaign. On April 4, 1981, Henry Cisneros won handily with 62 percent of the vote, including almost half those in San Antonio's Anglo precincts.

Cisneros' election attracted wide media attention. Here was the first Mexican-American mayor of a major American city. Yet in fact the city's head did not wield great power. San Antonio had an appointed city manager who handled its routine day-to-day affairs; the elected mayor's $4,000 annual salary reflected the mayor's limited powers. The only way that Cisneros could afford the job was by continuing to teach at the university. Though he was little more than the first among equals on the City Council, he made his mark on city policy by his intelligence, moral force, public support, and his ability to establish the council's agenda.

Cisneros' administration was a resounding success. He managed to lower fuel prices for consumers, get the legislature to establish a school of engineering in San Antonio, and draw industry to the city. In some ways his most important achievement was to give the city's Mexican-American majority a sense of participation in the political process and reduce ethnic conflict. When he ran for reelection in 1983, Cisneros won an astounding 94 percent of the total vote.

Cisneros' success gave him national visibility. Here was a well-spoken, personable—and moderate—Mexican-American who demonstrated the willingness of American society to reward merit from any group. In July 1983 President Reagan selected him as a member of the National Bipartisan Commission on Central America to consider American policy in El Salvador and toward the Sandinistas of Nicaragua. Here he served as a balance wheel to the conservatives who favored a hardline policy toward the Central American left. In the end, the commission report reflected many of the mayor's concerns for human rights violations by the far right in both countries. In a number of dissenting footnotes he also proposed a dialogue with the Marxist Sandinista group to discourage them from exporting revolution to their neighbors.

On July 4, 1984, Henry Cisneros, with his wife and two small daughters, faced the national press in front of Walter Mondale's home in St. Paul, Minnesota. Mondale had virtually won his campaign for the Democratic presidential nomination and was interviewing potential vice presidential candidates. Mondale said that Cisneros would make a "superb vice president"; he had "the ability, the strength, the values, the drive." Although at home his Hispanic background had come to seem irrelevant, the mayor himself recognized that he filled a special niche in a Mondale election strategy. When questioned by the reporters about his possible contribution to a Democratic ticket, Cisneros declared that he thought he would bring to the vice president's job important special values—values "related to our country's relationship to the south, values that relate to how people are living in the central cities of America, values that relate to the problems of those who lose by the transitioning American economy."

In the end, Mondale's choice fell on Congresswoman Geraldine Ferraro of New York, a person who represented an even larger "minority" than the nation's 14 million Hispanic-Americans. Yet for the first time it was clear that there was an American with a Spanish name and a Spanish heritage waiting in the presidential wings. Once more, it seemed, the promise of American life was on its way to being fulfilled.

---

self-perpetuating. People asked: "Why wait to buy when the price will only be higher tomorrow?" This attitude sent millions of Americans rushing off to department stores and discount houses to snap up appliances, clothing, sports equipment, and goods of every kind with their credit cards. The buying spree added fuel to the inflationary surge. It also reduced personal savings. There was little incentive to put money into savings accounts when the gain from interest earned was certain to be more than offset by its loss of value. The drop in personal savings in turn reduced the pool of funds available for building new houses, factories, and equipment and thus slowed the rate of growth in output. It also made the United States increasingly dependent on foreign sources of capital for financing private industry and even to help service the large federal debt.

Experts puzzled over the causes of the inflation. Many pointed to the skyrocketing energy costs that entered into the prices of all goods and services. Others emphasized rising wages. Labor was able to extract higher wages from employers without commensurate increases in labor productivity, and these costs could be simply passed along to consumers because in many areas competition was purely nominal. Still others took their cue from the conservative economist Milton Fried-

The handsome, articulate mayor of San Antonio, Henry Cisneros, a symbol of Hispanic-American progress.

man, who insisted that an excess of cheap money and credit, permitted by the Federal Reserve system and reinforced by large federal deficits, explained the powerful inflation surge.

One difficulty in dealing with inflation was that keeping prices low seemed to depend on keeping unem-

ployment high. Cutbacks in government spending would reduce overall demand for goods and services. Increases in interest rates would discourage investment and consumer buying. Both together should push up the jobless rate, but at the same time reduce inflation. Many liberals opposed such policies for that very reason. Better higher prices than mass unemployment, they argued.

But the argument seemed pointless. Inflation versus unemployment was a formula that no longer seemed to work. At the end of the 1960s the unemployment rate had been less than 4 percent. By 1975 it was up to almost 8 percent. Thereafter it fell, but in 1980 it rose again, averaging over 7 percent of the labor force. In past eras, with so many wage earners out of work, prices would fall or at least remain level. Now, however, unemployment was accompanied by continued inflation.

The combination of high inflation and high unemployment, called *stagflation* by phrase-makers, could not easily be explained. Some experts claimed it was a false problem. Unemployment was actually not as great as it seemed. Many of the unemployed were now women who moved into and out of the job market with great frequency. This flux raised the unemployment figures, but the joblessness of such workers did not affect prices as would unemployment among high-salaried workers who were the chief support of their families.

Another explanation of the high unemployment

A combination of "Pacific Rim" competition and the tight money policies after 1979 to stop inflation produced long lines at the unemployment insurance offices. Detroit, the nation's auto capital, was especially hard hit.

rates in the face of rising prices emphasized the poor fit between skills and the kind of jobs available. The complex economy of the 1970s and early 1980s required highly trained people—men and women who could operate computers, perform experiments, write reports, design equipment, do market research. By the late 1970s there were some 25 million people classified as "technical, professional, managerial, and administrative" workers. This "new class" was affluent and enjoyed a low unemployment rate. But millions of Americans, especially among minorities, lacked these skills and could find no place in the new "high-tech" economy no matter how much demand consumers displayed for goods and services.

Liberals advocated major government retraining programs to teach the new technical skills. Conservatives pointed out that such programs were certain to be expensive, and because deficit spending was one source of inflationary pressure, the process might be self-defeating. Clearly the nation faced a dilemma: It could have full employment, but apparently only at the expense of more severe inflation.

The Carter Years

Jimmy Carter would be forced to shoulder much of the blame for the economic troubles of the late 1970s. Yet when he took office in January 1977, many people were optimistic that this ex-peanut farmer, who had come from nowhere to win the presidency, would be an effective leader. They would be disappointed.

Carter as President. Americans at first were impressed by Jimmy Carter. Though a Washington outsider, he opted for experienced people in selecting his cabinet: Cyrus Vance at the State Department, Harold Brown at the Defense Department, and Joseph Califano at

The election of 1976

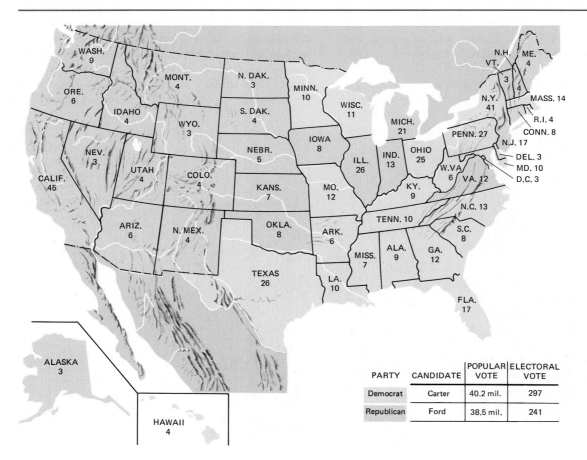

PARTY	CANDIDATE	POPULAR VOTE	ELECTORAL VOTE
Democrat	Carter	40.2 mil.	297
Republican	Ford	38.5 mil.	241

the Department of Health, Education, and Welfare. His choice for treasury secretary went to Michael Blumenthal, president of the Bendix Corporation. The White House inner circle, however, would be made up mostly of outsiders like Carter himself.

The Carter style at first seemed refreshingly informal. He broke with precedent by walking in his own inaugural parade with his wife, Rosalynn, and his daughter, Amy, by his side. From the White House he answered citizens' phoned-in questions on TV and wore blue jeans and old sweaters around the Oval Office. Amy went to a Washington public school, like other unpretentious residents of the District of Columbia, rather than a private school. Carter also tried to reduce the number of White House officials, and he cut back on staff limousines and television sets.

The politicians on Capitol Hill found him less pleasing. Having run against the Washington "establishment," Carter had trouble achieving a working relationship with Congress. He also experienced the congressional backlash against presidential leadership following Watergate and the abrasive years of the imperial presidency. Inexperienced in the ways of Washington, he and his staff often fumbled badly.

Carter's first mistake was to attack a congressional sacred cow by cutting off federal funding for eighteen dams and other water projects in the West. His arguments were valid, but he had not reckoned with the importance of these "pork barrel" projects to members of Congress. Faced with a storm of protest, he retreated. He did little better in his early relations with key congressional leaders, failing to consult Senate Majority Leader Robert Byrd on which senators to brief on energy policy, and announcing federal appointments in House Speaker Thomas ("Tip") O'Neill's own Massachusetts district without first informing him. Eventually, Carter and his advisers improved relations with Congress, but they were never able to establish an effective partnership with those who enacted the nation's laws.

Domestic Policies. The gravest domestic policy question Jimmy Carter faced was how to end the nation's dependence on foreign oil. The challenge aroused all the president's considerable moral fervor. At one point he called the battle to make the United States oil-independent (borrowing a phrase from philosopher William James) "the moral equivalent of war."

Unfortunately, his actual recommendations to Congress in February 1977 were disproportionately modest: a federal tax on crude oil imports and on "gas-guzzling" cars. Given the president's grave tone

Jimmy and Rosalynn Carter walk to the White House from the Inauguration—happy as two larks.

and dire warnings, this program struck many Americans as ludicrous. Humorist Russell Baker abbreviated the "moral equivalent of war" to MEOW. Congress was similarly unimpressed and acted slowly, though eventually giving the president much of what he asked for.

In March 1979, with oil supplies once more in jeopardy because of a new Middle East crisis, and with the Three Mile Island accident raising new doubts about nuclear power, Carter again turned his full attention to the energy problem. Additional modest recommendations followed: a standby gasoline rationing plan, a program to develop synthetic fuels, and $10 billion for energy-conserving mass transit. It was a case once again of too little, too late. In the summer, near-disaster was triggered by the turmoil in Iran. During the confusion of the Islamic fundamentalist revolution that overthrew the Shah, Iranian oil production, a major source of American energy, dropped drastically. The oil-importing nations were soon bidding against one another for the reduced world supply, thereby tripping off a panic that left Americans fuming in long gas lines through June and July. By now many citizens had concluded that here, as in other areas, Carter was an ineffectual leader.

The oil crisis of 1979/80 accelerated the inflation surge. In 1979, prices leaped 13.3 percent in a single year. In early 1980 they rose still faster, threatening to reach an astronomical 18 percent for the year if not stopped. The Federal Reserve, under its new head, Paul Volcker, raised interest rates to discourage spending with borrowed money. The president established a Council on Wage and Price Stability to monitor wage and price guidelines. Neither move worked at first. Interest rates were pushed to 20 percent in early 1980, but prices continued to rise. The council proved ineffective. Its orders were unenforceable and its fruitless "jawboning" only made the administration again seem feeble and incompetent.

Foreign Policy. Carter's foreign policy was not an outstanding success either. Liberals, who shared his sense that America must distance itself from aggressive Vietnam-era policies, endorsed his treaty with Panama ending exclusive American control of the Canal Zone. This agreement, they believed, was necessary to avoid a dangerous confrontation with Panamanian nationalists and to raise American stock in Latin America. Liberals also applauded his "human rights" campaign to use America's good offices to support victims of government oppression around the world. They endorsed his strong support for the new strategic arms limitations talks (SALT II) with the Soviet Union, which promised to slow the nuclear arms race.

Most conservatives saw these initiatives in a different light. The human rights policy, they said, all too often offended conservative foreign leaders who were friends of the United States and opponents of the Soviet Union. The Panama Canal treaties had weakly surrendered American rights of seventy years standing. SALT II was a Soviet trick. Its predecessor, SALT I, had lulled America to sleep, enabling the Soviets to catch up and then pass the United States in conventional weapons. The Soviet navy, for example, had become a global fleet able for the first time to challenge the United States in every corner of the high seas.

There was one foreign-policy area, however, namely Arab-Israeli relations, where everyone agreed that Carter deserved praise. In November 1977 Egyptian president Anwar Sadat had made an unprecedented visit to Jerusalem, the Israeli capital. For the

Probably the high point of Carter's presidency: the hand clasp confirming the Camp David accord between Egypt's Anwar Sadat (on left) and Israel's Menachem Begin.

first time the head of an Arab state had recognized the legitimacy of the Jewish nation and it looked as though peace between Egypt and Israel might be at hand. Unfortunately, the peace process soon bogged down over the thorny problem of Palestinian self-rule, and it seemed that Sadat's bold initiative would come to nothing. To break the impasse, in September 1978 Carter induced both Sadat and Israeli Prime Minister Menachem Begin to come to Camp David, the president's hideaway in the Maryland mountains, to discuss the remaining differences between the two countries. Carter used every means to get these two stubborn men to agree and finally succeeded in squeezing a joint peace statement from them. As a result of the Camp David accords, in March 1979 Israel and Egypt signed a peace treaty that bound the two nations to full diplomatic relations, to Israeli phased-evacuation of the Sinai Peninsula, conquered during the 1967 war, and to some form of autonomy for the Palestinians living in the West Bank and Gaza Strip. However, the treaty did not bring peace to the Middle East. None of the other Arab nations followed Egypt's lead and the Palestinian issue continued to fester. But for the first time in its history Israel was at peace with one of its Arab neighbors.

The Hostage Crisis.

Whatever credit Carter earned from the Camp David accords was squandered by his handling of the hostage crisis with Iran. Iran was a distant, exotic place to most Americans in 1979, an Islamic—though not Arabic—nation located on the oil-rich Persian Gulf. It was ruled despotically by Shah Mohammed Riza Pahlevi, a close friend of America. The United States had helped the Shah gain his throne and considered him a bulwark of stability in the Middle East. In January 1979 he was ousted by internal enemies who despised his repressive methods, his friendship with the West, and his attempts to modernize his backward land. The Shah fled to Mexico, leaving behind a nation in turmoil. In October he was admitted to a New York hospital for treatment of cancer. This show of American hospitality outraged the faction now dominant in Iran, the Islamic fundamentalists led by the ultraorthodox religious leader, the Ayatollah Ruhollah Khomeini. On November 4, 1979, a group of pro-Khomeini Iranian students, probably with the Ayatollah's approval, invaded the American embassy in Teheran and took hostage over sixty American citizens, mostly embassy employees.

Weeks of protest, negotiation, and maneuver would follow, but to no avail. Seizing the embassy of a country that one was not at war with was contrary to all civilized practice and no government could have condoned it. But America found itself dealing with a regime ruled by fanatics. The Islamic fundamentalist government considered America "the Great Satan" and demanded ransom to release the hostages. The United States must surrender the Shah to his enemies, apologize for supporting him in the past, and agree to turn over to the Iranian government all the assets that the Shah supposedly had taken with him when he fled his homeland. If it did not, not only would the hostages be kept prisoner, but they might well be tried for espionage, and if convicted, executed.

The United States could not possibly accept such conditions and did not. The administration froze billions of dollars of Iranian assets in the United States, cut off all trade with Teheran, and appealed to the United Nations and the World Court to condemn the hostage-taking. Nothing worked. As the weeks passed Americans became obsessed with the hostage crisis. Public frustration and anger at American impotence grew and voices were soon raised demanding retalia-

The blindfolded man is an American held hostage by the students of the Iranian Islamic Revolutionary Committee. They seem rather older than most students.

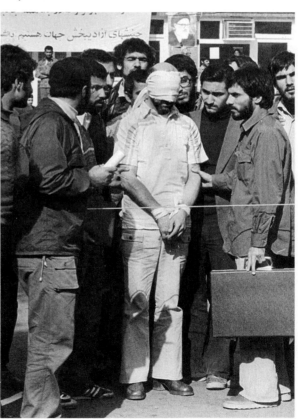

Americans became obsessed by the Iranian hostage crisis. Here grade school pupils are writing letters to the American prisoners.

Africa, and it seemed to many people that the Soviets could not be trusted. All hope of SALT II ratification disappeared when, in late December 1979, Soviet troops and tanks poured across the border into Afghanistan, the Islamic country tucked between Iran and Pakistan, to keep a Soviet puppet leader from being toppled by opponents.

The Soviet invasion shocked Carter. The president indignantly announced that Soviet premier Leonid Brezhnev had deceived him. He now told the American people that the United States must once more seek to contain Soviet expansionism and be prepared to defend the free flow of oil to the West from the Persian Gulf region. To implement this policy (quickly labeled "the Carter Doctrine"), he cut off sales of wheat and advanced technology to the Soviet Union, withdrew the United States team from the 1980 summer Olympics in Moscow, shelved SALT II for the foreseeable future, and asked Congress to enact legislation requiring all nineteen- and twenty-year-olds to register for the military draft.

The 1980 Election. Despite this vigorous response, with each passing week the public came to perceive the Carter administration as feckless and impotent. Americans listened to the president's homilies about energy belt-tightening, "malaise," and international morality, and felt irritated and depressed. They watched events abroad and saw only a growing American powerlessness. The public's gloomy mood helps explain the outcome of the 1980 election.

Carter won renomination easily despite the misgivings of many Democrats. The Republican nominee was Ronald Reagan, spokesman for the Republican ideological right. The former California governor appealed to the same backlash voters who had supported George Wallace and Richard Nixon in 1968. He too disliked the social changes of the 1960s and denounced "big government." Reagan and his constituency accused the Carter administration of being weak in its response to Soviet aggression and allowing American military strength to fall behind Soviet strength. During the campaign Reagan received the strong support of conservative political action committees (PACs) and fundamentalist Protestant groups, called the Moral Majority, led by the Reverend Jerry Falwell. Both were new forces on the political scene.

The Carter administration hoped for a breakthrough on the Iranian hostage issue to give it an electoral boost. But the Iranians toyed with the American negotiators, reinforcing the impression of administration weakness. When election day arrived the hostage

tion. Some people called for a declaration of war against Iran and a blockade of the Persian Gulf. Irate citizens attacked Iranian students attending American universities. The administration too became consumed with the hostage crisis to the neglect of other important matters. In late April 1980 the president ordered a military rescue operation from U.S. naval vessels in the Persian Gulf against the advice of Secretary of State Vance. This maneuver failed dismally and eight men died in the attempt. Vance resigned. The public's level of frustration rose to new heights.

The Cold War Resumes. The Middle East troubles undermined Soviet-American relations and threatened to destroy détente beyond repair. From the time Carter became president the relations between the Soviet Union and the United States had seesawed. In June 1979 the president had finally signed the SALT II agreement, placing further limitations on Soviet and American nuclear arsenals, but the treaty awaited ratification by the Senate. By now many Americans felt the Soviets were no longer truly interested in détente. The Soviet Union was becoming increasingly aggressive in the Arabian peninsula and, through its Cuban surrogate, in

WASH.
MONT.
N.D.
MINN.
ORE.
IDAHO
S.D.
WIS.
MICH.
N.H.
VT.
ME.
N.Y.
MASS.
R.I.
CONN.
N.J.
DEL.
MD.
D.C.
NEV.
WYO.
IOWA
NEB.
UTAH
COLO.
PA.
OHIO
IND.
ILL.
W. VA.
VA.
CALIF.
KAN.
MO.
KY.
N.C.
ARIZ.
N.M.
OKLA.
ARK.
TENN.
S.C.
MISS.
ALA.
GA.
TEXAS
LA.
FLA.
HAWAII
ALASKA

Carter 49
Reagan 489

The electoral vote, 1980

Reverend Jerry Falwell, founder of the fundamentalist Moral Majority, speaking out for conservative positions during the 1980 presidential campaign.

crisis remained unresolved. The result was an impressive Republican victory. Reagan received 43 million popular votes to 35 million for Carter. Going down to defeat along with the president were a flock of liberal Democratic senators and representatives. Reagan would have a Republican Senate to work with and, though the House of Representatives would continue to have a Democratic majority, it would be less liberal than in the recent past.

Conclusions

The defeat of Hubert Humphrey in 1968 promised an enormous swing in the American political pendulum. America, it seemed, had repudiated one of its most liberal political leaders and embraced one of its most conservative.

But those who hoped for a major swing to the right in public policy would be disappointed. Richard Nixon would turn out to be a less doctrinaire man than his opponents had feared. He would support some of the environmentalists' policies, endorse a guaranteed annual income, and end the American quarantine of

Communist China. Nixon was scarcely a liberal, and during a second full administration might have devoted more attention to the conservative agenda. But his character failings and his political limitations would erupt in the form of Watergate and prevent him from achieving anything after 1972.

His successor, Gerald Ford, though also a conservative, had little prestige and standing, and he damaged whatever moral authority he might have had by pardoning the ex-president. Though in 1976 the public repudiated Ford for a more liberal man, it did not betoken an ideological shift. Carter nonetheless might have reversed the conservative current if he had been adept and likable. He was neither, and in 1980 the voters turned him out of office to try once more to get what they had failed to do in 1968. In the end it was Ronald Reagan, rather than Richard Nixon, who would launch the real conservative experiment.

For Further Reading

Richard Nixon. *Six Crises* (1962)

Published just before Nixon's defeat in his 1962 race for the California governorship. Tells Nixon's own version of major crises in his life, including the Hiss case, the Checkers Speech, Eisenhower's heart attack, Nixon's near-catastrophic visit to Caracas, the "kitchen debate" with Khrushchev, and the 1960 presidential contest with Kennedy.

Gary Wills. *Nixon Agonistes: The Crisis of the Self-Made Man* (1970)

One of the best analyses of Richard Nixon and his place in American political history. It is also a valuable comment on the contradictions and illusions of the liberal tradition in twentieth-century American history.

Theodore White. *Breach of Faith: The Fall of Richard Nixon* (1975)

An excellent summary of Watergate by a master of political journalism who once admired Nixon.

Richard Nixon. *Memoirs* (1978)

This book illustrates the importance of looking at both sides of almost any story. Not ultimately convincing, but it does make it clear that Nixon was a fallible human being, not some inhuman monster.

Henry Kissinger. *The White House Years* (1979)

A fascinating inside report on the making of American foreign policy during Nixon's first four years, by his national security adviser at the time. Kissinger gives Nixon generally high marks as a diplomat, but also reveals this president—and himself—to be poor administrators and rather devious men.

John Osborne. *White House Watch: The Ford Years* (1977)

A moderate appreciation of the Ford administration by a liberal journalist.

Robert Shogan. *Promises to Keep: Carter's First Hundred Days* (1977)

A journalist's favorable report on the Carter administration's first three months in office. Shogan was allowed to attend cabinet meetings to write this book. A curiosity in light of the later course of the Carter administration.

Haynes Johnson. *In the Absence of Power: Governing America* (1980)

A thoughtful indictment of the Carter administration for its feebleness and lack of competence.

Studs Terkel. *Working People Talk about What They Do All Day and How They Feel about What They Do* (1974)

Terkel turned on his tape recorder and interviewed 130 people from a wide range of occupations, socioeconomic groups, and ethnic communities. Here they talk about the frustrations and gratifications of earning a living in the 1970s while maintaining their sense of individual worth.

Barry Commoner. *The Politics of Energy* (1979)

An indictment of American energy policy by a man of the political left. Commoner believes that most of the nation's energy difficulties have been caused by big-business groups greedy for profits. Central planning, he says, can solve them.

Robert B. Stobaugh and Daniel Yergin, editors. *Energy Future: Report of the Energy Project at the Harvard Business School* (1978)

The authors of the essays that make up this study *do* take the energy crisis seriously. It is real, not manufactured. They recommend various solutions, but say that the most effective way to deal with the crisis is strict conservation of energy resources.

William Quandt, *Decade of Decision: American Policy Toward the Arab-Israeli Conflict* (1977)

The single best volume on this important subject.

Christopher Lasch. *The Culture of Narcissism: American Life in an Age of Diminishing Expectations* (1979)

A pessimistic and somewhat carping book about what has gone wrong with American culture in the 1970s. Like so many other contemporary studies of American culture and society, this book is both a diagnosis and a symptom of the problem it diagnoses.

Ralph E. Smith, editor. *The Subtle Revolution: Women at Work* (1979)

A survey of the enormous changes that have taken place in women's roles in the American economy since 1945, with special emphasis in the 1970s.

Paul Freiberger and Michael Swaine. *Fire in the Valley: The Making of the Personal Computer* (1984)

The best single-volume history of a subject so new that the ancient past is 1975. Good reading if you've got an Apple or PC.

Kirkpatrick Sale. *Power Shift: The Rise of the Southern Rim and Its Challenge to the Eastern Establishment* (1975)

A good analysis of the political rise of the Sun Belt and its significance for national affairs.

Chapter 31

The "Reagan Revolution":

What Was It? What Did It Accomplish?

1980   Ronald Reagan elected president • Republicans gain control of Senate

1981   Beginning of Reagan era • Conservative agenda put into place • Cutbacks in domestic social programs • Huge increases for defense • Tax cuts seen as stimulus to economic growth • Deregulation of industries • Reagan fires striking air traffic controllers

1982   Budget deficits mount • Breakup of AT&T • Midterm elections see Democrats pick up seats in House while GOP retains Senate control • Contra aid a political issue

1983   Reagan continues to stress military buildup; adds new missiles in Europe • American marines sent to Lebanon • President pushes Star Wars to counter Soviet missile threat • 241 marines killed in Beirut terrorist attack • Soviets shoot down Korean airliner killing 269 • US-Soviet relations worsen

1984   Reagan reelected in landslide • AIDS crisis grows ever larger

1985   Stock Market continues to be bullish

1986   Space shuttle disaster • Trade imbalance worsens • US jets attack Libya • Reagan-Gorbachev summit in Iceland ends on chilly note • Iran-Contra scandal breaks

1987   Congress probes Iran-Contra affair; televised hearings begin • Bork nomination to Supreme Court defeated in Senate • Stock Market crash • Reagan and Gorbachev meet in Washington and sign agreement eliminating medium-range missiles from Europe • Scandals beset religious right

1988   Reagan era winds down • Jesse Jackson shows surprise strength in Democratic primaries • Economy experiences upswing

R onald Reagan came to office as spokesman of the same forces that had supported Richard Nixon in 1968 only to see their hopes dashed by Nixon's political downfall. When sworn in on January 20, 1981, the new president emphasized one central theme. "Government," he said, was "not the solution to our problem. Government is the problem." Above all, he would "get the government back within its means and . . . lighten our punitive tax burden." In 1989 a new president would stand in the same place, making *his* pledges of change. Those intervening eight years have sometimes been called the "Reagan Revolution," implying major shifts in the course the nation was traveling.

Was there a "Reagan Revolution"? What did Reagan accomplish in his two terms? Did the nation benefit or lose by the efforts of the administration that came to office in January 1981?

The First Term

Taxes. As Reagan's Inaugural Address made plain, the conservative critique of recent America focused on the abuses of "big government" and especially its dangerous power to tax. This emphasis was not new among conservatives. As far back as the late 1970s they had made drastic tax reduction a critical part of their agenda. The passage in 1978 of Proposition 13 in California by a coalition of conservatives had signalled the political right's revival in the 1980s. This measure sharply reduced property taxes. In one year California state taxes fell by almost 40 percent. However, Proposition 13 also severely reduced the state's ability to support social programs and education.

The coalition of forces behind Proposition 13 included defenders of the laissez-faire teachings of Adam Smith and his eighteenth- and nineteenth-century collaborators. It also included "libertarians" who opposed virtually all government as a violation of personal freedom. Many libertarians were disciples of Ayn Rand, a writer and pop philosopher who expressed her frank elitist views through novels like *The Fountainhead* and *Atlas Shrugged*, which glorified the lone hero fighting the ignorant and conformist mob. To such philosophical conservatives, cutting taxes was part of a larger ideological whole. It meant shrinking the entire welfare state system to the point where it no longer, they said, forced the enterprising and the successful to carry the lazy and the incompetent on their backs.

Not all tax reducers were moved by ideology. High taxes indeed shackled enterprise and discouraged innovation. Arguably, they encouraged tax evasion. Many people were "working off the books," taking money in cash that they did not declare as income for services or goods, and creating a whole "underground economy." There was also the real problem of "bracket creep," the effect produced by steeply progressive tax rates during an inflationary era. As wages and prices rose, the tax system took an ever larger proportion of personal income without any increase in tax rates. One very powerful force behind the tax-reduction drive was frankly self-serving: High-income people simply wanted to keep a larger share of what they earned. Yet by 1980 the tax-reduction issue had become entwined in a conservative political philosophy.

The conservative tax cutters had foreseen one serious problem in their program. Slash taxes but continue to spend and the result would be federal deficits of enormous size. For years Republican conservatives had denounced the Democrats' deficit spending. It had produced an enormous national debt of over $900 billion by 1980, almost $4,000 for every man, woman, and child in the country. This was a colossal burden on enterprise and must be reduced, conservatives argued. The Reagan administration fully intended to cut programs to offset the lower tax revenues, but what if the administration could not get all the cuts it wanted? There was a convenient answer at hand. Borrowing from the "supply-side" theories of Arthur Laffer, administration experts claimed that a major tax cut, by unleashing the country's creative energies, would expand the economy so rapidly that the government's total revenues would actually grow—automatically—without pain to anyone. During the 1980 Republican primary campaign, George Bush, Reagan's chief rival, would call this theory "voodoo economics," a tag he of course repudiated when he secured second place on the ticket.

Inevitably, after the dust of the inauguration had settled, the administration's first order of business was a tax-cutting bill. Prepared by David Stockman, head of the Office of Management and Budget, a cocky young former congressman from Michigan, the proposed cuts were the most extensive in the country's history. The Democrats controlled the House of Representatives and might have defeated the measure, but Reagan proved an enormously effective parliamentary leader. Using cajolery, personal charm, and liberal patronage promises, he won over enough conservative Democrats, primarily from the South (the "Boll Weevils"), to his side to get his bill through.

The Economic Recovery Act of 1981 mandated a 25-percent cut in everyone's personal income tax over a three-year period and a sharp reduction, from a 70 percent to a 50 percent maximum, of taxes on unearned income. It also authorized what one Reagan official described as "the largest tax cut in the history of American business" to stimulate investment.

Conservatives hailed the measure as a long-overdue unleashing of the nation's innovative energies. But there were deep private doubts within the administration itself. Stockman admitted in a frank 1981 magazine article that "greed" had been a key motivating factor in writing the tax bill. After he resigned as budget director, Stockman wrote a best-selling book on his administration years in which he described the White House staff as "illiterate when it came to the essential equation of policy." These were people who "never read anything," and "lived off the tube." The president himself was "a kind, gentle, and sentimental man," but he was incapable of understanding "the complexities, intricacies, and mysteries involved in the tax breaks."

Actually, according to Stockman, although the administration professed to believe the supply-side doctrines, it had a secret agenda. Many administration officials hoped, he said, that if the deficits following the tax cuts grew too fast, the liberals would be compelled to cut their wasteful domestic programs. Thus the threat of soaring budget deficits could be put to good use in the conservative war against the welfare state. Liberals would later claim that it was this desire that actually was at the heart of the administration's tax policy.

The Economy. At first the tax cut failed to produce the economic stimulus its proponents had promised. But these early months were not a fair test. Toward the end of the Carter administration, Paul Volcker, head of the Federal Reserve System, had tightened the

David Stockman, the Reagan administration's conservative budget adviser, apparently expressing a skeptical opinion of several liberal "entitlement" programs.

money supply and raised interest rates to take the steam out of inflation. By the time Reagan came to office the "Fed's" policies had slowed private spending and investment and produced a business recession. By December 1982, unemployment soared to 10.8 percent of the labor force; 12 million Americans were out of work. This was the largest percentage of jobless since the Great Depression. It was worse among blacks and teenagers: 20.2 percent and 24 percent, respectively.

But the "Fed's" tight money policies finally began to affect prices as well. In 1980, Carter's last year, consumer prices had risen by over 13 percent. By 1983 price rises had slowed to a little over 3 percent. Toward the end of Reagan's second term pessimists would warn that inflation was still an untamed dragon, but in fact it would never become the frightening monster of the late 1970s.

Volcker and the president would be given credit for ending the socially and economically ruinous inflation of the 1970s. Actually, many forces contributed to the advent of relative price stability. Clearly one major price deflator of the Reagan years was the end of the oil shortage. By the early 1980s conservation measures had begun to ease world petroleum demand, while at the same time total world oil output, stimulated by high prices in the 1970s, began to grow. Before long the world was awash in oil reserves. Dramatic oil price declines would not come until mid-decade, but by 1982 the decade-long price increases had ceased, removing a major force behind the powerful inflation thrust of the seventies.

Reagan and Labor

Ronald Reagan, though at one time a trade-union leader himself, was not organized labor's closest friend. His coolness toward the trade-union movement showed itself in many ways, but one of the most dramatic was his firing of all the members of PATCO, the Professional Air Traffic Controller Organization, for striking against the government. The strike was indeed illegal, but it is hard to believe that a pro-labor president would not have shown more forebearance.

The following is a report of a press conference held August 3, 1981, in which Reagan and his attorney general announced their plans to clamp down on the striking air controllers.

The President. This morning at 7 A.M. the union representing those who man America's air traffic control facilities called a strike. This was the culmination of 7 months of negotiations between the Federal Aviation Administration and the union. At one point in these negotiations agreement was reached and signed by both sides, granting a $40 million increase in salaries and benefits. This is twice what other government employees can expect. It was granted in recognition of the difficulties inherent in the work these people perform. Now, however, the union demands are 17 times what had been agreed to—$681 million. This would impose a tax burden on their fellow citizens which is unacceptable.

I would like to thank the supervisors and controllers who are on the job today, helping to get the nation's air system operating safety. In the New York area, for example, four supervisors were scheduled to report for work, and 17 additionally volunteered. At National Airport a traffic controller told a newsperson he had resigned from the union and reported to work because, "How can I ask my kids to obey the law if I don't?" This is a great tribute to America.

Let me make one thing plain. I respect the right of workers in the private sector to strike. Indeed, as president of my own union, I led the first strike ever called by that union. I guess I'm maybe the first one to ever hold this office who is a lifetime member of an AFL–CIO union. But we cannot compare labor-management relations in the private sector with government. Government cannot close down the assembly line. It has to provide without interruption the protective services which are government's reason for being.

It was in recognition of this that the Congress passed a law forbidding strikes by government employees against the public safety. Let me read the solemn oath taken by each of these employees, a sworn affidavit, when they accepted their jobs: "I am not participating in any strike against the Government of the United States or any agency thereof, and I will not so participate while an employee of the Government of the United States or any agency thereof."

It is for this reason that I must tell those who fail to report for duty this morning they are in violation of the law, and if they do not report for work within 48 hours, they have forfeited their jobs and will be terminated.

Q. Mr. President, are you going to order any union members who violate the law to go to jail?

The President. Well, I have some people around here, and maybe I should refer that question to the Attorney General.

Q. Do you think that they should go to jail, Mr. President, anybody who violates this law?

The President. I told you what I think should be done. They're terminated.

The Attorney General. Well, as the President has said, striking under these circumstances constitutes a violation of the law, and we intend to initiate in appropriate cases criminal proceedings against those who have violated the law.

Q. How quickly will you initiate criminal proceedings, Mr. Attorney General?

The Attorney General. We will initiate those proceedings as soon as we can.

Another important inflation-easing force was the declining bargaining power of American labor. Here, the rising unemployment rates of 1980 to 1983 were significant. Wage earners do not threaten strikes to force wage increases from their employers when business is bad and there are thousands of unemployed ready and willing to take their jobs. In the early 1980s, with over 10 percent of the labor force jobless, wage pressures inevitably eased. Unions were compelled not only to moderate their wage demands to avoid further layoffs but they were often forced to "give back" wage and fringe benefits they had previously won for their members.

If organized labor had been a more powerful force in America during the 1980s, the wage-depressing effects of the slump might have been more limited.

But organized labor was weak and defensive by the time Reagan took office.

Several factors explained labor's decline. During the 1950s unions had lost prestige because of Communist infiltration and connections with organized crime. They had also suffered from the changing nature of the labor force. Unions had always been strongest among male workers and, since the 1930s, within heavy industry, especially steel, coal, and automobiles. By the 1980s the proportion of male to total workers had declined. So had the proportion of industrial workers to the total. By 1980 the coal, steel, and automobile industries—the "smokestack" industries—were all in trouble owing to foreign competition and had cut back on their labor force. It is true that the service trades had simultaneously ballooned. But white-collar service workers were more resistant to union organizing than were blue-collar workers. The shift of industry to the South, the section most resistant to the trade union movement, led to further membership losses. Unions made valiant attempts to organize the new groups and, in fact, made some inroads among public employees. But overall they were less successful with them than with the northern male craftsmen and industrial workers of the past.

The Reagan administration helped to make these trends worse. Reagan's appointees to the National Labor Relations Board, the New Deal–created agency that supervised union collective-bargaining elections, drastically slowed the process of authorizing elections, putting an effective damper on unionization. Union membership dropped sharply during the Reagan years.

In 1960, 24 percent of American workers belonged to unions. As late as 1980 this figure remained at 23 percent. By 1987 it was down six more percentage points. All told, during the period from 1980 to 1984, total trade union membership dropped by over 2.7 million members.

The president also took a tough line toward work stoppages. In August 1981, when the air traffic controllers called an illegal strike against the government, Reagan fired all 11,000 members and refused to hire them back when they relented. The lesson of all this was clear: This president did not "sup at labor's table," and it would be wise for the unions to pull in their horns and modify their demands.

Reagan and the Poor.   As we have noted, the administration hoped to use the tax cut to justify cutting domestic social programs. But its opposition to the welfare state was not merely fiscal. Reagan and his advisers were passionately convinced that the welfare programs of the 1960s, many still flourishing in 1980, had only made poverty and dependency worse. As conservative social thinker Charles Murray would write in 1984, the nation's poverty programs had "tried to provide more for the poor and produced more poor instead." In 1968, 13 percent of Americans had been classified as "poor." The proportion of poor in 1980 was exactly the same: 13 percent. And all this had cost billions of dollars! How could better results be achieved—and at less expense? Their views were also influenced by their class affiliations. There is no question that a substantial portion of Reagan supporters were successful

The smiles did not last. President Reagan soon fired the striker air traffic controllers.

middle-class people who, whatever their attitudes during the 1960s, by the 1980s had ceased to feel much sympathy with those who had been left behind in the "race of life."

Liberals denounced the proposed cuts in welfare as selfish and cruel. The president assured the public that his policies would maintain a "safety net" for the most vulnerable and disadvantaged groups in society. He would, however, get rid of the "welfare cheats" who received money, though actually unqualified under the law; he would eliminate programs that had proved ineffective; he would reduce high administrative costs. Wherever possible he would demand that the able-bodied work rather than receive handouts. Liberals were not reassured.

Spurred by the administration's goading, Congress cut back substantially on federal social programs. It reduced the food stamp program by 14 percent; the child nutrition program by 28 percent, Aid to Families with Dependent Children by 14 percent, Supplemental Security Income by 11 percent, Low Income Energy Assistance by 11 percent, financial aid for needy students 16 percent, job-training programs 37 percent, health block grants 24 percent, and many others in similar proportions. The president and his colleagues claimed that none of this seriously harmed the poor; his critics claimed that its effects were devastating.

Cutting through the rhetoric to the truth is not easy. There can be no question that the poor were hurt. One estimate suggests that between 1983 and 1985 the tax- and services-cutting policies together reduced the income of households earning less than $20,000 a year by a total of $20 billion and increased that of families making more than $80,000 by $35 billion. By 1984 the Census Bureau reported that income distribution in the United States was more unequal than at any time since 1947, when the bureau first began to collect accurate figures on the subject. By 1984 the proportion of Americans living below the official "poverty line" had grown from 13 percent in 1980 to 14.3 percent. Nor was the loss felt only by the poorest. In 1986 the "middle fifth" of income recipients, those people dead center economically, were receiving a lower proportion of total national income than at any time since 1947.

But there was another side of the coin as well. By the late 1980s unemployment had fallen below 6 percent nationally, and in states like Massachusetts, where hi-tech industries had taken deep root, it was even lower. In Massachusetts the "trickle down" process, whereby overall prosperity helped even the poor, did not work too badly. But Massachusetts and a few other high-tech states were not typical, and the poor suffered. Clearly the educated middle class was flourishing and its own prosperity made it insensitive to the plight of the poor. The new class of yuppies seemed unashamed of greed and cared little about those who had dropped by the economic wayside.

But even if the poor had gotten poorer under Reagan, clear answers to chronic poverty were not obvious. The existing welfare system was not very effective. The programs were necessary, perhaps, to keep people from starving, but they were obviously incapable of transforming society's unsuccessful and their children into self-supporting members of the community. Merely throwing money at poverty would never, it seemed, create confident, independent men and women capable of self-support. People will only sacrifice when they think it will lead to some positive goal. By 1981, the whole welfare "mess" seemed so intractable that it is easy to understand why most middle-class citizens tried to put it out of their minds.

Yet we must not assume that the Reagan administration was able to demolish the entire welfare state constructed since the 1930s. The administration did not get more than a portion of the domestic program cuts it proposed. Behind every "entitlement"—whether useful and economical, or ineffective and wasteful— was a powerful constituency that resisted elimination or drastic cuts. A Democratic House, and even the Republican-controlled Senate, often refused to give the president what he wanted. Despite its efforts, the administration was unable to secure the domestic budget cuts it pushed for. The feeling seemed to be: "Cut the other fellow's program; it's a waste of money. But leave mine alone." The administration's efforts to slash programs it believed expendable met fierce resistance and achieved only modest success.

None of these programs was as sacred, or as untouchable, as Social Security. As the decade progressed, it became ever clearer that the aged were no longer an underprivileged group. The income of people over age sixty-five, owing to private pension plans and Social Security payments, was now greater than average. The poor were now primarily families with young children, especially those headed by single parents. Children, in effect, were the new poor. Why continue to cosset the elderly when so many of them were well off? the critics asked. Why not limit the benefits of those over sixty-five in the name of social equity?

The Social Security system was also becoming enormously expensive and economically unsound. And yet well-organized lobbies for "senior citizens" were able to prevent most attempts to cap Social Security

A "Gray Panther" lady defending her income against Reagan administration efforts to economize.

payments or tax Social Security income. When the president proposed revisions to hold down soaring Social Security outlays and make the system fiscally workable, the outcry from elderly voters forced him to drop the issue like a hot potato. Eventually it required a bipartisan congressional commission to add some common sense to the system by increasing Social Security taxes, skipping some projected increases, and mandating a gradual rise in the minimum retirement age.

All told, then, the administration was forced to retain much of the welfare state it had inherited from its predecessors.

Defense Policy. An even worse budget-buster was defense appropriations. Like many conservatives, Reagan considered Carter's foreign policies feeble and believed his predecesor had allowed the Soviet Union to leap ahead of the United States. During the 1980 presidential campaign he described a "window of vulnerability" in nuclear arms as well as deficiencies in conventional arms that had to be corrected if America was to remain strong. Reagan came to office pledged to a massive arms build-up that would increase American military power relative to the Soviet Union. Though a one-time liberal who had deplored Cold War antagonisms for a time after World War II, during the 1960s and 1970s Reagan had become intensely suspicious of the Soviets and wary of their aggressive policies around the world. At one point during his presidency he would call the Soviet Union an "evil empire," and "the focus of evil in the modern world."

In the first news conference of his administration the president attacked détente. It had been "a one-way street" that the Soviet Union had "used to pursue its own aims." Among his earliest proposals as president was a five-year, $1.7-trillion increase in defense spending to catch up with the Soviets. Congress scaled down the administration's military shopping list despite the determined resistance of Secretary of Defense Caspar Weinberger, but overall defense outlays leaped from $135 billion in 1980 to $210 billion in 1983 to $231 billion in 1984. All told, the Reagan administration would engineer the largest military build-up in peacetime American history.

Budget Deficits. The explosion in defense spending more than offset the moderate cuts in domestic programs and, combined with the giant tax cuts, produced the largest budget deficits Americans had ever experienced. The results were ironic. As Democratic critics quickly pointed out, for decades the Republicans had denounced their opponents as wild spenders who had mortgaged the nation's future to gratify their urge to throw money at problems. Now, under a Republican president, the annual deficit went from Carter's $60 billion in 1980 to over $180 billion in 1984. By the final year of his first term, Reagan had increased the national debt by an additional $650 billion, a sum almost as great as the total deficits run up by every president from Franklin Roosevelt to Jimmy Carter.

The deficits frightened many people. Some of the criticism was clearly motivated by politics. Democrats, though seldom bothered before by large government shortfalls, now warned of financial catastrophe if the deficits were not reduced. More disturbing, the deficits created uneasiness in the business community and among academic economists. Heavy government borrowing, they said, would quickly exhaust the limited supply of domestic savings and propel interest rates still higher. In fact, this did not happen. Instead, billions of dollars from abroad—especially from Japan and Western Europe—flowed into American treasury coffers to meet the government's needs. But this process only raised other questions. Such foreign capital was volatile. It would be available only as long as American interest rates were relatively high and foreign investors had confidence in America's fiscal soundness. If interest rates fell, or if investors lost their faith in America's economic solvency, they might well pull their money out abruptly, causing a severe financial crunch. Mean-

During the 1980s Americans began to see a new economic phenomenon: Japanese-operated, Japanese-owned factories in the United States.

while, Congress and the president argued bitterly over cutting expenditures, with the Democrats determined that defense outlays must be reduced, and the administration demanding domestic budget cuts. During Reagan's first term, nothing was accomplished; the national debt continued to grow.

Deregulation and the Environment.

An important part of the president's economic program was deregulation of industry and business. Conservatives believed that the federal government should give business free rein to compete. All too often in the past, they argued, government regulation had condoned legal monopolies that only added to the public's costs. The process of deregulation had already begun in the Carter administration. In the communications industry, for example, the American Telephone and Telegraph Company (AT&T) had enjoyed virtually a legal monopoly of telephone services. In 1982, acting on a Justice Department lawsuit, the courts ordered the breakup of AT&T into twenty-two local Bell Companies plus a scaled-down AT&T, allowing the parent firm to enter the computer field and authorizing new firms to provide long-distance telephone service.

Even more thorough was the deregulation of the airline industry. This move brought many new discount companies into the airline business and reduced fares. But it also forced several major airline bankruptcies, the abandonment of some less popular routes, and the deterioration of service in the airline industry as a whole. By the end of the decade there were major complaints from airline passengers and deep concern about airline safety.

Under Reagan the hands-off process accelerated. The government reduced its consumer product supervision, cutting the budget for the agency that administered consumer safety laws from $41 million to $34 million, to the dismay of consumer advocates. Reagan's secretary of interior, James Watt, opened to private exploitation areas in national forests hitherto closed to mining and timber companies. He sought to weaken federal rules against strip mining and regulations to protect wildlife. Under Watt, the number of "emergency exemptions" for restrictions on pesticide use more than tripled. The secretary also proposed to sell off millions of acres of federal land to private interests.

Even more controversial was the administration's attempt to reduce the government's role in environmental protection. Many in the administration deplored what they considered the excesses of the environmentalists. By the 1980s, they said, every project to increase the country's energy output, improve the country's roads and highways, provide new office space, lower the cost of raw materials, or exploit natural resources inevitably crashed into a wall of environmental regulation or encountered a wave of environmental lawsuits. The presence of some obscure "endangered species," like the snail darter, could bring to a grinding halt a major dam project; the claim that a new building might cast a shadow over a park could stop a skyscraper from going up. Every major construction scheme was invariably burdened with reams of "environmental impact" statements and other elaborate documentation that added to costs. The administration claimed, then, that its chief concern was to lower costs and raise productivity. Its critics insisted that its anti-environmentalism was primarily a payoff to the business groups whose support it counted on. When criticized, the administration responded that its opponents were elitists who wished to preserve pristine environments that only a few could appreciate at the expense of jobs and growth that would benefit the many.

Although liberals claimed that the American voter still supported liberal causes, the public mood was undoubtedly more conservative than in the recent past. But environmental concerns still had powerful support. Many Americans remained deeply worried about water and air pollution from radioactive and chemical poisons, and they were willing to incur expense, and risk interference with private profit, to avoid exposure to these hazards.

The chief federal agency for safeguarding the public health against pollution and contaminants was the Environmental Protection Agency (EPA), established under Nixon in 1970 and given jurisdiction over a wide range of environmental concerns. During the Reagan administration, EPA's budget was steadily cut, falling from $5.6 billion in fiscal 1980 to $4.1 billion in fiscal 1984. Reagan's appointee as EPA head was Anne Burford, who administered a $1.4-billion "superfund" to clean up toxic waste dumpsites that dotted the nation and menaced the health of many Americans. Burford, however, was not an effective guardian of the public's health. Her sympathies seemed to lie primarily with the firms accused of pollution, and she came under attack for delaying the vast task of ridding the environment of places where chemical companies and industrial firms had disposed of dangerous substances over the years. In February 1983, Rita Lavelle, Burford's subordinate in charge of the clean-up program, resigned under fire from critics who charged that she had deliberately dragged her feet to protect various business groups from incuring the expense of paying for the clean up. The following December, she was convicted of perjury for denying knowledge of Burford's violation of waste-dumping laws. In March 1983, Burford too had resigned. Secretary of Interior Watt himself did not last much longer than Burford. In October 1983, after a crude remark that managed to insult Jews, the handicapped, blacks, and women simultaneously, the secretary quit and was replaced by William Clark.

First-Term Foreign Policy. Reagan's first term coincided with a gap in the leadership of the Soviet Union. In November 1982 Leonid Brezhnev, long-time head of the Soviet government, died of a heart attack. Brezhnev was seventy-six at the time of his death and for years had clung to conventional Soviet hard-line policies. His successor was the sixty-eight-year-old Yuri Andropov, a former head of the KGB, the Soviet security police. Neither Andropov's age nor his past associations raised any hope for changes in Soviet policies, and in fact his appointment seemed a mere stopgap while the Soviets sought a more permanent head of state. Less than two years later Andropov died and was succeeded by the sickly Konstantin Chernenko, who himself lasted a little more than a year. Not until the elevation as Communist Party Chairman in March 1985 of Mikhail Gorbachev, a vigorous man of fifty-four, did the prolonged Soviet succession crisis end.

In the interim Soviet-American relations had deteriorated. In September 1983, a Soviet fighter plane shot down a Korean airlines passenger jet that had wandered off course en route to Seoul, Korea, killing 269 passengers and crew. International opinion was outraged by the deed, and the Reagan administration used it as another occasion to condemn the Soviet regime.

More dangerous, many people believed, was the accelerating arms race with the Soviet Union. Besides the American arms build-up, the president and his advisers wanted to base additional intermediate-range Pershing missiles on the soil of our NATO allies in Western Europe to protect them against a similar Soviet missile arsenal. Anti-nuclear and peace groups in Britain, Holland, and West Germany protested this move as a revival of the arms race and another danger to peace. Despite this opposition, the missiles were emplaced.

The Soviets, predictably, were even more hostile to the Pershings and, in response, the Soviet negotiators in late 1983 walked out of the ongoing arms limitations talks in Geneva. The Soviets were concerned with more than the intermediate missiles, however. In March 1983 Reagan had proposed a Strategic Defense Initiative (SDI), soon labeled "Star Wars" by its opponents, to counter the Soviet nuclear threat. The United States, the president said, should develop a system of laser-equipped space satellites that could destroy enemy missiles after launch so that none could hit America. A successful SDI system, he declared, would render nuclear missiles obsolete and held out "the promise of changing the course of human history."

Until now both nations had relied on the principle of *mutual assured destruction* (MAD, its critics called it) to deter superpower nuclear war. If each superpower

Secretary of Interior James Watt against the sort of western scenery his opponents said he was determined to ruin.

could be certain that it possessed the nuclear arsenal to destroy an attacker, then, said the theory, no one would try an attack. In one way, MAD had worked. Although the Soviet Union and the United States had been fierce rivals for a generation or more, neither had pushed the other to the point of war. Now, the president was saying, we would abandon MAD with all its uncertainties and simply try to guarantee that any Soviet attack must fail.

The Soviets found the Star Wars scheme deeply disturbing. America was far ahead of the Soviet Union in the advanced computer and laser technology that Star Wars required. It would take an immense Soviet catch-up effort to avoid being placed in a position where the United States could destroy the Soviet Union and at the same time intercept and shoot down all retaliatory missiles directed at her. Star Wars, if successful, would end MAD as a stabilizing principle and shift the advantage to the United States. Some Americans found the Star Wars idea attractive for that very reason, but others, including many scientists and computer experts, believed it to be a grave mistake. It would create new uncertainties and dangers for international order, they said. It was also probably not workable. It was simply impossible, opponents claimed, to devise any system that could destroy in space all the hundreds of missiles that would be launched at us in the event of nuclear war, and even if only a few got

This is the way an artist imagined the starwar (SDI) system would work. In all likelihood the whole Strategic Defense Initiative will never be more real than this.

through the destruction would be enormous. Also, the system would be incredibly expensive, its costs running into the hundreds of billions of dollars.

Yet despite the objections, Congress voted preliminary funding for Star Wars research. Some members did so because they believed the scheme was feasible; others felt that Star Wars was a splendid bargaining chip with the Soviet Union. If the Soviets were sufficiently frightened by it they would be encouraged to make concessions on nuclear arms and other matters. Star Wars did not actually have to work to further America's vital interests.

Reagan was equally aggressive in other corners of the world, although when real danger appeared, prudence often overcame his hard line. In the Middle East the president maintained close ties with Israel and was rumored to have encouraged the Israeli invasion of Lebanon in 1982. In September 1983, in the hope of pacifying that chronically chaotic country, Reagan sent American marines to Lebanon. Rather than bringing peace, the marines themselves became targets of warring Lebanese factions, several of them representing violently anti-American, pro-Iranian groups. Earlier in the year a Muslim fanatic had detonated an explosives-laden truck next to the American embassy in Beirut, killing forty-seven people, including sixteen Americans. In October 1983, soon after the marines arrived, another Muslim terrorist carried out a similar attack against the marine barracks in Beirut, killing 241 American servicemen. In February 1984 the president decided that the marines were too exposed and removed them from the scene of the violence. Many Americans questioned whether the entire affair had not betrayed impulsiveness mixed with weakness, a disastrous combination in the conduct of international affairs. Meanwhile, ominously, the same anti-American Muslim groups in Lebanon had begun to take hostages among the Americans residing in Beirut, and the media, as well as the victims' families, began to pressure the administration to do something to recover the kidnapped men.

Reagan's foreign policy mistakes did not affect his standings in the public opinion polls. Somehow, Americans considered even his failures acceptable. The president's personal charm, his relaxed manner, and his good looks sugar-coated his actions. The "great communicator" was able to convey a verbal message of no-nonsense toughness toward America's enemies that conflicted at times with his timid actions. He was able to seem like a "good guy" while cutting programs for the poor. A generation raised on images seemed to take his words and manner more seriously than his deeds. Exasperated opponents would dub him the "Teflon president," because nothing adverse seemed to stick to his political skin.

Nicaragua. Reagan's policies in Central America and the Caribbean were in tune with his general anti-Soviet views. The president and his advisers saw the hands of the Soviets and their Western Hemisphere surrogate, Cuba's Fidel Castro, behind much of the social and political unrest in Latin America. They feared the Marxist powers might establish another beachhead in the Americas that, like Cuba, would threaten America's interests in the Western Hemisphere. In El Salvador the administration intervened to help the conservative-to-moderate regime of Napoleon Duarte against a Marxist-led insurgency. In October 1983, American troops invaded the tiny island republic of Grenada, ostensibly to ensure the safety of several hundred American students studying for their medical degrees on the island, but actually to keep the Cubans from getting a toehold. The action satisfied the American public's yearning for redress after the inglorious Lebanon fiasco, but peace groups and a number of America's allies condemned it as unnecessary aggression.

The most inflamed point in the Americas was Nicaragua, like El Salvador, a small republic in Central America. The country was ruled by the Sandinistas, a leftist group responsible for the overthrow in 1979 of the American-supported strongman, Anastasio Somoza. Since coming to power, the Sandinistas, led by Daniel Ortega, had established a one-party political system and had governed by increasingly dogmatic and authoritarian Marxist principles. Observers disagreed over whether the Sandinistas were inherently anti-American and pro-Soviet, or whether the United States had pushed them in that direction. The administration had no doubt that the Sandinistas were allied with Castro and the Soviet Union and accused them of aiding the Salvadorean rebels and stirring up general anti-American discontent in Latin America.

Reagan tried to topple the Sandinista regime and replace it with one to America's liking. The administration undertook spying operations in Nicaragua, conducted intimidating military and naval maneuvers near the Nicaraguan border in Honduras and off the Nicaraguan coast, and, early in 1984, began to mine Nicaraguan harbors to prevent the delivery of Soviet and Cuban arms to the Sandinistas.

But the administration's chief weapon against the Nicaraguan leftists was the "Contras," anti-Sandinista exiles, some of them Somoza supporters, but many of them moderates, who despised Ortega and

his regime as repressive and pro-Soviet. The American government provided arms, logistical support, and intelligence to the Contras, hoping they would overthrow Ortega and establish a government friendly to the United States.

Americans had mixed feelings about the civil war raging in Nicaragua and about America's role in it. Most deplored another Marxist bridgehead in the Americas, but many also feared a repetition of the Vietnam quagmire with the locale shifted to our own hemisphere.

The debate over Nicaragua in the media and Congress would simmer slowly through the president's first four years. Then, in mid-October 1984, expressing majority opinion in the nation at large, Congress would cut off military aid to the Contras. Within the National Security Council, the action would set in motion forces that would precipitate a major political crisis.

Reelection. In 1982 the administration had faced, and failed, its first electoral challenge. The midterm congressional elections found the country still lagging economically, with the unemployment rate at 9.7 percent. The Republicans blamed the recession on their predecessors: Carter and the Democrats were responsible for the hard times. The maneuver failed, and the Democrats made substantial gains in the House of Representatives, though losing one seat in the Senate.

By 1984 the economy had sprung back. There remained many soft spots, especially in the old Snow Belt industrial areas, but the South and West were booming, and those parts of the Northeast that had made the successful transition to computers, hi-tech, and the "information revolution" had recovered remarkably. Although the poor were still poor, middle-class America had begun to feel flush and confident.

As the 1984 presidential election approached, then, the Democrats faced a popular president who claimed to have ended the decade-long inflation surge and brought renewed prosperity. Yet the Democratic nomination attracted a wide field of competitors, including Senator Gary Hart of Colorado, a former aide to George McGovern; Senator John Glenn of Ohio, the former astronaut; the Reverend Jesse Jackson, an associate of Martin Luther King, Jr., and the first serious black presidential candidate; and Carter's vice president, Walter Mondale. The colorless Glenn quickly fell by the wayside, but the other three were soon battling fiercely for delegates.

Each represented a different option for Democratic voters. The handsome, breezy Hart appealed to younger, "yuppie" voters, with his talk of getting away from the tired ideas of the Great Society and the need to stimulate economic growth and make America competitive in the world. Jackson attracted support from blacks and from the party's most liberal wing. His goal, he proclaimed, was to establish a "Rainbow Coalition" of all the nation's outsiders and dissenters, including racial and ethnic minorities, homosexuals, and feminists. No one expected Jackson to actually win the nomination, but he promised to gather enough support to be a major Democratic power broker. Unfortunately for the Rainbow Coalition, Jackson made some off-the-record anti-Semitic remarks during the campaign that offended many Democrats and threatened to divide the party.

Mondale represented the party's mainstream. His supporters included most of the party's traditional blue-collar, trade-union voters and the surviving old New Dealers, but his opponents accused him of being the candidate of the liberal "special interests" such as Social Security pensioners, racial minorities, and organized labor.

By the time the Democratic convention assembled in San Francisco, Mondale, with trade-union money

The volatile Democratic presidential candidate Gary Hart in a pose imitative of Adlai Stevenson—though Stevenson's shoes had only one hole.

and support, had a clear majority and won on the first ballot. The convention itself was a brilliant media performance. Jackson gracefully apologized for his divisive remarks; the keynote speaker, governor Mario Cuomo of New York, eloquently celebrated the Democrats' traditional ability to make one "family" of many diverse American strains. Mondale himself boldly chose a woman, Congresswoman Geraldine Ferraro of New York, as his running mate, and just as boldly promised, if elected, to support a tax increase to bring down the escalating budget deficits. For a few brief days in late summer the polls showed the Mondale-Ferraro ticket neck-and-neck with the Reagan-Bush ticket, reconfirmed without opposition at the August Republican convention in Dallas.

In the end, the contest was no contest. By the early fall of 1984 the economy was booming and most Americans felt that Ronald Reagan had restored America's standing in the world. Underscoring the new pride was the sweep by the Americans at the summer Olympic games in Los Angeles, for which the president somehow gained credit. As the election contest reached the home stretch, one Reagan adviser noted that he "almost felt sorry for Mondale, . . . it's like running against *America.*"

A Reagan victory was certainly a foregone conclusion, but the Democrats did their cause little good. The promise of higher taxes proved a mistake. The out-of-control budget deficit was a serious problem, but as yet no one felt its effects, and the Democratic candidate's proposal seemed to many Americans another example of the Democratic commitment to heavy taxation. Geraldine Ferraro proved a liability rather than an asset when her financial disclosure created the impression that there was something shady about the sources of her family's income. Mondale did little to appease the South, the core of Democratic strength for over a hundred years and now uneasy with the party's liberal leadership. In fact, by first appointing and then firing Bert Lance, a Georgian, as head of the Democratic National Committee, the candidate offended many southern voters.

Mondale's chief hope lay in winning the televised presidential debates. A smarter and better-informed man than the president, he might tip the balance by putting the "great communicator" to shame. In the first of the two debates, the challenger clearly bested the incumbent, making Reagan appear old and bumbling. But the president recovered in the second debate, and this showing restored the public's confidence in him.

On election day it was a Reagan landslide; the

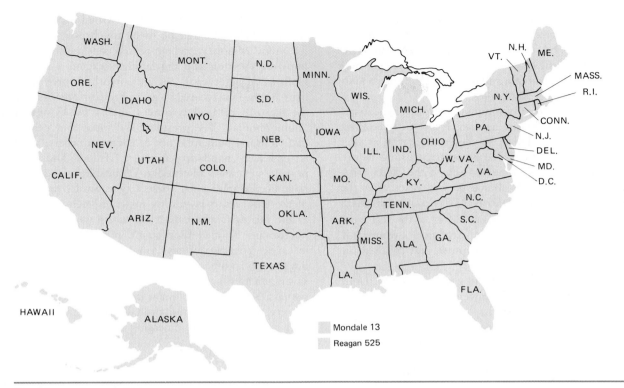

The electoral vote, 1984

Republican ticket won every state except Minnesota, Mondale's home state, and garnered 59 percent of the popular vote. The Republicans had done well in almost every electoral sector. Despite Ferraro, a large majority of women had voted Republican; so had a majority of Catholics and many more Jews than in the past. Young and old had gone for the president. The Moral Majority, Reagan's allies on the religious right, had managed to register more voters than the Rainbow Coalition, and its success showed, especially in the South and West. There was one bit of good news for the Democrats, however. Despite the Reagan landslide, the new House of Representatives would remain under Democratic control.

The Second Four Years

Few presidents have accomplished as much in their second term as in their first. By the beginning of its fifth year a successful administration has achieved most of its agenda and has depleted its energies. Besides, all its tricks have become familiar and easy to counter. In Reagan's case the problems were compounded by

the 1986 midterm elections, when the Democrats regained control of the Senate, making it even more difficult for the administration to win congressional cooperation than before.

The administration's second-term problems were aggravated by the president's age and health. Reagan was already seventy when he became president, the oldest man to hold the presidential office. In addition, he had survived an assassination attempt in 1981, and by 1987 he had undergone surgery for colon cancer and an enlarged prostate. At times in his second term he seemed to be tired, distracted, and forgetful. He still read prepared speeches well, but did poorly at extemporaneous press conferences where he had to think on his feet, and so avoided them. Some Americans would believe he had lost his grip.

The AIDS Crisis. Troubles and conflicts would come in shoals during Reagan's second four years. In 1981 the calamity of AIDS burst on the scene when scientists discovered that a hitherto unknown agent was attacking the immune systems of thousands of victims and destroying their resistance to cancer and infectious diseases. It soon became apparent that the afflicted were predominantly homosexual males and the disease was transmitted through infected bodily fluids including semen and blood. In 1984 French and American scientists identified the disease-causing agent as a virus that entered the bloodstream and destroyed the body's ability to manufacture antibodies.

AIDS (Acquired Immune Deficiency Syndrome) was not a "gay" disease as such. It also infected drug users who shared heroin needles with others, as well as people who had received blood transfusions before techniques were developed to screen the AIDS virus from blood donations. But even five years after the first data became available, over 70 percent of all AIDS victims remained homosexuals. Most of the rest were intravenous drug users. The great majority were adult men, though the number of women and children infected with AIDS was growing.

The disease ravaged the gay community. Until its advent, homosexuals, concentrated primarily in a few large, cosmopolitan cities like New York, San Francisco, Chicago, and Los Angeles, had developed a confidence and assertiveness beyond anything in the past. The mood fed a sexually permissive lifestyle that provided the perfect environment for the AIDS virus to flourish and spread. AIDS ran through New York's Greenwich Village, the Castro district in San Francisco, and other gay communities like the Black Death, cutting down young men in the thousands and undermining the hard-won self-confidence that gays had acquired since the late 1960s. It also produced a sharp upsurge of anti-gay feeling. Though the disease obviously afflicted other groups, social conservatives, including many of the Moral Majority, saw it as a sign of God's displeasure at homosexuality.

Although medical experts insisted that the disease could not be transmitted by casual contact, many people feared any contact with AIDS victims, however they had acquired the disease. People began to avoid contact with gays; they demanded that AIDS-infected children be kept from school. Medical personnel took to wearing masks and gloves when in the presence of AIDS patients. Some surgeons even declared they would not perform major operations on people infected with the AIDS virus. Fear of AIDS also began to affect relations between heterosexual men and women; experts claimed that all sexual contact with infected people created the risk of infection. Combined with a surge of genital herpes and other sexually transmitted diseases, the advent of AIDS brought to a quick end the permissive Sexual Revolution of the 1960s and 1970s.

The president was caught in the middle of the controversies and the anger that swirled around the AIDS scourge. Though he owed much politically to the Moral Majority, and supported conservative positions on abortion and the family, Reagan, a former Hollywood actor, was not an unworldly, provincial man. Yet he was accused by gays of resisting mobilizing the nation's medical resources against AIDS out of "homophobia." The president did insist that people had "a moral obligation not to endanger others," and he endorsed mandatory testing of federal and state prisoners, patients admitted to VA hospitals, and marriage-license applicants. These suggestions fell far short of the enforced mass-testing programs demanded by a few far right advocates, but many gays and civil libertarians claimed they would place the jobs and insurance coverage of gays in jeopardy and were preliminary to an official policy of quarantine. Some even saw it as a harbinger of concentration camps for homosexuals. Never highly popular in the homosexual community, the administration probably lost whatever support it had among an emerging self-conscious social minority.

Retreat of the Religious Right. As his second term approached its end Reagan also found his support among the religious right less sustaining. The rapid growth of fundamentalist Protestant groups and their increasing self-confidence and political activism, as we have seen, had benefited Reagan and political conservatism generally. Since his election, the Moral Majority coalition and similar groups had applauded the president's pronouncements on abortion, on school prayer, on traditional family values. They had been less impressed with his actions. Reagan, some said, talked a good game but did little to implement it.

In 1987, following Justice Lewis Powell's decision to retire from the Supreme Court, the President sought to appease his supporters on the religious and political right by nominating Judge Robert Bork to succeed Powell on the High Court. Bork, a federal appeals court justice and former law professor, had opposed the judicial activism of many of his liberal predecessors on the bench. He had also attacked the Court's recent tendency to uphold the right of privacy against state interference and to expand civil liberties protections and the scope of affirmative action. Liberals, civil libertarians, even many middle-of-the-road citizens saw Bork as an extremist, outside the conservative mainstream, and they feared having him and his views entrenched for life at the nation's judicial center. After widely watched televised hearings, the Senate rejected him.

Angry at the defeat the administration defiantly nominated another far right-judge, Douglas Ginsburg. The hasty choice represented a victory for Attorney General Edwin Meese against the advice of Howard Baker and other White House moderates. Ginsburg soon confessed to having smoked marijuana while a law professor, and in a matter of days agreed to withdraw his name. The president then nominated Judge Anthony Kennedy of Sacramento, a man closer to the center, whom the Senate finally confirmed. But the ill-conceived initial selections underscored for many social conservatives how little the administration had accomplished in actually reversing the liberal trends of the day.

By 1987 the religious right itself was in retreat, a victim of its own excesses. The chief culprit in the reverse was Jim Bakker, a fundamentalist preacher who, along with his blonde wife, Tammy Faye, had become an evangelist media star on the flourishing religious right TV network. Bakker was one of a number of fundamentalist preachers who used the electronic media effectively to disseminate their messages of good works, salvation, righteous living, and antimodernism. He and other "televangelists" had vast followings who responded enthusiastically to their appeals for funds "to continue the good work." The Bakkers, in addition to their TV ministry (called PTL, "Praise the Lord") were sponsors of a large resort in Fort Mill, South Carolina, that combined the features of Disneyland, a revival camp, and a country club. There the devout, who paid a substantial sum, could spend their vacations soaking up the sun and God's word at the same time.

In March 1987 Bakker resigned as head of PTL after the media published stories that he had paid over $100,000 to a former PTL employee to keep her from revealing that he had sexually assaulted her. Soon after, he was also accused of having made homosexual advances to several young men.

Bakker's associates, unwilling to see PTL dismantled, called in Jerry Falwell, the Virginia preacher who in 1979 had founded Moral Majority, to rescue the organization. Falwell quickly uncovered serious financial irregularities in the management of PTL. He also revealed how the Bakkers had used the contributions of the faithful for their own private advantage.

The Jim and Tammy caper hurt the evangelical movement as a whole. Many sincere followers of fundamentalist preachers became disillusioned. Contributions to TV evangelism dropped; membership growth in fundamentalist churches slowed. Falwell, discouraged by the unchristian squabbling and infighting that had erupted over his handling of PTL, announced in

The smile on Judge Robert Bork's face did not last long. He was not confirmed by the Senate as Associate Supreme Court Judge.

late 1987 that he was abandoning political activism and would hereafter focus on his pastoral duties as minister at the Thomas Road Baptist church in Lynchburg, Virginia.

The Space Shuttle. Reagan's second term was also marred by a space shuttle disaster that highlighted the administration's fecklessness and lack of direction

The wildly successful TV evangelist Jimmy Bakker and his slightly over madeup wife, Tammy—before the fall.

Seven brave Americans—men and women—died when the *Challenger* space shuttle exploded after takeoff on a cold January day in 1986 from Cape Canaveral, Florida. The tragedy set back the American space program by more than two years.

satellites. When these failed with dismaying frequency, many informed Americans lamented the parlous state of American technology. Meanwhile, the Europeans and the Soviets forged ahead in their satellite programs, making America seem a has-been in space. Having promised to restore America's world prestige and pride, the space policy fiasco once again made the administration look bad.

The Economy Flattens. During Reagan's second term the economy remained spotty. Unemployment continued to decline, reaching 6.6 percent in December 1986. The inflation rate remained low. During the first quarter of 1986 prices were rising at the rate of only 2.2 percent per year, the lowest figure since 1953. Most spectacular of all was the stock market boom. In 1985 the Dow Jones Index of leading industrial stocks, the most common measure of stock performance, rose by over 20 percent; in 1986 it leaped by another 15 percent; in the first half of 1987 it soared into the stratosphere.

The bull market following 1985 could be dismissed as a shaky speculative phenomenon. But some parts of the economy were clearly flourishing. The United States had pioneered the personal computer revolution in the late 1970s and early 1980s and, though the Japanese and other East Asians were closing fast, still retained the lead. By mid-decade almost every aspect of life was affected by the little box with keyboard and monitor—the way people banked, made travel reservations, kept accounts, wrote letters, and even spent their leisure time.

But overall prosperity was uneven. Among minorities, unemployment far exceeded the average, with inexperienced, uneducated young black and Hispanic men and women finding it particularly difficult to find jobs in an economy that required sophisticated skills in communication, finance, and services.

On the nation's farms, times were also hard. In May 1985, prices for farm commodities were 11 percent below those of a year before. Farm prices had been rising in the 1970s and many farmers had, as in past inflation eras, borrowed heavily to finance expansion. Now they were again caught in a squeeze when prices fell. The administration responded to farm distress by lifting the embargo on American wheat exports to the Soviet Union, which President Carter had imposed after the Soviets invaded Afghanistan. But when Congress passed a measure to provide farmers with debt relief, the administration called it a "budget-busting" bill and the president threatened to veto it. More serious, both to reduce federal farm outlays

in its commitment to space exploration. Although January 28, 1986, was unusually cold, National Aeronautics and Space Administration (NASA) officials, following several previous postponements, authorized the space shuttle *Challenger* launch from Cape Kennedy. Shortly after takeoff the shuttle exploded in a ball of flame, killing all seven crew members including Christa McAuliffe, an appealing Concord, New Hampshire, school teacher who had come along on the launch to help publicize the shuttle program among the nation's school children.

The tragedy crippled the American space program. The investigation that followed showed that, to hold costs down, NASA had ignored repeated warnings that the O-ring seals on the shuttle's solid-state rockets were defective and had also authorized the launch against expert advice that icing on the rocket might create a problem. To prevent a repetition of the catastrophe, NASA stopped all shuttle launches until the fuel-seal problem was solved. It quickly became clear that the country had invested too many of its space eggs in the shuttle basket. With the space shuttle out of service for the foreseeable future, the United States was forced to turn to older rockets to launch needed civilian and military communications

and encourage "market" forces in agriculture, the administration pushed and succeeded in passing a farm bill that sharply reduced federal price supports and took farm land out of production. Farmers felt that they needed more, not less, federal help, and discontent in the agricultural Midwest continued to fester.

The most worrisome aspect of the economy from the mid-eighties on was America's international economic position. For the previous three-quarters of a century the United States had sold floods of farm and manufactured goods abroad, far more than we bought. The trade surplus had been offset by large American exports of capital, so that the United States for many years had been the world's largest creditor nation. In 1971, for the first time since 1914, we ran a trade deficit. It was not until the 1980s, however, that this trade gap began to expand at a dangerous rate. By 1984 the American trade shortfall had reached $107 billion a year. In 1986 it had gone to $170 billion, by far the largest in history.

No nation can continue to run trade deficits for very long unless other nations are willing to lend it money. And so it went now. By 1984, for the first time since World War I, seventy years before, the United States had become a debtor nation, owing its creditors billions more than they owed us. By 1990, one estimate held, Americans would be paying out interest to foreign lenders of over $100 billion a year. Increasingly, foreigners came to own ever larger amounts of American assets—stocks, bonds, treasury notes, real estate, manufacturing establishments. Bit by bit, critics said, Americans were converting pieces of their property and their heritage into Sonys, Toyotas, and Nikons.

The reasons for the sweeping change in America's international economic position were complex. Clearly it had something to do with the quality of American products, especially manufactured goods. By the mid- and late-seventies, while American laboratories continued to lead the world in new, cutting-edge research, American engineering and management skills had fallen behind those of Germany and Japan. We no longer produced the best-quality products at low prices. Americans had invented the VCR, but it was Japan that developed it into a cheap and reliable consumer product that quickly made its way into almost every middle-class American living room. The cheap family car had been an American innovation, but the Japanese and now the Koreans had developed low-priced, high-mileage automobiles that outclassed American models. American automobile manufacturers soon lost their markets abroad and quickly found themselves besieged by foreign imports at home.

But the growing trade deficit represented more

The faces of America's competitors. Young Korean women producing electronic gear at Samsung Electronics near Seoul.

An Historical Portrait

Stephen Wozniak and Steven Jobs

Stephen Wozniak and Steven Jobs did not invent the personal computer; what these two young men from northern California did was to create the personal computer revolution. It was in Jobs's garage in Los Altos that the two assembled the first computer that could be used by anyone capable of inserting a plug and pressing a key. In the process they put unprecedented power to access information and manipulate data on the office desks and kitchen tables of millions of ordinary Americans.

The first electronic computers were built during World War II to process complex numbers for calculating gun trajectories and for similar military purposes. These were monster contraptions. ENIAC (Electronic Numerical Integrator and Calculator), unveiled in 1946, just after V-J Day, filled a large room. It had 18,000 vacuum tubes that produced so much heat that the machine had to be air conditioned to keep it from melting. Because vacuum tubes had a high failure rate, it was also subject to frequent breakdowns. Yet for its day, ENIAC was a wonder. It could multiply 97,365 by itself 5,000 times in half a second. The press described its operations as "faster than thought."

Actually, the machine was an electronic dinosaur. Despite its huge size ENIAC had a tiny memory and could be programmed for specific tasks only with great difficulty. Yet it offered such immense computational advantages over everything then known that it set off a research and development drive that quickly brought a flood of improvements. During the late 1940s scientists at Cambridge University and the University of Pennsylvania built ma-chines that could be programmed to perform a wide range of operations. By the early 1950s large American companies, including IBM, Bell Telephone, and Sperry-Rand, were designing expensive vacuum-tube computers for use by government and industry.

Although computers were still bulky and slow by our standards, most scientists were content with the new machines; others, however, believed that smaller, more powerful computers would revolutionize the scientific and business worlds. The big hurdle was the fragile and imperfect vacuum tube. The breakthrough came at the end of the 1940s when, at Bell Labs in New Jersey, John Bardeen, Walter Brattain, and William Shockley invented the transistor, a device made of a semiconducting material that, like the vacuum tube, could amplify current. The transistor was much faster, less bulky, and produced almost no heat. It promised enormous computing power in a small package. Impelled by the space race of the 1950s, by Cold War U.S.-Soviet rivalry, and by urgent business needs, the number of expensive, powerful, transistor-using computers expanded at a breakneck pace.

One other technical development was still needed to make the personal computer possible—the "integrated circuit." This device was a silicon wafer, or "chip," on which many small transistors were etched by machine. The integrated circuit replaced transistors laboriously linked together by wires, and it packed the computing power of many transistors into an even smaller space. In effect, a single chip became a "microprocessor" capable of lightening-speed switching and enormous memory storage in a very small space.

By the late 1960s most of the technology for the personal computer already existed. What was absent was the perception that a truly small, desktop computer could make a difference in people's lives. This perception found expression in one place—the artificial intelligence laboratory of the Massachusetts Institute of Technology. There, in Cambridge, as early as 1958/59, a group of undergraduates had coalesced into a little subculture of "hackers." These young men were almost obsessed with computers and the remarkable things they could do. Given the opportunity to use MIT's large mainframe machines after hours, they "scorned delights and spent laborious days" creating elaborate and ingenious computer programs. Many of these were for entertainment; the MIT hackers wrote the first video game programs. But others perceived the computer as a powerful information tool that could liberate humankind if its potential could be made widely available. Eventually the hacker culture spread beyond Cambridge to other centers of computer research. By the early 1970s it was firmly implanted in the San Francisco Bay area and the adjacent Santa Clara ("Silicon") Valley where a flock of small electronics firms had begun to mass-produce cheap microprocessor computer chips.

In 1975 many of the northern California hackers worked for Hewlett-Packard, Fairchild, or one of the other Silicon Valley electronics companies and were members of the Homebrew Computer Club. One of the club's charter members was Stephen Wozniak, an employee of Intel, a chip manufacturer; another was his younger friend, Steven Jobs, who worked for a new video game firm called Atari. The two had met while in school in Los Altos, and although five years apart in age, they had been drawn together by their shared fascination with electronic gadgets. Both were young men of their time and place: long-haired, socially nonconformist, and antiestablishment. Working together after hours, Jobs and Wozniak had first constructed a "blue box," a device that enabled the user to call anywhere in the world without paying a fee to the telephone company. When the phone company cracked down on blue-box users, the two friends turned their energies elsewhere.

By this time a few small, out-of-the-way firms had begun to produce primitive "microcomputers" for electronic hobbyists. These machines had no keyboards, screens, or data storage devices. Yet they sold briskly to skilled hackers who knew how to add their own equipment to make them usable. Many of the Homebrew Club's meetings were devoted to exchanging information about how these primitive contraptions could be made to do something useful or interesting.

Jobs and "the Woz" were as excited as anyone by the advent of these simple machines, but they believed they could make something better. During the latter half of 1975 they worked evenings putting together a microcomputer in Jobs's bedroom and garage with components picked up here and there for a few dollars. Unlike its predecessors, the new computer had a keyboard and a substantial amount of memory. Wozniak, who did most of the technical work, also added a device that would enable it to use BASIC, an important, "high-level" programming language. To get the prototype model into production, Jobs sold his Volkswagen bus; Woz-

niak sold his expensive Hewlett-Packard calculator. With the $1,300 they raised, they managed, along with Jobs's sister, Patty, to build a few dozen machines. These they advertised in hobbyist magazines at $666.66 apiece.

Although the new devices were little more than circuit boards, the hackers and hobbyists were delighted with the new machines, and the young entrepreneurs soon had many more orders than they could fill. At this point they turned for financial help to various "venture capitalists" willing to risk their money in the new "high-tech" industries proliferating in the 1970s. One of the people Jobs approached, noting his long hair, dismissed him as "a renegade from the human race," but mentioned him to another financial whiz, "Mike" Markkula, a former marketing expert for several Silicon Valley electronics firms. Markkula eventually gave Jobs and Wozniak $250,000 in exchange for a part interest in the enterprise.

Markkula insisted on introducing rational methods into the business and induced the reluctant founders to incorporate. But Jobs and Wozniak exacted their small counterculture revenge. While considering one day what to name the new firm, Jobs started to munch on an apple. The act inspired the name: Henceforth the enterprise would be called Apple Computers. The name and the accompanying logo captured the fresh image of nature and good health that suited the mood and attitudes of the two young founders. At about this time the young firm acquired a new advertiser, Regis McKenna, which soon made the Apple image into a major marketing asset.

The Apple Corporation was soon making lots of money. In 1977/78 the company introduced the Apple II, a machine with a disk drive to record and store data. The new computer was an amazingly powerful contriv-

ance for its size, with a memory capacity equal to the IBM model 1401, a machine that had sold for $120,000 in 1966 and required an air-conditioned room with 600 square feet of floor space. The Apple II was also a relatively "open" machine that, true to the "hacker ethic," could be "upgraded" easily by anyone with a little electronic or programming skill. Before long, scores of people were writing "software" programs for the Apple II so that it could calculate, keep records and accounts, teach academic subjects, and act as a supertypewriter. When the Apple Corporation offered its stock for sale to the public, the major stockholders—Jobs, Wozniak, and Markkula—found themselves instant millionaires. In 1981 their fortunes ranged from $137 million for Wozniak, who had generously handed out stock to friends and associates, to $260 million for Jobs, who had held on to all his shares.

The success of the Apple II launched the personal computer revolution. Every office worker could now have his or her machine to write reports, manipulate business data, or access company records. For a time it looked as if there would also be a machine in every private household to do word processing, keep accounts, play electronic games. Apple was soon joined in the personal computer field by Commodore, Tandy, Atari, and several others. In 1981 "Big Blue," the mammoth IBM Corporation, introduced its own personal computer. Even more than the Apple II, the firm's "PC" was an open machine that invited programmers and makers of auxiliary hardware to supplement the manufacturer's basic equipment. This proved to be a wise marketing strategy. With the giant of business machines behind personal computing, the providers of "peripherals," upgrade "boards," and software programs poured out hundreds of new products for every conceiv-

An Historical Portrait (*continued*)

able use. Though it was late on the scene, by the mid-1980s IBM had outdistanced all its rivals including Apple.

The success of Apple changed the lives of its founders. Wozniak got divorced and, tired of being called a college "dropout," returned to the University of California under an assumed name to get his B.S. degree in computer science. He was never happy with the business side of computers and for a time dropped out of active participation in the firm. During this period, as if to recapture the 1960s, he sponsored a festival of rock music and science in San Bernardino. He returned to Apple in 1984 but announced the following year that he was finished with computers. He would now devote his attention to the latest electronic gadget, video transcription devices.

Jobs tried for a time to conform to the new corporate atmosphere. He cut his hair and began to sound less like a flaky 1960s visionary. But he was not an especially good businessman, and by 1980 Apple sales began to falter. In 1981 the firm hired John Sculley, a Pepsi-Cola executive, as chief executive officer to improve its balance sheet. Jobs, meanwhile, remained as chairman of the board, devoting most of his attention to developing a new machine, the Macintosh, that gave Apple a big financial boost. But then Apple's fortunes once more began to flag, in part, many said, because of Jobs's inconsiderate, confrontational, and inconsistent managerial style. Before long Jobs and Sculley were at war.

In late 1985, to Sculley's relief, Jobs decided to establish his own firm to develop educational comput-

ers, though staying on as chairman of Apple's board of directors. He had hoped that the parting might be amicable, but when he gave Sculley a list of Apple personnel he intended to take with him, Sculley was outraged. The list included some of Apple's most creative engineers and programmers. Sculley and the Apple board members decided to fire Jobs and file suit against him for going into competition with Apple.

As the 1980s began to wind down, both Jobs and Wozniak were no longer associated with Apple. But they had, at the ages of twenty-one and twenty-six, respectively, become historical figures, as important in molding how Americans did business and amused themselves as were Henry Ford or Thomas Edison three generations before.

This is ENIAC, one of the first electronic computers. The power of this vast machine is greatly exceeded by the simplest desk top computer of today.

than the slippage of American manufacturing quality and efficiency. America, as suited the leader of the free world, remained an open market for foreign goods. Our competitors, critics said, did not play by the same rules. The Japanese, for example, placed effective obstructions in the way of American imports, including tariffs and burdensome licensing requirements. In addition, Japanese consumers, who were also compulsive savers, bought few consumer goods relative to their income. At the same time Japanese companies sometimes "dumped" products in the United States below actual cost in order to eliminate American firms and then gain control of the American market.

The administration placed enormous pressure on the Japanese to import more American commodities, but they proved stubborn and evasive. Japan's apparent unwillingness to play fair angered many Americans. Labor unions and business groups pressured Congress to hit back with tariffs and punitive legislation, but by and large, moved by the desire to preserve Japanese-American friendship and avoid the dangerous economic effects of a tariff war, the government resisted the temptation. There were times when the administration's patience wore thin, however. In late March 1987, under standby legislation, the administration imposed duties on a wide range of Japanese electronic goods in response to Japanese dumping of computer microchips.

Not only did foreign debts rise, but so did domestic debt. By the mid-1980s many Americans were living beyond their personal means, taking advantage of credit cards and the equity they had accrued in their homes during the era of soaring real estate prices to borrow and buy. Consumer debt rose at a tremendous rate during the decade, leaping from $300 billion in 1980 to over $500 billion by 1986.

But private indebtedness was puny compared to the indebtedness of the federal treasury. No one liked these deficits and debts, and virtually everyone believed that they must be brought down. But liberals continued to insist that the path to fiscal balance lay through raising taxes and cutting the defense budget; conservatives continued to claim that cutting spending, especially for domestic programs, was the only course to take. In May 1986 Congress passed a major tax reform bill, closing tax loopholes, eliminating deductions for interest charges, removing many poor people from the federal income tax rolls, and establishing a maximum tax bite, even for the richest, of 28 percent. The bill represented a hard-fought tradeoff of lower tax rates for an end of special deductions and loopholes. Conservatives now insisted that any tax hikes would be a betrayal of the bargain made in hammering out the new tax bill.

"Irangate." In 1986/87 Ronald Reagan finally lost his Teflon coating. The event that changed his luck was a secret arms-for-hostages deal with Iran with the profits from the sale of weapons secretly shunted to the Nicaraguan Contras. Reagan himself may not have known about the "Irangate" actions undertaken by his National Security Council, but if he had not himself broken the law and violated the Constitution, he had displayed a shocking ignorance of events taking place just a few hundred feet from the Oval Office. Many critics said the Iran arms deal revealed the serious decline of the president's personal capacity.

Two motives apparently moved the chief Irangate instigators: William Casey, head of the CIA; and Lt.-Col. Oliver North of the National Security Council (NSC), and his chief at the NSC, Vice Admiral John Poindexter. All three men believed the Nicaraguan Sandinistas were a dangerous threat to United States' interests in the Americas. But Congress was begrudging in supplying the Contras with the funds they needed and for a time had cut these off entirely. The end of American aid would assure a Marxist victory in Central America, the small circle at the CIA and the NSC believed. They also believed, apparently, that they could make some sort of contact with "moderate" elements in Iran, leaders who might be induced to take a more friendly position toward the United States than had the Khomeini regime.

The key to this policy was arms sales to Iran. The Iranians were desperate for military weapons to help defeat the Iraqis, with whom they had been at war since 1980. They would pay any price to get guns, missiles, and aircraft parts, and perhaps in gratitude, the Casey-North-Poindexter theory went, they would adopt a more reasonable view of the United States. Making contact with the Iranians might serve several other purposes as well. The Iranians, it was clear, had influence over the Muslim fanatics who had taken Americans hostage in Lebanon, if they had not in fact sponsored them directly. President Reagan and other Americans, deluged for months with pathetic media stories about the victims' plight, had become excessively concerned about freeing them. Though for months the president had been proclaiming that the United States would never pay ransom for hostages, he apparently did not object when North, Poindexter, and others suggested that the Iranians might be induced to use their influence to get the hostages released in return for sorely needed arms.

There was an additional element in the complicated covert Irangate scheme. The profits from the deal did not have to be made public. Why not just transfer these funds to the Contras, thus getting around Congress' unwillingness to fund the "freedom fighters" struggling to overthrow the Marxist Nicaraguan regime?

The Irangate deals were conceived in mid-1985 when the president authorized the then National Security Adviser, Robert McFarlane, to contact Iranian officials and offer to sell them arms. Soon after, he approved sending American missiles in Israeli possession to the Iranians, the first of several shipments. At the end of 1985 National Security Council aide Lt.-Col. North told the Israelis that he intended to use the profits from future sales to the Iranians to secretly fund the Contras.

In May 1986 North and McFarlane, now a private citizen, secretly flew to Iran to meet with Iranian "moderates" and make a deal for further arms sales in exchange for the Lebanon hostages. They quickly found that there were no real "moderates" in the Iranian government and they did not manage to secure the release of any of the captives. In fact, shortly after, Muslim extremists in Lebanon took several new American hostages. Finally, on November 2, the day before a Lebanese magazine published details of the arms sales and McFarlane's visit to Teheran, the extremists released the first of a small group of kidnapped Americans.

The actual arms deals took place through intermediaries, who took a share of the profits. An uncertain portion of the remainder ended up in the coffers of the Contras where it paid for arms and supplies in the anti-Sandinista guerrilla war, though by this time Congress had relented and had agreed to resume military aid.

Most Americans were shocked when they learned of the Iran-Contra deal at the end of 1986. The public had counted on Ronald Reagan to be tough on terrorists and America's enemies generally. He had repeatedly denounced the Libyans and the Iranians and held them accountable for bombings and hostage-takings. In April 1986, after a number of airplane hijackings, airport bombings, and an attack on an American servicemen's discotheque in West Berlin that implicated the Libyans, Reagan ordered an air attack against the Libyan cities of Tripoli and Benghasi from carriers and from air bases in Britain. One of the attacks almost killed Libyan strongman Muammar Qaddafi. Over 77 percent of the American public endorsed the attacks, although they feared the volatile Qaddafi would retaliate and, in droves, canceled plans to travel in Europe and the Mediterranean during the summer of 1986.

But after this bold strike what was the public now to make of the deal with the worst terrorists in the entire Mideast? It seemed hard to believe that the Ronald Reagan who had authorized the arms-for-hostages trade was the same man who had ordered the Libyan and Grenada attacks. The deal would come to seem especially ironic when, in late 1987, the United States and the Iranians became involved in a minor shooting war in the Persian Gulf following the administration's risky decision to place Kuwaiti oil tankers under American protection to fend off attack by the Ayatollah's forces.

Americans from all parts of the political spectrum were appalled by the Irangate affair. What antiterrorist credibility did America have left now that it had made a deal with Iran to ransom hostages? And who was running American foreign policy? Congress had cut off funds for the Contras. Did the administration or, more accurately, a small cabal within the administration have the right to ignore the nation's constitutional policy-making processes?

At first the president denied that there had been an arms-for-hostages deal. He acknowledged that the United States had sent "defensive weapons" and spare parts to Iran but refused to concede that the purpose had been to buy the hostages' freedom. Few people believed him. A week or so later Attorney General Meese admitted that profits from the arms sales had been diverted to the Contras, and soon after the president announced that he had fired Oliver North and accepted the resignation of Admiral Poindexter.

Through the weeks of new revelations that followed, the president seemed confused and ill-informed about what had been done under his very nose. Chief of staff Donald Regan, to save his own reputation, soon disclosed a White House where confusion reigned and where, he said, only his own rearguard actions had prevented open scandal.

Moderates and liberals were especially dismayed. As more information surfaced, it became clear that a rogue operation, without supervision by constitutional authorities, had been mounted by quite junior officials in the government, in violation of federal law. Once again, as under Nixon, an administration had violated public trust and ridden roughshod over the Constitution. In mid-December Reagan authorized a special prosecutor, as in the Watergate affair, to investigate the Iran-Contra matter. The president also appointed a commission headed by former Republican Senator John Tower of Texas to investigate what had happened.

Meanwhile, Congress established its own investigating committee to look into the affair.

In late February 1987 the Tower Commission issued a report condemning the administration's operations as "chaotic" and "amateurish." It expressed dismay at Reagan's "personal management style" and criticized him for allowing his concern for the hostages to get in the way of his good sense, but it absolved him of actual wrongdoing. The chief Tower Commission Report culprit was Donald Regan, who was blamed for not keeping the president informed of White House operations. Regan, now under heavy attack, fought to keep his job, but the First Lady, Nancy Reagan, highly protective of her husband, turned against him and helped force him out. Soon after, Howard Baker, the respected former senator from Tennessee, assumed the role of White House chief of staff. Many people, skeptical of the president's grasp, applauded the change. At least now the aging chief executive would have a skilled and savvy man to back him up.

The congressional hearings on the Iran-Contra affair began in early May 1987 with a parade of witnesses who told of the complex negotiations and intrigues that constituted the operation. The two chief witnesses were Colonel North and Admiral Poindexter, both of whom appeared under grant of partial immunity from legal prosecution. CIA director Casey could not be examined; he had died of a brain tumor, taking his knowledge of Irangate to the grave.

During the televised hearings, Poindexter did not make a favorable impression, but the young, crisp, articulate North made a powerful case for his actions and managed to indict his critics as people of dubious patriotism. The public at first ate it up. For a week or two the nation found itself in the grip of "Ollimania," an uncritical acceptance of North at his own word, as a patriot and a hero.

Meanwhile, the president's reputation and standing had slipped badly. A December 1986 poll showed that Reagan's approval rating had dropped from 67 percent to 46 percent in one month. In late April 1987, 65 percent of those asked by a *Washington Post*-ABC poll believed the president was not telling the truth about his role in the Iran-Contra fiasco. The Teflon, it seemed, had finally begun to wear off the country's chief executive.

Nicaragua. The polls also showed that the public remained unwilling to become deeply involved in Nicaragua. In early 1986, 62 percent of those questioned by the pollsters opposed giving aid to the Contras.

To millions of Americans he was a hero; to others a dangerous adventurer. Lt. Colonel Oliver North testifying to a Congressional investigating committee on his role in the Iran-Contra affair.

Even among those who considered themselves Reagan partisans, only 35 percent favored Contra assistance.

Yet the president and his advisers continued to seek the overthrow of Daniel Ortega and his government. Liberals, as well as activists on the left, meanwhile continued to liken Nicaragua to Vietnam and warned against becoming bogged down in another military and political swamp, this one nearer home.

Toward the end of 1987 it began to look as if a peaceful solution might emerge in Central America after all. Five Central American nations, led by president Oscar Arias-Sanchez of Costa Rica, agreed on a peace plan designed to bring the Contras and Sandinistas together, to introduce democratic practices into Nicaragua, and end the threat of superpower intervention in that country. The plan was hailed around the world as a model of local self-determination, and president Arias won the 1987 Nobel Peace Prize for his role in its conception. In the United States, most Democrats also approved of it as a way out of the Central American impasse, but the administration remained skeptical. The plan, it said, did not guarantee Soviet exclusion from Nicaragua, did not hold Ortega to strict enough account for fulfilling his part of the bargain, or sufficiently protect the interests of the Contras. It looked for a time as if the peace plan had stalled. Then, in late March 1988, the Sandinistas and the Contras signed a cease-fire. Perhaps a peaceful settlement in Nicaragua was possible after all.

The Soviet Union and Disarmament. During 1985 and 1986 the United States and the Soviet Union continued to snipe at one another, mostly over spying activities. In August 1986, after the FBI arrested a suspected Russian spy in Washington, the Soviets jailed an American correspondent in Moscow, Nicholas Daniloff, charging him with espionage. In the end a deal was arranged releasing both men simultaneously.

The Daniloff affair underscored continuing Soviet-American mutual suspicion, but the antagonists did not allow these squabbles to stand in the way of improved relations. In November 1985 the two superpowers had resumed cultural relations, consular exchanges, and airline connections severed by the Afghanistan invasion. By early 1987 both the Soviet and American governments were anxious for a major disarmament agreement and a substantial lessening of Soviet-American tensions. Each had its own reasons for desiring an accommodation. After the bruising Iran-Contra fiasco, Reagan was clearly seeking to rescue some part of his second term from disaster. A major arms agreement with the Soviet Union would enable him to leave office on an upbeat note. The Soviets, for their part, were afraid to allow the arms race to continue. Mikhail Gorbachev, the vigorous and personable new General Secretary, had pledged to modernize and liberalize the Soviet system. Through *glasnost* (openness) and *perestroika* (economic restructuring) he would bring the Soviet Union into a more competitive position in the world. The new Soviet chief did not intend to turn his country into a Russian version of the Western democracies, or to allow it to be over-whelmed by the United States, but he did recognize how Soviet economic and political rigidities had handicapped his nation in world economic competition. Any reform of the Soviet system, however, required avoiding a major arms race with the United States.

At first, Star Wars proved a stumbling block. At a Gorbachev-Reagan summit conference at Reykjavik, Iceland, in October 1986, the Russians agreed to substantial nuclear cuts, but only if the Americans were willing to drop all SDI (Star Wars) work outside of laboratory research. Reagan refused to yield, and the meeting broke up in mutual recriminations.

But the arms-reduction process did not end. At the ongoing Soviet-American arms negotiations in Geneva, the Russians proposed nothing less than getting rid of all medium-range missiles. This time they did not link their proposals to ending SDI development. If accepted, this would be the first time the superpowers had actually eliminated a whole weapons system, and the plan promised to be a landmark in post–World War II international relations.

There were critics of the proposals on both sides. In the Soviet Union, hardliners fought many of the Gorbachev reforms, including disarmament. In the NATO countries there were many who believed that eliminating mid-range missiles would give the Soviet Union a great military advantage in Europe because its conventional ground and air forces were far superior to the West's. Secretary of Defense Caspar Weinberger considered the treaty a dangerous concession to the Soviet Union and, using his wife's health as his excuse, decided to resign rather than defy the president.

The "Evil Empire" did not look so evil this day. Gorbachev and Reagan signing the INF nuclear arms reduction treaty in the White House.

Still, in early December 1987, Gorbachev and Reagan met in Washington and signed an arms agreement eliminating the medium-range missiles from Europe. The American public was impressed with Gorbachev, who seemed a frank and open man who told jokes and stopped his limousine on the way to an appointment at the White House to shake hands with ordinary Washington pedestrians. They even liked his wife, Raisa, the first Kremlin "first lady," one wag remarked, who weighed less than her husband. Despite misgivings on the political right, people around the world hailed the arms agreement as the dawn of a new era in superpower relations. Many of his critics had to concede that Reagan had recouped some of the ground lost after the debacle of the Iran-Contra affair.

"Black Monday." But to offset this gain, the president left office with an economic cloud hanging over his head. On October 19, 1987, "Black Monday," the stock market Dow-Jones averages dropped over 500 points, the most catastrophic one-day decline in the history of Wall Street. Elsewhere around the world the other major stock exchanges experienced similar catastrophic deflation. In the United States alone, experts estimated, a trillion dollars in paper value had been wiped out between August 25, when stocks had reached their all-time peak, and October 20, most of this on Black Monday itself. Over the next several months the market fluctuated, first regaining some of its losses, but then dropping again. For a time investors, speculators, and the public remained apprehensive that, as in 1929, the stock market crash of 1987 foreshadowed a major depression.

The reasons for the bull market collapse of 1987 were unclear. Stocks had dropped as mysteriously as they had soared. Some experts believed that Japanese and European money, seeking profitable outlet, had fueled the bull market to begin with, and that the drop in the value of the dollar relative to their own currencies had led foreign investors to pull out of American stocks. Others claimed that all investors, foreign and American, had become increasingly worried over the continuing American trade deficits and the inability of the American government to bring revenue in line with expenditures. The ever-growing national debt, they said, hung like a sword over the economy and had finally caused a panic. Still other observers believed that Black Monday was merely another case of the universal law of speculative markets: What goes up must come down.

Whatever had caused the drop, once it happened it was widely believed that, to avoid a worse market decline followed by a severe depression, the American government must send investors a signal that it was willing to deal with the budget deficit. For a time it looked as though the major players on the budget scene understood the stakes. Soon after Black Monday, the president's aides and congressional leaders met in intense bargaining sessions seeking a formula to reduce future budget deficits. Days passed while Republicans and Democrats argued over what appropriations should be cut and what taxes should be raised or imposed, with the usual disagreement: The Democrats wanted new taxes, cuts in defense spending, but entitlement programs and Social Security left untouched; the Republicans wanted as few tax increases as possible and sharp cuts in most domestic programs, though they too were reluctant to take on the politically potent senior citizen army. Finally, on November 20, 1987, the two sides announced a reduction-tax package of about $30 billion for 1988 and a somewhat higher amount for the year after. The agreement was clearly better than nothing, but many observers said that it scarcely touched the major sources of imbalances and left the international economy still jittery.

The Election of 1988. By 1987 Reagan was a lame duck. But besides the normal loss of authority that came with the winding down of an administration, the Republican loss of the Senate in 1986, Irangate, prosecutions of former Reagan aides for influence peddling, the president's own aging—all had further reduced his ability to govern. For much of 1987 and 1988 the president and Congress remained deadlocked over Star Wars, the budget, aid to the Contras, and many other important issues.

The Democrats should have profited from the administration's slippage. Many observers also expected them to be the beneficiaries of the normal twenty- to thirty-year liberal-to-conservative cycle in American politics. Instead, from the early beginning of the presidential election season, they seemed determined to squander their advantage. The Democratic frontrunner at the outset was Gary Hart, the young former senator from Colorado who had given Walter Mondale such a close race for the presidential nomination in 1984. During the primary battle four years before there had been some talk that Hart was a womanizer and a man given to deception. In the summer of 1987 Hart virtually dared the media and the press to investigate his private life. They did, and the *Miami Herald* caught him spending the night alone with a Miami model-actress in his Washington townhouse.

No black man ever got so close to the White House as the Reverend Jesse Jackson, here seen at the beginning of the presidential primary season in New Hampshire.

These and accusations of other romantic peccadilloes forced him to leave the race in May.

This left the field to seven other Democratic hopefuls. Senator Joe Biden of Delaware soon withdrew when he was caught plagiarizing other politicians' speeches. The frontrunners now were Governor Michael Dukakis of Massachusetts, Senator Albert Gore of Tennessee, and Jesse Jackson. Jackson represented the party's black and most liberal voters but, the smart money said, was unlikely to win the broad middle needed for victory in November 1988. The other Democratic candidates—senators, governors, and former governors—suffered from lack of public recognition. During the early months of the primary battle the Democratic candidates jockeyed to establish some preeminence through an extended series of televised debates.

The public proved rather cool, and wits were soon calling them the "seven dwarfs." Then, in December 1987, Hart startled everyone by announcing that he had decided to return to the race. The move dismayed many Democrats. Hart could only damage the party's chance in 1988; he certainly could not win.

Meanwhile, the Republican battle for the nomination quickly turned into a horserace between Vice President George Bush and Senate Minority Leader Robert Dole of Kansas. Both men were conservatives and each claimed the mantle of Ronald Reagan. By late March, Bush had forged so far ahead of Dole in the primary contests that Dole was forced to withdraw. Bush would be the Republican presidential nominee with the young Republican senator from Indiana, J. Danforth Quayle, as his running mate.

On the Democratic side the field soon narrowed to Dukakis and Jackson. By late spring the contest had become a battle between the moderate supporters of the Massachusetts governor anxious to shake off the Democrats' liberal taint and the Jackson enthusiasts representing a large new black constituency intent on gaining full recognition and respect in national politics for the first time. After the New York primary, Dukakis took a decisive lead and, along with conservative Texas senator Lloyd Bentsen, chosen to help carry Texas and the South, was nominated at Atlanta in July. But the Jackson people, aware of their new strength, insisted on, and secured, a major Jackson role in the contest ahead. Jackson and his followers, it was clear, would now be a major factor in Democratic politics. Obviously there was no way they could be denied a key role in the party's affairs, but Democratic moderates wondered if the Republicans would again be able to convince middle-of-the-road voters that their opponents represented "special interests" rather than the nation as a whole. Only the campaign to come would tell.

Conclusions

Ronald Reagan and his supporters hoped to launch a "revolution," a conservative revolution. The president got at most only a modest part of what he wanted.

The conservative program called for an unleashing of enterprise by tax changes and simultaneous cutting back on various entitlement programs that, supposedly, encouraged sloth and reinforced poverty. The president got his tax cuts. He even got some of the cutbacks. In Reagan's two terms a portion of the Great Society effort to engineer greater economic equality came to a halt. Between 1981 and 1989 there was a sharp scaling down of welfare outlays and a shift of income from the bottom to the upper half of the income scale.

The president claimed that the changes would bring prosperity to all. He was mistaken. After a stretch of high unemployment early in his administration, joblessness fell. Well-trained, well-educated people generally felt prosperous, but millions of Americans who did not meet the requirements of an "information society" found themselves permanently shut out of a booming economy. In the eight years of the Reagan administration the gap between the rich and the poor, which seemed to be diminishing during the sixties, widened.

Reagan came to power determined to make America once more competitive in the world economy. His success was limited. The massive tax cuts of the first months did not detectably release creative entrepreneurial powers. American business leaders were not abruptly made over into new Edisons or Carnegies. In fact, increasingly, the nation's best brains turned to arranging corporation takeovers and mergers and buying and selling stocks and other paper assets, neglecting, many experts said, the sort of creative innovation needed to restore America's sagging productivity.

With the rapid fall of the dollar against most foreign currencies during 1987, American goods became cheaper and more competitive in world markets. People were soon noting an export surge. Unfortunately, American goods still had not caught up in quality to much of what the "Pacific rim" and the Europeans produced. And the cheapness of American goods at the same time fueled the heavy buying up of American real estate, corporations, and any other assets. By 1988 some experts were beginning to worry about the takeover of the United States by foreign capital, as dramatic a reversal of economic circumstances as any in the past century.

Reagan and his supporters also proclaimed that,

after the humiliations of the Carter era, they would make America "stand tall" once more among the world's nations. They succeeded in launching the most massive arms build-up in the nation's history. The president, in the process, may well have frightened the Soviets into a major arms agreement, but he threw away much of the world's respect—and damaged his administration's domestic reputation—by an astoundingly inept exchange of arms for hostages with Iran, the Middle East's premier fomenter of terrorism and disorder. Meanwhile, against all the public opinion polls, he threatened to entangle the United States in a military quagmire in Central America reminiscent of Vietnam.

The president's agenda also included a return to traditional social values. Here his success was still more limited. Reagan talked law and order; he and his wife publicly denounced the drug traffic. The president also promised to stop abortion on demand and to strengthen the family. Yet by the end of his administration his war on drugs had evaporated; abortions were as frequent as ever; divorce rates remained high; illegitimacy continued unabated. Even his drive to shift the Supreme Court to the social right, though not a complete failure, had been blunted by the inept handling of the Bork and Ginsburg nominations.

Even measured by his own standards, then, Reagan accomplished less than he intended. To be fair, many of the nation's social pathologies and economic failings did not lend themselves to short-run solutions based on presidential initiatives. Most could only yield to slow processes of education, private initiative, and social evolution. Yet as the Reagan administration passed into history the judgment of most careful observers was that the president had accomplished less of a revolution than he and his eager followers had intended. Many of his disciples would be disappointed; his opponents would be grateful.

For Further Reading

Ronnie Dugger. *On Reagan: The Man and His Presidency* (1983)

> A highly critical view of Reagan and his administration by the publisher of the *Texas Observer*, a liberal magazine. Despite the bias, it is a useful source for Reagan's first term.

Elizabeth Drew. *Campaign Journal: The Political Events of 1983–1984* (1985)

> Theodore White no longer writes his quadrennial histories of American presidential elections. In their absence we will have to do with Elizabeth Drew. This volume is not as readable as White's *The Making of the President* series, but it is probably better reportage.

Charles Murray. *Losing Ground: American Social Policy, 1950–1980* (1984)

> Though this work deals with the years before Reagan's presidency, it expresses many of the conserva-

tive attitudes toward social policy that characterized the Reagan administration. It should be read as a document of conservative thought.

Sidney Blumenthal. *The Rise of the Counter-Establishment: From Conservative Ideology to Political Power* (1986)

A critical, liberal-oriented treatment of the conservative surge of the 1970s and 1980. Blumenthal focuses on the ideological foundations of conservativism in the 1980s and the intellectuals who created that foundation.

Thomas Ferguson and Joel Rogers. *Right Turn: The Decline of the Democrats and the Future of American Politics* (1986)

This is another critical appraisal of the Reagan administration. The authors conclude that Reaganism triumphed, not because public opinion shifted to the right, but because the Democrats collapsed politically and a new elite, composed of rich business people, manipulated the electoral process successfully to achieve their conservative ends.

Robert S. McElvaine. *The End of the Conservative Era: Liberalism After Reagan* (1987)

Placing his faith in a cycle theory of conservative-liberal swings, McElvaine believes the impetus behind the Reagan Revolution had waned by the mid-eighties. He warns the Democrats against conservative "me-tooism" in the mistaken quest for popular support.

Randy Shilts. *And the Band Played On: Politics, People, and the AIDS Epidemic* (1987)

A crack San Francisco reporter chronicles the AIDS plague, both as an unfolding human tragedy and as a story of folly and error. Shilts blames both the gay community and the government, especially the Reagan administration, for their failure to see the magnitude of the impending disaster and to act quickly to contain it.

Garry Wills. *Reagan's America* (1988)

An impressionistic, skeptical view of Ronald Reagan's life and career by a liberal scholar of the American presidency. Wills finds the key to much of Reagan's presidency in the illusory values Reagan acquired as a youth in the Midwest and as a young actor in Hollywood.

Jack W. Germond and Jules Witcover. *Wake Us When It's Over: Presidential Politics of 1984* (1985)

Germond and Witcover don't respect the way Americans now nominate and elect their presidents. This description of the 1984 election emphasizes the work of professional media and campaign advisers who package the candidates and brainwash, mislead, and deceive the voting public in the process.

Guy Sorman. *The Conservative Revolution in America* (1985)

A French writer examines the conservative tide of the 1980s and finds much of it good and all of it interesting. France, he says, will have to reckon with many of the same forces in the future.

David Stockman. *The Triumph of Politics: The Inside Story of the Reagan Revolution* (1986)

The Reagan Budget Director's account of how he sold the president and his advisers an economic policy that he himself was unsure of and how, in his estimate, it failed.

Martin Anderson. *Revolution* (1988)

A "Supply-side" true-believer's view of the Reagan "Revolution." Anderson believes it really was a revolution.

Donald Regan. *For the Record: From Wall Street to Washington* (1988)

Bitter at being made the scapegoat for the Iran-Contra fiasco, Reagan chief-of-staff, Don Regan, reveals the confusion in the White House, Nancy Reagan's influence on the president, and various astrologers' influence on her.

Appendix

In Congress, July 4, 1776
The Declaration of Independence
The unanimous Declaration of the thirteen United States of America

When in the Course of human events, it becomes necessary for one people to dissolve the political bands which have connected them with another, and to assume among the powers of the earth, the separate and equal station to which the Laws of Nature and of Nature's God entitle them, a decent respect to the opinions of mankind requires that they should declare the causes which impel them to the separation.

We hold these truths to be self-evident, that all men are created equal, that they are endowed by their Creator with certain unalienable Rights, that among these are Life, Liberty and the pursuit of Happiness.

That to secure these rights, Governments are instituted among Men, deriving their just powers from the consent of the governed.

That whenever any Form of Government becomes destructive of these ends, it is the Right of the People to alter or to abolish it, and to institute new Government, laying its foundation on such principles and organizing its powers in such form, as to them shall seem most likely to effect their Safety and Happiness. Prudence, indeed, will dictate that Governments long established should not be changed for light and transient causes; and accordingly all experience hath shewn, that mankind are more disposed to suffer, while evils are sufferable, than to right themselves by abolishing the forms to which they are accustomed. But when a long train of abuses and usurpations, pursuing invariably the same Object evinces a design to reduce them under absolute Despotism, it is their right, it is their duty, to throw off such Government, and to provide new Guards for their future security.

Such has been the patient sufferance of these Colonies; and such is now the necessity which constrains them to alter their former Systems of Government. The history of the present King of Great Britain is a history of repeated injuries and usurpations, all having in direct object the establishment of an absolute Tyranny over these States. To prove this, let Facts be submitted to a candid world.

He has refused his Assent to Laws, the most wholesome and necessary for the public good.

He has forbidden his Governors to pass Laws of immediate and pressing importance, unless suspended in their operation till his Assent should be obtained; and when so suspended, he has utterly neglected to attend to them.

He has refused to pass other Laws for the accommodation of large districts of people, unless those people would relinquish the right of Representation in the Legislature, a right inestimable to them and formidable to tyrants only.

He has called together legislative bodies at places unusual, uncomfortable, and distant from the depository of their public Records, for the sole purpose of fatiguing them into compliance with his measures.

He has dissolved Representative Houses repeatedly, for opposing with manly firmness his invasions on the rights of the people.

He has refused for a long time, after such dissolutions, to cause others to be elected; whereby the Legislative powers, incapable of Annihilation, have returned to the People at large for their exercise; the State remaining in the mean time exposed to all the dangers of invasion from without, and convulsions within.

He has endeavoured to prevent the population

of these States; for that purpose obstructing the Laws for Naturalization of Foreigners; refusing to pass others to encourage their migrations hither, and raising the conditions of new Appropriations of Lands.

He has obstructed the Administration of Justice, by refusing his Assent to Laws for establishing Judiciary powers.

He has made Judges dependent on his Will alone, for the tenure of their offices, and the amount and payment of their salaries.

He has erected a multitude of New Offices, and sent hither swarms of Officers to harrass our people, and eat out their substance.

He has kept among us, in times of peace, Standing Armies without the Consent of our legislatures.

He has affected to render the Military independent of and superior to the Civil power.

He has combined with others to subject us to a jurisdiction foreign to our constitution, and unacknowledged by our laws; giving his Assent to their Acts of pretended Legislation:

For quartering large bodies of armed troops among us:

For protecting them, by a mock Trial, from punishment for any Murders which they should commit on the Inhabitants of these States:

For cutting off our Trade with all parts of the world:

For imposing Taxes on us without our Consent:

For depriving us in many cases, of the benefits of Trial by Jury:

For transporting us beyond Seas to be tried for pretended offences:

For abolishing the free System of English Laws in a neighbouring Province, establishing therein an Arbitrary government, and enlarging its Boundaries so as to render it at once an example and fit instrument for introducing the same absolute rule into these Colonies:

For taking away our Charters, abolishing our most valuable Laws, and altering fundamentally the Forms of our Governments:

For suspending our own Legislatures, and declaring themselves invested with power to legislate for us in all cases whatsoever.

He has abdicated Government here, by declaring us out of his Protection and waging War against us.

He has plundered our seas, ravaged our Coasts, burnt our towns, and destroyed the Lives of our people.

He is at this time transporting large Armies of foreign Mercenaries to compleat the works of death, desolation and tyranny, already begun with circum-

stances of Cruelty & perfidy scarcely paralleled in the most barbarous ages, and totally unworthy the Head of a civilized nation.

He has constrained our fellow Citizens taken Captive on the high Seas to bear Arms against their Country, to become the executioners of their friends and Brethren, or to fall themselves by their Hands.

He has excited domestic insurrections amongst us, and has endeavoured to bring on the inhabitants of our frontiers, the merciless Indian Savages, whose known rule of warfare, is an undistinguished destruction of all ages, sexes and conditions.

In every stage of these Oppressions We have Petitioned for Redress in the most humble terms: Our repeated Petitions have been answered only by repeated injury. A Prince, whose character is thus marked by every act which may define a Tyrant, is unfit to be the ruler of a free people.

Nor have We been wanting in attentions to our British brethren. We have warned them from time to time of attempts by their legislature to extend an unwarrantable jurisdiction over us. We have reminded them of the circumstances of our emigration and settlement here. We have appealed to their native justice and magnanimity, and we have conjured them by the ties of our common kindred to disavow these usurpations, which, would inevitably interrupt our connections and correspondence. They too have been deaf to the voice of justice and of consanguinity. We must, therefore, acquiesce in the necessity, which denounces our Separation, and hold them, as we hold the rest of mankind, Enemies in War, in Peace Friends.

We, therefore, the Representatives of the united States of America, in General Congress, Assembled, appealing to the Supreme Judge of the world for the rectitude of our intentions, do, in the Name, and by Authority of the good People of these Colonies, solemnly publish and declare, That these United Colonies are, and of Right ought to be Free and Independent States; that they are Absolved from all Allegiance to the British Crown, and that all political connection between them and the State of Great Britain, is and ought to be totally dissolved; and that as Free and Independent States, they have full Power to levy War, conclude Peace, contract Alliances, establish Commerce, and to do all other Acts and Things which Independent States may of right do.

And for the support of this Declaration, with a firm reliance on the protection of divine Providence, we mutually pledge to each other our Lives, our Fortunes and our sacred Honor.

JOHN HANCOCK

NEW HAMPSHIRE
Josiah Bartlett
William Whipple
Matthew Thornton

MASSACHUSETTS BAY
Samuel Adams
John Adams
Robert Treat Paine
Elbridge Gerry

RHODE ISLAND
Stephen Hopkins
William Ellery

CONNECTICUT
Roger Sherman
Samuel Huntington
William Williams
Oliver Wolcott

NEW YORK
William Floyd
Philip Livingston
Francis Lewis
Lewis Morris

NEW JERSEY
Richard Stockton
John Witherspoon
Francis Hopkinson
John Hart
Abraham Clark

PENNSYLVANIA
Robert Morris
Benjamin Rush
Benjamin Franklin
John Morton
George Clymer
James Smith
George Taylor
James Wilson
George Ross

DELAWARE
Caesar Rodney
George Read
Thomas M'Kean

MARYLAND
Samuel Chase
William Paca
Thomas Stone
*Charles Carroll, of
  Carrollton*

VIRGINIA
George Wythe
Richard Henry Lee
Thomas Jefferson
Benjamin Harrison
Thomas Nelson, Jr.
Francis Lightfoot Lee
Carter Braxton

NORTH CAROLINA
William Hooper
Joseph Hewes
John Penn

SOUTH CAROLINA
Edward Rutledge
Thomas Heyward, Jr.
Thomas Lynch, Jr.
Arthur Middleton

GEORGIA
Button Gwinnett
Lyman Hall
George Walton

Resolved, That copies of the Declaration be sent to the several assemblies, conventions, and committees, or councils of safety, and to the several commanding officers of the continental troops; that it be proclaimed in each of the United States, at the head of the army.

The Constitution of the United States of America

Preamble

We the People of the United States, in Order to form a more perfect Union, establish Justice, insure domestic Tranquility, provide for the common defence, promote the general Welfare, and secure the Blessings of Liberty to ourselves and our Posterity, do ordain and establish this Constitution for the United States of America.

Article I

Section 1. All legislative Powers herein granted shall be vested in a Congress of the United States, which shall consist of a Senate and House of Representatives.

Section 2. The House of Representatives shall be composed of Members chosen every second Year by the People of the several States, and the Electors in each State shall have the Qualifications requisite for Electors of the most numerous Branch of the State Legislature.

No Person shall be a Representative who shall not have attained to the Age of twenty-five Years, and been seven years a Citizen of the United States, and who shall not, when elected, be an Inhabitant of that State in which he shall be chosen.

Representatives and direct Taxes shall be apportioned among the several States which may be included within this Union, according to their respective Numbers, [which shall be determined by adding to the whole Number of free Persons, including those bound to Service for a Term of Years, and excluding Indians not taxed, three fifths of all other Persons.][1] The actual Enumeration shall be made within three Years after the first Meeting of the Congress of the United States, and within every subsequent Term of ten Years, in such Manner as they shall by Law direct. The Number of Representatives shall not exceed one for every thirty Thousand, but each State shall have at Least one Representative; and until such enumeration shall be made, the State of New Hampshire shall be entitled to chuse three; Massachusetts eight; Rhode Island and Providence Plantations one; Connecticut five; New York six; New Jersey four; Pennsylvania eight; Delaware one; Maryland six; Virginia ten; North Carolina five; South Carolina five; and Georgia three.

When vacancies happen in the Representation from any State, the Executive Authority thereof shall issue Writs of Election to fill such Vacancies.

The House of Representatives shall chuse their Speaker and other Officers; and shall have the sole Power of Impeachment.

Section 3. The Senate of the United States shall be composed of two Senators from each state, [chosen by the Legislature thereof,][2] for six Years; and each Senator shall have one Vote.

Immediately after they shall be assembled in Consequence of the first Election, they shall be divided as equally as may be into three Classes. The Seats of the Senators of the first Class shall be vacated at the Expiration of the second year, of the Second Class at the Expiration of the fourth Year, and of the third Class at the Expiration of the sixth Year, so that one third may be chosen every second Year; [and if Vacancies happen by Resignation, or otherwise, during the Recess of the Legislature of any State, the Executive thereof may make temporary Appointments until the next Meeting of the Legislature, which shall then fill such Vacancies.][3]

No Person shall be a Senator who shall not have attained to the Age of thirty Years, and been nine Years a Citizen of the United States, and who shall not, when elected, be an Inhabitant of that State for which he shall be chosen.

The Vice President of the United States shall be President of the Senate, but shall have no Vote, unless they be equally divided.

The Senate shall chuse their other Officers, and also a President pro tempore, in the Absence of the Vice President, or when he shall exercise the Office of President of the United States.

The Senate shall have the sole Power to try all Impeachments. When sitting for that Purpose, they shall be on Oath or Affirmation. When the President of the United States is tried, the Chief Justice shall preside: And no Person shall be convicted without

---

[1] Bracketed material superseded by Section 2 of the Fourteenth Amendment.

[2] Bracketed material superseded by Clause 1 of the Seventeenth Amendment.

[3] Bracketed material modified by Clause 2 of the Seventeenth Amendment.

the Concurrence of two thirds of the Members present.

Judgment in Cases of Impeachment shall not extend further than to removal from Office, and disqualification to hold and enjoy any Office of honor, Trust or Profit under the United States: but the Party convicted shall nevertheless be liable and subject to Indictment, Trial, Judgment and Punishment, according to Law.

Section 4. The Times, Places and Manner of holding Elections for Senators and Representatives, shall be prescribed in each State by the legislature thereof; but the Congress may at any time by Law make or alter such Regulations, except as to the Places of chusing Senators.

[The Congress shall assemble at least once in every Year, and such Meeting shall be on the first Monday in December, unless they shall by Law appoint a different Day.][4]

Section 5. Each House shall be the Judge of the Elections, Returns and Qualifications of its own Members, and a Majority of each shall constitute a Quorum to do Business; but a smaller Number may adjourn from day to day, and may be authorized to compel the Attendance of absent Members, in such Manner, and under such Penalties as each House may provide.

Each House may determine the Rules of its Proceedings, punish its Members for disorderly Behaviour, and, with the Concurrence of two thirds, expel a Member.

Each House shall keep a Journal of its Proceedings, and from time to time publish the same, excepting such Parts as may in their Judgment require Secrecy; and the Yeas and Nays of the Members of either House on any question shall, at the Desire of one fifth of those Present, be entered on the Journal.

Neither House, during the Session of Congress, shall, without the Consent of the other, adjourn for more than three days, nor to any other Place than that in which the two Houses shall be sitting.

Section 6. The Senators and Representatives shall receive a Compensation for their Services, to be ascertained by Law, and paid out of the Treasury of the United States. They shall in all Cases, except Treason, Felony and Breach of the Peace, be privileged from Arrest during their Attendance at the Session of their respective Houses, and in going to and returning from the same; and for any Speech or Debate in either House, they shall not be questioned in any other Place.

No Senator or Representative shall, during the Time for which he was elected, be appointed to any civil Office under the Authority of the United States, which shall have been created, or the Emoluments whereof shall have been encreased during such time; and no Person holding any Office under the United States, shall be a Member of either House during his Continuance in Office.

Section 7. All Bills for raising Revenue shall Originate in the House of Representatives; but the Senate may propose or concur with Amendments as on other Bills.

Every Bill which shall have passed the House of Representatives and the Senate, shall, before it become a Law, be presented to the President of the United States; If he approve he shall sign it, but if not he shall return it, with his Objections to that House in which it shall have originated, who shall enter the Objections at large on their Journal, and proceed to reconsider it. If after such Reconsideration two thirds of that House shall agree to pass the Bill, it shall be sent, together with the Objections, to the other House, by which it shall likewise be reconsidered, and if approved by two thirds of that House, it shall become a Law. But in all such Cases the Votes of both Houses shall be determined by Yeas and Nays, and the Names of the Persons voting for and against the Bill shall be entered on the Journal of each House respectively. If any Bill shall not be returned by the President within Ten Days (Sundays excepted) after it shall have been presented to him, the Same shall be a Law, in like Manner as if he had signed it, unless the Congress by their Adjournment prevents its Return, in which Case it shall not be a Law.

Every Order, Resolution, or Vote to which the Concurrence of the Senate and House of Representatives may be necessary (except on a question of Adjournment) shall be presented to the President of the United States; and before the Same shall take effect, shall be approved by him, or being disapproved by him, shall be repassed by two thirds of the Senate and House of Representatives, according to the Rules and Limitations prescribed in the Case of a Bill.

Section 8. The Congress shall have Power To lay and collect Taxes, Duties, Imposts and Excises, to pay the Debts and provide for the common Defence and general Welfare of the United States; but all Duties, Imposts and Excises shall be uniform throughout the United States;

To borrow Money on the credit of the United States;

To regulate Commerce with foreign Nations, and among the several States, and with the Indian Tribes;

To establish an uniform Rule of Naturalization,

---

[4] Bracketed material superseded by Section 2 of the Twentieth Amendment.

and uniform Laws on the subject of Bankruptcies throughout the United States;

To coin Money, regulate the Value thereof, and of foreign Coin, and fix the Standard of Weights and Measures;

To provide for the Punishment of counterfeiting the Securities and current Coin of the United States;

To establish Post Offices and post Roads;

To promote the Progress of Science and useful Arts, by securing for limited Times to Authors and Inventors the exclusive Right to their respective Writings and Discoveries;

To constitute Tribunals inferior to the supreme Court;

To define and punish Piracies and Felonies committed on the high Seas, and Offences against the Law of Nations;

To declare War, grant Letters of Marque and Reprisal, and make Rules concerning Captures on Land and Water;

To raise and support Armies; but no Appropriation of Money to that Use shall be for a longer Term than two years;

To provide and maintain a Navy;

To make Rules for the Government and Regulation of the land and naval Forces;

To provide for calling forth the Militia to execute the laws of the Union, suppress Insurrections and repel Invasions;

To provide for organizing, arming, and disciplining, the Militia, and for governing such Part of them as may be employed in the Service of the United States, reserving to the States respectively, the Appointment of the Officers, and the Authority of training the Militia according to the disciplie prescribed by Congress;

To exercise exclusive Legislation in all Cases whatsoever, over such District (not exceeding ten Miles square) as may, by Cession of particular States, and the Acceptance of Congress, become the Seat of the Government of the United States, and to exercise like Authority over all Places purchased by the Consent of the Legislature of the State in which the Same shall be, for the Erection of Forts, Magazines, Arsenals, dock-Yards, and other needful Buildings;—And

To make all Laws which shall be necessary and proper for carrying into Execution the foregoing Powers, and all other Powers vested by this Constitution in the Government of the United States, or in any Department or Officer thereof.

Section 9. The Migration or Importation of such Persons as any of the States now existing shall think proper to admit, shall not be prohibited by the Congress prior to the year one thousand eight hundred and eight, but a Tax or duty may be imposed on such Importation, not exceeding ten dollars for each Person.

The Privilege of the Writ of Habeas Corpus shall not be suspended, unless when in Cases of Rebellion or Invasion the public Safety may require it.

No Bill of Attainder or ex post facto Law shall be passed.

No Capitation, or other direct, Tax shall be laid, unless in Proportion to the Census or Enumeration herein before directed to be taken.[5]

No Tax or Duty shall be laid on Articles exported from any State.

No Preference shall be given by any Regulation of Commerce or Revenue to the Ports of one State over those of another: nor shall Vessels bound to, or from, one State, be obliged to enter, clear, or pay Duties in another.

No Money shall be drawn from the Treasury, but in Consequence of Appropriations made by Law; and a regular Statement and Account of the Receipts and Expenditures of all public Money shall be published from time to time.

No Title of Nobility shall be granted by the United States: And no person holding any office of Profit or Trust under them, shall, witout the Consent of the Congress, accept of any present, Emolument, Office, or Title, of any kind whatever, from any King, Prince, or foreign State.

Section 10. No State shall enter into any Treaty, Alliance, or Confederation; grant Letters of Marque and Reprisal; coin Money; emit Bills of Credit; make any Thing but gold and silver Coin a Tender in Payment of Debts; pass any Bill of Attainder, ex post facto Law, or Law impairing the Obligation of Contracts, or grant any Title of Nobility.

No State shall, without the Consent of the Congress, lay any Imposts or Duties on Imports or Exports, except what may be absolutely necessary for executing its inspection Laws: and the net Produce of all Duties and Imposts, laid by any State on Imports or Exports, shall be for the Use of the Treasury of the United States; and all such Laws shall be subject to the Revision and Controul of the Congress.

No State shall, without the Consent of Congress, lay any Duty of Tonnage, keep Troops, or Ships of War in time of Peace, enter into any Agreement or Compact with another State, or with a foreign Power, or engage in War, unless actually invaded, or in such imminent Danger as will not admit of delay.

[5] Modified by the Sixteenth Amendment.

Article II

Section 1. The executive Power shall be vested in a President of the United States of America. He shall hold his Office during the Term of four Years, and, together with the Vice President, chosen for the same Term, be elected, as follows.

Each State shall appoint, in such Manner as the Legislature thereof may direct, a Number of Electors, equal to the whole Number of Senators and Representatives to which the State may be entitled in the Congress: but no Senator or Representative, or Person holding an Office of Trust or Profit under the United States, shall be appointed an Elector.

[The Electors shall meet in their respective States, and vote by Ballot for two Persons, of whom one at least shall not be an Inhabitant of the same State with themselves. And they shall make a List of all the Persons voted for, and of the Number of Votes for each; which List they shall sign and certify, and transmit sealed to the Seat of the Government of the United States, directed to the President of the Senate. The President of the Senate shall, in the Presence of the Senate and House of Representatives, open all the Certificates, and the Votes shall then be counted. The Person having the greatest Number of Votes shall be the President, if such Number be a Majority of the whole Number of Electors appointed; and if there be more than one who have such Majority, and have an equal Number of Votes, then the House of Representatives shall immediately chuse by Ballot one of them for President; and if no Person have a Majority, then from the five highest on the List the said House shall in like Manner chuse the President. But in chusing the President, the Votes shall be taken by States, the Representation from each State having one Vote; A quorum for this Purpose shall consist of a Member or Members from two thirds of the States, and a Majority of all the States shall be necessary to a Choice. In every Case, after the Choice of the President, the Person having the greatest Number of Votes of the Electors shall be the Vice President. But if there should remain two or more who have equal Votes, the Senate shall chuse from them by Ballot the Vice President.][6]

The Congress may determine the Time of chusing the Electors, and the Day on which they shall give their Votes; which Day shall be the same throughout the United States.

No Person except a natural born Citizen, or a Citizen of the United States, at the time of the Adoption of this Constitution, shall be eligible to the Office of President; neither shall any Person be eligible to that Office who shall not have attained to the Age of thirty-five Years, and been fourteen Years a Resident within the United States.

[In Case of the Removal of the President from Office, or of his Death, Resignation, or Inability to discharge the Powers and Duties of the said Office, the Same shall devolve on the Vice President, and the Congress may by law provide for the Case of Removal, Death, Resignation or Inability, both of the President and Vice President, declaring what Officer shall then act as President, and such Officer shall act accordingly, until the Disability be removed, or a President shall be elected.][7]

The President shall, at stated Times, receive for his Services, a Compensation, which shall neither be encreased nor diminished during the Period for which he shall have been elected, and he shall not receive within that Period any other Emolument from the United States, or any of them.

Before he enter on the Execution of his Office; he shall take the following Oath or Affirmation—"I do solemnly swear (or affirm) that I will faithfully execute the Office of President of the United States, and will to the best of my Ability, preserve, protect and defend the Constitution of the United States."

Section 2. The President shall be Commander in Chief of the Army and Navy of the United States, and of the Militia of the several States, when called into the actual Service of the United States; he may require the Opinion, in writing, of the principal Office in each of the executive Departments, upon any Subject relating to the Duties of their respective Offices, and he shall have Power to grant Reprieves and Pardons for Offences against the United States, except in Cases of Impeachment.

He shall have Power, by and with the Advice and Consent of the Senate, to make Treaties, provided two thirds of the Senators present concur; and he shall nominate, and by and with the Advice and Consent of the Senate, shall appoint Ambassadors, other public Ministers and Consuls, Judges of the supreme Court, and all other Officers of the United States, whose Appointments are not herein otherwise provided for, and which shall be established by Law: but the Congress may by Law vest the Appointment of such inferior Officers, as they think proper, in the President alone, in the Courts of Law, or in the Heads of Departments.

The President shall have Power to fill up all Vacancies that may happen during the Recess of the Sen-

---

[6] Bracketed material superseded by the Twelfth Amendment.

[7] Bracketed material modified by the Twenty-fifth Amendment.

ate, by granting Commissions which shall expire at the End of their next Session.

Section 3. He shall from time to time give to the Congress Information of the State of the Union, and recommend to their Consideration such Measures as he shall judge necessary and expedient; he may, on extraordinary Occasions, convene both Houses, or either of them, and in Case of Disagreement between them, with Respect to the Time of Adjournment, he may adjourn them to such Time as he shall think proper; he shall receive Ambassadors and other public Ministers; he shall take Care that the Laws be faithfully executed, and shall Commission all the Officers of the United States.

Section 4. The President, Vice President and all civil Officers of the United States, shall be removed from Office on Impeachment for, and Conviction of, Treason, Bribery, or other high Crimes and Misdemeanors.

Article III

Section 1. The judicial Power of the United States, shall be vested in one supreme Court, and in such inferior Courts as the Congress may from time to time ordain and establish. The Judges, both of the supreme and inferior Courts, shall hold their Offices during good Behaviour, and shall, at stated Times, receive for their Services, a Compensation, which shall not be diminished during their Continuance in Office.

Section 2. The judicial Power shall extend to all Cases, in Law and Equity, arising under this Constitution, the Laws of the United States, and Treaties made, or which shall be made, under their Authority;—to all Cases affecting Ambassadors, other public Ministers and Consuls;—to all Cases of admiralty and maritime Jurisdiction;—To Controversies to which the United States shall be a Party;—to Controversies between two or more States;—between a State and Citizens of another State;—between Citizens of different States;—between Citizens of the same State claiming Lands under Grants of different States, and between a State, or the Citizens thereof, and foreign States, Citizens or Subjects.[8]

In all Cases affecting Ambassadors, other public Ministers and Consuls, and those in which a State shall be Party, the supreme Court shall have original Jurisdiction. In all the other Cases before mentioned the supreme Court shall have appellate Jurisdiction, both as to Law and Fact, with such Exceptions, and under such Regulations as the Congress shall make.

The Trial of all Crimes, except in Cases of Impeachment, shall be by Jury; and such Trial shall be held in the State where the said Crimes shall have been committed; but when not committed within any State, the Trial shall be at such Place or Places as the Congress may by Law have directed.

Section 3. Treason against the United States, shall consist only in levying War against them, or in adhering to their Enemies, giving them Aid and Comfort. No Person shall be convicted of Treason unless on the Testimony of two Witnesses to the same overt Act, or on Confession in open Court.

The Congress shall have Power to declare the Punishment of Treason, but no Attainder of Treason shall work Corruption of Blood, or Forfeiture except during the Life of the person attainted.

Article IV

Section 1. Full Faith and Credit shall be given in each State to the public Acts. Records, and judicial Proceedings of every other State. And the Congress may by general Laws prescribe the Manner in which such Acts, Records and Proceedings shall be proved, and the Effect thereof.

Section 2. The Citizens of each State shall be entitled to all Privileges and Immunities of Citizens in the several States.

A Person charged in any State with Treason, Felony, or other Crime, who shall flee from Justice, and be found in another State, shall on Demand of the executive Authority of the State from which he fled, be delivered up, to be removed to the State having Jurisdiction of the Crime.

[No Person held to Service or Labour in one State, under the Laws thereof, escaping into another, shall, in Consequence of any Law or Regulation therein, be discharged from such Service or Labour, but shall be delivered up on Claim of the Party to whom such Service or Labour may be due.][9]

Section 3. New States may be admitted by the Congress into this Union; but no new State shall be formed or erected within the Jurisdiction of any other State; nor any State be formed by the Junction of two or more States, or Parts of States, without the Consent of the Legislatures of the States concerned as well as of the Congress.

The Congress shall have Power to dispose of and make all needful Rules and Regulations respecting the Territory or other property belonging to the United States; and nothing in this Constitution shall be so

---

[8] This paragraph modified in part by the Eleventh Amendment.

[9] Bracketed material superseded by the Thirteenth Amendment.

construed as to Prejudice any Claims of the United States, or of any particular State.

Section 4. The United States shall guarantee to every State in this Union a Republican Form of Government, and shall protect each of them against Invasion; and on Application of the Legislature, or of the Executive (when the Legislature cannot be convened) against domestic Violence.

Article V

The Congress, whenever two thirds of both Houses shall deem it necessary, shall propose Amendments to this Constitution, or, on the Application of the legislatures of two thirds of the several States, shall call a Convention for proposing Amendments, which, in either Case, shall be valid to all Intents and Purposes, as Part of this Constitution, when ratified by the Legislatures of three fourths of the several States, or by Conventions in three fourths thereof, as the one or the other Mode of Ratification may be proposed by the Congress; Provided that no Amendement which may be made prior to the Year One thousand eight hundred and eight shall in any Manner affect the first and fourth Clauses in the Ninth Section of the first Article; and that no State, without its Consent, shall be deprived of its equal Suffrage in the Senate.

Article VI

All Debts contracted and Engagements entered into, before the Adoption of this Constitution, shall be as valid against the United States under this Constitution, as under the Confederation.

This Constitution, and the Laws of the United States which shall be made in Pursuance thereof; and all Treaties made, or which shall be made, under the Authority of the United States, shall be the supreme Law of the Land; and the Judges in every State shall be bound thereby, any Thing in the Constitution or Laws of any State to the Contrary notwithstanding.

The Senators and Representatives before mentioned, and the members of the several State Legislatures, and all executive and judicial Officers, both of the United States and of the several States, shall be bound by Oath or Affirmation, to support this Constitution; but no relgious Test shall ever be required as a Qualification to any Office or public Trust under the United States.

Article VII

The Ratification of the Conventions of nine States, shall be sufficient for the Establishment of this Constitution between the States so ratifying the Same.

DONE in Convention by the Unanimous Consent of the States present the Seventeenth Day of September in the Year of our Lord one thousand seven hundred and Eighty seven and of the Independence of the United States of America the Twelfth. IN WITNESS whereof We have hereunto subscribed our Names.

GEORGE WASHINGTON—President
and deputy from Virginia

NEW HAMPSHIRE
John Langdon
Nicholas Gilman

CONNECTICUT
William Samuel Johnson
Roger Sherman

NEW YORK
Alexander Hamilton

NEW JERSEY
William Livingston
David Brearley
William Paterson
Jonathan Dayton

PENNSYLVANIA
Benjamin Franklin
Thomas Mifflin
Robert Morris
George Clymer
Thomas FitzSimons
Jared Ingersoll
James Wilson
Gouverneur Morris

DELAWARE
George Read
Gunning Bedford, Jr.
John Dickinson
Richard Bassett
Jacob Broom

MASSACHUSETTS
Nathaniel Gorham
Rufus King

MARYLAND
James McHenry
Daniel of St. Thomas
   Jenifer
Daniel Carroll

VIRGINIA
John Blair
James Madison, Jr.

NORTH CAROLINA
William Blount
Richard Dobbs Spaight
Hugh Williamson

SOUTH CAROLINA
John Rutledge
Charles Cotesworth
   Pickney
Charles Pinckney
Pierce Butler

GEORGIA
William Few
Abraham Baldwin

Attest: William Jackson,
Secretary

The Amendments

ARTICLES in addition to, and Amendment of the Constitution of the United States of America, proposed by Congress, and ratified by the Legislatures of the several States, pursuant to the fifth Article of the original Constitution.

Article I

[Articles I through X, now known as the Bill of Rights, were proposed on September 25, 1789, and declared in force on December 15, 1791.]

Congress shall make no law respecting an establishment of religion, or prohibiting the free exercise thereof; or abridging the freedom of speech, or of the press; or the right of the people peaceably to assemble, and to petition the Government for a redress of grievances.

Article II

A well regulated Militia, being necessary to the security of a free State, the right of the people to keep and bear Arms, shall not be infringed.

Article III

No Soldier shall, in time of peace be quartered in any house, without the consent of the Owner, nor in time of war, but in manner to be prescribed by law.

Article IV

The right of the people to be secure in their persons, houses, papers, and effects, against unreasonable searches and seizures, shall not be violated, and no Warrants shall issue, but upon probable cause, supported by Oath or affirmation, and particularly describing the place to be searched, and the persons or things to be seized.

Article V

No person shall be held to answer for a capital, or otherwise infamous crime, unless on a presentment or indictment of a Grand Jury, except in cases arising in the land or naval forces, or in the Militia, when in actual service in time of War or public danger; nor shall any person be subject for the same offence to be twice put in jeopardy of life or limb; nor shall be compelled in any criminal case to be a witness against himself, nor be deprived of life, liberty, or property, without due process of law; nor shall private property be taken for public use, without just compensation.

Article VI

In all criminal prosecutions, the accused shall enjoy the right to a speedy and public trial, by an impartial jury of the State and district wherein the crime shall have been committed, which district shall have been previously ascertained by law, and to be informed of the nature and cause of the accusation; to be confronted with the witnesses against him; to have compulsory process for obtaining witnesses in his favor, and to have the Assistance of Counsel for his defence.

Article VII

In Suits at common law, where the value in controversy shall exceed twenty dollars, the right of trial by jury shall be preserved, and no fact tried by a jury shall be otherwise re-examined in any Court of the United States, than according to the rules of the common law.

Article VIII

Excessive bail shall not be required, nor excessive fines imposed, nor cruel and unusual punishments inflicted.

Article IX

The enumeration in the Constitution, of certain rights, shall not be construed to deny or disparage others retained by the people.

Article X

The powers not delegated to the United States by the Constitution, nor prohibited by it to the States, are reserved to the States respectively, or to the people.

Article XI

[Proposed March 4, 1794; declared ratified January 8, 1798]

The Judicial power of the United States shall not be construed to extend to any suit in law or equity, commenced or prosecuted against one of the United States by Citizens of another State, or by Citizens or Subjects of any Foreign State.

Article XII

[Proposed December 9, 1803; declared ratified September 25, 1804]

The Electors shall meet in their respective states and vote by ballot for President and Vice-President, one of whom, at least, shall not be an inhabitant of the same state with themselves; they shall name in their ballots the person voted for as President, and in distinct ballots the person voted for as Vice-President, and they shall make distinct lists of all persons voted for as President, and of all persons voted for as Vice-President, and of the number of votes for each, which lists they shall sign and certify, and transmit sealed to the seat of the government of the United States, directed to the President of the Senate;—The President of the Senate shall, in the presence of the Senate and House of Representatives, open all the certificates and the votes shall then be counted;—The person having the greatest number of votes for President, shall be the President, if such number be a majority of the whole number of Electors appointed; and if no person have such majority, then from the persons having the highest numbers not exceeding three on the list of those voted for as President, the House of Representatives shall choose immediately, by ballot, the President. But in choosing the President, the votes shall be taken by states, the representation from each state having one vote; a quorum for this purpose shall consist of a member or members from two-thirds of the states, and a majority of all the states shall be necessary to a choice. [And if the House of Representatives shall not choose a President whenever the right of choice shall devolve upon them, before the fourth day of March next following, then the Vice-President shall act as President, as in the case of the death or other constitutional disability of the President.][10] —The person having the greatest number of votes as Vice-President, shall be the Vice-President, if such number be a majority of the whole number of Electors appointed, and if no person have a majority, then from the two highest numbers on the list, the Senate shall choose the Vice-President; a quorum for the purpose shall consist of two-thirds of the whole number of Senators, and a majority of the whole number shall be necessary to a choice. But no person constitutionally ineligible to the office of President shall be eligible to that of Vice-President of the United States.

Article XIII

[Proposed January 31, 1865; declared ratified December 18, 1865]

Section 1. Neither slavery nor involuntary servitude, except as a punishment for crime whereof the party shall have been duly convicted, shall exist within the United States, or any place subject to their jurisdiction.

Section 2. Congress shall have power to enforce this article by appropriate legislation.

Article XIV

[Proposed June 13, 1866; declared ratified July 28, 1868]

Section 1. All persons born or naturalized in the United States, and subject to the jurisdiction thereof, are citizens of the United States and of the State wherein they reside. No State shall make or enforce any law which shall abridge the privileges or immunities of citizens of the United States; nor shall any State deprive

any person of life, liberty, or property, without due process of law; nor deny to any person within its jurisdiction the equal protection of the laws.

Section 2. Representatives shall be apportioned among the several States according to their respective numbers, counting the whole number of persons in each State, excluding Indians not taxed. But when the right to vote at any election for the choice of electors for President and Vice President of the United States, Representatives in Congress, the Executive and Judicial officers of a State, or the members of the Legislature thereof, is denied to any of the male inhabitants of such State, being twenty-one years of age, and citizens of the United States, or in any way abridged, except for participation in rebellion, or other crime, the basis of representation therein shall be reduced in the proportion which the number of such male citizens shall bear to the whole number of male citizens twenty-one years of age in such State.

Section 3. No person shall be a Senator or Representative in Congress, or elector of President and Vice President, or hold any office, civil or military, under the United States, or under any State, who, having previously taken an oath, as a member of Congress, or as an officer of the United States, or as a member of any State legislature, or as an executive or judicial officer of any State, to support the Constitution of the United States, shall have engaged in insurrection or rebellion against the same, or given aid or comfot to the enemies thereof. But Congress may by a vote of two-thirds of each House, remove such disability.

Section 4. The validity of the public debt of the United States, authorized by law, including debts incurred for payment of pensions and bounties for services in suppressing insurrection or rebellion, shall not be questioned. But neither the United States nor any State shall assume or pay any debt or obligation incurred in aid of insurrection or rebellion against the United States, or any claim for the loss or emancipation of any slave; but all such debts, obligations and claims shall be held illegal and void.

Section 5. The Congress shall have power to enforce, by appropriate legislations, the provisions of this article.

Article XV

[Proposed February 26, 1869; declared ratified March 30, 1870]

Section 1. The right of citizens of the United States to vote shall not be denied or abridged by the United States or by any State on account of race, color, or previous condition of servitude.

[10] Bracketed material superseded by Section 3 of the Twentieth Amendment.

Section 2. The Congress shall have powere to enforce this article by appropraite legislation.

Article XVI

[Proposed July 12, 1909; declared ratified February 25, 1913]

The Congress shall have power to lay and collect taxes on incomes, from whatever source derived, without apportionment among the several States, and without regard to any census or enumeration.

Article XVII

[Proposed May 13, 1912; declared ratified May 31, 1913]

The Senate of the United States shall be composed of two Senators from each State, elected by the people thereof, for six years; and each Senator shall have one vote. The electors in each State shall have the qualifications requisite for electors of the most numerous branch of the State legislatures.

When vacancies happen in the representation of any State in the Senate, the executive authority of such State shall issue writs of election to fill such vacancies: *Provided,* That the legislature of any State may empower the executive thereof to make temporary appointments until the people fill the vacancies by election as the legislature may direct.

This amendement shall not be so construed as to affect the election or term of any Senator chosen before it becomes valid as part of the Constitution.

Article XVIII

[Proposed December 18, 1917; declared ratified January 29, 1919; repealed by the Twenty-first Amendment December 5, 1933]

Section 1. After one year from the ratification of this article the manufacture, sale, or transportation of intoxicating liquors within, the importation thereof into, or the exportation thereof from the United States and all territory subject to the jurisdiction thereof for beverage purposes is hereby prohibited.

Section 2. The Congress and the several States shall have concurrent power to enforce this article by appropriate legislation.

Section 3. This article shall be inoperative unless it shall have been ratified as an amendment to the Constitution by the legislatures of the several States, as provided in the Constitution, within seven years from the date of the submission hereof to the States by the Congress.

Article XIX

[Proposed June 4, 1919; declared ratified August 26, 1920]

The right of citizens of the United States to vote shall not be denied or abridged by the United States or by any State on account of sex.

Congress shall have power to enforce this article by appropriate legislation.

Article XX

[Proposed March 2, 1932; declared ratified February 6, 1933]

Section 1. The terms of the President and Vice President shall end at noon on the 20th day of January, and the terms of Senators and Representatives at noon on the 3d day of January, of the years in which such terms would have ended if this article had not been ratified; and the terms of their successors shall then begin.

Section 2. The Congress shall assemble at least once in every year, and such meeting shall begin at noon on the 3d day of January, unless they shall by law appoint a different day.

Section 3. If, at the time fixed for the beginning of the term of the President, the President elect shall have died, the Vice President elect shall become President. If a President shall not have been chosen before the time fixed for the beginning of his term, or if the President elect shall have failed to qualify, then the Vice President elect shall act as President until a President shall have qualified; and the Congress may by law provide for the case wherein neither a President elect nor a Vice President elect shall have qualified, declaring who shall then act as President, or the manner in which one who is to act shall be selected, and such person shall act accordingly until a President or Vice President shall have qualified.

Section 4. The Congress may by law provide for the case of the death of any of the persons from whom the House of Representatives may choose a President whenever the right of choice shall have devolved upon them, and for the case of the death of any of the persons from whom the Senate may choose a Vice President whenever the right of choice shall have devolved upon them.

Section 5. Sections 1 and 2 shall take effect on the 15th day of October following the ratification of this article.

Section 6. This article shall be inoperative unless it shall have been ratified as an amendment to the Constitution by the legislatures of three-fourths of the several States within seven years from the date of its submission.

Article XXI

[*Proposed February 20, 1933; declared ratified December 5, 1933*]

Secton 1. The eighteenth article of amendment to the Constitution of the United States is hereby repealed.

Section 2. The transportation or importation into any State, Territory, or possession of the United States for delivery or use therein of intoxicating liquors, in violation of the laws thereof, is hereby prohibited.

Section 3. This article shall be inoperative unless it shall have been ratified as an amendment to the Constitution by conventions in the several States, as provided in the Constitution, within seven years from the date of the submission hereof to the States by the Congress.

Article XXII

[*Proposed March 24, 1947; declared ratified March 1, 1951*]

Section 1. No person shall be elected to the office of the President more than twice, and no person who has held the office of President, or acted as President, for more than two years of a term to which some other person was elected President shall be elected to the office of the President more than once. But this Article shall not apply to any person holding the office of President when this Article was proposed by the Congress, and shall not prevent any person who may be holding the office of President, or acting as President, during the term within which this Article becomes operative from holding the office of President or acting as President during the remainder of such term.

Section 2. This article shall be inoperative unless it shall have been ratified as an amendemnt to the Constitution by the legislatures of three-fourths of the several States within seven years from the date of its submission to the States by the Congress.

Article XXIII

[*Proposed June 16, 1960; declared ratified April 3, 1961*]

Section 1. The District constituting the seat of Government of the United States shall appoint in such manner as the Congress may direct:

A number of electors of President and Vice President equal to the whole number of Senators and Representatives in Congress to which the District would be entitled if it were a State, but in no event more than the least populous state; they shall be in addition to those apointed by the States, but they shall be considered, for the purposes of the election of President and Vice President, to be electors appointed by a State; and they shall meet in the District and perform such duties as provided by the twelfth article of amendment.

Section 2. The Congress shall have power to enforce this article by appropriate legislation.

Article XXIV

[*Proposed August 27, 1962; declared ratified February 4, 1964*]

Section 1. The right of citizens of the United States to vote in any primary or other election for President or Vice President, for electors for President or Vice President, or for Senator or Representative in Congress, shall not be denied or abridged by the United States or any State by reason of failure to pay any poll tax or other tax.

Section 2. The Congress shall have power to enforce this article by appropriate legislation.

Article XXV

[*Proposed July 6, 1965; declared ratified February 23, 1967*]

Section 1. In case of removal of the President from office or of his death or resignation, the Vice President shall become President.

Section 2. Whenever there is a vacancy in the office of the Vice President, the President shall nominate a Vice President who shall take office upon confirmation by a majority vote of both Houses of Congress.

Section 3. Whenever the President transmits to the President pro tempore of the Senate and the Speaker of the House of Representatives his written declaration that he is unable to discharge the powers and duties of his office, and until he transmits to them a written declaration to the contrary, such powers and duties shall be discharged by the Vice President as Acting President.

Section 4. Whenever the Vice President and a majority of either the principal officers of the executive departments or of such other body as Congress may by law provide, transmit to the President pro tempore of the Senate and the Speaker of the House of Representatives their written declaration that the President is unable to discharge the powers and duties of his office, the Vice President shall immediately assume the powers and duties of the office as Acting President.

Thereafter, when the President transmits to the

President pro tempore of the Senate and the Speaker of the House of Representatives his written declaration that no inability exists, he shall resume the powers and duties of his office unless the Vice President and a majority of either the principal officers of the executive department or of such other body as Congress may by law provide, transmit within four days to the President pro tempore of the Senate and the Speaker of the House of Representatives their written declaration that the President is unable to discharge the powers and duties of his office. Thereupon Congress shall decide the issue, assembling within forty-eight hours for that purpose if not in session. If the Congress, within twenty-one days after receipt of the latter written declaration, or, if Congress is not in session, within twenty-one days after Congress is required to assemble, determines by two-thirds vote of both Houses that the President is unable to discharge the powers and duties of his office, the Vice President shall continue to discharge the same as Acting President; otherwise, the President shall resume the powers and duties of his office.

Article XXVI

[*Proposed March 23, 1971; declared ratified July 5, 1971*]

Section 1. The right of citizens of the United States, who are eighteen years of age or older, to vote shall not be denied or abridged by the United States or by any State on account of age.

Section 2. The Congress shall have power to enforce this article by appropriate legislation.

Presidential Elections

Year	Candidates Receiving More Than One Percent of the Vote (Parties)	Popular Vote	Electoral Vote
1789	GEORGE WASHINGTON (No party designations)		69
	John Adams		34
	Other Candidates		35
1792	GEORGE WASHINGTON (No party designations)		132
	John Adams		77
	George Clinton		50
	Other Candidates		5
1796	JOHN ADAMS (Federalist)		71
	Thomas Jefferson (Democratic-Republican)		68
	Thomas Pinckney (Federalist)		59
	Aaron Burr (Democratic-Republican)		30
	Other Candidates		48
1800	THOMAS JEFFERSON (Democratic-Republican)		73
	Aaron Burr (Democratic-Republican)		73
	John Adams (Federalist)		65
	Charles C. Pinckney (Federalist)		64
	John Jay (Federalist)		1
1804	THOMAS JEFFERSON (Democratic-Republican)		162
	Charles C. Pinckney (Federalist)		14
1808	JAMES MADISON (Democratic-Republican)		122
	Charles C. Pinckney (Federalist)		47
	George Clinton (Democratic-Republican)		6
1812	JAMES MADISON (Democratic-Republican)		128
	De Witt Clinton (Federalist)		89
1816	JAMES MONROE (Democratic-Republican)		183
	Rufus King (Federalist)		34
1820	JAMES MONROE (Democratic-Republican)		231
	John Quincy Adams (Independent-Republican)		1
1824	JOHN QUINCY ADAMS (Democratic-Republican)	108,740	84
	Andrew Jackson (Democratic-Republican)	153,544	99
	William H. Crawford (Democratic-Republican)	46,618	41
	Henry Clay (Democratic-Republican)	47,136	37
1828	ANDREW JACKSON (Democratic)	647,286	178
	John Quincy Adams (National Republican)	508,064	83
1832	ANDREW JACKSON (Democratic)	687,502	219
	Henry Clay (National Republican)	530,189	49
	William Wirt (Anti-Masonic)	33,108	7
	John Floyd (National Republican)		11
1836	MARTIN VAN BUREN (Democratic)	765,483	170
	William H. Harrison (Whig)		73
	Hugh L. White (Whig)	739,795	26
	Daniel Webster (Whig)		14
	W. P. Mangum (Anti-Jackson)		11
1840	WILLIAM H. HARRISON (Whig)	1,274,624	234
	Martin Van Buren (Democratic)	1,127,781	60
1844	JAMES K. POLK (Democratic)	1,338,464	170
	Henry Clay (Whig)	1,300,097	105
	James G. Birney (Liberty)	62,300	0
1848	ZACHARY TAYLOR (Whig)	1,360,967	163
	Lewis Cass (Democratic)	1,222,342	127
	Martin Van Buren (Free Soil)	291,263	0
1852	FRANKLIN PIERCE (Democratic)	1,601,117	254
	Winfield Scott (Whig)	1,385,453	42
	John P. Hale (Free Soil)	155,825	0
1856	JAMES BUCHANAN (Democratic)	1,832,955	174
	John C. Frémont (Republican)	1,339,932	114
	Millard Fillmore (American)	871,731	8

Year	Candidates Receiving More Than One Percent of the Vote (Parties)	Popular Vote	Electoral Vote
1860	ABRAHAM LINCOLN (Republican)	1,865,593	180
	Stephen A. Douglas (Democratic)	1,382,713	12
	John C. Breckinridge (Democratic)	848,356	72
	John Bell (Constitutional Union)	592,906	39
1864	ABRAHAM LINCOLN (Republican)	2,206,938	212
	George B. McClellan (Democratic)	1,803,787	21
1868	ULYSSES S. GRANT (Republican)	3,013,421	214
	Horatio Seymour (Democratic)	2,706,829	80
1872	ULYSSES S. GRANT (Republican)	3,596,745	286
	Horace Greeley (Democratic)	2,843,446	—*
	Other Candidates		63
1876	RUTHERFORD B. HAYES (Republican)	4,036,572	185
	Samuel J. Tilden (Democratic)	4,284,020	184
1880	JAMES A. GARFIELD (Republican)	4,453,295	214
	Winfield S. Hancock (Democratic)	4,414,082	155
	James B. Weaver (Greenback-Labor)	308,579	0
1884	GROVER CLEVELAND (Democratic)	4,879,507	219
	James G. Blaine (Republican)	4,850,293	182
	Benjamin F. Butler (Greenback-Labor)	175,370	0
	John P. St. John (Prohibition)	150,369	0
1888	BENJAMIN HARRISON (Republican)	5,447,129	233
	Grover Cleveland (Democratic)	5,537,857	168
	Clinton B. Fisk (Prohibition)	249,506	0
	Anson J. Streeter (Union Labor)	146,935	0
1892	GROVER CLEVELAND (Democratic)	5,555,426	277
	Benjamin Harrison (Republican)	5,182,690	145
	James B. Weaver (People's)	1,029,846	22
	John Bidwell (Prohibition)	264,133	0
1896	WILLIAM McKINLEY (Republican)	7,102,246	271
	William J. Bryan (Democratic)	6,492,559	176
1900	WILLIAM McKINLEY (Republican)	7,218,491	292
	William J. Bryan (Democratic; Populist)	6,356,734	155
	John C. Wooley (Prohibition)	208,914	0
1904	THEODORE ROOSEVELT (Republican)	7,628,461	336
	Alton B. Parker (Democratic)	5,084,223	140
	Eugene V. Debs (Socialist)	402,283	0
	Silas C. Swallow (Prohibition)	258,536	0
1908	WILLIAM H. TAFT (Republican)	7,675,320	321
	William J. Bryan (Democratic)	6,412,294	162
	Eugene V. Debs (Socialist)	420,793	0
	Eugene W. Chafin (Prohibition)	253,840	0
1912	WOODROW WILSON (Democratic)	6,296,547	435
	Theodore Roosevelt (Progressive)	4,118,571	88
	William H. Taft (Republican)	3,486,720	8
	Eugene V. Debs (Socialist)	900,672	0
	Eugene W. Chafin (Prohibition)	206,275	0
1916	WOODROW WILSON (Democratic)	9,127,695	277
	Charles E. Hughes (Republican)	8,533,507	254
	A. L. Benson (Socialist)	585,113	0
	J. Frank Hanly (Prohibition)	220,506	0
1920	WARRAN G. HARDING (Republican)	16,143,407	404
	James M. Cox (Democratic)	9,130,328	127
	Eugene V. Debs (Socialist)	919,799	0
	P. P. Christensen (Farmer-Labor)	265,411	0
1924	CALVIN COOLIDGE (Republican)	15,718,211	382
	John W. Davis (Democratic)	8,385,283	136
	Robert M. La Follette (Progressive)	4,831,289	13
1928	HERBERT C. HOOVER (Republican)	21,391,993	444
	Alfred E. Smith (Democratic)	15,016,169	87
1932	FRANKLIN D. ROOSEVELT (Democratic)	22,809,638	472
	Herbert C. Hoover (Republican)	15,758,901	59
	Norman Thomas (Socialist)	881,951	0

Year	Candidates Receiving More Than One Percent of the Vote (Parties)	Popular Vote	Electoral Vote
1936	FRANKLIN D. ROOSEVELT (Democratic)	27,752,869	523
	Alfred M. Landon (Republican)	16,674,665	8
	William Lemke (Union)	882,479	0
1940	FRANKLIN D. ROOSEVELT (Democratic)	27,307,819	449
	Wendell L. Willkie (Republican)	22,321,018	82
1944	FRANKLIN D. ROOSEVELT (Democratic)	25,606,585	432
	Thomas E. Dewey (Republican)	22,014,745	99
1948	HARRY S. TRUMAN (Democratic)	24,179,345	303
	Thomas E. Dewey (Republican)	21,991,291	189
	J. Strom Thurmond (States' Rights)	1,176,125	39
	Henry Wallace (Progressive)	1,157,326	0
1952	DWIGHT D. EISENHOWER (Republican)	33,936,234	442
	Adlai E. Stevenson (Democratic)	27,314,992	89
1956	DWIGHT D. EISENHOWER (Republican)	35,590,472	457
	Adlai E. Stevenson (Democratic)	26,022,752	73
1960	JOHN F. KENNEDY (Democratic)	34,226,731	303
	Richard M. Nixon (Republican)	34,108,157	219
1964	LYNDON B. JOHNSON (Democratic)	43,129,566	486
	Barry M. Goldwater (Republican)	27,127,188	52
1968	RICHARD M. NIXON (Republican)	31,785,480	301
	Hubert H. Humphrey (Democratic)	31,275,166	191
	George C. Wallace (American Independent)	9,906,473	46
1972	RICHARD M. NIXON (Republican)	45,631,189	521
	George S. McGovern (Democratic)	28,422,015	17
	John Schmitz (American Independent)	1,080,670	0
1976	JAMES E. CARTER, JR. (Democratic)	40,274,975	297
	Gerald R. Ford (Republican)	38,530,614	241
1980	RONALD W. REAGAN (Republican)	42,968,326	489
	James E. Carter, Jr. (Democratic)	34,731,139	49
	John B. Anderson (Independent)	5,552,349	0
1984	RONALD W. REAGAN (Republican)	53,428,357	525
	Walter F. Mondale (Democratic)	36,930,923	13

* *Greeley died shortly after the election; the electors supporting him then divided their votes among other candidates.*

Chief Justices of the Supreme Court

Term	Chief Justice
1789–1795	John Jay
1795	John Rutledge
1795–1799	Oliver Ellsworth
1801–1835	John Marshall
1836–1864	Roger B. Taney
1864–1873	Salmon P. Chase
1874–1888	Morrison R. Waite
1888–1910	Melville W. Fuller
1910–1921	Edward D. White
1921–1930	William H. Taft
1930–1941	Charles E. Hughes
1941–1946	Harlan F. Stone
1946–1953	Fred M. Vinson
1953–1969	Earl Warren
1969–1986	Warren E. Burger
1986–	William Rehnquist

Presidents, Vice Presidents, and Cabinet Members

President and Vice President	Secretary of State	Secretary of Treasury	Secretary of War	Secretary of Navy	Postmaster General	Attorney General	Secretary of Interior
1. George Washington (1789) John Adams (1789)	Thomas Jefferson (1789) Edmund Randolph (1794) Thomas Pickering (1795)	Alexander Hamilton (1789) Oliver Wolcott (1795)	Henry Knox (1789) Timothy Pickering (1795) James McHenry (1796)		Samuel Osgood (1789) Timothy Pickering (1791) Joseph Habersham (1795)	Edmund Randolph (1789) William Bradford (1794) Charles Lee (1795)	
2. John Adams (1797) Thomas Jefferson (1797)	Timothy Pickering (1797) John Marshall (1800)	Oliver Wolcott (1797) Samuel Dexter (1801)	James McHenry (1797) John Marshall (1800) Samuel Dexter (1800) Roger Griswold (1801)	Benjamin Stoddert (1798)	Joseph Habersham (1797)	Charles Lee (1797) Theophilus Parsons (1801)	
3. Thomas Jefferson (1801) Aaron Burr (1801) George Clinton (1805)	James Madison (1801)	Samuel Dexter (1801) Albert Gallatin (1801)	Henry Dearborn (1801)	Benjamin Stoddert (1801) Robert Smith (1801) J. Crowninshield (1805)	Joseph Habersham (1801) Gideon Granger (1801)	Levi Lincoln (1801) Robert Smith (1805) John Breckinridge (1805) Caesar Rodney (1807)	
4. James Madison (1809) George Clinton (1809) Elbridge Gerry (1813)	Robert Smith (1809) James Monroe (1811)	Albert Gallatin (1809) George Campbell (1814) Alexander Dallas (1814) William Crawford (1816)	William Eustis (1809) John Armstrong (1813) James Monroe (1814) William Crawford (1815)	Paul Hamilton (1809) William Jones (1813) Benjamin Crowninshield (1814)	Gideon Granger (1809) Return Meigs (1814)	Caesar Rodney (1809) William Pinckney (1811) Richard Rush (1814)	
5. James Monroe (1817) Daniel D. Thompkins (1817)	John Quincy Adams (1817)	William Crawford (1817)	Isaac Shelby (1817) George Graham (1817) John C. Calhoun (1817)	Benjamin Crowninshield (1817) Smith Thompson (1818) Samuel Southard (1823)	Return Meigs (1817) John McLean (1823)	Richard Rush (1817) William Wirt (1817)	
6. John Quincy Adams (1825) John C. Calhoun (1825)	Henry Clay (1825)	Richard Rush (1825)	James Barbour (1825) Peter B. Porter (1828)	Samuel Southard (1825)	John McLean (1825)	William Wirt (1825)	
7. Andrew Jackson (1829) John C. Calhoun (1829) Martin Van Buren (1833)	Martin Van Buren (1829) Edward Livingston (1831) Louis McLane (1833) John Forsyth (1837)	Samuel Ingham (1829) Louis McLane (1831) William Duane (1833) Roger B. Taney (1833) Levi Woodbury (1834)	John H. Eaton (1829) Lewis Cass (1831) Benjamin Butler (1837)	John Branch (1829) Levi Woodbury (1831) Mahlon Dickerson (1834)	William Barry (1829) Amos Kendall (1835)	John M. Berrien (1829) Roger B. Taney (1831) Benjamin Butler (1833)	
8. Martin Van Buren (1837) Richard M. Johnson (1837)	John Forsyth (1837)	Levi Woodbury (1837)	Joel R. Poinsett (1837)	Mahlon Dickerson (1837) James K. Paulding (1838)	Amos Kendall (1837) John M. Niles (1840)	Benjamin Butler (1837) Felix Grundy (1838) Henry D. Gilpin (1840)	
9. William H. Harrison (1841) John Tyler (1841)	Daniel Webster (1841)	Thomas Ewing (1841)	John Bell (1841)	George E. Badger (1841)	Francis Granger (1841)	John J. Crittenden (1841)	

President and Vice President	Secretary of State	Secretary of Treasury	Secretary of War	Secretary of Navy	Postmaster General	Attorney General	Secretary of Interior
10. John Tyler (1841)	Daniel Webster (1841) Hugh S. Legaré (1843) Abel P. Upshur (1843) John C. Calhoun (1844)	Thomas Ewing (1841) Walter Forward (1841) John C. Spencer (1843) George M. Bibb (1844)	John Bell (1841) John McLean (1841) John C. Spencer (1841) James M. Porter (1843) William Wilkins (1844)	George E. Badger (1841) Abel P. Upshur (1841) David Henshaw (1843) Thomas Gilmer (1844) John Y. Mason (1844)	Francis Granger (1841) Charles A. Wickliffe (1841)	John J. Crittenden (1841) Hugh S. Legaré (1841) John Nelson (1843)	
11. James K. Polk (1845) George M. Dallas (1845)	James Buchanan (1845)	Robert J. Walker (1845)	William L. Marcy (1845)	George Bancroft (1845) John Y. Mason (1846)	Cave Johnson (1845)	John Y. Mason (1845) Nathan Clifford (1846) Isaac Toucey (1848)	
12. Zachary Taylor (1849) Millard Fillmore (1849)	John M. Clayton (1849)	William M. Meredith (1849)	George W. Crawford (1849)	William B. Preston (1849)	Jacob Collamer (1849)	Reverdy Johnson (1849)	Thomas Ewing (1849)
13. Millard Fillmore (1850)	Daniel Webster (1850) Edward Everett (1852)	Thomas Corwin (1850)	Charles M. Conrad (1850)	William A. Graham (1850) John P. Kennedy (1852)	Nathan K. Hall (1850) Sam D. Hubbard (1852)	John J. Crittenden (1850)	Thomas McKennan (1850) A. H. H. Stuart (1850)
14. Franklin Pierce (1853) William R. King (1853)	William L. Marcy (1853)	James Guthrie (1853)	Jefferson Davis (1853)	James C. Dobbin (1853)	James Campbell (1853)	Caleb Cushing (1853)	Robert McClelland (1853)
15. James Buchanan (1857) John C. Breckinridge (1857)	Lewis Cass (1857) Jeremiah S. Black (1860)	Howell Cobb (1857) Philip F. Thomas (1860) John A. Dix (1861)	John B. Floyd (1857) Joseph Holt (1861)	Isaac Toucey (1857)	Aaron V. Brown (1857) Joseph Holt (1859)	Jeremiah S. Black (1857) Edwin M. Stanton (1860)	Jacob Thompson (1857)
16. Abraham Lincoln (1861) Hannibal Hamlin (1861) Andrew Johnson (1865)	William H. Seward (1861)	Salmon P. Chase (1861) William P. Fessenden (1864) Hugh McCulloch (1865)	Simon Cameron (1861) Edwin M. Stanton (1862)	Gideon Welles (1861)	Horatio King (1861) Montgomery Blair (1861) William Dennison (1864)	Edward Bates (1861) Titian J. Coffey (1863) James Speed (1864)	Caleb B. Smith (1861) John P. Usher (1863)
17. Andrew Johnson (1865)	William H. Seward (1865)	Hugh McCulloch (1865)	Edwin M. Stanton (1865) Ulysses S. Grant (1867) Lorenzo Thomas (1868) John M. Schofield (1868)	Gideon Welles (1865)	William Dennison (1865) Alexander Randall (1866)	James Speed (1865) Henry Stanbery (1866) William M. Evarts (1868)	John P. Usher (1865) James Harlan (1865) O. H. Browning (1866)
18. Ulysses S. Grant (1869) Schuyler Colfax (1869) Henry Wilson (1873)	Elihu B. Washburne (1869) Hamilton Fish (1869)	George S. Boutwell (1869) William A. Richardson (1873) Benjamin H. Bristow (1874) Lot M. Morrill (1876)	John A. Rawlins (1869) William T. Sherman (1869) William W. Belknap (1869) Alphonso Taft (1876) James Cameron (1876)	Adolph E. Borie (1869) George M. Robeson (1869)	John A. J. Creswell (1869) James W. Marshall (1874) Marshall Jewell (1874) James N. Tyner (1876)	Ebenezer R. Hoar (1869) Amos T. Akerman (1870) G. H. Williams (1871) Edwards Pierrepont (1875) Alphonso Taft (1876)	Jacob D. Cox (1869) Columbus Delano (1870) Zachariah Chandler (1875)

President and Vice President	Secretary of State	Secretary of Treasury	Secretary of War	Secretary of Navy	Postmaster General	Attorney General	Secretary of Interior
19. Rutherford B. Hayes (1877) William A. Wheeler (1877)	William M. Evarts (1877)	John Sherman (1877)	George W. McCrary (1877) Alexander Ramsey (1879)	R. W. Thompson (1877) Nathan Goff, Jr. (1881)	David M. Key (1877) Horace Maynard (1880)	Charles Devens (1877)	Carl Schurz (1877)
20. James A. Garfield (1881) Chester A. Arthur (1881)	James G. Blaine (1881)	William Windom (1881)	Robert T. Lincoln (1881)	William H. Hunt (1881)	Thomas L. James (1881)	Wayne MacVeagh (1881)	S. I. Kirkwood (1881)
21. Chester A. Arthur (1881)	F. T. Frelinghuysen (1881)	Charles J. Folger (1881) Walter Q. Gresham (1884) Hugh McCulloch (1884)	Robert T. Lincoln (1881)	William E. Chandler (1881)	Timothy O. Howe (1881) Walter Q. Gresham (1883) Frank Hatton (1884)	B. H. Brewster (1881)	Henry M. Teller (1881)
22. Grover Cleveland (1885) T. A. Hendricks (1885)	Thomas F. Bayard (1885)	Daniel Manning (1885) Charles S. Fairchild (1887)	William C. Endicott (1885)	William C. Whitney (1885)	William F. Vilas (1885) Don M. Dickinson (1888)	A. H. Garland (1885)	L. Q. C. Lamar (1885) William F. Vilas (1888)
23. Benjamin Harrison (1889) Levi P. Morgan (1889)	James G. Blaine (1889) John W. Foster (1892)	William Windom (1889) Charles Foster (1891)	Redfield Procter (1889) Stephen B. Elkins (1891)	Benjamin F. Tracy (1889)	John Wanamaker (1889)	W. H. H. Miller (1889)	Jon W. Noble (1889)
24. Grover Cleveland (1893) Adlai E. Stevenson (1893)	Walter Q. Gresham (1893) Richard Olney (1895)	John G. Carlisle (1893)	Daniel S. Lamont (1893)	Hilary A. Herbert (1893)	Wilson S. Bissel (1893) William L. Wilson (1895)	Richard Olney (1893) Judson Harmon (1895)	Hoke Smith (1893) David R. Francis (1896)
25. William McKinley (1897) Garret A. Hobart (1897) Theodore Roosevelt (1901)	John Sherman (1897) William R. Day (1897) John Hay (1898)	Lyman J. Gage (1897)	Russell A. Alger (1897) Elihu Root (1899)	John D. Long (1897)	James A. Gary (1897) Charles E. Smith (1898)	Joseph McKenna (1897) John W. Griggs (1897) Philander C. Knox (1901)	Cornelius N. Bliss (1897) E. A. Hitchcock (1899)
26. Theodore Roosevelt (1901) Charles Fairbanks (1905)	John Hay (1901) Elihu Root (1905) Robert Bacon (1909)	Lyman J. Gage (1901) Leslie M. Shaw (1902) George B. Cortelyou (1907)	Elihu Root (1901) William H. Taft (1904) Luke E. Wright (1908)	John D. Long (1901) William H. Moody (1902) Paul Morton (1904) Charles J. Bonaparte (1905) V. H. Metcalf (1906) T. H. Newberry (1908)	Charles E. Smith (1901) Henry Payne (1902) Robert J. Wynne (1904) George B. Cortelyou (1905) George von L. Meyer (1907)	Philander C. Knox (1901) William H. Moody (1904) Charles J. Bonaparte (1907)	E. A. Hitchcock (1901) James R. Garfield (1907)
27. William H. Taft (1909) James S. Sherman (1909)	Philander C. Knox (1909)	Franklin MacVeagh (1909)	Jacob M. Dickinson (1909) Henry Stimson (1911)	George von L. Meyer (1909)	Frank H. Hitchcock (1909)	G. W. Wickersham (1909)	R. A. Ballinger (1909) Walter L. Fisher (1911)
28. Woodrow Wilson (1913) Thomas R. Marshall (1913)	William J. Bryan (1913) Robert Lansing (1915) Bainbridge Colby (1920)	William G. McAdoo (1913) Carter Glass (1918) David F. Houston (1920)	Lindley M. Garrison (1913) Newton D. Baker (1916)	Josephus Daniels (1913)	Albert S. Burleson (1913)	J. C. McReynolds (1913) T. W. Gregory (1914) A. Mitchell Palmer (1919)	Franklin K. Lane (1913) John B. Payne (1920)

President and Vice President	Secretary of State	Secretary of Treasury	Secretary of War	Secretary of Navy	Postmaster General	Attorney General	Secretary of Interior
29. Warren G. Harding (1921) Calvin Coolidge (1921)	Charles E. Hughes (1912)	Andrew W. Mellon (1921)	John W. Weeks (1921)	Edwin Denby (1921)	Will H. Hays (1921) Hubert Work (1922) Harry S. New (1923)	H. M. Daugherty (1921)	Albert B. Fall (1921) Hubert Work (1923)
30. Calvin Coolidge (1923) Charles G. Dawes (1925)	Charles E. Hughes (1923) Frank B Kellogg (1925)	Andrew W. Mellon (1923)	John W. Weeks (1923) Dwight F. Davis (1925)	Edwin Denby (1923) Curtis D Wilbur (1924)	Harry S. New (1923)	H. M. Daugherty (1923) Harlan F. Stone (1924) John G. Sargent (1925)	Hubert Work (1923) Roy O West (1928)
31. Herbert C. Hoover (1929) Charles Curtis (1929)	Henry L. Stimson (1929)	Andrew W. Mellon (1929) Ogden L. Mills (1932)	James W. Good (1929) Patrick J. Hurley	Charles F. Adams (1929)	Walter F. Brown (1929)	W. D. Mitchell (1929)	Ray L. Wilbur (1929)
32. Franklin D. Roosevelt (1933) John Nance Garner (1933) Henry A. Wallace (1941) Harry S. Truman (1945)	Cordell Hull (1933) E. R. Stettinius, Jr. (1944)	William H. Woodin (1933) Henry Morgenthau, Jr. (1934)	George H. Dern (1933) Harry H. Woodring (1936) Henry L. Stimson (1940)	Claude A. Swanson (1933) Charles Edison (1940) Frank Knox (1940) James V. Forrestal (1944)	James A. Farley (1933) Frank C. Walker (1940)	H. S. Cummings (1933) Frank Murphy (1939) Robert Jackson (1940) Francis Biddle (1941)	Harold L. Ickes (1933)
33. Harry S. Truman (1945) Alben W. Barkley (1949)	James F. Byrnes (1945) George C. Marshall (1947) Dean G. Acheson (1949)	Fred M. Vinson (1945) John W. Snyder (1946)	Robert P. Patterson (1945) Kenneth C. Royal (1947) *Secretary of Defense* James V. Forrestal (1947) Louis A. Johnson (1949) George C. Marshall (1950) Robert A. Lovett (1951)	James V. Forrestal (1945)	R. E. Hannegan (1945) Jesse M. Donaldson (1947)	Tom C. Clark (1945) J. H. McGrath (1949) James P. McGranery (1952)	Harold L. Ickes (1945) Julis A. Krug (1946) Oscar L. Chapman (1949)
34. Dwight D. Eisenhower (1953) Richard M. Nixon (1953)	John Foster Dulles (1953) Christian A. Herter (1959)	George M. Humphrey (1953) Robert B. Anderson (1957)	Charles E. Wilson (1953) Neil H. McElroy (1957) Thomas S. Gates (1959)		A. E. Summerfield (1953)	H. Brownell, Jr. (1953) William P. Rogers (1957)	Douglas McKay (1953) Fred Seaton (1956)
35. John F. Kennedy (1961) Lyndon B. Johnson (1961)	Dean Rusk (1961)	C. Douglas Dillon (1961)	Robert S. McNamara (1961)		J. Edward Day (1961) John A. Gronouski (1963)	Robert F. Kennedy (1961)	Stewart L. Udall (1961)
36. Lyndon B. Johnson (1963) Hubert H. Humphrey (1965)	Dean Rusk (1963)	C. Douglas Dillon (1963) Henry H Fowler (1965) Joseph W. Barr (1968)	Robert S. McNamara (1963) Clark M. Clifford (1968)		John A. Gronouski (1963) Lawrence F. O'Brien (1965) W. Marvin Watson (1968)	Robert F. Kennedy (1963) N. deB Katzenbach (1965) Ramsey Clark (1967)	Stewart L. Udall (1963)

President and Vice President	Secretary of State	Secretary of Treasury	Secretary of War	Secretary of Navy	Postmaster General	Attorney General	Secretary of Interior
37. **Richard M. Nixon** (1969) Spiro T. Agnew (1969) Gerald R. Ford (1973)	William P. Rogers (1969) Henry A. Kissinger (1973)	David M. Kennedy (1969) John B. Connally (1970) George P. Schultz (1972) William E. Simon (1974)	Melvin R. Laird (1969) Elliot L. Richardson (1973) James R. Schlesinger (1973)		Winton M. Blount (1969)	John M. Mitchell (1969) Richard G. Kleindienst (1972) Elliot L. Richardson (1973) William B. Saxbe (1974)	Walter J. Hickel (1969) Rogers C. B. Morton (1971)
38. **Gerald R. Ford** (1974) Nelson A. Rockefeller (1974)	Henry A. Kissinger (1974)	William E. Simon (1974)	James R. Schlesinger (1974) Donald H. Runsfeld (1975)			William B. Saxbe (1974) Edward H. Levi (1975)	Rogers C. B. Morton (1974) Stanley K. Hathaway (1975) Thomas D. Kleppe (1975)
39. **James E. Carter, Jr.** (1977) Walter F. Mondale (1977)	Cyrus R. Vance (1977) Edmund S. Muskie (1980)	W. Michael Blumenthal (1977) G. William Miller (1979)	Harold Brown (1977)			Griffin B. Bell (1977) Benjamin R. Civiletti (1979)	Cecil D. Andrus (1977)
40. **Ronald W. Reagan** (1981) George H. Bush (1981)	Alexander M. Haig, Jr. (1981) George P. Schultz (1982)	Donald T. Regan (1981)	Caspar W. Weinberger (1981)			William French Smith (1981)	James G. Watt (1981) William Clark (1983)
41. **Ronald W. Reagan** (1985) George H. Bush (1985)	George P. Schultz (1985)	James B. Baker III (1985)	Caspar W. Weinberger (1985)			Edwin Meese III (1985)	Donald P. Hodel (1985)

Writing About History

Dr. Robert Weiss

What is "history"? We employ the word constantly to refer to everything from the "history" of the world to an individual's "history." But how often do we stop to think about what the word means? The following essay addresses this question, and provides some fundamental principles for reading, researching, and writing historical reports and essays.

What is History?

History can best be defined as a record and interpretation of past events. This statement is not very complicated, yet it is not as simple as it may appear. Let us examine it more carefully.

The "record" part is straightforward. Since the purpose of history is to inform us about what happened in the past, it must include substantial data, or "facts" (a troublesome word that some social scientists avoid). Names, dates, places, and events are the essence of history. But historical writing is not a compendium of facts. It consists of facts placed in a sequence to tell a connected story. A work of history is not merely a story, however. It also must analyze what happened and *why*—that is, it must interpret the past for the reader in a useful and informative manner. It is not sufficient, for example, to state that the American Revolution began in 1775–76, and then give an account of the relevant individuals and events, such as George Washington, Thomas Jefferson, Lexington and Concord, and the Declaration of Independence. The historian must proceed to the next step: Why did the Revolution occur in 1776? Here again, historians must resort to concrete data, including the Proclamation of 1763, the Boston Massacre, the Boston Tea Party, and the Intolerable Acts. Rather than simply composing a catalog of events, however, the historian must weave the material into a well-integrated narrative that analyzes the *process* whereby the American colonies severed their political ties to the mother country. To accomplish this task, historians must make certain value judgments concerning the role and significance of these events. Which were more important, and which were less important? What was the relationship of each event to the others, and what does each tell us about the behavior of the American colonists?

To address questions like these, historians must place their material within an appropriate historical context. An account of a past event is not very instructive unless it is analyzed as a component of a larger sequence of events within a specific social, political, and economic setting. The Boston Tea Party, for example, would be analyzed in relation to such factors as British financial expenses incurred during the French and Indian War, colonial views regarding commerce and taxation, Britain's relationship with its empire, and the role of merchants in American colonial society. Only by examining such factors can we hope to understand why both sides behaved as they did.

Historical interpretation takes place on many levels. Some historians focus on the "larger forces" in history, such as the industrial revolution of the nineteenth century and the communications revolution of the twentieth century. Obviously these developments exerted a profound effect on the way we live. The emphasis on context, however, also acknowledges the human element in history. Human beings are the actors in the historical drama, and an effective historical work attempts to explain why people behaved as they did. A history of the American Revolution, for example, would be incomplete if it documented the events leading up to American independence, but offered no insights as to *why* formerly loyal subjects of the British crown took up arms against their mother country. To understand human behavior, the historian, like the psychologist or psychiatrist, must examine the effects of "larger forces" and specific events on people as well as the ways in which the people themselves perceived these forces and events. To appreciate the American desire for independence in 1776, one must view the events of the 1700s through eighteenth-century, not twentieth-century, eyes.

A note of caution should be introduced here. To understand the behavior of various groups is not necessarily to endorse it. By using the proper resources, the historian can understand such phenomena as the Reign of Terror during the French Revolution, the development of slavery in the American South, and the ascendancy of Hitler in Germany. But this claim does not imply that the historian approves of guillotines, slavery, or Nazism. Rather, it asserts the historian's responsibility to analyze all facets of history, even those that he or she finds personally reprehensible.

The preceding paragraphs indicate the "subjective" nature of the interpretive process. When historians make the transition from recording data to interpreting that data, they are imposing an order and a meaning on a set of circumstances that they usually did not experience firsthand. Moreover, historians' interpretations often differ from those of various parties who *did* experience the events. While historians' interpretations should always be based on evidence, there comes a point at which they must transcend that evidence and rely on their own insights, values, and experiences in forming conclusions. Historians collect facts, and when they feel they have mastered them, they draw conclusions as to their significance and their relationship to one another. This process is not unique to the history profession, but is characteristic of all the natural and social sciences. Like all scientists, historians must pursue the maximum feasible "objectivity" in forming their conlusions, while acknowledging the impossibility of total objectivity. Historians must be aware of their personal biases and values so they can monitor the effects of these biases on their interpretations of the past. At the same time, writers of history should never allow the fear of "subjectivity" to stifle the creative process.

Reading History

An understanding of the fundamentals of historical writing will make the student of history a more discerning and selective reader. Although no two historical works are identical, most contain the same basic elements and can be approached in a similar manner by the reader. When reading a historical monograph, concentrate on the two basic issues discussed in the preceding section: facts and interpretation.

Interpretation.　The first question the reader should ask is: What is the author's argument? What is his theme, his interpretation, his thesis? A theme is not the same as a topic. An author may select the Civil War as a *topic*, but he then must propose a particular theme or argument regarding some aspect of the war. (The most common, not surprisingly, is *why* the war occurred.)

Discovering the author's thesis is usually easy enough because most writers state their arguments clearly in the preface to their book. Students often make the crucial error of skimming over the preface—if they read it at all—and then moving on to the "meat" of the book. Since the preface indicates the manner in which the author has used his data to develop his arguments, students who ignore it often find themselves overwhelmed with details without understanding *what* the author is attempting to say. This error should be avoided always.

The more history you read, the more you will appreciate the diversity of opinions and approaches among historians. While each author offers a unique perspective, historical works fall into general categories, or "schools," depending on their thesis and when they were published. The study of the manner in which different historians approach their subjects is referred to as *historiography*. Every historical subject has a historiography, sometimes limited, sometimes extensive. As in the other sciences, new schools of thought supplant existing ones, offering new insights and challenging accepted theories. Below are excerpts from two monographs dealing with the American Revolution. As you read them, note the contrast in the underlying arguments.

1. "Despite its precedent-setting character, however, the American revolt is noteworthy because it made no serious interruption in the smooth flow of American development. Both in intention and in fact, the American Revolution conserved the past rather than repudiated it. And in preserving the colonial experience, the men of the first quarter century of the Republic's history set the scenery and wrote the script for the drama of American politics for years to come."[*]

2. "The stream of revolution, once started, could not be confined within narrow banks, but spread abroad upon the land. Many economic desires, many social aspirations were set free by the political struggle, many aspects of colonial society profoundly altered by the forces thus set loose. The relations of social classes to each other, the institution of slavery, the system of landholding, the course of business, the forms and spirit of the intellectual and religious life, all felt the transforming hand of revolution, all emerged from under it in shapes advanced many degrees nearer to those we know."[†]

What you have just read is nothing less than two conflicting theories of the fundamental nature of the American Revolution. Professor Jameson portrays the Revolution as a catalyst for major social, economic, and

[*] Carl N. Degler, *Out of Our Past*, rev. ed. (New York: Harper and Row, Harper Colophon Books, 1970), p. 73.
[†] J. Franklin Jameson, *The American Revolution Considered As a Social Movement* (Boston: Beacon Press, 1956), p. 9.

political change, while Professor Degler views it primarily as a war for independence that conserved, rather than transformed, colonial institutions. The existence of such divergent opinions makes it imperative that the reader be aware of the argument of every book and read a variety of books and articles to get different perspectives on a subject.

All historical works contain biases of some sort, but a historical bias is not in itself bad or negative. As long as history books are composed by human beings, they will reflect the perspectives of their authors. This need not diminish the quality of historical writing if historians remain faithful to the facts. Some historians, however, have such strong biases that they distort the evidence to make it fit their preconceived notions. This type of history writing (which is the exception rather than the rule) is of limited value, but when properly treated can contribute to the accumulation of knowledge by providing new insights and challenging the values—and creative abilities—of other historians.

Evidence. Once you are aware of the author's central argument, you can concentrate on his use of evidence—the "facts"—that buttress that argument. There are several types of questions that you should keep in mind as you progress through a book. What types of evidence does the author use? Is his evidence convincing? Which sources does he rely on, and what additional sources might he have consulted? One strategy you might adopt is to imagine that *you* are writing the monograph. Where would you go for information? What would you look at? Then ask yourself: Did the author consult these sources? Obviously no writer can examine *everything*. A good historical work, however, offers convincing data extracted from a comprehensive collection of materials.

As you begin to ask these questions, you will develop the skill of critical reading. Used in this sense the word *critical* does not mean reading to discern what is wrong with the narrative. Rather, it refers to analytic reading, assessing the strengths and weaknesses of the monograph, and determining whether the argument ultimately works. All historical works should be approached with a critical—but open—mind.

One important point to remember is that you need not accept or reject every aspect of a historical monograph. In fact, you most likely will accord a "mixed review" to most of the books you read. You may accept the author's argument but find his evidence inadequate, or you may be impressed by his data but draw different conclusions from it. You may find some chapters tightly argued, but others unconvincing. Even if you like a particular book, almost inevitably you will have some comments, criticisms, or suggestions.

Researching History

Most history courses, especially advanced ones, require some type of research project. Research skills are vital to history, and can be developed by observing certain rules.

The first rule is to know exactly what you are researching. Every history project begins with a question or problem. Thus the first step is to select a manageable question. Remember, a question is different from a topic. You may choose the American Revolution as a topic, for example, but you then must choose some aspect of the Revolution that interests you. Obviously a project such as "Discuss the American Revolution in all its aspects" is not realistic. You may be interested in the causes of the Revolution. This is a legitimate question, but still a broad one, more appropriate for a book than a paper. You would do better to select a more specific question, such as "Was the American Revolution really a revolution?" This question poses a specific problem, which will require you to collect data and then formulate a definite argument.

Once you have chosen the question, you begin the search for information. There are several possible sources you may wish to explore. First, you might want to consult your professor, who should be familiar with the relevant literature. This approach could be productive; on the other hand, the professor may want you to develop research skills on your own. In that case, a good encyclopedia, such as the *Encyclopaedia Britannica*, will provide a brief but useful overview of a topic and will cite the works from which the information was collected. Even more valuable is an American history textbook. The bibliography section for the appropriate chapters—and, if included, a list of recommended readings—will direct you toward the appropriate literature.

The library card catalog constitutes another vital source of information. It contains three types of cards, which may be filed separately or together, but are always in alphabetical order: author, title, and subject cards. Author cards are filed according to the author's last name; title cards, according to the book's title (excluding "the"); and subject cards by major topical groupings. Obviously subject cards are the most appropriate when you are looking for sources and ideas. If you are uncertain as to *how* your particular topic is filed, choose a heading that sounds appropriate. To come back to our sample topic, possibilities include: "American Revolution"; "Revolution—United States"; "United States—History—Revolution." If you should pick the wrong heading, the catalog will usually have one card under that heading referring you to the proper subject category. If you already have compiled a list of names and/or authors, you can save much time by going directly to the author and title cards.

The following is the card for a famous work in American history. Note the diversity of information that the card contains. (See below.)

This information not only helps you to locate a book, but can indicate whether the book is relevant to your topic. Often, however, you cannot determine a book's usefulness until you have examined its table of contents and perhaps skimmed through a chapter or two.

As you search for materials, you should be aware that historical sources are divided into two general categories: primary and secondary. Primary sources are those produced by the historical characters themselves or their contemporaries: correspondence, diaries and journals, autobiographies, government publications, newspapers, and similar documents. Secondary sources include books, magazine articles, and Ph.D. dissertations written by later scholars or writers. In most cases, primary sources are more impressive, since they provide a firsthand account of the events in question. Unfortunately they are often more difficult to locate. In the case of the American Revolution, for example, much primary information does exist, including correspondence, newspapers, and government materials. While some of these materials, such as the letters of Washington and Jefferson, are available in printed form in many university libraries, other materials exist only in the original manuscripts and are confined to special libraries, state historical societies, and similar institutions. Fortunately primary materials are not required for all assignments. Consult your professor and use your own judgment to determine what types of sources are most appropriate for your project.

Once you have selected your sources, the task of note taking begins. Thorough notes are the key to successful research. When you locate a source on the library shelves, the first step is to fill out a note card listing the author, title, publisher, and publication date. You might also note the library call number, in case you need to consult the book again. Once you have recorded this information, the next step is to read the appropriate sections of the book or article, and to jot down any information that may be helpful to you on additional cards. The general rule is one idea per card. Following this procedure allows you to arrange and rearrange your notes in the course of your writing. As you are taking notes, rephrase the data in your own words. Or, if you use the author's language, be sure to put quotation marks around it to indicate it is a direct quote. Always include on your card the author, title, and the page(s) on which you found the inforation. This will be useful when you wish to cite the material in a footnote. Remember, if you are using a book, you need not read the entire book, but only those sections relevant to your topic. Magazine articles generally should be read in their entirety.

Writing History

Once you have collected your data, you face the often difficult task of putting your ideas on paper. Composing

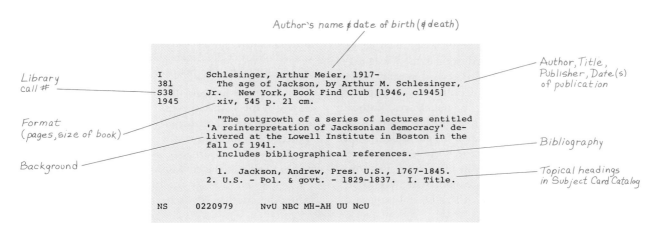

Author's name & date of birth (& death)

Library call #

```
I
381
S38
1945
```

Author, Title, Publisher, Date(s) of publication

Schlesinger, Arthur Meier, 1917-
    The age of Jackson, by Arthur M. Schlesinger,
Jr.   New York, Book Find Club [1946, c1945]
    xiv, 545 p. 21 cm.

    "The outgrowth of a series of lectures entitled
'A reinterpretation of Jacksonian democracy' delivered at the Lowell Institute in Boston in the
fall of 1941.
    Includes bibliographical references.

    1. Jackson, Andrew, Pres. U.S., 1767-1845.
2. U.S. - Pol. & govt. - 1829-1837. I. Title.

```
NS      0220979    NvU NBC MH-AH UU NcU
```

Format (pages, size of book)

Background

Bibliography

Topical headings in Subject Card Catalog

a history essay allows for few legitimate shortcuts. By adhering to a particular set of procedures, however, you can minimize difficulties while enhancing the quality of your writing.

The first step in writing a paper is to create an outline. Although students often avoid this stage in their haste to "get started" on their project, the outline performs a critical role in the creative process. Not only does it contribute to a more logical and coherent development of ideas, but it also helps you see and eliminate many structural problems before you become engrossed in the actual writing. As a general rule, the earlier you can spot any problem, the easier it is to resolve. The outline may be as general or as specific as you wish. It serves not as an ironclad script for you to follow, but as a general framework to provide direction for the narrative. It can be modified later to accommodate ideas that occur to you as you proceed.

After you complete the outline, you should begin your paper with a clear statement of your argument. For example, if you are addressing the question of whether the American Revolution really was a revolution, you should begin by taking a clear position on the question. It is important to note that the position need *not* be a simple "yes" or "no"; it may be more complicated than that. History is seldom black and white; most often it consists of many gray areas. Whatever position you take, it should be made explicit. If you fail to do this, the effectiveness of your writing will be diminished, since your readers may not be aware of the point of your essay. A common mistake students make is to treat a paper like a mystery story, giving readers the "clues" first and supplying the "solution" at the end. This style is not conducive to good history. State your argument in the beginning so that your readers will be able to follow—and assess—your narrative.

From your introduction you should move smoothly into your narrative. It is here that you develop your argument, using your evidence in a convincing manner. The narrative should exhibit a logical sequence of ideas, not a random collection of data. While evidence is crucial, the key to successful writing is in the elaboration of evidence. Contrary to a popular slogan, the facts do not speak for themselves. Rather, the author must explain the relevance of his facts to his central argument. Few people, for example, would dispute the statement that George Washington crossed the Delaware River to surprise the Hessians at Trenton. The author, however, must explain why this event was significant to his topic. Otherwise it becomes a mere fact of passing interest, without any greater meaning.

History involves the process of change over time, and an effective narrative must illustrate this process. To do so, the narrative must connect diverse facts so that they form a cohesive story. Each sentence should follow logically from the preceding one, and lead into the next one; each paragraph should do the same. To accomplish this, you must pay particular attention to *transition*; that is, moving from one topic to a related topic. Too often students shift from one topic to another without explaining the connection between the two. A historical essay that shifts immediately from Washington's crossing of the Delaware to Jefferson's authorship of the Declaration of Independence creates confusion as to the course of the narrative. A successful transition can be effected by inserting a sentence such as "While some individuals fought for independence on the battlefield, others pursued it in the halls of the Continental Congress." This sentence establishes a concrete relationship between the two events.

In addition to elaborating your evidence, you must cite the sources of this evidence. Any information that is not "common knowledge" should be demarcated by a footnote. If you are uncertain as to proper footnote use and form, consult a stylistic manual such as Kate Turabian's *A Manual for Writers*. Although some footnotes can be complicated, the basic forms for books and articles are illustrated below.

For books:

Robert E. Brown, *Middle-Class Democracy and the Revolution in Massachusetts, 1691–1780* (Ithaca, N.Y.: Cornell University Press, 1955), p. 27.

Notice that the footnote includes the author, title, publisher, date, and page on which the information was found. As mentioned earlier, it is essential that you record this information when taking notes.

Articles are footnoted as follows:

Jesse Lemisch, "Jack Tar in the Streets: Merchant Seamen in the Politics of the American Revolution," *William and Mary Quarterly*, 3rd Series 25 (July, 1968): 347–381.

This footnote includes the author, title, the journal in which the article appears, and the date and edition of publication. The pages indicated are those from which the information was taken. Note that the title of the book or journal is underlined, while the title of the article is placed within quotation marks.

For an article by one author appearing in a work edited by another:

Gordon S. Wood, "Rhetoric and Reality in the American Revolution," in *Essays on the American Revolution*, ed. David L. Jacobsen (New York: Holt, Rinehart and Winston, 1970), p. 50–52.

This form combines various elements of the previous two styles (all forms are based on Turabian's *Manual*.)

In addition to knowing *how* to footnote, you must learn *when* to footnote. All specific data that are not common knowledge, as well as all direct quotes, should be cited. Never use historians' words or ideas without giving them credit in a footnote. To do so constitutes plagiarism, which is a serious offense within the academic world. For stylistic purposes, most readers prefer one comprehensive footnote at the end of a paragraph to a footnote at the end of each individual sentence. (A single footnote may cite several sources.) In the case of a direct quote, however, a footnote must appear at the end of a sentence. If you use a series of quotations, one multiple footnote may suffice. The word *footnote* implies that the citations should appear on the bottom of the page on which the cited material appears. While this is the most convenient arrangement for the reader, it complicates the typing of the paper substantially. Therefore, most professors will accept a separate footnote section at the end of the narrative.

One final word regarding footnotes. While you must cite a source every time you take data from it, you need only give the full citation the *first* time you cite the source. After that, an abbreviated footnote form is acceptable. For example:

Brown, *Middle-Class Democracy*, p. 11.

Adopting this form can save you considerable time in the typing of your paper.

Although all individuals must develop their own style of presenting evidence, a few basic rules should be observed. Keep your language clear and succinct. Avoid wordiness and redundancies. Expressions such as "a determined, headstrong, ambitious, unyielding, perservering individual" are repetitious and stylistically unacceptable. Make sure you have command of your vocabulary; do not employ "impressive" words if you are unsure of their precise meaning. Avoid excessive quoting. Quotes are a highly effective means of illustrating ideas and attitudes, but when used excessively, they *become* the narrative, rather than highlighting the narrative. Let your characters speak for themselves, but remember that the final argument must be yours.

Learn to employ active rather than passive verbs in your writing. "Congress passed a law" reads better than "A law was passed," and is also more informative since it reveals *who* passed the law. Since history is a record of the past, it should be written in the past tense.
Incorrect: "Hitler invad*es* Russia in June of 1941"
Correct: "Hitler invad*ed* Russia in June of 1941."
Since you are, in a sense, telling a story, humorous anecdotes and interesting asides, when used properly, can make your narrative more readable. If your writing includes extensive quantitative (numerical) data, you might want to incorporate the information into charts or appendices to avoid interrupting the flow of your narrative.

When you have completed the actual narrative, you should summarize your argument *briefly* in your conclusion. Just as your introductory paragraph prepares your readers for your argument, your conclusion reaffirms the major ideas that you want to communicate to your readers.

After the narrative comes the bibliography, which is a list of all the sources you have used in the course of your work. Several differences distinguish a bibliography from footnotes. While the sequence of footnotes is determined by your narrative, the bibliography is arranged in alphabetical order. Most bibliographies are divided into primary and secondary sources, and subdivided into general categories, such as books, articles, newspapers, and government documents. Moreover, the bibliographic form differs slightly from that of footnotes. Examples of proper bibliographic forms follow:

Brown, Robert E. *Middle-Class Democracy and the Revolution in Massachusetts, 1691–1780*. Ithaca. N.Y.: Cornell University Press, 1955.

Lemisch, Jesse. "Jack Tar in the Streets: Merchant Seamen in the Politics of the Revolutionary America." *William and Mary Quarterly*. 3rd Series 25 (July, 1968): 371–407.

Wood, Gordon S. "Rhetoric and Reality in the American Revolution." In *Essays in the American Revolution*, pp. 43–65. Edited by David L. Jacobsen. New York: Holt, Rinehart and Winston, 1970.

Although the form differs from that of footnotes, most of the information is the same. Note that in the case of articles, however, the bibliography gives the page numbers for the entire article, while the footnote gives only those pages from which information has been extracted. Note also the way the author's last names stand out in a bibliography, enabling the reader to see at a glance which sources you have used. (The bibliographic form used here comes from Turabian's manual. If you have any questions regarding the bibliography, consult Turabian or some other manual.)

The final state in writing a paper is proofreading. Ideally, you should compose a first draft, proofread it carefully, and then rewrite the paper where necessary. If you write only one draft, make your corrections as neatly as possible. Unless otherwise instructed, papers should be typed, double-spaced.

Finally, pay strict attention to deadlines. Allot adequate time for each project, including time for typing and proofreading. If you encounter any difficulties, inform your professor immediately. Do not wait until the due date to reveal that you cannot submit your paper on time.

Photo Credits

Index

Associated Press, 601
Atlanta Compromise (1895), 626
Atlanta University, 431
Atlantic, Battle of the, 744
Atlantic Charter, 744
Atlantic Monthly, 585, 587
Atlas rocket, 785
Atlas Shrugged (Rand), 868
Atomic bomb, 760–61
Atomic Energy Commission, 785
Attitudes during Reconstruction, 416–17
Attlee, Clement, 780
Austria, opposition to emigration, 474
Automobile, impact of, 678–79
Automobile industry, 883
  unionization of, 726
Avranches, Battle of (1944), 757
Axis powers, 745
Ayer, Beatrice, 756
Ayers, Bill, 816

Babbitt (Lewis), 689–92
Baby boom, 813, 847
Backlash vote, 836–38
Back-to-Africa movement, 686–87
Baer, George F., 630
Baez, Joan, 808
Baker, Howard, 889
Baker, Ray Stannard, 619, 621
Baker, Russell, 859
Bakke, Allan, 847
Bakke decision, 847
Bakker, Jim, 881
Bakker, Tammy Faye, 881
Baldwin, James, 809
Ball, George, 804
"Ballad of the Harp Weaver, The" (Millay), 692
Ballinger, Richard A., 634–35
Ballinger-Pinchot controversy, 634–35
Ballot, secret, 625
Baltimore and Ohio (B and O) railroad, 446
Bankhead-Jones Farm Tenant Act (1937), 728
Banking Act (1935), 727
Banking Acts, 639
Banks and banking
  farmers and, 522
  Great Depression and, 704–5
  international, 777
  investment, 444–45
  national system, 444
Bannock Indians, 505
Baptist, Ebenezer, 810
Baptists, 431
Bara, Theda, 596, 663
Barbed wire, 519
Bardeen, John, 884
Bargaining, collective, 460, 715
Barnes, Clive, 800
Barnett, Ross, 804
Baruch, Bernard, 660
Baseball, 593, 776
BASIC, 885
Basic training, 747
Basie, Count, 708
Bastogne siege, 757
Bataan, 752
Bauer, Kate, 466
Bay of Pigs, 801
Beard, Charles A., 605, 617
Beat generation, 793, 796, 808
Beatles, the, 808
Beecher, Henry Ward, 449, 609
Begin, Menachem, 861
Belgium, 741
Bell, Daniel, 483, 766
Bellamy, Edward, 462
Belleau Wood, 665
Benghazi, air attack against, 888
Bennett Law, 544
Berger, Victor L., 467, 664
Berkeley, University of California at, 813–14
Berkman, Alexander, 463
Berlin, Irving, 595
Berlin Accord (1971, 1972), 833
Berlin Airlift, 784
Berlin crises, 802
Berlin wall, 802
Bernstein, Barton J., 702
Bernstein, Carl, 840

Berrigan, Daniel, 825
Berrigan, Philip, 825
Bertillon, Alphonse, 619
Bethmann-Hollweg, Theobald von, 653, 654, 655
Beveridge, Albert, 558, 631, 634
Bicentennial celebration, 843
Bicycle, 593
Biden, Joe, 892
Big-Band Music, 708
Big business
  mining and, 512–14
  T. Roosevelt and, 630
Bigness, fear of, 614
Bilbo, Theodore G., 626
Bill(s)
  force, 541
  strike, 537
Bill of Rights, 425, 808
Biograph, 596
Birmingham, 811
Birth-control information, 482
Birth of a Nation, The (film), 596–97, 694
Black Codes, 423–24
Black convention (1865), 419
Blackfoot Indians, 500
Black Hills, 498, 512
Black International, 462
Black Kettle, Chief, 504
"Black Monday" on stock market, 891
Blackmun, Harry, 838, 848
Black Muslims, 812
Black Panther movement, 809
Black Power, 809–13
Blacks
  Slavery
    aftermath of Civil War and, 414–15
    disappointment in Seventies, 843–44
    economic gains in World War I, 661
    education of, 431
    family structure, 844
    gold miners, 499
    grassroots protests by, 776–77
    Great Depression and, 706–7
    lynching of, 617, 627
    music, 595
    1920s and, 686–87
    Northern migration of, 680, 686
    Populist Party and, 547
    Progressivism and, 616–17, 626–27
    during Reconstruction, 419, 431
      attitudes toward, 416–17
      cultural change, 430–31
      politics, 431
      tenantry and sharecropping of, 428–30
    segregation of, 431, 594, 617, 775, 776
    settlement of Great Plains, 500
    in spectator sports, 594
    support of F. Roosevelt, 720
    two-tier social structure, 844
    wages of industrial workers, 454
    Warren Court and, 776
    Wilson presidency and, 640
    World War I and intolerance of, 664
    World War II social stresses on, 748–49
    World War II changes for, 775–76
Black Shirts, 707
Blaine, James G., 530, 536, 538–40, 544–45, 562
Bland, Richard ("Silver Dick"), 549
Bland-Allison Act (1878), 534
Blatch, Harriot Stanton, 655
Bliss, William, 609
Blitzkrieg, 741
Blount, James H., 567
Blues, the, 595
Blumenthal, Michael, 859
Bly, Nellie, 601
Bohemians of Twenties, 689
Bohr, Niels, 760
Boissevain, Eugen, 692
Bok, Edward W., 602
Boker, George, 585
Bolshevik Revolution (1917), 658–59, 683
Bolshevism, 467
  fear of, 683–85
Bonds
  government, 445
  war, 751

Bonnie and Clyde (film), 819
Bonus Army, 710
Bonus Expeditionary Force (BEF), 710
Booth, William, 609
Borah, William E., 631
Bork, Robert, 840, 880
Borman, Frank, 822
Bosque Redondo reservation, 503
Bossism, 484–90
Boston
  the poor in, 479
  transit system, 492
Boston Red Sox, 593
Bourbons, 547
Bourgeoisie, 461
Boxing, 593–94
Bradley, Omar, 757
Brain Trust, 713
Brandeis, Louis D., 638, 640–41, 680, 723
Brannan Plan, 770
Brattain, Walter, 884
Brazil, 648
Bretton Woods Agreement (1944), 777–78
Brezhnev, Leonid, 862, 875
Briand, Aristide, 675
Bristow, Joseph, 631
Britain, Battle of, 741
British Guiana, 567
Brooklyn Bridge, 590–91
Brotherhood of Locomotive Firemen, 466
Brotherhood of Sleeping Car Porters, 748
Browder, Earl, 719
Brown, Edmund, 826
Brown, H. Rap, 809
Brown, Harold, 858
Brown v. Board of Education of Topeka, 776
Bruce, Blanche K., 431
Bryan, William Jennings, 466, 533, 549–54, 576–77, 633, 651, 696
  resignation, 654
  as secretary of state, 646–47
Bryce, James, 484, 650
Bryce Report, 650
Buck, Pearl S., 708
Budget, defense, 785
Budget deficits, 824
  Black Monday and, 891
  under Reagan, 873–74
Buffalo herds, 500–501
  destruction of, 505–6
Bulge, Battle of the, 757, 758
Bull Head, Lieutenant, 510
Bull Moose party, 636–38
Bull Run, Second Battle of (1862), 504
Burchard, Samuel, 540, 545
Bureaucratization, 807
Burford, Anne, 875
Burgess, John W., 563
Burleson, Albert S., 664
Burnham, Daniel, 590
Burns, Tommy, 594
Burroughs, William, 792, 808
Bush, George, 868, 892
Business
  See also Big business; Industrialism
  deregulation of, 874–75
  labor and, 679–80
Busing, 837
Butler, Ed, 488
Butler Law (1925), 696
Butterfield, Alexander, 840
Buying on margin, 704
Byrd, Robert, 859
Byrne, Jayne, 846

Cable, George Washington, 585
Cable cars, 491
Cagney, James, 707
Califano, Joseph, 858–59
California
  agriculture, 521
  anti-Chinese movement in, 475–76
  gold in, 499
  Proposition 13, 868
California Fruit Growers' Exchange, 521
Calley, William, Jr., 824
Call of the Wild, The (London), 588